EBURY PRESS

RAMA

Priya Arora is a spiritual seeker and a devoted follower of Advaita Vedanta. Delving into this ancient civilizational philosophy for many years was an eye-opening experience for her, dispelling many misconceptions. Vedanta's profundity and continuing relevance today inspire her writing.

Priya was born and raised in India and later graduated from Oxford University with a degree in English literature. She lives in the San Francisco Bay Area with her husband, children and beloved French bulldog, Humphrey.

RAMA

A MAN OF DHARMA

A Retelling of Valmiki's Ramayana

PRIYA ARORA

EBURY
PRESS

An imprint of Penguin Random House

EBURY PRESS

Ebury Press is an imprint of the Penguin Random House group of companies
whose addresses can be found at global.penguinrandomhouse.com

Published by Penguin Random House India Pvt. Ltd
4th Floor, Capital Tower 1, MG Road,
Gurugram 122 002, Haryana, India

Penguin
Random House
India

First published in Ebury Press by Penguin Random House India 2024

Copyright for text and illustrations © Priya Arora 2024

Illustrations by Surojit Bhattacharjee

ISBN 9780143468608

Typeset in Adobe Garamond Pro by MAP Systems, Bengaluru, India
Printed at Replika Press Pvt. Ltd, India

www.penguin.co.in

MIX
Paper | Supporting
responsible forestry
FSC™ C016779

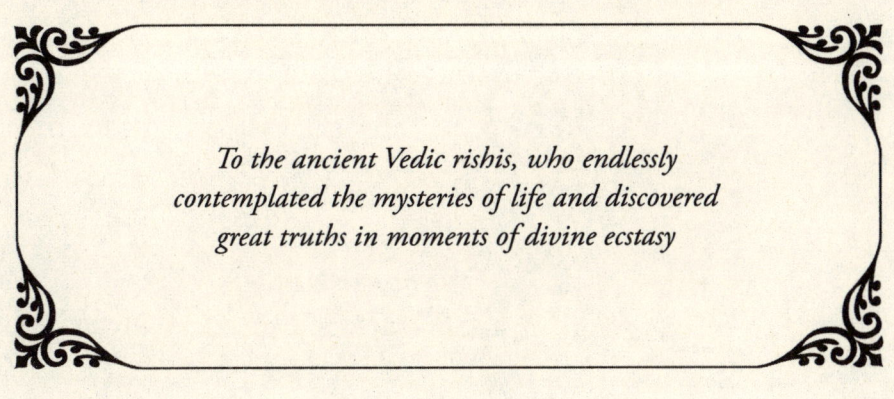

*To the ancient Vedic rishis, who endlessly
contemplated the mysteries of life and discovered
great truths in moments of divine ecstasy*

Contents

Contents

om sarve bhavantu sukhinah
sarve santu niramayah
sarve bhadrani pasyantu
ma kascid duhkha bhagbhavet
om santih santih santih

Om, may everyone be happy
May everyone be healthy
May everyone only see auspiciousness
May no one experience suffering
Om peace, peace, peace

Brihadaranyaka Upanishad

Preface

> You are what your deep, driving desire is
> As your desire is, so is your will
> As your will is, so is your deed
> As your deed is, so is your destiny
> —Brihadaranyaka Upanishad IV.4.5

Valmiki composed his epic biography of Rama eons ago, and since then, many versions of the story have been told and retold through the ages. Aside from these, there are numerous translations of the original and several abridged versions in almost every world language. It is natural, then, to question the value of one more. In response, I would like to reiterate Valmiki's stated purpose, which is largely lost today. The Ramayana is viewed chiefly as a mythological fantasy or a devotional piece about Vishnu's seventh avatar, but neither interpretation is compatible with the poet's original intention. While acknowledging that Rama took birth to destroy evil, Valmiki asserts his mission in the opening verses of his magnum opus to depict the remarkable life of an exceptional human being. He does not attribute Rama's eminence to divinity but to high ethics, which made him choose righteous action in every circumstance, no matter how adverse the outcome was to him. In Vedic philosophy, each person is divine, a manifestation of infinitely existing consciousness, so Rama felt pain and suffering in human form, just as we all do. The difference was that he did not take birth due to past karma like everyone else, but as an avatar, solely for the benefit of humanity.

I am not detracting from the godliness of Rama or his worship by those who deify him. After all, I am a devotee myself, but I see his life as a shining example of righteousness, as therein lies his greatness. Valmiki's Ramayana is about a historical character, who lived in ancient times and ruled from Ayodhya, a great king whose reign was marked by peace and prosperity, still remembered today as the golden age of Ramrajya. His monarchy left such a lasting impression that Deepavali, the festival of lights, is still observed every year, commemorating Rama's return home when his people celebrated his victory over evil by lighting oil lamps throughout the city. I have elaborated on Rama's historicity at the end of the book, which readers can refer to for more information, so I will not repeat the details here.

Trials and tribulations beset Rama throughout his life, yet he bore his hardships with equanimity, never compromising his lofty principles for personal gain. His exemplary character and unshakable adherence to ethical conduct bestow him with the title 'Maryada Purushottam'—the perfect man. There is much to learn from his fortitude, as suffering is an inevitable part of the human condition. Rama's journey through life expresses the high philosophy of the Vedas stemming from an inherent belief in harmony, which I have referenced in footnotes throughout the book. The entirety of the Vedic outlook can be distilled to 'Aham Brahmasmi', that the consciousness within me is God, the same that pervades all matter. Therefore, in seeing creation as inseparable from the creator, unity is the central principle of the Vedas. Rama was a realized person, who had liberated himself from a narrow identity, seeing oneness instead of division.

The Ramayana does not speak only to a particular group of followers; its message is all-embracing, illustrating everlasting values accepted by humanity as a whole. Since it expounds eternally applicable ethics focusing on dharma, not religious persuasion, its lessons apply to everyone regardless of ethnicity or personal faith. As an exemplar of timeless dharma, Rama is truly a man for all ages. Sadly, he is mainly viewed as a religious figure in recent years, embroiled in politics and communal strife, an association that has distanced him from what he symbolizes. I hope my rendition of Valmiki's story will show the reader Rama's value as a noble ancestor of humankind, worthy of universal respect and emulation, not limited to a deity venerated by some.

Although this is an abridged version, I have stayed reasonably close to the original story so that none of Valmiki's intent is lost. After much internal debate, I included some of the Puranic-style tales in Books 1 and 7. Scholars claim that many are later-day interpolations; nevertheless, I have added them as they feature in the complete edition. In this regard, I would like to acknowledge Gita Press Gorakhpur's excellent English translation, *Srimad Valmiki Ramayana*, which I used as the template for my book. I have also included supplemental information with essays discussing various Vedic terms and concepts pertinent to a proper appreciation of the story, as there is considerable misinformation about many of these ideas.

Valmiki says that a person who listens to the Ramayana benefits greatly, and from personal experience, I would like to say this is indeed true. It teaches courage and fortitude to handle problems that are the inevitable result of birth, and many valuable lessons to help lead a more peaceful existence. The Ramayana instills leadership, forbearance, loyalty, respect, equality, forgiveness and humility, but most of all, selflessness. Rama demonstrates the path to enlightenment through conscious selfless action, Karmayoga. He illustrates how one can attain liberation from suffering not by renunciation but by engaging fully in life, yet rising above it, by the purity of our choices. A spiritual attitude may not remove difficulties, but it makes them easier to overcome by building resilience to handle unavoidable situations.

In Vedic philosophy, just as every wave is an expression of the ocean, so too, every aspect of creation arises from the same consciousness. If we see this inherent harmony in nature, we do not view anyone else as 'the other', and therefore live unselfishly in fellowship. Cultivating a detached attitude towards the individual body–mind complex by identifying with the indwelling spirit helps alleviate current pain, while assuring peace in the hereafter. By spiritualizing daily activity, every act becomes one of worship and is the highest form of prayer. It gets rid of selfishness, replacing 'I' and 'my' with 'us' and 'ours'. Can you imagine a world where everyone acts for the greater good, rather than only in self-interest? That was the world of Rama's Ayodhya. In today's materialistic society, perhaps such a utopia is too lofty a goal, but great good is wrought if we each try to do the right thing, driven by conscience rather than automatically veering towards personal profit.

I hope those who read this book will enjoy the entertaining story, and at the same time, benefit from its immense wisdom. Rama has inspired people through the ages, and the example he set for righteousness is eternally valid. I take this opportunity to thank my friends and family for poring over my initial drafts and for their valuable feedback. In this regard, my late father-in-law, Sham Lal Arora, deserves special mention for his insightful comments that helped improve my manuscript enormously. Also, I must appreciate my husband Mohit's support in this endeavour and his patience as I locked myself away for hours on end! Above all, I would like to express deep gratitude to my online gurus, Swami Sarvapriyananda and Dr Karanam Aravinda Rao, for their outstanding lectures on Vedanta, which changed my outlook on life and inspired me to write this book.

Prologue

This enduring narrative is about events that took place many centuries ago in an ancient land we now call India. It portrays the Vedic[1] civilization's noble values, depicting a surprisingly advanced society that flourished to great heights in culture, philosophy and science in the distant past. The story is an inspiring account that explores love and duty, extolling ethical conduct: the honour of word, deed and principle. It sings the praise of integrity, courage, fortitude and selflessness in the face of life's greatest adversities, glorifying the remarkable devotion of a son, a wife and a brother. Above all, it is an uplifting tale that celebrates the victory of good over evil, the ultimate triumph of righteousness, which the ancients called dharma,[2] over wrongdoing or adharma.[3] This magnificent saga venerates Rama of Ayodhya, whose heroic life embodied the highest universal values of humanity—of all people, of all faiths, of all times.

A long time ago in the distant past,[4] it happened thus:[5]

---

[1] The Vedic civilization was founded on the principles expounded in the sacred Vedic texts. See Appendices.

[2] There is no word in English that adequately describes 'dharma'. The closest is 'righteousness', though it does not explain it fully. Refer to the detailed explanation in the Appendices.

[3] Adharma is unrighteousness, the opposite of dharma.

[4] Dating of the Ramayana and evidence for Rama's historicity is discussed in the Appendices.

[5] The Valmiki Ramayana is referred to as 'itihas', which means 'it happened thus', and is therefore regarded as historical.

The hermit Valmiki posed a question to his guru,[6] Narada,[7] foremost among sages, known for his supreme eloquence and deeply contemplative mind. 'Does a person of exemplary virtue, aptly considered a paragon of perfection, exist on Earth at present?[8] Does there walk amongst us, a righteous, resolute man, who is true to his word and full of gratitude even for the smallest service he receives? One who displays the highest character in every action, striving tirelessly for the welfare of others? While being eminently learned, is there a person in this world who is also singularly pleasing in appearance and attitude? Do you know anyone who exhibits such extraordinary self-control that he never falls prey to sensual desires? Is there a high-souled man alive today, who has conquered anger and is never envious or captious? An individual who shines with the brilliance of his goodness. Besides possessing all these fine qualities, I wonder if a human being equally ferocious in battle lives among us. A person who makes his enemies shake so that even the mighty Devas[9] marvel at his unfailing valour?'

After pondering for a moment, Narada replied enthusiastically, 'A king known as Rama, born into the Ikshavaku[10] clan of the Suryavanshi[11] dynasty, is the epitome of human goodness. He displays many extraordinary qualities rarely found together in one individual, bringing delight to all who encounter him. He is an exceptionally principled human being; disciplined, learned, valorous, resolute, eloquent, brilliant, with great fortitude, enormous

---

[6] A guru is a path illuminator and far more than the English dictionary definition of a teacher or expert. In Sanskrit, the word 'guru' means one who removes the ignorance that obscures our true reality. In addition to imparting knowledge, a guru is an exemplary individual; a moral guide who has achieved spiritual enlightenment.

[7] Narada was a revered celestial sage, one of the mind-born sons created by Brahma.

[8] Valmiki uses the word 'sampratam', which translates as 'at present', so he is clearly asking about a contemporary figure, not a fictional character.

[9] The offspring of Aditi and Rishi Kashyapa. Benevolent beings of light with higher powers than humans, associated with the elements.

[10] The eldest son of Manu. Manu was the progenitor of mankind after the deluge and his name is the root word for man in English.

[11] The Solar dynasty.

willpower and a sharp wit. His proficiency in the Vedas[12] and the Vedangas[13] makes him sagacious. Although he holds an influential position as a monarch, he remains humble, considering himself a servant of his people. He always abides by dharma, relentlessly fighting against unrighteousness, and is benevolent to everyone, fearlessly protecting the welfare of his subjects. He is respectful to elders and deeply introspective; coupled with this, he has admirable self-control and a focused mind. Since he grasps the essence of the shastras,[14] he lives scrupulously by their philosophy.

'Sporting a handsome appearance as beautiful as his inner nature, Rama is broad-shouldered with powerful arms, a wide chest, a sturdy conch-shaped neck, muscular clavicles and a firm jaw. This fearless man is puissant enough to handle even the mightiest bow, vanquishing his enemies with ease. His long arms extend almost to his knees, yet he is perfectly proportionate without a hint of ungainliness, evidenced by his majestic gait. His head is well-shaped, his eyes are large and his forehead is broad. He is tall, though not unduly so, and while he has the look of a mighty warrior, he bears a gentle demeanour. His complexion is radiant, and he is blessed with all the bodily characteristics considered auspicious in the Samudrika Shastra.[15] Rama is renowned as pious, unbiased and high-minded in all three worlds.[16] His ability to handle any situation life throws at him with rock-like endurance makes saintly people seek his company like the rivers seek the ocean. He is a role model of exalted conduct, an "arya"[17] endowed with all the noble qualities fit to be emulated, and the depth of his personality is only comparable to the vastness of the sea. Rama, his mother Kaushalya's pride, never sways in courage, standing

---

[12] Ancient Sanskrit texts of knowledge containing hymns, philosophy and guidance. The four Vedas are: Rig Veda, Sama Veda, Yajur Veda and Atharva Veda.

[13] The six auxilliary disciplines that assist in the study of the Vedas. They are: 1. Siksha (Learning)—phonetics and pronunciation; 2. Nirukta—etymology of words; 3. Vyakarana—grammar and syntax; 4. Chandas—prosody/poetic meter; 5. Kalpa—instruction on rituals and sacrifices; 6. Jyotisha—astronomy and astrology.

[14] The word shastras refers to the various fields of knowledge.

[15] This literally means 'knowledge of body features' and was a study of what bodily characteristics indicated.

[16] Bhuloka (Earth), Devaloka (abode of the Devas) and Patalaloka (abode of the Asuras).

[17] 'Arya' in Sanskrit refers to a cultured or refined person, not to a race. A racial connotation was falsely ascribed to the word by nineteenth-century European Indologists. Refer to the Appendices, 'Who Were the Vedic People?', for more details.

as firm and unshakeable as the Himalayas. In bravery, honestly, he equals Vishnu;[18] in aspect, he is as handsome as Chandra.[19] Unrivalled in archery,[20] he is unbeatable on the battlefield like the all-consuming fire at the end of creation, while his forbearance is like that of Mother Earth. He resembles Kubera[21] in his propensity to give away wealth, and Dharmaraja[22] in his adherence to truthfulness.'

Narada narrated Rama's life story to Valmiki to illustrate why he considered him an exceptional human being, who exemplified dharma through his deeds. Having done this, Narada took his leave, and musing on what he had just heard, Valmiki proceeded to the river Tamasa[23] with his disciples to bathe and perform his midday worship. As he stepped into the clear waters of the river, his gaze fell on a pair of Sarus cranes mating. Then all at once, an arrow unexpectedly pierced the male bird, obliterating their bliss. The female squawked in pain and overcome by grief at the ill-timed slaughter of innocent life, Valmiki involuntarily uttered a curse, crying, 'Fie on you, hunter! May the one who committed the heinous crime of killing a creature in a union have no peace.' The spontaneous admonishment escaped his lips in the form of a verse, a poetic meter comprising four lines, each with eight syllables, called a shloka.[24]

When Valmiki returned to his hermitage, his mind continued to linger on the incident of the cranes, and as he brooded, Brahma[25] appeared before him, to his astonishment. Valmiki welcomed his guest with reverence and told him about the curse he had uttered. He was troubled by the female

---

[18] Embodiment of the power of preservation in the Vedic Trinity.

[19] The moon.

[20] Rama was an expert in Dhanur Veda, the knowledge of archery and missiles that existed at the time.

[21] The Vedic guardian of wealth and protector of the northern quarter.

[22] Yama, lord of death and reckoning.

[23] A tributary of the Ganga.

[24] The Sanskrit word 'shoka' means sorrow; and since this poetic verse was a result of Valmiki's sorrow, it was called a 'shloka'.

[25] The Creator in the Vedic trinity—Brahma, Vishnu, and Mahesh/Shiva. The three deities depict the three cosmic functions of creation, preservation and dissolution, respectively. Brahma symbolizes the Vedas, so his appearance figuratively asserts that the story is a dramatization of Vedic philosophy.

crane's pathos and his outburst of anger towards the hunter, which showed a lack of restraint. Brahma advised him not to dwell on what had happened but to make the best use of the beautiful poetic meter he had accidentally created while making his pronouncement. He asked Valmiki to compose a biography of Rama's life based on what he had just heard from Narada, as it illustrated a praiseworthy journey in dharma. Brahma promised that every detail of what had transpired would be divinely revealed to Valmiki through his yogic powers as if he were witnessing the events as they took place. He added that it would be an enduring story that would abide for as long as there were mountains and rivers on the Earth, and so saying, he disappeared. Thus, from the outpouring of sorrow, the Ramayana was born[26] and first memorized and sung by Valmiki's gifted young disciples, Lava and Kusha.

---

[26] The Ramayana is about handling suffering.

satyameva jayate

Truth alone triumphs

Mundaka Upanishad

brahma veda brahmaiva bhavati

The knower of Brahman (the divine) becomes
Brahman (the divine)

Mundaka Upanishad

BOOK 1
Prince Rama

Chapter 1

The Birth of the Princes of Ayodhya

Many thousands of years ago, a new day was about to dawn, with the sun rising in the east, as it had done from time immemorial. In a dense forest on the banks of the Sarayu,[1] in the renowned kingdom of Kosala,[2] the last watch of a rainy monsoon night would soon give way to the first rays of early morning, its gentle light filtering down through the canopy onto the denizens below. The hunters stalked their prey, while the hunted were ever mindful of the slightest danger in the eternal struggle of life and death. The leaves rustled as young Prince Dasharatha[3] made his way astride his magnificent horse, engrossed in the royal pastime of hunting.

A gurgling by the river broke the silence. 'Ah,' thought Dasharatha, 'An animal for sure, a large one that sounds like an elephant; what a big prize!' Lifting his bow, he aimed his arrow towards the slurping noise. The arrow whizzed through the air and swiftly met its mark. It had to; after all, Dasharatha was an expert marksman, who could pierce a target unaided by vision and guided by sound alone. A piteous cry rang out as he made his way towards his prey, with his heart pounding and beads of sweat running down his forehead. Approaching the river's edge, to his horror, he saw a young hermit boy severely wounded, a pitcher lying by his side, and his topknot undone. Dasharatha's bow slipped from his clammy hands as he trembled,

---

[1] The river is still called the Sarayu today, as is the city of Ayodhya.

[2] Kosala was a large and powerful kingdom in northern India with many vassal states.

[3] Dasharatha was a name given to him because he could ride his chariot in all ten directions, including in the sky and to the underworld. The ten directions were uttar/north, dakshin/south, poorav/east, paschim/west, ishanya/north-east, agneya/south-east, nairutya/south-west, vayavya/north-west, urdhwa/skywards and adastha/downwards. His birth name was Nemi.

overcome with guilt and grief. He felt sick to the stomach, his thoughts raced and his pulse quickened as he came to grips with what had happened. If only he could turn back time!

Though dying, the boy asked sharply, 'Why did you shoot an ascetic like me who caused you no harm? All I was doing was drawing water for my parents. Now, not only is the vitality ebbing fast from my body, but you have extinguished three lives with one deadly arrow, as my parents depend on me entirely for their survival. Please confess your wrongdoing to my father, and ask for his forgiveness, so he does not curse you too harshly for your misdeed.' Pointing to a footpath, he added with a groan, 'You will find his hermitage yonder.' Dasharatha was not only overwhelmed with remorse at committing the egregious act of murdering an innocent person, but also profoundly unsettled by the demise of a man of learning and the consequent loss to society. Then, almost as though the boy read his mind, he said, 'I am not a *dvija*;[4] education was not expected of me since my mother is a Shudra,[5] and my father is a Vaishya,[6] so you will not incur the additional sin of slaying one who is a repository of knowledge.'

---

[4] Dvija means twice born, or one who was initiated into scholarship under a guru. Anyone with an orientation to scholarship could choose to be a dvija, but it was a prerequisite to being a Brahmin. Hence, all Brahmins were dvijas, though all dvijas were not necessarily Brahmins. Brahmins devoted their lives to learning and piety, serving society with their knowledge. They lived on charity, dedicating themselves solely to scholarship. Since they were storehouses of wisdom, killing a Brahmin was like burning a library and considered extremely sinful. The profession like all others was passed down from father to son but not restricted to birth; and in Vedic literature there are numerous instances of people acquiring knowledge and becoming Brahmins. The boy states he is not of Brahmin parentage, indicating he was not expected to be a dvija, but we later learn he was a student engaged in scholarship, showing he had the choice of attaining Brahminhood if he wished.

[5] Shudras were the workers who served in jobs that did not necessarily require a formal education. Therefore, they were generally not 'dvijas' or twice born like the Brahmins, Kshatriyas and Vaishyas, who were considered 'born again' when they were initiated into schooling. Shudras were not looked down upon; they formed most of society, providing their services for a wage or fee. For instance, artisans, charioteers, engineers, actors, musicians, carpenters, potters and even physicians were Shudras.

[6] Vaishyas were traders, and included anyone who engaged in business and commerce, including cowherds and farmers.

By now, writhing on the ground in agony, he mumbled weakly, 'Take some water to my parents who are waiting for me.' With this last utterance, the boy's spirit left his body. Tears of contrition streamed down the prince's face as he filled the narrow-mouthed earthen pot that had fallen by the water's edge. He reprimanded himself over and over for mistaking the sound of water filling the vessel for an animal drinking, but alas, he could not undo what he had done. Dasharatha, the Crown Prince of Kosala, who had the world at his feet, was completely helpless in this instance. His royal power and limitless riches were futile in the face of death.

The hermitage was a short distance away, and Dasharatha heard the old couple call out as he approached. Hearing footsteps, the boy's father exclaimed in relief, 'There you are, dear son! What took you so long? Your mother and I were getting worried about you. Why don't you speak? I hope you are not annoyed by something we said. Remember, you are our eyes and our only support.' Being blind, at first, they did not recognize that it was not their son bringing them water. Dasharatha stood frozen in his tracks, unable to say anything. He stared dolefully at the helpless couple, who looked pathetic like a pair of birds with clipped wings. Then mustering his courage, he said in a faltering voice, 'Forgive me, I am not your son; I am a Kshatriya[7] prince called Dasharatha. While hunting, I killed your son, mistaking him for an elephant. I am full of regret for my crime and beg you for mercy.' His words pierced the aged parents' hearts, and tears filled their eyes. However, instead of pronouncing a terrible curse, the father said, 'Had you not admitted your fault, your head would have shattered into a thousand pieces this very instant. A Kshatriya is a protector who must never kill a blameless person, much less a hermit living in austerity, engaged in the scholarship[8] of the Vedas. Still, you will incur a lesser punishment since you are guilty of an unintentional crime and not one of evil design. You will not die prematurely, and your bloodline will not become extinct. Now, please take us to our son so we can be with him one last time.'

---

[7] Kshatriyas were warriors and were responsible for the protection of the realm and enforcing justice. The king was a Kshatriya.

[8] This statement confirms the study of the Vedas was available to everyone, not exclusive to a privileged few. The status of a Brahmin was earned not inherited. Manusmriti (2.28) states that the body is made fit to be called Brahmin through study of the Veda, recitation of shastras, keeping religious observances, offering libations to the holy fire (homa), noble selfless deeds and meritorious actions, as the young boy was doing.

When Dasharatha led them to the dead body, they fell on it, weeping inconsolably, and the whole forest rang with their heart-rending lamentations. 'Now that you are gone, we will never again hear you melodiously chanting the Vedas in the early morning! Who will perform the Sandhya Vandana[9]? Who will offer oblations to the holy fire? Who will look after us? Dear child, you served us selflessly! Like heroes who die in battle, may you attain the highest plane of heaven.'[10] Then, as Dasharatha prepared a pyre to perform the boy's last rites, overcome by grief, the sage said with folded hands, 'Young prince, you have thousands to serve you, but we had only one son. We are deprived of him and left helpless, so you will necessarily reap the consequences of your folly in this lifetime. Like us, you too will die of heartache, experiencing the pain of separation from your son, and in your suffering, you will come to understand the intense misery you have caused us today.' With these anguished words, the old couple gave up their bodies in the blazing pyre to join their son in the other world.

There is no better healer than time, so as the years rolled by, the incident in the forest faded into a distant memory. The prince regent ascended the throne of Ayodhya,[11] Kosala's grand capital city. He came from a noble line of kings and proved himself worthy of his illustrious lineage that traced its ancestry back to Surya,[12] the Sun Deva. Dasharatha was a mighty warrior, but, at the same time, a kind and benevolent ruler, who cared for his people like a father. He was well versed in the Vedas and virtuous like all his predecessors. His people loved him dearly and compared his piety to that of a sage. Eight exceptionally competent ministers of the highest integrity assisted him in administration—Dhrishti, Jayanta, Vijaya, Siddhartha, Arthasadhaka, Ashoka, Mantrapala and Sumantra. Two sagacious spiritual

---

[9] 'Sandhya Vandana' is a salutation to the sun. Through it, the sun is worshipped as a glorious manifestation of the Supreme Consciousness, the giver of life. It is a reminder of one's higher nature and of universal oneness; conducted three times a day—at dawn, midday and dusk. 'The Self in man and in the Sun is one. Those who understand this see through the world and go beyond the various sheaths of being to realize the unity of life.' Taittiriya Upanishad 2.8.1

[10] In Vedic philosophy, heaven is a temporary plane of existence with many levels. The nobler one's karma or deeds, the higher the realm achieved as a resting state between births.

[11] Ayodhya is in northern India in the state of Uttar Pradesh.

[12] The Deva associated with the sun.

counsellors, Vasishta and Vamadeva, provided moral guidance and helped him rule with complete impartiality. No one was above the law, no matter their position in society, and the ministers did not hesitate to punish even their offspring for any transgression. An assembly called the Parishad[13] made governance democratic, comprising representatives of the people, who deliberated on the welfare of the citizens. Kosala's supremacy as a prosperous kingdom spread far and wide, enriched by numerous vassal kingdoms that paid taxes as tribute in recognition of its suzerainty.

Ayodhya, its very name meaning 'unconquerable', was the capital; a shining jewel, a sprawling city twelve yojanas[14] long and three yojanas wide, built by Manu on the southern banks of the river Sarayu. It had well-laid-out streets, and a broad tree-lined avenue sprinkled with water daily ran through it. There were rows of neatly constructed houses and many multi-storeyed buildings of eclectic design, studded with precious gems. Demarcated areas housed busy marketplaces that bustled with traders from all over the world. The artisans were of the highest skill, and their craftsmanship was unparalleled. Jewellers sold gems by weight and displayed precious metals piled up like straw; such was the abundance of riches in the land. Although densely populated, it was a beautiful paradise dotted with arches, gateways, and lush gardens with mango trees. The city was kept sanitary by an underground drainage system. Fresh water was never in short supply, thanks to large storage tanks, and it was said to be sweet like sugarcane juice. The people, like their king, were upright and led contented lives. They knew no poverty, dressed in the best attire and always adorned themselves with jewellery. Every household lit a holy fire, and every person maintained the highest level of cleanliness. Culturally, the city had the most talented dancers and musicians, and there were many schools for music and theatre, some entirely composed of women. The town was alive, with the vibrant melody of *mridangams*,[15] veenas[16] and *panavas*[17] filling the air.

---

[13] This was the earliest form of democratic government as representatives of the people were involved in decision making. Notably, all four varnas were included.

[14] A 'yojana' was a unit of distance. Scholars are not certain exactly how much it measured at the time of the Ramayana because it varied over the ages from 4.5–10 miles.

[15] A percussion instrument still played today.

[16] A string instrument similar to a lute.

[17] Cymbals.

Ayodhya was safe from intruders, surrounded by high walls, encircled
by an impregnable moat and protected from danger by a formidable army
consisting of four divisions: elephants, horses, chariots and foot soldiers. The
soldiers were well trained in warfare, equipped with the most potent weapons
available and scrupulously observed ethics in combat. The horses were of
the best breeds from Kambhoja,[18] Bahalika[19] and Vanayu.[20] Similarly, the
elephants were the mightiest from the Vindhya,[21] Sahyadri[22] and Himalaya[23]
regions. People in society were divided into four categories called varnas,[24]
based on their function and duty. The Brahmins were learned men, who spent
their time exclusively in the pursuit of scholarship and spiritual attainment.
The Kshatriyas were the warriors, responsible for protecting the realm. The
Vaishyas were the tradesmen, who conducted commerce and business for
profit, responsible for the land's economic prosperity. The Shudras were the
workers, who served with their hands, the backbone of the community on
whom the other varnas relied. Though it was the norm for a profession to pass
on from father to son, the division was functional and not hereditary; hence,
movement between social classes was not unusual. Society was egalitarian
and discrimination was unknown; each occupational class or varna was clear
about its duty and valued for its contribution. Wealth was abundant, and
the granaries were full. The people were content, conscientious and always
practised righteous conduct. Women walked freely during the day or night

---

[18] Located in Central Asia beyond Afghanistan—Tajikistan, Uzbekistan and surrounding
areas.

[19] Central Asian region of Balkh, Afghanistan.

[20] Arabia.

[21] The Vindhya mountains in India separate the Deccan Plateau from the Gangetic
Plain.

[22] The Sahyadri mountains are the Western Ghats that run parallel to the western coast
of India.

[23] The Himalayas are to the north of India. They are spread over five countries today:
India, China, Nepal, Pakistan and Bhutan.

[24] 'Varna' in Sanskrit indicates classification, grouping or description. It pointed to a
group of people who followed a similar profession but was mistranslated as caste by
European Indologists. This had serious repercussions, felt to the current day, as the two
words are not interchangeable; caste has negative connotations, while occupation does
not. Also, varna in its original form was not based on birth but on aptitude and what a
person did for a living. Refer to the Appendices for more details.

without fear of any threat to their safety, and even if a jewel were dropped in the street, it would lie untouched.

Wars were waged and won, territories subjugated, the arts flourished, and wealth abounded. King Dasharatha had everything the material world could offer him, including 350 wives and three principal queens. However, his happiness was incomplete as he did not have an heir to perpetuate his line. His first queen was Kaushalya, princess of the kingdom of Dakshina Kaushala.[25] She was a sweet-natured, prayerful woman, devoted to her husband, but unfortunately unable to give him a son. Dasharatha then married Sumitra, princess of Kashi,[26] who also failed to produce an heir to the throne. Finally, he wed Kaikeyi, the beautiful and feisty princess from the mountain kingdom of Kekaya.[27] The only sister amongst seven brothers, Kaikeyi trained with them and was a skilled warrior in her own right. Soon, she became the king's favourite wife, and he spent all his time in her company. Dasharatha hoped that Kaikeyi would give him an heir, but sadly, she too proved barren. The most remarkable of the three was Sumitra, the middle queen. She was wise and even-tempered, and held the family together with her sacrificing nature. Although Sumitra was neither the senior queen nor the favourite, she was never resentful, which perhaps explained why the three queens coexisted without too much of the natural strife that arose from being co-wives.

Dasharatha ruled for many years, during which his kingdom reached great heights. However, the longing for a successor weighed heavily on his mind. One day, he was struck with the idea of performing a fire sacrifice for the prosperity of his kingdom. He thought the Ashwamedha[28] Yagna[29] might result in the blessing of an heir, so he summoned his ministers and counsellors to discuss the matter. When everyone concurred with his plan,

---

[25] Modern-day Chhattisgarh.

[26] Modern-day Varanasi.

[27] Kekaya was the area extending into Afghanistan from north-west Pakistan.

[28] The Ashwamedha was a horse sacrifice described in the Rig Veda. A stallion was let loose to roam and was followed by an army. The lands it passed through unobstructed accepted the authority of the king performing the ritual. If it was captured, a battle ensued to establish supremacy. The Ashwamedha was prohibitively expensive, so it was performed only by the mightiest kings.

[29] Yagna was a fire ritual/devotional ceremony where oblations were offered to a sacred fire.

he ordered preparations to begin. Dasharatha's charioteer[30] Sumantra, who also happened to be one of his ministers and a close confidant, called him aside privately and suggested inviting the sage Rishyashringa to perform the yagna. He had demonstrated his great yogic powers by helping the king of Anga[31] bring rain to his land. Rishyashringa was raised in the woods by his father, Vibhandaka, in complete isolation from society, acquiring extraordinary mystical abilities through an unrelenting focus on his spiritual quest. King Romapada of Anga once faced a severe drought in his kingdom and was advised to bring Rishyashringa to alleviate it. He was doubtful Rishyashringa's overprotective father would grant him leave from the hermitage, so he sent a bevy of attractive courtesans[32] to entice the young sage away. Unknown to Vibhandaka, Rishyashringa fell for their charms. The women succeeded in their endeavour not only because he was celibate, but also unacquainted with the fairer sex. They escorted him to Anga, and miraculously, as soon as he stepped on the land, showers of rain greeted them. Romapada ultimately made amends to Vibhandaka and gave his daughter Shanta in marriage to Rishyashringa in gratitude. Romapada and Dasharatha shared a close association. In fact, Shanta was Dasharatha's biological offspring, whom he had given to his dear friend in adoption when she was a small child.

Romapada agreed wholeheartedly to help Dasharatha and immediately sent Rishyashringa and Shanta to him. Once the ceremonial Ashwamedha horse was released to roam, Ayodhya got busy with elaborate arrangements that lasted a whole year. The king's priest, Vasishta, prepared a long list of invitees from many kingdoms, north, south, east and west, to be treated with the highest honour. Engineers, builders and artisans began constructing a satellite town on the northern banks of the Sarayu. Mansions and lodges sprang up to house thousands of guests, and dancers and singers practised day and night to provide entertainment for the occasion. Chefs assembled provisions and procured massive cooking vessels for large-scale community feeding. The craftsmen, priests and royal guests were given generous gifts

---

[30] Being a service provider, Sumantra was a Shudra by profession but also the king's closest adviser, which shows that Shudras were not considered lowly in Vedic times. Moreover, there was no hierarchy in the varna system as each group was considered important for what they contributed to society.

[31] Anga covered parts of eastern Uttar Pradesh, Bihar and West Bengal.

[32] Courtesans were not considered fallen women in Vedic society. They were respected members of the community, intelligent and talented in sixty-four different fine arts.

with a staggering one million cows, a 100 million gold coins, and 400 million silver coins distributed. Workers received appropriate remuneration commensurate with their effort,[33] and all the attendees were rewarded handsomely for their presence at the occasion. The yagna pavilion was constructed in strict adherence to prescribed Vedic ordinances. It had twenty-one octagonal pillars, twenty-one spans high: six each of bilva,[34] khadira[35] and palasa[36] wood; one sleshmataka[37] and two deodar.[38] These pillars stood precisely six feet apart, clad in gold and decorated with flowers and sandalwood paste. The shastras delineated the brick measurements, and the altar arrangement was in the shape of Garuda.[39] It was three times the regular size, with eighteen fire pits rather than the usual six, and every detail was planned to perfection.

The grand yagna took place after a year, when the Ashwamedha horse returned. Then, Rishyashringa conducted a special Putrakameshti[40] ritual for the king to beget a son. As Rishyashringa poured ghee into the sacrificial fire, accompanied by the chanting of sacred hymns, the flames leaped into the air, reaching for the heavens. The king and his three wives were seated solemnly in veneration, when a resplendent celestial being emerged from the fire. He handed Dasharatha a small golden bowl with a silver lid that kept its contents at a perfect temperature[41] and said, 'Share this divine rice pudding amongst your wives, and your wish will be fulfilled.' Dasharatha gave half the contents of the bowl to his first queen Kaushalya, a quarter to Sumitra and half of the balance to Kaikeyi. He still had one-eighth left over, so he pondered for a moment and intelligently gave the remaining portion once again to his wise wife, Sumitra.[42]

---

[33] Slavery was unknown in Vedic times. The Greek envoy Megasthenes noted its absence when he visited the court of Chandragupta Maurya.

[34] Also called bael and used in Ayurveda; botanical name *Aegle marmelos*.

[35] Cutch tree or *Acacia catechu* also used in Ayurveda.

[36] Also called Kimsuka. Flame of the Forest in English because of its red blossoms.

[37] Lasora or *Cordia dichotoma*, which has medicinal benefits.

[38] Cedar or *Cedrus deodara*.

[39] A giant eagle, the mount of Vishnu.

[40] Prayer for a son.

[41] Silver being a better conductor than gold, the excess heat escaped from the lid.

[42] The rice pudding did not result in immaculate conception. It was a potion that aided fertility.

In the meantime, the Devas looked down from their abode[43] in the sky and went to Brahma with a complaint. They were concerned about the havoc caused by a particular boon he had granted. They spoke to Brahma of the harassment everyone faced in the three worlds from the Rakshasa[44] Ravana, who had become a menace because a benediction of invincibility protected him from death. In his audacity, he continually oppressed the sages, outraged the modesty of women and bullied the meek, safeguarded from demise at the hands of all beings except humans, whom he considered too puny to be a threat. Brahma directed the Devas to seek the help of Vishnu, so they implored him to incarnate on Earth as a human to vanquish the evil that Ravana and his followers were perpetrating, thereby re-establishing righteousness. Vishnu agreed to their request and decided that he would divide himself and be born as the four sons of Dasharatha. In doing this, his main avatar would benefit from the support of three brothers. The Devas were relieved, and as Brahma instructed, they begat sons in the form of Vanaras[45] or forest men to further assist in the divine plan. Thus, Indra[46] fathered Vali, Surya[47] fathered Sugriva, Agni[48] fathered Nila, Vishwakarma[49] fathered Nala, the Ashwinis[50] fathered the twins Mainda and Dwividha, Varuna[51] fathered Sushena, and Vayu[52] fathered the mighty Hanuman. These Vanaras would have the blessing of unique attributes from their fathers. They would also be valiant, have tremendous physical strength, the ability to assume any form and would play a crucial role in the battle with Ravana.

---

[43] The Devas lived in a world called Swargaloka or Devaloka.

[44] The Rakshasas were beings with a proclivity for wickedness, though not all were evil.

[45] The Vanaras are mistakenly thought to be monkeys, but Vanara means forest man. They were probably a tribe that were ape-like in appearance.

[46] The king of the Devas and the guardian of the eastern quarter.

[47] The Sun Deva.

[48] The Deva of Fire.

[49] The architect of the Devas.

[50] The twin Devas of health and medicine.

[51] The Deva of water and the Vedic guardian of the western quarter.

[52] The Deva of the wind.

Six seasons[53] of the Vedic calendar went by, and on the ninth day of the waxing moon in the month of Chaitra,[54] as the day began to advance,[55] Kaushalya gave birth to a beautiful baby boy they named Rama. The star Punarvasu[56] was in the ascendant; the sun was in Aries; Mars was in Capricorn; Saturn was in Libra; Jupiter was in Cancer and Venus was in Pisces; all in exalted positions. Cancer was rising in the east and Jupiter above the horizon. Next, Kaikeyi had a son, Bharata, born under the ruling star Pushya.[57] And finally, Sumitra, who had eaten two servings of the pudding, was blessed with twins, Lakshmana and Shatrughana, born under Aslesha.[58] Dasharatha was ecstatic! He had not one but four heirs to the throne, and overjoyed at his good fortune, gave away vast sums of wealth in charity to express his gratitude.

The princes felt a solid filial bond from their early childhood and treated each of the three queens as their mother. Likewise, the queens made no difference between the boys. The brothers were devoted to each other, and the younger ones looked up to Rama with reverence. However, Rama and Lakshmana shared a special attachment from the start, as did Bharata and Shatrughana. In time, they would all turn out to be brave like lions among men, masters of the Vedas, exceptional warriors and devoted followers of dharma.

---

[53] The six Vedic seasons were: vasant—spring, grishma—summer, varsha—monsoon, sharad—autumn, hemant—pre-winter and shishir—winter.

[54] The month associated with the coming of spring.

[55] Noon.

[56] The brightest star of Gemini, Pollux. Valmiki has date stamped Rama's birth and other major events in the Ramayana with the star positions in the sky. More details are given in the chapter on Rama's historicity.

[57] Pushya is Altaraf. Based on the star formation, Bharata was born the next day, sixteen hours after Rama.

[58] The main star in the constellation Hydra.

Chapter 2

Student Life—Vasishta and Vishwamitra

In due course, the boys' schooling began away from the palace at the hermitage of their family priest, the venerable guru Vasishta. He was a luminary of his time, an outstanding scholar and one of the seven distinguished sages who had attained the highest level of spiritual enlightenment that gave him the title of Brahmarishi.[1] Vasishta was a great yogic master, who had achieved complete self-control, conquering anger, desire, attachment, greed, envy and pride. The spiritual treatise Yoga Vasishta[2] that expounds on the truth about existence is a dialogue between him and Rama. He ran his gurukul[3] with his wife Arundhati, where he educated hundreds of students, including the royal princes of Ayodhya.

Dasharatha suffered deeply from the separation. Perhaps the old curse welled up in his mind, making it impossible to snuff out the terrible fear that engulfed him? However, brahmacharya[4] was a prerequisite; the princes needed the education to be good monarchs, so the aged king had no choice but to bear their absence stoically. Under Vasishta's expert tutelage, they mastered

---

[1] The highest level of spiritual enlightenment. The knower of Brahman, who is established in the Supreme Consciousness.

[2] A philosophical treatise on existence, in the form of a dialogue between young Rama and Vasishta. It has six sections that cover the following subjects: 1. Dispassion; 2. The qualities and longing of a spiritual seeker; 3. Creation, origin of the universe, time and space; 4. The ego and human nature; understanding the Self and true existence; 5. Dissolution; 6. Understanding Brahman, the supreme consciousness and liberation.

[3] A gurukul was a residential school where the student served his guru while gaining knowledge.

[4] Vedic life was divided into four stages. The first was brahmacharya or student life, dedicated exclusively to learning.

16

all the skills required to make them able rulers, including horsemanship, charioteering, archery and the use of various weapons. Alongside these talents went the most significant teaching of the Vedas and Vedangas, as proficiency in the shastras[5] was the hallmark of an erudite person.

The Vedas are not just compilations of hymns, prayers and rituals but divine revelations of universal truths. They are a repository of wisdom gleaned by great minds in deep contemplation from time immemorial that expound on the reality of the inner self and man's relationship with the cosmic consciousness viewed as God.[6] Besides, the Vedas are also a compendium of knowledge that served to inspire all walks of ancient life, including medicine, astronomy, science, mathematics, politics, human conduct, yoga and meditation. Above all, they are a discourse on the abiding philosophy of Sanatana Dharma.[7] This high ideology has no association with any religious dogma or icon of worship. It does not have commandments of prescribed action or dictates demanding faith in a specific deity, for the Vedas perceive God as the supreme reality that resides in every living being. God is seen as an omniscient, omnipotent, omnipresent, formless, all-pervading power that can be worshipped in any manifestation, as all prayers ultimately reach the same divinity. The belief holds loving, selfless actions as the highest expression of devotion, for such noble deeds are an act of worship in themselves. In essence, Dharma stands for a set of immutable values, including strength of character, a reverence for principles and ethical action.

The profound spiritual concept of one almighty power pervading all creation formed the basis of Vedic culture. Hence, harmonious living with each other and the planet was considered fundamental to the purpose of dharma. Righteous action depended on the circumstance at hand. Therefore, dharma was intricate and necessarily varied, based on the context of the specific events faced relative to one's role in life. Guru Vasishta always emphasized working for the benefit of others, never causing unnecessary harm and dutifully upholding dharma in every situation encountered. It was believed that this eternal path would always bring victory in the end, even if it seemed contrary to one's personal interests.

---

[5] See Appendices on eighteen branches of the Shastras.

[6] See Appendices for more on the Vedic concept of God.

[7] 'Sanatana Dharma' means everlasting truth—that which is eternally valid. This concept is discussed in detail in the Appendices.

The four boys achieved excellence in every field, and their education imbued them with many admirable qualities. Each was brave, well-versed in the Vedas, and devoted to their people's welfare while remaining firmly rooted in dharma. Students served in the gurukul by doing all the daily chores regardless of their status. As a result, when Vasishta sent the princes back, they were accomplished in the art of ruling a kingdom as well as wise, humble and kind human beings. Dasharatha's heart swelled with pride when the princes returned. He adored all his sons, but always had a special affection for Rama, his pride and joy—tall and handsome, a fierce warrior and yet, a gentle soul. He had beautiful eyes like the lotus flower and thick wavy locks. His quick intelligence ensured that he excelled at everything he did, yet he was never arrogant. Always unfailing in righteousness, Rama was indeed endowed with every desirable attribute a person could hope to have. The old king had nothing left to wish for in life except to find suitable brides for his sons.

One day, as he discussed the topic of their marriage with his spiritual counsellors Vasishta and Vamadeva, the great sage Vishwamitra appeared at the palace gates. Vishwamitra had a commanding presence and a forbidding reputation. Through countless years of austere yogic mediation, he had attained immense spiritual powers that earned him veneration throughout the land. The doorkeepers rushed to announce his arrival, and in the tradition of the day, Dasharatha welcomed Vishwamitra with great honour and hospitality. With folded hands, he said reverently, 'Holy master, most exalted rishi, I am fortunate to be graced by your esteemed presence just as the parched land is by rainfall.' After exchanging pleasantries,[8] the king unreservedly offered Vishwamitra anything he desired, saying, 'Please let me know what I can do for you. Ask for whatever you wish without hesitation, as it would be my privilege to grant you your desire.'

Pleased to hear these words, Vishwamitra replied, 'I need a small favour. No one is more generous than you, O king, so I am sure you will fulfil your promise. I am performing an important yagna but two powerful Rakshasas, Maricha and Subahu, rain flesh and blood on my altar, interfering with my fire ritual. They act instigated by their chief, Ravana, the brother of Kubera and son of Rishi Vishrava. I cannot deal with them myself, for once I begin my yagna, I must not interrupt it, so please allow me to take your eldest son

---

[8] Vishwamitra particularly asked if Dasharatha's vassals were sending their tributes in a timely manner, and if he was performing all his royal responsibilities dutifully.

for ten days to help me destroy them. He will benefit by learning useful skills from me, and I promise no harm will come to him. Rama is capable of doing the job I ask, and I am sure his guru, Vasishta, will endorse that.'

Hearing his request, Dasharatha was stupefied and shuddered in panic. Once again, perhaps the old curse came flooding back, and he grew disconcerted, wondering how his young boy, though gallant, could be a match for powerful Rakshasas. Despite Vishwamitra's assurance of safety, he was anxious that something untoward would happen to his beloved child and swooned in fear.

When he regained his composure, the mighty king exclaimed in dismay, 'My lotus-eyed Rama is a child not yet sixteen[9] and is far too inexperienced for this dangerous task. Ravana is impossible to defeat, and Rakshasas are deceitful, infamous for disregarding the rules of battle and resorting to all kinds of trickery. Instead of my son, I will come myself with a full Akshauhini[10] army of 21,870 chariots, 21,870 elephants, 65,610 horses and 1,09,350 foot-soldiers to rid you of this threat. Eminent Brahmin, please do not ask for Rama! He was born to me in my old age, begotten with great hardship, and I cannot bear to lose him.'

Vishwamitra's eyes blazed with anger like a fire well-fed with ghee,[11] as he ranted, 'The excessive sentimentality you have for your son is mawkish. Unfortunately, your cloying parental affection makes you go back on your pledge to me. O king, you are a descendant of the great Raghu, and your ancestors prided themselves on keeping their word, no matter the consequence. It is a disgrace that honour is not important to you, and you are forcing me to leave empty-handed. Anyway, be that as it may, I wish you every happiness with your family.'

The air was thick with tension, and all present trembled at Vishwamitra's wrath. Vasishta, the family priest, was alarmed to see the eminent sage

---

[9] Rama's age here is much-debated because the statement could indicate that he was under sixteen or a few years younger. However, later in the story, Sita tells Ravana that Rama was exiled at twenty-five, after they had been married for twelve years; so, taken in conjunction with this, he was thirteen here. Dasharatha protests that Rama is not yet sixteen as that was the age a Kshatriya was considered ready for war.

[10] An Akshauhini was a battle formation that consisted of a specific number of chariots elephants, horses and infantry—21,870 chariots, 21,870 elephants, 65,610 horses and 1,09,350 foot-soldiers.

[11] Clarified butter.

storming out and quickly intervened. He advised, 'Dasharatha, don't go back on your word and bring shame to your family name. Vishwamitra is a learned man, who has attained the pinnacle of yogic abilities, and I can assure you that no one is more familiar with his mystic powers than I am. He knows the use of every kind of weapon in the three worlds, so Rama is perfectly safe with him. You must understand he is entirely capable of dealing with the fiends himself and is asking for Rama for his good. Any consternation on your part is unwarranted, so do not be reluctant in giving your consent to send Rama with the rishi as he has requested.'

Despite Dasharatha's unease, his guru's counsel somewhat reassured him, so he finally relented to Vishwamitra's demand. Kissing Rama on the forehead, he entrusted him to the sage, and knowing that Lakshmana could not stay apart from his brother, he sent him along on the quest, too.

Vishwamitra was an imposing man, who radiated splendour. He had the mental strength of a yogi[12] and the physical prowess of a warrior. This unusual combination was because he was not always a Brahmin; he was born Kaushika, son of Gadhi, a Kshatriya king of the Kusha dynasty. Under his guidance, the second chapter in the princes' education began. Rama and Lakshmana followed Vishwamitra close at his heels as they walked along the southern banks of the river Sarayu. They had covered about twelve miles when the sun began to set and Vishwamitra said, 'Take some water in your hands. I will teach you two powerful mantras, the fountainhead of success: Bala[13] and Atibala.[14] If you chant these, you will not feel hunger, thirst or fatigue. Recite these every day, and no one will be able to defeat you.' This instruction was just the beginning of many valuable teachings Vishwamitra imparted to them.

That night, the princes slept under the stars on a bed of grass, remarkably at ease on the hard ground as if they were in their palace beds. The next day, Vishwamitra woke them up at the crack of dawn with the words, 'Arise, O Rama, glorious son of Kaushalya, tiger amongst men. It is time to take a dip in the river and do your duty of morning worship.' So, after chanting the

---

[12] A practitioner of yoga, not the exercise programme as it is understood today, but attaining union with the cosmic consciousness. Yoga is the path to achieving communion with God/universal consciousness in samadhi or bliss.

[13] Bala means strong.

[14] Atibala means very strong.

Gayatri Mantra[15] and performing their Sandhya Vandana, the trio continued their journey, walking until they reached the confluence of the Sarayu and the Ganga. There they came upon a holy hermitage and halted for the night. Vishwamitra told them that this was the very spot where Kama,[16] the Deva of love, was burnt to ashes by Shiva's third eye when he disturbed the great Lord's penance with his flowery arrows.[17] The following day, they crossed the Ganga, and as they made their way, Vishwamitra entertained them with fascinating stories associated with the rivers, mountains and cities they passed. Then, all at once, before them stretched a terrifying forest inhabited by the mother of Maricha and Subahu, a villainous woman called Tataka.

Vishwamitra told the princes about her wickedness. He explained, 'This forsaken place where no birds sing was once occupied by people and home to many animals. In happier times, there used to be two kingdoms here: Malad and Karush. A brave Yaksha[18] called Suketu lived here with his beautiful daughter, Tataka, but she became cruel over the years and started harassing innocent people. When she made the mistake of attacking Agastya's ashram,[19] he cursed her to take on a hideous form, and she developed rakshasa qualities. Due to her devastation, only deadly insects and vicious predators remain in this sinister forest. All others have fled in fear of her reign of terror. Tataka is immensely powerful and has the strength of a thousand elephants. Since she is a man-eating ogress, who does not abide by dharma, you must kill her, as it is your Kshatriya duty to protect the innocent and punish the unrighteous. Do not hesitate to challenge her on account of her gender. She is evil personified, and it is not a crime to kill someone who is a scourge to society, even if it happens to be a woman. This righteous execution has precedence, and no sin accrues when an action is performed selflessly for humanity's welfare. Tataka cannot continue hiding her impiety behind her womanhood, so show her no mercy.'

---

[15] The Gayatri Mantra is the most revered Vedic hymn. It is a prayer dedicated to the sun, a glorious manifestation of the supreme consciousness. It demonstrates the unity of all creation and was contributed to the Rig Veda by Vishwamitra.

[16] Kama is the Vedic deity of love, like Cupid.

[17] This refers to the story in which the Devas try to get Shiva to break his penance to marry Parvati.

[18] Yakshas were nature spirits.

[19] One of the seven great Vedic sages. He features in greater detail later in the story.

Rama replied, bowing reverently, 'My father ordered me to obey you, so I will do as you ask. It is my solemn duty to carry out your command as my guru to further the good of the people.' He knew he would have to choose the higher dharma in this moral conflict.[20]

To draw Tataka out of her lair, Rama pulled his bowstring sharply, and a deafening twang resounded through the forest. So loud was the sound that Tataka was stunned for a moment. Then, incensed with rage at the audacious provocation and maddened by the scent of human flesh, she came rushing out, kicking up vast clouds of swirling dust. Gigantic in size, with an ugly, contorted face, Tataka began her frenzied attack, creating various illusions, changing into horrible forms and turning invisible from time to time. A fierce battle ensued, but still unable to bring himself to kill a woman, Rama decided to maim her into submission instead. He shot two arrows that struck Tataka's arms, hoping to stop her, but the mutilation only served to enrage her further, and she resumed her attack with renewed fury. Lakshmana then sent an arrow that cut off her ears and the tip of her nose, but Tataka was unfazed, because Rakshasas were demonic and far more powerful than humans. They also had magical powers and could shapeshift at will, so sometimes she was there and sometimes not.

The princes found themselves blinded by dust and assailed with a shower of stones from all sides. Realizing the vulnerability of the situation, Vishwamitra cautioned, 'Your hesitation is dangerous! Cast aside your tenderness and get rid of her quickly. She already has the strength of 1000 elephants; twilight is fast approaching, and Rakshasas gain greater vigour as darkness falls.' Rama could not see Tataka clearly, but he was an excellent archer, and like his father, was skilled at piercing a target hidden from view. So, he lifted his bow, aiming carefully in the direction of the sound, and with one swift arrow shot Tataka in the breast, felling the monstrous creature to the ground. Vishwamitra was overjoyed! He embraced his protege and said warmly, 'I am very pleased with you, O glorious prince. You have shown great courage for one so young. May you always be victorious in battle, and

---

[20] Dharma is complicated because it does not involve specific commandments. The right thing to do is determined based on context and conscience. The killing of Tataka is one of the many situations where conflicting dharmas are depicted in the Ramayana. Manusmriti 9.232 says: 'Those who kill women, children or scholarly people should be given the strictest punishment.' Although killing a woman was considered a sin in Vedic times, in this case, Vishwamitra argues it is a just action.

to that end, I will impart to you my knowledge of the most sought-after supernatural weapons. Now let us rest for the night, for you must be weary from your effort. Tomorrow, my teaching will begin.'

Ancient weapons were classified as 'shastras',[21] handheld physical devices like the sword, bow or mace; and voice-controlled 'astras', which were projectile weapons. Astras functioned as missiles but were not material objects; they were extraordinary energies harnessed and imbued into any ordinary weapon by chanting special incantations called mantras.[22] Vishwamitra gave Rama the knowledge of fifty such missiles that invoked powerful forces, like fire by the Agniastra, deluge by the Varunastra and storms by the Vayuastra. He gave him the Danda Chakra, the Kala Chakra, the Vishnu Chakra, the Indra Chakra and the two mighty javelins presided over by Narayana[23] and Mahadeva.[24] The Gandharva missile could stupefy the enemy, the Praswapana had a hypnotic effect and the Prasamana created passivity. The Varsana, Sosana, Santapana and Vilapana could, in turn, produce rain, dry up moisture, bring on conditions of excessive heat and generate extreme distress. Rama learned to call the Madana of Kamadeva, which inebriated the enemy, the Manava of the Gandharvas[25] and Mohana, which brought on a sense of infatuation. He also received instruction on summoning numerous other weapons, including the invincible Brahmastra, which had the energy of the entire universe and the potential to destroy the whole world. The knowledge of invoking these powerful weapons on demand and directing them in times of need made Rama undefeatable. He even learned the use of Aishikha to weaponize innocuous objects like a blade of grass, so that he was never without a means to protect himself.

Once Vishwamitra had armed Rama with a formidable arsenal of weapons, he said it was time for them to proceed to his hermitage, so he could resume his fire sacrifice. Soon, they reached Siddhashrama, deep in the forest. Ashrams were remote from civilization; they were peaceful

---

[21] Not to be confused with the branches of Vedic knowledge, pronounced 'shaastras'.

[22] A mantra was an utterance that utilized sound technology to create specific effects.

[23] Another name for Vishnu. In Sanskrit 'Nara' means water, which is symbolic of consciousness. 'Ayana' means resting place. Narayana is literally one who rests on water and philosophically, all pervading consciousness.

[24] Another name for Shiva, meaning the greatest deity.

[25] Supernatural beings known for their musical abilities.

retreats where sages practised austerities and engaged in yogic meditation, scholarship and lofty spiritual pursuits. Siddhashrama was a serene spot where Vishnu, in his Vamana[26] avatar, had rid the Asura king Bali of his pride, dispatching him to the netherworld of Patala.[27] It was in this tranquil sanctuary that Vishwamitra practised his penance. His disciples greeted them warmly, and the yagna commenced without delay. Vishwamitra reminded the princes about Tataka's sons, Maricha and Subahu, and asked them to keep a constant vigil for six days and six nights so he could complete the yagna without hindrance.

The two youths dutifully guarded the holy proceedings for five days and five nights without a break as the sacrificial fire blazed and sacred hymns were recited. Finally, on the sixth day, Rama remarked to Lakshmana, 'It has been uneventful so far, but we must be especially cautious now as the yagna is nearing completion.' As soon as he uttered this, Maricha and Subahu appeared with a band of demons, attempting to attack the sanctum and defile the sacrifice with flesh and blood. Though vastly outnumbered, the princes found Vishwamitra's training beneficial. Rama sent a shower of arrows at once to form a canopy over the altar, protecting it from harm. He then called upon the missile of Manu, the Manavastra, which struck Maricha in the chest, flinging him a great distance of 100 yojanas into the sea. Next, he used the weapon of Agni, the Agniastra, which instantly incinerated Subahu and his followers, reducing them to ashes. Thus, Vishwamitra was able to conclude his sacrifice successfully without interference.

---

[26] The fifth avatar of Vishnu, when he incarnated as a dwarf to chasten the powerful Asura king Bali.

[27] Lowest realm of existence.

Chapter 3

The Marriage of Rama and Sita

Everyone slept peacefully that night, untroubled by the nuisance of the Rakshasas. The next day, Rama said humbly to Vishwamitra, 'Holy master, greatest among sages, my father deputed me to your service, so please let me know if there is any other task you have for me.' Smiling kindly, Vishwamitra replied, 'Janaka, the saintly king of Mithila,[1] is performing a fire sacrifice. He has a special bow in his custody that I would like you to see. The Lord of the Universe, the great Shiva, gifted it to Janaka's ancestor Devarata. It is a splendid weapon, enormous and exceedingly heavy. In fact, it is so unwieldy that no one—even among the Devas, Gandharvas or Asuras[2]—has been able to lift it. I would like you to accompany me to view it, and once our purpose there is done, you can return to Ayodhya, while I continue to the Himalayas to perform further austerities.'

Accordingly, they left for Mithila, which lay north of the Ganga, with all of Vishwamitra's disciples in a long train of bullock carts. After the day's travel, they stopped by the banks of the Sona for the night, where they came upon a charming garden in a lush forest. Rama asked Vishwamitra if there was any specific history associated with the spot, so he told them the story of his family, who had lived in this area. 'A great king called Kusha had four sons, Kushamba, Kushanabha, Asoortarajasa and Vasu. They founded four cities Kausambi, Mahodaya, Dharmaranya and Girivraja. Kushanabha lived in this area with his wife, the Apsara[3] Ghritachi. They had 100 daughters, all

---

[1] Located in northern Bihar, bordering Nepal.

[2] The offspring of Diti and Rishi Kashyapa. Supernatural beings who were half-brothers of the Devas.

[3] Apsaras were celestial beauties who were dancers in the court of Indra.

attractive and talented. The girls would sing and dance in the royal garden and one day, Vayu Deva saw them and fell in love with their beauty. He asked them to marry him, but the dutiful girls replied that they would only marry the man chosen by their father. Vayu was angry at being rejected and cursed them to lose their beauty, deforming their limbs. When the girls told their father what had happened, he was impressed by their obedience and arranged for them to marry the pious king Brahmadatta of Kampila. Miraculously, as soon as Brahmadatta touched them, his saintliness restored them to their original beautiful forms. After getting his daughters married, Kushanabha performed a yagna for an heir. In time, he had a son, who came to be known as Gadhi. He was my father. My name is Kaushika, because I am a descendant of Kushanabha. As you can see, my family history is associated with this place, but now the stars and moon are shining, telling us it's time to sleep.'

The next day, as they travelled along the banks of the Ganga, Vishwamitra continued to regale them with tales of the places they passed through. One story was of the Ganga, and how the celestial river was brought down to the plains safely in streams through the matted locks of Shiva. This incredible feat achieved by the perseverance of Rama's ancient ancestor Bhagiratha[4] was undertaken to liberate his predecessors' souls. Bhagiratha succeeded where so many generations of kings before him had failed, and his doggedness gave sustenance and life to the lands the Ganga flowed through. His story is symbolic of how persistent human endeavour can overcome any obstacle, no matter how daunting it appears. In the evening, they stopped at Vishala. Vishwamitra told them that this was where Diti, the mother of the Asuras, had done penance for many years in antiquity to avenge the killing of her sons. King Sumati of Vishala welcomed the travellers as honoured guests and was full of admiration for Rama and Lakshmana when he heard about their victory over the Rakshasas. Then, after partaking of his hospitality overnight, Vishwamitra and the princes resumed their journey.

Just before they reached Mithila, they came upon an eerily deserted hermitage, and when Rama inquired about it, Vishwamitra narrated the tragic story of Ahalya.[5]

---

[4] Therefore, the Ganga is also called the Bhagirathi.

[5] Ahalya was created by Brahma as a flawless woman of great beauty.

He said that for many years, this place served as the ashram of Rishi Gautama,[6] where he practised austerities with his young wife, Ahalya. She was bewitchingly beautiful, and Indra was hopelessly smitten by her. Once, when the sage had stepped out, he appeared in the guise of her husband. The disguise did not fool Ahalya; however, she was flattered that someone as powerful as Indra was interested in her and found herself overcome by uncontrollable desire.

'Beautiful woman,' Indra said, 'I cannot help being enamoured by your loveliness and must consort with you to extinguish the lust burning within me. Since our union is for passion alone, we do not have to wait for the time of the month that facilitates conception, so let us engage with each other right away.' Ahalya felt gladdened by the attention lavished on her and agreed to the tryst. When their passionate encounter ended, she expressed satisfaction with the experience, but asked Indra to leave quickly before her husband returned.

Unfortunately for Ahalya, Rishi Gautama arrived just as Indra was making a hasty retreat. Seeing their guilty faces, he instantly realized what had taken place, and his anger knew no bounds. Gautama cursed Indra to become a eunuch for his crime of seduction. He then turned to his wayward wife and punished her for her infidelity to endure a life of penance for many years in complete isolation. 'You will reside here in solitude,' he said, 'unnoticed by anyone, living on air, without food, and sleeping on ashes. You will live like this in the atonement of your unchecked desires until the high-souled one called Rama comes to see you. His purity will be your redemption, and once you absolve yourself of your indiscretion, you can return to live with me as my wife.'

Vishwamitra concluded that Ahalya was a decent woman, but she lacked self-control, and that one fatal flaw caused her to transgress from the path of dharma. Rama was moved by Ahalya's rigorous penance, for he believed that even the greatest of sins were forgiven by sincere repentance. When they entered the ashram, they found her seated in prayer, shining brightly as a result of the many years of strict austerity she had undergone. Rama and Lakshmana touched her feet, and Ahalya redeemed herself through her austerity as predicted. Rishi Gautama appeared, and the husband and wife reunited once again.

---

[6] Gautama was one of the seven great Vedic rishis.

Mithila was the capital of the kingdom of Videha,[7] a centre of culture, learning and scholarship. Seeradhwaja, who held the title of Janaka like every king before him, was its sapient and selfless ruler. He was known as the 'Hermit King' because he was more a seeker of enlightenment than a warrior. Although he was the monarch of a great kingdom, Janaka had freed himself of worldly attachments and interested himself in spiritual discourse rather than material aggrandizement. He would keep just enough means to satisfy his basic needs and give away the rest of his wealth to charity. Mithila was an intellectual hub for sages who came from far and wide to discuss and debate high philosophy. Janaka often held marathon sessions that ran into days, even weeks, where proponents of various schools of thought fervently argued their case. In the end, a grand prize was awarded to the one who proved himself most learned.

When Janaka heard that the venerable sage Vishwamitra had arrived at the yagna grounds of his kingdom, he was overjoyed and went out immediately with his family priest, Shatananda, welcoming him with great respect and reverence. Noticing the two striking youths who accompanied him, Janaka could not help being impressed and asked, 'Who are these gallant young men? They look like a pair of Devas, as if the Ashwinis[8] have descended on Earth.' Vishwamitra introduced them as the students of Vasishta, the sons of King Dasharatha of Ayodhya, and narrated how they had killed Tataka and helped him get rid of the Rakshasas that threatened the peace of his hermitage. Janaka was fascinated by the youths, their bravery, dazzling good looks and regal bearing, and was especially taken by Rama. He secretly thought this extraordinary young man would make an excellent match for his precious daughter Sita. Vishwamitra also spoke about the redemption of Ahalya, to the great joy of Shatananda, King Janaka's priest, for he was none other than the son of Ahalya and Gautama. On hearing the news, he exclaimed thankfully, 'May people remember my mother for her life of penance, and not as a fallen woman defined by her unfortunate lapse in judgement.' Then, praising the part Vishwamitra played in reuniting his parents, Shatananda told Rama how lucky he was to have such a great mentor; and to substantiate his assertion, he recounted the incredible story of Vishwamitra's life.

The sage's journey from a mighty Kshatriya warrior called Kaushika to a Brahmin called Vishwamitra, who attained supreme knowledge, was

---

[7] Videha covered north-eastern Bihar and southern Nepal.

[8] Devas who were twin horsemen, known for their healing powers and good looks.

remarkable. King Kaushika and his retinue had once stopped during an expedition at Vasishta's ashram, where they were honoured with a sumptuous feast. The lavish banquet contained foods of all flavours considered necessary to satisfy the taste buds: sweet, salty, bitter, sour, spicy and bland. All this was made possible by the grace of a wish-fulfilling cow called Sabala,[9] a gift from the Devas. Kaushika began to covet the cow of plenty, feeling that he had more use for it as a king than Vasishta, who had renounced worldly pleasures. He offered a 1,00,000 cows in exchange for Sabala, but Vasishta refused, saying that the cow was not for sale no matter the price, as she was inextricably associated with his life of religious practices, and he was dependent on her. Kaushika was undeterred by the denial and increased the payment, offering 14,000 elephants with gold chains, 11,000 prize horses, and 10 crore cows of every breed, but Vasishta still did not budge. In the end, Kaushika, who was not used to being turned down, was incensed, and driven by avarice, ordered his men to take the cow by force.

Sabala was distressed at being grabbed for worldly purposes, so shaking off the soldiers, she ran crying to Vasishta, asserting that her powers were meant to fulfil the disciplined needs of sages, not the unrestrained desires of kings. When Vasishta said that the king with his colossal army was stronger than him, Sabala reminded him that the yogic strength of a Brahmin was far greater than the physical power of a Kshatriya and asked him to use it to command her to resist Kaushika. Vasishta agreed, and Sabala produced legions of warriors who defeated Kaushika's indomitable army in a bitter battle. Seeing this, Kaushika's sons rushed towards Vasishta to kill him; but save one, he turned them all into ashes with a single utterance. It was a tremendous blow to Kaushika's pride, and he was stunned that Vasishta's spiritual energy was more potent than his Kshatriya might.

Shattered by defeat, Kaushika left his kingdom to his remaining son and retired to the Himalayas, vowing to achieve the same powers as his adversary. Invoking Lord Shiva, he meditated in a quest to acquire knowledge of the most powerful weapons in existence to avenge his humiliation. After many years when Kaushika learned the use of every missile, his arrogance swelled, and he was sure his nemesis was now as good as dead. He returned to Vasishta's ashram to seek revenge and assuage his wounded pride. There, he used his newly obtained arsenal of missiles to burn down the ashram,

---

[9] Daughter of Kamadhenu, the celestial cow. Kamadhenu, also called Surubhi, fulfilled every desire and was considered the mother of all cows.

causing all the disciples to flee in terror. However, Vasishta himself could not be killed, as his spiritual energy as a Brahmarishi was so immense that with his humble staff alone, he countered Kaushika's weapons one by one, rendering them ineffective. Forced to accept defeat again, Kaushika realized that even the most formidable weaponry was insignificant compared to the strength attained through yogic meditation. Dejected at his failure, he decided to embark on an even more rigorous penance than before to become like Vasishta.

To this end, Kaushika practised austerities dedicated to Brahma for many years, earning the title of Rajrishi or royal sage. Although commendable, he had fallen short of the spiritual level of Brahmarishi, as he was beset by negative emotions of krodha[10] and kama,[11] and had a long way to go. It disappointed Kaushika that he had not reached his goal; he could not stomach being spiritually inferior to Vasishta, so he decided to work towards his target more zealously than before. Meanwhile, one of Rama's ancestors, a king called Trishanku, came to him for help. He was unnaturally attached to his corporeal form and wanted to go to heaven with his body intact. This desire was an unrealistic expectation that contravened the laws of existence, so when he asked his guru Vasishta to perform a yagna for the purpose, the rishi naturally refused. He then requested Vasishta's 100 sons to help him, but they also declined. When Trishanku told them he would seek another rishi to fulfil his desire, they chastised him for disrespecting his family guru's counsel and cursed him to lose his beautiful body and become a Chandala.[12] In dismay at his unfortunate transformation, Trishanku went to Kaushika for help.

Kaushika felt compassion for Trishanku's predicament, and Vasishta's refusal motivated him to take up the challenge immediately. He promised to send Trishanku to heaven in his body just as he desired, saying the job was as good as done. Kaushika arranged a yagna and sent his disciples to summon all the Brahmins from near and far to join him, telling them to

---

[10] Anger.

[11] Sensual gratification.

[12] Chandalas were not part of the four varnas. They lived in separate communities on the outskirts of the city and did not follow Vedic customs. For instance, they ate dogs, which was considered abominable. However, the difference was only at the physical level, because in spirit they were the same as anyone else. In Vedic philosophy the Brahmin, the dog and the dog-eater have the same divine Atman.

report back if anyone disregarded his request. When Kaushika's disciples approached Vasishta's sons, they laughed, mocking that a yagna performed for an inauspicious purpose by a Kshatriya for a Chandala defied all norms and could never be fruitful. Kaushika's eyes turned red with anger at hearing this. He cursed Vasishta's 100 sons to turn into ashes and condemned them to live on carcasses and dog flesh for seven lives to come. This haughty anger depleted much of Kaushika's spiritual power; nevertheless, he performed the yagna to send Trishanku to heaven with his body.

The Devas did not respond to the prayers offered in the yagna, so Kaushika used his yogic abilities to make Trishanku rise to heaven. However, when Indra saw him ascending, he intervened and pushed him back to earth. Tumbling down headlong, Trishanku shouted for help, and Kaushika arrested his fall, promising to create an alternate heaven for him. The Devas were now perturbed, so they appeared before Kaushika and explained that Trishanku's wish was against the natural order. Even so, Kaushika insisted on keeping his word, so the Devas made a compromise and agreed to keep Trishanku[13] as a star shining brightly in the heavens forever. Though the matter concluded there, Kaushika had expended all the spiritual merit he had previously earned due to his anger and arrogance, so he went to the Pushkara Lakes in the west to perform further austerities to regain what he had lost.

Unfortunately, Kaushika kept getting distracted by various interferences and could not concentrate with a single-minded focus. After overcoming many interruptions, his attention was diverted again when he chanced to see a beautiful Apsara called Maneka bathing in a lake. Her beauty was electrifying like lightning, and overwhelmed by passion, Kaushika invited her to live with him at his hermitage. They remained lost in love for many seasons as the years rolled by like a single day, without realizing whether it was day or night. Suddenly, after ten years had elapsed, Kaushika felt guilty that he had allowed himself to become distracted from his objective by physical desire. So, he sent Maneka away and went to the Himalayas to resume his quest to become a Brahmarishi. Years passed, and Brahma conferred the title of Maharishi[14] on him.

Kaushika was still not in complete control of his senses; since the title of Brahmarishi eluded him, he now strove even harder to attain it. His focus was so intense that Indra decided to test the immense spiritual merit he was

---

[13] Trishanku is the triple star system Alpha Centauri—The Southern Cross.

[14] Maharishi means great seer.

earning and devised a plan to distract him. As Kaushika was meditating, he approached in the form of a cuckoo bird, along with a beautiful Apsara called Rambha and the Deva of Love, Kama. While Indra melodiously cooed, Rambha sang and danced seductively. However, Kaushika sensed the entrapment and flew into a rage, cursing Rambha to turn to stone. He had successfully controlled sexual desire, but anger that negated spiritual merit still plagued him. Kaushika realized that this shortcoming was impeding his spiritual progress. He took an oath to rid himself of all negative emotions by practising extreme austerities, living on air alone, facing the elements, rain, heat and cold unprotected, with his arms clasped in prayer over his head.

He proceeded to the east and remained in deep yogic meditation for years without food, never wavering, although his body became emaciated like a stick. When he finally broke his fast, Indra appeared again just as he sat down to eat, this time in the guise of a Brahmin begging for food.[15] Kaushika gave away his meal without hesitation, and though he knew who the Brahmin was, he felt no anger towards him. After this, Kaushika embarked on the most arduous penance of all, putting himself in a deep spiritual trance and suspending respiration until not a single flaw remained. Eventually, the time came when he finally conquered the six impediments to spiritual illumination: kama—desire, krodha—anger, moha—attachment, lobha—greed, madha—pride, and matsarya—envy.[16]

At last, Kaushika had achieved complete perfection, and Brahma welcomed him as a Brahmarishi. He had transformed himself into an enlightened being by gaining the highest knowledge[17] and became Vishwamitra, literally a friend of the whole world. He was cleansed of all toxic emotions and had gained total control of his senses, rid of the very impetus that initially drove him to pursue his goal. His pride was humbled, and with all traces of hostility gone, he sought Vasishta's forgiveness, leading the life of an ascetic from that time onwards. Vishwamitra listened to the narration of his life story without displaying any emotion as Shatananda recounted both the good and the bad he had done. He had genuinely evolved in his inner journey and had gained complete mastery over his senses.

---

[15] Brahmins lived on charity, begging for their food, so it was considered a sin to refuse them alms.

[16] Vishwamitra's progress is one from *rajas* (passion) to *sattva* (purity).

[17] The highest knowledge is understanding that one consciousness pervades the whole universe.

The company retired for the night, and the following day, Vishwamitra took Rama and Lakshmana to Janaka, saying that they were eager to see Shiva's bow. Janaka was delighted, and explained how the bow came into the possession of his ancestor Devarata. He also happily narrated the story of Sita's adoption. King Janaka and his queen, Sunaina, had been childless for many years when Sita came into their life most unusually. There was a period when the kingdom of Videha was afflicted by severe drought, resulting in a terrible famine that caused great suffering. King Janaka was distraught; he could not bear to see his people go through such adversity and sought the advice of the sages. They instructed him to plough the land himself as an act of penance to usher the much-needed rainfall to his kingdom. While tilling the field, Janaka struck a hard object. When he moved the soil aside and reached down into the furrow, to his amazement, he found a box. Lying inside was a beautiful baby girl! King Janaka was captivated; his heart overflowed with affection for the tiny infant. At once, he declared the abandoned child his own and named her Sita, which means 'furrow' in Sanskrit. Later, Sita came to be known by many names: Janaki, because she was Janaka's daughter; Maithili, the princess of Mithila; Vaidehi, because she was from the kingdom of Videha; and Bhumija, one born of the earth.

Sita grew into an exquisitely beautiful and accomplished young woman. She was her father's darling, raised with great tenderness and staunch adherence to dharma, along with her sister Urmila, born a year after her discovery in the field. Her cousins Mandavi and Shrutakirti, daughters of Janaka's brother Kushadhwaja, were also close companions. Tidings of Sita's beauty spread far and wide, and suitors came from many lands to seek her hand in marriage. However, King Janaka wanted her to marry someone genuinely worthy, an outstanding person unequalled in valour. Therefore, he decided to give her hand in marriage only to the man who could lift and string Lord Shiva's great bow, knowing this feat was impossible for an ordinary person. From time to time, kings and princes came to Mithila with great aspiration to try their luck with the bow. Each left disappointed; no one succeeded in moving it even one inch, let alone lifting and stringing it. In fact, at one point, the frustrated suitors, aggrieved by their futility, even banded together and waged war on Mithila for an entire year to soothe their wounded pride.

Vishwamitra was sure that Rama could accomplish the task, so he said, 'O king, my students, the two glorious sons of Dasharatha, are keen to see the grand bow that is in your safekeeping. Please show it to them.' Janaka gladly obliged and commanded the bow to be brought out. It took 5000 well-built men to propel the large iron[18] chest mounted on eight wheels, containing the bow. Janaka spoke of how princes from all races—the foremost amongst the Devas, Yakshas,[19] Gandharvas, Asuras, Kinnaras[20] and Nagas[21]—had tried and failed at his challenge to string it. Hearing this, Vishwamitra turned to Rama and said, 'Open the chest and behold the venerated bow adorned with sandalwood paste and flowers.' Rama dutifully walked towards the chest, and asked if he could lift and string the bow. Janaka was only too happy to give his permission, and to the astonishment of all those present, Rama grasped it in the middle and picked it up effortlessly. He then proceeded to string it, pulling it to his ear, when suddenly there was a loud noise that reverberated like a crash of thunder, and the giant bow snapped in half. King Janaka looked on in delight and utter disbelief at the extraordinary feat. Rama, a mere youth, had succeeded when so many seasoned warriors in the past had failed. Then, with great pleasure, he announced, 'My pledge for my Sita to be married only to a man of great courage stands redeemed today. I feel reassured that my treasured child, who is dearer to me than life itself, will wed someone exceptional.'

Riders were dispatched immediately to Ayodhya, bearing the good news of Rama's incredible achievement in winning Sita's hand in marriage. Dasharatha was overjoyed, and set out with Bharata, Shatrughana and a large entourage, including his counsellors and ministers, on the four-day journey to Mithila. An army protected the long procession of palanquins and chariots as they travelled, carrying abundant gifts and precious jewels. Simultaneously, grand arrangements were in full force in Mithila as the city prepared for the royal guests. Janaka sent for his brother Kushadhwaja, the king of Sankashya, and he arrived immediately for the auspicious event.

---

[18] The Iron Age ostensibly began around 1200 BCE, but the reference to iron in the Ramayana dated to the fifth millennium BCE indicates that it was already known. Recent dating of iron artefacts in Egypt, China and Iran go back to the fourth millennium BCE. Also, excavations in Tamil Nadu, India have unearthed iron artefacts dating back 4200 years, so the 1200 BCE date needs to be revisited.

[19] Nature spirits—followers of Kubera, the Vedic guardian of the northern quarter.

[20] Supernatural beings who were musicians like the Gandharvas. Kinnaras often had a human body and an animal head, or vice versa.

[21] Supernatural beings who were part-human and part-snake but could assume either a wholly human or serpent form.

Dasharatha was received with high honour when he reached Mithila, and was elated to see his sons again.

The family priests from each side, Vasishta and Shatananda, presided over discussions on the wedding arrangements, exchanging the bride and groom's noble ancestry. Rama traced his line to Ikshavaku,[22] eldest son of the progenitor Manu, and Sita from King Nimi,[23] celebrated for his piety in all three worlds. Nimi was succeeded by Mithi, after whom Mithila got its name. He was the first Janaka, and after him, every king in the line bore that title. During the talks, Janaka offered his daughter Urmila in marriage to Lakshmana. Dasharatha gladly accepted the proposal, and when Vishwamitra and Vasishta jointly suggested that it would be even more advantageous to see Bharata married to Mandavi and Shatrughana to Shrutakirti, he agreed to this, too. Not only were the families well matched, but this would further strengthen the alliance between the two kingdoms. With much jubilation, it was decided that the four princes would be married to the four princesses on the same day.

The celebrations were magnificent! Blessings were elicited on auspicious occasions by charitable giving, which was considered meritorious. Dasharatha, the doting father, gave away 4,00,000 cows with gold-capped horns in the name of his four sons. Janaka had a grand pavilion erected for the ceremony, decorated with beautiful flowers. In the centre was the sacred altar smeared with sandalwood paste. The wedding arrangements were conducted very precisely according to Vedic scriptural ordinance. Jars and platters of gold were filled with various ingredients like holy water and turmeric-stained rice needed to perform the sacred rites. Vessels of incense were provided, and long ladles made of Palasa wood to pour oblations into the fire. The venerable Vasishta officiated at the four weddings. As he fed the fire[24] with copious quantities of ghee and chanted verses from the Rig Veda, the couples, hand in hand, circled the sacrificial fire clockwise.

Seven steps together representing seven vows tied the couples in holy matrimony. The first step was a prayer for nourishment in married life. The bridegroom promised to provide adequate sustenance in his duty as a householder, and the bride gave her word that she would share in the

---

[22] The lineage of the Solar dynasty is given in the Appendices.

[23] The story of Nimi is told in the Epilogue.

[24] Fire is considered sacred because it can never be polluted and is central to the Vedic wedding ceremony. All marriage vows are solemnized before the fire to be binding.

responsibility of their household. The second step signified a commitment of strength and togetherness in sickness and health, in good times and bad. The third step was an invocation for prosperity in family life and a pledge of loyalty to each other. The fourth step taken was for happiness and an oath to love and serve each other and their family elders. The fifth step sought blessings for virtuous progeny and was a vow to be caring parents. The sixth step was a wish for a long life together, good health and freedom from disease. The seventh and final step was an assurance to each other of everlasting love and friendship and an undertaking to live together in harmony forever, not only in this lifetime but in all future lives. As Janaka put Sita's hand in Rama's in the ritual of Panigrahana,[25] he said fondly, 'Take my virtuous daughter Sita to be your steadfast companion in good times and bad. I am placing her hand in yours in this sacred rite that signifies she will always be your faithful partner in dharma.'[26] Thus, the wedding ceremony solemnized Rama and Sita's union in a marriage where they would be like kindred souls.[27] Rama was so captivated by his lovely princess that he never took another wife, in deviation from the convention of the age. In fact, over the years, their deep attachment would become immortalized as one of the greatest love stories of all time.

Once the celebrations concluded, having played his part in arranging the marriages of the princes of Ayodhya with the princesses of Mithila, Vishwamitra said to Rama, 'I have achieved my mission here and must now retire to the Himalayas to continue my meditation.' Rama bowed low and touched his feet in obeisance. He would remember the great sage's teachings in the lifetime of accomplishments that lay ahead. No matter what obstacle came his way or what trials and tribulations he faced, he never wavered from his Kshatriya dharma, fighting tirelessly to protect the innocent and destroy the wicked. The next day, the hour arrived for the princesses to bid farewell to Mithila, leaving behind everything they had known so far to start a new life. King Janaka sent them to Ayodhya loaded with gifts that included cows, horses, elephants, chariots, carpets, delicate silk fabrics, cotton, silver, gold and gems. He also sent a hundred handmaidens to care for their every need. Janaka knew he would miss the girls, especially Sita, but he felt comforted in

---

[25] Literally 'taking the hand'.

[26] The word used by Valmiki is 'sahadharmacharini', partner in dharma.

[27] In Vedic belief, a husband and wife are considered two indivisible halves of a whole.

the knowledge that they would continue to receive the same love and respect he had showered on them, in their new home.

A strange event took place on their return journey to disturb the peace. All appeared to be going well when suddenly the sky darkened; a storm seemed to approach, and the earth shook as an imposing figure loomed before them. He had matted locks, an axe in his right hand and an enormous bow slung over his left shoulder. This fearsome character was the powerful sage Parasurama.[28] The king of the Haihayas, Kartaviryaarjuna, had wrongly killed his father, and from that day, Parasurama vowed to eradicate all Kshatriyas. He deemed them corrupt and would kill them indiscriminately. Many years of rigorous yogic penance gave him enormous strength and the ability to transport himself anywhere instantly.

The sight of Parasurama unnerved Dasharatha, and fearing for his sons' safety, he pleaded with the sage not to harm them. However, Parasurama ignored the king, and singling out Rama, arrogantly challenged him. 'I have heard of your prowess and recent accomplishment of breaking Lord Shiva's bow. It was no minor achievement, but Vishwakarma, the engineer of the Devas, had fashioned two identical bows. You broke the one that belonged to Shiva, and I have the other owned by Lord Vishnu and given to his devotee, my grandfather Richika. If you can string it and shoot an arrow, I will believe you are truly valorous and will give you the privilege of duelling with me.'

Rama noted Parasurama's provocative tone but did not want to be discourteous. He replied firmly, yet politely, 'I, too, have heard of your prowess and fearsome reputation of exterminating all Kshatriyas to avenge your father's death. While I understand your feelings, I am proud to be a Kshatriya, so do not think I am afraid of you.' He confidently seized Lord Vishnu's bow and marked it with an arrow, declaring, 'An arrow once drawn must not go in vain. I cannot harm you because you are the grandnephew of my guru Vishwamitra. Where then should I aim it; at your accumulated powers of penance or the power by which you transport yourself instantly anywhere you wish?' Parasurama could not afford to lose his teleportation ability because of a promise he had made to retire from habitation at night, so he gave up all the spiritual merit he had earned in a chastening of his arrogance. Humbled by his defeat, he acknowledged Rama's heroism, and giving his blessings, left for his abode in Mount Mahendra. Rama then

---

[28] Parasu is an axe, so the name Parasurama means Rama who bears an axe.

handed Vishnu's bow to Varuna by immersing it in water, and thenceforth, they continued uneventfully to Ayodhya.

The people of Ayodhya rejoiced and gave the princes and their brides a hearty welcome amidst great pomp and splendour. Conches blared in fanfare, and flags fluttered proudly on tall poles. Their path was sprinkled with rose water and strewn with flowers. The citizens lined the streets to catch a glimpse of their beloved princes, especially Rama, whom they adored. Kaushalya, Sumitra and Kaikeyi received their sons and new daughters-in-law with the aarti[29] ritual. There was much happiness all around as the princes settled into married life and royal duties. The bond between Rama and Sita grew stronger every day, and they lived in the harmony of wedded bliss. Each dwelled in the other's heart, and their companionship was so deep that they could communicate without the need for words. They were indeed like a single soul housed in two bodies. People said that Sita's love was twice as much as Rama's, and his adoration for her was double hers for him! He was an ideal husband, and she was a model wife. They were a devoted couple like Vishnu and Lakshmi,[30] completely contented in their relationship.

Since Rama was the eldest son, he was the crown prince, and Dasharatha began to instruct him on various state matters, including the citizens' welfare. The old king felt gratified that his son was praiseworthy in every way. Rama respected everyone equally regardless of their station in life. He had the rare combination of physical power and strength of character, never straying from the path of righteousness. A harsh word did not escape his lips, nor was he upset by any unkindness shown to him. Rama was always calm and soft-spoken, showing tremendous gratitude even for the tiniest favour he received, taking no one nor anything for granted. Mendacity was unknown to him, and he always remained steadfast to his word. His ability to stay humble was commendable, given his charming appearance and great intellectual prowess. He was a master of debate, and no one could match his wit or eloquence; yet he was never arrogant or disrespectful towards his opponents.

A talented musician himself, Rama was a great connoisseur of the arts. He was never envious and always compassionate, thinking of the well-being

[29] A ritual performed with incense and a flame, either done to worship a deity or to honour someone.

[30] Vishnu and Lakshmi are aspects of the supreme consciousness referred to as God. Vishnu is the sustainer of life, and his divine consort, Lakshmi, is associated with good fortune or prosperity. Together, they symbolize the ideal couple.

of others above his interests. The company of erudite people was a source of delight to Rama, and his deep spirituality coupled with a strong sense of Kshatriya duty made him worthy of his noble lineage. He had mastered the Vedas and had a command over the Vedangas, its six auxiliary branches: phonetics, grammar, prosody, etymology, astronomy and liturgy. He was pragmatic and knowledgeable in all aspects of ruling a kingdom, including warfare, jurisprudence, politics, economics and international relations, and was always resourceful in dealing with problems. In a nutshell, Rama was a person of stellar qualities rarely found in one individual, which earned him universal admiration. True to the meaning of his name, Rama was a delight to everyone, and Dasharatha felt secure that his beloved kingdom would be protected after him.

BOOK 2
Ayodhya

Chapter 4

Dasharatha Chooses an Heir

Many moons went by in peace and tranquillity. Then one day, Queen Kaikeyi's brother Yudhajit unexpectedly arrived in Ayodhya. He said that his father, King Ashwapati, was ailing and wished to see his grandson Bharata, so he had come to fetch the young prince. Since Shatrughana was very attached to Bharata, he decided to go along. When they left for Kekaya, no one could have imagined that this mundane event would be of such great consequence!

After ruling for many years, Dasharatha began to feel his age and decided to plan his succession. The burden of the crown had become tiresome, and seeing how adept Rama was at managing his royal duties, it felt appropriate to proclaim him heir apparent officially. Wearied by his long reign, the ageing monarch now looked forward to spending his final years in retirement, free from the cares of the kingdom. Moreover, crowning Rama would ensure that he could ascend to heaven peacefully when the time came, knowing that his beloved Ayodhya was in good hands.

So, one beautiful spring morning in the month of Chaitra, Dasharatha called a special session of his assembly to ask for their approval in naming Rama his successor. Invitations went out to prominent kings and tribal chieftains from all over—but strangely, his close allies, Ashwapati and Janaka, were not called. He rationalized that they would be happy with the news and would not feel offended at being left out.

Addressing the assembly in his deep baritone voice, Dasharatha proposed Rama's name as next in line. He said, 'I have ruled for a long time, during which I have lovingly served the people, always prioritizing their well-being above all else. But now I am getting old, and the responsibility of governing needs to pass to the next generation. I think the time has come

43

for me to hand over my crown, and I would like to suggest my eldest son Rama's name as my replacement. The kings in my lineage have always put the people's welfare before themselves, and I feel Rama has proved himself worthy of taking on this responsibility. In archery, his skills are unmatched, and he has never lost a battle. Although Rama is a mighty warrior and an expert commander of the troops, he is never boastful of his accomplishments.

'Additionally, I find he has shown great wisdom in all matters of administration, including prudent fiscal management of the treasury. He is especially adept at collecting taxes without putting an undue burden on the subjects. People look up to Rama, and he commands respect on account of his noble deeds, not because he is feared. No one is a more persuasive debater than he is, yet he never belittles his opponents. Aside from Rama's aptitude as a leader, he has a sparkling personality and many extracurricular talents, including proficiency in music and sports. I am confident that he will be a just and able king as he is righteous, truthful, free from envy, and above all, he is altruistic, never driven by self-interest. Please let me know if you agree with my proposal, and if not, feel free to advise me on an alternative that might be for the greater good.'

The council members applauded and agreed unanimously to the proposition, for everyone admired Rama; but Dasharatha was careful not to force his decision on his subjects. He did not want to thrust his bias as a fond father on anyone inadvertently. To make sure that his people had not given their concurrence merely to please him, Dasharatha pressed them further. 'I feel Rama is eminently qualified to take over from me because he exudes both power and grace to do the job competently. But I trust your agreement is not solely to satisfy my wishes? Please give me the reasons for your consent because I hope you have given it freely without constraint.'[1]

The assembly replied enthusiastically, 'We have been waiting to hear this announcement for so long! Rama is supreme among men in every noble trait, the very embodiment of truth and integrity. He is so accomplished that he could be entrusted with ruling all three worlds, not just one kingdom. It is truly praiseworthy that Rama always keeps dharma in mind while pursuing artha.[2] Despite his high position, he is courteous to everyone, never treating

---

[1] A Vedic king was not a despot; he had a responsibility to his people, believing his happiness lay in their welfare. Therefore, a good king was not an autocrat and ruled by consensus.

[2] Wealth and prosperity. Refer to Purushartha, described in the Appendices.

anyone as inferior. While exuding natural charisma, Rama is as brilliant as Brihaspati[3] and as fearless as Indra. Besides this, he is proficient in the arts and has a superior knowledge of the Gandharva[4] Veda. There is no one more powerful than Rama, always returning victorious from every expedition. Yet, the noble prince is empathetic and compassionate; when he is out in the city riding on an elephant or in his chariot, he makes it a point to stop and ask about people's concerns. Rama is so approachable that he has endeared himself to all and is constantly in everyone's prayers, wishing him a long life, health and happiness.'

Dasharatha was pleased to hear their response and asked Sumantra to fetch Rama, so he could formally proclaim his coronation. Everyone in the assembly looked on in admiration as he arrived, announcing himself and bowing respectfully. The king declared with great pride, 'You are my eldest son, born of my senior wife, and not only are you my favourite, but you are also the darling of the people. The Parishad has consented without exception to your nomination, so I want to declare you my heir officially. Once you are king, remember to always remain in control of your senses. Stay away from addictions like womanizing, gambling, hunting and drinking. You will have enormous power at your discretion, so always use it discerningly. Be a wise ruler, and never give anyone too harsh a punishment or indulge in wasteful expenditure.'

After the larger assembly dispersed, Dasharatha met with his inner circle of ministers and spiritual counsellors to discuss details of the upcoming ceremony. He decided to have the coronation performed without delay the following day, when Pushya was in the ascendant,[5] so he sent for Rama again to talk about the matter more informally. Rama entered his father's presence once more, bowing low with his hands folded, showing deep regard for his aged parent. Being in a more private setting than the larger assembly, Dasharatha affectionately pulled him to his bosom and said, 'I have lived life to the fullest and have achieved everything I set out to do. All my obligations as king are complete, and I only have one task left in life: to place you on the throne. Unfortunately, I have been plagued by bad dreams recently, and

---

[3] The learned guru of the Devas known for his intelligence.

[4] One of the four Upavedas or applied knowledge derived from the four Vedas. It covers the art of music.

[5] Pushya is the eighth star in the zodiac and was Rama's birth star. Since Pushya was in the ascendant the following day, it was an auspicious time for him.

the stars do not bode well for me, as malevolent influences shadow my birth planet. I have a strange premonition of impending misfortune, so even though it may seem unduly hasty, I want to install you as my successor without delay tomorrow morning. The astrologers say Pushya is an auspicious hour, and I am keen to crown you prince regent quickly before any unanticipated impediment comes in the way.'

Then, Dasharatha made an unusual comment that Rama did not quite understand until much later. He added, 'I realize Bharata is not here at present to share in this joyful occasion, but perhaps it's for the best. I do not doubt his virtue, but even so, human nature can be unpredictable.' He concluded by instructing, 'You need to prepare for the ceremony with your wife, sanctifying your minds through fasting and prayer. In accordance with the tradition of practising humility, tonight you must sleep on the floor on a bed of darbha[6] grass with a stone slab for a pillow. Depart now and begin your preparations, as time is short.'

Rama felt honoured by his father's confidence in him and proceeded to his mother Kaushalya's residence to inform her about his new responsibility. Hearing about the upcoming event, Sumitra arrived with Lakshmana and Sita at Kaushalya's palace,[7] and the two mothers shed tears of joy in anticipation of the forthcoming consecration. Then Rama turned to Lakshmana and said, 'This fortune bestowed upon me belongs to you, too, dear brother. You are my life, and I intend for you to rule this land with me.' Lakshmana's heart was filled with gratitude, love and admiration for his elder brother, while Sita looked dotingly at her husband, pleased that he had been justly rewarded.

Dasharatha handed over the coronation arrangements to his priests, Vasishta and Vamadeva. The month of Chaitra marked the season of new beginnings, and it seemed nature, too, was celebrating the big event, resplendent with brightly coloured blossoms that covered the trees. Each minister had a specific area to organize, and the coronation would strictly follow stipulated Vedic guidelines. Everything needed for the ceremony had to be procured by the following day, including garlands of white flowers, parched rice, honey, curds, ghee, 100 gold pitchers, several cows and a bull with gold-plated horns. In addition, they required a white umbrella and a ceremonial elephant from amongst the best. The army's four divisions would

---

[6] Also called kusha grass. It was considered sacred and used in Vedic rituals, and to make prayer mats. Darbha also has healing properties and is used in Ayurveda.

[7] Each queen had her own residence.

salute their new king with uniformed soldiers standing at attention. The main street was sprinkled with water to settle the dust, and the whole city was decorated with flags and garlands. Incense filled the air with a sweet fragrance. Food and gifts were organized, and seating arrangements made for 1,00,000 Brahmins. At dawn, the deities in the temples and at the crossroads were to be worshipped. Hymns of purity would be sung, and dance performances would provide entertainment for the grand occasion.

The news of the coronation circulated quickly, spreading like wildfire through the city, and there was great exuberance amongst the people. After all, their beloved prince was going to be their king! However, there was one inhabitant who was not rejoicing like everyone else. Manthara was an old hunchback maidservant of Queen Kaikeyi, with a cantankerous nature and quarrelsome reputation. She had mysterious antecedents, and little was known about her except that she had come to Ayodhya with Kaikeyi when she accompanied her as a new bride. She was Kaikeyi's caregiver from childhood and was like a mother to her, so they shared a special relationship. That afternoon, it so happened that Manthara looked out of a high balcony and noticed the festivities in the city. She was surprised to see Kaushalya giving away cows in charity and was curious about the reason for this, when she spotted one of Kaushalya's maids dressed in celebratory silk. Manthara stopped her and inquired about the enthusiasm outside and why Kaushalya, who was usually tight-fisted, was suddenly so free with her wealth that day. The maid burst out in delight that the excitement was because of Rama's coronation as the crown prince the following day. Her words about the upcoming event made Manthara burn with envy, as she could not bear the thought of her beloved Kaikeyi losing her exalted position to Kaushalya once the latter became queen mother. In that instant, she decided that she had to do everything possible to prevent the coronation from taking place; but how could she, a humble servant, achieve this?

Manthara hobbled furiously to her mistress, barging unceremoniously into her chamber as she lay reposing on her bed and cried out, 'Wake up, foolish girl! You lie here blissfully unaware of a great peril that awaits you. Your crafty husband, who professes to love you most amongst his wives, is deceiving you, my guileless child. He sent Bharata to his grandfather to get him out of the way and is now planning to make Rama his heir.'

Manthara took the liberty of talking to the queen in this insubordinate manner because of the close association they shared, and Kaikeyi was not offended by her disrespectful tone. Springing up from her bed in delight, she looked at her incredulously and exclaimed, 'What calamity are you prattling about so hysterically? You have given me the most welcome news! Whether my son Bharata or my son Rama is crowned king, it is all the same. I make no difference between them, so the information you have brought that Rama is to be declared the king's successor gives me great joy.'

Manthara scoffed, 'The one you call your child is your stepson, your rival Kaushalya's son, not yours.'

Irked by her remark, Kaikeyi retorted sharply, 'He may not have been born of my womb, but he is as dear to me as my own son Bharata. Since you have come with such good tidings, I would like to reward you with an ornament.' Saying this, she unclasped her necklace and affectionately gifted it to her.

Manthara hurled it aside in indignation, and mocked her mistress's simplicity, remarking sardonically, 'You are far too trusting and naïve, my dear child. What you call good news is a harbinger of doom. Clearly, you fail to see the changing tide in your fortunes. Quite honestly, your joy is so misplaced that it is ludicrous, and your gullibility is pitiful. Once Rama is king, you will have no status in this palace. As queen mother, Kaushalya will wield the immense power of that position. Undoubtedly, she has held a grudge against you for every time you have slighted her in the past. Do not forget you replaced her when the king married you, and she surely resents you being the recipient of his undivided attention all these years. In Kaushalya's new position of authority, you will be subservient to her and effectively become her servant. Also, Bharata will have reason to fear danger, for everyone knows that Rama only loves Lakshmana. Rama is politically shrewd and may see Bharata as a threat with equal merit to the throne. He might turn him out of the kingdom, or even worse, put him to death.'

Kaikeyi felt exasperated. Upbraiding Manthara's cynicism, she extolled Rama's virtues at length. Moreover, she explained he had every right to be king, not just because he was the eldest son, but because he also had all the qualities of an exemplary ruler. Then, in irritation, she chided, 'You have no reason to be distressed, Manthara; Rama has always served me more than he has served his own mother, Kaushalya; moreover, he treats his younger brothers like a father would his children. After Rama, I am sure Bharata will get his turn to rule. Today is a day to celebrate, yet you are sullen-faced, burning with hate and jealousy.'

Manthara was not distracted from her intention of sowing distrust; she sighed heavily in annoyance and retorted wryly, 'How can you harbour such foolish expectations that the kingdom will ever go to Bharata? If Rama is king, the kingdom will naturally pass on to his son. Besides, you have kept Bharata isolated from the family by sending him to Kekaya for months. This separation was a mistake because goodwill is only generated by proximity. Dasharatha has no affection for him, and while Lakshmana and Rama are as close to each other as the Ashwini twins, Bharata does not share this bond. Rama is likely to consider Bharata a contender to the throne due to the closeness of his birth, and though he may speak sweetly, he is sure to cause Bharata harm like a snake that feels threatened. You are too trusting and do not see it, but this coronation is a carefully orchestrated conspiracy to cheat Bharata and deprive him of his rights. Why else would they not wait for him to return? It is troubling that such a momentous event is being arranged so clandestinely that the king did not even discuss it with you. After all, you are supposedly his favourite queen. You did not know about it until I told you, yet the whole of Ayodhya is celebrating outside. It seems you are already losing your position in this palace. I dread to think what will befall you after the coronation. I have nurtured you from babyhood, and you know my only interest is your welfare. I implore you to heed my words, as they are solely for your benefit.'

All this while, Kaikeyi had been dismissive of Manthara, but she was suddenly gripped by panic that there was a nefarious plan afoot. Manthara seemed right; the king had not discussed anything with her, and his motives appeared dubious. Furthermore, the apparent subterfuge in the secrecy of the coronation was disconcerting. Dasharatha had coddled and cosseted Kaikeyi all these years, indulging her every whim, and now she feared being relegated to the background. She would be a nobody rotting in her chambers, while Kaushalya would lord over everyone in her new authority. Kaikeyi was not an evil woman; it would be more accurate to say that she did not have the blessing of good sense or a sacrificing nature like Sumitra. She was self-absorbed and led a pampered life of prettying herself, preoccupied with sartorial elegance. The insecurity of losing her status in the palace worried her, and Manthara artfully exploited this weakness. A relentless pursuit of material pleasures and an over-attachment to the physical body leaves a person open to manipulation, especially if their personal gratification and well-being are threatened. It is an unfortunate aspect of the human condition that negative emotions arising from crushed desires lead to anger, resulting in one's undoing.

Provoked by insecurity and the fear of being sidelined from the exalted position she enjoyed, Kaikeyi heaved a sigh and said gratefully, 'O Manthara, best among hunchbacks, you are like the stalk of a beautiful lotus[8] bent in the breeze. You have opened my eyes and are indeed a wise woman and a true well-wisher. Strangely, my right eye has been twitching[9] all morning, indicating an impending misfortune, and now I see what it portends. Tell me what I should do.' Feeling vindicated, Manthara smiled in satisfaction, exhaled sharply, and coached Kaikeyi on her poisonous plan. 'Listen to me carefully!' she said. 'The king is besotted with you and will never refuse you anything. He would gladly give up his life for you, so exert the influence you have over him and ask him to give the crown to your son Bharata, and exile Kaushalya's son Rama to the forest to live there as a hermit for fourteen years, so that he is not a threat.' Kaikeyi was astounded by her audacious suggestion and replied that the king would never agree to such a request.

Manthara then reminded Kaikeyi of two boons King Dasharatha had granted her that she had reserved for the future. Many years earlier, Dasharatha had helped Indra, Lord of the Devas, fight against an Asura king called Sambara. Kaikeyi had accompanied him to the battle because she was a skilled warrior. Dasharatha fought bravely but was seriously injured, and his body was riddled with arrows. He was on the verge of death when Kaikeyi, an excellent charioteer, sped him away from the battlefield. She tended to his wounds and stayed by his bedside, tirelessly nursing him back to health. Dasharatha was so pleased with her devotion that he granted her two boons. At the time, Kaikeyi said she had nothing to wish for and would save the favours for later. Manthara declared that the time had now come to use those two boons. The king would not refuse because his illustrious predecessors' tradition dictated that a word, once given, was sacrosanct and could never be violated.

She hissed venomously, 'O beautiful daughter of Ashwapati, go to your inner quarters to the chamber of anger[10] and prepare to feign a tantrum. Cast off your jewellery and fine clothes; wear the garb of mourning, and lie down on the bare floor, your hair bedraggled and face smudged with tears. When Dasharatha enquires why you are so sorrowful, make him promise to

---

[8] The lotus was considered auspicious, so this simile indicates how favourably Kaikeyi regards Manthara's advice.

[9] The right eye twitching was a bad omen for a woman.

[10] It appears there were chambers for specific purposes, including sulking rooms!

grant you your two wishes. Stand firm; do not get taken in by paltry offers of gold and jewels in place of your demands. Stick to the purpose of ensuring Bharata is crowned king and Rama is sent to the forest. Rama must go to the forest because the people love him too much and will not accept Bharata as their king unless he is gone. Fourteen years is long enough for Bharata to establish himself as the legitimate ruler. You must stop this coronation by pressuring the king today, for if Rama inherits the kingdom, both you and our son will suffer greatly.' Kaikeyi was now totally under Manthara's spell, and like a little girl walking down the wrong path, the misguided queen obediently put her perfidious plan into action.

Chapter 5

Kaikeyi Makes a Demand

After a hectic day at court, Dasharatha made his way to Kaikeyi's palace, driven by his passion for her and bursting with eagerness to tell her about Rama's coronation. It was a splendid white mansion with extensive grounds that sported charming bowers and arbours with ivory, silver and gold seats. Soft music added to the ambience, and the call of peacocks, parrots, swans and cranes reverberated throughout. There were fruit trees and flowers of every description, and an assortment of refreshments always laid out for guests to enjoy. Dasharatha was sure Kaikeyi would be overjoyed to hear the good news, for he knew she loved Rama as her son. But to his surprise, she was nowhere to be seen on this occasion. 'How unusual! My favourite queen is always there to greet me,' he thought. Then, a maid stepped forward to inform him that the queen was distraught and had retired to the chamber she went to when she was angry, to be in solitude.

Dasharatha found his beautiful young wife lying on the ground in a dishevelled state with her jewellery scattered around. Sobbing pitifully, she looked like a forlorn nymph. He rushed to her side in alarm, and stroking her hair gently, asked in a tender voice, 'Why has your face lost its lustre, dearest one? Surely your anger is not directed towards me, my love, so tell me what is causing you such intense sorrow? Who has dared to upset you? Speak, dear beloved, so that I can dispel your grievances. As you know, you are very precious to me, and I cannot bear to see you suffer in any way, so ask whatever you want, and I will grant it to you, even at the cost of my life. My power extends on this earth as far as the chariot rolls, so there is nothing that I am incapable of giving you. In addition to Kosala, the prosperous lands of Dravida, Sindhusauvira, Saurashtra, Dakshinapatha, Vanga, Anga, Magadha, Matsya, Kashi and umpteen others bow to me, so let me know what you desire.'

Anger clouded Kaikeyi's pretty face, and she resembled a dark, starless sky. Wiping her tears, she replied sullenly, 'I have no complaint for you to redress, but there is indeed something I want that only you can fulfil. However, before I tell you what it is, I want you first to promise that you will grant me what I am yearning to have.'

Dasharatha affectionately assured her, swearing in the name of Rama, whom he loved so dearly, that he would give her anything her heart desired. Then, feeling satisfied that she had trapped him, Kaikeyi reminded the king of the two boons he had given her years ago when she nursed him back to health, stating that she wanted to redeem them now. Utterly unaware that he was caught like a deer in a snare, Dasharatha smiled indulgently, thinking his queen was getting upset over some trifling matter. But of course, he would grant her whatever she asked. He was an almighty emperor, and nothing was beyond his power. Kaikeyi spoke coldly without any feeling. 'The thirty-three Devas[1] led by Agni are witnesses to your oath, which I am sure you will honour since you are a virtuous king, who strictly upholds dharma. After all, the sages say that truth is the only thing that matters in life. As mentioned, the time has come for me to claim the two boons you so kindly granted me years ago. I believe that you have planned to coronate Rama as your successor tomorrow. My first demand is to use the same arrangements to appoint my son Bharata as your heir instead. As for my second boon, I would like Kaushalya's son to live as an ascetic in the Dandaka Forest, dressed in bark clothes with matted hair, for a period of nine and five years. I want him to leave today itself, so that Bharata can rule without the hindrance of a thorn pricking him in his side. You are a celebrated monarch from a prestigious line, so I am sure you will be true to your word and family name by granting me what I ask.'

The words she spoke struck like arrows piercing the old king's heart. Kaikeyi's wish for Bharata to be crowned and Rama to be exiled to the forest to live as a hermit for fourteen years echoed in his ears long after they were uttered, filling him with waves of anger, bewilderment and despair all at once. Indeed, this was a bad dream! Dasharatha could not believe what he had just heard, especially from his most cherished wife. Sick to the stomach, he fell to the ground in a faint. When he recovered, he could not control his

---

[1] Thirty-three Devas are mentioned in the Vedas. They are: twelve Adityas—sons of Aditi, eleven Rudras—manifestations of Shiva, eight Vasus—elemental deities, and the two Ashwinis.

rage and lashed out bitterly, 'O cruel woman, what wrong has Rama done
to you? He has loved you as if you were his own mother and served you
even more dutifully than your son Bharata. Why are you betraying him in
this manner and bringing ruin to our family? Alas, I did not see the venom
behind your loveliness! The whole world extolls Rama's virtues, yet you
want me to forsake him for no good reason? How can I commit the sin of
banishing my blameless son to please you? Have you thought of the agony
this will cause the delicate Maithili? How will my sweet boy, raised in the lap
of luxury, bear the hardship of roaming in the forest as a mendicant? Here
in the palace, cooks compete to feed him with delicacies, but there in the
wilderness, he would have to forage for fruits and roots to satisfy his hunger.
I fall at your feet and ask you not to make me do this terrible deed. It is
against dharma in every way, so I beg you to reconsider your request. If you
want me to crown Bharata king, I am willing to concede that; he is also my
son, but do not make me send my Rama away. The world may continue to
exist without the sun, and the crops may thrive without water, but I cannot
live without Rama.'

Despite Dasharatha's ardent pleas, Kaikeyi was unmoved. The seeds of
distrust that Manthara had sown in her mind had firmly taken root, and
she remained obstinate in her demands, replying angrily, 'This wailing does
not befit you, Maharaja! You made a contract, and now you are bargaining
with me to amend it because it does not suit you. You must keep your word
and grant me what I have asked. Why are you behaving as though you are
sinning by keeping your oath to me? Honouring your pledge is the path
of righteousness, for the principled know that truth is the highest form of
dharma. If the king's word cannot be trusted, what can be expected of an
ordinary person? For the sake of dharma, I repeat it three times and ask you
to send Rama away. It is an anathema for me to see Kaushalya promoted
to the position of the queen mother, so if you go back on your word, I will
consume poison and kill myself before your eyes.'

Caught in the noose of dharma, Dasharatha tried all night desperately to
convince Kaikeyi to change her mind. He struggled in the face of conflicting
duties. As a king, he had given his word to the assembly, yet the promise to
his wife tugged him in the opposite direction. Dasharatha used every means
of persuasion; he coaxed, pleaded and rebuked, but through it all, Kaikeyi
remained unrelenting. Even abandoning his pride, he beseeched her to show
mercy to an old man whose life had almost come to an end. He stood before

her wretchedly with folded hands, blabbering incoherently, 'Don't make me exile Rama!' But Manthara had so corrupted Kaikeyi that in a few hours, her lifelong affection for Rama was entirely replaced by hatred. 'I will not be satisfied with anything other than the banishment of Rama,' she spat back viciously. 'It appears your word is not as important to you as you so proudly claim. Your family boasts of honouring an oath no matter the consequence, even at the cost of life itself. You seem to have forgotten your noble ancestors' sacrifices to uphold their vows. Shibi cut the flesh from his thigh to keep his promise to a hawk. King Alarka unhesitatingly plucked out his eyes and handed them to a Brahmin. The honest Harishchandra gave away his kingdom and put himself in servitude to abide by his word. However, in your case, this meritorious tradition is nothing but an empty vaunt, as you are quibbling so much about fulfilling a simple undertaking to me.'

Having spoken thus, she was silent and resolute, bent on getting her way, while the old king lamented loudly. 'Who has influenced you with such malicious thoughts? You were so sweet-natured, and I cannot understand how you have suddenly turned so heartless! The august assembly is in favour of Rama becoming king. Furthermore, his reputation is spotless, so what will the people of Ayodhya think of me if I allow myself to be misled by you? Forsaking my faultless son just to satisfy my wife stands in brazen defiance of the behaviour of an "arya", and in forgoing my royal dharma, I will surely be treated as a pariah and shunned; disgraced like a Brahmin who drinks liquor! As a king, I am a role model to society; if I practise adharma, the people will do likewise. O wicked woman, you have beguiled me and brought joy to our enemies in bringing about the destruction of our clan! Rama's exile will surely spell my death, and that will be the price you will pay for your avarice of ruling this kingdom with your son.

'I was happy to have a devoted boy like Rama all these years, but today I feel dejected that he has such an obedient nature. I know he will follow whatever I command, and ironically this has turned out to be my greatest sorrow. I curse the day I held your hand and took those seven steps around the sacred fire. I was so infatuated by your outward beauty that I gave you the position that rightfully belonged to Kaushalya. What a colossal error in judgement I made! How foolish I have been! From this day forward, I disown you and sever our relationship forever. You mean nothing to me anymore, and if Bharata accepts the crown, I do not want him to come anywhere near my body at my funeral.' Then, quivering in anguish at his inability to resolve the conflict of opposing dharmas, he dropped to the ground like a felled tree and lay in a motionless stupor.

The morning brought a flurry of activity. Unaware of the tragedy that had struck, Rama dressed in fine silk clothing and performed his rituals of worship at dawn, chanting the Gayatri Mantra and following the other special observances instructed by their guru, Vasishta. He and Sita had been told to fast until the ceremony, and at night they slept on kusha grass with a hard stone pillow at the feet of Vishnu on the floor of their family temple. A king's obligation was to serve his people, and this austerity symbolized that duty.

The people swept and cleaned the city from top to bottom. Every house was decorated with flags, and the streets were covered with flower petals. Oil lamps were arranged in rows, ready to be lit in celebration at dusk. Ayodhya looked so beautiful that it vied in splendour with Indra's magnificent capital, Amravati. Meanwhile, the appointed hour arrived, and Vasishta needed the king's presence so the ceremony could commence before the auspicious time passed. Strangely, Dasharatha was missing, so his able minister Sumantra went in search of him.

When Sumantra found him, he was bewildered to see the king looking morose on the day he had awaited so eagerly. Nevertheless, conveying the message he was told to deliver, he said, 'O great king, the arrangements for the coronation are complete; Vasishta and the priests are ready to start the ceremony. All that is needed now is your presence to begin the rituals.' The king looked gaunt and tired; he stared vacantly into the distance and muttered, 'Your words torture me.' So, Kaikeyi decided to reply on his behalf. She said curtly, 'The king is feeling emotional about the coronation and is tired because he did not sleep very well last night. He wants to see Rama, so please bring him here from his palace immediately.' Suspecting something was amiss, Sumantra rushed to Rama's palace, pushing past the crowd thronging outside in anticipation of the grand event. He had free access to the residence, being the king's most trusted adviser, and hurrying beyond the security gates, the elephants, horses, peacocks and deer on the grounds, he made his way to Rama's inner quarters. The mansion was a magnificent building with massive doors and numerous balconies. The main entrance was heavily embellished with gems and corals, and adorned with statues of gold. There were intricate carvings in sandalwood and aloe throughout. Their scent wafted through the air, and hundreds of servants stood in attendance, contributing to the opulence.

When Sumantra was announced, Rama invited him to enter his chamber, where he was seated on a magnificent golden couch with Sita. On hearing that his father and Kaikeyi wished to see him urgently, Rama rose immediately, remarking jovially that his youngest mother, Kaikeyi, had a soft spot for him, so perhaps she was planning a special surprise. Telling Sita to expect him back soon, Rama left with Sumantra, looking glorious like a majestic lion exiting his mountain cave.

As they reached the first gate, they saw Lakshmana waiting, and he too climbed into the chariot. Followed by a retinue of soldiers on horseback, they proceeded to the king's palace, cheered by citizens lining the streets on both sides, waiting eagerly to catch a glimpse of their beloved prince. As the chariot rolled past the beautiful decorations that adorned the city, the people called out praises and sang Rama's glory, showering him with flowers. Though he gratefully acknowledged their compliments, he never allowed their adulation to make him feel egotistical, as vanity was unknown to him.

Soon, Rama arrived at the royal palace. Going past the three outer courtyards and walking across two more, he stood before his father. He was shocked to see him sitting in silence, looking distraught; his face was wan with reddened eyes blinded by tears. Dasharatha resembled the sun shaded by an eclipse or a sage tormented by the guilt of telling a lie. Rama touched his feet and then those of Kaikeyi, but all the king could say was 'Rama'. His voice was weak and shaky. No other words followed, nor did he look up. Rama was taken aback! 'What is wrong,' he asked, addressing Kaikeyi, 'My father does not speak. Is he ill or unhappy about something untoward that has taken place? I hope Bharata and Shatrughana are alright? I have never seen him like this, and it pains me deeply to behold him in this miserable condition. I hope I have not unwittingly done something to cause him distress?'

Kaikeyi snapped brusquely, 'Nothing is wrong; the king is neither ill nor angry. Your father has something on his mind that he finds difficult to communicate, because he is afraid of displeasing you. It is a simple matter; he wants to forsake his promise like a commoner. In trying to back away from his commitment to me despite giving his word, he attempts to build a dam after the water has flowed out. Truth is the cornerstone of dharma, and since the king hesitates to honour his contract, it is up to you to ensure he follows the path of righteousness. I do not wish to waste my breath, so I will only tell you what he is unable to voice if you agree to fulfil his pledge.'

Rama, ever virtuous, naturally agreed without hesitation to uphold his father's oath. He added that it was unfortunate that any doubt should arise in this regard, stating that he would do anything his father wished, even jump into the fire, eat poison or drown in the ocean. He assured Kaikeyi that he was not in the habit of equivocating; once having spoken, his word was final.[2] This resoluteness was his noble ancestral tradition, as it constituted dharma. Relieved that Rama was willing to follow through on Dasharatha's promise, Kaikeyi recounted the story of her two boons and what she had claimed to redeem them.

Though the same words had destroyed his father, there was no change in Rama's expression, not even the slightest hint of disappointment; his countenance remained one of complete equanimity.[3] When he entered the room, his face had shown no undue exuberance about his good fortune, and similarly, he now appeared as inscrutable, exhibiting no overt dejection at the reversal of his circumstances. With unshakeable self-control so characteristic of his nature, Rama continued to bear a calm demeanour. Moments from inheriting the greatest kingdom on Earth, he was suddenly stripped of everything, and worse still, for no specific fault. Despite the unfairness of Kaikeyi's demands, Rama displayed no anger, no resentment, no pain at the unexpected turn of events, just a deep desire to act according to dharma, keeping the sanctity of his father's promise.

'So be it,' he said, 'Without question, I must uphold my father's word, so I will depart immediately for the forest and take up abode there as a hermit. Bharata is accomplished in all aspects of ruling and is dearer to me than life itself, so I am pleased for him to replace me as the new king. For the good of the kingdom, the transition of power must happen swiftly and smoothly, so messengers need to be dispatched immediately to call him back. The only sorrow I have is that you did not approach me directly. Since you are my

---

[2] The Vedas refer to the importance of truth as dharma in multiple passages. Brihadaranyaka Upanishad 1.4.14: 'Dharma is but truth only. Therefore, when a person speaks truth, he speaks dharma.' Taittiriya Upanishad 1.11.1 says: 'Speak truth, practise dharma.' And, in the Chandogya Upanishad 7.16.1: 'But truly he is an excellent speaker, who excels in speaking the truth.'

[3] Equanimity comes from disinterest either in pleasure or pain associated with the perishable body. In the Katha Upanishad 2.2, Yama the teacher says: 'Perennial joy or passing pleasure? This is the choice one is to make always. Those who are wise recognize this but not the ignorant.' In 3.1 Yama says again: 'In the secret cave of the heart, two are seated by life's fountain. The separate ego drinks the sweet and bitter stuff, liking the sweet, disliking the bitter, while the supreme Self drinks the sweet and bitter, neither liking this nor disliking that.'

mother, it was unnecessary to go through my father to fulfil your wishes, as your command itself would have been sufficient for me.'

Kaikeyi felt pleased with her victory, but she was not satisfied merely with Rama's agreement to leave. Wanting him to depart without delay, she pressed, 'As long as you remain here, your father will not bathe or eat, so you should go right away.' In response, Rama confirmed that he would depart that very day, for he had no attachment to worldly pleasures; his only request was for a few moments to bid farewell to his mother and his wife, Sita. Saying this, he circled[4] Dasharatha and Kaikeyi, respectfully taking leave of them.

The inability to extricate himself from entrapment was more pain than the old king could bear, and he slumped down unconscious, crying, 'Shameful woman!'

---

[4] Circling a person was done to show respect.

Chapter 6

Farewell to Ayodhya

When Rama left the palace after his audience with Kaikeyi and his father, he declined the use of the chariot that had brought him there, feeling he did not have the right to royal privileges anymore. Just the previous day, he had trodden these steps to give his mother Kaushalya the happy news of his coronation; now, he walked the same path to deliver the sad news of his exile. His devout mother was conducting a ritual for his well-being, and Brahmins chanted prayers, pouring oblations into the holy fire. He knew she would be devastated to hear what had transpired; nonetheless, she had to be informed about the new developments. When Rama approached, Kaushalya rushed exuberantly to greet him like a mare reuniting with her lost foal, but soon her joy turned to sorrow.

Overwhelmed with grief, she wailed, 'Even childlessness did not cause me as much agony as I am suffering from hearing this awful news. The king has never given me my rightful position as his senior queen. He always put Kaikeyi above me, but I never complained. Through all my suffering, I had you, my glorious son! I have waited patiently the last seventeen years from your thread ceremony[1] for your anointment as the king. Now, that happiness is also denied to me! How can I live without seeing your beautiful face every day? Kaikeyi has always been condescending towards me. I was hoping all my worries would be over today, but it looks like they are just beginning. Alas! My austere life has been in vain. I cannot bear to be separated from you and feel heartbroken like an old cow bereft of its calf.'[2] Sobbing inconsolably, she collapsed to the ground like the bough of a tree severed by an axe, imploring

---

[1] The thread ceremony marked the initiation into learning and was considered a second birth on becoming a dvija.

[2] The comparison of deep love with that of a cow for her calf is a recurring motif.

Rama not to obey Kaikeyi's command, insisting that following his mother's wishes was his highest duty.[3]

Life rarely presents easy options. Rama had to choose between his mother's order and his father's promise. Often one is pulled in contrary directions by conflicting dharmas, and it is precisely in such times that strength of character determines the right course of action. In this case, for Rama, the path of dharma led to the forest and not to the throne.

He declared firmly, 'Mother, I have to fulfil my father's vow because it is the right thing to do, so I beg you to give me your permission to leave. Remember how Sagara's sons dutifully obeyed their father's command despite it resulting in their tragic end, and how Parasurama beheaded his mother Renuka to honour his father's word? The virtuous sage Kandu even killed a cow[4] because his father ordered him. Like them, I feel bound to carry out my father's wishes because righteousness must always be upheld no matter how difficult the path.'

Kaushalya pleaded, 'Take me with you, my son, or I will fast to death, unable to endure your absence for so many years.'

However, Rama reminded her of her duty as a wife, pointing out that his father was old and suffering terribly at Kaikeyi's betrayal. He stressed that Dasharatha needed comfort from her now more than ever and requested that she bear his exile stoically. Begging his mother for her good wishes, he pleaded, 'Give me your blessings to go to the forest and do my duty as a son. I promise to return to you after I complete fourteen years.'

Lakshmana had accompanied Rama, and though silent throughout, was fuming with rage inside at Kaikeyi's iniquitous demand. Like a virulent serpent in a hole, he erupted in impassioned anger, expostulating loudly, 'I cannot accept the injustice of your banishment! By what authority has our father given the kingdom to Bharata? Obviously, his base actions are driven by lust and senility, and you must stand up to him and take back what is rightfully yours. Every person is accountable for their actions without exception, so anyone who commits a transgression must be punished, even if he happens to be a guru, parent,[5] or respected elder. I will remain firmly

---

[3] 'The teacher (acharya) is more important than ten instructors (upadhyayas), and the father more than a hundred teachers, but the mother more than a thousand fathers.' Manusmriti 2.145

[4] Refer to the Appendices on why killing a cow was considered a sin.

[5] Manusmriti 8.335

by your side and kill anyone in Ayodhya who supports Bharata over you or defies your right to the throne, including our royal father. Intoxicated by the charms of his favourite wife, the king has been led to behave in a contemptible manner, abandoning his godlike son to gain her favour. You have no reason to follow the dictates of someone acting irresponsibly in his dotage. Bharata cannot be allowed to have what is yours, like a hyaena that steals a lion's kill.'

Lakshmana was hot-tempered and easily provoked, so hearing his tirade, Rama put his hand on his shoulder and said soothingly, 'You must shed your anger! I know you speak out of supreme affection for me but cast aside this ignoble attitude of violence and help me uphold the path of virtue. A promise, once given, cannot be broken. Do not blame our father or even Mother Kaikeyi, who has been kind to me until today. We must put this misfortune down to divine will, as destiny cannot be overturned[6]. Life is full of twists and turns, and expecting uninterrupted happiness for our entire existence is unrealistic. Unexpected occurrences like this often happen because of past karma[7]. Adversity is part of the human condition, and we must learn to deal with ups and downs that arise with resilience and acceptance. I am not attached[8] to the trappings of kingship, and it matters little to me whether I sit on the throne or go to the forest. It is paramount to do the right thing, even if it seems unpleasant, rather than falling for the temptation of fleeting enjoyment.[9] I am determined to keep our father's promise, as dharma dictates that a word once given cannot be violated. I intend to leave today, but I assure you I will return to Ayodhya after fourteen years.

Lakshmana was unconvinced and continued to rage. Glancing obliquely, with his head thrust forward and bent slightly to the side, he shook his forearm like a bull elephant would its trunk. Glowering, he rebuked, 'Your decision

---

[6] This is not fatalism because in Vedic belief destiny is self-created by our free will.

[7] The word karma means deed, and the doctrine of karma was central to Vedic belief. It indicates both the action as well as the consequence. Destiny is therefore considered the result of a person's own doing and not an arbitrary happening. See Appendices on karma.

[8] The value of detachment is discussed using the analogy of two birds in the Mundaka Upanishad. 'Like two golden birds perched on the selfsame tree, intimate friends, the ego, and the Self dwell in the same body. The former eats the sweet and sour fruits of the tree, while the latter looks on in detachment.' Mundaka Upanishad 3.1.1

[9] The concept of Shreya (ultimate good) over Preya (temporary happiness) is explored in the Katha Upanishad of the Yajur Veda. This is what Rama is referring to here.

is meek and fatalism[10] is not becoming of a valorous Kshatriya. Kaikeyi and our father are exploiting your kind nature, and the whole story about boons given and granted is, in my opinion, a complete hoax. Excuse me for saying this, but your adherence to piety has made you timid and deluded you from taking the right action. Only weak people talk about providence, while the strong defy destiny with their efforts. I intend to show the world that human effort is more powerful than fate by ensuring that nothing interferes with your coronation. You can retire to the forest and take up Vanaprastha[11] after you have finished ruling and handed the kingdom to your successor, but it is not appropriate for you to do so now. I suggest you go ahead with the ceremony and take the reins in your hands as planned. The people want you to be king, and I cannot tolerate anyone else taking your place. No one knows what has transpired yet, and the priests are waiting, so before the word gets out, install yourself as prince regent. My strong shoulders and arms are not for show, and my weapons are not decorative ornaments, so I can assure you no one in the world will be able to disrupt the proceedings. Once I wear my finger guards and stand with my bow, I am enough to safeguard you without assistance from anyone else.'

Rama wiped Lakshmana's tears and said calmly, 'You have worked yourself up into a highly agitated state, but do not be angry and vengeful on my behalf. I feel no sorrow at giving up my claim to the throne and stand by our father's word, as this alone is the most honourable course of action. Artha and kama[12] must always be pursued within the bounds of dharma, or we become hateful creatures. It is unworthy to go against righteousness, disregarding our father's commitment and forcibly wresting the kingdom for myself, just to enjoy material pleasures.'

By now, Kaushalya grudgingly realized that nothing would dissuade Rama, so she kissed his forehead and embraced him tightly. Then, blessing

---

[10] Lakshmana seems to have misunderstood Rama or perhaps his anger is clouding his mind, because acceptance of karma is not the same as fatalism. Karma is self-determined and driven by choice, whereas fate assumes impotence and an uncontrollable predetermination.

[11] Vanaprastha literally means going to the forest. It was the third stage of Vedic life marked by retirement from responsibilities.

[12] A virtuous person pursues prosperity and desire only within the boundaries of dharma. This is the basis of 'Purushartha' or the purpose of life. Refer to the Appendices for more details.

him, she said, 'Since I cannot change your mind, I have no choice but to bid you farewell. May God be with you, for my sorrow will only end when you return. May dharma that you have followed so scrupulously protect[13] you and let the merit you have earned by your obedience keep you from harm. May the weapons Vishwamitra gave you safeguard you from danger. May the Devas and the forces of nature, the stars and planets always smile on you. May no wild animal or Rakshasa in the forest hurt you in any way.' Then Kaushalya requested a Brahmin to perform a fire ritual to ensure his safety, and once it was done, Rama touched his mother's feet reverently and went to Sita.

Sita was unaware that things had gone awry and was busy with her preparations, eagerly looking forward to the consecration as she waited for Rama to return after meeting with his father. He entered the room with his gaze lowered, not quite sure how to break the unfortunate news or how he would console Sita, knowing it would be tough for her to accept being apart from him for fourteen years.

Seeing Rama's troubled countenance, Sita sprang from her seat and asked anxiously, 'What happened? Today is a day of great joy when the auspicious constellation of Pushya is in the ascendant, so why then do you look so crestfallen, dear husband? Where is your white umbrella, and what happened to all the pomp and splendour that accompanied you when you left?'

As he had told his mother Kaushalya, Rama narrated the story once more, except with Sita, his life partner, his face displayed the emotion he had controlled so well before everyone else. Enjoining her to wait for his return, he said, 'You are from a noble-minded family,[14] cognizant of righteousness, so you will understand that the two boons claimed by dharma cannot be disregarded. I must leave for the forest today to keep my father's promise, but I would like you to stay here and wait for my return. While I am away, continue with your prayers and sacred observances, dutifully caring for our father and three mothers. Remember always to be courteous to Bharata and respect him as the new king. Never praise me excessively in his presence or offend him in any way, as I do not want you to forfeit his goodwill. Fourteen years will go by quicker than you think, and before long, I will return to you.'

---

[13] 'Dharmo rakshati rakshitah': Manusmriti 8.15. 'Dharma violated, destroys; dharma upheld, preserves. Therefore, those who follow dharma are protected by it.'

[14] Janaka was considered the most pious king to ever exist. He was known for his detachment from materialism and was called Rajrishi, the Philosopher King.

Although Sita was shocked to hear about the setback, like Rama, she felt no angst at the loss of his kingship. She was not upset that Bharata would be the new monarch or that she would not be queen. Her only wish was to remain by her husband's side, so out of an outpouring of love, she replied crossly, 'O Rama, what are you saying? I find your instruction to stay back completely absurd and impossible to follow. While every person has their destiny, a wife alone shares her husband's fortune, whether good or bad. If you have been commanded to the forest, then so have I, for my place is with you. I am quite aware of my duties as my parents taught me dharma, so I insist on going with you. I will be of assistance in your exile and promise not to be a burden. To me, even the joys of heaven are meaningless without you, let alone the worldly pleasures of palace life.'

Rama felt moved by his wife's devotion but knew the forest was no place for a delicate princess, so he argued, 'Sita, I spoke for your well-being, not because I felt you would be a burden. I do not think you know the dangers that lurk in the forest. It is infested with vicious creatures: mosquitoes, snakes, scorpions and savage wild animals. Besides, there are other perils; the path is thorny, the winds are furious and the rivers are full of alligators. Forest life involves extreme hardship and exposure to the elements, devoid of the amenities you are accustomed to here. Not only will we have to sleep on a bed of fallen leaves and wear rough clothing, but there may be periods of hunger, eking out an existence, foraging for fruit and edible roots to satisfy our bellies. How can I expose you to this adversity, my sweet princess?'

Sita was undeterred; with tears welling up in her eyes, she said adamantly, 'I am alive to the hardships in the forest and am not concerned about any discomfort I may face there. I am confident that you can protect me from wild animals. Not even the mighty Indra[15] can harm me when you are with me. Besides, I have been prepared mentally for this eventuality for a long time. When I was a child, sages prophesied that I would spend a large part of my life in the forest, and now I see that prediction coming true. We have a joint destiny, and my place as your partner in life is with you. Heaven is where we are together, and hell is where I am without you. With you, the forest is preferable to me than living in paradise; the fallen leaves more comfortable than my royal bed; the meagre sustenance superior to the fine delicacies of the palace, and the thorny paths more pleasing than one strewn with petals.'

---

[15] Indra was considered the pinnacle of strength and power.

Despite her pleas, Rama continued to dissuade her, insisting it was not practical for her to accompany him. Still, Sita, a very assertive woman, grew indignant and exclaimed sarcastically, 'Why are you so afraid of taking me with you? It appears my father, King Janaka, gave my hand in marriage to a woman in the guise of a man.[16] I have lived with you since I was a young girl, and I cannot live apart from you, relegated to the custody of others. I promise I will not complain about any deprivation, and on the contrary, I know I will enjoy forest life because I love nature. If you leave me here, I will not be able to bear the separation, and you will not find me alive when you return.' She clung to him and cried helplessly as a female elephant assailed with several poisoned darts.

Rama, who rarely lost an argument, could not stop Sita from joining him. In this instance, he had to concede defeat, for just as he was upholding his dharma as a son, she was following her dharma as a wife to stand by him, whether he was wealthy or impoverished. Finally, capitulating to her wish, he said, 'O Maithili, since you refuse to stay behind, let us prepare to leave for the forest together. Without you, heaven has no meaning for me either. We will start by giving away all our jewels, fine clothing and other possessions that we have no use for anymore.'

Lakshmana was standing at the door, listening to their exchange. He touched Rama's feet and said, 'If you plan to leave, I will accompany you, too. I have always been your shadow and have never been apart from you, so I cannot stay here in your absence. I will walk ahead with my bow clearing the path for you. You had asked me to rule the kingdom with you; now, I ask to join you in your exile. Please do not prevent me from following you; I will do everything to serve you during your fourteen years in the forest.' Rama tried his best to discourage Lakshmana, saying that their mothers Sumitra and Kaushalya would be left unprotected if he left. However, Lakshmana refused to consider this a problem, arguing that Bharata would be kind to their mothers; besides, he insisted Kaushalya did not need to depend on any handouts.[17] She was not beholden to anyone; she was financially independent and wealthy in her own right, with control over 1000 villages, so leaving her alone would not be negligent on his part. Bent on accompanying his brother,

---

[16] This shows that women were not afraid to speak their mind.

[17] This comment indicates women were not merely dependents and had financial means of their own.

he said, 'While you spend time with Sita in the forest, I will serve you both by doing all the chores during the day and guarding you at night.'

Rama knew Lakshmana would not stay back, so he conceded and asked him to get the two bows of Varuna, the two inexhaustible quivers, and the two swords he received as wedding gifts from Janaka that were left in Vasishta's safekeeping. In order to donate his possessions, Rama also asked Lakshmana to invite their guru's son Suyajna and other deserving Brahmins; and bowing to his brother, Lakshmana went to do his bidding.

Lakshmana's sacrifice was immense. There was no reason for him to give up fourteen years of his marriage and princely privileges in the prime of his life to take on unnecessary hardship, but he was devoted to Rama and did not stop for a moment to think of himself. All he wanted was to be by his brother's side in his time of need.

Rama and Sita gave away everything they owned in preparation for their departure. They donated ornaments, silks, beds, couches, horses, elephants, gold and silver to those who served them and to needy Brahmins, who depended on charity for a living. Rama even prepaid all his servants' wages for fourteen years from his personal means, not the state treasury. An impoverished Brahmin with many children called Trijata heard about the charitable giving and requested assistance. In response, Rama jokingly asked Trijata to throw his staff as far as he could and gifted him the number of cattle that fitted into the distance covered by the stick, not only showing his immense generosity but his ability to be light-hearted in a time of personal calamity. Once they had distributed all their wealth, Rama, Sita and Lakshmana bid farewell to King Dasharatha. They had shed all traces of their royalty, and Sita, who had hitherto lived a pampered existence sheltered behind palace walls, now walked like an ordinary citizen on the street. The news of Rama's exile was out by this time, and crying at his plight, the people cursed Kaikeyi and mourned his exile, determined to follow him to the forest. Rama himself, however, showed no hint of discomfiture; he remained composed, his face a picture of tranquillity despite the enormous storm that had turned his life upside down.

When they reached Dasharatha's palace, he said to Sumantra, 'Please announce my arrival to the king.' Sumantra hurried in and declared that Rama had come after distributing his wealth to all those who petitioned him. Dasharatha was in abject misery; his cheerlessness resembled a blazing fire reduced to ashes. However, despite his frayed emotional condition, he had the presence of mind to ask Sumantra to call all his wives, so that Rama could have their blessings. They arrived quickly, and all were red-eyed with weeping, except for Kaikeyi. Dasharatha was surrounded by his consorts and courtiers when Rama entered the room, his hands folded in salutation. Seeing his beloved son, he jumped up excitedly and rushed to greet him, but feeble with sorrow, he did not get far before stumbling weakly to the ground. Rama and Lakshmana lifted him gently, and after helping him to his seat, Rama said, 'Father, I am here to say goodbye and seek your blessings as I am leaving for the Dandaka Forest today. Please permit Sita and Lakshmana to go with me, for despite my best efforts to dissuade them, they refuse to stay behind.' Dasharatha was torn with grief and replied woefully, 'It is not my wish for you to leave; I was deceived into it by Kaikeyi. You do not have to go! You have taken on this hardship only to protect me from transgression and save me from hell. Throw me in prison instead and take over the kingdom.'

Firmly established in dharma, Rama replied, 'Father, do not be sad about giving the kingdom to Bharata or about my going to the forest. There is good in every situation, no matter how bleak the outlook. I look forward to the serene experience of communing with nature and the serendipitous opportunity of enjoying the lakes, rivers, hills, forest fauna and flora. I must go! In my duty as your son, propriety dictates that I uphold your vow, but I promise to return after fourteen years to clasp your feet once more.'

Unable to come to terms with the finality of Rama's departure, Dasharatha pleaded with him to stay one more night, but Rama was adamant about leaving immediately, insisting that a delay would not help mitigate the pangs of separation. Dasharatha then expressed a desire to make Rama's exile as comfortable as possible. He asked Sumantra to send a store of grain, along with an army, a team of attendants and enough riches from the exchequer, so Rama could live a life of ease during his exile. Hearing this, Kaikeyi pursed her lips and objected vociferously, complaining that Bharata would be left with an empty shell to inherit. Dasharatha grew angry that she had taken exception to his command, reminding Kaikeyi that she had not made these preconditions, but she argued, citing precedence in their clan, quoting that Sagara had banished his son Asmanjas from the kingdom, turning him out with nothing.

A highly respected minister called Siddhartha bristled at the false analogy, interjecting to correct her misconception. Stating that it was not a comparable situation, he clarified that Asmanjas was a wicked person, who delighted in drowning children for fun, whereas Rama was blameless and devoid of evil. Furthermore, he asserted that punishing an innocent person was such a heinous crime that it would even burn the mighty Indra. Siddhartha begged Kaikeyi to give up her madness, but no amount of persuasion would get her to change her mind. However, before there was any more debate on the subject, Rama himself refused any assistance; he said that having already given away all his possessions in preparation for an ascetic life, he had no use for the proposed comforts anyway.[18] Then, he added pragmatically, 'Only a foolish person holds onto the tether after he has given away his prize elephant,' and agreed only to ride in a chariot to the outskirts of the kingdom, from where they would proceed on foot.

Sumantra was incensed by what was happening and stood shaking his head, wringing his hands, and grinding his teeth. Being Dasharatha's closest confidant, he erupted in a fury, admonishing[19] Kaikeyi. 'Shame on you! You seem to have no compunctions about killing the king and destroying this clan. Dasharatha has always been unshakable like Indra, but look at the miserable state to which you have reduced him! You are focused solely on yourself and your son, and your callousness towards the rest of the family is shocking. According to the law of primogeniture, it is customary for the eldest son to inherit the kingdom, and it is shameful of you to overturn this tradition. We are all prepared to leave Ayodhya with Rama. What happiness can you expect from an empty kingdom?' In a final attempt to get her to withdraw her demands, he implored, 'The king is bound by his word, but you have the power to free him by taking back your unfair demand.' However, Kaikeyi was beyond reason and remained obdurate, determined for Rama to leave as quickly as possible.

Sumantra was disgusted at her obstinacy and exclaimed in revulsion, 'You are just like your mother in your indifference to your husband's well-being.' He was referring to an incident where Kaikeyi's mother exhibited similar selfishness. Once, when her parents were enjoying a quiet moment together, her father, King Ashwapati, chuckled as his glance fell on two tiny ants. His wife asked what he found so funny, and Ashwapati replied that he was amused by what the ants were saying to each other. Filled with curiosity, the queen asked what they had said. The king responded that he could not divulge their conversation, because the benediction by which he understood the speech of animals forbade him from disclosing what he heard. If he did,

---

[18] Detachment from material possessions was considered necessary for spiritual progress. The Varaha Upanishad in the Yajur Veda says: 'Man is bound by "mine", but he is released by "not mine".'

[19] Sumantra scolds the queen publicly, showing that Shudras were not inferior in status.

his head would burst open. Instead of leaving the matter to rest, Kaikeyi's mother insisted on knowing the details, regardless of the consequences. Her callousness enraged the king so much that he sent her back to her parents' house. This was also how Manthara became Kaikeyi's surrogate mother.

Kaikeyi was happy to hear Rama say he did not need any comforts and intended to go to the forest as promised. Pleased with his unyielding resolve to leave immediately, she quickly fetched the bark clothes worn by hermits for the three young people. Everyone in the court was incredulous, gasping as Sita tried to wear the humble attire. Vasishta was outraged and burst out, 'Evil woman, you have crossed all limits of decency and have brought ruin to our kingdom by disgracing your family with your uncultured behaviour. Sita is not a party to your bargain, and there is no reason for her to wear the clothes of an ascetic or forgo her jewellery. If Bharata has any decency, he will abandon you and not accept the kingdom, so I suggest Sita should stay and rule in the spirit of Rama, for man and wife are two equal parts of a whole.'[20] However, Sita insisted on leaving with her husband, and although Dasharatha could not stop her, he objected to his daughter-in-law being clad in beggarly garments. Admonishing Kaikeyi, he clarified that she had exceeded her authority, saying, 'Vaidehi is a tender girl and the daughter of a great king. Besides, she was not included in the promise I gave you. You only asked for Rama to go to the forest as an ascetic, so Sita will leave properly ornamented and suitably dressed in silk as befits her position as a princess.'

With no option to prevent Rama's exile, Dasharatha instructed Sumantra to bring a chariot suitable for long-distance travel, yoked with the finest horses, to conduct the trio safely to the forest. He also summoned the treasurer and asked him to arrange for enough clothes and ornaments for fourteen years, so that Sita could dress in the manner she was accustomed to thus far. While saying goodbye, Kaushalya embraced her daughter-in-law and advised, 'It is the natural tendency of women in their graciousness to disregard the small foibles of their husbands, but they rarely tolerate major catastrophes. Some fickle ones walk away in hard times, especially when faced with destitution. I hope you will always stay true to Rama even though he is impoverished now and has nothing to offer you.'

Sita folded her hands respectfully and said resolutely, 'I know my responsibilities as a wife and will never deviate from dharma. Do not equate

---

[20] This statement points to the equality women enjoyed.

me with unchaste women! Just as moonshine cannot be divorced from the moon, my heart can never be separated from Rama. A veena has no purpose without its strings, and a chariot is useless without its wheels; similarly, a good wife can never be happy without her husband, even if she has 100 sons. I can never abandon dharma, so how can I possibly disavow my duty to stand by Rama?'

Kaushalya felt reassured by Sita's words and hugged her close in gratitude. Rama added, 'Mother, be kind to father; fourteen years will be over before you know it, so please do not fret anymore.'

Meanwhile, Lakshmana was saying goodbye to Sumitra. She was not only a strong woman but a veritable ocean of wisdom. Instead of weeping, Sumitra offered words of encouragement, saying magnanimously, 'My son, I permit you to go because I know you are devoted to your brother. Your actions comply with dharma, so keep up your selflessness and never be negligent in your service. Treat Rama as you would your father, Dasharatha, Sita as you would me, your mother, and consider the forest as Ayodhya. Remember to be happy wherever you find yourself.'

The sight of the princes leaving with Sita to begin their exile was harrowing for everyone in Ayodhya. Rama and Lakshmana took nothing but their weapons as they embarked on their journey. The forest was a dangerous place, and they needed to have the means to protect themselves. As they ascended the chariot driven by Sumantra, the people crowded the streets with tears streaming down their faces. Ayodhya plunged into mourning, and the sound of musical instruments that always filled the air was replaced by wailing. The day that had dawned with celebration metamorphosed into one of grief as melancholy took the place of the earlier festivity. The oil lamps remained unlit at dusk, and that evening the city was shrouded in gloomy darkness. The people were filled with such emptiness that they made up their minds to follow Rama into the forest. They decided they would construct a new city where he went and leave a deserted Ayodhya for Kaikeyi to give to her son. Their love for their prince was so great that they were willing to give up their prosperous lives to share in his misfortune.

As the chariot pulled away, citizens young and old ran behind. Even Dasharatha staggered after it, calling out 'Wait!'; but soon, all that could be seen was a cloud of dust. Rama had glanced back, and not wishing to prolong the agony, asked Sumantra to drive faster. Dasharatha kept staring ahead, long after the chariot was out of sight, till the last specks of dust settled. At that moment, he felt his heart would break into a million pieces and fell to the ground, haunted by the incident in the forest so many decades ago as if it were yesterday. The old king realized that karma had caught up with him.[21] Every action inevitably has its consequence in this lifetime or another, and none can escape the destiny they have ordained for themselves. We shape our future by what we set in motion by our own deeds, and there are no exceptions to this law. Dasharatha's three queens rushed to his aid and tried to lift him, but as Kaikeyi came near, he pushed her away in disgust. 'Do not touch me, selfish woman,' he said, 'Begone from my sight forever. I never want to see you again in this world or the next. I renounce you as my wife from this day; may your greed to rule be fulfilled as a widow. As for your son Bharata, if he accepts this kingdom, I disown him too and forbid him from making any offerings at my funeral.' Having spat out this biting rebuke, he left with Kaushalya for her palace, feeling he could only find solace in her company.

They grieved late into the night as the king felt his life slowly slipping away, and Kaushalya, inconsolable like a cow separated from her calf, lamented that her pain was excruciating. She cursed destiny for dealing her such a hard blow, and weeping with tears running down her face in torrents, bemoaned that death would not come to her before its appointed time. Sumitra was the only one who displayed fortitude. Despite the sad parting from her son, she had remained remarkably composed through the events of that fateful day. Consoling Kaushalya with inspiring words, she said, 'Stay strong for Rama's sake and be proud of giving birth to someone as virtuous as he. By upholding his father's promise and placing dharma over personal interest, he has set a shining example to the world. His noble actions have delivered him the highest victory, and with the flag of his glory fluttering so high, how can you grieve like this? Keep your faith; pray for his well-being and safe return, knowing that he will be back with Sita in fourteen years, and there will be joy in Ayodhya once again.' Hearing Sumitra, Kaushalya was comforted and wiped her tears.

---

[21] In the Brihadaranyaka Upanishad IV. 4–5, the Sage Yagnavalkya discusses karma:
'You are what your deep driving desire is.
As is your desire, so is your will.
As is your will, so is your deed.
As your deed is, so is your destiny.'

Chapter 7

Exile to the Forest

Rama's fourteen years of exile commenced as the chariot sped out of the city. Many citizens of Ayodhya refused to stay behind and faithfully followed their prince in solidarity. Advising them to turn back and return to their families, Rama said, 'Accept Bharata wholeheartedly as your new king; he is kind and heroic and deserves the same respect that you give me.' However, the people were undeterred and tirelessly trailed the chariot all day till they reached the banks of the river Tamasa. There they tethered the horses and set up camp. Soon dusk turned to night, and everyone prepared to rest, exhausted by the long day of travel.

After their evening worship, Lakshmana made a bed of leaves for Rama and Sita, and while they slept, he kept vigil with Sumantra through the night. The following day, Rama arose early, before any of the others. He looked at the sleeping subjects who had given up everything to be with him, and his heart filled with compassion.[1] Whispering to Lakshmana, he said, 'I cannot permit these people to suffer on my account, sacrificing the comforts they have worked so hard for all their lives. Let us leave this place before they awaken. If they cannot follow us anymore, they will be forced to go back to Ayodhya.' He instructed Sumantra to drive the chariot in various directions; north, south, east, west and in circles to confuse their trail. Then they set off in haste and were far gone before anyone awoke. With no discernible tracks to follow, the people had little choice but to return to the city in despair.

Sumantra drove the chariot a great distance that day as they sped through villages and fields traversing Kosala's lush lands. When they reached the

---

[1] Compassion—karuna is one of the four attitudes a yogi cultivates, along with unconditional friendliness—maitri, joy in the happiness of others—mudita, and tolerance of people's faults—upeksha.

border, Rama turned back nostalgically to take a last look at his beloved
homeland before taking his leave of it. Travelling southwards, they crossed
the rivers Vedashruti, Gomti and Syandika, and by nightfall, they reached
Shringaverapura.[2] This little habitation stood by the Ganga, the blessed river
that flowed in all three worlds, which had been brought to earth by the
penance of Rama's ancestor, Bhagiratha. Here, its banks were dotted with
hermitages hidden in the thick forests that lined it on both sides, and its
crystal-clear waters thronged with a variety of creatures: sharks, crocodiles,
snakes, swans and cranes, who made it their abode. Finally, Rama spotted
a place where they could camp for the night and asked Sumantra to halt,
saying, 'Let's stop here; I see a large ingudi[3] tree with shady branches covered
in flowers, where we can take shelter and rest till dawn.'

This area was home to the nishada[4] tribe. They were forest dwellers
who lived off the land, hunting and fishing, and their chieftain was Guha.
Although he was not of the same social standing as Rama, they shared a
close association, so when Guha learned that his dear friend had arrived in
his domain, he felt highly honoured and immediately rushed to meet him.
Embracing[5] Rama warmly, he said, 'Welcome to our land! The entire Earth
is yours, including my kingdom, so consider me your servant. You may stay
here as long as you like and rule as king.' Warmed by Guha's generosity,
Rama embraced him back, saying, 'Thank you, dear friend, for your affection
and kind offer, but I have made a promise to live as a hermit, forsaking all
luxuries for fourteen years. I am content to sleep on a bed of grass and will
not partake of food today as I am fasting. However, I would be grateful if

[2] The place is twenty-two miles from Allahabad (recently renamed Prayagraj) and is still
visited today. The spot where Rama crossed the Ganga is marked by a dais called Ram
Chaura. The area was excavated by Professor B.B. Lal, Sarvashri K.V. Soundararajan,
and K.N. Dikshit, of the Archaeological Survey of India. The book *Excavations at
Sringaverapuram 1977–86* by B.B. Lal contains details of their findings, which included
tanks for rainwater harvesting.

[3] Botanical name *Balanitis aegyptica* or desert date.

[4] The tribe still exists in Uttar Pradesh, and its members continue to follow their
traditional water-centric occupations of boating and fishing.

[5] An instance that shows there was no class distinction at the time because Guha feels
comfortable enough to embrace Rama. This fact may seem surprising to the modern
reader, but non-discrimination is the very basis of Vedic philosophy; more on the subject
in the Appendices.

you could provide my horses with water and fodder, for they have ferried us a long distance.'

Everyone settled down for the night, but Lakshmana refused to rest and stood guard, unwearied despite the tedious journey. Noticing this, Guha said, 'Please rest, dear prince. Rama is very dear to me, too, so I assure you that my people and I will keep watch and ensure no harm comes to him. No one knows this forest better than us, and we are confident of thwarting even the slightest danger that might arise.' Lakshmana's mind was still churning over the events that had led to Rama's exile, and an uncontrollable rage was boiling inside him. Warmed by Guha's words, he unburdened himself, saying, 'I do not doubt your ability to protect my brother and his wife, but unfortunately, sleep eludes me tonight. I cannot bear to see their suffering as they lie on the hard ground, and my mind is restless, recalling the sorrow in Ayodhya when we left. My mother Sumitra has Shatrughana for support, but I fear my father and mother Kaushalya are so broken that they may not survive till we return, and we may never see them again.' Seeing the brave warrior so distraught, Guha felt warm salty tears run down his face.

On the morrow, sunrise was heralded by the call of the cuckoo bird, announcing that it was time to move on. That day they would cross the swift-flowing Ganga in search of a suitable place to set up home. Thanking Sumantra for his service and bidding him farewell, Rama said, 'We have crossed the borders of Kosala, so we should abandon the chariot and proceed on foot. I am grateful to you for bringing us here, but now it's time for you to return to Ayodhya.' Although Sumantra found it hard to tear himself away, he reluctantly agreed when Rama managed to convince him of the need to confirm to Kaikeyi that her orders had been followed. Then, reminding him of his duty to the kingdom as Dasharatha's trusted adviser, he requested Sumantra to assuage his father's sorrow by reassuring him that all was well with the three of them and to assist Bharata in ruling the land.

Rama then asked Lakshmana to join him in collecting sap from a banyan tree, and using it, they matted their hair in completion of their guise as hermits, shedding the last vestiges of royalty. Soon, the two princes, like rishis resplendent in their virtue, headed towards the Ganga with Sita. Then they took their leave of Guha, who had arranged a boat and a helmsman to ferry them across the mighty river. As they crossed, Sita prayed fervently, 'O sacred river, carry us across safely and protect the sons of Dasharatha, so that we may return unharmed after fourteen years. When we are back,

I vow to show my gratitude with generous donations of clothes, food and 1,00,000 cows.'

The other side of the river was thickly forested and dangerous, infested with many predatory animals. Concerned for Sita's safety, Rama warned Lakshmana, 'We are now truly on our own and without friends in an unknown place. Peril could await us at any instance, so we must be alert to any possible threat, especially ensuring Sita's safety. I suggest you walk ahead, clearing the path with her in the middle while I bring up the rear.' They journeyed in this manner all day and by evening, found themselves in the kingdom of Vatsa. Not having eaten for two days, they hunted a deer[6] and prepared to rest for the night after consuming its roasted meat.

Rama could not sleep, tormented by thoughts of their family in Ayodhya. Sharing his concerns with Lakshmana, he said, 'I feel unsettled, worrying about our mothers Kaushalya and Sumitra. The king looked weak and worn when we left. The influence of kama[7] is overpowering and even forced our father to give me up though I was always obedient to him. He will not protect our mothers in his current state of mind if Kaikeyi uses her newly acquired position to treat them unkindly. I would feel more at ease if you returned to Ayodhya tomorrow morning to care for them. I see no problem in proceeding with Sita from this point.'

Lakshmana's eyes teared up. He was devoted to Rama beyond expression in words, and refusing to be parted from him, pleaded, 'You know I cannot live without you, my dear brother, so do not make me leave your side. If I were to go back, I would die gasping for breath just like a fish pulled out of water.' Seeing his intense love, Rama conceded and agreed that Lakshmana could stay.

The next day, the three of them continued walking along the banks of the Ganga till they reached its confluence with the Yamuna at Prayag.[8] When they saw the swirling smoke of a sacrificial fire from a hermitage in the distance, they headed towards it. By sunset, they arrived at a clearing

---

[6] Rama was a Kshatriya, so he would have eaten meat and Valmiki mentions this in the early stage of his exile. However, over his stay in the forest he appears to give it up. Later, when Kabandha tells him about plump fish in the Pampa Lake, there is no mention of consumption. Also, in describing Rama's sorrow to Sita, Hanuman says he eats only a few roots and fruit once a day.

[7] Sensual desire.

[8] Modern-day Allahabad, recently renamed Prayagraj.

in the forest, where the revered Sage Bharadwaja lived with his disciples. Introducing himself to the holy man, Rama said, 'Venerable master, I am Rama, son of King Dasharatha of Ayodhya, and am accompanied by my brother Lakshmana and my wife Sita, the Princess of Videha.[9] We have been exiled for fourteen years and are looking for a place to settle and make our home. I would be grateful for your advice on where to stay.'

Welcoming them, Bharadwaja said warmly, 'I have been awaiting your arrival! I heard about the unfortunate incident that resulted in your exile and can see how painful it must be for you, especially since you did no wrong. You may reside in my ashram if you wish. It is a peaceful place sanctified by the confluence of two great rivers, and you will find comfort here.'

Rama thanked him but accepted his hospitality only for the night. He felt the ashram was too close to Ayodhya and enquired if there was a more isolated spot, fearing that the people would not let him fulfil his vow to live in seclusion. Bharadwaja reflected for a moment and told him about the Chitrakoota[10] Mountain, south of the Yamuna. He said, 'Chitrakoota, a few yojanas away, is the perfect place for you, so I suggest you proceed there. It has an abundance of trees bearing all kinds of edible fruit; also, you will have no trouble finding honey and tubers to eat. The river Mandakini flows nearby, and herds of gentle animals, like elephants and deer, roam the sylvan mountain slopes. There is music in the air from the call of birds like the cuckoo and waterhen. Moreover, it is home to many great sages, a holy place where much austerity has been practised over the ages, and I am sure you, too, will find solace there.'

At first light the following day, the three began the journey to Chitrakoota, setting out on a large raft they built out of logs and bamboo. Loading it with their weapons and Sita's clothes and jewellery, they crossed the swift-flowing Yamuna. When they reached the other bank, they came across a holy site with a giant Banyan tree that Bharadwaja had mentioned. He said it was a hallowed spot from the accumulated energies of the many sages who had meditated beneath it. Sita joined her palms and circled the tree clockwise, once again praying for their safe return at the end of fourteen years. Then,

---

[9] Rama's introduction shows women retained their own identity. Sita was also called Vaidehi because she was from the kingdom of Videha.

[10] A famous pilgrimage centre that lies in Madhya Pradesh today. It has several temples including the Bharat Milap temple marking where Bharata tried to persuade Rama to return to Ayodhya.

they continued towards Chitrakoota, following the path indicated to them. As they approached, they marvelled at the beautiful fauna and flora amidst the vast forest ablaze with the flagrant red blossoms of kimsuka[11] trees. The mountain loomed ahead, with its peak rising high as if to pierce the sky, and its bucolic wooded slopes were a serene haven of tranquillity, just as Rishi Bharadwaja had described. The air was crisp, and the waters of the Mandakini were clear. Multitudes of swans, cranes, deer and elephants thronged the river, frolicking gleefully in it. Dancing waterfalls dotted the fascinating landscape, painting a pretty picture. The trees were covered in divinely fragrant flowers and laden with fruit like mangoes, jackfruit, jamuns[12] and pomegranates. Rama was enchanted; surveying the breathtaking beauty of their surroundings, he exclaimed happily, 'This will be our home! Think of this mountain as Ayodhya and the river as the Sarayu.'

Valmiki's ashram was nearby, so they went to pay their respects to the sage. In the meantime, Lakshmana, always at his brother's service, collected wood, leaves and reeds and built a lovely little thatched cottage by the river. They offered prayers of purification[13] before moving in and put aside their grief to begin a new life in communion with nature. Rama felt at peace; he was satisfied he had done his duty in upholding his father's promise and happy with the sacrifice he had made by giving the kingdom to Bharata. He asked Sita and Lakshmana to join him in finding joy in their exile; it would be an opportunity to spend time in the excellent company of sages, further educating themselves and leading an existence of self-discipline.

Vedic sages, known as rishis,[14] were scholars who had abandoned worldliness for a life of learning and contemplation. They were enlightened people, and the accumulated revelations of the greatest amongst them were compiled in the Vedas,[15] the sacred repository of knowledge that influenced

---

[11] *Butea monosperma*. Commonly called palash, or flame of the forest.

[12] *Syzygiumjambos* or Malabar plum

[13] This purification ritual, one that welcomes positive energy into a dwelling, is still practised before people move into a new home.

[14] There is no English word that fully captures the meaning of the word rishi, as they did not exist outside Vedic culture. Rishis were extraordinarily enlightened people who had given up material life. Peculiarly, they were both scientists and philosophers at the same time.

[15] Rishis were not priests or religious preachers. The various rituals described in the Karmakanda section of the Vedas deal with lower knowledge. The Vedic sages ignored ceremonial observances and sought higher knowledge of the Universal Consciousness described in the Upanishads.

all aspects of human life. Rishis achieved extraordinary powers through the unusual combination of academic pursuit and spiritual concentration. They did not propound religion, but engaged themselves in scholarship and intense yogic meditation, through which they received profound wisdom on universal truths. These spiritual masters made discoveries about the world in a transcendental state of higher consciousness, delving into the depths of the mind and beyond. The attainment of samadhi[16] allowed yogis to find the truth about life and the fundamental reality of the self.[17] Due to the might of their intense mental focus, they even developed supernatural powers, like teleportation and the ability to see the future. While they were distinguished philosophers, rishis were also eminent scholars on subjects like medicine, astronomy, mathematics, physics, chemistry, engineering, botany, literature and even the art of warfare. They embodied the unique union of science and spirituality, and Rama was looking forward to broadening his intellectual horizons in their elite company.

---

[16] State of yogic union with the cosmic consciousness.

[17] The knowledge of the inner self is the ultimate truth discussed in the Upanishads. It is the enlightenment that the real self is no different from the universal consciousness called Brahman that pervades all of creation. Four cryptic lines called Mahavakyas, or great utterances, express this:

1. Prajnanam Brahma – Consciousness is Brahman. Rig Veda—Aitareya Upanishad 3.3
2. Aham Brahmasmi – I am Brahman. Atharva Veda—Mandukya Upanishad 1.2
3. Tat Tvam Asi – That (Brahman) thou art. Sama Veda—Chandogya Upanishad 6.8.7
4. Ayam Atma Brahma – This self is Brahman. Yajur Veda—Brihadaranyaka Upanishad 1.4.10

Chapter 8

The Death of Dasharatha

Unknown to Rama, Sita and Lakshmana, they were followed the whole way by spies sent by Guha. Sumantra had not yet left Shringaverapura and was waiting for their return before departing. Only once informed that the three were safely ensconced in Chitrakoota did he set out for Ayodhya. When Sumantra reached the city, he found it still in mourning, its vibrance replaced by lassitude. The people nurtured a faint hope that Rama might have a change of heart and return, so some rushed forward as Sumantra's chariot sped by to inquire why he had not brought their beloved prince back. However, Sumantra did not stop; he made his way directly to Dasharatha, anxious to inform him of all that had transpired since Rama left. He hoped to put the king's mind at rest with the comfort that his children had established residence in Chitrakoota and sent their respects to him and their mothers.

Sumantra conveyed Rama's request to Kaushalya to forgive Kaikeyi and look upon her kindly. He delivered the special message for Bharata to treat all their mothers like his own and spoke about Sita's devotion to her husband and stoic acceptance of their circumstances. Lakshmana, he said, had come to terms with Rama's exile though his anger had not abated. He had sent an unusual message that Sumantra conveyed to the king with significant discomfort. Lakshmana wanted his father to know that he could not forgive him for mistreating his brother. Therefore, he did not consider him his parent anymore and would now look upon Rama to fulfil that role. Much to everyone's surprise, Dasharatha was not upset when he heard this pronouncement. On the contrary, although Lakshmana had rejected him, he felt relieved at his words, knowing that Rama had his undiluted support.

Sumantra had hoped to ease Dasharatha's pain, but his anguish was unabated. He wailed pathetically, 'I can't imagine how my beloved children will endure living in the wilderness in those harsh conditions? They were used to resting on the softest silken bedding, but now sleep on the cold ground. After dining on the finest food all their lives, they eke out meagre sustenance from measly scraps they find. The best horse-drawn chariots were at their command, but they are now condemned to walk endlessly on foot instead. I feel unbearable agony at the hardship my blameless children are forced to suffer. This tragedy is all my fault! I acted in haste at the insistence of my wicked wife, Kaikeyi. Caught between my promise to her and my duty to my people, I acted impetuously without counsel. I should have discussed the matter with my advisers before summoning Rama; they might have guided me otherwise. Take me to Rama so I can beg him to return, for I cannot bear the sorrow of his absence any longer.' With his energy spent in this outburst, Dasharatha lost consciousness.

When he regained his senses, he saw Kaushalya in a distressed state. She, who was always so gentle and understanding, scolded him sharply. 'Maharaja, your generosity is well known, yet your compassion did not extend to your son. My heart aches to imagine the suffering the delicate Vaidehi is going through right now. I have no idea when I will see Rama's beautiful face again, and I am so devastated that it is surprising I am still alive. It was cruel of you to exile your blameless son. He is so righteous that he did not attempt to take the kingdom by force, even though he could easily have done so. How could you perpetrate such an injustice on one so virtuous? Despite being his father and protector, you betrayed him like a fish that eats its offspring. When he returns after fourteen years, I doubt Bharata will give the kingdom back to him. Your favourite wife bewitched you, bringing about the ruination of this kingdom solely for her happiness and that of her son.'

Dasharatha folded his hands and begged for forgiveness, pleading that he was already suffering enough. Seeing her glorious husband in such abject misery, Kaushalya felt ashamed about losing her self-control and quickly apologized, 'Please forgive me; grief plays great havoc! It has warped my mind and destroyed my fortitude. It was wrong of me to lash out at you so harshly.'

That night before sleeping, as Dasharatha pined for Rama, he unburdened himself of his long-held secret. He confided in Kaushalya about the terrible misdeed he had committed as a young prince and how the same anguish he caused the aged parents decades ago had now come back to haunt him. The old king knew in his heart that he could not escape his past karma and sensed he would not live much longer. Feeling his vision and all his faculties failing slowly, he exclaimed, 'Those who live for the next fourteen years should consider themselves fortunate, as they will see Rama return.' These were the last words Dasharatha spoke.

It had been six days since Rama left when King Dasharatha succumbed to his sorrow in his sleep, passing away in the night like a lamp that had run out of oil. In the morning, the royal panegyrists tried to wake him in the custom of the day, singing his glory, but he was unresponsive. Kaushalya and Sumitra, who were suffering from their sons' separation, were now dealt another blow, widowhood. The king's demise had come on the heels of Rama's exile, resulting in much weeping in the palace already in a state of gloom. Without a leader at the helm, Ayodhya was now like a rudderless boat drifting in the ocean without direction. Dasharatha was blessed with four sons, yet not one was present at his death; Rama and Lakshmana were in exile, and Bharata and Shatrughana were far away in Kekaya.

Seven wise Brahmins—Markandeya, Maudgalya, Vamadeva, Kashyapa, Katyayana, Gautama and Jabali—came together to caucus with Vasishta on the proposed course of action in this precarious time of political uncertainty. They asked Vasishta to select a king to take charge urgently, for a kingdom without a leader ran the risk of rapidly descending into a lawless state. Society faced the danger of disintegrating, with the law of fish taking over, the strong inevitably devouring the weak. Moreover, the risk of invasion by hostile nations posed a serious concern, and internally, law and order could crumble to the point where it would be unsafe for women to step outside after dusk. However, Vasishta said picking someone to fill the empty throne was unnecessary because the king had already chosen his replacement. All that was required was to summon Bharata from Kekaya, so five messengers were dispatched immediately. Siddhartha, Vijaya, Jayanta, Ashoka and Nandana set out on the swiftest horses with gifts for King Ashwapati and the charge to bring the prince home. They were particularly instructed not to mention Rama's exile or the king's death, only conveying that Bharata was needed in Ayodhya urgently due to a pressing matter.

They rode furiously through many lands and made their way across the Ganga at Hastinapur.[1] Continuing north-westwards, they galloped

---

[1] Hastinapur is modern-day Meerut.

through Panchala,[2] Kurujangala,[3] and past the gently flowing Sharadanda River frequented by birds. Next, they reached the city of Kulinga and the village of Abhikala, crossing the sacred Ikshumati, associated with Rama's ancestors, flowing from the Bodhibhavana Mountain.[4] After that, they rode towards the Sudama Mountains,[5] passing through Bahalika. Then, from the mountain peak, the messengers beheld the river Vipasa[6] and an area called Vishnu Padam[7] before eventually arriving at their destination. They took the most expeditious route, riding through forests almost without a break, and by nightfall the riders and their tired horses reached Rajagriha, the capital of Kekaya.

Bharata was enjoying his visit with his grandfather, but strangely the very night the messengers arrived, he had ominous nightmares. In his dream, he saw his father in a crazed state, with his head shaven, falling from a cliff into a heap of cow dung. Then, he saw the ocean turning dry, the moon falling to the ground, a blazing fire and burning trees. He also had visions of people dressed in black and the king driving a chariot drawn by donkeys heading southwards.[8] While he was narrating his unsettling dream to Shatrughana and his other companions in the morning, the messengers came to see him. As instructed, they told him that he was needed back in Ayodhya for some urgent business. Surprised at the abrupt summons home, Bharata asked, 'I trust my noble father is fine and that Rama and Lakshmana are in good health? How about Rama's pious mother, Kaushalya, and my virtuous middle mother, Sumitra? Is there a special message from my own mother? She tends to be selfish, arrogant and peevish, so I hope all is well with her?'

The messengers replied that there was no cause for concern as good fortune shone on him, so, reassured, Bharata and Shatrughana prepared to

---

[2] Western Uttar Pradesh.

[3] Located in Haryana.

[4] Ikshumati is perhaps the Swat River described as flowing down from Bodhibahavana, the Hindu Kush. It was called the Ikshumati, alluding to the Ikshavaku dynasty and Shibi who ruled the area. (Jayashree Saranathan blog, 11 November 2017: *Swat River Valley—The Region of Rama's Ancestors!*)

[5] Could be the Sulaiman Mountains.

[6] Vipasa is called the Beas today.

[7] Vishnu's feet.

[8] Yama, the god of death, was the guardian of the southern quarter.

leave immediately, without any further ado. King Ashwapati provided them with a grand chariot, sending them home with generous gifts, including carpets, deer skins, 2000 gold coins, many majestic elephants, 1600 prize horses and several well-trained hunting dogs[9] with large fangs, as powerful as tigers.

Travelling eastwards, Bharata and his party crossed the Sudama and Hladini; then, finally, the mighty rivers Shutudri,[10] Saraswati,[11] Yamuna and Ganga. The journey back was via a much longer circuitous route and took a week, because they could not go through the forest with the large entourage that followed. Then, at last, they approached Ayodhya, and seeing it again in the distance, Bharata felt a warmth surge through his body. He had missed his home and family more than he realized and was looking forward to being with them again. However, as they entered the city through the western gate, Vaijayanta, the place appeared eerily quiet. It was lifeless, with none of the usual hustle and bustle; no chatter of people busy with their daily activities; no sound of Brahmins chanting sacred hymns; no musical notes of the veena and kettledrums echoing in the streets; and even the beautiful pleasure gardens were bereft of lovers. The shops were shuttered and the place seemed deserted, as if abandoned by the people. The houses looked neglected, and the front courtyards were unswept. There was no sign of oblations offered to the holy fires and no worship conducted at the temples. Bharata hurried quickly to his father's palace with great apprehension, worrying why he had been called back without being given a reason. To his surprise, the king was nowhere in sight, so he went to his mother. He was sure his father would be there with his favourite queen.

Kaikeyi was reclining on her golden couch and excitedly sprang to her feet at the sight of her son. She embraced him tightly, kissed his forehead and pulled him to sit beside her. Then she inquired tenderly about his journey home, eagerly asking about his stay at Kekaya and her father and brothers' well-being. Bharata assured her that they were all in good health, but was impatient to know his father's whereabouts. He expressed concern that the city looked unusually gloomy and wondered why he was asked to come back

---

[9] Mastiffs/Molossers are one of the oldest breeds, of which the Afghan Tiger Dog is found in this area.

[10] Sutlej.

[11] The mention of the river Saraswati indicates that the Ramayana was composed when it was still a mighty river, well before it completely dried up in 1900 BCE.

in such haste. Kaikeyi spoke without emotion, omitting to mention her role in her husband's demise. She said matter-of-factly, 'Sadly, everyone has to embrace death at some point. Unfortunately, the noble king met the fate that is the inevitable destiny of all mortals and has gone the way of all flesh.'

Bharata was grief-stricken to hear his mother's words and fell to the floor, where he lay weeping for a long time. Previously he had conjectured that the sudden order back to Ayodhya was to attend Rama's coronation; after all, he was the eldest son, and everyone expected his ascension to the throne sometime soon. Irritated at his distress, Kaikeyi said in a vexed tone, 'Get up; it doesn't become a king to give in to excessive emotion and roll despondently on the floor.'

Bharata never imagined he would not see his father ever again, and ignoring her instruction, asked incredulously, 'How did the king die, and what were his last words? Where is Rama? He should have taken our father's place by now?'

Recounting Dasharatha's final moments, Kaikeyi said, 'The king died of sorrow, calling out to Rama, Sita and Lakshmana; he said those who lived for the next fourteen years to welcome them back from exile should consider themselves lucky.'

Bharata was aghast to hear the word exile; feeling an uncomfortable knot in his stomach, he asked in disbelief, 'Why was Rama exiled? I find it impossible to believe that he could have done anything egregious enough to warrant banishment or even that he could have exiled himself in atonement for a crime. I cannot imagine Rama would ever stray from dharma by stealing someone else's property, unfairly killing an innocent person or appropriating another man's wife, so why was he sent away?'

Kaikeyi then enthusiastically recounted the events that had taken place and how she had so expertly paved the way for Bharata to inherit the throne. Gloating over her achievement, she said, 'I asked for the two boons that your father had once granted me and used them to make you king, and as for Rama, he went away of his own accord to uphold the king's promise. Dasharatha died of sorrow, and the throne is vacant, waiting for you. Now please go and see Vasishta so that your coronation can happen as quickly as possible.'

Unfortunately, Kaikeyi did not know her son! She had seriously misjudged him, thinking Bharata would be overjoyed to hear of his good fortune; instead, he was appalled and lashed out sharply. 'You are a treacherous and despicable woman; after carrying out one evil deed after another, you are now rubbing salt in my wounds by asking me to become king! What is the use of this kingdom without my father and brother? Your malicious actions have destroyed our family, killing my father and committing my brother to the life of an ascetic. Only a wicked demoness would stoop so low, abandoning dharma to perpetrate something so sinful, and I am thoroughly ashamed to be your son. I forsake my relationship with you this instant. You have humiliated your father, King Ashwapati, with your greed and are a blot on your noble lineage. Rama always treated you with love and respect, so how could you repay him with such heartlessness, depriving mother Kaushalya of her only son? I will never accept the crown, so I can assure you that your evil plan is doomed to fail. You know the rule in our family is for the eldest son to be king, so how can you expect me to flout tradition and bring infamy to my name?

'I do not want the kingdom; I intend to bring Rama back and redeem my honour by retiring to the forest in his place. Let it be your son who lives in exile! I must do everything I can to undo the damage you have done and restore dharma with sincere repentance for your misdeeds. Your evil conduct has placed a terrible burden on me, and I cannot rest till the wrong you have done is righted. I need to establish my innocence and salvage my reputation in the eyes of the world, for I am sure everyone thinks I am complicit in your scheming machinations. Hell is the only fitting place for a deplorable person like you, so you should immolate yourself in shame or, at the very least, voluntarily leave this kingdom in disgrace. There is no other way you can redeem yourself from your villainous behaviour, and I cannot bear to stand here in your presence a moment longer.'

Appalled by Kaikeyi's callousness towards Rama, after spitting out this scathing rebuke, Bharata rushed to see Kaushalya. He found her with Sumitra, looking haggard, a shadow of her former self. Kaushalya did not express her characteristic joy at seeing him and instead said sarcastically, 'You and your mother have cleverly conspired to obtain the kingdom. Now you have it to enjoy; the path has been cleared for you at the expense of my son, so go rule happily and leave me to my sorrow.'

Bharata felt mortified at Kaushalya's misjudgement of him, and falling at her feet, professed deep regret for his mother's unethical actions. Protesting tearfully, he pleaded, 'O noble lady, O arya, do not censure me. Unfortunately, the blood of a wicked woman runs in my veins, but I had no knowledge of her corrupt ambitions, or I would have surely stopped her. Rama is dearer to me than life itself, and I cannot imagine taking his rightful place as king. If I had any designs on the kingdom or played any part in my mother's evil conspiracy, may I be deprived of all my knowledge of the Vedas and suffer the harsh consequences of sinful actions,[12] like the one who keeps bad company. The one who ill-treats animals, kicking a sleeping cow. The one who overburdens those who serve him. The one who kills a good king. The one who breaks a promise. The one who commits money to a priest for a ritual and quibbles when paying him. The one who does not follow ethics in warfare. The one who does not show respect to his parents or lets down a friend in need. The one who disrespects his guru. The one who does not make offerings to the Devas. The one who talks behind a person's back. The one who eats without sharing food with his guest. The one who eats fresh food with his family and gives stale leftovers to his servants. The one who kills a Brahmin, a child, a woman or an aged person. The one who makes money from selling liquor, meat, iron or poison. The Kshatriya who deserts the battlefield. The one who gambles a woman. The one who steals. The one who sleeps at sunrise or sunset instead of offering due worship. The one who does not perform 'shraddha' for his departed parents. The one who does not offer water to a thirsty person. The one who milks a cow that has calved less than ten days ago. The one who pollutes water or commits arson. The one who turns a blind eye to wrongdoing. The one who ignores his wife and lusts after another's. The king who collects one-sixth in tax from his subjects and does not protect them.'

Bharata's sincerity was abundantly clear, and seeing his great love for Rama, Kaushalya regretted her unwarranted accusation. So, begging forgiveness for her harsh words, she lovingly embraced and comforted him.

In the meantime, Vasishta was anxious to conduct the king's funeral. The embalmed body lay preserved in a trough of oil, and the cremation was long overdue.[13] Now that Bharata was back, it was time to perform the last rites without delay. The ashen corpse was lifted out and placed on a luxurious bed decorated with jewels as the officiating priests prepared a sandalwood pyre. It was then taken on a palanquin in a large procession, with gold and silver coins scattered in its path. The fire blazed as oblations were poured, and the body was consigned to flames to the chanting of Vedic hymns. The royal women

---

[12] The sins mentioned by Bharata point to the values of the society.

[13] A corpse was ideally supposed to be cremated within two muhurtas (ninety-six minutes), to free the spirit from attachment to the body and help its onward journey.

circumambulated the pyre[14] anti-clockwise, weeping inconsolably. While Ayodhya mourned, a teary Bharata performed the water-rites for his father's departed spirit on the banks of the Sarayu. Ten days later, as the eldest son present, he performed the shraddha ceremony, a ritual to pay homage to his father's memory and pray for the peace of his spirit in the other world. On the twelfth day, he donated a large amount of wealth to charity, and on the thirteenth day, he collected the mortal remains from the cremation ground and immersed them in the Sarayu. 'O father,' Bharata cried out, 'You have abandoned us and sent Rama to the forest. Shatrughana and I are alone now and in terrible agony.' Seeing Bharata weakened by grief, Vasishta consoled him, explaining the necessity of accepting what cannot be changed. Taking him by the shoulders, he spoke about the inevitability of death and reminded him that leaving the body was not the end but a necessary stage in the spirit's ongoing journey.[15] While Vasishta spoke to Bharata, Sumantra comforted Shatrughana, explaining that departure from the world is inescapable and must be accepted just like all other milestones.[16]

The following day, fourteen days after the king's passing, the counsellors headed by Vasishta broached the topic of the vacant throne. They pleaded with Bharata to assume power immediately, expressing grave concern that the kingdom was dangerously unattended without a ruler. But Bharata would not hear of it; turning them down very firmly, he said, 'I am troubled that you have misjudged me to such an extent that you think I will accept what is not

---

[14] Women were clearly not forbidden to go to the cremation grounds, so this practice must have sprung up later.

[15] In Vedic belief while the body perishes, the real inner self (the Atman) never dies. The Mandukya Upanishad from the Atharva Veda, discusses four states of consciousness. We fear death because we are aware only of three states: waking, dreaming and deep sleep. However, our real existence is in the fourth state called 'Turiya' or pure consciousness, which is eternal. It is the witness to the other three states, which are just a reflection of it. 'Verily indeed this body dies when deprived of the living self, but the living self does not die. That which is the subtle essence of this whole world, that which is the true reality, is the self. That thou art Svetaketu.' Chandogya Upanishad 6.11.3

[16] Vedic philosophy does not see death as a finality, but a necessary stage in an endless journey of reincarnation till liberation (moksha) from wandering (samsara) is achieved. 'On this ever-revolving wheel of life, the individual self goes round and round, through life after life; believing itself to be a separate entity until it sees its identity with the Lord of Love and attains immortality in the indivisible whole.'—Svetasvatara Upanishad 1.6–8

rightfully mine. Like me, you are all painfully aware that my mother acted in an unprincipled manner by going against our family's custom of the eldest son inheriting the throne. Snatching the kingdom from Rama contravenes the righteous conduct of an arya and forsakes tradition. I plan to bring him back to Ayodhya to rule while I live in the forest in his place. Summon the engineers to build a highway up to the Ganga. I want to take along a large army so that Rama can be anointed king right there and brought home with all the honour that befits a monarch.'

Following Bharata's instructions, the construction began, and he eagerly awaited the road's completion.

Meanwhile, Shatrughana was still bewildered by all that had happened and could not come to grips with Rama's exile. One day while conversing with Bharata, he remarked, 'Lakshmana has great strength and valour; I am surprised that he did not restrain our father when he knew he was under Mother Kaikeyi's evil spell. It is perplexing that he did not prevent him from sending Rama away.' At that very moment, Manthara happened to be strutting around outside, basking in the success of her victory, slathered in perfume, dressed in finery and decked in expensive ornaments lavished on her by Kaikeyi. The guards seized her and pushed her into the room, shouting, 'Here is the wicked wretch who brought about this great calamity. She is the one who poisoned the queen against Rama and should be punished for her chicanery.'

The sight of the hunchback filled Shatrughana with an insurmountable rage. He grabbed her wrist and dragged her violently along the ground with such force that her ornaments broke and scattered all around, clinking as they fell. Manthara shrieked for help at the top of her voice, rightly fearing her life was about to end that day. Hearing the commotion, Kaikeyi arrived to mediate, but the sight of Shatrughana's fury sent her cowering behind her son. Bharata quickly intervened, holding Shatrughana back. Then, sternly admonishing him, he said, 'Stop! I want to remind you that it is against dharma to kill a woman. If this were not the case, I would have done away with my mother by now! Rama would never approve of you straying from righteousness, so for his sake alone, you must calm yourself.' Chastened by his brother's words, Shatrughana released his vice-like grip on Manthara and flung her aside in disgust.

Chapter 9

The Greatness of Bharata

The construction of a road to the Ganga was a massive infrastructure project, but it served to bring the people together with a common purpose that helped shed their despondency. In addition to the highway, rest stops needed to be set up along the way and wells dug to provide water. Unavoidably, numerous trees had to be cut down in the process, but care was taken to plant new ones elsewhere in restitution.[1] When the land was levelled and the road was ready, Bharata set out to fetch Rama, accompanied by Shatrughana, their mothers, the counsellors, ministers, representatives of all four varnas and a large battalion of the army.

They traced the exact steps that Rama had taken that miserable day when he left the city, and like him, they too arrived in Shringaverapura, where they decided to set up camp. When Guha saw Bharata's emblem, a giant kovidara[2] tree fluttering on his chariot, accompanied by a vast army as endless as the ocean, he became concerned about the prince's intentions. He feared Bharata had come to seek Rama out to eliminate him as a contender for the throne. So, Guha told his men to stand ready with expert archers and 500 boats pending his investigation. To verify his suspicion, he went to find out the purpose of Bharata's arrival, determined to prevent his army from crossing the Ganga if they had come in hostility.

---

[1] Vedic culture placed great emphasis on living in harmony with nature. Cutting trees was frowned upon, as it damaged the environment, and if removed, they had to be replaced with new planting. 'Whatever I dig from thee, O earth, may that have quick regrowth again. O purifier, may we not injure thy vitals or thy heart.' Atharva Veda 12.1.35

[2] Botanical name *Bauhinia purpurea* or Orchid tree. It has medicinal properties and is used in Ayurveda.

Guha took baskets of forest produce as homage and proceeded to the camp to better assess the situation. When Sumantra introduced him to Bharata as Rama's friend, who had been so hospitable to him, Guha said politely, 'Our land is in effect the backyard to your kingdom, and we are your servants, so please accept the offerings I have brought to honour you.' After they exchanged cordialities, Bharata asked the best way to reach Rishi Bharadwaja's ashram. Guha said reluctantly, 'We tribal people have an intimate knowledge of every inch of this land and can certainly guide you, but first, I must ask your reason for seeking Rama. I see your big army and fear for his safety.'

Bharata was crushed that Guha suspected him of disloyalty to his brother, and replied woefully, 'I feel wretched that you accuse me of evil intentions. However, your apprehension is unnecessary. My elder brother, Rama, is like a father to me, and I have come with an army only to take him home with due honour as the rightful ruler of Ayodhya, so please assist me in finding him.' Guha was relieved that he was mistaken about Bharata, and recognizing his greatness of heart, praised his integrity and extended his full support.

That night after everyone fell asleep, Bharata paced restlessly and said to Guha, 'Tell me about my brother's night here. Where did Rama, Sita and Lakshmana sleep, and what did they eat?' Guha replied, 'I offered Rama the comforts of my palace, but he refused to stay there and even declined the delicacies I served, satisfying himself with water alone. Instead, he and Sita slept on a bed of grass under an ingudi tree. Lakshmana was so tormented by the injustice done to your brother that he stayed awake with me, ever-vigilant with his bow, constantly watching over them all night.' Bharata went to the ingudi tree and noticed that the grass bed still bore indentations where Rama and Sita had lain. All at once, emotion at the hardships they suffered overwhelmed him. Bharata found it torturous to picture Rama, accustomed to sleeping on a luxurious bed, resting on the bare earth.

Broken-hearted, he took the same vows of austerity, proclaiming, 'From today, the ground will be my bed, roots and fruit my food and hermit's garb my clothing. Rama will return to rule Ayodhya, and I will take his place in exile.'

Karma, the greatest leveller of all, forced Kaikeyi to endure the same pain she had inflicted on Kaushalya when her son voluntarily shed his royal robes and reduced himself to a mendicant.

At sunrise, Guha's men readied more than 500 boats marked with the auspicious swastika[3] sign of well-being, as well as numerous rafts. Then,

---

[3] The Swastika is the Vedic symbol for auspiciousness, denoting peace and well-being. Its four limbs represent the four Vedas, the four Vedic stages of life, the four aspects

after cleaning up their campsite so that no trace of their presence remained, Bharata and his entourage navigated the Ganga and travelled towards Prayag. Some crossed on boats and rafts, others climbed onto the backs of elephants and horses, while the adventurous ones swam across. Leaving the army and the rest of the party a short distance away, Bharata went on foot with Vasishta and Shatrughana to meet Rishi Bharadwaja, dressed simply in a silk dhoti, devoid of his ornaments and weapons.[4] The sage welcomed them cordially, but like Guha, he too had misgivings about Bharata's motives. Questioning his intentions, Bharadwaja said, 'I am concerned about your reason for coming here. I hope you do not intend to do any harm to Rama. His character is spotless; he has given up his claim to the kingdom to uphold his father's word and is not a threat to you in any way.'

Bharadwaja was a great luminary, deeply respected for his extraordinary scientific knowledge. He was not only an eminent physician who had made many contributions to Ayurveda,[5] but was also esteemed for his theories on aeronautics. His Vaimanika Shastra[6] delineated detailed technical specifications of different kinds of aircraft, including the various alloys employed in their construction. He had documented the types of fuel used and advanced mechanisms like cloaking and uncloaking. He had even gone as far as to describe three types of craft capable of flight: those used for travel on Earth, those utilized to get to another planet and those that could go to a different universe.

Bharata felt extremely disconcerted that someone of this immense stature had such a poor opinion of him. Looking visibly downcast, he said sorrowfully, 'Most respected rishi, my heart sinks to hear your words. I cannot imagine harming Rama; I never coveted the throne and had no part in my mother's intrigue to secure it for me. If I was involved in any way, may I lose all the knowledge I have acquired from my gurus this very instant! I am here

---

of Purushartha, the four varnas or professions, the four directions, the four yugas or Vedic epochs and the four seasons. It was found in the excavated sites of the Indus-Saraswati civilizations, the oldest of which dates back as far as the eighth millennium BCE. Unfortunately, Hitler distorted its meaning when he used it to symbolize the Nazi party in propagating his twisted theory of racial supremacy.

[4] Bharata went simply attired as a mark of respect.

[5] Ancient knowledge of well-being; the Vedic science of healing.

[6] Ancient science of aeronautics consisting of 3000 verses in eight chapters.

to express deep remorse at the despicable actions that were carried out in my absence and to beg Rama to return.'

Bharata's genuineness impressed Bharadwaja, and his mistrust was replaced by admiration. He not only agreed to tell Bharata the route to Chitrakoota Mountain, but invited everyone in the royal party to stay the night so that he could host them a dinner. Bharata did not want to impose on the sage's kindness or have his army invade the peace of the ashram since there were so many of them, but relented on Bharadwaja's insistence.

Bharadwaja went before the holy fire; sipping water thrice, he chanted a special mantra and used his yogic powers[7] to invoke Vishwakarma. Through the grace of the divine architect, grand whitewashed houses were erected miraculously, and arrangements were made for an elaborate feast. All the guests were entertained to the hilt as they sipped well-aged wine made of dates and various refreshing drinks made of jaggery, honey and sugarcane. The Gandharvas staged a music recital, and all enjoyed the Apsaras' dance performances. Kubera's magnificent garden manifested itself there with trees bearing the choicest fruit. A pleasant breeze akin to that around Mount Malaya filled the air with the scent of sandalwood. Luxurious couches and seats materialized. Bharadwaja showed Bharata to a throne as his honoured guest, but the virtuous prince did not sit on it. He felt it was improper to take Rama's place, so he circled it respectfully and took a seat next to it as a minister. Beautiful hostesses massaged the guests' feet and served them a sumptuous banquet. There were all kinds of fruit and vegetables, rice and lentils, buttermilk flavoured with cumin seeds and saffron, curds, and a spread of well-roasted meat: goat, jungle fowl and wild boar. The soldiers felt they were in heaven and did not want to leave that incredible paradise. Even the elephants, donkeys, bullocks and horses were pampered and well-fed. Bathing arrangements were made by the riverside, with fresh clothing, footwear, combs, mirrors, sandal paste and various toiletries. The night passed in much revelry, but by dawn, everything was gone as mysteriously as it had appeared. When Bharadwaja asked if everyone had

---

[7] Superhuman abilities were achieved through advanced spiritual practice. These siddhis/yogic powers were 1. Anima—ability to reduce the size of the body; 2. Mahima—ability to expand the size of the body; 3. Garima—ability to make the body heavier; 4. Laghima—ability to become weightless; 5. Prapti—ability to reach any place instantly at will; 6. Prakamya—ability to achieve any desire; 7. Istva—achievement of supremacy; 8. Vastva—control over the panchabhoota or five elements.

enjoyed themselves and if the hospitality was to their satisfaction, Bharata thanked him for his generosity, but was eager to continue his journey. When he expressed a desire to leave for Chitrakoota at the earliest, Bharadwaja gave him directions, explaining that it was only three-and-a-half yojanas away.

The three queen mothers joined Bharata in taking leave of the sage. Kaushalya, full of sorrow and quite emaciated from fasting, went forward first and touched his feet. Sumitra followed, and then Kaikeyi, shamefaced and flushed with embarrassment, knowing how much she was reviled. When Bharadwaja asked Bharata to introduce him to his mothers, he said, 'The noble lady who looks gaunt and grief-stricken is the mother of the tiger among men, Rama. Leaning on her left shoulder is the goddess-like Sumitra, pious mother of Lakshmana and Shatrughana. The third one is the woman I had the misfortune of being born to, responsible for all the turmoil in our family. She is the spiteful person who exiled my blameless brother and caused our father to die in the agony of separation from him. Although she outwardly presents a noble appearance, she is short-tempered, inane, arrogant and full of vanity. Sadly, her behaviour does not befit an arya, and I consider it my tragedy to be her son.'

Bharadwaja saw that Bharata was drawing deep breaths, hissing like an angry serpent when talking about Kaikeyi. Counselling him on his attitude, the sage advised, 'Don't show any further animosity to your mother. I know you see Rama's banishment as a catastrophe, but in the end, it will be for the greater good of humanity.'

After receiving this guidance, Bharata circled Bharadwaja clockwise and left, eager to see Rama. As the enormous army approached Chitrakoota, it kicked up massive clouds of dust, and a thunderous sound resonated for miles as the soldiers marched through the forest. Adding to the ruckus was the clamour of terrified herds of animals scattering hither and thither as they ran for cover. Meanwhile, Rama and Sita were revelling in the natural beauty of their peaceful surroundings. Rama had just remarked on the simple joys they were experiencing, when they were startled by the din. Surprised by the disturbance, he asked Lakshmana to investigate what disrupted the usual serenity of the place. Lakshmana obediently climbed a flowering sala[8] tree and saw a large force of chariots, horses, elephants and infantry looming ahead in the northern direction. 'Hide Sita in a cave and ready your bow and

---

[8] Botanical name *Shorea robusta*.

arrow. A hostile army is heading towards us,' he cried in alarm. Rama asked if he could tell from the markings on the flags whose army it was.

On spotting Bharata's standard displaying a large Kovidara, Lakshmana's temper flared. Seething with rage, he bellowed, 'The enemy is none other than the son of Kaikeyi, on whose account this whole calamity has unfolded. Now that he has obtained the kingdom with his ruthless mother's help, I think he is here to kill you to secure it forever. I will not allow him to succeed in his objective, so do not worry; I will rout him and his entire army, and the slopes of Chitrakoota will be drenched in their blood.'

Rama was perturbed by Lakshmana's rash tirade; trying to placate him, he said, 'Do not let mere conjecture allow you to jump to such harsh conclusions impetuously. If our brother Bharata is coming here, why do you need your bow and arrow? He has always nurtured a great love for us in his heart, and there is no reason to suppose otherwise today. I consider any unkind words spoken about Bharata an affront to me, so put aside this bellicose mood and drop your unnecessary rhetoric about slaying our dear brother, who means more to me than life itself. Bharata is probably visiting because he feels apologetic about my exile, and my heart aches to embrace him. I now see father's old elephant Shatrunjaya in the lead, so maybe he is here too, though I am troubled that I do not see him under the white umbrella.' Admonished by Rama for his outburst, Lakshmana felt ashamed and his anger subsided.

Bharata ordered the army to camp at the foot of the mountain to cause as little damage to the environment as possible. Then he set out with Shatrughana, Sumantra and Guha to locate Rama, declaring he would not have any peace till he convinced his brother to return to Ayodhya. Scanning the area, Bharata clambered up a sala tree, and when he spotted a smoke spiral rising from a fire near a cottage made of leaves, his heart exulted with joy like that of a shipwrecked person seeing the shore. He rushed to Rama, sending word to Vasishta to fetch the three mothers, ministers and advisers. As Bharata neared the thatched hut, he saw strips of bark tied to branches to mark the way. Although the cottage was in a peaceful sanctuary, it looked forbidding, like a lion's den. Hanging outside were arrows with blazing tips, two quivers, two swords, two shields, finger guards and body armour. Heaps of dried dung from deer and buffaloes had been piled up to use as protection from the cold. There was a stack of firewood; flowers were gathered for worship, and a sacrificial altar blazed brightly in the north-east. Inside the dwelling, Rama sat cross-legged with his matted hair, broad shoulders and mighty arms. Beside him were Lakshmana and Sita.

Bharata felt a terrible pang of guilt at being the cause of Rama's unfortunate predicament. Instead of being surrounded by courtiers in Ayodhya, he was now amidst animals in the forest. Blinded by tears and unable to contain himself, Bharata threw himself at his brother's feet, and at a loss for words, kept repeating, 'O arya, O noble one.' Tired and jaded, his face had lost its brilliance; with his hair matted and dressed in hermit's clothes, Bharata was almost unrecognizable. So far, he had been in the unenviable position of being viewed with suspicion by everyone, but Rama did not doubt him even for a moment. Rama was the only one who really knew him and had complete faith in his character. Lifting Bharata and embracing him lovingly, he said tenderly, 'I am happy to see you, but how did you come away leaving your royal duties, and why are you dressed like an ascetic with matted hair? I hope our father is well? And everyone else in Ayodhya, including our mothers?' He did not wait for an answer but continued to ask a series of rhetorical questions to assure Bharata that he had conceded the kingdom without malice. Rama's monologue was a masterpiece on good governance, serving as an instruction on the tenets of an ideal administration, known as 'Ramrajya'.[9]

He began by asking if Bharata held certain critical people in the administration in high esteem. 'I hope you are giving due regard to the valuable guidance of our preceptor? The revered Vasishta has been the Ikshavaku family guru[10] for generations. He is a person of the highest calibre, devoted to dharma, and knowledgeable in all matters. Be assured that our guru will always give you unbiased advice so you can rely on his counsel implicitly. He never has a personal agenda to advance or ulterior motives, so you can be confident his only intent is to ensure your welfare. Guru Vasishta deserves your highest respect because he will ensure that you are always on the right track. His son Suyajna, your personal priest, is equally sagacious. He is an

---

[9] Rule of Rama, marked by justice, equality, peace and prosperity.

[10] A guru was the highest level of teacher and commanded great respect in Vedic culture. Gurus never forced their views on their students. They acted as path illuminators, and it was up to the student to find his way. Therefore, most Vedic teachings are in the form of a dialogue. The following hymn shows the status given to a guru: 'Gurur Brahma, Gurur Vishnu, Gurur Devo Maheshwara. Guru saksat param Brahman, tasmai sri gurave namah'—'Guru is Brahma the creator, Vishnu the preserver and Shiva the destroyer. I offer obeisance to that guru who is the absolute.'—Guru Gita from Skanda Purana

eminent scholar of the Vedas and proficient in all the rituals you must perform for the kingdom's well-being. I trust you honour him, and Sudhanva, your teacher in archery who is astute in political matters? Always show respect to the Devas,[11] unexpected guests, elders, physicians, the learned, as well as your servants. I must warn you, however, to be wary of Brahmins who are worldly-minded and stray from their duty of devoting themselves to the pursuit of learning. Some are superficial in their scholarship but pretend to be pundits, and their advice is of little value. In this regard, I hope you make sure that the holy fire rituals conducted for the prosperity of the people are being performed only by those knowledgeable of the Vedas and well versed in the sacred traditions?'

Then, underscoring the importance of selecting the right team to secure sound counsel, Rama asked, 'I hope that you have appointed upright ministers on whom you can depend so that you benefit from good advice when taking decisions. Support from those who are cultured, learned and righteous, with shared values, forms the basis of a king's success. I trust your private deliberations with your advisers always remain confidential before implementation. Hopefully, your ministers are discreet and can be counted on to keep their silence so that important state matters are not leaked to the public or your vassals prematurely? I am sure you know that it is better to discuss important issues with one wise man who steers you in the right direction, rather than a thousand foolish sycophants who lead you astray. Remember, it is not appropriate to act unilaterally without guidance, or, conversely, have too many people offering nebulous advice on critical matters. You must beware of those with an unclean purpose, like an avaricious physician who fleeces his patient without curing the malady; a disloyal person who conspires against his employer, or a traitorous commander with an eye on power.'

Stressing the importance of equity in criminal jurisprudence, Rama inquired if the law applied uniformly to everyone and if Bharata ensured its application was always fair and unbiased. He questioned, 'When you try an offender, I hope the sentence meted out is neither too harsh nor too lenient for the type of crime committed? Never prosecute anyone without adequate

---

[11] The Devas here are symbolic of the various aspects of nature. Rama is saying that nature, when respected, nourishes human life in turn. The environment in which we live, the earth, air and water must never be polluted, nor should we ever take more from nature than we put back.

deliberation, as the false conviction of an innocent person is a grave offense. Your ministers must be incorruptible enough to arbitrate impartially. If a dispute occurs between a rich man and one who is poor, there must not be a miscarriage of justice due to the exchange of a bribe. Keep in mind that a kingdom cannot prosper unless the laws enacted are egalitarian and the dispensation of justice is even-handed. Remember, being the king, you are ultimately accountable for whatever happens in your domain. In the end, it is your responsibility to ensure that all punishments are meted out fairly, or the tears of those who face injustice will destroy you and your family.'

Rama pointed out that a robust economy coupled with prudent fiscal management of the exchequer laid the foundation for a prosperous society. He asked, 'I hope milk-cows are in abundance because they are your wealth. You must ensure that you have an honest and fiscally competent treasury head. The treasury needs to have a balanced budget that shows income well above expenditure. You must complete infrastructure projects economically as planned so public money is not wasted. Do not procrastinate on implementation once a plan is ready, as delays often result in cost overruns. The Vaishyas must be adequately encouraged in their trade, so that their businesses prosper, increasing the land's wealth. Ensure farmers and cowherds are particularly supported, as they are a vital part of the economy, and their efforts provide succour to everyone. I hope you are careful that charity only goes to those truly in need. Be circumspect about giving donations to any undeserving Brahmins who are greedy or addicted to worldliness.'

Highlighting the personal qualities that are the hallmark of a good leader, Rama said, 'I hope you do not fall victim to indiscipline in your personal life and rise and sleep following a proper routine. It is not appropriate to stay up late into the night dwelling on matters pertaining to the acquisition of wealth.'

Advising Bharata on human relations, he continued, 'Be sure you are accessible to your people by appearing well-attired every morning in the assembly hall to hear their concerns. You must make yourself available to your subjects to address their smallest problems. Foster an atmosphere of free speech, where citizens never hesitate to speak their minds while showing you due deference. The middle path between aloofness and over-familiarity is the best to adopt in your approach. Amongst your subjects, treat children, the elderly and physicians with special consideration, and show great veneration to teachers, ascetics, Devas, unexpected guests and learned Brahmins. I hope you balance your worldly pursuits and spiritual aspirations by avoiding overindulgence in personal pleasures. Greed and over-gratification of the senses only serve to lead one astray, so keep in mind the rule that artha and kama must always be pursued within the boundaries of dharma.[12]

'A disciplined ruler abandons the fourteen sins that kings often succumb to: impiety, falsehood, anger, arrogance, sloth, lust, procrastination, dereliction of duty, disregard for wise advice, obsessive pursuit of wealth and desires, accepting impolitic counsel, being despotic, being loose-lipped and attempting to do too many things at the same time. Seven weaknesses are known to bring about the downfall of even the most firmly established ruler, so avoid engaging in them. They are: womanizing, gambling, hunting, drunkenness, harsh rhetoric, wasteful expenditure and handing out onerous punishments. In addition to avoiding these seven deadly vices, there are ten kinds of people whose company a king should never keep, as they do not follow dharma. Stay away from those who are intoxicated, delusional, insane, enervated, acrimonious, voracious, impulsive, pusillanimous, avaricious or lascivious.'

On internal and external affairs of the kingdom, Rama elaborated, 'I hope that nepotism is never involved in allotting jobs, and that they are assigned solely on capability, based on the skill and merit of the individual. With its sturdy gates, mighty elephants, swift horses, grand chariots and beautiful mansions, the city of Ayodhya has been lovingly nurtured by our ancestors, and you must ensure that it continues to be well protected. You must provide the people with peace to go about their daily business without worrying about their safety. I presume you have chosen a patriotic, valorous, and loyal commander-in-chief to lead your army and that you make sure the warriors and your servants get paid a fair wage, which they receive on time. Delay in payment to salaried individuals causes them significant hardship, and if they are disgruntled, it diminishes their loyalty to you. Soldiers lay down their lives for the land and deserve your highest respect. If you face war with an enemy, be cognizant of six considerations. You must first carefully weigh the circumstances before launching an attack that leads to unnecessary bloodshed. Marching against your adversary right away may not always be the best option. There are four other strategies worth considering: coming to terms with the other party through a peace treaty, biding your time for a

---

[12] Purushartha, discussed in the Appendices.

favourable opportunity, weakening your opponent by causing dissension in the enemy ranks and seeking the support of a powerful ally.'

Regarding external affairs, Rama emphasized keeping a close watch on other kingdoms. He asked, 'I trust that you have selected an intelligent person who is an expert in diplomacy to be your ambassador? Your envoy should not only be tactful, with the presence of mind to assess a situation at hand, communicating an appropriate strategy to you, but must also be one who was born in your land. It is vital not to underestimate your enemies, so you should have a robust intelligence system in place to gather information on their activities. Depute spies to keep an eye on your adversaries, for even those whom you think are vanquished can unexpectedly return to cause you harm. There are eighteen functional heads of an enemy kingdom whose actions always need surveillance: 1. The chief minister; 2. The king's family priest; 3. The crown prince; 4. The principal army commander; 5. The head warder; 6. The chamberlain; 7. The superintendent of jails; 8. The head of the treasury; 9. The herald; 10. The government advocate; 11. The judge; 12. The assessor of taxes; 13. The officer who disburses salaries; 14. The officer who distributes money from the exchequer; 15. The Kotwal in charge of the city; 16. The person who oversees border security; 17. The magistrate; 18. The officer who manages the conservation of natural resources, water, and forests. Fifteen of the eighteen just mentioned (disregarding the first three) are equally essential to monitor internally with secret agents. While you trust your officials, it is necessary to verify their actions. The best way is to have three different sources of the same intelligence from people acting covertly who are unknown to each other so that you get accurate feedback.

'When dealing with other kingdoms, there are twenty situations in which you should never enter an alliance. First, avoid associating yourself with a king who is still a child or very aged, as his decision-making power is questionable. Also, forgo making a pact with someone terminally ill or who has been rejected by his subjects, is a coward or surrounded by faint-hearted people. Second, please stay away from a monarch who is avaricious or has greedy associates. Never conduct any dealings with one who lacks the confidence of his ministers, is excessively pleasure-loving, relies on fickle-minded advisers, or disrespects the Devas and Brahmins. Third, be cautious of a ruler in the throes of adversity, or if he is a fatalist lacking drive, his kingdom is afflicted by famine, he has too many enemies or is affected by several military reversals. Also, beware of a king who ignores the duties of his kingdom. Finally, and most importantly, watch out for the untruthful ruler who does not adhere to dharma.'[13]

Rama said about urban and rural development, 'I hope you are protecting the environment and that the provinces are prosperous with fertile lands and lots of cattle. I trust you have good breeding programmes for elephants and horses in your kingdom and that you are conserving the forests, the home of wild animals, for the continuity of their kind. I pray Ayodhya flourishes and has temples and altars laid throughout for worship. I hope learned men abound in the city, bringing well-being to all with their lofty thinking. I trust there are sufficient water reservoirs and lakes to avoid dependence on rain. It is best to celebrate festivals enthusiastically to bring people together in kinship. Domestic animals must never be abused and should be housed humanely in suitable shelters. You must aim for the kingdom to be well-stocked with grain, water, wealth and weapons at all times.'

He concluded by saying, 'I hope you are following the teachings of the Vedas? Emulate the governing practices that our father and forefathers observed, as they were righteous and always in accordance with dharma. Though vested with unlimited power, they never acted as sovereigns, but only as administrators for whom the welfare of the people was their greatest concern.'[14]

After delivering this lengthy speech, Rama asked Bharata if he agreed with these views and questioned once more why he had come to the forest dressed as a hermit, when he ought to have been back in Ayodhya performing his royal duties. Bharata folded his hands and replied, 'Noble brother, my conniving mother maliciously influenced our mighty-armed father to disinherit you, and sadly, after committing the unthinkable deed of sending you away, he was inconsolable and ascended to heaven.'

Rama felt like a thunderbolt had hit him, and he swooned as if struck by Indra's vajra. When he recovered, he lamented that his father had died of grief because of him and felt guilty that he could not discharge his duties as the eldest son at the funeral. Extolling Dasharatha's greatness as a ruler,

---

[13] Later in the story, Rama allies with Sugriva rather than the more powerful Vali. He did this because Vali had abandoned dharma.

[14] Kautilya details this duty of the Vedic king in his Arthashastra: 'In the happiness of his subjects lies the king's happiness; in their welfare his welfare. He shall not consider as good only that which pleases him, but treat as beneficial to him whatever pleases his subjects.' Arthashastra 1.19.34

Rama mourned never seeing him again. Then recalling his father's valorous deeds, he prepared to perform the necessary obsequies for the departed spirit.

Accompanied by Lakshmana and Sita, Rama stepped into the river Mandakini, and facing southwards, made a water offering. Then, he used ingudi fruit pulp to create a benefaction of food and laid it out on a bed of darbha grass by the riverbank to complete the death rituals. The four brothers hugged each other and cried loudly in sorrow. Their wailing carried to the party waiting at the foothills, and they quickly rushed in the direction of the sound. As Vasishta led the queens to the hut, they passed the offerings on the riverbank, and Kaushalya shed tears when she saw the measly little date cakes neatly laid out on the grass. It hurt her deeply to see that her son was so impoverished now that he had nothing better to offer his illustrious father's spirit. When they reached the hut, there was an emotional reunion, and the mothers wept in joy. Rama, Lakshmana and Sita touched their feet and then paid their respects to Vasishta. Kaushalya hugged Sita like her own child and commiserated with her unfortunate circumstances. 'O daughter of a great king, what terrible misfortune has befallen you! You remind me of a beautiful lotus scorched by the sun and the bright moon covered by clouds.' The night passed in mourning, grieving Dasharatha's demise, and the following day, after offering sacred oblations to the fire and performing their Sandhya Vandana by the river, they sat down to talk.

Bharata was determined to convince Rama to return to Ayodhya. He desperately pleaded, "My mother's unconscionable wickedness must be remedied. She manipulated our father into committing a great sin by playing on his infatuation with her. If you return and take back the kingdom, you will redeem him from his wrongdoing. The representatives of all four varnas[15] of the people, the ministers, and even our mothers are here to implore you not to forsake us. I bend my head to your feet and ask your forgiveness for being the cause of all that has transpired and beg you to come back home.'

Rama looked at him lovingly and replied, 'There is no reason for you to ask for forgiveness as you have done no wrong and have no culpability in what has happened. You are a highly virtuous person, and your character is beyond reproach. I do not have an iota of doubt about your integrity because I know that you are strongly grounded in morality. Do not speak ill of your mother; honour her as you honoured our father. A mother has full right to

---

[15] The repeated reference in the Ramayana to the inclusion of all four varnas shows that each one was important.

command her children, so she had the authority to send me to the forest. Parents are entitled to distribute their wealth and property amongst their offspring as they desire, and it is not our place to question their decisions. Before departing from this world, the king made a promise that directed you to rule the kingdom and obligated me to live in the forest. We must obey his dictates, so you need to perform your kingly duties in Ayodhya while I remain here as an ascetic.'

Bharata was not ready to give in so quickly and continued his desperate appeal. 'Please do not talk to me about royal duties. How can a younger brother be king when his virtuous elder brother still lives? Father's command violates the law of inheritance followed by our family from its inception. I entreat you to return to Ayodhya! I do not wish to rule; my mother's misdeed has sullied my reputation. The people love you, and you alone have the legal right to be king.' Bharata's selflessness touched Rama, but dharma made it impossible to agree to his wishes. Sticking firmly to his conviction, he said, 'I cannot go back on my undertaking to uphold our father's vow. Do not blame yourself, Mother Kaikeyi, our father or anyone else. I am here because a word once given is sacrosanct and must be honoured even at the cost of one's life.' Bharata was distraught and beseeched him to reconsider, insisting that the kingdom needed him because their father's demise had left the realm defenceless and insecure.

He cried, 'Father kept his word; he granted my mother her wish, and accordingly, I inherited the kingdom. Now that it is mine, I choose to give it back to you. Our father's death has been a blow to the kingdom, leaving it vulnerable. I do not have your competence; a donkey cannot be swift as a horse, and no ordinary bird can soar like an eagle. My mother realizes her mistake and sincerely regrets her actions, so please come back, dear brother. Father always intended for you to rule after him, and the people want to see you on the throne, so don't deprive Ayodhya of your leadership.'

Bharata's appeal was heartfelt and drew admiration from the crowd, but Rama remained firmly committed to his promise. 'We have no control over events that occur due to providence, but we always have the free will to follow the right path in our actions. Just as a ripe fruit eventually drops to the ground, death is the inevitable result of birth. You should not mourn our father's passing excessively by allowing dejection to overpower you into inaction. He led a just and pious life adhering to dharma, so I am sure he has attained Brahmaloka, the highest plane of heaven, and we honour his memory by obeying his commands. While all material things in life are transitory, the consequences of our actions alone are abiding. Since we carry our karma with us when we die, we must always follow the path of truthfulness. You were mandated to be king to rule under a white umbrella, and I was ordered to the forest to live under a green canopy. This is how it must be, so go to Ayodhya and govern as a just and noble king. Do not berate Mother Kaikeyi or dwell on why she acted, whether out of greed or an abundance of affection for you. Despite all that has happened, I request that you care for her and treat her with respect.'

Still adamant about persuading Rama to return, Bharata protested, 'No one in the world is as equanimous as you! Your ability to be unaffected by adversity, transcending the vagaries of joy and sorrow, is truly remarkable. It is a pity for a competent person to waste his governing skills living as a recluse in the forest. I am disgusted by my mother's vile actions in my absence. I have not killed her only because dharma prevents me from committing an unrighteous act. Our father was a great man, but he was responsible for horrible wrongdoing in pandering to a woman out of passion. Delusion made him act out of character, and it is our duty as his sons to rectify his mistake, not perpetuate his bad judgement. You will redeem father of his offense by returning to Ayodhya and, in doing so, save my mother and me from the stain of immorality. Remember, you are a Kshatriya, and your dharma demands that you rule and take care of the people, not retire to the forest as a renunciate. Your current stage in life is Grihastha,[16] that of a householder, not a retiree in Vanaprastha. I am inferior to you, not only in seniority of birth but also in every respect, whether in knowledge, experience, intellect or virtue. Allow us to crown you here in the forest because everyone who needs to approve is present. Unless you accept the kingdom, the blemish tarnishing our father's reputation and that of my mother and myself cannot be removed. You must save our father from the demerit he has accrued by sending you away! If you refuse to listen to me, I will join you in the forest.'

Everyone marvelled at the two brothers who displayed the highest integrity, each arguing for the other's benefit. In response to the compelling case Bharata presented, Rama said gently, 'I understand your feelings, and while your reasoning has merit, you are not privy to the information that you were always meant to be king. It has been brought to my attention that when our father married mother Kaikeyi, he did not have an heir and had promised

---

[16] Grihastha was the second stage of Vedic life. It was marked by professional and family responsibilities. Vanaprastha, the third stage marked by retirement, only came after this.

your grandfather King Ashwapati that the son born to his daughter would be the ruler of Ayodhya. Now that father is no more, it is our responsibility as his sons to repay his debt to save his soul from torment. Truth is the foundation of all virtue, so we cannot deviate from it. While your duty demands that you rule the kingdom, mine requires me to reside in the forest. Shatrughana will assist you just as Lakshmana is assisting me. I am confident of your abilities; our gurus have trained you well, and I know you will make a fine king. Return to Ayodhya under father's white umbrella with the assurance that I will be back after fourteen years to be with you once again.'

Jabali was one of the sages in Dasharatha's advisory circle. Hoping to assist Bharata in his argument, he interjected with advice from a materialistic philosophy called Charvaka[17] that believed only in the perceivable world of the here and now. He propounded that it was not worth forgoing present happiness for the dubious fantasy of a better afterlife. In a desperate attempt to convince Rama to accept the crown, he said, 'You speak like an ordinary man, not one who enjoys high status and prosperity. Everything we experience as humans is limited to what we see around us, and there is no life after death to safeguard. Birth results from the union of a sperm and an egg, and when we die, we disappear into oblivion. Therefore, live in the present without worrying about protecting your father from hell. There is no reckoning after the body turns to dust, so keeping a promise to someone who is not in this world anymore is pointless. The grand city of Ayodhya awaits you, so accept the material pleasures that go with being its ruler. Seize the moment and make the most of your short time on this Earth without the fetters of dharma because there is no existence after death.

'One must pity those who dwell excessively on righteousness, ostensibly to secure a future paradise in another world. They miss out on enjoying what is at hand for a celestial bliss that is entirely fictitious. The immortality of a spirit outside the body is a hoax perpetuated by wily Brahmins to exercise control and benefit from the charity of credulous people. Performing any austerity for the departed is futile and a waste of time because the dead do not benefit from it. Reality only comprises what you see around you, so trust in what exists before your eyes and enjoy life to the fullest before you die. Give up all your talk about adhering to dharma; instead, accept the kingdom and find happiness.'

---

[17] Ancient Indian philosophy of materialism.

Furious to hear Jabali's shallow views, Rama firmly dismissed his worldly philosophy. He said indignantly, 'I am surprised that my father trusted you as an adviser in his court. His misjudgement is truly stunning, since you do not accept the teachings of the Vedas. Every word you have said deviates from righteousness and serves to disrupt social stability. Truth is the highest goal, so though you think you are speaking for my benefit, your advice only serves to lead me astray. Although your logic may seem alluring to some, it is unworthy, and the path you advocate is a dangerous one to follow. The unbridled pursuit of enjoyment imposes no boundaries on conduct and destroys character. What you propagate is degenerate and unbecoming of an arya. A man's good breeding is judged by his behaviour alone; if I follow your guidance, I will be reviled by society! People are as repulsed by a liar as they are by a serpent. What kind of example would I set by breaking my promise? What credibility would I have if I were untruthful? A leader sets the standard for his people, and if he is corrupt, the people follow suit. Your argument is purely opportunistic and selfish, and I strongly condemn it as improper. Thought, word and deed must always be in harmony with dharma, so there is nothing noble about what you suggest. I am not driven by the self-serving desires that provide temporary enjoyment.[18] In this human form, we have the opportunity to liberate ourselves from endless rebirth[19] by generating good karma through righteous actions. Please know that no material temptation will ever make me deviate from abiding by the truth.'

Pushing Jabali aside, Vasishta quickly came to his rescue, and asked Rama to forgive him. He insisted Jabali did not believe in abandoning dharma and was just using an intellectual argument to persuade Rama to return home. Vasishta continued that as the Ikshavaku family guru for many generations, it was his earnest request that Rama follow tradition as the firstborn and accept the crown. He held forth on the importance of a prince's duty to his family and his people, but it was to no avail; Rama remained adamant about fulfilling his father's promise, insisting it was a higher obligation.

---

[18] 'The only friend who follows people even after death is dharma; for everything else is lost at the same time when the body perishes.' Manusmriti 8:17.

[19] Humans alone exercise free will through which they can be liberated from the cycle of birth and death. Animals do not create karma as they act on instinct. For instance, a lion cannot choose to shun violence and become a vegetarian.

Acknowledging his debt[20] to Dasharatha for his existence, Rama said that children could never repay parents for their dedication in raising them and reiterated that he could therefore not allow his father's word to be proven untrue. With no other means of convincing Rama, Bharata declared that he was ready to take his place and live in the forest for fourteen years, but Rama reminded him that a substitute would falsify their father's words. He asserted that his decision was final, stating categorically, 'Even if the moon loses its lustre, the Himalayas became devoid of snow or the ocean crosses over the shore, I can never go back on my commitment.' The sages realized that it was impossible to persuade Rama to change his mind, and seeing that the debate was at an impasse, they advised Bharata to accept his decision.

On Vasishta's recommendation, Bharata laid the golden coronation sandals at Rama's feet and asked him to step into them. Then, he knelt before him, picking them up reverently, and said, 'Noble brother, I will rule the kingdom only in your place, and these sandals will sit on the throne to represent you. I will not live the comfortable life of royalty while you live one of hardship. Like you, I will wear matted hair and live abstemiously on fruit and roots. I will reside in a hut outside the palace practising austerities, waiting for your return. You have given me your word to be back after fourteen years, so if I do not see you to the very day, I vow to consign my body to flames.'

Bharata returned to Ayodhya disappointed, carrying the sandals under the white umbrella atop Dasharatha's big elephant. On the way, he stopped at Bharadwaj's ashram with the news of Rama's refusal. He told the sage that he would carry his brother's sandals back to Ayodhya and administer his kingly duties as Rama's representative. Then, crossing the Yamuna and Ganga once more, he reached the city. True to his resolve, saying goodbye to the three mothers, Bharata moved out of his royal residence to Nandigram on the outskirts. Placing his brother's sandals reverently on the throne, he ruled just as Rama had instructed, but only in proxy as his regent.

---

[20] It was held that a child is born with a debt to his parents and therefore, serving them is one of the highest duties.
'See the divine in your mother, father, teacher and guest.'—Taittiriya Upanishad 1.11.2
'The travails parents go through to raise a child cannot be repaid in 100 years.'—Manusmriti 2.227

yastu sarvani bhutanyatmanyevanupasyati
sarvabhutesu catmanam tato na vijugupsate

Those who see all creatures in themselves and
themselves in all creatures do not hate or harm anyone.

Isha Upanishad

sarvam kalvidam brahma

All this is Brahman (Universal Consciousness)

Chandogya Upanishad

BOOK 3
Forest Life

Chapter 10

Life amidst Rishis and Rakshasas

After Bharata left, life continued uneventfully at Chitrakoota for several months. Then, Rama noticed that the sages started leaving the area in droves and would whisper strangely to each other in hushed tones when he approached. He was concerned about this new development and asked one of the elderly hermits if he had unwittingly caused them some offence. The old recluse assured him that this was not the case and explained that a man-eating Rakshasa called Khara was harassing them. He inhabited a part of the forest called Janasthana some distance away but had suddenly appeared in this hitherto peaceful spot to persecute them. He would attack unexpectedly, taking on various frightening forms and disrupt their rituals, dousing their holy fires with water and smashing the pots that contained sacred offerings. Rama volunteered to drive Khara away, but the sage insisted that Chitrakoota was not safe any more. They were afraid for their lives and had already decided to move to an ancient hermitage some distance away, where fruit and roots were plentiful. He advised Rama to join them with his wife and brother, but he was insistent on remaining, and thanking the sage, said he did not fear the Rakshasa.

However, once the sages had departed, Rama reconsidered his decision as Chitrakoota was not the same in their absence. Also, it was associated with too many painful memories of Bharata's visit and the unhappiness caused by his refusal to return to Ayodhya. Additionally, there was the concern that his whereabouts were no longer secret, and he did not want the people to continue visiting him out of allegiance, thereby undermining Bharata's position as their ruler. Furthermore, despite the care taken, the large army camped there had trampled the area and damaged the forest's delicate ecosystem by its presence; now, the place needed to be left uninhabited to regenerate itself. With this rationale, the trio abandoned their little cottage and walked southwards through the forest until they reached the hermitage of Rishi Atri.

The hoary old sage Atri was one of the seven great rishis in the land and had contributed to the fifth mandala of the Rig Veda. He lived in the forest with his pious wife Anasuya,[1] with whom he had spent many years in contemplation, practising intense yogic austerities. The elderly couple welcomed Rama, Sita and Lakshmana with much fondness. Anasuya was an aged woman, grey-haired and wrinkled, with trembling limbs. Having reached a very high level of spiritual perfection, she was so pure that she saw nothing but good in everyone, and Sita felt honoured to be in the company of such an esteemed lady. Anasuya felt a motherly affection for Sita and commended her selflessness in sacrificing the comforts of the palace to follow her husband. Complimenting her, she said, 'You are indeed a virtuous woman. By joining your husband in exile, you have kept your marriage vow to be his companion through fortune and misfortune alike. It is a wife's duty to be her husband's best friend, guiding him through life with good counsel. Your fidelity will be an inspiration for generations to come.'

Sita replied graciously, 'My parents taught me to be righteous, but honestly, it is quite easy for me to be devoted to Rama, for he is compassionate, disciplined and brave. Moreover, he is steadfast in his love for me, his family, the people, and above all, the principles of dharma. When my father put my hand in his, my mother instructed me to be faithful to my husband, no matter his circumstances, and your words remind me of her.' Anasuya took Sita's hands, kissed her forehead and said tenderly, 'I am so pleased with your high standard of morality. What can I give you as a token of my affection?' Sita replied that she did not desire anything as she was happy to be there for her husband. Her response further impressed the old anchoress, and determined to show her appreciation, she bestowed on her a divine garland that would never wither, a garment that would never get soiled, beautiful jewellery to adorn her person, and various scented creams. Anasuya then asked Sita about her wedding, saying she had heard that Rama had won her hand by performing a challenging feat and was keen to know the details. Sita happily narrated the events of her life, giving a complete description starting from the day Janaka found her in the field while ploughing the land. Anasuya was delighted to hear the story, but by this time, they had talked for a long

---

[1] Anasuya means one who is devoid of spite or envy and does not see fault in anyone.

while, and it was nightfall, so she said, 'It's getting dark now, and moonlight is spreading like a blanket over the Earth, but before we rest, I would like to see you dressed in what I gave you.' Sita obliged; looking radiant, she went excitedly to show Rama. Admiring how lovely she looked, he told her how lucky she was to be honoured by such a great lady.

The following day, they took their leave of the revered couple and set out again, deeper into the Dandaka Forest. The rishis at Atri's ashram indicated a path that they said would be relatively safe, as the forest was very thick and inhabited by several dangerous Rakshasas. They walked in single file, with Rama in the lead this time and Lakshmana at the back, keeping Sita safely in the middle. As they wended their way, they came upon a badly trampled spot with fallen trees and mangled branches, and the damage did not look like the work of elephants. Then without warning, a frightening creature suddenly leaped out before them. He was humungous in size, attired in a tiger skin dripping with blood; he had long legs, bloodshot eyes, protruding razor-like teeth and a big belly. To add to the terrifying picture, he held a long spear on which he had skewered three lions, four tigers, ten deer and a giant elephant head.

'Who are you?' he bellowed. 'What brings you to Dandaka? Since you are armed and in the company of a beautiful woman, it is clear you are not real sages. My name is Viradha, and you have trespassed into my territory.' Then he looked leeringly at Sita and continued, 'I will eat the two of you and make this slender-waisted lady my wife.' Saying this, he snatched Sita and placed her on his shoulder.

Aghast at the sudden mishap, Rama cried out in horror, 'Alas! Lakshmana, look at the hapless condition of my chaste wife, who was hitherto protected in the palace and used to every comfort! I was sent here by Kaikeyi to suffer, so this misfortune will undoubtedly be to her satisfaction. When I lost my kingdom, I bore it without sorrow; when my father died, I accepted it stoically, but I cannot tolerate anything untoward happening to my lovely Sita.' To reassure him, Lakshmana said, 'Brother, I came here to serve you; I will not allow any harm to come to Sita. I have bottled up my anger ever since your exile, and this evil fellow will soon face my pent-up wrath.' He warned Viradha that he would put an end to him unless Sita was returned, and Rama added that he should beware as they were from the valorous Ikshavaku clan.

Viradha responded with a hearty laugh. Guffawing loudly, he said, 'Your threats are in vain; I have a benediction from the almighty Brahma, by the grace of which no weapon can kill me. So, give up this pretty lady to me, and in return, I will spare your lives. Now run along!'

Outraged at Viradha's temerity, Rama sent a volley of seven gold-shafted arrows, which pierced the monster's grotesque body, but he merely flexed his muscles, and they fell off, doing little harm. Rama then broke his spear, so putting Sita down, Viradha picked him up along with Lakshmana and began to run away. Afraid for their lives, Sita wept, 'O Rakshasa, take me instead and spare them.' Rama decided something needed to be done fast, so he swiftly cut off Viradha's left arm while Lakshmana lopped off the right one. As the giant creature fell to the ground, to their surprise, he began telling Rama a strange story. 'I now realize that you are not an ordinary mortal. You said you are an Ikshavaku, so you are probably Rama, son of King Dasharatha, and I have been waiting for you. I was not always a Rakshasa; previously, I was a Gandharva called Tumburu in the court of Kubera. I was cursed to take this form for dereliction of duty and was told I would only return to my former self once you killed me. I want to be freed from the imprisonment of this repulsive body, but weapons cannot kill me, so please bury me in a pit. A powerful rishi called Sarabhanga lives about one-and-a-half yojanas from here. Once you inter me, go to him, and you will get useful guidance.' After liberating Viradha, Rama embraced and comforted the frightened Sita, saying, 'This forest is impenetrable and dangerous, so we should go quickly to the seer called Sarabhanga and ask him to recommend a safe place to stay.'

As they approached Sarabhanga's ashram, they saw the sage standing by a sacrificial fire, deep in conversation with a radiant being seated in a divine chariot hovering in the air. The individual the sage was speaking to was attended upon by powerful bodyguards and beautiful Apsaras, youthful in appearance with svelte bodies. Rama realized it was Indra with his entourage. However, as he neared them, Indra noticed him and hurriedly took his leave of the sage, saying, 'Rama is here, but I don't want to meet him prematurely. I need to wait till he completes the mission for which he was born.' When Rama, Lakshmana and Sita came forward to touch Sarabhanga's feet, his face lit up. He told Rama that he was expecting him and said cordially, 'Welcome, dear guests! I have earned a place in Brahmaloka[2] through years of severe penance, and Indra had come to take me, but I knew you were on your way, so I waited to receive you. I have accumulated much spiritual merit and would like to share my benedictions with you.' Rama thanked him but

[2] The highest heavenly realm.

said that it would not be proper for him to benefit from anything without effort, it being more appropriate for him to earn any such distinction by himself. However, he welcomed a suggestion on where they could settle. Sarabhanga told him to follow the path up the river Mandakini where they would come upon a holy seer called Suteekshna, who would direct them to a suitable place. Then, with his desire to see Rama fulfilled and his current lifetime's karma exhausted, Rishi Sarabhanga gave up his body just as a snake sloughs off its old skin for which it has no more use; and his soul rose to the highest plane in heaven.

Sages of many sects engaged in gruelling austerities nearby flocked to see Rama after Sarabhanga ascended to heaven. Some lived only on leaves or water, while others, in extreme renunciation, survived on air alone. They endured rigorous penance while performing yogic meditation, subjugating their bodies to severe heat surrounded by fire or exposing themselves to frigid temperatures standing neck-deep in water. Imploring Rama for his help, they pleaded, 'You are a Kshatriya, a descendant of the noble Ikshavaku, and a strong upholder of dharma, renowned in all three worlds for your valour. Kings receive one-sixth of the revenue from the land as tax and benefit from one-fourth of the spiritual merit attained by rishis, so it is your Kshatriya duty to protect us. We hermits are being slaughtered mercilessly by man-eating Rakshasas, and you are our only hope.' Rama acceded to their request without any reservation. He promised unhesitatingly, 'Say no more; I will carry out your wish as if it were a command. You have my assurance that my brother Lakshmana and I will end your torment by killing all the Rakshasas in the area who are a scourge to you.' Giving the rishis this solemn pledge of safety, they went on to find Suteekshna.

On the way, Sita felt perturbed by a moral conflict and voiced her concern to Rama as they walked.[3] Issuing a word of caution on his promise to the rishis, she remarked, 'I feel your judgement was clouded when you committed to wiping out the Rakshasas. There are three actions a person who upholds dharma must avoid: false speech, unfaithfulness and causing harm without justification. You are incapable of speaking an untruth, and

---

[3] A wife was considered a partner in dharma, a moral compass for her husband.
'O woman you are as strong as earth and on a very high pedestal. Protect the world from the path of vices and violence.' Yajur Veda 13.18
'O brilliant woman (symbolized by dawn), remove ignorance with your bright intellect and provide bliss to all.' Rig Veda 4.14.3

it is impossible to conceive of you coveting another man's wife, but I am concerned that you agreed to kill those who have not done anything to hurt you. I am reminded of a rishi who lived peacefully with the birds and beasts in the forest until he suddenly turned violent. It so happened that one day, Indra, disguised as a soldier, decided to test him by leaving a great sword in his safekeeping. The rishi began to carry the sword with him everywhere he went, and it had a polluting effect on his mind. His placid personality slowly changed, turning him away from living harmoniously with others. He started killing creatures who had not done him any injury, and by abandoning dharma, he descended into hell. Dearest husband, carrying weapons has a tainting effect on the purity of the mind as it incites aggression. I feel worried when you talk about eradicating all the Rakshasas in the area, because you have no personal enmity with them. Remember, you have come here as a hermit, not as a Kshatriya, so you should adopt the dharma of ahimsa. A Kshatriya is like fire, and a weapon is like firewood, so a conflagration occurs very easily when the two come together. I do not intend to preach to you; I speak out of love and respect only to remind you of righteous action.'

Rama patiently listened while Sita spoke. Then, complimenting her on her adherence to dharma, he replied, 'I appreciate your advice, and I understand your concern. Your point of view on ahimsa has merit, but dharma is intricate and rarely black or white. Often, we need to decide between two righteous actions, both worthy, choosing which one to pursue. In this case, I cannot abandon the rishis as the Rakshasas are massacring them. You are justified in advocating that I avoid violence, because a weapon must never be used to harm an innocent person, but that does not apply in this case. Dharma enjoins a Kshatriya to heed a cry of distress. The rishis spend their lives engaged in meditation, practising severe austerities, and cannot fight back. Since they are pacifists, who exercise rigorous self-control over their emotions, they came to me begging for protection, and it would be against dharma to turn them away. Therefore, I gave them my word and must fulfil it. While every Rakshasa is not evil, the ones here delight in cruel deeds and are involved in all kinds of knavery. You have rightly pointed out that they have not personally caused me harm, but they inflict pain on those seeking refuge in me, which warrants my intervention. Since you are grounded in righteousness as my companion in Kshatriya dharma and one who is dearer to me than my own life, I hope you understand my reasoning.' Hearing Rama's explanation, Sita felt reassured about the sanctity of his actions, and her doubts about him committing any wrongdoing were dispelled.

The three of them traversed the forest a great distance, crossing rivers, hills and lakes, passing by various ashrams. Then, they came upon a large lake covered with beautiful lotuses. A mesmerizing melody of musical instruments mysteriously emanated from its depths. This strange phenomenon roused their curiosity, so they inquired about it from a rishi called Dharmabhrat, who lived nearby. He told them that the lake was called Panchapsara,[4] and was the home of a sage called Mandakarni, an ascetic who once lived in the forest performing exacting penance. The accumulation of spiritual merit made him extremely powerful, which did not go unnoticed by the Devas. Realizing that Mandakarni would soon surpass them in his abilities, they decided to test him by breaking his concentration. To this end, they sent five beautiful Apsara maidens to distract him from his purpose. The women appeared before Mandakarni and enticed him into a life of amorous dalliance. Intoxicated by sensuality, the rishi abandoned his meditation for the company of the Apsaras in a house under the lake, the source of the unusual music.

Finally, after covering a considerable distance, the trio reached a tall mountain with densely forested slopes, where they found the ashram of the ascetic Suteekshna. Here, as everywhere else they had stopped, the three received warm hospitality, and when Rama asked about a place to set up home, the rishis generously invited them to stay. However, they accepted the offer only for the night and then roamed from one hermitage to another, visiting many rishis, offering them protection and in turn gaining wisdom from them. They stayed one month in some places, two or three, and even up to eight months in others, and in this manner, ten years passed.

One day, Rama revisited Suteekshna and asked, 'O illustrious one, I have heard the supreme sage Agastya lives somewhere nearby in this forest. I wish to pay him my respects, so please direct me to his hermitage.' Suteekshna was happy to hear this, knowing that Rama would benefit from meeting the eminent rishi. He instructed the group to travel four yojanas south to the ashram of sage Agastya's brother, where he suggested they stop overnight. From there, he said it would be easy to go on to Agastya's hermitage as it was only a yojana away, in a level clearing surrounded by a plantain grove and a thicket of flowering trees.

---

[4] Lonar Crater Lake in the Buldhana district of Maharashtra. See Pande, Vikrant, and Kulkarni, Neelesh. *In the Footsteps of Rama: Travels with the Ramayana* (Gurugram: HarperCollins, 2021).

Agastya was a short husky man, with an aura that shone resplendently like the sun. He was a Brahmarishi, greatly respected and considered one of the foremost amongst the great sages. He and his wife Lopamudra, the erstwhile princess of Vidarbha, were celebrated scholars whose insights are found in many Vedic hymns.[5] He was also a scientist par excellence, who compiled the Agastya Samhita, which included details on making an electric battery,[6] the method of electroplating metals, splitting water into hydrogen and oxygen, and even the use of hydrogen in aerodynamics. He was a towering figure, skilled in martial arts[7] with extensive knowledge of weapons. His spiritual powers were immense, and he even arrested the growth of the Vindhyas, which gave him the name Agastya, meaning 'one who stopped the mountain'.

As they walked towards his ashram, Rama told Sita and Lakshmana a fascinating story of how Agastya once saved the rishis who lived in Dandaka from the dreadful harassment of two Rakshasa brothers, Ilava and Vatapi. The pair had a predilection for human flesh and had found a novel way of obtaining their delicacy. Ilava would assume the form of a Brahmin, and Vatapi would turn himself into a goat. Then Ilava would invite unsuspecting sages to feast with him and cook the goat. After the meal, Ilava would shout, 'O Vatapi, come out!' and Vatapi would resume his form and emerge, ripping the body of the guest, instantly killing him. In this manner, they ate thousands of sages till they encountered Agastya. Like the others who had fallen prey to the brothers, he too ate the goat cooked by Ilava. However, as soon as he finished, he rubbed his belly and smilingly said, 'Be digested!' When Ilava called for Vatapi to come out, this time, nothing happened. Incensed with rage, he tried to attack Agastya but was no match for the mighty sage and was instantly incinerated by the fire of his glare. Agastya also once helped the Devas defeat the Asuras who had hidden themselves in the sea, ridding them of their cover. Therefore, the Rakshasas feared him and stayed away from his hermitage.

When they reached the ashram, Rama told Lakshmana to ask Rishi Agastya for an audience. Lakshmana accordingly informed one of the

---

[5] Rig Veda 1.165–1.191.

[6] Agastya's battery has been recreated in modern times and it works! It uses an earthen pot, copper plate, copper sulphate, wet sawdust as a separator and zinc amalgam. Today's battery cell follows the same principle.

[7] Agastya developed Kalarippayattu, considered the source of all martial arts.

disciples about their arrival. When Agastya heard who was at his door, he was elated and instructed that they be brought to him immediately. The ashram was extensive and beautifully laid out, with deer roaming around peacefully. It had many sacred shrines dedicated to the Supreme Consciousness that manifested in different forms: Brahma, Vishnu, Shiva and other deities, to whom the young people offered obeisance as they passed.[8] When they reached the presence of Agastya, Rama prostrated himself before him, clasping his feet in veneration. The great sage gave his blessings and offered them a traditional welcome and refreshments. He was very impressed with Sita's loyalty in standing by her husband through difficult times. Despite being brought up delicately, she had voluntarily undertaken the hardship of accompanying Rama to the inhospitable forest. Her devotion was commendable and Agastya praised her supreme sacrifice, asking Rama to take good care of her. He said Sita's presence blessed his ashram because she was noble, virtuous and flawless in character. Then knowing what the future[9] had in store for Rama, he presented him with some unique gifts: a divine bow that once belonged to Indra, two inexhaustible quivers, a mighty sword in a large silver sheath and a fiery arrow from Brahma that never missed its mark.

Rama expressed his most profound gratitude for the weapons bestowed and then asked the sage if he could direct them to a suitable place to stay. Since they still had a few years of exile to complete, he explained that they were looking for a peaceful spot with a plentiful water supply and fruit trees, somewhere amidst rishis whom they could serve and protect. Agastya pondered for a while and said, 'Two yojanas from here is a perennially flowering grove blessed with abundant fruits and roots. It is called Panchavati[10] because five banyan trees anchor it. The Godavari, with its crystal-clear waters, runs nearby. It is an enchanting place with lots of beautiful birds and gentle deer that the princess of Mithila will enjoy. The sages living there will be grateful for your protection and glad to have you amongst them. The fourteen years of exile you undertook are almost over, and I foresee you returning after keeping your promise.'

Agastya wished them a safe journey, and following his directions, the trio proceeded to Panchavati. On the way, they came upon a giant eagle

[8] See Appendices on the Vedic Concept of God as the one consciousness worshipped in many forms.

[9] Rishis had divine vision resulting from their high spiritual attainment.

[10] Nashik in Maharashtra.

sitting on a banyan tree. He was so enormous that Rama suspected he might be Rakshasa in the guise of a bird and asked, 'Who are you?' The bird replied, 'My name is Jatayu, Garuda's[11] nephew, the younger son of his brother Aruna, Surya Deva's charioteer. I have an elder brother, Sampati, who lives by the coast further south, but I live here in the forest. Now tell me about yourselves and what brings you here?' When he heard that Rama and Lakshmana were sons of king Dasharatha, he was overjoyed and said warmly, 'Son, I knew your noble father well and was his friend. I must warn you that this area is infested with dangerous Rakshasas, so you must be very careful residing here. However, do not be concerned; I will assist you in every way I can to help ensure Sita's safety.' With these words, Jatayu accompanied them to Panchavati.

In Panchavati, Lakshmana found a spot that was flat and surrounded by numerous blooming trees: ashoka,[12] champaka,[13] tilaka,[14] and ketaka.[15] Beautiful vines clung to the branches, and not far was a pond covered in lotuses that filled the air with an intoxicating fragrance. The nearby Godavari was visited by many flocks of birds, including elegant swans and cranes. The call of peacocks rang sweetly, and large herds of gentle deer grazed peacefully on the verdant landscape. It was a truly scenic place with sandalwood trees and others heavily laden with fruit. Soon Lakshmana constructed a large cottage with bamboo and leaves for Rama and Sita to set up home. However, as in Chitrakoota, he never slept inside, feeling it improper to stay in proximity to his sister-in-law. Rama was very appreciative of his service. He hugged Lakshmana and exclaimed in gratitude, 'You tend to me with the devotion of a father caring for his child. I feel deeply indebted to you! It is uncanny how you read my mind and anticipate my needs, never straying from dharma in anything you do. You make me feel father is still here looking after me.'

---

[11] Garuda is Vishnu's vehicle.

[12] *Sarada asoca*—The sorrowless tree.

[13] *Magnolia champaca*—Known for its fragrant flowers.

[14] *Cinnamomum iners*—Dalchini or cinnamon.

[15] *Pandanus tactorius*—Kewra.

Chapter 11

Surpanakha's Infatuation and the War with Khara

Since the first day of their exile, thirteen years had elapsed experiencing the simple pleasures of forest life. Time slipped by, the seasons continually changing in their ongoing cycle—winter yielding to the gentle warmth of spring, the sweltering summer relieved by heavy monsoon rains, followed by the mellow autumn, succumbing in turn to the chilly winter again. It was now the season of Hemant just before winter, as the pleasant autumn made way for colder and drier weather. One dewy dawn, as the three went to the Godavari for their morning worship, Lakshmana remarked to Rama, 'This golden season is your favourite time of year, when granaries everywhere are full after the harvest. The air is crisp, the water is frigid and the fire's warmth is inviting. The sun has moved over the southern hemisphere, and its blistering heat no longer oppresses us. Like us, the elephants and birds are skittish about immersing themselves in the icy river, and the lotuses are reduced to stalks without the bright light to warm them. My mind is filled with thoughts of Bharata in Ayodhya. He must be practising austerities in his anguish of being separated from you, and like us, he is perhaps taking a dip at this very moment in the cold waters of the Sarayu. Bharata is truly a high-souled person! It is said that men take after their mothers, but our noble brother has proved that untrue. He is nothing like his vicious mother, Kaikeyi.'

Rama quickly interrupted, delivering a gentle reprimand: 'Dear brother, don't say anything uncharitable about Mother Kaikeyi. Let us limit our comments to the greatness of Bharata. He is a sweet, affectionate and righteous person, and I long for the day when we four brothers are united again.'

123

After they had finished their ablutions and morning worship of the Almighty symbolized by the rising sun, by happenstance, they were spotted by a widowed Rakshasa woman lurking in the trees. Her gaze fell on Rama; enthralled by his handsomeness, she could not take her eyes off him. His dark skin glistened with droplets of water, and his complexion had the luminescence of the moon. He was tall and well-proportioned, with a narrow waist, flat stomach, broad shoulders and long arms. Although he was muscular and powerfully built like a lion, he had a gentle countenance. His thick hair fell in curls by his ears, and his eyes, beautiful as lotus petals, captivated her. Though he was dressed as an ascetic, he had a regal bearing and an elephant's majestic gait. Infatuated by him, the Rakshasi[1] found herself overcome by irrepressible desire!

In stark contrast, the woman herself was the very antithesis, both in appearance and personality. She was haggard and advanced in age, while Rama was virile and in the prime of life. She was ugly, and he was extraordinarily handsome. She had a potbelly and an unattractive figure like a pillar, while he was toned with rippling muscles. Her brassy voice was jarring compared to his, which had a deep resonance. As for their eyes, hers were small and beady, while his were large and mesmerizing. She had thin coppery hair in contrast to his mop of thick black wavy locks. Crookedness was intrinsic to her demonic nature, while he was straightforward and blessed with every divine quality. She was lustful, and he was the very embodiment of self-discipline. Aware of the discordance between them, the Rakshasi transformed herself into a beautiful maiden, hoping to entice him.

Approaching Rama, she asked curiously, 'Who are you? I notice you are attired like an ascetic, yet you have a warrior's physique and carry weapons. Tell me about yourself and what you are doing in this forest?' Rama introduced himself, Lakshmana and Sita in his habitually affable manner. He told her the story of his exile that had brought them to Dandaka and asked her about herself. The demoness replied, 'I am a Rakshasi called Surpanakha, the sister of the famous king of the Rakshasas, Ravana, whom you have no doubt heard about as he is the most powerful being in all the three worlds. I also have two other brothers, a mighty one called Kumbhakarna, who is under a spell and sleeps continually, and a pious one called Vibhishana, who unfortunately is a misfit in our family. I live here in the forest with my cousins, Khara and Dushana, who are known for their valour.' Then looking

---

[1] Female Rakshasa.

into Rama's eyes, she confessed that she was hopelessly attracted to him, proclaiming adoringly, 'From the moment I set eyes on you, I decided to make you my husband. I am a more suitable partner than that ugly, skinny woman with a sunken belly who is your wife. Therefore, you should accept me; I have many superior abilities, including magical shapeshifting powers, that make me worthy of you.'

Rama was taken aback by Surpanakha's boldness. Slightly amused, he smiled and responded politely, 'Good lady, I have to turn down your kind offer as I am already married to Sita, whom I love dearly to the exclusion of anyone else. Furthermore, I am sure a woman of your high status would not relish being a junior wife. Perhaps you can ask my prepossessing brother Lakshmana if he is interested in your proposal? He is more handsome than I am by far and on his own here.'

Surpanakha was so full of lust that she immediately turned to Lakshmana to satisfy her ardour. However, when she propositioned him, Lakshmana laughed and said in jest that he was Rama's servant, so she would be a servant too, if they married. Instead, he suggested she go back to Rama and ask him again. When Rama refused her a second time, Surpanakha felt slighted. Believing the brothers were toying with her, she charged in a frenzy towards Sita with her long, sharp, claw-like nails that indicated the meaning of her name. Shrieking viciously, she cried, 'I will kill and eat this loathsome woman you are married to, who is an impediment to our union, and once she is gone, you will be free to marry me.' The mood had darkened, and the atmosphere ceased to be convivial. Rama exclaimed in alarm that they had exercised poor judgement in their facetious banter, because Sita was now in danger. Lakshmana realized this, too, and ever vigilant, acted like lightning. Before Surpanakha could do any harm, he unsheathed his sword and cut off her nose and ears[2] in a flash. Disfigured and humiliated, the Rakshasi wailed demonically and quickly disappeared into the forest from whence she came, leaving a trail of blood in her path.

Surpanakha ran to Janasthana, the domain of her cousin Khara, and fell at his feet, bleeding profusely. Seeing her ghastly state, he roared, 'Who did this to you? Who is the fool who has unwisely dared to instigate a black cobra tying the noose of death around his neck? I will have him killed to avenge

---

[2] It was a sin to kill a woman, but cutting off the nose and ears was acceptable punishment according to the norms of the time.

your insult, and vultures will eat his flesh. No power on Earth can save him from my wrath.'

Choking back tears, Surpanakha blurted out the sorry tale of her ignominy, telling Khara about the two extraordinarily handsome men she chanced upon and the beautiful, ornamented woman who accompanied them, crying that she would have no peace till she drank their blood. Khara immediately summoned fourteen of his strongest generals, ordering them to go with her and bring back Rama's head. When they arrived in Panchavati, Surpanakha pointed out her foe. Seeing the generals advancing toward him, Rama instructed Lakshmana to guard Sita so he could deal with them. Then, standing tall, he questioned, 'Why are you here to attack us unprovoked? You may instil fear in the hermits with your atrocities, but I am not afraid of you. I advise you in your interest to turn back so that you do not meet an untimely end.'

The Rakshasas haughtily replied that Khara had sent them to punish him for his impudence, so they had no intention of leaving until they accomplished their purpose. They hurled their mighty spears at Rama, but he countered them with his lethal arrows. In the blink of an eye, fourteen deadly iron shafts flew swiftly through the air and struck each general in the heart, killing them all simultaneously, soaking the earth in their blood.

Surpanakha was thunderstruck as she watched the dauntless warriors drop to the ground, felled like trees cut at the base. Once again, she ran back to Khara, falling at his feet, crying bitterly. 'Why are you weeping now?' he asked in an irritated tone. 'I have sent my best men to avenge you. They are my mightiest and cannot be killed. I assure you they will return with Rama's head soon, so stop writhing on the ground like a snake and wipe your tears.' Surpanakha sneered, 'You sent fourteen fearsome Rakshasas armed with deadly weapons, but they were all killed by the arrows of one puny mortal in the blink of an eye. He is even more powerful than you, so although you think you are a mighty warrior, I know you will not be able to settle the score for me. I am filled with shame today and feel like giving up my life in humiliation.'

Khara's ego was bruised, and he could not believe that a mere human had bested his invincible generals. He called upon his brother Dushana, his commander and other valiant fighters—Mahakapala, Sthulaksha, Pramathi and Trishira—to join him. They gathered their most fearless men—Sheyenagami, Prithugriva, Yajnashatru, Vihamgama, Durjaya,

Karaviraksha, Parusha, Kalakarmuka, Meghamali, Mahamali, Sarpasya and Rudhirashana—and a force of 14,000 fierce combatants. Promising to resolve Surpanakha's problem before the day was out, Khara advanced determinedly towards Panchavati. On the way, he felt his left eye throb, and several other unfavourable omens appeared before him. However, he brushed them aside, thinking that only timid people feared such indications, marching on supremely confident of his strength. The sun was eclipsed by a halo, black in the centre and red at the edges like a ring of fire, and though it was afternoon, darkness enveloped them.[3] Meteors flashed across the sky, a stormy cloud rained blood, a giant vulture alighted on the flagpole of Khara's chariot, jackals howled menacingly and his left arm throbbed, all auguring his doom.

Rama saw the intimidating Rakshasa army approaching, with Khara menacingly in the lead. He too observed nature's warnings but felt confident of success, for in his case, his right eye twitched propitiously. He told Lakshmana not to argue about accompanying him and instead, take Sita to a hidden cave on higher ground to keep her safely out of the fray. The 14,000 ferocious Rakshasas forged ahead in what seemed to be a sure victory against one virtuous albeit ordinary human. The deafening sound of their battle cries and the tumult of war drums rent through the forest as the animals ran pell-mell in terror.

When Khara and his troops reached the vicinity of the cottage, they saw Rama standing resolutely with his bow, battle-ready with his armour and finger guards. He looked ferocious like a blazing fire devoid of smoke, and though he faced the Rakshasas alone, he was composed and confident, resembling Rudra[4] with his Pinaka.[5] Khara commanded his army to begin their attack, sending forth a shower of arrows, but they were not a match for Rama. Unperturbed by the assault, Rama retaliated with fury and, turning his bow horizontally for maximum coverage, neutralized every arrow that came his way. As a result, the enemy was consumed as effortlessly as the ocean absorbs the great rivers that flow into it. Rama's fierce counter-offensive devastated thousands of Rakshasas, while others scattered in fear. Dushana rallied some of his men and rushed forward to quell the damage,

---

[3] Solar eclipse seen from Panchavati on 7 October 5077 BCE.

[4] Another name for Shiva.

[5] The bow of Shiva.

uprooting sala trees and hurling rocks, but once again, Rama dispatched them to death's door, his arrows shooting out in all directions like the rays of the sun. Finally, in desperation, Dushana picked up a giant mace, but before he could hurl it, Rama severed his arms, sending him to the ground club in hand, as he breathed his last.

Mahakapala, Sthulaksha and Pramathi mounted a joint attack on Rama, but they too were vanquished; Mahakapala's head was severed, Sthulaksha's body lacerated and Pramathi was shot gruesomely through the eyeballs. The ground was saturated in blood as Rakshasa bodies lay strewn all over in disarray like grass clippings. Now, the only ones still left standing were Khara and Trishira. Khara, seething with rage, prepared his reprisal, but Trishira intervened, asking for the opportunity to prove his valour. He drove his chariot intimidatingly towards Rama, and there was a fierce clash between the two formidable warriors, like a lion and an elephant battling. Rama was wounded but remained undaunted, declaring heroically to Trishira that his arrows were falling on him like flowers. He then responded with fourteen potent shafts as virulent as serpents. Four of them brought down Trishira's horses, eight his chariot, one severed his standard, and the last tore open his chest. Khara was astounded! He could not believe that one measly human had single-handedly wiped out his entire army, leaving him the sole survivor. He attacked with all his might, but Rama's responded to his onslaught valiantly. Flames and sparks shot through the sky as the two titans fought relentlessly, one on his chariot and the other on foot.

The Devas watched anxiously from above, showering their blessings on Rama. So many arrows and counter-arrows flew back and forth that they formed a canopy in the sky, obliterating the sun. Khara broke Rama's bow, but unruffled by the setback, Rama strung the special one presented to him by Agastya, and with his gold-tufted arrows, brought down Khara's standard. Khara fought back, striking Rama repeatedly, wounding him severely all over his body. Despite bleeding profusely from deep gashes, Rama kept up his ferocious assault, releasing six deadly arrows from his Vishnu bow. One struck Khara's head, two his arms and three crescent-shaped ones hit his chest, but protected by his armour, he did not perish. Rama then released thirteen more arrows, shattering Khara's bow and chariot wheels, killing his charioteer and horses. As Khara leaped to the ground, seizing a mace, Rama shouted, 'You came here with a big army of elephants, horses and chariots, but they are all destroyed. Unrighteousness can never win! You have spent your entire life committing abhorrent and wicked deeds, tormenting the innocent, but your evil actions have caught up with you. Today justice will be served, so be warned that your end is nigh.'

Khara yelled back, grimacing, 'Don't be so quick to boast; thus far, you have only slain ordinary soldiers. Valorous persons don't crow about themselves, so all you have proved is your petty nature.' Then, hurling his mace, he shouted, 'Watch me end your life and avenge the death of my 14,000 brave Rakshasas.' Rama broke the weapon into tiny fragments while it was still whirling in the air towards him, exclaiming, 'Your club has been smashed to smithereens, so now you have no choice but to surrender! Janasthana needs to be made safe so that the rishis can roam peacefully again!'

Khara had no intention of yielding. Looking for another weapon, he uprooted a giant sala tree, but it too was cut to pieces. Next, a thousand arrows flew from Rama's hand and pierced Khara from head to toe. Blood gushed out of his body like a waterfall cascading down a steep mountain, but he was still not ready to accept defeat, Khara threateningly staggered forward. Finally, Rama drew Agastya's fiery arrow, and bending his bow, released it with a sound like a clap of thunder. That very instant, it was all over. Khara went down like Andhaka[6] in his battle with Rudra.

Sita was watching anxiously from her vantage point, and her eyes met Rama's as he looked up at her, smiling in vindication.[7] Her heart overflowed with emotion, seeing his lacerated body dripping with blood. In less than two muhurtas,[8] Rama had destroyed 14,000 mighty Rakshasas! Running down the hill breathlessly, Sita threw her arms around her brave husband, hugging him dearly. She was proud of Rama for fulfilling his promise to the rishis by exterminating the Rakshasas and ridding Janasthana of their tyranny.

---

[6] Andhaka means darkness; he was a malevolent Asura who coveted Shiva's wife Parvati.

[7] Sita had called him a woman, an affront to his manhood, when he refused to take her with him to the forest.

[8] A muhurta is 48 minutes or 1/30th of a day.

Chapter 12

Ravana, Lord of Lanka, and the Golden Deer

Every Rakshasa in Khara's army was killed except one who slunk away unharmed; his name was Akampana. He hastened to Lanka to inform his king, Ravana, of the terrible calamity that had befallen his people. Apologetic about being the bearer of bad news and trembling with fear, he narrated the story of their humiliating defeat, describing how Rama, the son of King Dasharatha, had single-handedly vanquished every mighty Rakshasa in Janasthana, including the invincible Khara. Ravana was outraged at Rama's brazenness and resolved to deal with the insult immediately, not wanting anyone who offended him to get away with it. However, Akampana cautioned him, extolling Rama's enormous prowess and matchless strength. Praising[1] his valour and powerful build, Akampana insisted Rama was the best archer he had ever seen and was convinced that no one could kill him. He believed that Rama's might was so immense that he could stop the ocean tides and even pull down the sky and stars with his golden arrows. Then, suggesting a devious way to affect him, Akampana said, 'Capture Sita, his beautiful wife, and bring her to Lanka. I believe they are a devoted couple, and Rama will languish without her. Once he is reduced to an emotional wreck, he will be an easy target.'

Ravana liked this strategy and went to his uncle Maricha for help. After his encounter with Rama years ago, Maricha had given up his Rakshasa ways for a life of penance and now lived a solitary existence as a recluse in a remote cave. Since he had personally experienced Rama's might, fear gripped him when he heard the plan to abduct Sita. Cautioning his intemperate nephew, he said nervously, 'I must dissuade you from this reckless venture. Whoever

---

[1] Rama was such a skilled warrior that even his enemies could not help praising him.

advised you to do this did not have your interest at heart, as it is a foolhardy plan akin to jumping into a fire. I suggest you continue to live happily with your wives in Lanka and let Rama live peacefully in the forest. Nothing constructive is achieved by rousing a sleeping lion.' Surprisingly, Ravana took Maricha's advice and returned home.

Meanwhile, Surpanakha reached Lanka, smouldering with rage and smarting at the indignity meted out to her. The death of her dear cousins Khara and Dushana further fuelled her animosity, and harbouring deep resentment for all that had happened, she now sought comfort in her indomitable brother Ravana. He was one of the mightiest beings ever to exist in all the three worlds, and she was sure he would be able to exact the retribution she so desperately sought. Surpanakha's confidence was not misplaced; Ravana had the reputation of being unequalled in strength. He was born from two different races;[2] his Brahmin father, Vishrava, was human, and his mother, Kaikesi, was a Rakshasa princess. In fact, Kaikesi had married Vishrava with the precise intention of producing offspring with extraordinary abilities, and accordingly, Ravana was blessed with many talents. His father taught him the Vedas, and he mastered them with a high degree of competence. While he inherited a love of scholarship from Vishrava, he obtained his enormous physical strength and shape-shifting ability from Kaikesi. He spent his early life gaining proficiency in Vedic shastras and studying astronomy and the sciences, including Ayurveda. He was a maestro at the veena and a talented musician, who created many famous compositions. He was so learned that he had the knowledge of ten heads and was called Dashagriva. Blessed with so much aptitude, Ravana had the potential for great good, but unfortunately, he was also self-absorbed, egotistical and arrogant. His maternal grandfather, Sumali, encouraged these negative qualities that slowly pulled him away from the path of righteousness to one of wrongdoing. At his instruction, Ravana usurped Lanka, the glorious kingdom ruled by his half-brother Kubera, and later commandeered his golden flying chariot, the Pushpaka Vimana, which enabled him to reach any place he wished at will. Driven by overwhelming lust, he used it to carry off any woman he fancied with or without her consent. He delighted in cruelty and gave sanction to his Rakshasa followers to wreak havoc on innocent people, especially sages, whom they tormented mercilessly.

---

[2] The details of Ravana's lineage feature in the Epilogue.

Everyone feared Ravana because he had even crushed the almighty Devas. His chest bore the scars of Indra's Vajra and Airavata's[3] tusks, which he sported with pride. He was a mountain of a man, so strong that he had the might of twenty arms. A divine benediction completed his invulnerability, making him unbeatable in any contest. After performing years of intense yogic penance to please Lord Brahma, Ravana asked for the boon of immortality. Brahma could not grant this wish because it was against the natural order of the world, where every creature born must eventually die, but he gave Ravana a blessing that was almost as good. Ravana had modified his demand requesting invincibility against any Deva, Yaksha, Gandharva, Kinnara, Asura, Rakshasa, Naga, bird or beast. Interestingly, he did not mention humans because, in his arrogance, he felt they were too weak to be a threat to him.

Surpanakha burst into Ravana's court as he sat on his golden throne surrounded by his ministers, and screeched, 'You sit here happily immersed in sensual pleasures, completely unaware of what is happening in your kingdom. Do you have any idea about what has just taken place at Janasthana? All our kinsmen there, including Khara and Dushana, have been slaughtered at the hands of one man called Rama. Dandaka Forest is not ours any more and now belongs to the rishis. This calamity is just the beginning; if you do not rouse yourself into action, you may lose your entire kingdom and even your life. How can you ignore the outrage against our brethren with your arms crossed? You must act without delay!'

Ravana was troubled by the development at Janasthana and intrigued by what Surpanakha said about Rama, as she echoed what he had heard from Akampana earlier. He was bewildered by how a single human could destroy 14,000 Rakshasas, especially a champion fighter like Khara, and asked incredulously, 'How was Rama able to achieve this? What weapons did he use, and who disfigured your face in this manner?' Surpanakha recounted how Rama's placid appearance belied his ferocity as a warrior and how his valour outrivalled the supremacy of the Devas. She spoke of his golden arrows that blazed forth from his bow so fast that they could barely be seen before they destroyed everyone in their path, just like pelting hailstones ravage a field of crops.

Then Surpanakha insidiously aroused her brother's lust. Knowing Ravana's weakness for women, she praised Sita's incomparable beauty,

---

[3] Indra's famous white elephant with four tusks and seven trunks.

dwelling on her flawless features, golden complexion, large black eyes, full red lips, long luxurious hair, slender waist, ample bosom and wide hips. Comparing her to Devi Lakshmi, Surpanakha asserted that she had never seen such a lovely woman, and cleverly playing to Ravana's lechery, added that any man she held in her embrace had to consider himself fortunate. She insisted that Sita would make a perfect wife for her brother and cunningly twisted the facts of her encounter in the forest to gain his favour. Pretending that she had tried to bring Sita for him as a prize, she said she regretted that Lakshmana had foiled her plans. Surpanakha moaned that Lakshmana had cut off her ears and nose, and stated that he had only spared her life because of her gender. She artfully impressed on Ravana the urgency of acting immediately to avenge both her insult and the wanton massacre of their people by killing Rama and acquiring the lovely Sita for himself.

Ravana had just put aside the plan to abduct Sita, but now found himself burning with passion. Kindled by his sister's fascinating description of her loveliness and egged on by uncontrollable desire, he summarily dismissed his ministers, lest they counsel him otherwise, and set about formulating a plan by which he could obtain the woman of ethereal beauty. He went surreptitiously to his aircraft hangar and asked for a flying chariot to be readied, setting out once again for Maricha's abode. It was a beautiful gem-studded vimana drawn by golden mules with devilish faces; boarding quickly, he flew over the sea, along the coast over prosperous cities, mountains and plains. On the way, Ravana passed ascetics in forests engrossed in penance, but since he was possessed by irrepressible passion, they did not inspire any piety in him.

When he alighted again at the remote ashram, Maricha was surprised to see him return so soon and asked anxiously if all was well in Lanka. Surpanakha had given Ravana an additional reason to justify retaliation. Relating everything she had said, he insisted that he could not merely stand by without chastising those who had no qualms about mutilating his innocent sister's face. Ravana thundered furiously, 'Rama is a villainous person, who was expelled by his own father. He has sealed his fate by picking enmity with me, and his end is near. Rama mercilessly slaughtered all our fellow Rakshasas in Janasthana unprovoked and is a disgrace to all Kshatriyas in his needless cruelty. It is abundantly clear that he has no control over his senses and absolutely no respect for dharma. I consider him a bully who likes to show off his strength because he even had the temerity to disfigure my blameless sister. I have decided to abduct his wife Sita to teach him a lesson, and I need your help to carry her away. You are skilled in the art of magic, so I want you to attract Sita by assuming the form of a golden deer with silver spots that she will no doubt find impossible to resist. Tempted by you, she is sure to ask Rama to capture you for her, and when he attempts to do this, you must elude him and draw him far away. If Lakshmana is left behind to protect Sita, call out for help, mimicking Rama's voice so that he leaves her side. Once Sita is alone, it will be easy for me to abduct her, and when Rama is languishing in misery without his wife, he will be easy to defeat.'

Maricha stared at Ravana, quaking in fear; his throat went dry, and his lips quivered as he recalled how Rama had killed his brother and flung him into the sea when they had interfered with Vishwamitra's rituals. Licking his parched lips and folding his hands in supplication, he stammered, 'I cannot do this! I implore you to listen to my advice, for you are not acquainted with Rama's strength, and I do not think you have weighed your decision carefully or considered all the odds. By offending Rama, you are inviting death. Just as a patient does not relish the bitter medicine that cures him, my advice to point you in the right direction may not appeal to you, as it is perhaps not what you want to hear. Regardless, I consider it my duty to give you my honest opinion by begging you to give up this foolish enterprise! Remember, you have only heard one side of the story. Akampana and Surpanakha may be motivated by self-interest in baiting you to make an adversary of Rama. Tread cautiously, for you cannot be sure of the veracity of what they have told you or the actual reason behind their instigation.

'There is no greater sin than coveting another man's wife, so you are committing a grave misdeed. Moreover, let me remind you that the one you dismiss as an ordinary human has wiped out your entire army of fearsome Rakshasas. This accomplishment shows his power, and it is not prudent to cross him. It is well known that Rama loves his wife more than he does his own life and will surely destroy every Rakshasa on Earth if you touch her. Besides, I do not think you have appointed good spies, as you seem to have been fed a lot of misinformation. Rama is equal to Indra in strength and can easily eliminate the entire Rakshasa race. I wonder if Sita was born to bring about your downfall and mine, too? I fear your unbridled desires will cause Lanka to perish.'

'I suggest you go back and consult with your ministers, including the righteous Vibhishana, carefully weighing the merits and demerits of your plan before rushing into any impetuous action. Although Rama is our enemy, I must concede that he is the very embodiment of dharma. He was not turned out for any misdeed; on the contrary, Rama nobly left Ayodhya of his own accord to uphold his father's promise. His reputation is spotless[4]; he is known for keeping his word and strictly adhering to decorum in every instance. Rather than being mercurial, as you allege, he is always judicious in his actions. It is a fallacy to believe he is greedy or a disgrace to the Kshatriyas, so I must tell you that you have heard false reports about him. Many flatterers dance around you, saying things pleasing to hear, but few will tell you the hard truth. Please pay attention to my words as I have personally experienced Rama's strength. He reduced my brother Subahu and his followers to ashes with a single arrow. It is a miracle that I am alive today, but I can never forget how I was hurled 100 yojanas away into the ocean by him, that too when he was a mere youth. In the early years of his exile, I foolishly tried to avenge our defeat by attacking him with two companions, but they were both killed, and I narrowly escaped with my life. Although I now spend my days in meditation, I still shudder at the thought of him. Our encounter years ago haunts my dreams to this day, and even the sound of the first syllable of his name fills me with dread. I entreat you as your well-wisher not to embark on this madness or ask me to be a party to it, for it will ruin us both.'

Maricha's warning was wise and presented earnestly, but it fell on deaf ears. This time Ravana did not accept his advice; conversely, it inflamed him further because he did not take kindly to the eloquent praise of his enemy. Loath to hear that someone could equal or surpass him in valour, he was even more determined to destroy Rama and extinguish any possible competition posed by the exiled prince. Driven by arrogance and the intense desire to possess a beautiful woman, he threatened menacingly, 'I have not come here to be schooled by you. I am here to seek assistance, not unsolicited advice that I consider as useless as a seed sown in barren soil. Nothing you say will deter me from my objective of making Rama suffer the pain of losing his beloved wife, so do not waste your breath trying to convince me to change my mind. You are a master of disguise, and I command you to go to Panchavati as a decoy. Your refusal to help me is blatant ingratitude, especially since you have availed yourself of my charity all these years and owe me your allegiance. If you do as I say, I will reward you with half my kingdom, but if you decline, I will cut you into pieces this very moment.'

Maricha had no option but to agree. He knew Ravana would not spare him, so it was better to take his chances with Rama. Resigned to his fate,

---

[4] Another example of where Rama is praised by an enemy.

he replied miserably, 'I still hold that whoever gave you this ill-considered advice is your enemy and does not have your well-being at heart. A minister who offers unsound guidance is like a dim-witted charioteer who drives the chariot[5] and his master into a ditch. Dharma flows from the top down; a tyrant who is a slave to his senses cannot be an effective king, and his people are bound to suffer. In such circumstances, good people often come to grief for no fault of their own. Unfortunately, this misfortune has come upon me today. I know my death at Rama's hands is imminent if I assist you with this foolhardy plan, but I would prefer to be killed by the enemy than by my own relative. Sadly, though you do not see it, neither you nor your family will survive for very long after you commit this self-destructive deed. Nevertheless, since you are adamant about going ahead despite my best efforts to counsel you otherwise, let us proceed.' Ravana beamed with satisfaction to have Maricha's consent and ignored his misgivings. Embracing him, he said enthusiastically, 'Now you are talking like the valorous Maricha I know! Get in the vimana and let us depart for Janasthana.'

Ravana set off for the Dandaka Forest with Maricha and landed his flying chariot a short distance away from the cottage in Panchavati. Maricha transformed himself into an enchanting golden deer, and Ravana took the guise of a sage. The illusory deer frolicked playfully in the vicinity of the cottage, romping around animatedly, drawing attention to itself. Sita was picking flowers for worship when she looked up and noticed the endearing animal gambolling about, nibbling tender shoots. Mesmerized by its incredible beauty, she could not help being enamoured by its lively antics. Her eyes dilated in wonder, and she called out excitedly to Rama and Lakshmana to

---

[5] In the Katha Upanishad, Yama uses the metaphor of a chariot to explain the relationship of the Self/Supreme Consciousness with the body–mind complex/human being. The inner Self is the master of the chariot. The body is the chariot. The intellect/power of discrimination is the charioteer. The mind is compared to the reins. The sense organs are the horses and the roads traversed are the various desires pursued. 'When a person lacks discrimination and his mind is undisciplined, the senses run hither and thither like wild horses. But they obey the rein like trained horses when one has discrimination and has made the mind focused. Those who lack discrimination, with little control over their thoughts, reach not the pure state of immortality, but wander from death to death. But those who have discrimination with a still mind and a pure heart, reach the journey's end.' Katha Upanishad 1.3.5–8.
'A wise person should be self-controlled like a charioteer in control of his horses, and not allow the sense organs to run wild after alluring sensual objects.' Manusmriti 2.88

come and see the captivating creature with its snow-white belly, silver spots, sapphire antlers and eyes that sparkled like diamonds. They, too, admired the deer, but Lakshmana was instantly suspicious and warned, 'We must be cautious; this deer smacks of falsity. Do you see how the others of its kind are shunning it? Rakshasas can assume any form they like, and I think this beguiling creature might be one of them in disguise, no doubt with some mischief in mind.' However, Sita was smitten and filled with an intense desire to possess the deer. She pleaded with Rama, 'I am sure it is real! It is the most charming animal I have ever seen and has stolen my heart. O arya, forgive me for my greed and bring it to me. It would be so nice to play with, and I would love to have it as a pet. Our exile is almost over, and we can take it to Ayodhya with us, where I know it will bring delight to everyone in our palace gardens, not just to me but also to our mothers.'

Rama agreed that it was indeed a lovely creature, but like Lakshmana, he too felt it was fake, so he asked her to give up her craving for the deer. However, Sita was uncharacteristically obstinate, and pouting in disappointment, implored him once more. Rama pondered on her request and finally decided to accede to her wish. He reasoned that Sita had borne the hardship of life in the forest for so many years without complaint, never asking him for anything, and he thought this small favour would bring her immense happiness. Tying a belt around his waist to hold his sword and picking up his bow and quiver, he said, 'Lakshmana, I would like to get the deer for Sita. If it is real, she will have a companion to play with, and if it is a Rakshasa like the wicked Vatapi that Agastya killed, I will shoot it with my arrow. Please guard Sita vigilantly and do not leave her side no matter the provocation. I will chase the deer and capture it, or else if it turns out to be an agent of darkness, I will kill it.'

Rama followed the deer as it ran deeper and deeper into the forest, darting back and forth as if to tease him, appearing suddenly and then disappearing entirely from view. Just when it seemed he could easily catch it, it would be gone like a puff of smoke. Rama began to feel the futility of the pursuit but did not want to go back empty-handed and disappoint Sita, so he kept up with the chase. The deer led him far away from the cottage, and no matter how hard Rama tried, he could not capture it. Finally, after pursuing the animal a considerable distance, he got fed up and concluded that Lakshmana was correct in his assessment. This deer could not possibly be real; it had to be a Rakshasa in disguise. He lifted his bow and shot it with such impact that it flew up into the air and landed back on the ground with a colossal thud.

As soon as the arrow found its mark, the deer immediately reverted to its original form. In the throes of death, Maricha garnered the little energy left in his writhing body and did as instructed, crying out in Rama's voice, 'O Sita, O Lakshmana!' Rama was filled with apprehension, instantly realizing this was a ruse to lure him away from the cottage. Although he was confident that Sita was safe in Lakshmana's care, he worried that his brother might have heard the cry and would come searching for him. Fearing the worst, he hastened back to the cottage as fast as he could with his heart pounding in his chest.

Sita was excited at the prospect of Rama returning with the golden deer, but the hours passed and there was no sign of him. She felt it was unusual for her powerful husband to be taking so long to capture a little deer and was beginning to fret about his safety when the plaintive cry 'O Sita, O Lakshmana!' wrought by Maricha's magic echoed through the forest. Hearing it, she trembled in apprehension, thinking her beloved husband was in grave danger. Why else would he call out like that? Overcome by panic, Sita exclaimed, 'Lakshmana, I fear something terrible has happened to Rama. He might have fallen victim to an evil Rakshasa. Please go to his aid immediately. You must leave at once!'

Lakshmana, however, was not perturbed by the cry and replied calmly, 'Sita, the voice sounds like Rama, but I am quite sure it is not him. O princess of Videha, no harm can befall him; your husband is stronger than the strongest warriors in all three worlds put together. I can assure you he is too powerful to be in any trouble. So please calm yourself and wait patiently for his return. I am very sure he will be here in no time with the deer you wanted.'

Sita was filled with dread and regretted pestering Rama for the deer. In her anxiety, she lost her composure and scolded Lakshmana, 'How can you ignore your brother's desperate call for help? Obviously, you have no affection for him, and it doesn't matter to you if he dies.'

Lakshmana remained adamant about obeying his brother's instructions not to leave Sita unprotected and replied firmly, 'Don't worry yourself needlessly in this manner, Sita. I am very certain that was not Rama calling out. I honestly think it is a trick by some Rakshasa, because they have become our sworn enemies ever since their humiliating defeat. Rama has entrusted me with your safety, so I cannot leave you here alone and go looking for him.' Sita was livid at his refusal. Her concern for Rama drove her to distraction, and she hurled unthinkable insults at Lakshmana in anger. 'You are ignoble and cruel, an enemy in the guise of a friend. I view you as a complete disgrace to your noble lineage. You supposedly accompanied Rama to help him, but you refuse to assist him now that he needs you. Perhaps you came here as an agent of Bharata, or worse, followed your brother to the forest with corrupt intentions to get him out of the way because you covet me. I think you secretly want him to die, but please know that I will kill myself if anything happens to my lotus-eyed husband, for I cannot live a moment in his absence.'

Lakshmana was stunned at the unfair accusations and could not believe what he had just heard. How could Sita, whom he had served so dutifully, treating her as a mother all these years, utter such uncharitable words? He was astounded at her churlishness and the dreadful aspersions she cast on his character. Reeling in shock, he said with tears in his eyes, 'I have always held you in the exalted position of a goddess; I have thought of you as my mother, so I have no response to your baseless allegations except that your denigrating words feel like molten arrows piercing my ears. Alas! Women can sometimes be so cruel and capricious! I hope you realize the unfairness of what you have said and regret what you have expressed so harshly to one who has always had your welfare uppermost in his mind. Unfortunately, now you have left me with no choice but to disobey Rama's orders for the first time in my life. Despite my grave concerns about your safety, I am forced to go in search of him as you have instructed and can only pray that the forest deities take care of you in my absence. I am leaving with great unease, fearing you may not be here when I come back with Rama.'

Saying this, he perfunctorily joined his palms together to take his leave, and left boiling with anger.

Chapter 13

Sita's Abduction

The trees suddenly became eerily still; the wind stopped blowing, and the Godavari began flowing ever so slowly as if nature was expressing its trepidation at the events that were to follow. Now, the stage was set and the moment that Ravana was eagerly awaiting had finally arrived. Rama and Lakshmana were both out of the way, and he had the perfect opportunity to seize Sita and carry her off. All this time, he was staring at her spellbound, hidden from view in a thicket. Despite her tear-stained face, she was even more alluring in person than expected; dressed in yellow silk with the countenance of a beautiful full moon, she evoked in him a maddening ardour.

Like a malevolent planet shadowing the star Rohini, Ravana promptly appeared at the cottage, muttering Vedic chants. He perfectly recreated the persona of a wandering hermit, clad in saffron robes, with wooden slippers on his feet and an umbrella in his hand. His disguise was convincing and he even had a water pot dangling from a staff on his left shoulder for authenticity. Hermits roamed the forest; they were revered and it was customary to treat them with respect, so Sita was not alarmed to see him. Quickly wiping her tears, she said unsuspectingly, 'Welcome, holy master!' It was a grave sin in Vedic culture to turn away a guest[1] without extending due hospitality, so Sita poured water to wash his feet and offered him some fruit they had in the hut. Her appearance

---

[1] 'Atithi Devo Bhava'—May an unexpected visitor be considered a Deva. Taittiriya Upanishad 1.11.2. Atithi means without date, so the term refers to an uninvited guest. 'One should offer a guest, as soon as he arrives, a seat, some water and food that has been ritually prepared and perfectly cooked to the best of one's ability. If a Brahmin visits and is not honoured, when he departs, he takes away all the credit for one's good deeds...' Manusmriti 3.99–100

enthralled Ravana, and unable to take his eyes off her, he asked, 'Who are you, lovely lady of superlative beauty? Your complexion is golden, and you are as beautiful as a full moon; are you an Apsara or a celestial being? Your limbs are comely and your lissom body is very fetching, with its slender waist, full hips and pert breasts like the fruit of the palmyra tree. Without a doubt, you are the most exceptional woman I have seen! You ought to be enjoying the comforts of a palace, not living alone with the animals and ascetics in the forest, so I must ask what you are doing here?'

Sita found it very out of character for a holy man to be speaking about her appearance in this manner—but he was a sage, and she did not want to annoy him. Replying that her name was Sita, she said she was the daughter of the pious Janaka, king of Videha, and the beloved wife of Rama of Ayodhya. Sita then narrated the story of her marriage and her happy life in Ayodhya, enjoying every conceivable luxury for twelve years. She explained at length how her husband was exiled to the forest at the age of twenty-five, the day he was to be crowned king, adding that she had followed him with his brother Lakshmana, and they had been wandering in the forest ever since. 'Rest here on this seat of darbha grass,' she said guilelessly, 'My husband and brother-in-law should be returning soon and would be very happy to meet you. In the meantime, tell me about yourself. Where is your ashram, and why are you roaming alone without the company of other sages?'

Ravana lost no time in getting to the point. He said, 'I am not really a hermit. I am Ravana, king of Lanka, and I strike fear in the hearts of all creatures, including the mighty Devas. You have captivated me with your beauty, and though I have a gynaeceum filled with many beautiful women from different lands, they all pale in comparison to you. I want to offer you the position of my principal queen. Come rule my island kingdom with me, and live in the lap of luxury, adorned with ornaments, waited on by five thousand servants.'

Ravana thought Sita would be tempted to elope with him hearing about his enormous wealth, but to his chagrin, she felt repulsed by his indecent proposal. Going pale, she shook in horror like a delicate banana tree buffeted by the wind. Then, filled with revulsion, she spat out in disgust, 'I am a chaste wife and my devotion to my husband is unshakeable. How dare you speak to me in this offensive manner! Rama is brave like a lion; on the other hand, you are a thieving jackal attempting to proposition someone else's wife. I warn you that you are courting death because my husband has immense power. He is mighty like the ocean, whereas you are like a tiny brook; he is as pure as gold, and in contrast, you are corrupt like a base metal; he is majestic like the eagle Garuda, and you are pathetic like a crow. Do not harbour any false hopes of making me your wife because I will never allow you to come near me. Your desire to possess me is as fruitless as trying to cross the sea with a stone tied to your neck or attempting to lift a blazing fire with a piece of cloth. If my husband returns now, he will reduce you to dust, so leave this instant and never come back.'

Ravana's eyes narrowed in annoyance and his honeyed tone turned choleric. 'Don't compare me with Rama. He is a humble hermit, whereas I am the invincible lord of Lanka, the glorious son of Rishi Vishrava. I am so powerful that the Asuras, Devas and Gandharvas quake in terror before me; the wind blows gently in my presence; trees and rivers stand still; even the sun becomes mellow in deference to me. Fearing my enormous might, my half-brother Kubera surrendered his magnificent city and treasured aerial chariot, the Pushpaka, to my possession. My kingdom, which lies on the other shore of the ocean, is more beautiful than Indra's famous Amravati.[2] The houses are built of gold and decorated with precious jewels; the gates are lapis lazuli and the lovely gardens abound with fruit trees of every kind. Come live with me there and relish unimaginable pleasures instead of wasting your time here in the forest in the company of a vagabond. Your husband is a weakling who accepted his exile without a fight. I implore you not to reject me, for I have come here besotted by you, craving your love. Aside from that, consider it your good fortune that I am drawn to you as you have so much advantage to gain.'

Sita was beside herself with rage and shouted angrily, 'Go away, you monstrous wretch! How can one who claims to be the noble Kubera's brother be so odious? I will never submit myself to you. A man may survive Indra after he lays his hands on Sachi[3] but let me warn you, it is impossible to escape Rama's wrath if you touch me. So, if you are as brave as you say you are, wait till my husband returns and duel with him. I can assure you he will shred you to pieces.' Ravana was outraged by the affront, and realizing Sita was not going to relent, he assumed his actual form, towering malevolently before her. His brows furrowed, and his eyes reddened as he roared, 'Foolish woman, clearly you have not been listening to me, or you

---

[2] The capital of Indra, the king of the Devas, built by Vishwakarma with gold and precious gems.

[3] Indra's wife, a woman of great beauty.

would have appreciated my pre-eminence. I can lift the Earth, swallow the sea and destroy the sun with my arrows.' He looked intimidating, like a gigantic dark cloud, as he bellowed, 'I am the fittest partner for you! Marry me, and you will have a husband celebrated in all three worlds. It is time to give up the silly sentimentality that keeps you foolishly clinging to someone who has lost his kingdom. So far, I have tried patiently to convince you to come away with me, using every reasonable argument, but it has not worked. Now I have no choice but to take you with me by force.' Before Sita could react, Ravana grabbed her; then, holding her hair with one hand and her thigh with the other, he carried her into his flying chariot.

As Ravana bore Sita away, she struggled furiously, calling out desperately for help, pleading for someone to assist in her hour of need. She shouted out to Rama and Lakshmana, and when they did not hear her, she begged the animals in the forest and even the trees and the sacred river to tell them her plight, but it was in vain. Then suddenly, there was a glimmer of hope; the old eagle Jatayu was resting on the branch of a tree and heard her cry out in distress. 'O noble bird, O arya, hasten to Rama and let him know that his beloved wife is being spirited away by the sinful Ravana.' Since the situation warranted an immediate response, Jatayu did not go in search of Rama; instead, he flapped his giant wings and soared up to Ravana's vimana, hoping to reason with him. 'How can a king of your stature stoop so low and abduct another man's wife?[4] What merit will you gain from this disgraceful act that violates the norms of decency?[5] O grandson of Pulastya, all conduct ultimately flows from the leader down to his people, so remember you are a role model whose example others emulate. If a king does not tread the path of virtue, he sets a bad example for his subjects to follow. Rama has not harmed you; he was not the initial aggressor. When Khara attacked him, he was forced to retaliate in self-defence. By abducting Sita, you have taken on more than you can handle, like tying a poisonous snake to your garment. In provoking Rama, you have unavoidably placed the noose of death around your neck. Desist from committing this misdeed that will bring shame to your noble lineage, because there is nothing to gain from it except grief.'

---

[4] Manusmriti 8.323 advocates the death penalty for anyone who commits the heinous crime of abducting a woman.

[5] 'For in this world there is nothing more detrimental to a long life than the seduction of another man's wife.' Manusmriti 4.134

Ravana ignored him and continued on his way, so Jatayu threatened, 'I may be advanced in years, but I will not hesitate to fight you if you do not release Sita immediately. You can be sure I will resist your misconduct until my last breath.'

Ravana had a volatile nature and was not open to logic; his eyes blazed like fire, and he lashed out, viciously striking Jatayu. A fierce battle followed; it was an extraordinary clash in the sky between an eagle and a Rakshasa, like two rain clouds propelled by opposing winds. Jatayu had no weapons except his sharp beak and talons, which he used with great ferocity, puncturing Ravana all over his body. Ravana fought back with arrows that soaked Jatayu in blood. Despite being badly injured, he continued to fight valiantly, shattering Ravana's bow, shredding his armour, decapitating his charioteer and ultimately forcing his vimana down.

Ravana put Sita aside and fought Jatayu on the ground, duelling for an hour. For a while, it seemed the bird was winning as he kept up his ferocious assault, gouging Ravana repeatedly on his back and tearing out clumps of his hair. Eventually, however, Jatayu started to tire as his age began to take its toll. The much younger Ravana had greater endurance, and seizing an opportune moment, he slashed off Jatayu's wings and feet with his sword, leaving him incapacitated and clinging to life. Sita felt overcome by guilt that Jatayu had given his life in the valiant attempt to save her. Grief-stricken at his plight, she cradled him in her arms, sobbing bitterly, 'O Rama, you are unaware of the dreadful calamity that has taken place and how this great bird has sacrificed himself to save me!' With Jatayu debilitated and unable to help, she clung to a tree as Ravana approached, desperately trying to resist being carried away, but he yanked her from it by her hair and took off, holding her squirming body firmly on his lap. All that remained were the signs of a dreadful scuffle; scattered flowers, a solitary bejewelled anklet and a broken gold chain.

On the one hand, the Devas looked on with sadness to see Sita in anguish; and, on the other, they were relieved that Ravana's end was inevitable, as the impetus for his destruction was now set into motion. As they flew through the sky, Sita chastised Ravana bitterly. 'You pride yourself on being brave, but you shamelessly killed an old bird; O spineless coward, who did not dare face my husband. You abducted me like a rogue while he was deceitfully led away and are reprehensible; your wicked deed will be remembered forever, bringing disgrace to your clan for all time to come. If you think you can coerce me to submit to you, you are mistaken. Let me restate that you will never win my heart, as it is firmly with Rama, and I cannot live without him. My heroic husband killed 14,000 of your Rakshasas unassisted, so I know he will not spare your life when he sees you. Therefore, reconsider your actions carefully; you still have the chance to repent and take me back. Rama is very forgiving and will excuse your immoral conduct if you are penitent; otherwise, be warned, you are surely inviting your destruction.' Rama could not hear her cries, and Ravana paid no attention to her, no matter how much she inveighed against his misconduct. Dismissing her protests, he said sternly, 'O Maithili, lovely lady with a beautiful smile, you have no alternative but to agree to be my wife.'

Sita felt helpless in her predicament, but fortuitously as they sped along, she saw a group of Vanaras, ape-like forest men, on a mountain below. Unnoticed by Ravana, she took off her jewellery, making a bundle of it with her upper cloth, and threw it down, praying that Rama would find it. The vimana travelled swiftly like an arrow shot from a bow, proceeding southwards over forests, rivers, mountains and lakes. Soon they reached the end of the land and crossed over the ocean to Lanka. On arrival, Ravana took Sita through many gated passageways to a secret chamber in his palace's inner quarters. He summoned a troop of female attendants, instructing them to tend to her with the utmost care, providing her with fine jewellery, expensive clothing and any convenience she desired, all the while keeping a close watch and not allowing anyone near her. He then left, planning his next move.

Ravana called eight savage Rakshasas and ordered them to go to Janasthana, armed with powerful weapons to re-establish his supremacy there. In addition, their mission was to keep an eye on Rama and wait for an opportunity to kill him. Feeling confident that his warriors would be victorious now that Rama was weak with grief, he returned to Sita. She was a miserable sight, like a cornered doe beset by hounds after being singled out from her herd.

Ravana was unused to facing rejection; it hurt his pride, and his ego could only be soothed if he won her over. He felt confident that it would be impossible for Sita to resist the temptation of sharing in the glory of his exalted status once she saw his abundant wealth with her own eyes. Hoping to seduce her with a display of all that he owned, he marched her through his palace complex, flaunting its unsurpassed grandeur. It was indeed as marvellous as he had boasted, even more magnificent than Indra's Amravati. Many seven-storeyed buildings, each reeking of luxury, housed thousands of women. The majestic pillars were ivory, inlaid with gold, crystal and silver, studded with precious jewels like diamonds, pearls and lapis lazuli. Everything glittered with gold, including the massive gates, the staircases and the long rows of seats. The windows were decorated with gold netting, and the floors were made of a gleaming white marble set with gems. In the manicured grounds outside were charming waterfalls, serene pools and lovely birds, and the sound of kettledrums sounded throughout the palace, paying homage to its opulence.

Blinded by hubris, Ravana bragged, 'I am not only lord and master of all this, but I also have 320 million Rakshasas who answer to my every command. Be my wife, and all this will be yours as well; rule by my side, and you will enjoy a life of unparalleled comfort beyond your wildest imagination. We can even travel together worldwide, exploring exciting places in my Pushpaka Vimana. Lanka is a hundred yojanas wide and completely protected by the sea on all sides. It is unassailable, and no one can come here. Rama is a mendicant with no kingdom, and remember, your youth is fleeting, so make the most of it while you can. The time that is lost can never be reclaimed! Your impoverished husband has nothing to offer you; besides, you will never see him again.'

Sita covered her face and cried in misery, tears streaming down her cheeks, which Ravana mistook for shyness. So, twisting the shastras to suit him, he said, 'Don't hide your face coyly from me or have any concern about violating dharma. The union of lovers who elope is sanctioned by the shastras, as it is the result of passion[6].' Then bending down, he touched his head to her feet and begged, 'Show me your favour as I am a slave to your love, and desire burns like a fire within me. Ravana has never bowed to any woman before, so let it not be in vain.'

Sita drew strength from her undying devotion as a wife, quelling her fear though she was in the depths of despair. Ravana so revolted her that the sight of him was repugnant. Plucking a blade of grass and fixing her gaze on it, she delivered a withering admonishment, averting her eyes from him altogether. 'I am the daughter-in-law of Dasharatha, who was always inextricably associated with righteousness. My husband Rama, true to his noble lineage, is devoted to dharma, and he will forever remain the object

---

[6] Ravana is referring to Gandharva Vivah—Marriage between lovers resulting from passion, without the consent of their families. It is one of the eight types of marriage described in Manusmriti 3.20–30. However, Gandharva marriage does not apply if the woman is abducted and is an unwilling participant.

of my everlasting affection. Just as a female swan[7] sports exclusively with her glorious mate amidst the lotuses in a lake, without a scintilla of interest for the diver bird standing in the reeds, I have no regard whatsoever for a sinner like you. Rama is strong and valiant, and I know he will come here with his brother Lakshmana and destroy you and all your evil supporters, just as he did Khara. You think the sea is an obstacle for him in your conceit, but I know that he will come for me even if an ocean of stars separated us. Lanka will be soaked in blood, and the pitiful wailing of widows will replace the sound of the kettledrums. If you had dared to approach me in Rama's presence, you would not be standing here today; nevertheless, be warned that your wickedness has marked your time. Nothing you have flaunted today evokes even the slightest temptation in me. My heart remains steadfastly with Rama, and whether you torture me, put me in chains or even kill me, please know that I will never submit to you as long as I live.'

Ravana was exasperated at his failure. His earlier persuasive tone became harsh, and he replied testily, 'O beautiful princess of Mithila, I warn you that if you do not accept me within twelve months, my cooks will slice you into pieces and cook you for my breakfast.' Peeved at being snubbed, Ravana summoned the female attendants again and instructed, 'Take Sita to the Ashoka Grove[8] and keep her prisoner there. Use every means available to you to bring her under control as one does with a wild she-elephant. Break her will and make her yield to me by alternately using threats and kind words to wear down her resistance slowly.'

The women joined their palms in obedience to his command, and seizing Sita, took her to a beautiful park covered in flowers of myriad hues and trees of every kind that fruited in all seasons. Ironically, as its name suggests, the Ashoka[9] Grove was meant to be a pleasure garden that dispelled sorrow, but Sita, who loved nature, did not find any joy there. Plunged in grief, all she dwelled on was her beloved Rama and her terrible treatment of Lakshmana. Overcome by heartache and remorse, she lost consciousness.

---

[7] In Vedic literature the swan (hamsa) is a symbol of intelligent discrimination and self-realization, as it was believed to be able to separate milk from water, or good from bad.

[8] Believed to be Sita Eliya in Nuwara Eliya, Sri Lanka. See Bala, Saroj, *Ramayan Retold with Scientific Evidences* (Prabhat Prakashan, 2019).

[9] Ashoka literally means devoid of sorrow.

Chapter 14

Rama's Grief

Back in the Dandaka Forest, Rama was deeply troubled by the incident of the deer. In the convulsions of death, it had disturbingly called out in his voice, and he felt sure it was part of a diabolical ploy to draw him away. Rama fervently prayed that Lakshmana would not fall for the deception and leave Sita unprotected. As he raced towards the cottage as fast as he could, jackals howled and his left eye[1] twitched inauspiciously, adding to his discomfiture. Then his worst fears were realized when he saw Lakshmana hurrying towards him with knitted brows and a stressed countenance. Alarmed by the potential repercussions of his disobedience, Rama chastised him severely. 'Why did you leave Sita and come here? I left her in your care, and you betrayed my trust. The cry you heard was a cunning trick, perhaps designed specifically to entice you away so that Sita would be alone. The deer I chased and finally killed was a Rakshasa, and it was he who called out to delude you. How could you let me down like this? I am petrified that some evil creature may have gotten hold of my beloved wife, and you know I cannot live without her. Even the kingdom of the Devas is meaningless to me without her by my side. O Lakshmana, you have committed a terrible blunder leaving Sita alone.'

The reprimand filled Lakshmana with guilt, as his brother had never scolded him like this before. Remonstrating that he had not come looking for him voluntarily, he recounted Sita's unbearable accusations, complaining that her taunts were so intolerable that they provoked him to leave. However, Rama was not pacified and said sternly, 'Sita's distress drove her to madness and she said irrational things because she was not in her senses. Her words were the raging of a temporarily unhinged mind, but you should have

---

[1] The twitching of the left eye was auspicious for a woman, but inauspicious for a man.

known better than to take umbrage and act impulsively on her imprudent instructions. I am very disappointed that you failed to obey me and allowed your judgement to be clouded by anger.'

When they reached the cottage, it was deserted and in disarray; things were strewn around haphazardly, indicating a struggle. Rama's heart sank in despair, and an icy chill ran down his spine. He was sure Sita had been abducted, maybe even killed by now, and devoured by a despicable Rakshasa. For the first time in his life, he felt driven to distraction and lost his usual composure, looking frantically for Sita everywhere. Rama scoured the forest, searching every bush, tree, cave and hollow, but she was nowhere to be found. He called out helplessly to the forest's fauna and flora in a crazed state. 'O kadamba[2] tree, my Sita so loved your flowers, did you see her? O arjuna,[3] O bilva,[4] O tilaka, do you know where my lovely wife is? O deer with beautiful eyes like those of my beloved, did she come this way? O elephants and tigers, did you chance upon a woman with a face as radiant as the full moon?' Considering various scenarios, he questioned anxiously, 'Perhaps she has gone to pick flowers for worship or to bathe in the Godavari? Maybe she is hiding because she is upset with me or playing a prank to tease us?' And they searched on and on.

Sadly, all efforts to find Sita were for naught, and they were forced to return to the cottage in utter despair. Tears of dejection streamed down Rama's face and his mouth was dry as he wept. 'Lakshmana, we have looked everywhere, but there is no sign of my darling Sita. I fear she may be dead, captured and eaten, and we will never find her. My head is full of morbid thoughts of her delicate neck being severed and some vile Rakshasa drinking her blood. Our exile is almost over, but how can we go back to Ayodhya without her? I can never face king Janaka again, having failed miserably in my duty as a husband to keep his daughter safe. Leave me here, Lakshmana, and go home because I cannot return without Sita. Inform Bharata that he should continue to rule and tell my mother my tragic story and take care of her for me. Alas! There is no one more blighted than I am! I continue to be assailed by one sorrow after another and must believe that I am reaping the result of some terrible misdeed I committed in a previous life.'

---

[2] *Neolamarckia cadamba*: burflower tree

[3] *Terminalia arjuna*: arjuna tree

[4] *Aegle marmelos*: bael

Lakshmana put his hand on his brother's shoulder and said tenderly, 'I know an ineffable sadness engulfs you, but I implore you to cast off your dejection and focus your attention on recovering Sita. Give your grief a purpose and continue looking for her. I am confident we will find her if we persist in our efforts.' His words encouraged Rama, and together they resumed the search. As they hunted for clues, they passed a stone slab on the banks of the Godavari that brought back poignant memories of happy times at that spot, listening to Sita tell stories.

Rama begged the river to inform him where she had gone, but it was dead silent. He pleaded with the sun and the wind to help him. 'O sun, you witness everything that happens on Earth; did you see Sita? O wind, you pervade the world; where is my Sita?' Then, by chance, he noticed a herd of deer heading southwards, and recalling the deep communion Sita had with nature, said to Lakshmana, 'Maithili shared a special bond with the deer, so they may be able to give us an inkling of her whereabouts.'

They followed the deer, and a short distance away, they came upon some scattered flowers. Rama exclaimed, 'These are the flowers I gave Sita this morning to adorn her beautiful hair, so she must have trodden this way. They lie here undisturbed, protected by Mother Earth as a sign for me. The sun has not wilted them, and the wind has been kind enough not to disperse them.'

A little further, they saw small footprints overtaken by larger ones, a humungous bow decorated with gems that lay in pieces, broken armour made of gold with beads of lapis lazuli, a dead charioteer, and drops of blood smattered here and there. Cast to one side was a broken umbrella and a shattered standard. Rama was sure that two Rakshasas had fought over Sita, and these remnants were the signs of their tussle. His grief unexpectedly turned to anger as he threatened to annihilate all three worlds. Shedding his mild demeanour, he roared in a temper, 'There is no value for gentleness in this world! If the Devas do not come to my assistance and Sita is not restored to me, I will destroy every semblance of life in all three worlds. Today I shake with such fury that nothing can restrain me.'

Lakshmana was alarmed to see his brother so disoriented by sorrow that he was not himself any more. He had assuaged Rama's grief, but now the earlier anguish had taken on a more frightening form, so he folded his hands reverently and pleaded, 'O brother, your virtuous deeds have always shone brightly like the sun. You are charming like the moon in your attitude and as patient as the Earth in your forbearance; do not forsake your true self now.

The righteous never harm the innocent, so how can you stray from dharma by talking about punishing all creatures for the crime committed by one individual? I beg you to check yourself from succumbing to anger, as it is a base emotion that only impairs good sense. You have the reputation of being judicious in your actions. It is clear from the vestiges of the battle that no army was involved here. It seems two beings fought over Sita; one got killed, and the survivor took her. If we can locate him, undoubtedly, we will find her too. Remember, we were taught that suffering is the inevitable consequence of birth, and hardship comes to everyone in one form or another. Character is revealed by how the vicissitudes of life are handled, so even if by some unfortunate chance Sita has perished, do not let it provoke you into doing something wrong. Recall the misfortune by which our guru Vasishta lost all his sons in a single day. The very Earth we live on undergoes repeated upheavals. Every so often, the sun and moon endure eclipses that obscure their light, and problems even afflict the Devas, who are more powerful than us.

'Please garner your courage and do not let your grief goad you into tarnishing your unblemished reputation in the world. Is it not unrighteous to wreak destruction on the innocent because of your own misery? This behaviour goes against everything you have stood for all your life. So, heed my advice and let us resolve this problem intelligently, using our brainpower to track down the person who stole Sita. Together we will hunt every corner of the Earth to find the rogue who has brought about this awful calamity. If a great person like you becomes downhearted in the face of difficulties, how can ordinary people be expected to deal with them? A mountain does not topple over no matter how rough the winds blow, and I know you have the same resilience. You are equal to Brihaspati in wisdom, so please forgive me for my audacity in counselling you. All I am trying to do is to remind you of your quintessential nature, because at this moment, you are so overcome by emotion that your mind is confused.'

Lakshmana's words had a profound effect on Rama. He realized that he had succumbed to grief and anger, which were detrimental to any constructive action. Recognizing his lapse, he instantly reigned in his unruly instincts with new determination and resumed the search with Lakshmana.[5]

---

[5] Valmiki depicts emotion as natural to human beings, even in great avatars like Rama. However, those who are enlightened are able to check themselves from acting impetuously in a fit of passion.

Once again, they combed every corner of Janasthana; the woods, gorges, caves, hills, valleys and even the habitat of the Gandharvas and Kinnaras. Then suddenly, they came upon a giant eagle in a pool of blood. Rama thought it must be the Rakshasa resting after catching and consuming Sita. He rushed towards the creature with his bow drawn, but as he approached, he realized it was Jatayu. Life was ebbing from his body, and his mouth oozed blood and froth. Sighing laboriously, he said, 'My child, the noble lady you are seeking was snatched by Ravana, the son of Vishrava and brother of Kubera. I saw him carrying her off southwards and tried to stop him, but age was not on my side, and I failed in my endeavour when he cut off my wings and feet. I have clung to life only to tell you who took her, so now I can die in peace. Take solace that Ravana abducted Sita during the hour of Vinda,[6] a time that indicates you will regain what you have lost, whereas he will ultimately perish like a fish that has swallowed a baited hook. Sita is terrified; go rescue her with the confidence that your success is assured.' Uttering these final words, the great eagle breathed his last.

Rama cradled Jatayu's lifeless body, overwhelmed with sorrow that he had died while selflessly trying to save Sita, without any thought for his own life. Praising his bravery, he said to Lakshmana, 'My grief at the heroic sacrifice of this most honourable bird is hitting me even harder than my pain at the loss of my beloved wife. Nobleness is not just a human quality; animals have it too! I am deeply indebted to Jatayu for trying to help Sita and telling me who took her, and I feel the same reverence for him that I felt towards our father. The least we can do to express our gratitude to this dharmatma[7] is to cremate his body in accordance with the shastras, so he attains the highest plane of heaven.' They gathered logs and consigned Jatayu's body to the flames,[8] chanting Vedic hymns. After performing the water and food offering to his departed spirit, they set out towards the south with renewed vigour.

Janasthana was now behind them, and they approached the Krauncha Forest. Like Janasthana, it was thick with trees and shrouded in creepers,

---

[6] An inauspicious time. According to the calculation of muhurtas in the Shatapada Brahmana, this would be between 2.00 p.m. and 2.48 p.m.

[7] One who upholds dharma.

[8] This place is called Sarvateerth today and is 58 kilometres from Nashik. There is a Jatayu Rama temple there.

but even more perilous for being home to many dangerous creatures. They had not gone far when a thunderous roar resounded through the forest. The brothers drew their swords as a gigantic ogre appeared in their path. His name was Kabandha; devoid of a head or neck, he was the most hideous-looking creature they had ever seen. He had an enormous torso covered in bristles and a single massive eye with tawny lashes. His gigantic mouth, lined with sharp fangs, was so big that he could devour bears, lions and even elephants whole. In an instant, he extended his long tentacle-like arms and grabbed Rama and Lakshmana, one in each hand, bringing them together and holding them firmly in a vice-like grip. Then, glaring at them as they wriggled to free themselves, he asked, 'Who are you hermits, oddly bearing bows and swords? I don't know what brings you here, but I am hungry, and you are welcome fare for my voracious appetite.'

Lakshmana quivered to hear him; his mouth went dry, and he said to Rama, 'Leave me here as his food and free yourself so that you can continue the search for Sita.' However, despite the dangerous situation, Rama remained composed and replied calmly, 'We are in a precarious position for sure. Look at the power of time that can change one's fortune in a moment! Even the mightiest people succumb to its vagaries, but before this ogre can eat us, let us act quickly and cut off his arms with our swords.' Rama severed his right arm and Lakshmana his left one in a flash. Kabandha emitted a loud, agonized scream and suddenly became meek, to their amazement. He asked who they were, so Lakshmana narrated their story.

When Lakshmana questioned how he had come to be a headless torso, Kabandha replied, 'There was a time when I was not deformed as I am now. This hideous body is the result of a curse because I lacked humility. I was once a Danu, a messenger of the Devas with a handsome appearance, but I was haughty about my abilities. Being a Deva, I could alter my shape and enjoyed assuming frightening forms to oppress the rishis in the forest. One day, I bothered a maharishi called Sthulashira, ignorant of his powers. Enraged that I had disturbed his meditation, he cursed me to forever remain in the ugly body I had adopted. When I begged him to forgive me, he reduced the severity of his pronouncement, saying that I would be released the day my arms were cut off and I was burnt alive. However, I was still not rid of my bumptiousness, and one day I needlessly picked a quarrel with Indra. He struck me with his thunderbolt, the Vajra, and I got further deformed, with my head pushed into my body. I have roamed this forest ever since then, but now that you have

severed my arms, please burn me so that I can be freed from the rishi's curse
and regain my former self. If you do me this favour, you can ask for something
in return.'

Rama recounted his misfortune and said the only thing he wanted was
information about Ravana and where he had taken Sita. Kabandha stated he
had no knowledge about Ravana in his current condition but was sure he
would be able to give him some insight once his divine vision was restored.

Following Kabandha's wishes, they cremated him. As his grotesque body
perished, a dazzling figure in a vimana drawn by swans arose from the flames.
Ascending into the sky, he advised them to seek out a valiant Vanara[9] called
Sugriva, for, like Rama, this forest dweller was also suffering the sorrow of
separation from his wife. His brother Vali had appropriated her after wrongly
ousting him from his kingdom, and he was hiding on Rishyamukha Mountain
with four close associates ever since he had been cast out. Kabandha praised
Sugriva as strong, brave, noble, truthful, intelligent and capable, adding that
his fighting spirit would help recover Sita. He urged, 'Go in haste and make
friends with Sugriva, the son of Surya, sealing your friendship with Agni as
your witness.[10] Although he is a Vanara, there is nothing lowly about him,
and he will prove to be a powerful and loyal friend to you. Sugriva is familiar
with every quarter of all three worlds because he ran from place to place when
Vali pursued him before finally finding refuge on Rishyamukha.'

Kabandha emphasized that one of the six strategies[11] recommended for
kings facing an enemy was to join forces with someone in a similar situation.
He said he was positive Sugriva, who knew every possible hiding place,
would assist him in finding Sita no matter where she was being held captive,
be it at the top of Mount Meru or in the depths of the netherworld. Then

---

[9] Vanara in Sanskrit means forest dweller (vana/forest + nara/man), so Valmiki clearly
indicates they were not monkeys as depicted in other versions of the Ramayana.

[10] Fire symbolized purity and was regarded as the universal witness. In the body it is
represented by the eyes. The first hymn in the Rig Veda praises Agni/fire as fire is characterized
by truth and perfection. A pact made with fire as witness was therefore rendered sacred. 'To
you Agni who shines upon darkness, we come day after day, bringing our thoughts and
homage.' Rig Veda 1.7

[11] The six strategies are: 1. Sandhi—making a truce; 2. Vigraha—continuing the
hostility; 3. Yaana—waging war; 4. Aasana—Biding time till it is suitable to strike;
5. Dvaidhi Bhava—creating dissent in the enemy ranks; 6. Samashraya—joining forces
with someone in a similar situation.

he instructed them to travel westwards till they reached an area prolific with fruit trees. At that point, they were to turn south, crossing one hill after another till they reached a lake called Pampa.[12] He described it as an idyllic spot with clear waters, fragrant with the scent of lilies and lotuses. Birds of all kinds—swans, cranes, curlews and kingfishers—frequented the place; it was home to many varieties of fish, plump like pots of ghee, that could be caught and roasted.[13] The gently sloping banks were covered in fine white sand and the lake's bed was not slippery or marred by moss and pebbles, making it easy to wade in. Nearby, he said, they would find the ashram of the departed Rishi Matanga, where his old disciple, the pious Shabri, was waiting for them. After stopping to see her, he advised them to go onwards to Rishyamukha, where Sugriva lived in a cave hidden by a large rock. Rama thanked Kabandha and bade him farewell, and turning around as he left, Kabandha called out, 'Make friends with Sugriva!'

Shabri was a devout woman who had lived an austere life. As a young tribal[14] girl, she had sought Rishi Matanga's protection and had been his faithful follower ever since, participating in spiritual discourse with the rishis and becoming a siddha.[15] When the sage was ready to give up his body, Shabri begged to join him, but he prophesized Rama's visit and instructed her to wait for the prince's arrival, so she could serve him. Shabri dutifully obeyed her guru's bidding, living as the custodian of the ashram, sweeping and cleaning it as she had always done. Every day, she collected the sweetest fruit in case Rama arrived. So, when he finally came, she was overwhelmed with joy and welcomed him with great affection, extending all the traditionally prescribed courtesies. Shabri had achieved 'Brahmagyana'[16]

---

[12] Lake Pampa is in the Koppal district near Hampi, south of the river Tungabhadra. Hindus consider it a sacred lake. Interestingly, filled with lotuses, the lake continues to be a very picturesque spot even today.

[13] However, there is no mention of Rama catching and eating them. He appears to be living on roots and fruits now.

[14] Shabri was from the Bhil tribe, one of the oldest in India; as per genetic studies, the Bhils go back more than 10,000 years. See Bala, Saroj, *Ramayan Retold with Scientific Evidences* (Prabhat Prakashan, 2019).

[15] A siddha is a person who has achieved spiritual perfection.

[16] Brahmagyana is the highest knowledge by which one is liberated from the cycle of birth and death. It is understanding the unity of all creation. As the Mundaka Upanishad 3.2.9 says: 'The knower of Brahman becomes Brahman.' Brahmagyana is

or divine knowledge through her dedicated service and teacher's grace, which had freed her from earthly bondage. Seeing that she was the epitome of devotion, Rama said, 'I heard about your great spiritual eminence from Kabandha, and I would very much like to see your ashram.'

Matanga[17] was the son of a Shudra and had become a Brahmin when he attained enlightenment after years of penance, standing on one leg till his body was reduced to skin and bone. The ashram continued to bear the effulgent energy of the sage, with its sacred altars that still glowed, flower garlands that had not withered, and ascetic robes that were still damp with water from the seven oceans that he had invoked to pool there by his yogic power. After showing Rama around, Shabri said that her work in the world was done, having hosted him, and it was time for her to cast away her body. She prepared a pyre and, offering herself to the burning flames, disengaged her spirit from her mortal frame. Then, consumed by the dazzling fire, she rose with the brightness of lightning to join her guru in heaven.[18] Rama and Lakshmana were in awe of Shabri's piety and continued to marvel at the holiness of Matanga's ashram as they set out in search of Sugriva. As they walked, Rama remarked to Lakshmana, 'The spiritual eminence of the sages seems to have influenced the temperament of the wild animals here because, in these sacred precincts, even the tigers and deer live in harmony. We were lucky to have seen the waters of the seven seas, and I am grateful that we could make an offering with it to our forefathers. My mind feels much more positive now as we head to Rishyamukha.'

---

the true understanding of the Self/Atman as Brahman or pure consciousness, the same consciousness that pervades the universe. 'Those who see all creatures in themselves and themselves in all creatures know no fear. Those who see all creatures in themselves, know no grief. How can multiplicity of life delude the one who sees its unity?' Isha Upanishad 6–7. A person who sees himself in all beings and all beings in himself is a Brahmagyani, who attains oneness with Brahman. Such a person, though embodied, is not affected by the weaknesses of the body.

[17] Matanga became a Brahmin through acquiring knowledge, an example showing varna was not assigned by birth. A profession was acquired and not conferred through birthright.

[18] Giving up the body voluntarily after life's work is completed is not the same as suicide. Suicide is frowned upon as an escape from responsibility, but Shabri had completed her karma and was ready to embrace the next stage of existence.

On the way, they stopped at Pampa Lake to bathe in its limpid waters, aromatic with sweet-smelling lotuses and lilies. It was the month of Chaitra, and Vasant, the season of renewal, was in full bloom. The trees were thick with blossoms. Worker bees buzzed about noisily, peacocks danced, birds called to their mates and stags frolicked with does. Heralding spring, the inebriated cuckoo bird sang in euphoria and the trees swaying gently like a swinging garland looked like they were dancing to its tune. The bleakness of winter had given way to vigorous new beginnings. There was an explosion of colour in the landscape, and the pleasant breeze scented with wildflowers made Rama's heart ache with an intense longing for Sita.

The beauteous surroundings reminded him of how much she loved nature and filled with a deep yearning for his beloved wife, Rama exclaimed sorrowfully, 'O Lakshmana, I have lost what is most precious to me in this world. Whenever I felt troubled, Sita was my emotional support. I miss her more than ever!' Everything around him brought back memories of her. He saw her gentle eyes in those of the deer, he smelled her fragrance in the beautiful lotus flowers, and even the mildness of the breeze was redolent of the softness of her speech. Saddened to his core, he lamented that the vibrancy of nature that filled lovers with the joy of togetherness only served to intensify the anguish of those separated. Parted from his dear wife, Rama's mind was full of torment, and his whole body burned in agony as if it were on fire. As he wondered where Sita was and worried about her condition, Lakshmana commiserated with him to lift his spirits. Boosting his morale with encouraging words, he said, 'Don't allow melancholy to enervate you. Even the impossible can be achieved with a spirit of enthusiasm and an indomitable will to succeed. Now is the time to cultivate unflinching determination, so we spare no effort to recover Sita.'

BOOK 4

The Alliance with
the Vanaras

Chapter 15

Sugriva

As Rama and Lakshmana approached Rishyamukha, Sugriva spotted them. The sight of two tall, strapping men armed with weapons heading purposefully in his direction filled him with terror. He lived in constant dread of Vali and feared they were assassins sent at his behest. Sugriva knew Vali could not come to Rishyamukha himself because Rishi Matanga had cursed him to drop dead if he set foot there, but it was not inconceivable for him to send mercenaries on his behalf. Since it was uncommon for anyone to enter this remote area, he reasonably assumed that the majestic-looking bowmen were Vali's agents, sent in disguise to complete a task he could not accomplish himself.

Sugriva worked himself up into a highly agitated state and took off in fright, jumping from crag to crag to the top of the mountain with his followers. Counselling him to calm down, his trusted minister Hanuman said, 'You are exhibiting the monkey aspect of your nature with your skittishness! Rishyamukha is a holy place where your safety is assured because neither Vali nor any other dark force can enter here. As a leader, you ought to use your intelligence and powers of analysis before jumping to conclusions so quickly. Observe the men closely; their disposition and body language show no sign of aggression, and the concerned expression on their faces seems to indicate that they have problems of their own.' However, Sugriva was not pacified and replied anxiously, 'They have weapons, long arms and strong shoulders; they look as powerful as a pair of Devas, so I can't help being afraid of them. Vali could easily have sent them; you know he is ruthless in dealing with his enemies and has many allies to call upon in times of need. Disguise yourself as an ordinary human and befriend them; you are a skilled orator, so find out who they are and why they have come here. I want you to face me while talking to them, so I can determine from your countenance whether they are friends or foes.'

The Vanaras were forest dwellers whose appearance bore a resemblance to apes. They lived in communities like humans, wore clothing, followed Vedic customs and communicated using language. However, like apes, they lived in caves, had sloping foreheads and protruding lower jaws. In addition, they could leap long distances and had tails and muscular hirsute bodies. Hanuman was exceptional among them and stood apart from the other Vanaras in his abilities. He was born through divine intervention when his mother Anjana was blessed with a gifted child, biologically seeded by Vayu, the wind Deva. The son of the wind was a beautiful little boy named Sundara. From birth, the child was superior to his peers; once, he even leaped towards the sun, mistaking it for a ripe mango. Indra felt threatened by his advance and struck him with his thunderbolt, knocking little Sundara to the ground, where he lay unconscious with a broken jaw. From then on, he came to be known as Hanuman, the one with the disfigured jaw. His father, Vayu, was furious with Indra and withdrew from the world. This action caused an extinction-level event, so the other Devas rallied to appease him.

Brahma resuscitated Hanuman and gave him the benediction of invincibility, adding that the Brahmastra[1] he presided over would never harm the boy. Also, each Deva gifted him extraordinary powers. Hanuman had already inherited the ability to fly anywhere he wished from Vayu, and now had even greater capabilities. Indra was contrite, and in recompense, gave him a body of iron as strong as his thunderbolt, the Vajra. Agni, the Deva of fire, granted him immunity from being burnt. Varuna, the Deva of the ocean, ensured water would not harm him, and Vishnu presented him with a mighty mace. Surya promised to be his teacher, and under his tutelage, Hanuman mastered the Vedas, nine works of Sanskrit grammar and the yogic technique by which he could increase or reduce his size and acquire any shape.[2] He was immensely grateful to his guru and asked what he could give him in return as a fee. Surya said it was satisfying enough to have an exemplary student, but if Hanuman wished to provide him with something

[1] Missile with the power of Brahma. It had the ability to destroy the world, similar to an atomic weapon judging by its effects. Remarkably, J. Robert Oppenheimer, the father of the atomic bomb, appears to have alluded to its ancient origin when he remarked that his invention was the first in modern times.

[2] Advanced yogic technique. See Appendices.

more, he could promise to protect his earthly son Sugriva. Hanuman kept his word, and that is how he came to be Sugriva's loyal adviser.

In deference to Sugriva's bidding, Hanuman went to investigate, appearing before the hermits in the guise of a wandering mendicant. Bowing reverently and extolling them with high praise, he courteously inquired about the purpose that brought them to Rishyamukha. 'Who are you, and what brings you here? Handsome men with powerful bodies and eyes like lotus petals, I am perplexed by the contradictions you present. Although you are armed like mighty warriors, you are dressed as ascetics with matted hair. You wear no jewellery, yet you radiate splendour as though you are ornamented. Your appearance suggests you could be protectors of the world from the land of the Devas, yet your feet touch the ground. Let me introduce myself; I am Hanuman, the son of Vayu, a Vanara minister of Sugriva. He is a righteous prince who has unfortunately fallen into hard times. Though brave and virtuous, Sugriva was unjustly banished from his homeland by his brother, and now he lives in hiding. He saw you approaching and sent me as his emissary to say he seeks your friendship.'

Rama was instantly drawn to Hanuman and whispered to Lakshmana, 'It is indeed fortunate that the very person we have come here searching for has himself extended his hand in friendship to us. I feel tremendous admiration for his messenger. His command of the Sanskrit language is a testament to his scholarship. He conveyed a great deal; yet did not ramble on needlessly in his communication. Only someone who has imbibed humility from the Rig Veda, memorized the Yajur Veda thoroughly and has a mastery of the knowledge inculcated by the Sama Veda would be able to conduct himself in such a creditable fashion. There was not one misplaced word in his impeccable speech. His diction was perfect, and his grammar faultless. His tone was well-modulated, with every word correctly enunciated, and he only divulged what was relevant, remaining succinct and to the point. From the commendable way he presented himself, both in his fluency and manner, there is no doubt that he is eminently well-read. Even an enemy with a raised sword would be impressed by such a skilled orator, and the master he serves would necessarily achieve success in all his ventures when he is represented by one so articulate.'

On Rama's instructions, Lakshmana said, 'O learned Vanara, we were told about the virtues of Sugriva and have come here looking for him, so we gladly accept his offer of friendship.' Probing further, Hanuman asked, 'What exactly is the reason you have come to this woodland seeking Sugriva?' Rama gestured to Lakshmana to tell their story, so he narrated it in detail.

Starting with their exile from Ayodhya and describing Sita's abduction, he explained how Kabandha had advised them to ally with Sugriva. Then, his eyes moistening, Lakshmana concluded by saying, 'I am Rama's younger brother, but I serve him not merely out of duty but out of enormous admiration for his integrity. He is the very embodiment of dharma, and though he has always been the refuge for anyone in need, now this noble person himself seeks the grace of Sugriva.'

Hearing about Rama's plight convinced Hanuman beyond doubt that the two gallant men were not a threat. He said that their arrival was opportune because Sugriva also needed help. Then, remarking that they could be of mutual benefit, he placed Rama and Lakshmana on his shoulders and leaped to the top of the mountain with great alacrity.

When they reached the presence of Sugriva, Hanuman briefed him privately about the encounter. 'The two visitors you asked me to interrogate are Rama and his younger brother Lakshmana. They are the sons of Dasharatha of the Ikshavaku dynasty. Rama has come here in amity to seek your help recovering his wife Sita, who Ravana has carried off. I have thoroughly vetted them and have concluded that they are honourable and valorous, so I advise you to receive them respectfully.'

Sugriva heaved a sigh of relief to hear that the strangers had come in peace and not in hostility. He also felt gratified that an exalted Ikshavaku prince had sought a humble forest dweller's fellowship. Approaching Rama with his hand held out, he said warmly, 'Hanuman has spoken very highly of you. Please know that I am honoured that you have been gracious enough to seek my friendship, and I extend my hand to you in a pact of brotherhood.'

Rama clasped Sugriva's hand and returned the gesture by embracing him. Since they both faced a similar problem, they agreed to assist each other, sealing their alliance with the ritual Kabandha had advised. Hanuman kindled a fire by rubbing two sticks and the pair solemnly circumambulated it, pledging undying partnership. At the very moment of their agreement, Sita, Vali and Ravana all felt their left eyes twitch[3] as an indication of the future!

Sugriva broke off a branch from a sala tree to use as a seat, inviting Rama to join him. Hanuman noticed that Lakshmana was left standing, so he tore off another branch for him and sat on the ground beside him.

---

[3] The left eye twitching indicated that Sita would be rescued, and that Vali and Ravana were doomed.

Then, addressing Rama, Sugriva said, 'Now, my dearest friend, your grief is mine, and mine is yours. I live in fear of my brother Vali every day. He stole my wife after unfairly ostracizing me from our community, and I now look to you for assistance in righting these wrongs.' Rama assured him that it was a friend's duty to help when needed and promised unconditional support. Pleased with his assurance of help, Sugriva continued, 'Hanuman has informed me about your misfortune. I can empathize with your distress at the loss of your wife and can also imagine how miserable she must be without you. I promise to do everything in my power to help you find her, so you are reunited. I am sure I saw her being carried away by Ravana some months ago. One day, while sitting on the mountain slope with my four advisers, I heard a commotion in the sky. When I looked up, I saw a woman struggling frantically and shrieking loudly as she was carried off. She noticed us and dropped a bundle containing some ornaments. I have them in my possession. Perhaps you should check if they belong to your wife.'

Rama could not control his tears when he saw the bundle. He picked it up and pressed it to his chest repeatedly as he inquired, 'Sugriva, where did the terrible roamer of the night take my beloved Sita? Please tell me in which direction he went so that I can dispatch him to Yama, the Lord of Death.' Rama opened the bundle, and after scrutinizing the ornaments, asked ruefully, 'Lakshmana, these look like Sita's jewels, don't they?' Lakshmana, who had a profound veneration for his sister-in-law, replied that he did not recognize the armlets or earrings, but was sure that the anklets were Sita's. They sparked his memory because he had seen them every day when he paid her his respects by touching her feet.

Sugriva felt deep sympathy for Rama's anguish, and tears welled in his eyes as he spoke. 'Unfortunately, I do not know where Ravana lives or anything much about him, except that he is a vile being. However, I can unequivocally commit to you that we will find him wherever he may be, so cast aside your misery, knowing that every effort will be made to recover Sita. My wife has also been abducted, but I have not allowed myself to submit to melancholy. While I am not trivializing your pain, I urge you not to succumb to sorrow. Excessive grief is enervating and robs one of action; remember, a boat capsizes when water floods it, so be bold, never allowing your unhappiness to weigh you down. I hope you will forgive me for sermonizing, but I am only saying this as a fellow sufferer who has your welfare at heart.'

Rama wiped his tears with the end of his garment and regained his equilibrium once again. He thanked Sugriva for his counsel, saying, 'You have acted just as a good friend should by steering me in the right direction with your wise words. I am as grateful to you for this as I am for your promise to help me find Sita. Your advice has revitalized me and my optimism is renewed.'

The two sat down on the branch again, and Rama asked Sugriva to frankly recount the events that led to his estrangement from Vali, precisely stating what he wished done. It was important for Rama to know the specific details of the rift between the brothers to be sure that Vali was indeed in the wrong.

In a choked voice, Sugriva spoke of how he had come to live on the mountain. 'My elder brother Vali and I once shared a close fraternal bond. When our father died, he naturally ascended the throne of Kishkindha.[4] Vali is mighty and admired by everyone as an able ruler. I served him with devotion as his younger brother, dutifully assisting with the kingdom's administration. We lived happily; he with his beautiful wife Tara and I with my lovely Ruma, till the night when an Asura called Mayavi came clamouring at the palace gates. He and Vali apparently had their eyes on the same woman, and he had come to challenge him. Also, Vali had killed Mayavi's younger brother Dhundhubi sometime earlier, so perhaps he was also motivated by revenge. Vali could never refuse a dare and immediately rushed out to confront him. I followed because I was concerned for Vali's welfare, but when Mayavi saw the two of us, he took off running.'

'We pursued him for a long time, till finally, he disappeared into a large hole in the ground. Vali was determined to follow Mayavi, and though I was keen to go along, he insisted that I stay behind and wait for him at the entrance of the opening. A whole year passed, and I patiently stood by as instructed. With no sign of my brother for so long, I began to worry and paced restlessly, wondering what to do. Suddenly, I heard a spine-chilling scream followed by a torrent of fresh foamy blood gushing out of the hole. I did not recognize the voice as Vali's, so I concluded that it had to be Mayavi crying out in victory after killing him. Since he had done away with our king, I was sure he would now come after everyone in Kishkindha. To prevent this, I pushed a giant boulder over the hole, thereby blocking the exit. Grief-stricken, I wept profusely at the death of my brother and performed the sacred water-rites for his departed spirit.'

---

[4] Hampi in modern Karnataka.

'When I returned to Kishkindha, the ministers anointed me as the new king, insisting it was imprudent to leave the throne unoccupied. I ruled justly in my brother's footsteps, till one day, to everyone's astonishment, Vali, who was presumed dead, walked into the court. Initially, I thought he was an apparition, but lovingly welcomed him home in delight when I realized it was really him. I knelt before him and handed back the royal umbrella, offering him my services as his servant once more. I expected everything to revert to how it had been previously, but to my dismay, Vali flew into a rage. Ranting and raving furiously, he accused me of treachery. Elaborating on what had happened after I left, Vali said the hole led to a long subterranean cavern, and apparently, after pursuing Mayavi for a long time, and finally killing him, he could not return because I had sealed off the egress. He added that pushing the boulder away was a near-impossible task, but he eventually dislodged it by kicking it repeatedly. To my consternation, he insisted that I had purposely closed the opening to usurp the kingdom for myself.'

'Nothing could have been further from the truth, but Vali turned a deaf ear to all my protestations of innocence. Despite my sincerity, he drove me out of Kishkindha with nothing but the single cloth I was wearing. Even worse, he snatched my precious wife, who is dearer to me than my life, and made her his own. In exile, four faithful companions followed me: Hanuman, Nala, Nila and Jambavan. Since then, we have been hiding on Rishyamukha Mountain because Vali cannot set foot here. Now that you have heard about my misfortune, I beseech you to help me by killing Vali, as this is the only way I can recover my wife and return to my kingdom.'

Rama was moved by Sugriva's tale and empathized with his sorrow at losing his wife. Vali had rejected Sugriva's heartfelt apology, and the undue punishment meted out to him was disproportionate to the small error in judgement he had made. Like the rishis in Dandaka, Sugriva begged Rama to set an injustice right, and Rama never refused anyone who sought refuge in him. They were already bound in friendship, as allies, with the sacred fire as their witness; so, he assured Sugriva his fullest assistance in regaining everything that had been lost.

Although Sugriva was grateful, he was not entirely convinced that Rama would succeed in defeating Vali. His brother wore a magic gold chain gifted to him by Indra through whose blessings he was born, and it gave him immense strength by transferring his opponent's power to him. Vali could stride from ocean to ocean without fatigue, snap a giant tree as if it were a twig, and even toss mountains in the air in sport. Sugriva pointed to the massive skeleton of Dhundhubi, Mayavi's younger brother, that lay on the hill and narrated how Vali had killed him when Dhundhubi threatened him in the form of a humongous buffalo that had the strength of a thousand elephants. Vali had grasped Dhundhubi by his horns and, twirling him around, hurled him a yojana away, where his body burst open, spewing blood in all directions, desecrating Matanga's ashram. The sage was furious and pronounced a curse that the culprit who had polluted his sacred hermitage would die instantly if he ever set foot in its vicinity. This fear kept Vali away from Rishyamukha as it was the only place he was vulnerable.

Considering Vali's enormous strength, Sugriva was unsure of Rama's ability to deal with him. He said apologetically, 'I hope you do not misunderstand me because I truly consider it my good fortune to have your friendship, and it is not my intention to underestimate you, but you are unacquainted with Vali's abilities. While I do not mean to denigrate your strength in any way, I am afraid Vali may be too powerful for you.'

When Lakshmana asked how Rama could prove his competence, Sugriva replied that he would feel reassured if he could throw Dhundhubi's skeleton a distance of 200 bow lengths.[5] Rama obliged and with a flick of his toe, hurled it even further, ten yojanas away. Sugriva was impressed by the feat but still had a nagging doubt, because when Vali threw the carcass, it was not just a pile of bones but much heavier with flesh and blood. He pointed to a large sala tree and asked if Rama could cut it down with a single arrow, saying that Vali was able to divest it of every leaf just by shaking it with his bare hands. Rama noticed that the tree was one of seven in a row. Smiling indulgently, he picked up his bow and aimed. One golden arrow pierced all seven trees at once, tearing through a mountain and boring deep into the earth before returning to its master's quiver. Seeing Rama's incredible prowess, Sugriva fell at his feet, finally confident of his expertise. He could not help being awestruck at the exceptional skill demonstrated and announced that all his trepidation was gone with such a powerful friend by his side.

---

[5] A bow length was six feet.

Chapter 16

Vali

Sugriva wanted to settle the score with Vali without delay; so, it was agreed that he would challenge his brother to a duel that very day. To circumvent the unfair advantage of the necklace, Rama would help kill Vali. Sugriva went to Kishkindha, hollering with loud whoops outside Vali's window to incite him. Vali rushed out in a rage, and the brothers battled furiously, exchanging deadly blows with open palms, fists and knees. Sugriva was battered black and blue by Vali's powerful onslaught but held out for as long as he could, waiting for Rama's arrow. When help did not come, he gave up and fled for his life to the Matanga Forest. There, feeling betrayed, he said bitterly to Rama with his eyes downcast, 'Why did you ask me to confront Vali when you had no intention of helping me? I put my trust in you, and now look at me, injured and bleeding while he thrives.' Rama reassured Sugriva of his commitment and told him of a dilemma that prevented him from shooting his arrow. Sugriva was a replica of Vali, identical in appearance since they were twins, and it was difficult to tell them apart. Each time Rama drew his arrow, he feared killing Sugriva instead of Vali. Promising unswerving faithfulness to his word, Rama urged Sugriva to challenge Vali once more, this time wearing a garland of bright Gajapushpa[1] flowers, so that the brothers were easily distinguishable.

On the way to Kishkindha for the second time, they passed a grove thick with plants and fruit trees. When Rama inquired about the place, Sugriva said, 'Seven great sages once resided here practising gruelling yogic austerities. They would do penance standing on their heads in the position

---

[1] The name means elephant flower.

of shirshasana[2] all day, and at night they would rest floating on water. They did this for years, eating only once a week, before they eventually ascended to heaven. Their intense self-mortification has sanctified this spot, and their holy fires still burn, even though the rishis are long gone. So let us pay our respects here and take their blessings.' After the brief stop, Sugriva went once again to Vali's door, roaring for him to come out and fight. In the meantime, Rama, Lakshmana and Sugriva's four companions lay in wait behind a clump of trees. When Vali heard Sugriva's war cry, he was livid that his brother had come back so soon, and infuriated at his impertinence, prepared to confront him right away.

Vali's wife, Tara, was a very astute woman and tried her best to prevent him from acting rashly in an irate state of mind. She wisely advised Vali to defer any action until the following day, after his emotions had died down. Also, she remarked that it was atypical of Sugriva to return so quickly after facing such a humiliating defeat, especially since he had narrowly escaped with his life. Warning Vali that Sugriva's sudden confidence was suspicious, Tara added that their son Angada had heard from spies that two valiant princes of Ayodhya, Rama and Lakshmana, had allied with Sugriva, and their support was probably the source of his unusual courage. She cautioned that it was imprudent to antagonize Rama, who was known to fight against injustice, and pleaded with her husband to reconcile with his brother and avoid unnecessary bloodshed. She begged, 'If you love me and wish to make me happy, take my advice and be merciful to Sugriva. I believe Rama always protects the innocent, like a tree shelters those in need.'

However, Vali, in his hot-headedness, spurned Tara's sensible advice. Reprimanding her sharply, he said, 'How can you ask me to tolerate my brother's impudence and do nothing? I have never been afraid to accept a challenge, nor have I ever been defeated, so you have no reason to worry about my safety. As for Sugriva's new friend, Rama, he has a reputation for upholding dharma and will not harm me by interfering in a domestic quarrel that is none of his concern, especially since I have not done him any wrong. However, I appreciate that you have spoken out of love for me, and I do not want to upset you by disregarding you completely, so I will not kill Sugriva. Stay here with the other ladies while I teach him a lesson, bringing him to his knees once and for all.' Tara could not stop Vali, so she wished him good

---

[2] The yogic headstand.

luck as a devoted wife would, walking clockwise around him and reciting sacred Vedic mantras for his victory.

Red-faced with rage, his golden splendour eclipsed[3] by emotion, Vali strode purposefully towards Sugriva, breathing heavily and snorting in a fury. When he spotted him in a clearing surrounded by trees, his anger only intensified. Tightening his loincloth, Vali rushed towards Sugriva with his mighty fists clenched, and soon the two were engaged in a fierce battle. They fought, kicking and punching each other mercilessly, even uprooting trees as weapons to inflict heavy blows. Both fighters were covered in blood, but Sugriva soon began tiring as Vali's charmed necklace sapped his strength. Knowing he could not stand up to the assault much longer, he looked around nervously, wondering if Rama had failed him yet again, when an arrow sailed swiftly through the air and pierced Vali in the chest, felling him to the ground like a hewn tree. The indomitable Vanara lay on his back with his limbs outstretched, mortally wounded, but surprisingly his face still looked fresh as he clung to life by the grace of his magic necklace.

When Rama emerged with his bow from the foliage, Vali had harsh words for him, and though he delivered them courteously, his rebuke was stinging. 'You have shamed your noble father, Dasharatha, with your conduct, killing me unfairly when I was battling someone else. What merit have you earned by this unjust action that goes against dharma? People speak highly of you; they say you are compassionate, restrained, forgiving, valorous and judicious; so, when my wife Tara warned me to be careful of you, I ignored her. I believed you to be a man of integrity who followed the path of righteousness, but sadly your villainy has proved me wrong. Today's treachery belies your reputation; rather than being virtuous, you are, in fact, totally impious. You are nothing but a sinner in the garb of a saint, deceitful like a smouldering fire hidden by ashes or like a bottomless pit covered by grass. What justification do you have for killing me when I have not caused you any offense?

'Killing an innocent[4] being is as much of a sin as killing a Brahmin, a cow, or your king. Why would you end the life of a peaceful creature

---

[3] Vali is described as resembling the reddened sun, a reference to the solar eclipse that was visible from Kishkindha 3 April 5076 BCE. See Bala, Saroj, *Ramayan Retold with Scientific Evidences* (Prabhat Prakashan, 2019).

[4] 'Whoever does violence to harmless creatures out of a wish for his own happiness does not increase his happiness anywhere, neither when he is alive nor when he is dead.' Manusmriti 5.45

who has no quarrel with you? I am an ordinary vanara living in the forest on fruits and roots, while you are a famous prince from the city who eats cooked food; we are worlds apart, and there is no reason for any contention between us. Disputes typically occur over land or wealth, but I have never attacked your kingdom, so I am unsure what you stand to gain by killing me. As an educated person well versed in the shastras, you know that punishing someone without just cause is iniquitous. Kshatriyas are sworn upholders of righteousness and are not supposed to have a whimsical attitude; they protect the innocent and are expected to act only after careful consideration. You have shown yourself to be selfish and belligerent by compromising this rule. Therefore, I assert that you have indiscriminately engaged in a malicious murder driven solely by the immoral urge for self-gratification.

'What is the rationale for your reprehensible behaviour towards me? If you hunted me because you consider me an animal,[5] you killed me for no good reason. Vanaras are not among the five nailed animals[6] fit for human consumption. Our shastras frown on eating the flesh of my kind, and my skin and bones are of no use to you, so killing me was a wanton act that was totally unwarranted. The world degenerates into a terrifying place with deceitful people like you in power. I have been viciously struck down for no fault of mine. Further, you acted like a coward by not facing me directly. If you had done so, you would be the one lying here now instead of me. I believe you killed me as recompense to Sugriva for his promise to help you recover your wife, but this was unwise on your behalf. I am far more powerful than he is; if you had come to me directly, I would have brought Sita to you in a single day. Now my death is inevitable, and Sugriva will have the kingdom, but what you just did was wrong, and I demand to know why you have behaved so unjustly with me?'

After listening patiently while Vali spoke, Rama responded methodically to each of his accusations. He said, 'You have delivered a bitter reproach to me for not adhering to dharma, but your arguments are specious. Your

---

'If punishment is properly dispensed, it makes all people happy but if it is inflicted without consideration, it destroys everything.' Manusmriti 7.19

[5] Vali likens himself to an animal and yet is conversant with Manusmriti. He perhaps uses the term to mean forest dweller or unsophisticated.

[6] Manusmriti 5.17 mentions which five-nailed animals are fit for consumption, and Vanaras are not amongst them. Vali's arguments indicate that he is very familiar with the shastras, so he is clearly not an animal.

censure is prompted by ignorance because you lack clarity on the concept of dharma. You charged me with interfering in a private matter when you were fighting with your brother and added that I have no personal grievance with you. In this context, I would like to remind you that the authority of Ayodhya extends over the whole world. Kishkindha falls under the jurisdiction of the Ikshavakus, so you bow in allegiance to my brother Bharata. This sovereignty gives him the right to reward, punish and enforce justice when deemed necessary, and in this regard, I acted as his servant.

'You have accused me of violating dharma, when to the contrary, by the very act of punishing you, I have established righteousness.[7] According to the accepted social code, a younger brother is like a son; therefore, his wife must be considered a daughter-in-law.[8] Just as it is morally corrupt to engage in inappropriate relations with a sister or daughter, it is perverted of you to sleep with Ruma. Moreover, I must firmly state that it is unconscionable to take your brother's wife as your own while he is alive, as they are still married. Although you think you did no wrong in cohabiting with Ruma, you committed the abominable sin of incest, which carries the death penalty according to our laws. As you said, a Kshatriya is duty-bound to protect the virtuous and discipline the unrighteous, so with my arrow, I enforced justice; and by punishing you for your wrongdoing, I performed my Kshatriya dharma.[9]

'Our shastras say that a Kshatriya who stands by and watches an injustice without doing anything to correct it is as guilty as the one perpetrating it. Manu has made a clear statement in this regard, which confirms that castigating the wicked is the sacred duty of a Kshatriya. A king has the solemn obligation to deliver appropriate punishment for a crime committed, and if he fails in his responsibility to administer the law, he accrues sin upon himself. Legitimate and righteous chastisement serves to redeem the offender by holding him accountable and making him pay for his wicked deed. By killing you, I have

---

[7] 'Men stealing from a virtuous family, especially taking women and the most valuable gems, deserve capital punishment.' Manusmriti 8:323

[8] 'The wife of an elder brother is for his younger brother like the wife of a guru, but the wife of the younger is declared to be the daughter-in-law of the elder.' Manusmriti 9.57

[9] 'A Kshatriya who has undergone his transformative Vedic ritual in accordance with the rules should protect the whole world.' Manusmriti 7.2. This is to prevent the law of fish—'matsya nyaya', where the bigger fish eat the little fish who are smaller and weaker.

enforced justice[10] on behalf of Bharata, so consider yourself expiated of your wrongdoing by paying the price for your transgressions in this very life. Do not be under the illusion that I behaved unfairly or that my action against you was unwarranted. Instead, try to understand that your heinous crime thoroughly deserved the death penalty.

'As for your assertion that I am a neutral party who has no conflict with you, that statement as it is inaccurate. I have sworn undying friendship with Sugriva before the holy fire as witness, so his troubles are now mine. The harm he caused you was inadvertent and without malice, and despite his begging for forgiveness, you spurned him and cast him out. Anyone who harms my friend also hurts me. If you argue that you are not subject to human laws because you are an animal, you should not feel peeved that I did not openly invite you to fight. As you are aware, when an animal is hunted, the hunter conceals himself and does not suggest they battle. However, I did not kill you in sport, but as a punishment to enforce justice, so I do not think I have done anything wrong in meting out appropriate retribution to one who deserved it.'

Vali listened to Rama's reasoning, and his anger was replaced by contrition. He accepted culpability and realized that Rama had not acted for any selfish end. To recover his wife, it would have been far more beneficial for Rama to have allied with Vali than with Sugriva, but he did not do so because Vali had abandoned dharma. As Vali lay dying, he regretted his actions and begged for forgiveness, filled with shame at how he had treated his brother and sister-in-law. With folded hands, he said remorsefully, 'I now see the truth of everything you have stated. I transgressed and strayed from the path of dharma, so my death is well deserved.' Then, heaving like an elephant stuck in a bog, he continued, 'I am not concerned about dying, nor am I worried about Tara or my other relatives, but I am very anxious about what will happen to my son Angada, whom I have raised so fondly. Although he is an exceptional warrior, he is still of tender age and needs protection. I earnestly request you to fulfil this role for me and help promote a good relationship between him and his uncle. Please consider Sugriva and Angada like your family; show them the same love you have for your brothers to foster a bond between them. Also, I hope you will ensure that Sugriva does not disrespect Tara as she was in no way responsible for his ill-treatment. I foolishly did not

---

[10] 'For punishment has great brilliant energy, and for those who are undisciplined it is hard to maintain; it strikes down the king who swerves from his duty, along with his relatives.' Manusmriti 7.28

listen to my wife's counsel. You are a kingmaker, so Sugriva will now rule Kishkindha, and I accept my end at your hands because of my misbehaviour.'

Rama consoled Vali, saying that he was purged of his sins in repentance, and assured him of his support in protecting Tara and Angada.

When Tara heard that Vali had fallen, she rushed to the scene from her rocky cave with Angada, beating her head and chest in grief. She saw Rama leaning against his bow and the Vanara warriors scattering in fear of him, so she called them back admonishingly, 'Why are you running away? One brother has killed the other for the kingdom, and none of you are targets.' However, they were not placated and replied, 'Rama has brought down the great Vali who was invincible, so protect yourself and Angada. We must defend the city from assault and crown Angada king immediately. Let us do this right away before hostile forces take over the kingdom.' Though Tara was overwhelmed with grief, she was alive to the political ramifications of Vali's death and was concerned for Angada's safety in the event of a struggle for succession. To protect her child, she cried out expediently, 'Why are we fighting about the kingdom at a time like this when my husband lies dying?'

Falling on Vali, she pressed his head to her bosom and wept inconsolably, chiding him for not listening to her. 'O arya, O tiger among Vanaras, a warrior like you can't lie here helplessly. How can you forsake your beloved wife for the embrace of the cold earth? Alas! This fate has befallen you because of the evil you committed when you drove your brother away unjustly and snatched his wife. Why did you ignore all the good advice I gave you? Now you will ascend to heaven to be the darling of the Apsaras while I am left alone here as a helpless widow.'

Beckoning Angada to join her, she lamented to Vali, 'We raised our son with so much affection that I fear he will not be able to handle life in case Sugriva shows him any unkindness.' Then addressing Angada, she said, 'Look at your father for the last time, for you will not see him again.' Requesting Vali to give their son his parting guidance before dying, she continued sorrowing. 'Rama has fulfilled his promise to his friend and is redeemed of his indebtedness. O Sugriva, your desire has been fulfilled! You will get back your wife Ruma and have the kingdom to enjoy without any impediment.' Then, turning to Vali again, she cried, 'Why aren't you speaking? All your wives are here with me; how can you abandon us?'

Tara looked like a star that had fallen from the sky, and seeing her miserable state, Hanuman tried to console her. Philosophizing on life, he said, 'We all reap the fruit of our karma, both good and bad. Do not grieve for the loss of the body, as its existence is momentary, like a bubble. Now it is important to consider the future of your son. We pray that Vali achieves a higher plane in heaven based on his just rule and past good deeds, but the thousands of Vanara warriors under his authority now look to you for direction. So put aside your own sorrow; wipe your tears and offer Sugriva and Angada solace in their bereavement. We should start making arrangements both for your husband's funeral and your son's coronation.'

Hanuman was politically astute and was testing Tara's reaction by speaking about Angada becoming king. He knew the Vanaras would not accept Sugriva unless his succession had her blessings. But Tara was no fool and quickly clarified that Angada was not a contender for the throne. She was a protective mother who did not want any threat to her son's life, so she replied, 'Even if I had a hundred sons like Angada, I still would have no desire for the kingdom and prefer to die with my husband. Sugriva is the ruler now, and Angada is not competing with him for the position, so do not entertain any ideas about him becoming king.'

By this time, Vali was in great pain, breathing laboriously. Yet he observed all that was going on and spoke his last words. He said affectionately to Sugriva in a feeble voice, 'Forgive me for banishing you and appropriating your wife. Unfortunately, I did not see the perversity of my actions earlier, but now I realize how mistaken I was. Take my gold necklace, which has protected me all this time, and rule Kishkindha. I entreat you not to punish my family for my sins, as they are blameless. Look kindly upon my son Angada and treat him as if he were your own child; he is valiant and will help you in your battle with the Rakshasas. Take care of my beloved wife Tara—the sagacious daughter of Sushena—who is blessed with exceptional intelligence and great political acumen. She always tried to prevent me from treading the wrong path, so let her serve you and be your guiding light. You can trust her counsel implicitly and follow it blindly as it will always be wise.'

Vali then addressed Angada and said lovingly, 'Always act carefully according to the situation at hand, enduring both the good and bad that life presents with equanimity.[11] I have indulged you like a doting father, but do not expect the same from Sugriva as it may lead to feelings of disappointment.

---

[11] 'Human life is like a turbulent stream, strewn with rocks and pebbles; the brave step into it, for by sitting on the shore and enumerating hurdles, you shall never get across. Leave behind the burden of your fears, guilts, weaknesses and cumbersome attachments. Thus, freed from all negative forces, smoothly cross over the stream.' Atharva Veda 12.2.26

While keeping this in mind, always work for his benefit and never betray him. At all times, be loyal and cordial in your relationship with your uncle, neither too close nor too distant. To stay on good terms, moderation is always best in such a relationship.'

On delivering these final words, Vali's eyes rolled up, his mouth fell open and he breathed his last as the vital force left him. Through his sincere repentance in death, he expunged his sins. The Vanaras shed tears, recalling Vali's past glories and eulogized his victories. Tara clutched on to him like a creeper clinging to a tree, scolding him once again for not listening to her. 'Woefully, you lie dead, and Sugriva is now in power. A wise man should learn from seeing me and never give his daughter's hand in marriage to a brave warrior.' Looking at the arrow, she wept, 'I can't even hug you closely because Rama's deadly arrow is still stuck in your chest.' Hearing her lament, Sugriva's general Nila came forward and dexterously pulled out the offending weapon, causing blood to gush out like lava spewing from an erupting volcano. Tara sobbed so much that her tears washed Vali's body as she moaned, 'The enmity resulting from your sinful actions has ended in a terrible disaster.'

Angada, too, cried bitterly, falling at his father's feet. Seeing Tara and his nephew submerged in an ocean of sorrow, Sugriva also began weeping. He had wanted Vali killed all this time but felt miserable after hearing his last words. Though they had fallen out with each other, Vali was, after all, his brother, and he could not help thinking that things did not have to turn out the way they did. Turning to Rama, he said, 'You kept your promise to me, but strangely at this moment, I feel intense pain instead of pleasure. I think my brother must have loved me deep down because he always stopped short of killing me every time we fought, though he could easily have done so on many occasions. Witnessing the suffering I have caused Tara and Angada, I regret asking you to kill Vali. He handed me the kingdom, but I feel no joy in accepting it. I do not deserve to be king because I obtained the throne unethically, plotting to kill my elder brother. I fear I have sinned and am full of regret because Tara and Angada may not survive their sorrow. If anything happens to them, I, too, will immolate myself, as I will not be able to live with the guilt of destroying my clan. Nevertheless, be assured that I will not let you down; my valiant Vanaras will keep my pledge and help you find Sita.'

Rama was moved to tears as he looked at Tara, and directed by his glance, everyone rushed to assist her. Noticing Rama closely for the first time, Tara staggered towards him. She fell at his feet and said, 'You are a person of great eminence with many divine qualities, so I beg you to do me the favour of killing me with the same arrow you used to kill my husband. I know Vali will not be at peace till I join him in heaven. Since I am sure you understand the grief of parting only too well, end my life too, so Vali does not have to pine our separation any more. You will not accrue the sin of killing a woman as I am essentially half his body. The Vedic texts say a man receives no gift more treasured than a wife because she is his other half. In marriage, a man and a woman are two inseparable parts of a whole,[12] so I implore you to reunite me with Vali, for without him, my life is meaningless.'

Consoling Tara, Rama said, 'O wife of an intrepid warrior whose heroism was known to all, be courageous and don't speak of giving up your life. The dead derive no benefit from the grief of the loved ones they leave behind. It is appropriate now to direct all our energies towards arranging Vali's cremation without delay for the benefit of his onward journey. Be strong for the sake of your son Angada, who will be prince regent. As you know, nobody is exempt from the laws of karma. The fulfilment of desires and attainment of prosperity are natural endeavours of everyone on Earth, but these pursuits always need to be within the boundaries of righteousness. The actions we perform to attain our goals form our destiny, and by chasing desire and prosperity without dharma, Vali duly reaped the consequences.[13] However, be brave, taking comfort in the fact that he exonerated himself in death and will surely attain heaven.'

Lakshmana then gently advised Sugriva to take the initiative in arranging Vali's funeral, encouraging him to show leadership by procuring all the necessary materials for the cremation while assisting Tara, Angada and the other Vanaras in dealing with their sorrow. Lakshmana also reminded Sugriva that the kingdom was now his responsibility, so he needed to assume charge of it, putting himself in a position of control. Accordingly, Sugriva organized a grand funeral, and they carried Vali's body decorated with ornaments and garlands on a bier, scattering coins and gems in its path. Tara and Vali's other wives followed the mournful procession, and the mountain

---

[12] In Vedic philosophy, a husband and wife are considered equals in the marital relationship. 'The husband and wife being equal parts of one substance, are equal in every respect; therefore, both should join and take equal part in all works, religious and secular.' Rig Veda 5.61.8–9

[13] The doctrine of karma, which is fundamental to Vedic philosophy, is reiterated.

range reverberated with their cries. After Angada performed the last rites in full adherence to Vedic rituals under Rama's supervision, he went to the river with his mother Tara, uncle Sugriva and the rest of the Vanaras, and offered water to his father's spirit.

With the funeral completed, preparations began for the coronation. Hanuman said gratefully to Rama, 'The kingdom was delivered to Sugriva by your grace, so we would like to show our appreciation to you with garlands and gifts of precious gems and gold. Please come with us to Kishkindha and honour us with your presence at the enthronement ceremony.'

However, Rama declined politely because the terms of his exile precluded him from entering a town or village for fourteen years. Giving Sugriva his best wishes, he reminded his friend of his promise to Vali, saying, 'Take care of Angada and make sure you install him as the crown prince. He is fit to be your successor, not only as your elder brother's son but also because he is noble and a mighty warrior. The month of Sravana[14] is about to commence, and the rainy season will be in full force for the next few months. It is unwise to embark on any endeavour during inclement weather, so I will wait it out in a mountain cave with Lakshmana.[15] We can resume the search for Sita in the month of Karthika[16] when it is dry again. Meanwhile, devote yourself to your new duties and take the opportunity to enjoy the company of your near and dear ones.'

Thousands of Vanaras prostrated before Sugriva in a show of reverence for their new leader, and bidding them to arise, he addressed them as their king. Then, he entered his royal cave and took a ceremonial bath in preparation for the anointing. Elaborate arrangements were made for Sugriva's coronation; the paraphernalia included a royal white umbrella, two white whisk fans with gold handles, precious jewels, incense, aromatic scents, sandalwood paste, unbroken rice grains dipped in turmeric, honey, ghee, curds, a tiger's skin, a pair of fine shoes and the holy waters of rivers and oceans from all four quarters. Brahmins were invited to recite Vedic hymns at the ceremony.

---

[14] The four rainy months are Ashada—between June and July, Sravana—between July and August, Bhadra—between August and September, and Ashwina—between September and October.

[15] Climatological data corroborates that the monsoons were much heavier around 5000 BCE than they are today.

[16] Karthika is between October and November.

An altar with a sacred fire was lit, and Sugriva was sworn in with all the appropriate rituals as he sat on a grand throne with legs of gold draped in exquisite fabrics. At the same time, he warmly embraced Angada and made him the crown prince, quelling any dissidence from Vali's sympathizers. There was a grand celebration; flags and banners fluttered high, and Sugriva was overjoyed to have his kingdom and his wife back.

Chapter 17

Resuming the Search for Sita

Rama and Lakshmana took shelter from the incessant monsoon in a large cave near the summit of Mount Prasravana. The north-eastern side was low, and the western face elevated,[1] providing natural protection from strong winds and heavy rain. A rivulet that ran to the east supplied plenty of fresh water. The area was thickly forested, with several species of birds nesting in the trees, and it was home to tigers, deer and a host of other wild animals. Sweet-smelling shrubs grew abundantly on the slopes, filling the air with a pleasant aroma. There was a pond nearby with lovely lilies, and altogether it was a peaceful place frequented by rishis. Although Rama and Lakshmana were isolated from any habitation, Kishkindha was close enough for them to hear the merriment of the Vanaras as they celebrated with the music of mridangams and raucous cheers.

While the heavy downpours brought all human enterprise to a halt this time of year, nature busied itself with a spate of new activities. Thundering clouds saturated with moisture darkened the sky, vehemently emptying their contents on the parched land below. The life-giving rain provided a much-needed respite from the scorching sun, and all the forest creatures gleefully celebrated its arrival. Lightning flashed, and the howling wind bore the fragrance of ketaka flowers through the forest. The dust settled as the earth quenched its thirst and the rivers swelled with water. The jamun tree shared its bounty of juicy black fruit with the forest dwellers, and the animals consorted with their mates to continue their kind.

It was a challenging time for Rama. Every moment seemed to pass ever so slowly, and there was not a second when he did not think of Sita. The

---

[1] The monsoon winds blow from the south-west Indian Ocean.

beautiful moon reminded him of her when he slept, and on waking, she would be the first thought on his mind. As the days went by, Rama's face grew gaunt with sorrow, craving to be with Sita again. Lakshmana did all he could to make him feel better, telling him how important it was to be optimistic and stay focused on his goal. Whenever Rama received these valuable words of encouragement, he would shake off his despondency and direct his energies towards more positive thoughts as he bided time in what felt like an eternity.

Immobilized by the weather, Rama spent hours observing nature. Looking up at the heavens, he marvelled that for nine months the sun had beaten down, evaporating water from the oceans, making the sky pregnant with heavy clouds; and now that the gestation was over, it delivered rain to the earth in torrents. On another occasion, as Rama observed the clouds swirling on the top of a hillock, they appeared layered, like steps in the ether that could be climbed to the heavens. To his torn heart, the sun's redness at dusk resembled a bleeding wound bound with white bandage-like clouds, and its pale centre made it look as lovesick as he was. The hillside was full of ashoka trees, whose fallen flowers spread over the ground like a perfumed carpet wet with rain like the scented water with which Sugriva was recently coronated. The dark clouds that embraced the hill were suggestive of the black buckskins the rishis clad themselves in, and the sound of the roaring wind was reminiscent of their Vedic chants. The rumbling thunder made the sky seem like it was groaning in pain, struck by lightning akin to a golden whiplash. The bolts of bright light that repeatedly charged through the dark clouds evoked the image of Sita struggling to escape from Ravana's clutches. Graceful herons flying above in the formation of a white garland filled Rama with wonder, and he admired how they had waited so patiently for the rainy season to mate, tossed about by the winds amidst the clouds.

Rama reflected that while all human activities were at a standstill, with kings and their armies returning home to rest, there was a busyness in nature. The heavy rain caused flowers to fall, collecting in heaps, and the peacocks sipping their nectar danced in intoxicated joy. There was a grand symphony in the forest. The humming of the bees was redolent of string instruments like the veena. The croaking of frogs provided the rhythm, and the rumbling of the clouds was suggestive of a mridangam's drumbeat. The birds too appeared to participate in the concert, some singing, some dancing and others watching in delight. The rivers in full spate flowed swiftly to

meet the sea, like amorous women in the bloom of youth rushing to their
lovers in utter abandonment of modesty. Indra was happy, showering much-
anticipated rain, and the mighty bull elephants trumpeted to celebrate the
largesse he bestowed on them. The sparkling waterfalls that plunged with
great force from the top of the mountain bore a likeness to pearl necklaces
falling from the necks of celestial women in the heat of lovemaking.

As the days passed, Rama thought of Sugriva living happily in his
kingdom with his wives, in stark contrast to his own situation. However, he
knew he had to have patience while waiting out the weather. In anticipation
of Sugriva's help, he remarked to Lakshmana, 'I am glad my friend and his
wife are reunited. I am sure Sugriva will remember his promise and come to
my assistance as soon as the weather permits.' Lakshmana agreed, saying he
had no doubt Sugriva would keep his word once the rains stopped.

Meanwhile, back in Kishkindha, Sugriva was immersed in the pleasures
his royal position afforded him. Sadly, he had become negligent of his duties,
abdicating his responsibilities to his ministers, and indulging in the excesses
of wine and women, including the company of his erstwhile sister-in-law
Tara. He was so immersed in carnality that he was oblivious of how much
time had passed since he was crowned king, and seemed to have forgotten
his debt to Rama. Then, one autumn day, Hanuman looked up at the sky
and saw that the dreary rainy season was over. With every last drop of water
dispensed, the dark clouds had finally dispersed. He was concerned that
sensual desires had caused Sugriva to abandon his duties, so he approached
him to remind him of his promise. Using his expert communication skills to
nudge Sugriva into doing the right thing, Hanuman asked him to recollect
how Rama had helped him in his time of need and urged him to repay
the favour without prodding. He stressed the importance of gratitude and
advised Sugriva to summon the ten million Vanaras of their kind from all
over the Earth to search the three worlds for Sita. Sugriva agreed, ordering
his zealous commander Nila to work with Angada and assemble Vanaras
from near and far within fifteen days, on pain of death. Having issued this
instruction, he felt he had done his duty and promptly slipped back into a
profligate life of pleasure.

The four interminable months it took for the skies to clear felt like a
hundred years to Rama. He was restless to resume the search for Sita and
eagerly awaited Sugriva's assistance. In its glory, the beauty of autumn
tortured him ceaselessly with memories of Sita. The season reminded him of

her delight in the golden blossoms of the asana trees[2] back in their hermitage, and her joy at hearing the cranes and swans calling their mates. Rama was disappointed that Sugriva had made no attempt to reach out to him, and it seemed that having achieved his objective, Sugriva had forgotten about his friend's sorrow. Feeling let down, he said morosely to Lakshmana, 'The sky has cleared now, and the rains are behind us. Hark the sweet call of the cranes my beautiful wife loved so much. They are reminiscent of her melodious voice, and I cannot help wondering what she is doing now. I am constantly plagued with worry about her predicament and find myself getting emotional thinking about her.'

Seeing Rama's lugubrious mood, Lakshmana once again tried to raise his morale, urging him to muster his inner strength. 'It is important to remain positive, so do not give in to despair and lose heart. Sita is like a blazing fire; nobody can have her by force without being burnt to ashes.' Rama quickly pulled himself together and replied, 'You are right; now is the time for action, and it is not appropriate for me to wallow in self-pity. We must carefully plan our strategy to get Vaidehi back. Indra[3] has retreated after completing his work. The season has changed, and the slushy forest paths are baked dry by the sun. Now is the time that kings resume their expeditions and so must we. However, I do not see any action in this regard from Sugriva. To me, the rainy months have dragged on as if they would never end, and though I have waited patiently, I think my friend has forgotten me. I feel offended that he ignores our agreement after making a solemn promise, completely unmindful of his word. I would like you to go to Kishkindha and tell him that his ingratitude is immoral and deserves stern condemnation. Even vultures would refuse to eat the flesh of sinners who are so vile in their thanklessness. Tell Sugriva in no uncertain terms that I am displeased and advise him not to test my patience. He is abandoning dharma by failing to reciprocate the favour I did for him. Let him be warned by Vali's example and put him on notice that if he doesn't keep his end of our deal, he will face the power of my bow.'

Lakshmana could not bear to see Rama's distress. An uncontrollable rage erupted in him, and he exclaimed furiously, 'The ungrateful Vanara has abandoned righteousness by ignoring his obligations to his friend. He has lost his sense of judgement, absorbed in his new-found pleasures, and

---

[2] *Terminalia elliptica* or Indian Laurel.

[3] The Deva of rain.

such an unrighteous person does not deserve to be king. I cannot contain my anger at his appalling behaviour and will kill him this very day.'

Rama at once cautioned Lakshmana not to be impulsive and resort to violence without trying to reason with Sugriva first.[4] He asserted that Sugriva was their friend and had not gone back on his word yet. So far, he was only guilty of delay, and perhaps a reminder would coax him to follow through on his commitment. Advising Lakshmana, Rama said, 'There is no need to take the rash step of killing Sugriva. At this point, I think it would be enough to threaten him, so he is gently persuaded to do the right thing. Be tactful in your interaction with Sugriva and convey the importance of keeping his promise diplomatically.'

Lakshmana set off for Kishkindha fuming with rage, rehearsing what he was going to say the whole way. He strode through the forest, forsaking the mud path, knocking down branches and kicking aside boulders in a temper. Kishkindha was a pretty hamlet nestled on a hill, with handsome cave dwellings and wide pathways. A bubbly stream[5] ran by it; there were numerous fruit trees, and the scent of sandalwood wafted through the air, mingled with the delicate fragrance of flowers. The king's cave was built of white stone and had grand gates of gold adorned with garlands. When Lakshmana reached the entrance, the sentries sensed his hostility and ran quaking in fear to inform Sugriva of his arrival. However, the Vanara king was intoxicated with alcohol, and so engrossed in amorous dalliance with Tara, Ruma and his other consorts, that he ignored them.

Angada heard the Vanaras chattering in fear and came rushing out at the commotion. When he saw an incensed Lakshmana with flashing red eyes, he was filled with trepidation. However, Lakshmana was not annoyed with him, and said kindly, 'Son, inform your uncle Sugriva that I am here on behalf of Rama, who is sorely disappointed by his irresponsible behaviour. Tell him that I am waiting at his door and let me know what he says.' Accompanied by the Vanara ministers, Angada went hastily to deliver the message. First, he touched Sugriva's feet, next Ruma's and then those of his mother. Anxiously he informed them that Lakshmana was in a rage at the door, burning the Vanaras with his menacing looks. The ministers begged Sugriva to fall at

---

[4] Vedic philosophy advocates Ahimsa. However, Ahimsa does not mean pacifism, but rather choosing the least violent option in the circumstances. Violence is only sanctioned when all attempts at peaceful resolution fail.

[5] The Tungabhadra River.

Lakshmana's feet and calm him down by being truthful to his promise, but Sugriva was groggy and disconnected from reality in his inebriation. He was surprised to hear that Lakshmana was angry and asked what he could have done to cause a misunderstanding. He exclaimed in astonishment, 'It appears somebody has filled the princes with falsehoods about me to make them annoyed. I have not done anything wrong or spoken ill of them, so why is Lakshmana so angry? I speak out of incredulity rather than fear; alas, while friendship is easy to establish, it seems to break on flimsy grounds. Relationships are delicate and need careful nurturing, as feelings can easily change with misinformation. I know I am indebted to Rama for what he has done for me, and nothing I do in return can ever be enough to repay him, so I fail to understand why he thinks otherwise.'

Interjecting, Hanuman explained, 'I feel Rama is upset with you not out of animosity but because he loves you and is deeply disappointed that you have not tried to reciprocate his favour to you. Absorbed in sensual pleasure, you have lost all sense of time, ignoring your duty as a friend. The sky has cleared, and the rivers have resumed their normal flow. Now the time is ripe to set out on the undertaking you pledged. Rama is in a desperate situation, not knowing his wife's whereabouts, and despite this, he has waited patiently for your promised action. His anger is justified because you have aggrieved him with your indifference to his suffering. I urge you to fold your hands before him and ask for forgiveness. As your loyal minister, I say what you may not want to hear, but I assure you it is for your good. Follow through on your side of the bargain, so you do not bring an unnecessary calamity upon yourself. We have seen only a fraction of Rama's strength. If he is angered, he even has the power to subdue the mighty Devas, so it is my considered opinion that you placate him by showing your gratitude.'

Angada hurriedly returned to Lakshmana, pacing impatiently outside, and duly ushered him into Sugriva's residence. The palace was luxuriously furnished with seats of gold and silver. Melodious music played; and several young women flitted about, clad in fine clothing and decked in exquisite ornaments. Lakshmana passed through seven outer chambers making his way to the inner quarters. Nearing Sugriva's room, he heard anklets and girdle bells tinkling in the euphoria of lovemaking; being quite straitlaced by nature, his face reddened in embarrassment. Then, in a flash, his discomfiture was replaced by rage that Sugriva had ignored his message and gone back to his licentiousness again. He felt pushed to the end of his patience and angrily pulled his bowstring, emitting a loud twang that resounded terrifyingly through the cave. When Sugriva heard the sound, he trembled in fear, and turning to Tara, said with a bemused expression on his face, 'Lakshmana is a tender-hearted person, so I cannot fathom why he is so angry! Of course, I have not given him any reason to be annoyed with me, but even so, I think it would be best for you to go and pacify him with your tact and diplomacy. He is a gentleman and will not be discourteous to a woman. Once you calm him down, my dear, I will come out and see him.'

Reeling under the influence of the copious amounts of wine she had consumed, Tara went to meet Lakshmana, teetering unsteadily as she walked. Since she was fresh from Sugriva's embrace, her ornaments were askew, and her clothing was in disarray. Lakshmana turned scarlet at the sight of her and looked down at the floor in embarrassment, uncomfortably averting his gaze.

Tara bowed to him respectfully and asked in a genial tone, 'Why are you so angry, dear sir?' Surprisingly, despite her inebriation, she spoke cogently. 'We are all at your command. Rama is as powerful as a forest fire, so who would be foolish enough to upset him?' Lakshmana felt slightly reassured that the Vanaras still had regard for Rama, and relaxing a little, replied, 'Sugriva is caught up in enjoyment and has forgotten about his duties, including his promise to us. He is so drunk that he does not realize how much time has passed since he assured my brother of his help. You are a wise woman, so I am sure you will admit that his behaviour is unacceptable. While Rama is engulfed in sorrow, Sugriva is caught up in merrymaking, oblivious to his friend's unhappiness. His mind is befuddled by constant intoxication, and we all know that habitual drunkenness inevitably leads to a person's downfall. By defaulting on his commitment, Sugriva stands to lose a true ally. Being principled, you know right from wrong, so what is your opinion on this?'

Tara pleaded, 'O prince, do not be resentful of your friend. If there has been a small lapse on Sugriva's part, please excuse him. You are from a noble family, much more learned than us, and of a far higher status, so do not judge us by your lofty standards. While I can understand Rama's anger and appreciate all he has done for Sugriva, I request you to view the circumstances benignly since he fell prey only to irrepressible sensual desire and not to any ill intention. Although you are a man of eminent virtues, even you have shortcomings and are easily angered. Sugriva's failing is that physical pleasures swayed him, and he did not realize the passage of time while giving in to excess. Forgive him because the temptation of the flesh is often more alluring than greed for wealth. Even great rishis engaged in austere penance have been seduced by sexual desire and distracted from their goal by lust, let alone an ordinary Vanara!'

She paused to check Lakshmana's expression, and then continued. 'O noble sir, I assure you that Sugriva is very aware of his promise, so don't misconstrue his silence for negligence. Efforts are afoot to assist Rama; he has already issued orders a few days ago summoning Vanaras from all over the world to Kishkindha. In fact, many have arrived to report for duty. Let us go to Sugriva so he can reassure you personally. Although he is in his chamber with his wives, I don't think it is inappropriate for someone of your high calibre to meet him in their presence.'

Having soothed Lakshmana's temper, Tara led him to Sugriva. Adorned in garlands, he was seated on a golden couch surrounded by voluptuous women and locked in a tight embrace with Ruma. His shocking lack of gravitas, displayed in the salaciousness of the scene, irked Lakshmana, and his temper flared again. Startled, Sugriva leaped up in alarm and stood with folded hands, as Lakshmana admonished sternly, 'A good king has control over his senses and doesn't allow himself to fall prey to self-indulgence at the expense of dharma. Unfortunately, you have been remiss in your duty! By forgetting the service done by my brother, you have proved to be duplicitous, ignoble and untruthful to your word. Atonement is possible even for a sinner who kills a cow, a drunkard or a thief, but there is no redemption for an ungrateful person. Rama has been tolerant of you but if you do not honour your agreement, let me warn you that you will end up dead like Vali.'

Tara was worried when she heard Lakshmana's threat and, stepping in to mediate once again, said, 'I can assure you that Sugriva has not forgotten Rama's kindness to him, so please don't chastise him so severely. He is not thankless, cruel or deceitful; I request you empathize with his situation and condone his frailty. He was so exhausted hiding from Vali, living a life of deprivation for years and constantly on the run, that when the pressure lifted, he succumbed to overindulgence. Even someone as great as Vishwamitra lost track of time in his torrid passion for Menaka, and in her company, felt ten years were like the passing of a single day. You understand dharma better than anyone, so I beseech you not to let your anger over a small misunderstanding lead you to cast unfair allegations. Sugriva is so completely committed to helping Rama that he would gladly abdicate his kingdom and even abandon me, Ruma and Angada, if it were necessary to fulfil his pledge. Vali once told me that Ravana is exceedingly mighty; his control extends over vast parts of the Earth, and he rules over millions of Rakshasas, so we have already mobilized an extensive force to determine where he could have hidden Sita. We are waiting for reinforcements to arrive as we speak and several are expected today. Now I earnestly request you to shed your anger because the women standing around us are shaking in fear of your bloodshot eyes!'

On hearing Tara, Lakshmana's temper subsided and Sugriva heaved a sigh of relief. Tearing off his garlands, he said ashamedly, 'Please pardon my negligence, knowing everyone errs at some point in life. I acknowledge that everything I have today is on account of Rama. I am deeply indebted to him and will always be his faithful servant. I sincerely apologize for my tardiness. If I have inadvertently done anything to annoy Rama, I hope he will forgive me as I hold our friendship very dear.' Lakshmana was now completely mollified, his anger dying down as quickly as it had erupted. Speaking kindly to Sugriva, he said, 'Thank you for your assurance of support and above all your humility. There are very few people in this world other than my brother who can admit to their faults, and it shows great strength of character to apologize. I am sorry I spoke to you so harshly, and I sincerely ask for your forgiveness. Let us go and console Rama. He is in great anguish, and his emotional turmoil caused me to lose my mind.'

Sugriva turned to his most trusted minister Hanuman and asked him to send out a reminder once again to all races of Vanaras—black, brown, white and grey—ordering them to Kishkindha within ten days on pain of death. They were to convene immediately from their abodes in the forests of the Mahendra,[6] Himalayas, Vindhyas, Kailasha[7] and Mandara[8] mountains, including Udayagiri[9] and Ashtagiri.[10] Every able-bodied Vanara in the world, from the jungles of the north, south, east and west was summoned, and none was exempt from the decree. Soon, they would arrive in droves from distant lands, great multitudes marching to Kishkindha, bearing gifts of exotic fruits and medicinal herbs.

---

[6] Eastern Ghats of India.

[7] Abode of Shiva in the Himalayas.

[8] Some identify it with the Mandar Parvat in the Bhagalpur district of Bihar, but this remains unconfirmed.

[9] Where the sun rises in the east. Nilesh Oak, in studying the geography of the Ramayana, hypothesizes this to be the Andes.

[10] Where the sun sets in the west. Nilesh Oak hypothesizes this to be the Alps.

Meanwhile, Sugriva called for his royal palanquin and went with Lakshmana to see Rama so they could plan the next step. He parked a short distance from the cave and approached humbly on foot.[11] Rama was relieved to see him; he joined his palms in salutation and welcomed him warmly, while Sugriva fell at his feet begging for forgiveness. Rama raised him and commended Sugriva for not abandoning his dharma, saying, 'A true leader always balances the pursuit of wealth and pleasure with righteousness. A person who indulges in self-gratification without the guidance of dharma is like the one who falls asleep on a branch and wakes up only when he falls off, for he can never attain lasting happiness.' Sugriva reassured Rama that scores of exceptional Vanaras were arriving for his mission. He assured him of their competence and guaranteed that they would painstakingly scour the Earth and find Sita wherever she was hidden. Rama was overwhelmed with gratitude, and embracing Sugriva, exclaimed, 'I am blessed to have a magnanimous friend like you! I am sure the enemy will be conquered with your assistance, and Ravana will be brought to justice very soon.'[12]

---

[11] Sugriva goes on foot to show respect.

[12] Kshama or forgiveness was considered the noblest of virtues, an expression of dharmic action. It is one of the ethical guidelines to practise good conduct. Compare Rama with Vali, who did not pardon Sugriva, although he was repentant. Vali was full of ego, that results from an over identification with the physical body and mind, as opposed to the consciousness within.

Chapter 18

Search Parties Are Dispatched

In compliance with Sugriva's orders, Vanaras from all over the world assembled before Rama, resembling an endless lake of lotus buds as they stood with folded hands awaiting his command. Rama announced the assignment; to locate Ravana's kingdom and determine whether Sita was dead or alive. Since Sugriva had circled the globe[1] while trying to escape from Vali, Rama asked him to use his knowledge of world geography[2] to direct the troops and find out where Sita was being held captive. Ravana had a vast empire and could have hidden her anywhere; therefore, all four quarters of the Earth would need to be explored, not just the south. Sugriva divided the Vanaras into four groups to fulfil the task, giving them no more than one month to accomplish their mission.

The valorous Vinata, mountainous in size with a booming voice, was dispatched to the east[3] with a large contingent of 1,00,000 Vanaras. Giving detailed instructions, Sugriva said, 'Carefully search the territories of Videha, Brahmamala, Malawa, Kashi, Kosala, Magadha, Pundra and Anga. After exploring the areas along the banks of the Bhagirathi,[4] Sarayu, Yamuna,

---

[1] The Vedic people knew that the Earth was spherical and that it revolved around the sun.

[2] Sugriva's geography is not always easily matched with the place names today. Researchers have come up with various theories that are cited in these footnotes.

[3] Sugriva's directions are not given from Kishkindha as the starting point, but from Ujjain, through which the Prime Meridian ran in Vedic times.

[4] Ganga

Kausiki,[5] Saraswati, Sindhu[6] and Shona, go further to the Mahi and Kalamahi, proceeding eastwards to the land of silk and the regions famous for silver mines. The Mandara Mountains are home to grisly beings with odd physical characteristics, whose ears and lips are stretched to hang down. These tribes are very fierce and some of them are cannibals. Next, search the islands of the golden-complexioned Kiritas, who live on raw fish, and are also known as tiger men. You may reach the various islands by boat if it is not possible to leap across. I would like you to comb every forest, mountain, town, cave and riverside, including the island of Yawadwipa,[7] famous for its gemstones, and the seven other kingdoms in the vicinity rich in silver and gold. Continue beyond to Mount Shishira, whose peak touches the sky inhabited by Devas and Danavas.[8] Then search the islands of Plaksha and Ikshudwipa amidst the tempestuous Ikshu Ocean.[9] Proceed further east of that to the fearful red sea, Lohita. On an island in that ocean is the Shalmalidwipa, named after the kuta-shalmali tree. It has the mansion of Garuda constructed by Vishwakarma. After that, you will encounter fearful Rakshasas, the colour of stone, called Mandehas,[10] who live suspended from the rocky cliffs. They get scorched when the sun rises, falling into the water, only to re-emerge and hang downwards again.

'Beyond is a milky ocean called Kshiroda,[11] where there rises a gigantic white mountain called Rishabha.[12] It has many trees with fragrant blossoms and a lily-covered lake called Sudarshana[13] that the Devas, Kinnaras and Apsaras frequent. After passing Kshiroda, you will see the peaceful ocean[14]

---

[5] Kosi

[6] Indus. The mention of the Sindhu and Saraswati to the eastern group may seem odd but the Prime Meridian in Vedic times passed through Ujjain in the western part of India.

[7] Java

[8] Half-brothers of the Devas, the sons of Danu and Rishi Kashyapa.

[9] South China Sea

[10] Could allude to vampire bats (Nilesh Oak).

[11] This may be the Tasman Sea.

[12] This could be Mount Cook in New Zealand.

[13] Possibly Lake Pukaki.

[14] Pacific Ocean

with the fearsome Hayamukha fire.[15] The thousand-hooded Ananta sustains the world on his head in that region.[16] North of there, you will see a large golden mountain called Jatarupa, where the Devas marked the Earth's eastern quarter. Ananta's standard, a golden palmyra tree with three branches on a podium, is etched on its face like a flag.[17] The farthest east you can go is a mountain range 100 yojanas long called Udaya.[18] Finally, you will come across a peak called Soumanasa, where Vishnu placed his first foot in ancient times.[19] The sun rises daily above it and then circles over Jambudweepa.[20] Eminent sages called Valakhilyas practise austerities there. At the beginning of creation, this eastern mountain was developed as a gateway for those entering Earth or departing from it to higher worlds.'[21] Sugriva concluded by saying that no civilized land existed beyond that point and ordered the team to adhere strictly to the timeline of one month for their investigation.

Once Sugriva sent off the eastern search party, he commanded Angada to take a group to the south. He was careful to assign his most trusted followers—Nila, Nala, Hanuman and Jambavan—to accompany him, because he felt that Sita was most likely to be there. Also, he was somewhat insecure about his nephew's loyalty, having slain the boy's father, which could be the potential for disgruntlement. Giving precise instructions, Sugriva ordered, 'Explore the forested Vindhya Mountain range thoroughly and look for the daughter-in-law of Dasharatha, along the rivers Narmada, Godavari, Krishnaveni and Varada.[22] Meticulously cover the southern territories of

---

[15] Hayamukha means, 'shaped like a horse's face'. This appears to be a reference to the Pacific Ring of Fire.

[16] Chile; the southern tip of South America is associated with the head of the serpent, Ananta.

[17] Per Nilesh Oak, the flag appears to be the Paracas Candelabra in Peru, as the description is identical to it. Also, going eastwards from India, South America would be the furthest east.

[18] Presumed to be the Andes.

[19] Reference to the Vaman avatar of Vishnu.

[20] The Puranas speak of seven continents—Jambudweepa, Plakshadweepa, Shalmalidweepa, Kushadweepa, Kraunchadweepa, Shakadweepa and Pushkaradweepa. The Vedic world spread over a much larger area in Jambudweepa than just modern India.

[21] This statement is interesting in relation to the extraterrestrial activity associated with Peru.

[22] Wardha

Mekhala and Utkala, and the cities of Dasarna, Ambravati and Avanti.[23]
Make sure you check Vidarbha,[24] Rishika, Mahishaka, Vanga,[25] Kalinga[26]
and Kaushika. Scour every cave, river and mountain in the Dandaka Forest
moving south to Andhra, Pundra, Chola, Pandya and Kerala. Search the
Malaya Mountain covered in sandalwood trees and rich mineral deposits by
which the sparkling Kaveri flows. High above the summit, Agastya[27] shines
brightly like the sun.

'Then crossing the alligator-infested Tamraparni, you will see the golden
gem-studded gates of the Pandya[28] capital and the magnificent Mahendra
Mountain. You can leap across the ocean from there, depending on your
capability. On the other side of the sea, a 100 yojanas away, lies a forested
island inaccessible to human beings; nevertheless, try to reach it, for it is likely
to be the abode of Ravana.[29] When you cross over, exercise caution because
a terrible ogress lives in the sea there; she immobilizes her prey, catching the
shadow of anyone flying above. Beyond that, you will see the glorious islands,
Pushpitaka, Suryavan and Vaidyuta.[30] Past them is Bhogvati, the kingdom
of the snakes ruled by Vasuki, on a mountain called Kunjara. Agastya can be
sighted from there as well.'

'Further on, you will come to the mountain Rishabha, shaped like a bull,
replete with every kind of gemstone and many sandalwood trees. Please do not
touch them because Gandharvas called the Rohita guard them jealously. You
will not be able to go past that region, as beyond it lies the dark, inhospitable
land of Yama.[31] I do not advise you to search there, as the conditions are
treacherous, making it dangerous for Earthly beings. Once you see it, turn

---

[23] Ujjain

[24] Now in Maharashtra.

[25] Bengal (including Bangladesh).

[26] Odisha

[27] The star Canopus which could only be seen from the south of the Vindhyas in the
fifth millennium BCE.

[28] Madurai

[29] Earlier Sugriva had said he did not know where Ravana lived, so we must presume he
was unsure because the Rakshasa king had a vast empire.

[30] It is not clear which islands these are in present times. They may have submerged.

[31] Presumed to be Antarctica (Nilesh Oak's research).

back, and return quickly before a month elapses to avoid punishment. If you bring news of Sita, I will bestow on you great wealth equal to mine.'

Next, Sugriva respectfully approached Tara's father, the powerful Sushena. Bowing respectfully to his father-in-law, he asked him to take a unit to search the west. Elaborating on the brief, Sugriva said, 'Search all the towns and cities in the areas of Saurashtra,[32] Chandrachitra, Bahalika[33] and Kuksi.[34] Next, search the rivers, the desert regions and the high cliffs beyond which lies the sea with enormous fish. Explore the great western rivers, including the towns of Muravi, Jatapura, Avanti, Angalepa and the forest of Alaksita. At the juncture where the Sindhu meets the ocean,[35] you will come across a large mountain range called Hemagiri,[36] which you should check thoroughly. It has a hundred peaks and huge trees, and majestic lions and elephants roam on its plateaus. Travelling westwards, you will see the golden Pariyatra Mountain. Many powerful Gandharvas reside in the surrounding areas;[37] they guard the fruit growing there fiercely, so while searching for Sita, make sure you keep your distance, not to annoy them. Beyond that is the Vajra Mountain;[38] search its caves thoroughly and then go to a large circular range called Chakravan and check it carefully. After sixty-four yojanas, in the fathomless sea is another landmass called Varaha. There, in the city of Pragjyotishapura,[39] lives an evil-minded Rakshasa called Naraka, so make sure to hunt for Sita there. Keep traversing further to the Megha Mountains, the king of ranges associated with Indra. Continue heading west till you reach 60,000 golden hills, where you will find Meru Savarni, a most superior mountain, the abode of Lord Varuna. On its summit is an edifice constructed by Vishwakarma. Between Meru and the westernmost range, Ashtagiri,[40]

---

[32] Gujarat

[33] Balkh/Afghanistan

[34] Madhya Desha—middle country.

[35] The Arabian Sea called Sindhu Sagar in Vedic times.

[36] Possibly the Sulaiman Mountains.

[37] Appears to be Afghanistan.

[38] Could be the Zagros Range.

[39] Speculated to be in Iraq (Nilesh Oak's research).

[40] Speculated to be the Alps (Nilesh Oak's research).

where the sun sets, shines a palmyra tree of gold with ten branches supported on a base.[41] I do not know the area beyond there, so do not go any farther.'

Then addressing the team members, he warned, 'Do not spend longer than a month because anyone who procrastinates will face punishment. I have assigned my valiant father-in-law to go with you, so make sure you follow his command. It is imperative we find the princess of Videha so that we can repay our debt to Rama.'

Finally, Sugriva sent the great Vanara Shatabali to the cold regions of the north. He ordered him to carefully explore all areas, including the land of the Mlecchas[42] and Pulindas. The team was instructed to search the territories of the Surasenas,[43] Prasthalas, Bharatas, Kurus,[44] Kambojas, Yavanas,[45] Sakas[46] and Dardas.[47] Sugriva said, 'Scan the snowy Himalayas, including its cliffs and canyons, and the barren wilderness[48] that leads to Mount Kailasha, the white mountain abode of Lord Shiva. Nearby is the magnificent mansion of Kubera constructed by Vishwakarma. There is a lake frequented by swans there, thick with lotuses. It is also a favourite of the Apsaras. Make sure you hunt for Maithili in the forests of lodhra[49] and padmaka trees,[50] as well as the deodar[51] groves. Please ensure you investigate the Kala, Sudharshana and Devasaka Mountains. Next, go to the Krauncha Mountain, where you should look for Sita in its tunnel;[52] though challenging to access, high-souled sages live there. There are also two barren, treeless mountains, Kaama and

---

[41] Similar to the one in the east identified with the Paracas Candelabra, but the western one mentioned here is unidentified.

[42] Barbarians

[43] Area around Mathura.

[44] Areas of modern-day Delhi, Haryana and parts of Uttar Pradesh.

[45] Greeks

[46] Scythians

[47] The Gilgit region of Kashmir.

[48] The Tibetan Plateau.

[49] *Symplocos racemosa*, an evergreen tree used in Ayurveda.

[50] *Prunus cerasoides*, also known as Wild Himalayan Cherry, used in Ayurveda.

[51] *Cedrus deodara*, commonly known as Himalayan Cedar.

[52] This could be a reference to the Guoliang Tunnel area in the Taihang Mountains. Till 1972 (when it was improved), there was only a precarious ancient path cut through the rocks.

Manasa,[53] which should be scoured. If you go past Krauncha, you will reach the abode of Mayasura, which he constructed on a hill called Mainaka.[54] A tribe of horse-faced women also resides there. Beyond that are the hermitages of ascetics called Vaikhanasas and Valakhilyas; they are realized souls, so you can ask them if they have any knowledge of Sita. You will come across a lake called Vaikhanasa,[55] named after the ascetics.

Further on flows a river called Sailoda,[56] on the banks of which grow bamboos[57] called keechaka that make a whistling sound in the wind and are used to cross the river. The prosperous land of the Uttara Kurus[58] stretches from here. Travel far north till you come to the golden mountain in the northern ocean that marks the end of habitable land.[59] On the other side stretches an endless, dreary, sunless-starless realm[60] lit by an unusual brilliance. It is so unforgiving that even the Devas did not attempt to enter it. I do not know that land, so turn back and do not attempt to enter it, as you have a strict timeline within which to return.'

Each general was enthusiastic about achieving success, but Sugriva was confident Hanuman would be the one to accomplish the task. He remembered how Vali had pursued him to every corner of the world as he sought a safe place to hide, and that it was Hanuman who had advised him to seek shelter on Rishyamukha. Before the southern team left, Sugriva called Hanuman aside and said, 'O Hanuman, you are a bull amongst Vanaras. Like your mighty father, Vayu, you are unmatched in intellect, speed and agility. You know all three worlds; not only are you familiar with the land of humans, but you are also acquainted with the abode of the Devas, Gandharvas, Rakshasas and Nagas. I am sure that you will be the one to find Sita.' Rama, too, was optimistic about Hanuman's success. He took off his ring, which bore his insignia, and handed it to Hanuman, saying, 'Valorous one, I depend

---

[53] Possibly in the Qinling Mountains.

[54] Not the same mountain Hanuman encounters later in the story.

[55] Lake Baikal

[56] Angara River

[57] Siberian bamboo grass used by the locals to cross water bodies.

[58] North Kuru, inhabited by settlers who migrated out of India to Central Asia.

[59] The Urals

[60] Presumed to be the Arctic (Nilesh Oak) because Sugriva appears to be referring to the Aurora Borealis.

on your intelligence and competence in this difficult mission. In my heart, I believe you will find Sita, and when you do, give her this ring to assure her that I have sent you.'

After the Vanara teams left, Rama and Lakshmana waited eagerly on Mount Prasravana for them to return. The units earnestly swarmed the four quarters of the world like locusts, assiduously exploring every lake and river, field and habitation, slope and plateau. No mountain, cave, forest or grove was left unexamined. All day, they searched for Sita without a break, in every nook and cranny of the Earth; at night, they would find some fruit to eat and fall asleep exhausted. At the end of the month, Vinata returned dejected as there was no trace of Sita in the east. Shatabali made his way back crestfallen that luck had not favoured them in the north, and Sushena announced with disappointment that he was unsuccessful in the west.

There was no news of the southern team yet, and all hopes were now pinned on Angada's group. Like the others, the members of his team, too, had searched meticulously everywhere Sugriva had ordered. First, they looked along the rivers—Narmada, Godavari, Krishnanaveni and Varadha. Next, they explored the kingdoms of Vidarbha, Rishvikha, Mahishaka, Kalinga and Kaushika. They looked high and low in the Dandaka Forest and combed Andhra, Pandya, Chola and Kerala. Then they scrutinized the area around the river Kaveri and Malaya Mountains. South of the Vindhyas, no spot was left unturned, and though hope began to wane, they persisted. Then they came upon a barren place where the trees had no leaves or flowers, and the river had dried up. Eerily, no animals inhabited the region, nor was the buzzing of bees heard. It was a blighted spot because the ten-year-old son of a powerful rishi called Kandu had lost his life there. The rishi cursed the forest to turn into a wasteland shunned by all creatures, but the team searched it scrupulously, nevertheless. Not finding Sita there, they proceeded further to another forest where a colossal Rakshasa appeared before them, barring their path. Thinking he might be Ravana, Angada struck him with his fist so violently that blood gushed out of the Rakshasa's mouth, and he dropped dead. With him out of the way, they investigated the forest thoroughly, but there was no sign of Rama's dear wife there, either.

By this time, the Vanaras had slid into a state of despair, enervated both physically and mentally. However, Angada skilfully boosted their morale with words of encouragement that urged them to soldier on. He managed to get the Vanaras to continue searching, insisting that success could only be achieved with an undefeated spirit. Finally, after many peregrinations, tired, thirsty and on the verge of death, the team stumbled upon a large cave hidden in the undergrowth and noticed water-loving birds like swans and cranes emerging from it. Hanuman astutely concluded that a water body was inside, so they entered the cave. Since it was pitch dark, they walked holding hands, feeling their way, their hair standing on end, for about one yojana. Suddenly they were blinded by a bright light, and before them was a female sage sitting in meditation under a tree. She was dressed in black deerskin and shone with the radiance of her austerity. Next to her was a lake covered with lotuses. It was full of fish, giant turtles and numerous birds. Around the lake were beautiful dwellings made of gold and silver, decorated with precious gems and many golden vimanas. It was a paradise replete with trees bearing colourful flowers, juicy fruit and oozing honeycombs.

Hanuman approached the holy woman with his hands respectfully joined together and inquired curiously, 'Who are you, and to whom does this magnificent place belong?' She did not respond, so Hanuman went on, 'We entered this cave in search of water to quench our thirst and are surprised by the beauty we see here. Have your spiritual powers produced all this?' The woman replied, 'No, Mayasura, the architect of the Asuras, created this golden grove with his yogic powers. Many years ago, he fell in love with an Apsara called Hema from Indra's court and built this abode for her pleasure. However, she does not live here any more. My name is Swayamprabha, and I am the caretaker; you have my permission to refresh yourselves with food and drink to your heart's content.'

Once the Vanaras had eaten and felt revived, Swayamprabha asked them how they found themselves in such an isolated place. Hanuman narrated the story of Rama's exile, Sita's abduction, the alliance with Sugriva and their search for the princess. Thanking Swayamprabha for her hospitality, he spoke of their exhaustive efforts that had sadly yielded no results. When Hanuman asked if they could repay her kindness, she said she needed nothing, having given up all worldly desires. Hanuman then requested to be shown the way out of the cave to resume their undertaking. However, to his surprise, the woman said no one entering this magical place could return alive, but since their story elicited her compassion, she would use her spiritual powers to get them out safely. Giving her blessings, Swayamprabha directed them to search the southern shore where they might have some good fortune. The Vanaras closed their eyes as instructed; when they opened their eyes again, they were on the coast with the endless ocean roaring before them.

Gazing hopelessly at the vast sea with nowhere further to go, the Vanaras sat despondently on the soft sandy beach. By this time, even Angada had succumbed to pessimism. Addressing the team, he said despondently, 'More than a month has elapsed since we started exploring the south, yet we have not seen any sign of Sita. Sugriva will be annoyed with us for returning late, and our failure will further exacerbate his displeasure. Although you are all loyal to Sugriva, you know only too well that he is a tough taskmaster and will not hesitate to carry out his threat to punish us when we go back unsuccessful. Personally, I must admit that I have an inherent mistrust of him and feel I might become a scapegoat for his rage. After all, Sugriva installed me as crown prince only on Rama's insistence and not because he had any special affection for me. Therefore, I strongly advise that we do not return. Rather than going home to face condemnation, I think it is better to sit here on the shore and fast unto death.'

Most of the team agreed, preferring death to disgrace. Then a Vanara called Tara,[61] loyal to Vali, offered an alternative plan. He suggested that they go back to the magical cave and live there for the rest of their lives without fear of Sugriva ever finding them. The fickle mob cheered and switched camps at once, thinking this was a better idea.

Hanuman was concerned at the insurrection brewing amongst the Vanaras and was especially troubled by their animosity towards Sugriva. So, he called Angada aside, hoping to dissipate the tension and prevent a seditious conspiracy from taking root. Counselling him, Hanuman said, 'I regard you as a competent leader. You are even braver than your dauntless father, and Sugriva has fittingly chosen you as his successor. However, I am afraid I must disagree with the rebellious plan that has been mooted by Tara and advise you not to follow capricious creatures who think they can hide in a cave from Lakshmana's powerful arrows. Instead, stand with Nala, Nila, Jambavan and me, who are loyal to Sugriva. He is fair-minded, so you need not fear him. Sugriva believes in dharma and will not cause you or his people any harm. Besides, he is devoted to your mother and will never do anything to hurt her. Also, as you know, he has no children of his own, so there is no one to contest your position as his heir.'

Angada was unconvinced and replied dubiously, 'My uncle lacks integrity; he is cruel and crooked, and I do not trust him at all. I cannot forget that he blocked the exit when my father was battling Mayavi. He used

---

[61] Not Vali's wife. This is a male Vanara who shares the same name.

to treat my mother respectfully as his sister-in-law, but now he has made her his consort. He is unscrupulous and thinks solely of his interests. He even let down his friend Rama after making a solemn pledge to help him and only made good on his promise when Lakshmana forced him. I am the son of his enemy, so why would he be sympathetic to me? You are right that he does not have children, but that does not mean he will not have any in the future. When that happens, he will surely find a way to get rid of me. In any case, the resentment simmering inside me is public now, so it is dangerous for me to go back. Sugriva may secretly arrange to assassinate me for trying to disassociate from him without making it obvious. It is far better to die an honourable death here than a miserable one at home. I think the initial plan to end my life is the best option in the circumstances, and I swear not to return.' The rest of the Vanaras now went back to supporting Angada. Deriding Sugriva, they decided to embrace death and praised Vali, pledging allegiance to his memory.

As the Vanaras lay on the beach engulfed in a miasma of despair, lamenting their failure and preparing for death, unbeknownst to them, they were being observed from a cave on a hill by an eagle called Sampati. He was Jatayu's elder brother, who lived by the sea. Sampati's wings were burnt, a handicap that prevented him from hunting. The sight of the Vanaras made him ravenous, and he looked forward to eating them one by one as they dropped dead. Then he overheard Angada trying to persuade Hanuman to join him in his fast. 'We are laying down our lives for Rama, just as Jatayu did when he tried to stop Ravana from abducting Sita. He achieved great glory by his sacrifice and has undoubtedly ascended to the highest level in heaven. We, too, hope for the same.' When Sampati heard his brother was dead, he called out to the Vanaras, asking them to take him to the shore. 'My wings are scorched,' he said, 'and I cannot fly. Please help me down so that I can hear about what happened to my brother.' Initially, the Vanaras were worried about his sincerity. They suspected his request was a ruse to eat them, but agreed when Angada reminded them that they were planning to die anyway.

Angada told Sampati about all the events that had taken place thus far—how Jatayu had died trying to save Sita and how Sugriva had dispatched troops of Vanaras to search for her. Sampati was in tears to hear that his dear brother had lost his life. He wept that he could not avenge Jatayu's death because he was old and helpless with damaged wings. Narrating his story, he said, 'All birds do not ascend to the same height. Those like sparrows and songbirds stay close to the ground, searching for grain. Scavengers like crows, fruit eaters like parrots, and doves fly at the next level. Still higher go the waterbirds like herons, wild geese and cranes. Hawks attain the fourth level, but eagles rise to the highest altitude. Once Jatayu and I were vying to outdo each other and soared so high that our feathers began to get singed by the sun's rays. I protectively covered Jatayu with my wings but burnt myself in the process, never to fly again. I landed on this shore and have lived here ever since, while my brother fell by Janasthana. Unfortunately, I have had no contact with Jatayu since then, and the first news of him since our parting has been hearing you speak about his death.'

Continuing his tale, Sampati spoke of a strange prophecy that a rishi from a nearby hermitage made to him when he had regained consciousness six days after his fall. He had opened his eyes to see Rishi Nishakara, who foretold that Sampati would regrow his feathers when he provided helpful information to recover an Ikshavaku king's wife. Hearing this, Angada asked if he knew anything about Ravana that might assist in finding the Rakshasa king. Sampati replied that some months ago, a beautiful young woman was seen being carried away in a vimana, crying loudly and wriggling to free herself as her silken clothing fluttered in the wind. He continued, 'I am sure that was Sita, and her abductor was Ravana. He is the son of the Brahmin Vishrava and the half-brother of Kubera. Now please take me to the sea so I can offer water to my brother's spirit.'

After assisting Sampati with his request, Jambavan inquired if he had any additional information that might be helpful in their quest. Sampati said that since he was disabled, his son Suparshwa brought him food. One day, his son came to him empty-handed and explained that he had been hunting around Mount Mahendra for fresh meat, when he saw a lovely lady struggling with her captor as she was being carried off. Suparshwa thought he would seize them for food but decided against it when the man asked humbly for safe passage. He apologized to his father for not bringing him anything to eat that day but felt it was wrong to refuse someone who had pleaded so desperately. Sampati said he scolded his son for not helping the lady and added that Ravana lived on an island called Lanka, a beautiful kingdom built by Vishwakarma[62] with golden gates and tall mansions. He asserted, 'I am

---

[62] Vishwakarma is the architect of the Devas.

from the clan of Garuda;[63] blessed with acutely sharp vision, I see Sita held captive there.' Urging the Vanaras to rescue her, he added that he felt in his heart that they would be successful in their mission. As Sampati said this, his feathers miraculously grew back just as the rishi had predicted, and he flew off.

With new details of Sita's whereabouts, the Vanaras' mood lightened, and their despondency vanished. Although the ocean was vast like the sky, and reaching Lanka was a daunting task, they were optimistic of success and began to discuss the best way to make it across the sea. In keeping with his role as their leader, Angada asked how far each Vanara could jump. 'Who is the hero amongst us who will help Sugriva stay true to his word? Which one of you will be our saviour? By whose grace will we go home to our wives and children? Who is the brave one who will enable us to return to Kishkindha proudly with our heads held high? Someone, please step up to the challenge and give us back our lives!' Gaja said he could clear ten yojanas, and Gavaksha was confident of twenty, Sarabha thirty, Rishabha forty, Gandhamadana fifty, Mainda sixty, Dwividha seventy and Sushena[64] eighty.

The bear Jambavan claimed it would have been easy for him to jump the distance to Lanka in his youth when he was robust. However, now that he was old, he was not confident of his strength and could perhaps clear only ninety yojanas. Angada was reasonably sure he could leap a hundred yojanas but was unsure of his ability to return. Although he was the only one who could get across, Jambavan cautioned that it would not be advisable for him to go. Angada had the duty of a leader, and for the integrity of the mission, needed to safeguard himself from danger. Out of viable options, pessimism descended on the team again. Angada began to talk once more about fasting to death, lamenting that Sugriva was a strict disciplinarian with an erratic temperament that swung very quickly from kindness to harshness when provoked.

However, all was not lost! Jambavan noticed that Hanuman had not volunteered and was sitting silently, apart from the rest of the team. Knowing that Vayu's son could easily accomplish the feat of crossing the

---

[63] Some versions of the Ramayana refer to Jatayu and Sampati as vultures, but they are eagles because they are nephews of the eagle Garuda. Also, the references like hunting for fresh meat, soaring high into the sky, and excellent vision, are all typically associated with eagles.

[64] Not Tara's father, who went west. This is another Vanara with the same name.

ocean, Jambavan reminded[65] him of his competence. 'O Hanuman, why
haven't you come forward? Have you forgotten your strength? Those who
have the greatest abilities tend to be the most modest, so perhaps that is why
you have not spoken. I know you are eminently capable of performing this
task; not only are you brilliant, but your strength matches that of Sugriva.
I would even go so far as to say you are equal to Rama and Lakshmana. You
have the power of Garuda in your arms, so you must take up the challenge.
Brahma has granted you invincibility, and you are immensely swift like your
father, Vayu.

'Let me remind you about the story of your birth. Punjikasthala was a
beautiful Apsara, and Vayu was in love with her. However, because of a curse,
she left her celestial abode and was born as Anjana, a Vanara woman married
to Kesari. Once when Anjana was roaming on a mountain peak, Vayu blew
off her red-bordered yellow upper garment, exposing her beautiful body.
Being a devoted wife, Anjana asked who was trying to defile her. Vayu replied
that though he was deeply infatuated by her, his appreciation of Anjana's
beauty was mental, and he did not intend to violate her physically. He stated
that he had impregnated her with the power of his mind without offending
her chastity so she would have a son just like him. In time your mother gave
birth to you. Each Deva has given you a special power; even death cannot
claim you till you wish it. As a child, you leaped towards the sun, so I am sure
you will easily cross over to Lanka if you try. We are all counting on you, so
please don't ignore my request.'

As Jambavan spoke, Hanuman realized his true potential, and to the
delight of the Vanaras, began to increase his size to enormous proportions.
He climbed to the top of Mount Mahendra,[66] and standing on a grassy patch,
joined his hands in supplication to the Devas. He sought the blessings of his
guru Surya, the celestial king Indra, and his father Vayu, praying fervently
to the five elements[67] for their favour. Then inhaling deeply, he shook his
locks, lashed his tail and pressed his feet to the ground with his knees bent;
his massive head and shoulders stretched forward. In moments, the great
Hanuman sprang forth, hurtling through the air with the force of a comet.

[65] The Epilogue contains the full story about how Hanuman forgot his powers.

[66] Perhaps Gandhamadana Mountain near Rameswaram today. See Bala, Saroj, *Ramayan Retold with Scientific Evidences* (Prabhat Prakashan, 2019).

[67] Panchabhoota or five elements: 1. Prithvi—earth 2. Varuna—water 3. Agni—fire 4. Vayu—air and 5. Akash—space.

The mighty mountain shook violently, denuding the trees of their leaves and flowers as if to shower him with good wishes for the journey. The enormous pressure exerted on the earth when he lifted off forced metal ores to ooze out in coloured streams down the mountainside. Giant serpents emerged hissing from their holes with their hoods fanned out like flags. They struck at huge boulders, sending them crashing down into the sea, generating colossal waves. Gandharvas, merrymaking on the mountain, hastily dropped their golden goblets of wine and left hurriedly, as did the sages, in wonderment of his enterprise.

BOOK 5

The Golden Kingdom

Chapter 19

The Giant Leap

Hanuman flew at great speed, his immense body casting an enormous shadow on the salty sea below. As he coursed determinedly through the air like a gigantic ship propelled by the wind, the mighty ocean noticed him. Wishing to be helpful to Rama's envoy, Varuna pushed Mount Mainaka from the seabed to rise above the water to provide a rest stop. Hanuman was flying at high speed, so he hit the annoying obstruction with considerable impact, forcing the mountain to topple to one side. Then, to his surprise, it took a human form and spoke. 'Halt, most noble one among Vanaras! I did not intend to impede your journey, so do not be vexed at me. You are on an arduous quest, and I would like to offer you the opportunity to relax on my summit, so you can catch your breath before you continue. The ocean is indebted to the great Ikshavaku king Sagara,[1] and since you are on a mission for his descendant Rama, he would like to show his gratitude by being of service to you in your undertaking. Whereas dharma dictates that even an ordinary guest deserves to be treated with honour, as the eminent Wind Deva's son, you are worthy of the highest reverence. So, rest a while and enjoy the bounty of delectable fruits I have to offer.[2] You may not know this, but I am beholden to your father, Vayu. He did me a favour in the distant past, and it would give me great pleasure to be of assistance to his son.'

Hanuman appreciated the offer but politely declined, saying, 'Thank you for your concern, but I am on an important errand with no time to spare. I hope you will not take offence at my refusal to tarry, but I must reach

---

[1] This is a reference to the story of Sagara whose sons dug the Earth and extended the ocean.

[2] Mainaka represents comfort and material temptation, which challenge one's spiritual journey.

the other side before sunset. Even though I have not availed of your kind hospitality, please consider your debt repaid by your graciousness.' Saying this, he gently patted the mountain to show his gratitude and flew on.

A little further, Hanuman faced a second hurdle in his path when a frightening serpentine sea monster called Surasa posed a challenge. Towering above the waves, she blocked his passage, opening her massive jaws lined with menacing fangs. Then, threatening Hanuman, she said, 'It appears you have been sent here by providence to satisfy my hunger, so I order you into my mouth.' Hanuman told her about his important assignment, narrating the story of Sita's abduction. He promised with folded hands that he would allow her to eat him after he had reunited Rama and Sita, but the monster summarily rejected his request. She roared in annoyance, 'No one can escape me. I have a boon from Brahma, by which you can only continue on your way if you escape after entering my mouth.'[3] Hanuman thought quickly and devised a clever plan to outsmart her. First, he expanded himself, and seeing this, Surasa correspondingly stretched her jaws wider and wider. Then in a flash, he reduced himself to the minuscule size of a thumb and flew dexterously in and out of her mouth in a trice before she could shut it. Getting the better of Surasa, he declared in triumph, 'I entered your mouth, fulfilling the terms you stipulated, so you must allow me to go on my way.' Surasa was impressed with Hanuman's intelligence and blessed him with success. She revealed that she was the mother of the Nagas, sent by the Devas to test him in the form of a monster. The Devas were invested in Hanuman's victory and cheered his ingenuity. They were sure that one with such strong determination, quick thinking, clear judgement and artfulness could not fail in any job he set out to achieve.

As he neared Lanka, a third obstacle, unlike the other two but decidedly hostile in intent, waylaid Hanuman. A humungous Rakshasi called Simhika emerged from the ocean and grasped his shadow. Hanuman felt strangely powerless, like a boat facing a headwind in a storm, when he suddenly remembered Sugriva's description of a demoness, who trapped her victims by catching their shadow.[4] He was sure that this awful creature he had encountered was that same wicked female, and realized she was neither a

---

[3] Surasa is symbolic of the impediments that must be overcome with the intellect. They are threats to spiritual progress that are conquered with perseverance.

[4] Simhika represents the demons within that impede spiritual progress, like ego, envy and fear. These dangerous monsters must be destroyed to achieve success.

benefactor like Mainaka, who offered him support, nor a well-wisher like Surasa, who was merely testing him. As Simhika opened her cavernous mouth to consume him, Hanuman was able to look down her gullet; being intelligent and resourceful, he acted expeditiously. First, contracting his body to make it as hard as a diamond, he dove into her mouth. Then, using his sharp nails, he burst out of her belly, killing her instantly. The Devas, who were observing Hanuman's journey, could not help admiring his keen intelligence. He had successfully reasoned with Mainaka, cleverly outwitted Surasa and valiantly destroyed Simhika, so they showered him with abundant blessings.

Hanuman arrived on the island, landing on a mountain range that rose high into the sky, covered in thick forests, with rivers rushing into the ocean. He alighted on a peak called Lambashikara, abundant in coconut palms and fruit trees. Despite the considerable difficulties he had encountered along the way, surprisingly, he was not fatigued and remained intently focused on the task ahead. Hanuman immediately resumed his normal size to avoid drawing attention to himself, and carefully surveyed his surroundings from various aspects. Lanka appeared in the distance, high on a plateau amidst three peaks called Trikuta. The beautiful city built by Vishwakarma looked like a celestial town floating in the clouds and was completely protected from intruders by massive golden ramparts. In addition, it was surrounded by a wide moat, and heavily armed Rakshasas continuously guarded its four gates. From within rose tall, white-plaster buildings that seemed to kiss the sky. He could see beautiful gardens and lakes. Flags atop long poles fluttered proudly in the wind, and below there stood grand archways made of gold and adorned by creepers. Lanka presented an awe-inspiring sight, and as Hanuman neared the northern gates, he grew concerned. Looking at the high level of security, it seemed that even the wind would not be able to get past undetected. He could not help wondering how Rama and the Vanaras would breach the formidable fortifications, even if they accomplished the difficult task of crossing the vast ocean. The city looked so impregnable that Hanuman doubted it could be overpowered even by the mighty Devas.

Analyzing the four strategies[5] available to deal with an enemy, Hanuman began to feel increasingly dispirited, as it seemed none of them would be a viable option. He was sure that trying to negotiate using gentle persuasion or

---

[5] Four 'upayas'—approaches available to resolve a problem:
Sama: Conciliation. The first step to resolve a problem is by peaceful negotiation/discussion.

'sama' would not work with Rakshasas, as it was contrary to their bellicose nature. Winning them over monetarily through 'dana' was also unfeasible, as it was evident they already possessed abundant wealth. Creating dissension by employing 'bheda' within such a strong force didn't seem realistic, and attack or 'danda' appeared impossible, considering Lanka's impressive defences. He also arrived at the sad realization that out of the whole Vanara army, only Sugriva, Angada, Nila and he could cross over the sea, and this thought deepened his dejection.

Then, defiantly shaking off his negativity, Hanuman forced all errant fears about failure out of his mind and decided to focus exclusively on his task of finding Sita. He pondered for a while, planning how best to go about the search without being noticed. The mission had to be carried out with surgical precision, and he could not afford for it to be bungled at this critical stage, just as it was about to fructify. After deliberating at length, Hanuman decided that it would be best to wait till sunset so he could use the cover of darkness to jump over the boundary wall. To avoid being detected, he reduced his size further to that of a small cat. Satisfied that he had made himself inconspicuous, he waited patiently for dusk.

Soon, the moon rose as if ministering to him, and Hanuman proceeded cautiously towards the city walls. However, despite his vigilance, his presence did not go unnoticed as he had hoped. A frightening female guard called Lankini appeared before him, demanding to know the purpose of his intrusion. Hanuman said he would be glad to explain his visit but first asked her to introduce herself and state why she was unnecessarily hostile to someone who had come in peace. Lankini did not take kindly to Hanuman's audacious retort and bellowed angrily, 'O forest dweller, I am the guardian spirit of Lanka, Ravana's loyal servant, and I will have you know that no one can enter this city without my permission. It is my job to intercept and kill anyone who tries to sneak in, so prepare to die.'

Hanuman was not intimidated by the threat and replied calmly, 'I have heard a lot about the great city of Lanka and am here as a tourist to see its magnificent mansions, towers, ramparts, archways, gardens and groves. Once I have satiated my eyes with its beauty, I will return from where I came;

Dana: Compensation/buying peace. Giving payment or gifts to arrive at a resolution to conflict.
Bheda: Influencing the enemy's mind/manipulation.
Danda: Punishment/war. The final recourse when the first three fail.

so good lady, kindly let me pass.' Lankini was suspicious of his intentions and struck Hanuman with an open palm, sending him reeling, but he retaliated before she could inflict a second blow. Making his left[6] fist into a ball, he promptly struck her back, knocking her to the ground. As Lankini pleaded for her life, Hanuman spoke kindly, assuring her of clemency because she was a woman, and asked her once more to allow him entry to the city. This time she conceded, trembling, and spoke of Brahma's prophecy, which foretold that the day a Vanara defeated her, the destruction of Lanka was imminent. Then, with these prescient words, she hurriedly departed, giving Hanuman free access to enter.

Hanuman wisely avoided the heavily protected main gates. Instead, he jumped over the boundary wall, entering the city with his left foot forward, as this augured ill fortune for the place into which he stepped. He then climbed up a rampart, taking in the wondrous sights around him. It was night, but the city was well illuminated with blazing lamps that hung in golden archways. The weather was pleasant, cooled by a gentle ocean breeze. Wide, symmetrically laid-out roads stretched before him, with rows of seven- and eight-storeyed mansions of eclectic architecture. They were splendidly supported by golden pillars and flaunted pretty latticework windows studded with gems. As he leaped from one building to another, Hanuman noticed the extravagant doors of gold and floors of crystal inlaid with precious stones. The city was one of unparalleled beauty; it reminded him of a bejewelled woman and exuded luxury like nothing he had ever seen before.

The town was alive with all sorts of sounds. Hanuman could hear peals of laughter, the tinkling of anklets from the footfall of women climbing staircases and the melody of sacred Vedic chants emanating from the houses. He saw warriors slapping their biceps in an open ground as they wrestled, practising martial arts. The inhabitants who thronged the city centre were a diverse lot. Soldiers were stationed strategically on the streets, and spies mingled in the crowd, keeping an eye on everyone. Amidst the motley crew, some appeared to be warriors carrying weapons like clubs, spears, bows, slingshots and swords. Householders dressed in expensive garments, adorned with garlands, smeared with sandalwood paste and heavily ornamented with jewels, were seen alongside ascetics clad in bark robes with matted hair or tonsured heads. The inhabitants were of all kinds: some were malformed

---

[6] Hanuman used his left fist to avoid excessive force since Lankini was a woman, and he did not want to kill her.

with one eye, a single ear or disfigured mouths; there were tall ones and short ones, fat ones with hanging breasts and protruding stomachs and lean ones with chiseled bodies; there were those who were grotesque in appearance and others who were handsome and radiant. Leaving the city centre, Hanuman proceeded to the central garrison, which had a hundred thousand warriors protecting the royal enclave. He entered the golden portal high on the mountain that housed the nobility, with their horses and chariots, vehicles and vimanas, gentle peacocks and massive four-tusked elephants.

The full moon shone brightly in the sky, bathing the open terraces of the grand mansions in a muted glow. It illuminated the women seated on their lovers' laps, enjoying its soft radiance, and looked like a beautiful silvery-white swan swimming in a vast lake. In the courtyards of wealthy Rakshasas, there were men on horses and chariots; several were under the influence of alcohol, shoving each other and swearing as they quarrelled. Hanuman observed many beautiful women decked in jewellery in the inner quarters. Some were adorning themselves and applying perfumed creams; some rested on silken beds, and some lay in the arms of their husbands. There were those who were giggling and others who were sighing in irritation, but none amongst them matched the description of the delicate daughter of Janaka. The delightful sound of musical instruments filled the air. The melody of the lute and the beat of the mridangam were interrupted only by the blowing of the conch shell, as it was a full moon night, and the Rakshasas were duly conducting their worship.

Hanuman went from one house to another, creeping surreptitiously across gardens and walls, his diminutive size making him quite unnoticeable. He explored the lavish residences of Ravana's military commander Prahasta, his brothers Kumbhakarna and Vibhishana, as well as those of his sons and trusted advisers, before finally arriving at the mighty king's extensive private complex. Fearsome sentries stood guard over a collection of buildings, but Hanuman entered covertly without drawing attention to himself. The sweet fragrance of sandalwood filled the air, and flocks of peacocks flitted about peacefully. Housed in a giant hangar was the famous Pushpaka Vimana, as huge as a house, the magnificent aircraft exquisitely constructed by Vishwakarma. It had been gifted to Kubera by Brahma in recognition of his penance, and was adorned with a beautiful image of Devi Lakshmi, seated on a lotus, worshipped by two elephants with their trunks raised in homage. It could travel anywhere on command and was furnished with comfortable seating for long distances, a spectacular golden staircase to the upper deck and jewelled platforms. Every inch of it was elaborately decorated, replete with intricate carvings of birds, horses and serpents made of lapis lazuli, silver and coral. It had grand murals of forests and water pools, gold latticed windows and jewelled pillars with motifs of wolves. A plush carpet embellished with images of mountains, rivers and other topographical details mapping the Earth covered the floor. Hanuman stood spellbound, gazing in wonderment at the incredible beauty he beheld. Then, jolting himself back to reality, he leaped out, downhearted at not having come across Sita so far.

Ravana's spacious home stood grandiosely in the middle of the palace grounds, surrounded by an extensive network of smaller lodgings that housed his countless queens. It was the most striking among all the mansions and occupied an area half a yojana wide and one yojana long. Ferocious-looking armed guards patrolled outside, mounted on massive elephants with two, three and four tusks.[7] In addition, there were horsemen, chariots and an army unit stationed for extra protection. Inside, long corridors led to multiple chambers, each for a specific purpose. All opulently furnished, there were halls for sporting goods, bows, weapons, musical instruments, dining rooms, art galleries, day chambers and even spaces for amorous dalliances. Hanuman carefully searched as he passed the gem-studded pillars and golden staircases, the long rows of cushioned seats, the giant silver and ivory statues, the enormous jewel-encrusted gold vessels, the rich tapestries and the ornate gold windows inlaid with crystal. Gold was ubiquitous in Lanka, and Hanuman saw an ostentatious display of wealth everywhere he looked. Overflowing with these splendorous riches, Ravana's palace far surpassed Indra's acclaimed abode in its grandeur.

It was well past midnight when Hanuman entered the royal bedchamber. There lay sleeping hundreds of beautifully adorned women of every complexion from all over the world. They were the young daughters of kings, sages, Brahmins, Gandharvas and Rakshasas, whom Ravana had forcibly carried off as trophies. Hanuman saw them lying wasted on the floor wherever they could find a spot. After a night of drinking and cavorting, they resembled beautiful lotuses that had closed their petals at the end of the day, the excesses of their revelry plainly displayed in their disarrayed clothing, askew garlands, smudged tilaks and scattered jewellery. They looked dissolute in various stages of undress, obscenely entwined with one another, their limbs interlocked like a garland or carelessly draped over a companion. Some had

---

[7] Could be a reference to the now extinct Gomphothere. (Nilesh Oak)

even drifted into slumber while playing music, still clutching a drum, flute or string instrument, as if embracing a lover. Hanuman scrutinized them carefully, concluding that they looked contented to be co-wives despite the violence of their arrival there, and none resembled Sita. Surrounded by his many consorts, Ravana looked like the moon in the sky amidst a multitude of twinkling stars. The debauchery of the scene made Hanuman shrink in revulsion, but steadying himself, he stepped into the Lord of Lanka's private bedroom.

It was illuminated with the soft glow of four golden lamps, and the indomitable king was sound asleep. He lay spread-eagled with his massive arms outstretched and his palms with long, shapely fingers open. His high bed was on a dais made of crystal, decorated with gold, ivory and jewels, and upholstered with sheep's hide and luxurious fabrics. The royal white canopy with ropes of flower garlands was hung reverently overhead. His broad chest was smeared with red sandal paste, and its fragrance wafted through the room laced with the scent of the alcohol he had consumed. A delicate white silk garment was tied loosely to his waist, and a gold-threaded yellow silk cloth was draped around his upper body. Ravana looked majestic as he slept, adorned with a thick gold necklace with pearls and heavy earrings. Hanuman watched him lying satiated, sleeping peacefully after a night of heady passion, his breath hissing like a snake as he exhaled loudly. He looked invincible, like a great bull elephant in rut, whose supremacy all creatures in the forest accept without question. Hanuman climbed the steps of the platform to observe Ravana more closely. A sizeable gold crown lay to one side, and armlets adorned his muscular biceps. Deep scars on his chest were reminiscent of his battle with Indra, where Airavata had gored him. His brawny shoulders had the telltale marks of Indra's Vajra, and he looked imposing like a mountain even in repose.

Then suddenly, Hanuman noticed a couch apart from the others, and on it was a woman of exceptional beauty, who obviously enjoyed a special status. Hanuman was overjoyed! Her golden complexion and breathtaking features matched the description of Sita, and he was sure he had found her at long last. He could not contain himself; in jubilation, he kissed his tail and clambered up and down the pillars in simian delight. However, Hanuman's excitement was fleeting; while the woman shared a likeness to his mental image of Sita, he felt disconcerted by her tranquillity. There was no sign of distress on her face, and he slapped his forehead in admonishment for jumping to conclusions so impulsively. Hanuman realized that he had only noticed the superficial similarity of her appearance to Sita in his haste, without paying attention to her character. A chaste woman would not be merrymaking and sleeping so peacefully in the company of another man, so undoubtedly, this lady had to be one of Ravana's wives. Hanuman was right; the lovely woman was Mandodari, Ravana's chief queen.

The act of spying surreptitiously on Ravana's women in such flagrant positions made Hanuman feel discomfited. He asked himself if it was appropriate for him to be there, invading the privacy of the ladies. Then weighing his actions and rationalizing his presence in their private chambers, he concluded that righteous and unrighteous acts are differentiated by intention. Hanuman's reconnaissance mission was focused on finding a woman, so he had no choice but to search amongst members of the same gender, and though they appeared titillating in their half-nakedness, he had not cast a single impure glance at any one of them. His mind was firmly established in dharma,[8] fixed solely on doing his duty of finding Sita.

Leaving the bedchamber, Hanuman continued his search and found himself in a large banquet hall decorated with flower garlands. He saw the remnants of an elaborate feast in gold, silver and crystal vessels. There was a lavish spread of various roasted meats—venison, pork, goat, rabbit, wild buffalo, peacock, porcupine and fish—marinated in curds and well-seasoned with spices, accompanied by different chutneys. He noticed that some dishes were hardly touched. Large pitchers contained various beverages, and there were partly consumed jars of the best wines fermented from sugarcane and fruit juice.

By now, Hanuman was growing increasingly despondent. He had combed every inch of Lanka, searching mansions, bed chambers, gardens, streets, crossroads, galleries, halls, basements and even the Pushpaka Vimana, but had no luck finding Sita anywhere. Disappointment filled his mind with dark thoughts. Perhaps she was dead; maybe she had drowned while trying to escape from Ravana's clutches or been killed by his jealous wives. It was conceivable that she could have met her end protecting her chastity or perhaps had just perished in the terror of her horrible ordeal.

---

[8] The dharma of an action is determined by the intention with which it is done. In this case, Hanuman was performing a selfless duty with his presence in the bedchamber, so despite viewing naked women, his action was pure. 'The mind is chiefly spoken of as two kinds: pure and impure. The impure mind is that which is possessed of desire, and the pure is that which is devoid of desire.' Amrita Bindu Upanishad 1

Hanuman struggled with how he would break the awful news to Rama. His thoughts ran wild as his imagination conjured up the cascading chain of events that his failure would set off. He was sure Rama would die of sorrow on learning that he had lost his beloved wife forever. If he died, Lakshmana would follow out of devotion; and hearing about his brothers, Bharata would give up his life, and so would Shatrughana. Their mothers would surely die of grief without their sons. Sugriva, too, would kill himself in the shame of not keeping his word, and Tara, Ruma and Angada would follow. Given this, he decided that returning to Kishkindha would have dreadful consequences, so it seemed best not to go back and instead give up his life in Lanka.

However, as Hanuman wrestled with himself, he ultimately abandoned the idea of committing suicide since it was essentially a cowardly act,[9] and instead toyed with the more honourable plan of renouncing worldly life, retiring to the forest as a hermit. If he did not convey the bad news, at least Rama would live in hope. Plagued by a kaleidoscope of crazy thoughts, Hanuman argued back and forth with himself about his next move. After much internal debate, he finally decided that the right action would be to overcome his downheartedness and continue looking for Sita. Considering suicide or renunciation in this instance was irresponsible, as his team had entrusted him with a task, and escaping from it would amount to dereliction of duty. Hanuman correctly reasoned that success could only be achieved through perseverance, no matter the obstacles in his path. So, clearing his head, he composed himself and vowed either to find Sita or avenge her death by killing Ravana.

---

[9] Giving up the body as an escape from duty was considered a sinful act, not comparable with enlightened beings casting off their bodies because their life's work was done.

Chapter 20

The Ashoka Garden

Hanuman recalled that Sampati was confident about sighting Sita in Lanka, so he stepped outside, saying a fervent prayer for her to reveal herself. Adjoining the palace was a large grove of ashoka trees surrounded by a wall. He did not remember exploring this part of the city, so with renewed hope, he shot inside as quickly as an arrow. Jumping from branch to branch, shedding flowers and leaves in the process, he finally scrambled up a simsapa[1] tree with a large canopy and concealed himself in its thick foliage. It was just before dawn, and though it was still dark, the full moon was shining brightly, illuminating the beautiful garden around him. Looking around in admiration, Hanuman mused that this would be a perfect spot for Sita to perform her spiritual devotions as she loved nature so much, and he felt sure she would come there. The trees were in riotous colour, thick with blossoms, and many drooped down heavily laden with a bounty of fruit. Peacocks flitted about, and deer roamed peacefully. The lotus-covered ponds were a haven for flocks of noisy birds enjoying the placid waters. Besides the natural water bodies, there was an oblong-shaped artificial pool[2] with steps descending into it, surrounded by umbrellas and seats. There was a hill at one end, by which ran a clear stream that flowed away and then suddenly curved back, like a woman reconciling with her lover after a quarrel. A short distance from where Hanuman sat, he saw a tall white temple with a thousand pillars, steps of coral and platforms of gold on an elevated area.

A gentle scent-laden breeze blew as Hanuman surveyed his pleasant surroundings. Suddenly, his eyes fell on a young woman sitting cross-legged

---

[1] *Dalbergia sissoo*. A type of rosewood tree. Also called shisham.

[2] Artificial pools/baths also feature in the excavated sites of the Indus-Saraswati region.

on the bare ground like an ascetic under a tree. A group of grotesque-looking female guards surrounded her. One had a single ear; another had a mouth shaped like a conch; a third had a misshapen nose; some had bright red hair; some were bald, and others were as large as pillars with big bellies and hanging breasts. The woman was as lovely as Lakshmi to behold but looked tired and emaciated like a crescent moon. She wore a single soiled yellow garment, grimy with dust, and her pretty face lacked lustre, like a bright fire enveloped in smoke. From her unkempt state and lack of ornamentation, it was clear that she had not paid any attention to her appearance. Her thick hair fell in a single braid to her knees like a black serpent, and her large eyes, brimming with tears, had dark circles below. She presented such a bleak picture of hopelessness that Hanuman felt sure she was Sita. From her wistful expression, she appeared to be immersed in thought, sighing repeatedly; it was quite apparent that some deep sorrow dimmed her beauty.

Hanuman noticed that the pretty lady was a perfect match for Rama; also, she bore a strong resemblance to the woman he had fleetingly seen as she was being abducted. She and Rama were about the same age. Like him, she had a gentleness about her, and similarly, in the way she carried herself, the same refined bearing. Hanuman noticed that the ornaments thrown down on Rishyamukha corresponded to the ones missing on her person and that the cloth they had been tied in matched her garment. More significantly, unlike the other women he had seen in Lanka, she had a woebegone look that indicated a profound tragedy afflicted her. After careful analysis, Hanuman concluded that he had finally found Sita. This time he was sure he was not mistaken, as he had reached his verdict through a process of logical reasoning, evaluating all the evidence before him. Sita resembled a wilted lotus,[3] and for the first time, Hanuman was able to appreciate the intensity of pain that Rama was going through, separated from such a lovely woman. Seeing her pitiable condition, Hanuman was overwhelmed with emotion, simultaneously shedding tears of sorrow at her misery and tears of joy at having found her alive.

The morning was heralded by the sound of Vedic chants[4] emanating from the houses of Brahmin Rakshasas in the city. Ravana was awoken with music as panegyrists sang praises of his glory. As soon as he opened his eyes, Sita was the first thought on his mind, and overcome by desire, he dressed

---

[3] The lotus is sacred, a Vedic symbol of purity and prosperity.

[4] The inhabitants of Lanka followed the Vedic culture.

quickly to make his way to her. A bevy of a hundred adoring belles followed in procession, still sleepy and hungover from the previous night. One of them held the royal umbrella, while others reverently fanned him. They carried lamps, pitchers and rolled-up mats, sprinkling scented water in his path. Hanuman heard their anklets tinkling and jumped onto a lower branch to get a better view as he watched secretly from his leafy hideout.

As Ravana strode pompously before Sita, she shuddered and wept, sitting on the ground with her head buried between her knees. She had drawn them up to her belly to shield her body from view, holding her arms tightly around them. Her tearful face looked like the full moon shaded by an eclipse.[5] No woman had spurned Ravana before, so though Sita shrank from him, he was not dissuaded from trying to seduce her. Speaking gently, he cajoled, 'Why do you hide your pretty face and shy away from me, beloved lady? I am besotted by you, so there is no reason to be afraid of me. I abducted you out of an uncontrollable desire to possess you, not to do you any harm. Although custom permits a Rakshasa to take a woman he desires by force, I have been chivalrous, and do not intend to touch you without your consent. Lovely one, it is foolish to lie in the dirt like this in soiled clothes, marring your beauty by brooding and fasting. I cannot take my eyes off you because you are as gorgeous as a sparkling gem, every part of you exquisitely fashioned by the creator. O lady of broad hips,[6] accept my love and you will lead a royal life of comfort and luxury, dressed in costly attire and decked in precious jewels as you deserve.

'Dearest one with a beautiful smile and pearly teeth, you have stolen my heart! Even bedraggled, you look so ravishing that my mind is fixed on you to the exclusion of my stylish wives. Remember, youth and beauty are fleeting, so enjoy yourself while you can. All I ask is for your affection; I will even give you the honour of being my chief queen, and all my other consorts will serve you as underlings. Be favourably disposed to me, and along with you, your entire family will be honoured. I am prepared to conquer the whole world and offer it to your father as a token of my affection for you. My valour is unequalled in all three worlds. I am sure you know that the mighty Devas

---

[5] Valmiki inserts this reference to a lunar eclipse that occurred on 12 September 5076 BCE, which was visible from Sri Lanka according to sky data fed into Planetarium Software. This matches the Ramayana timeline. See Bala, Saroj, *Ramayan Retold with Scientific Evidences* (Prabhat Prakashan, 2019).

[6] Wide hips were a sign of beauty.

were forced to grovel before me. Forget Rama! He is a hermit living in the forest in tattered clothes, with nothing to offer you. He pales compared to me on all counts, be it wealth, prowess or even spiritual merit. Moreover, he may not be alive; even if he is, Lanka is inaccessible, and he will never be able to come near you again.'

Steadfast in her love for Rama, Sita cringed at Ravana's words. Picking up a blade of grass, she placed it symbolically before her like a curtain to distance herself from him. Suppressing the dread she felt within, Sita bravely rejected Ravana's imperious demands, retorting, 'Do not waste your time and effort trying to win me over. It is pointless; I am a virtuous woman and will always remain devoted to my husband. It would be best to lavish your attention on your own wives instead of trying to seduce one who is married to someone else. As a king, it is your dharma to protect all women,[7] including the wives of others. Show consideration and empathy; correct the wrong you are doing, as the wicked actions you have committed will cause your people to suffer on your account. It is perverted to steal another man's wife from him, but it appears you have no one in Lanka to counsel you appropriately. You have committed a grave offence[8] by abducting me, which will undoubtedly result in your downfall and that of your kingdom.

'Just as the sun and its rays cannot be separated, I can never be divorced from Rama. You cannot tempt me with anything—not wealth, praise, power or comforts. Having laid my head on Rama's shoulder, I cannot look at another. I am his wife and his alone! It is not too late to atone for your immoral actions by asking my noble husband for his forgiveness. Although Rama never rejects anyone who seeks his favour, be warned he also does not hesitate to punish those who violate dharma. Indra's vajra may fail to meet its mark, and it may even be possible to escape Yama's noose of death, but Rama's arrow is inescapable. You gloat about being all-powerful, but you cannot defeat Rama and Lakshmana any more than a dog pitted against a pair of tigers. You carried me away in a cowardly fashion like a thief, but I am

---

[7] A king, being a Kshatriya, was regarded as a protector. 'The king has been created to be the protector . . .' Manusmriti 7.35

[8] A good king was expected to have self-control. 'Day and night, he must strenuously exert himself to conquer his senses; for he alone who has conquered his senses, can keep his subjects in order.' Manusmriti 7.44

confident my husband will rescue me like Vishnu saved Bhudevi[9] with his three strides, and you will face his wrath no matter where you try to hide.'

Ravana turned red with rage.[10] His power and majesty had ultimately enticed every woman he had abducted, and he was not used to being rebuffed. He replied harshly, 'I have won over all the women I have wooed, but you snub me despite the ardent love I shower on you. It is a truism that the gentler one is with a woman, the more obdurate she becomes. I have offered you the world, yet you continue to reject me. O princess of Mithila, your insolence would normally be punishable by death! You are alive today only because I have a weakness for you, but I must warn you that my patience is running out. You have two months to come willingly to my bed. If you do not do so in that time, I will ask my cooks to chop you up and serve you to me for breakfast.'

While the other women present trembled, Sita's fear turned to anger, and her eyes flashed as she spoke. 'Is there no one in Lanka who has your welfare at heart? Nobody to tell you what is right and deter you from sinful actions? I suppose even if there were such a person, you would not pay any heed to him. Once again, let me remind you of Rama's valour. He has the strength of an elephant, while in comparison, you are puny like a hare. You only stand here boasting because you have not yet confronted him. If you had even one-quarter of the courage you brag about, you would have invited Rama to battle with you in Janasthana rather than deceitfully luring him away. I do not know how your wicked eyes have not fallen out of their sockets after laying them so indecently on me, or how your tongue still wags after you use it to utter such sleazy proposals to the daughter-in-law of Dasharatha. I have not cursed you to turn into ashes only because anger goes against my asceticism,[11] and I prefer to leave it to Rama to punish you with his arrows.'

Ravana's temper knew no bounds, and he erupted in rage. The veins in his neck bulged as he thundered, 'Foolish woman! Since you are determined to cling to an impoverished man against all good judgement, I might as well kill you today.' As he advanced menacingly toward Sita, Ravana's junior wife Dhanyamalini restrained him. Holding onto his arm, she pulled him away,

---

[9] Mother Earth.

[10] Ravana was well versed in the shastras, so he understood that he was on the wrong side of dharma. Yet, he was so deluded by ego that he could not help himself, and driven by desire, knowingly does the wrong thing.

[11] Anger results in demerit.

pleading, 'Don't waste your time with this wretched woman who spurns your affections. She is not worthy of you, and there is no pleasure in being with someone unwilling. Come with me instead and delight in the company of one for whom you are the whole world.' Ravana stormed out of the garden like a dark rain cloud dispelled by a gust of wind, pausing only to order the guards, 'Use all four prescribed strategies[12] to bring her under control, so she yields to me. First, try reasoning with her by appealing to her intellect; impress upon her that it is in her best interest to forget Rama and agree to share my bed. If that does not work, tempt her with expensive gifts. My ministers will put any amount of wealth at your disposal for this purpose. Even employ deception if necessary, and finally, in case she continues to be recalcitrant, punish her into submission. Work on her mind to wear down her resistance by alternating between being kind and harsh if you need to, but somehow rid her of her loyalty to Rama.'

Once Ravana was gone, the dour-faced guards gathered around Sita. They had been commanded to do a job and lost no time getting started. First, Ekjata tried to persuade her to relent by singing Ravana's glory. She spoke about his father Vishrava's distinguished ancestry, traced to Brahma, and his immense knowledge, equal to ten heads. Next, she praised Ravana's valour, extolling his conquests over the Devas, Nagas, Gandharvas and other Rakshasas, insisting on how beneficial it would be for Sita to agree to his proposal. Then Harijata, glowering with her cat-like eyes, talked about the great honour of being wedded to the most powerful person in the world. Besides, if Sita accepted Ravana, she would replace Mandodari as his head queen. Ravana was even ready to forsake all his wives for her company, and Sita would enjoy a prosperous life.

Vinata, the one with a big belly and protruding teeth, railed belligerently, rebuking Sita for rejecting her master's advances and directing her to transfer the love she had for Rama to Ravana, while another called Durmukhi shook her fist, threatening Sita with death if she refused to accept their ultimatum. The women kept repeating how lucky Sita was to be desired by their great king. They used every means of encouragement, alternating between gentle coaxing and severe threats as they implored her to forget Rama, but Sita did not waver.

----

[12] Sama—Dana—Bheda—Danda, the four possibilities that Hanuman had contemplated earlier.

She replied firmly, 'I am dismayed by your repugnant advice that directs a married woman to be unfaithful and abandon her husband for the greed of power and riches. I would not touch Ravana with my left foot, let alone marry him. Nothing in the world, not even your threats of death, can distance me from Rama. Walking in the footsteps of other faithful wives before me, I am steadfastly devoted to my husband, just as Sachi is to Indra, Arundhati to Vasishta, Rohini to Chandra, Lopamudra to Agastya, Savitri to Satyavan, Sukanya to Sage Chavana, Srimati to Kapila, Madayanti to King Saudasa, Keshini to King Sagara, and as Damayanti was to Nala.'

The women were angry at their failure, and Hanuman watched from his perch as they put persuasion aside and adopted a more macabre stance, threatening dire consequences if Sita refused to change her mind. Vikata, the one with pendulous breasts, said viciously, 'You don't deserve our king. We have indulged you thus far, but if you persist in your disobedience, I will not hesitate to pluck out your heart and eat it.' The hideous Chandodari brandished a huge spear, shouting chillingly, 'I will disembowel you and feast on your liver, and when I'm done, I will devour you, head and all.' Hearing her, Praghasa licked her lips in anticipation, saying, 'You are a heartless woman; I can't wait to squeeze your neck. Once we tell the king you are dead, he will let us eat you anyway.' Ajamukhi cheered at the gruesome plan and proposed dividing Sita's body equally to avoid discord. Surpanakha declared that all sorrows are drowned in wine, observing that it had been a while since they had eaten human flesh. She made the grisly suggestion that they bring drinks and dance before their Goddess Nikumbhila, who would be pleased with their sacrificial offering.

Sita found the torment unbearable and ran to the simsapa tree where Hanuman was hiding. Drawing deep breaths and sobbing loudly, she said, 'Even if you kill and eat me, I will never agree to marry your villainous king.' Then, holding onto a bough to support her unsteady legs, she continued wailing, 'O Rama, O Lakshmana, O Mother Kaushalya, the painful separation from my husband and the relentless harassment by these ghastly women is becoming more than I can endure. I feel like a boat[13] that has capsized in the sea. Although I have no wish to remain alive anymore, I have no choice, as death does not come to anyone before it is time. I must have committed a grievous sin in my previous life, for which my karma is

---

[13] The boat analogy is often used, indicating that India's maritime past dated back many millennia.

making me suffer today. Rama, why haven't you come for me? Surely you still care for your unfortunate wife. I know this island is remote, but you are invincible; nothing can stop you, and your arrows know no boundaries. I can only surmise that you do not know where I am, or you would have arrived here by now, and Lanka would have been reduced to ashes already. I pray that you and Lakshmana are safe and well. Ravana will put me to death very soon, and I fear I may not see you till we meet in heaven. Death is preferable to living without you, considering the hopeless circumstances. Blessed are those saintly ones who have risen above their experiences of joy and sorrow, enduring the vagaries of life with equanimity. Unfortunately, I am an ordinary human being without that kind of mental strength, so I feel I must end my life to be free from Ravana's wicked clutches. O Rama, I want you to know that even if you fail to rescue me and I am roasted in a fire or hacked to pieces, I remained true to you to the very end.'

Almost all the women who guarded Sita were obnoxious and enjoyed being spiteful to her. But there was an elderly one amongst them called Trijata, who was motherly and compassionate. Trijata had been asleep while Sita was being taunted and awoke to hear her lamentations. As a senior guard, she used her authority to admonish the others for their behaviour. 'Begone from here immediately! Eat each other if you must, but do not dare harm Sita. I just had a dream that does not auger well for Lanka.

'As you know, it is believed that early morning dreams are prophetic, so heed the words I speak.[14] First, I saw Sita reunited with Rama; he came here with Lakshmana, flying through the sky on an ivory palanquin. They picked her up as she stood on a mountain peak surrounded by the sea. Then I saw all three of them clad auspiciously in shining white garments, triumphantly seated on the back of a four-tusked elephant. After that, I saw them in the Pushpaka Vimana heading towards the north. Simultaneously, I saw inauspicious images of Ravana with a shaved head, smeared with oil and attired in red, indicating his fall is imminent. In yet another scene in my dream, he was dressed in black with a red garland; he was drunk and was being dragged through dung by a woman on a chariot drawn by donkeys. Finally, Ravana appeared gulping oil in a crazed state on the back of an ass

---

[14] Dreams were believed to provide a window into the future. Mentioned even in the Rig Veda 2.28.10 and 10.162.6. Chapter 7 of the Agni Purana gives details of the interpretation of various dreams.

as he sped in a southerly direction. Ultimately, I saw him fall to the ground, completely naked, uttering filthy words.

'Similarly, I saw Kumbhakarna and all of Ravana's sons with shaved heads going southwards to the land of Yama. They fell into a dung pit and vanished from sight. In my dream, Vibhishana was the only Rakshasa who appeared felicitously dressed in white, smeared with sandalwood paste and shaded by a royal umbrella, while our kingdom was annihilated and reduced to ashes. These visions are prescient of events to come. Rama will find Lanka and punish anyone who has caused Sita distress, so be careful of how you treat her, as she alone will have the power to save you from his wrath.' Shooing the guards away, Trijata warned them to beg Sita's pardon for their cruelty if they wanted forgiveness once Lanka was conquered.

Chapter 21

Hanuman Meets Sita

A bird in its nest began cooing sweetly as if to convey a favourable turn in fortune, and hearing it, Sita felt momentarily consoled. For an instant, she believed it was an indication that Rama would arrive soon before dismissing her optimism as wishful thinking. Although Trijata's intervention had drawn her tormentors away earlier in the day, giving Sita some respite, she was stricken by intense melancholy. The death sentence that Ravana had just pronounced loomed large, and she fretted that the two months' reprieve he had granted her would slip by very quickly. He would then chop her to pieces as a surgeon cuts up a dead foetus to extract it from the womb.[1]

Moreover, she was not sure if Rama was alive. If he were no more, she would never see him again, but even if he were alive, he might not be able to find her in this remote place within the short timeframe she had left to live. Thus, their reunion seemed uncertain at best, a thought that drove her to the depths of despair. She imagined that if Rama believed she was lost forever, he might return to Ayodhya at the end of fourteen years and remarry. Sita regretted her foolishness in sending him after the deer and was sincerely remorseful for her unkindness to Lakshmana. Filled with a sense of hopelessness, believing everything that had happened was her fault and that her death was imminent, Sita concluded it would not be sinful to end her life prematurely. So, she wrapped her long thick braid around her neck like a noose and proceeded to fasten it to the bough under which she was standing.

---

[1] This reference to a surgeon extracting a dead foetus shows the advanced knowledge of medicine at the time. The ancient Sanskrit text Sushruta Samhita on medicine and surgery, elaborates on the procedure to remove a dead foetus. Also remarkable is the groundbreaking method of rhinoplasty described by Sushruta, which is still practised today.

Hanuman had been watching the proceedings for hours from his vantage point in the tree as the day slowly gave way to dusk. The new development was alarming. He envisioned an awful calamity unfolding before his eyes; he had to stop Sita before it was too late but was unsure about how to do so without scaring her. There was a very narrow window of opportunity to act while the guards were away, but if he appeared suddenly in front of Sita, she would likely scream in fright and inadvertently alert them. Though Hanuman was confident about his ability to tackle the Rakshasas, he felt it was better to avoid undue risks. The outcome of an encounter is never predictable, and there is always the possibility, however slight, of getting killed. If something happened to him, who would convey the message to Rama that he had found Sita? No other Vanara could leap across the sea, so he needed to complete his job successfully. Hanuman pondered intently, in a quandary over his next step, weighing various options as he contemplated the most tactful way to present himself.

For a start, he was not sure in what language to communicate. If he addressed Sita in Sanskrit, the tongue of educated people, she might think he was Ravana disguised as a monkey. It was perhaps better to speak in the language of ordinary folk, but whatever language he chose, the problem of approaching her without causing alarm was hard to solve. Finally, after much deliberation, he had a brilliant idea: he would sing the praises of Rama very softly from his hidden perch in the tree so that only Sita could hear him. This ploy would distract her from her current endeavour by forcing her to look up; listening to the glory of her beloved husband would also put her at ease and help gain her trust. Yes, he thought, this would be the safest way to introduce himself.

Sita listened in surprise as Hanuman sang in hushed tones, 'There was once a noble Ikshavaku king called Dasharatha, known for his righteousness. His eldest son, who is as handsome as the full moon and the foremost archer in the world, is called Rama. People know him as a protector of the innocent and the destroyer of evil. Though faultless, he was forced into exile to honour his father's word and left for the Dandaka Forest with his wife, Sita, and brother, Lakshmana. There, he killed many Rakshasas and saved the rishis from persecution. One day he was spotted by Ravana's lovelorn sister, Surpanakha, and when she tried to get Sita out of the way, Lakshmana cut off her nose and ears. She complained to her cousin brothers Khara and Dushana, who attacked Rama, but they were vanquished handily. Angered by their death, Ravana used an illusory deer to trick Rama and Lakshmana into leaving Sita alone. He then carried her off to Lanka, where he thought no one would find her. Rama was heartbroken at the loss of his precious wife and walked with Lakshmana all the way from Panchavati in the west to Kishkindha in the south in search of her. There he made friends with Sugriva by helping him in his distress. Sugriva repaid Rama's favour by sending thousands of Vanaras to all parts of the globe in search of Sita. I am one of the Vanaras that went on the assignment. We were told by Jatayu's brother, Sampati, that the princess of Mithila was being held captive in Lanka, so I leaped across the sea, and now I think I am looking at the lovely lady Rama described to me.'

Sita's plan of suicide was interrupted. Thunderstruck, she glanced around incredulously, looking for the source of the melody. As she scrutinized the branches above, she saw the tiniest monkey she had ever seen camouflaged in the leaves. He was copper coloured with bright tawny eyes, dressed in a white dhoti, sitting on a branch with folded hands. Bewildered, she thought, 'Surely I must be seeing this apparition in my sleep!' and momentarily grew concerned because the Swapna Shastra[2] interpreted dreaming of a monkey as a bad omen.[3] Then, intrigued by what she had heard, Sita invoked Brihaspati, Indra, Brahma and Agni with a prayer, exclaiming, 'May this monkey's words be true and not my imagination.' Taking her words as a cue that she was receptive to him, Hanuman jumped down in front of her, and Sita realized that she was wide awake and that the monkey was real.

With his palms joined humbly above his head Hanuman said, 'Beautiful lady with eyes like lotus petals, I have been observing you, and it is obvious that you are of noble lineage. You look like a goddess, but from your plight, I have concluded that you must be Rama's wife, Sita, whom Ravana stole from Janasthana. Please confirm to me if my assessment is right.'

Sita replied, 'I am indeed Maithili, the daughter-in-law of the great king Dasharatha, daughter of the pious Janaka, the wife of the glorious Sri Rama. We lived happily in Ayodhya for twelve years after our marriage and left for the forest in the thirteenth year. His father's word meant more to Rama than the kingdom, and he accepted his exile wholeheartedly without complaint.' Sita narrated all that had happened to her thus far, informing Hanuman that she had two months before being put to death. Hanuman moved closer, telling her that he was Rama's messenger, saying how relieved he was to

---

[2] The study of dreams.

[3] Hanuman resembled a monkey more than a Vanara because he had reduced his size.

find her. He said reassuringly, 'Rama is alive and well, but his concern for you consumes him every moment. Your brother-in-law, Lakshmana, is also worried about your welfare and conveys his regards to you.'

Sita felt a surge of joy that she had not experienced for months, but suddenly it was overshadowed by distrust as Hanuman stepped toward her. She had been naïve in not seeing through Ravana's disguise when he came to her hut in the forest. She was determined not to be fooled once again. Interrogating Hanuman on his authenticity, she said, 'I cannot contain my happiness to hear you say that you are Rama's messenger, but how can I be sure that he sent you? I am wary because I was deceived by Ravana when he took the guise of a hermit, and for all I know, he may have sent you as a Vanara to dupe me again. Describe Rama to me, so I am satisfied that you are a bona fide messenger.'

Hanuman was not scant in his praise. 'Your noble husband Rama is as glorious and mighty as the sun and as gentle and delightful as the moon. He is as valiant as Vishnu and as well-spoken as Brihaspati, a man blessed with striking looks yet entirely devoid of arrogance. He never fails in his Kshatriya duty of protecting the innocent and punishing the wicked. As Rama's envoy, I would like to assure you that your sorrows are almost behind you. He will rescue you from incarceration soon, so do not be disheartened by your current circumstances anymore. Please trust me; I crossed the mighty ocean to find you and entered Lanka with my left foot to ensure Ravana's destruction. You have no reason to be suspicious of my intentions.' Hearing this, Sita felt more positively inclined towards Hanuman, but her doubts were not entirely allayed. She knew Rakshasas could take on any form and was sceptical of how a small creature like him could have crossed the vast sea.

She continued to interrogate him to assuage her mistrust. 'Tell me more; how did you meet Rama and Lakshmana? Describe their appearance to me.'

Hanuman replied, 'I am sure my description will match what you already know only too well. Rama's eyes are as beautiful as lotus petals, and his chiselled features make him as handsome as the moon. He is perfectly proportionate, standing eight feet tall, with a robust build, broad shoulders, muscular clavicles, a narrow waist, a flat stomach, strong arms, a conch-shaped neck, sparkling eyes, a resonant voice and a glowing dark brown complexion. His lips are full, his jaw is firm, his pearly teeth glisten and his nose is sharp. His chest, wrists and fists are as hard as a diamond. The corners of Rama's eyes and his nails, palms and soles are ruddy. He is long in the arms, eyebrows and scrotum. The toned muscles on his abdomen form three lines, and his body is smooth with fine hair. Your husband is handsome like a Deva, and his confident stride is akin to majestic animals like the lion, tiger, elephant and bull. He is kind and courteous to everyone, irrespective of their social status. Rama is known to handle difficulties with the forbearance of Mother Earth, never raising his voice, no matter the provocation. He is splendid like the sun and famous like Indra. Rama has a brilliant mind and is blessed with superior intelligence, comparable to the guru of the Devas. He has remarkable self-control, wisely apportioning his time between dharma, artha and kama, and everyone admires his devotion to righteousness. No one is a more skilled archer than Rama, and even his enemies, once defeated, cannot help but sing about his valour. While exceptionally skilled in warfare, he is also well trained in statecraft and respected by Vedic scholars for his extensive knowledge of the sacred shastras and their supplementary texts. Lakshmana is no less charming and resembles Rama in almost every way, except that he is fair.

'Ever since you were taken, the two brothers have been searching unceasingly for you, and their efforts finally brought them to Kishkindha, the kingdom of the Vanaras. In fact, we saw you being carried away by Ravana when you threw down a bundle of your ornaments. When we showed them to Rama, he swooned and fell, scattering the jewellery on the ground, and as I lifted him, he cried out repeatedly for you. Rama is burning in the anguish of separation and hardly sleeps. He is distraught with worry about you, and in his sorrow, looks shaken like a mountain in an earthquake. Search parties went out to the four quarters of the world to look for you. I arrived here yesterday; my name is Hanuman, the son of Vayu, and I am one of the Vanaras from the southern team. We met Jatayu's brother Sampati on the southern shore, and he told us you were in Lanka, so I leaped across the ocean to find you. Since then, I have been looking for you everywhere, and I had almost given up hope when I spotted you grieving in this garden. Please believe me when I say that I am Rama's messenger so my effort coming here is not in vain.' Then, handing Sita the ring, Hanuman continued, 'To prove my credentials to you, take this insignia that Rama asked me to give you.'

Rama's ring had a profoundly cathartic effect on Sita, and her face lit up. The mere sight of it filled her with euphoria as if she had been reunited with Rama in person. Her pallid countenance shone with fresh hope like the moon after an eclipse, and her unhappiness evaporated the instant she beheld the precious token. Any doubts she had about Hanuman were immediately obliterated, and gazing lovingly at the ring, she said, 'You are a jewel among

Vanaras! Only someone truly valorous, competent and intelligent could have accomplished the impossible feat of coming here. Not only have you crossed the ocean, which is a daunting task, but you show no fear of Ravana, so you are obviously no ordinary forest-dweller. How is my dear brother-in-law Lakshmana?[4] Tell me more about my beloved Rama; does he miss me as much as I do him? Why has he not burnt the Earth with his anger yet? I am perplexed that he has not come to my aid so far, as I had fully expected him to arrive here with Lakshmana by now. I hope his love for me has not dwindled or that he has been pushed into inaction by sorrow? Do you know when Rama plans to come and rescue me? What is his strategy? Is Bharata sending his mighty army, and is Sugriva going to assist? I know Rama loves me dearly and will not let me languish here, but he needs to come soon. I have a death sentence hanging over my head, and I may not be alive to see him if he delays much longer.'

Soothing her anxiety, Hanuman said, 'As soon as Rama hears where you are, he will bring a huge army of Vanaras to free you. His grief at being separated from you knows no bounds; he is restless, constantly consumed with thoughts of you. He barely sleeps and eats only a few fruits and tubers once a day.' Hanuman's words were bittersweet; Sita was comforted with the reassurance that Rama had not forgotten her but was also sad to hear about his state of mind. She replied anxiously, 'I have only two months to live. Vibhishana's daughter Kala mentioned that her father had advised Ravana to send me back to my husband, but he refused to listen. I do not doubt that he will kill me as he has threatened, so please tell Rama that if he does not rescue me within one month, I would rather give up my life than allow Ravana the pleasure of taking it from me.'

Seeing Sita's desperation, Hanuman offered to unite her with Rama right away. He suggested, 'I can liberate you from your misery this very moment, so you do not have to fear any delay in being saved from this unfortunate situation. Sit on my back, and I will take you across the ocean. I can return just as easily as I came here, and I assure you that no one will be able to stop me.' Looking at his diminutive size, Sita said in amusement, 'How can a tiny creature like you carry me such a long distance over the vast ocean?'

Hanuman was taken aback; no one had questioned his ability before, and he felt slightly miffed! He retreated a few steps, and using his yogic powers, expanded himself to show her that he was more than capable of carrying her.

---

[4] Sita feels Lakshmana might still be upset with her, so she asks about him first.

Sita looked at him in amazement, and though now convinced that Hanuman was indeed as powerful as his mighty father Vayu, she expressed misgivings about leaving with him. 'If I escape with you, we will be pursued by Ravana and his warriors. I might be snatched away again or fall off your back into the ocean in the attack to be devoured by sharks. I fear my deliverance from Lanka could be jeopardized if I try to make a getaway; the Rakshasas may kill me or hide me somewhere else even more difficult to find. In any case, I think Rama should recover me himself because his victory over Ravana is the only way to salvage my reputation. When I was forcibly carried away from Janasthana, my respectability was compromised. A stranger laid his hands on me, violating my sense of propriety, but I had no choice in the matter as I was a prisoner. In this case, it would be indecorous to agree to go on your back, voluntarily putting myself in intimate contact with a man who is not my husband. I hope you understand? When Rama and Lakshmana fight as a team, they are undefeatable like a fire fanned by the wind, so I am confident they will deliver me from my misery. It is my ardent plea that you bring them here at the earliest, as I see it as the only honourable means out of my terrible predicament.'

Marvelling at Sita's piety, Hanuman said, 'Your words speak of your great moral fortitude. O daughter of Janaka, the second reason you gave me is especially worthy coming from the lips of a faithful wife and consort of a great man like Rama. Only you could remain so high-minded despite your desperate circumstances. I offered to take you with me out of fidelity to Rama because it broke my heart to see you so unhappy. Also, since you expressed concern about the difficulty in reaching Lanka, I wanted to assure you that I could get you safely out of here. Please do not misunderstand my suggestion; you have great strength of character and your dedication to your husband is beyond question, so I will not insist anymore. I appreciate your point of view, so all I ask for is a token to convey to Rama as confirmation of our meeting.'

In a choked voice, savouring a memory of happier days, Sita said, 'I will tell you about a private incident that only Rama and I shared. Remind him about the crow that attacked me in Chitrakoota. One afternoon, after a dip in the river, as Rama was resting under a tree with his head on my lap, a crow swooped down and pecked my bosom, spilling a few drops of blood on him. Rama was infuriated when he saw the crow's offending beak and plucking a piece of kusha grass from his mat, infused it with the potency of the Brahmastra. The blade chased the crow, who was none other than

Jayanta, the son of Indra in disguise, and no matter where he went in the three worlds, it pursued him relentlessly. Finally, the crow collapsed at Rama's feet in repentance, at which point he was instantly forgiven.[5] However, the weapon once invoked could not be wasted, so Rama asked the crow where he should direct it, and, on his request, he took out one of his eyes instead of taking his life.'

'If Rama could use the power of the Brahmastra against a petty crow, ask him why he hesitates to use it to free me from Ravana. It is his duty to save me, both as a Kshatriya and as my husband. Rama is compassionate to everyone, so why does he not show the same consideration to me in my misfortune? He is familiar with every astra, and I fail to understand why he is reluctant to use them in this situation. I feel it is because of my bad karma that neither he nor Lakshmana is here yet.' By now, Sita was sobbing, so trying to console her, Hanuman said, 'I swear to you that they will come! Instead of despairing, be confident that the two tigers will soon rid you of your captors. Is there anything more you would like me to communicate on your behalf?'

Sita said, 'Give my salutations to Kaushalya's glorious son, who protects everyone in need. I would also like you to particularly convey to the son of Sumitra, my noble brother-in-law Lakshmana who gave up everything, including his wife, to serve his brother, that I truly commend his sacrifice. He looks upon Rama respectfully as a father and me as a mother. Although highly accomplished and blessed with every virtue, he never boasts about himself. Rama rightly loves him even more than he loves me. He is a virtuous person, pure in thought, speech and action. Now, Hanuman, everything depends on your skill as a messenger to be persuasive, so Rama sets out right away. I am in an ocean of sorrow, so although I want to live to see my husband, please emphasize to him that I do not intend to remain alive beyond a month. You would be doing me a great favour by expressing a sense of urgency that rouses Rama to take immediate action.'

From the end of her garment, she untied her chudamani,[6] a beautiful hair ornament, and handing it to Hanuman, said, 'Give Rama this hair clip; he will know it to be mine, as he saw my mother gift it to me in in the

---

[5] Forgiveness/Kshama is one of the ten principles of dharma, as stated in Manusmriti 6.92.

[6] Excavated artifacts found at Banawali (carbon dated to more than 5000 years ago) show this type of jewellery was in vogue in ancient India.

presence of my father-in-law Dasharatha on our wedding day.' Hanuman took the ornament and circled Sita three times to take his leave, promising that her sorrows would soon end. Concerned for his well-being, Sita asked him to rest before setting out, as he had been awake for two days, and added, 'I have a small doubt nagging me. How will Rama and the Vanara warriors get here, since it is challenging to cross the sea? Although I know you are competent enough to deal with the Rakshasas alone, I still feel it would be more appropriate for Rama to rescue me.'

To comfort Sita and reassure her that Rama would come for her at the earliest, Hanuman exaggerated the abilities of his fellow Vanaras, not to be deceitful in extolling them, but as an act of charity to someone who desperately needed encouragement.[7]

He said, 'Take heart; many others can make the leap. Moreover, Sugriva is very resourceful and will find a way here. He commands thousands of accomplished Vanaras, who can fly wherever they desire in the air, over water and land, unobstructed by any barrier. This battle would not be their first, and many have already travelled around the world. While several are superior to me, no one is inferior to me in the Vanara army. As you know, top-level commanders are not sent as messengers, so do not spend any more time fretting. I will bring Rama and Lakshmana here on my back if necessary. Just have patience for a short time more; you will see Vanaras arriving here in great numbers, and under Rama and Lakshmana's direction, they will be unstoppable.'

Sita was relieved and thanking Hanuman for his moral support, said, 'Be merciful to me by fulfilling your words. Please motivate Rama to come at the earliest, as I yearn for his touch. After you give him my hair clip and tell him the story of the one-eyed crow, also remind him that once when my tilaka[8] got smudged, he mischievously applied it on my cheek instead. As I mentioned, the hair clip was presented to me at my wedding, but now that I have given it to you, I have nothing left to savour that memory. Would you please explain to Rama that I am being harassed here every day and stress that he must rescue me within a month? May your return journey proceed auspiciously, and may you reach Kishkindha safely.'

---

[7] Here again, intention is considered the determining factor in judging whether an action is righteous or unrighteous.

[8] Mark on the forehead created by the application of a paste, usually of sandalwood or vermilion.

Chapter 22

Lanka Burns

It was late in the night when Hanuman left Sita's presence, mulling over the events of the last two days. He was satisfied that he had accomplished his mission of finding Sita, but there was an additional task he wanted to achieve. Competence is doing an assignment well, but excellence is overachieving the goal. Hanuman reviewed the four strategies for dealing with an enemy once again. As he had initially thought, the first three tactics still did not seem practical at this time. Rakshasas were not peace-loving by nature, so engaging in discussions was not a realistic expectation. Second, it was impossible to tempt them monetarily because Lanka abounded in wealth, and the Rakshasas were not needy. Third, there was no feasible way of infiltrating their ranks and encouraging defection. This left the fourth strategy, namely initiating war, as the only tenable option. Since conflict appeared inevitable, it was imperative to gauge the enemy's strength, so Hanuman decided to instigate a confrontation. Perhaps it would also allow him to come face to face with Ravana to know how his mind worked and anticipate his future moves better.

Hanuman thought to himself, 'If I destroy Ravana's pleasure garden, he will send his warriors to tackle me, and I will be able to estimate their ability. Besides, when I vanquish them, Ravana will get the message that my master Rama is not an ordinary adversary.' With this objective in mind, he expanded himself, and amidst deafening roars, began to break pillars, uproot trees and tear up creepers, muddying the clear water of the ponds. Once Hanuman was done creating mayhem, he stood leaning nonchalantly against the tall arched entrance to the garden. The ruckus woke up the alarmed residents of the city. The terrified guards who kept watch over Sita ran to Ravana with the news that a gigantic Vanara was on a rampage, wrecking his treasured garden. They added that it was curious that the only spot spared was the simsapa tree under which Sita was sitting; so, she knew more than she was letting on, though she refused to divulge anything. They were sure a powerful enemy had sent him: Indra, Kubera or maybe even Rama.

The breach of his kingdom's security was a blow to Ravana's ego, and he was furious. He sent a special battalion of 80,000 fierce Rakshasas of great might called Kinkaras[1] armed with iron mallets and clubs to deal with the cheeky Vanara. They confidently marched out, blissfully unaware that they were courting death like moths drawn to a flame. As they approached Hanuman, he lashed his tail and grew humungous in size, roaring, 'Victory to Rama, Lakshmana and Sugriva! I am Hanuman, the servant of Rama and the son of the wind; even thousands of Ravanas cannot stand before me in battle. Watch while I tear up hills, pluck out trees and destroy Lanka! Then I will fly back as easily as I came here.'

He pulled out an iron bar that functioned as a bolt in the archway, and wielding it menacingly, wiped out the entire Kinkara force within a very brief period. By now, Hanuman had worked himself into a fury, and spotting a grand edifice in the garden that was still standing, stomped on it and brought it down, demolishing it to rubble. A hundred giant Rakshasa guards rushed to stop the vandalism, but exulting in his success, Hanuman slapped his shoulders and cried victory to Rama once again. Then he picked up a gold-plated pillar which he whirled around with such force that it burst into flames. Hurling it at the flabbergasted guards, he shouted, 'Be warned, thousands like me will soon come here and destroy all of you and your king for making an enemy of Rama.'

Ravana was shocked that the Kinkaras had been routed and sent for Jambumali. He was the son of Prahasta, the army commander-in-chief, and had never lost a battle in his life. Jambumali's large canines gave him a ferocious appearance; he arrived with a flourish on a chariot drawn by mules, bearing a mighty bow and accompanied by a battalion of warriors. Hanuman was not intimidated by his menacing entrance and welcomed the opportunity to deal with him. Jambumali released several crescent-shaped arrows in the ensuing fight, hitting Hanuman on the forehead, which caused blood to run down his face. However, Hanuman was unmindful of his injuries, and picking up a boulder, he hurled it at his foe with considerable

---

[1] Kinkara means servant in Sanskrit, so in this case they are loyal warriors at Ravana's beck and call.

force. When Jambumali fragmented it, Hanuman plucked out a sala tree, but that was shattered, too. In exasperation, Hanuman grabbed the iron bar again and used it to pulverize Jambumali beyond recognition. The Rakshasa army ran in fear with the terrible news that their leader had met the same fate as the Kinkaras.

Ravana was now beside himself with rage and commanded the seven mighty sons of his chief minister to prevent the situation from getting out of hand. The well-trained warriors arrived on grand chariots, each boastfully vying with the other for superiority. They showered arrows on Hanuman like torrents of rain lashing a mountain, but he leaped around artfully, dodging injury as if in play. Then, he struck one of the warriors with his palm, stomped on another, used his fist on a third, and tore and killed the rest with his nails. Pleased with his handiwork, Hanuman dusted himself off and stood at the gate in anticipation of the next lot to come.

By now, Ravana realized that he was not dealing with an ordinary forest-dweller and sent for five of his powerful generals—Virupaksha, Yupaksha, Durdhara, Praghasa and Bhasakarna—who had delivered victories in previous encounters. Although he was troubled, he did not want to display his concern, so he was careful to express confidence despite suffering enormous losses. Briefing them, Ravana said, 'We do not appear to be dealing with a common Vanara, so I think someone influential like Indra or Kubera has sent him. While your orders are to subdue and capture the intruder, I must warn you not to underestimate his ability. I have encountered Vanaras like him in the past; one called Vali[2] had immense strength, but this one seems even more powerful. Nevertheless, I have the utmost trust in you; you are so competent that even Indra could not stand before you. Therefore, go forth single-mindedly focused on victory and take out this pest.'

Hanuman was standing in wait by the gate, shining like the rising sun. Once again, he was assailed by arrows, but immediately increased his size and jumped upon Durdhara, killing him. Then, he picked up a sala tree as a weapon and took out Virupaksha and Yupaksha. Praghasa and Bhasakarna came forward with spears, but Hanuman crushed them with a massive boulder. In no time, the five generals were out of the way, and Hanuman went to the gate and stood triumphantly like Yama, waiting for another batch of contenders to arrive.

---

[2] The Epilogue speaks more about this encounter.

Ravana was dumbfounded at the defeat of the five generals and their armies. He looked around his court, wondering who to send next, when his glance fell on his youngest son, Akshakumara. He was a mere boy at the time, but he jumped up enthusiastically like a flame in a yagna that leaps high when fed with ghee. He was eager to prove his mettle to his father and set out confidently to tackle the problem. Akshakumara looked impressive in his golden armour, armlets and earrings. He confronted Hanuman on his grand flying chariot, obtained by practising strict austerities. Expanding himself to the same size as Hanuman, the prince raised his bow, and soon the two were engaged in a fierce aerial combat. Akshakumara rejoiced when he pierced Hanuman with his arrows, and blood poured out from gaping wounds all over his body. Despite his tender age, Akshakumara fought valiantly, and Hanuman had to exert himself considerably to avoid being struck. He could not help feeling a tinge of admiration for the gallant youth and regretted having to kill someone who had his whole life ahead. But he knew any hesitation on his part would have lethal consequences. When Akshakumara made the miscalculation of coming a little too close, Hanuman swooped down on him and shattered his chariot with a mighty blow. Then grabbing him by the ankles, he twirled him around like a snake and dashed his brains to the ground.

The death of Akshakumara was too much for Ravana to bear, and the matter had now become personal. He summoned his valiant first-born son, Indrajit, and said, 'I have supreme faith in you because you have never faced defeat in battle. You are equal to me in every way. Your valour is famous in all three worlds, and you have even vanquished the invincible Indra. The many years you spent in penance have equipped you with extensive knowledge of missiles. That rogue monkey has vanquished your dear brother Akshakumara and all the warriors I sent before him, but I know he will not be able to stand up to you. As a father, having lost one son, I hesitate to send you, but as a king, I cannot allow the intruder to go unpunished. I want you to capture the Vanara and bring him to me so I can find out who sent him here.'

Indrajit folded his hands in obeisance and set out to face Hanuman. He was a towering figure, a peerless warrior, fittingly his father's pride and joy. At birth, he was named Meghnad, because his cry was like the rumble of thunder, but he became better known as Indrajit when he famously defeated Indra, the mighty king of the Devas. Indrajit made his appearance with the swiftness of Garuda, on a chariot drawn by four sharp-fanged tigers, proudly displaying Indra's fallen standard. Since both warriors were equally matched, an intrepid conflict followed. Though they attacked each other relentlessly, neither one was victorious. Hanuman expertly evaded Indrajit's arrows, and Indrajit masterfully avoided Hanuman's blows. Before long, Indrajit realized that he could not bring Hanuman down, so he decided to bind him using his most potent weapon, the Brahmastra. Hanuman saw it hurtling towards him but was not perturbed, knowing he would not be harmed. He had been granted immunity to it by its creator, Brahma himself, so, out of reverence, he offered no resistance to the weapon. Once the Brahmastra tightly bound Hanuman, the other Rakshasas, in their ignorance, brought ropes to secure him further, and Hanuman humoured their feeble efforts. To everyone's amazement, as soon as they did this, the Brahmastra released its hold on him, refusing to coexist with the other puny restraints. Indrajit was perplexed when he noticed that though Hanuman could easily have escaped, he did not attempt to get away. It would have been simple indeed for Hanuman to shake off his fetters, but he refrained, knowing he would be taken to see Ravana, and it suited his plan to have the opportunity of an audience with the Lankan king.

When Hanuman was dragged into the court, he could not help being wonderstruck by Ravana's magnificence. Surrounded by adoring minions, the Rakshasa overlord sat on a high throne, looking redoubtable. His head was adorned with a glittering gem-studded diadem of gold, embellished with strings of pearls, and he presented an awe-inspiring sight, regally clad in fine silk robes, his broad chest smeared with sandalwood paste. Despite his malfeasance, Ravana's majesty was undeniable. He evoked fear in his enemies, and even all the women he abducted ultimately fell for his charms. It seemed so unfortunate that his character was marred by a tragic flaw that would eventually result in his downfall. Regrettably, in straying from the path of righteousness, Ravana had thrown away his potential for greatness, and instead of achieving glory, he had descended into infamy.

As Hanuman entered the court, the noblemen cried out, 'Who is this foul creature? Who sent him, and what is his purpose here? We should put him to death at once.' A shiver ran down Ravana's spine as he wondered if Hanuman was Shiva's attendant Nandi,[3] whom he had once insulted. He asked himself if Nandi had perhaps come in disguise to seek vengeance, because clearly, this was not a run-of-the-mill Vanara. Commanding Prahasta to find out who had sent him, Ravana bellowed, 'Ask this perverse creature

---

[3] Discussed in more detail in the Epilogue.

where he has come from and why he is here. I would like to know the reason he has wilfully destroyed my garden, wantonly killing so many of my people.'

Prahasta inquired in a firm tone, 'Who sent you? Speak truthfully if you want to be set free. You are not an average Vanara and must be here at the behest of someone powerful. Who is your master? Is he Indra, Kubera, Yama, Varuna or Vishnu? We would like to know your motive in coming here and the reason for the unpardonable destruction you have wrought.'

Hanuman responded politely, 'Neither Indra nor any other Deva sent me. I am a Vanara, here at the command of my king Sugriva, and my actions were prompted by the desire to be brought before the Lord of Rakshasas. When your forces attacked me, I retaliated solely to protect my life, not to cause undue harm. Brahma has given me a boon by which no weapon can kill me, so let me tell you that I was only captured because I allowed myself to be subdued.' Then, adopting a diplomatic tone to see if he could convince Ravana to return Sita without the need for war, Hanuman continued, 'I am here as Rama's emissary, and I have an important message for you. I want to inform you that Vali, with whom you are acquainted,[4] has been killed by Rama, and his brother Sugriva now sits on the throne of Kishkindha. Sugriva sends you his greetings, as well as some friendly advice that is in your best interest. Rama, the virtuous son of the great king Dasharatha, went into exile for fourteen years to honour his father's word. In the last year, his wife Sita, the pious Janaka's daughter, was abducted. Rama and his brother Lakshmana arrived in Kishkindha looking for her and befriended Sugriva. Sugriva sent scores of Vanara warriors to all parts of the world in search of Sita; I—Hanuman—am one of them. I leaped across the ocean as we were informed she was here, and after much searching, I discovered her in your Ashoka Garden.

'It is immoral to steal another man's wife, and as you know, evil actions always come back to haunt the doer. You are powerful, enormously wealthy and extremely intelligent. It is well known that you have earned great blessings through years of penance, so do not throw it all away by committing a deed that is unworthy of your eminent stature. It is not too late to rectify your mistake; send Sita back respectfully to her husband and ask Rama for forgiveness. Remember, your benediction does not protect you from human beings, and no one can be more ferocious than Rama when he

---

[4] The story of Ravana being defeated by Vali is told in the Epilogue. By mentioning that Rama killed Vali, Hanuman is emphasizing Rama's strength.

is threatened. I am sure you recollect how he destroyed all your Rakshasa followers at Janasthana single-handed?

'Your past good deeds have blessed you with much good fortune, so why do you want to squander your hard-earned spiritual merit frivolously? So far, you have not reaped any retribution for your sins, but it is sure to come unless you take corrective action that negates the effects of your misconduct.[5] You would be wise to return Sita to her husband honourably. I can comfortably take on your entire army without assistance, but I do not have Rama's permission to do this. I am here only as a messenger to say he will destroy you if you do not send Sita back. You have tied Yama's noose of death around your neck by capturing her, so do not provoke Rama any further and hang yourself with your foolish deeds. Keeping Sita here against her will is as foolhardy as toying with a five-headed serpent, rushing into a dangerous conflagration or sipping poison, and will surely spell your downfall. I could have demolished your city and taken Sita with me, but I wanted to issue you a warning to save you from Rama's wrath. My cautionary advice is for your own good because you cannot win against Rama. You put Lanka and your people at risk of annihilation by your actions, actions that go against dharma. For the sake of your citizens, reconsider what you are doing and give Sita back. I want to reiterate that Rama is invincible. No one in all three worlds—Deva, Yaksha, Gandharva, Naga or Rakshasa—can defeat Rama, and by antagonizing him, you have put your life in danger. Once Rama marks you for death, no one can save you, not even Brahma.'

Ravana did not take kindly to being schooled by a petty Vanara. He shook with rage and ordered Hanuman to be executed immediately for his insolence. Ravana's brother Vibhishana, who always stood staunchly on the side of righteousness, was unsettled by this, as it was against the code of moral conduct to kill a messenger. He quickly stepped forward and, appealing to Ravana's ego, said in a humble voice, 'O king, excuse me for interceding, but swayed by anger, you have overlooked the fact that it is against diplomatic protocol to put an envoy to death. Be merciful! A distinguished monarch like you, well versed in statecraft, is undoubtedly aware of the ignominy of carrying out a prohibited act that contravenes the norms of civilized society.' Ravana, still seething, shouted, 'How can it be wrong to kill a sinner? Look at all the lives he has taken. Put an end to him at once.'

---

[5] 'Like seeds sown in the earth, adharma practised does not bear fruit on the same day, but in time it cuts out from the root (destroys completely) the perpetrator.' Manusmriti 4:172

Vibhishana continued suppliantly, 'Don't act in haste, O Lord of Lanka! You are knowledgeable of the shastras and have a superior intellect. I am not advocating that you let the Vanara go unchastised, as he has indeed caused great havoc. Although convention forbids you to take a messenger's life, you have the right to teach him a lesson. Punish him for his wrongdoing by disfiguring him, flogging him, shaving his head or branding him.

'A learned person cognizant of dharma must not act rashly or in an unrighteous manner. Your understanding of the shastras is unequalled,[6] and no one comes close to your might. I see no benefit to you in killing a mere messenger, who is not the brains behind the crime. The people who sent him are the ones you should concern yourself with punishing. An invincible person like you has no reason to fear confrontation. Order your mighty warriors to capture the two foolish princes and bring them before you; but first, I suggest you let the Vanara go back, exhibiting the shame of his punishment. Let him narrate your greatness to his masters! It befits one as illustrious as you to show your supremacy by vanquishing your enemies in battle rather than killing a petty representative.'

Vibhishana had managed to strike the right chord;[7] acceding to his advice, Ravana said, 'Since it is forbidden to kill a messenger, I will give him a punishment worse than death. A monkey is known to prize his tail, so wrap it with cloth and set it on fire. After that, parade him around the city to proclaim our victory, and then let him return to his friends disgraced, without his tail.'

Hanuman was not unduly concerned about the fate that awaited him because the benediction he had received from Agni protected him from being injured by fire. As his tail was bound with cloth rags dipped in ghee, he kept lengthening it, so that no amount of cloth was enough to cover it. With the tail growing longer and longer, the Rakshasas grew frustrated and finally decided to light it as it was. Then they paraded him through the streets amidst beating drums and blaring conches, jeering in glee, 'Come see the spy who tried to destroy Lanka.' As Hanuman was marched around the city, he cooperated with his jailers, taking the opportunity to carefully memorize the layout of Lanka and its fortifications, which he could see more clearly in the daylight. Sita's guards remarked snidely to her, 'Your friend, the Vanara

---

[6] Although Ravana was learned in the shastras, his knowledge did not find expression in his actions.

[7] He successfully appealed to Ravana's ego.

who destroyed this garden, has been apprehended, and his tail has been set on fire.' Hanuman's predicament pained Sita as much as the harrowing experience of being abducted from Janasthana, and she prayed to Agni not to harm him. In a fervent appeal, she implored, 'If I have been unswerving in my loyalty to my husband, let Hanuman be protected.'

At that very moment, Hanuman's tail felt as cool as a lump of ice. Surprised at not feeling the heat anymore, he attributed it to Rama's grace; after all, the Ocean Deva had come forward unsolicited to help him, so perhaps Agni was doing likewise. Suddenly outraged at the public humiliation he was being subjected to, Hanuman expanded himself, breaking free of his bonds. Once unfettered, he picked up an iron cudgel lying on the ground and promptly killed his captors. Then, on impulse, he decided it might be politically expedient to set fire to the city, thereby weakening it and making it easier to conquer. In minutes, Hanuman leaped from roof to roof, setting every building in Lanka ablaze. Finally, jumping to the top of Mount Trikuta, he observed his handiwork with satisfaction. Fanned by the winds, an immense fireball had engulfed the city, and dense columns of smoke rose from the blazing ruins. The only dwelling Hanuman had spared from the inferno was that of the honourable Vibhishana.

Chapter 23

The Southern Team Returns

After setting Lanka alight, Hanuman extinguished his fiery tail in the sea. Suddenly, he was gripped by panic. Regretting his recklessness, Hanuman worried whether Sita was safe in the fire that had consumed the city. Filled with contrition, he scolded himself: 'Anger[1] is so dangerous! Those who have the willpower to control their emotions are indeed blessed, because lack of restraint often results in irreparable damage. My foolishness may have defeated the very purpose for which I came here. Shame on me for acting rashly like a stupid monkey. If Sita has perished because of my madness, I will have to give up my life.'

Then, reasoning that Sita was pure like fire and protected by her spiritual merit, he reassured himself that fire could not burn fire. After that, he felt much better, concluding that Agni[2] did not hurt his tail, so he would not harm Sita.

Nevertheless, he needed to check that she was safe, so he hurried to the garden to confirm with his own eyes that all was well. Hanuman felt tremendously relieved when he saw Sita sitting at the foot of the simsapa tree, completely unscathed. Bowing reverently, he bade her farewell once more and, preparing to cross the ocean again, ascended Mount Arishta[3] covered in padmaka trees,[4] caverns and caves. As Hanuman sprang forward,

---

[1] Anger/Krodha is considered one of the deadliest vices due to its destructive power, and the absence of it, Akrodha one of the greatest virtues. Anger is one of the six dangerous enemies that need to be overcome, and often the most difficult.

[2] The Fire Deva

[3] Believed to be Nuwara Elya hill in Sri Lanka which has a network of caves and tunnels.

[4] *Prunus cerasoides*. Wild cherry.

the mountain sank under the enormous pressure exerted by his giant body. Eager to give Rama the excellent news, he shot through the sky with great jubilance, giving Mainaka a friendly pat as he passed. Soon he could see Mount Mahendra ahead and roared in victory. His anxious companions on the beach heard him and climbed onto higher ground, taking to treetops to get a better look, while Jambavan declared triumphantly, 'Hanuman has been successful!'

When he landed, the team excitedly gathered around, paying homage to their valiant hero with offerings of fruits and tubers. Hanuman bowed to Jambavan and the other elders in the group. Then addressing his leader Angada, he said, 'I have seen Sita! She is beyond reproach in her duty as a wife, pining for Rama, fasting and living in austerity, waiting for him to rescue her.'

The Vanaras could not contain themselves and leaped around, hugging each other, chattering in delight. Angada expressed his gratitude with high praise, saying, 'There is no one like you, Hanuman! You are truly unequalled in courage, strength, loyalty and determination, and in accomplishing this tremendous feat, you have given us all a new lease of life.' As the team sat around besieging Hanuman with questions about his trip, Jambavan said, 'Tell us everything so we can decide what is appropriate to report back.' Hanuman turned to the south, facing Lanka, and bowed to Sita. Then he recounted his experience of the past three days, giving them an exhaustive account of his exploits, especially highlighting how impressed he was by Sita's exemplary character. He extolled her great virtue and Ravana's inability to seduce her, despite offering to put the world at her feet, and concluded by saying, 'None of our efforts have been in vain. My mind bows to Sita's virtue, and even if we lay down our lives to save her, our sacrifice would be eminently worth it.'

When Hanuman completed his narrative, he made a suggestion. 'Sita has become painfully thin, sorrowing for Rama. Her condition is pitiable, reminiscent of a wilted lotus; furthermore, she has been sentenced to death by Ravana. Now that I have torched the city, we can easily conquer it and take Sita back to Rama. What do you think?' Angada readily agreed, saying, 'If Sita has been found, it is logical that we should go back to Rama with her and not just with the news of her whereabouts. We have so many powerful warriors amongst us, and since Lanka has already been made vulnerable, it will not require much effort to overpower the Rakshasas and kill Ravana.'

However, Jambavan did not think this was a good idea, and cautioned strongly against it. He said, 'O mighty Angada, while your intentions are noble, I must remind you that our assignment was only to find Sita, not to go beyond that. It would be wrong to disregard our orders and exceed our mandate. In my opinion, any sort of unilateral intervention on our part in rescuing Sita would not be appropriate. Rama took a vow before us all to recover his wife himself, and he may be upset with us if we deny him the opportunity to fulfil his promise. Therefore, we should return to Kishkindha with the wonderful news Hanuman has brought and act further solely under specific instructions.'

Angada accepted Jambavan's wise advice, and the elated Vanaras hastened towards Kishkindha, brimming with excitement.

As the Vanaras approached Kishkindha, they came across Sugriva's prized ancestral garden, Madhuvana. It was a tranquil haven he kept for his exclusive use, full of honeycombs, fruit trees and pots of choice liquor. To ensure that it was well maintained and protected from trespassers, he had installed his uncle Dadhimukha as its caretaker, and a few guards to assist him. The team members were in a celebratory mood, bursting with the exhilaration of their success, and requested Angada's permission to enjoy themselves there for a while. Although Angada did not have Sugriva's consent, he realized the search party's need to unwind from the excitement of their victory. So, after conferring with Hanuman and Jambavan, he granted his approval.

Descending on the garden en masse like a swarm of bees, the Vanaras drank to their fill, feasted on the luscious fruit and danced wildly, jumping around in drunken camaraderie. Unfortunately, their euphoria made them rambunctious, trampling the garden in their rowdiness. It was near ruination when Dadhimukha desperately tried to intervene. He begged them to stop, but the Vanaras were in such a frenzied state that they turned a deaf ear to his pleas. Finally, when Dadhimukha tried to restrain them physically, he got beaten black and blue and ran as fast as he could to Kishkindha, complaining bitterly to Sugriva. 'O king, the wild southern team is laying waste to your lovely garden. They are stripping the trees of fruit, drinking the honey and quaffing down all your wine with cupped hands. I tried to stop them but look at what they have done to me! They even had the impudence to show me their behinds in defiance and need to be thrashed severely for their atrocious behaviour.' Lakshmana did not understand the language[5] of their exchange and, curious to know what had transpired, asked Sugriva to explain.

---

[5] Dadhimukha probably spoke in the Vanara dialect.

Dadhimukha looked beseechingly at Sugriva, expecting him to fly into a rage and issue an order of strict disciplinary action. However, to his surprise, just the opposite happened. Sugriva grinned and exclaimed in joy, 'Arya Lakshmana, they have surely found Sita! The Vanaras would not dare take the liberty of raiding my garden if this were not so. I am certain that none but Hanuman could have achieved this task with his intelligence, determination and bravery. Take it from me; the team has been successful in its mission, undoubtedly with the benefit of Jambavan's wise counsel and Angada's expert leadership. I see my garden's destruction as a small price to pay for their success.' Turning to Dadhimukha, he said, 'I am so ecstatic that I am going to overlook the violation and forgive the errant Vanaras for trespassing. Go back and tell the lions who have achieved this great success to come here once they have expended their exuberance, as I can't wait to see them.'

When Dadhimukha reached the garden, the Vanaras were lying around indolently, their pent-up emotions spent. He told Angada that Sugriva was delighted with his team's success and was eager to see them. Addressing the group, Angada said, 'If Rama already knows the good news, we should go to Kishkindha without delay. I know you are all in a relaxed mood, but I must request you to rouse yourselves because propriety demands that we leave immediately.'

The Vanaras replied compliantly, 'We are at your command! You speak so kindly and never issue orders arrogantly. Despite your exalted position, you are devoid of conceit, so we are more than happy to obey you. Your humility is an indication of your bright future as a good king.' With that, they leaped enthusiastically into the sky like boulders hurled from a giant catapult. Sugriva beamed with pride as he saw them approach. Then, raising his tail high in delight, he said, 'I don't have an iota of doubt about their success; they look full of excitement despite having exceeded my strict time limit.'

When the team reached Mount Prasravana, Hanuman respectfully circled Rama and, standing before him with folded hands, delivered his message in his usual pithy style. 'Sita has been found!'

His words were sweet as nectar to Rama, and regarding Hanuman with admiration, he inquired anxiously, 'Where is my precious Sita being held, and how is she disposed towards me?' Hanuman replied comprehensively, but not before turning south and bowing reverently. He recounted every detail about his meeting with Sita: her outright rejection of Ravana, the daily harassment she faced, and her unflinching devotion as a chaste wife. However, out of modesty, he did not mention his own exploits. Sticking to the point, he said, 'I saw Sita living like an ascetic, sitting on the bare ground, unkempt and unadorned, with her hair in a single braid.[6] She keeps herself alive only with the hope that you will come for her. Although she is physically unharmed, she suffers deep mental anguish and spends all her time practising austerities in anticipation of your arrival. I won her confidence by singing your glory, and your ring further convinced her that I was a friend. Sita told me to tell you about the one-eyed crow and the incident of the smudged tilaka. She also gave me her hair ornament as evidence of our meeting, and expressly asked me to convey that she plans to give up her life if you do not rescue her within a month.'

When Rama received the jewel, he looked at it with deep longing. Then, holding it lovingly to his chest, he said with tears welling up in his eyes, 'My heart melts at the sight of this piece of jewellery, and I am filled with profuse love, like a cow when it sees its newborn calf. This ornament was given to Sita by her parents as a gift in my father's presence at our wedding, and when it was affixed to her hair, I remember she looked indescribably beautiful. Tell me more; what else did Sita say? I thirst to hear your every word.'

Hanuman related all that Sita had told him to report, particularly the limited timeframe for her rescue. He said, 'Sita was insistent that I convey the paucity of time to you as she has vowed to live only for a month.'

Rama cried out in pain, 'Take me there at once. Sita may have given me a month, but I cannot stay here a moment longer after hearing about her condition. She must be so frightened, being held prisoner by those terrible Rakshasas. Tell me her exact words without holding anything back; news of her is like therapy for a sick person.'

Hanuman once again stressed Sita's message of urgency, underscoring her request for Rama to rescue her quickly. He said, 'Sita praised you as the best amongst warriors, commending your physical strength as well as the mightiness of your character. However, she wonders why you have not yet used your extensive knowledge of astras to free her and particularly asked me to convey that you should come to her aid right away if you still love her. She was also concerned that Lakshmana had not attempted to reach Lanka and worried he might be upset with her. I reassured her that you would both set out as soon as you were informed of her location. Since she was so miserable, I even suggested bringing her to you right away on my back, but she refused, saying such an action on her part would be against dharma. She stated that it was not in her power to resist when Ravana laid his hands on

---

[6] A single braid/eka veni was a sign of austerity.

her, but she could not in good conscience voluntarily agree to touch another man.[7] Her explicit instruction was for me to state the importance of starting out immediately to rescue her from her sorrow. Regarding the matter of reaching Lanka, she was worried about the difficulty of crossing the ocean, so I assured her that there were many superior Vanaras in our army who would make it possible. In comforting Sita, I promised to bring you on my back if necessary, and this gave her some solace.'

Rama felt immensely grateful for all that Hanuman had done. He hugged the heroic Vanara affectionately and said, 'I am deeply indebted to you and cannot thank you enough for your service to me. In locating Sita, you have achieved the impossible. Other than you, only Garuda or Vayu would have been able to cross the ocean. You have returned successfully after courageously infiltrating the impenetrable city of Lanka, fulfilling your mission with the highest level of excellence. In finding Sita, you have not only saved me but also Lakshmana and my entire clan. I would have liked to reward you handsomely for your achievement, but sadly I own nothing at this point, so all I can offer you to show my appreciation is a heartfelt embrace.'

For Hanuman, the sincerity of Rama's gratitude meant more to him than anything in the world, and it brought him greater joy than any amount of wealth could have done.

---

[7] Dharma is about conscience and intention rather than rigid rules.

yasyamatam tasya matam matam yasya na veda sah
avijntam vijanatam vijnatamavijanatam

Brahman, the ultimate reality, is not known by those
who claim they know it. It is only attained by those who
realize they do not know it, as there is no
definition of the undefinable

na jayate mriyate va vipascin nayam kutascin na babhuva
kascit Ajo nityah sasvato yam purano na hanyate hanyamane sarire

The intelligent Atman is not born, nor does it die.
It does not come from anywhere nor is it anything
material. Unborn, eternal, everlasting, ancient;
it is not slain, though the body is slain

Katha Upanishad

BOOK 6
The Great War

Chapter 24

Preparations

Now that Sita's whereabouts had been identified, the first step in the rescue plan was achieved, but the more daunting task of recovering her safely still lay ahead. Voicing his concern about this, Rama said to Sugriva, 'Thanks to the valiant efforts of Hanuman, we now know where Sita is, but my heart sinks when I contemplate the formidable task of reaching her. A vast ocean inhabited by dangerous sea creatures separates us from Lanka, and it would be nearly impossible to get across it. Having determined Sita's location, we are so close and yet so far from realizing our objective.'

Sugriva replied reassuringly, 'Dear friend, do not feel disheartened. It was not easy to find Sita, yet we managed to accomplish it. Similarly, I am confident we will find a means to cross the ocean and destroy the enemy. You are a learned person who has studied the shastras, which teach us not to be distressed even in difficult times. Despondency is enervating and squashes initiative; it is a weakness associated with ordinary people, not someone as distinguished as you. Now, more than ever, we need to be positive, focusing our energies on devising a plan to reach Lanka. A dispirited person can never achieve his goal, so shake off your downheartedness for the indefatigable will to succeed. I am sure we will find a way across the sea if we adopt an unyielding attitude. Consider Ravana as good as dead, because no one in the three worlds is as powerful as you, and the Vanaras stand firmly by your side. I know that by working together, we will undoubtedly succeed in our endeavour.'

Rama was encouraged[1] by Sugriva's support. Regaining his confidence, he replied, 'You are right; I will try to build a bridge using my spiritual powers or else dry out the ocean with my mystic weapons.'

---

[1] One of Rama's strengths was his ability to recognize good counsel.

Then, turning to Hanuman, he asked, 'Tell me exactly what we are up against with the enemy. Describe Lanka to me in minute detail so that I can picture it clearly in my mind. Based on your reconnaissance, can you estimate the size of its army? Also, please share anything else that may be pertinent, especially regarding the kingdom's defences.'

Hanuman gave a detailed account of Lanka's fortifications. He said, 'I will gladly relate all I know. Lanka is a prosperous city, and its wealthy inhabitants are fiercely loyal to Ravana. High impregnable walls surround it, and its four gates are barricaded with massive bars. Powerful catapults or Shataghnis[2] are positioned on the ramparts. They discharge darts and boulders at any intruder and can kill hundreds simultaneously. Warriors armed with spiked iron clubs patrol day and night on chariots, elephants and horses to prevent unauthorized entry. A wide moat around the city is infested with giant alligators, so the only way inside is over one of the four drawbridges. The northern gate is the main entrance, majestic with golden pillars, and zealously protected by ten million[3] warriors handpicked for their valour. The eastern gate is guarded by 10,000 Rakshasas armed with spears and swords. A whole army of 1,00,000, including foot soldiers, horsemen, charioteers and an elephant brigade, is posted at the southern gate. Also, one million fighters equipped with all kinds of missiles keep watch over the western portal.

'Additionally, the central garrison is ten million-strong. Access to Lanka is cut off by the surrounding sea and further restricted by its elevation, high on Mount Trikuta. The mountain slopes outside the city walls are densely forested, providing yet another barrier to entry. Furthermore, Ravana keeps a watchful eye on everyone despite the high security measures and has spies mingling with the people to alert him of the slightest danger. However, the city is considerably weakened by the fire I set off; at your command, I can go back with stalwarts like Angada, Dwividha, Mainda, Jambavan, Panasa, Nala and Nila. It should be relatively easy for us to storm the city, so there would be no need to take a whole army to bring Sita back.'

Rama felt the onus was on him to free his wife, and it was not a duty he wanted to delegate. He said decisively, 'It is my responsibility as Sita's husband to recover her and protect her honour, so I am determined to do this task myself. Let us begin our march; the sun is at its zenith, and it is the

---

[2] A catapult that launched spiked cylindrical weapons to cause widespread damage.

[3] These numbers may be hyperbolic to indicate a large force.

auspicious hour of Abhijit.[4] Victory is assured when any venture is started during this time, so it is appropriate for us to leave now to ensure our success. I see good omens; my right eye twitches, and the stars smile on us, with the constellation Uttara Phalguni[5] in the ascendant. Sugriva, kindly give your consent for Nila to lead the way through the forests to the southern shore with an advance force of 1,00,000 The rest of the army will follow, protected by the most powerful Vanaras: Gaja, Gavaya and Gavaksha at the front; Rishabha on the right flank and Gandhamadana on the left. Jambavan and Sushena will defend the rear, while Lakshmana and I march in the centre on the shoulders of Angada and Hanuman. I think it would be prudent to send a preliminary search team to scout a suitable route where water is plentiful and where fruit, tubers and honey abound. The advance team can also watch out for the enemy lest they poison the water points or lie in wait to ambush us. If there are any assembled here who are not completely fit, they should stay back because we have a stiff battle ahead.'

Before long, the large army set forth, advancing zealously like a sea of warriors. Lakshmana, sitting atop Angada's shoulders, pointed out many encouraging signs as they made their way.[6] He remarked excitedly to Rama, 'It is promising that a favourable breeze is blowing in the direction that we are proceeding in, supporting us. Additionally, the sky makes me buoyant about our success. The sun is shining brightly, and Venus has risen behind us. Dhruva[7] is plainly visible, circled by the constellation of the seven rishis.[8] Notice how Trishanku[9] and Vishakha,[10] associated with our ancestors, are sparkling, while the star Moola[11] that is benevolent to the Rakshasas is tormented by a comet and in a weak position.'

---

[4] The star Vega.

[5] Denebola and 93-Leonis.

[6] This sky formation, according to results from the Planetarium software, was seen on 20 September 5076 BCE from Karnataka.

[7] The Pole Star.

[8] The seven brightest stars of the Great Bear—Ursa Major. The Vedic names are Atri, Angirasa, Pulastya, Pulaha, Kratu, Marichi and Vasishta.

[9] The Southern Cross which consists of three stars.

[10] Consists of four stars in the constellation of Libra: Alpha, Beta, Gama and Iota Librae.

[11] Nine stars representing the tail of a scorpion—Epsilon, Mu, Zeta, Eta, Theta, Iota, Kappa, Upsilon and Lambda Scorpii.

The Vanara troops marched enthusiastically onward without rest, walking day and night across the Sahaya and Malaya Mountains[12] till they reached Mount Mahendra on the southern shore. There they decided to set up a camp on the beach, and Nila prudently placed Mainda and Dwividha on guard duty to patrol all sides.

Once the army was settled, Rama climbed up a peak and surveyed his surroundings in the moonlight. Suddenly he was overwhelmed with emotion and couldn't help pouring his heart out to Lakshmana. 'The vast, fathomless ocean stretches before us, and we now face the daunting challenge of crossing it. People say that grief diminishes with the passage of time, but I do not find this to be true in my case. With every day that passes, my misery intensifies, and I miss my beloved wife even more. The breeze is blowing from south to north, so it has touched Sita, and as it wafts here, I feel as if it is carrying her gentle caress to me. I am sure she, too, is looking at the lovely full moon at this moment, and our eyes are united in the enjoyment of its beauty. I yearn for her so much that my body burns with a fever as if I have consumed poison. Knowing we both occupy the same Earth, and that Sita is waiting for me to rescue her, is the only thing that keeps me going. I think of her day and night, tormented that she is fasting and wasting away in sorrow. The day I hold her in my arms again cannot come soon enough, ending this terrible ordeal we are both suffering.'

Meanwhile, in Lanka, Ravana was perturbed by the grave security failure that had occurred when Hanuman breached his kingdom's well-fortified defences. So, he called an assembly of his advisers to assess the extent of damage in terms of loss of life and property and to decide on appropriate corrective measures. Mortified by the assault on his pride, he appeared visibly downcast. Addressing his ministers with considerable disquietude, Ravana said, 'I always took satisfaction in the thought that Lanka was impenetrable, but I was proved wrong by a mere Vanara. He entered unnoticed, discovered Sita and ravaged our city. How should we address this serious problem? The wise know that success depends on adopting the right strategy, and since I respect your intelligence, I would like your opinion.

'As you know, there are three kinds of leaders in the world: the adept ones, the mediocre ones and the ones who are inept. The most proficient consult competent advisers and develop a clear plan after discussion. The ruler who decides on a course of action solely based on his own deliberations ends

---

[12] The Western Ghats.

up only moderately successful. The least effective leader rushes impetuously ahead, without the benefit of wise counsel or ruminating on the crisis at hand himself to evaluate the pros and cons.

'Similarly, there are three types of guidance a king can choose to follow. Views that have unanimous consent and follow the rules of statecraft are the most beneficial. Suggestions that emerge from a heated debate between persons of opposing views, who eventually reach a compromise, are of middling value. The worst kind of counsel to act upon is when multiple opinions are proposed, but no consensus is reached, leaving the leader to choose a random path of his liking. I am concerned that Rama might come here with his brother and the Vanaras. He may use his weapons to dry up the ocean or find some other way across, and if that happens, we face a significant threat, so what should we do? Give me your recommendations on how best to safeguard Lanka.'[13]

Pandering to Ravana's ego, his advisers were quick to validate what they thought he would be pleased to hear without giving any real consideration to the peril posed by their adversary. Lavishing praise on their king to win his favour, they said with folded hands, 'You are the most powerful person in the world, and no one can defeat you. Besides, we have a massive army equipped with every weapon in existence. Be reminded of your past glories in battle. You attacked Bhogvati[14] and subdued the Nagas. You defeated the Danavas, although they held out for a whole year. Even your brother Kubera, who enjoys the great Shiva's protection and is endowed with so much might, bowed to you, surrendering his city and Vimana without contest. In awe of your high status, Mayasura gave his daughter Mandodari's hand to you in marriage to keep you on his side. You have easily overthrown numerous Kshatriya kings famous for their power. The Devas cower in fear when they see you, and even Indra quakes before you. Rama is nobody compared to you, so do not lose any sleep worrying about him. Your valiant son Indrajit even captured the almighty Indra, and he was freed only by Brahma's intervention; if required, he is more than capable of dealing with the Vanaras alone. What success can a couple of human beings and a band of monkeys hope to achieve against someone who has conquered the mighty Devas, Gandharvas and Nagas?'

Prahasta added, 'Do not be concerned, great king! The Vanara was successful only because he caught us off guard and escaped because we were

---

[13] Although Ravana knows the value of good counsel, he does not really seek it.

[14] Capital of the Nagas.

unprepared for him. Next time an intruder comes here, we will not let him live.' Prahasta's words incited the other stooges, and Durmukha shouted belligerently, 'We can never passively accept an assault on our city or tolerate any insult to our glorious monarch. The Vanaras will not escape us even if they hide in the depths of the ocean.' Brandishing his club, Vajradamshtra thundered, 'Let us not bother with Hanuman! It is more important to devise a strategy to destroy Rama and Lakshmana. I suggest our fighters infiltrate their army as soldiers from Bharata and kill them.' Kumbhakarna's son, Nikumbha, boasted he could kill Rama and his army unaided by anyone; and Vajrahanu, who was built like a mountain, said, licking his lips, 'Let there be business as usual in Lanka; eat, drink and make merry without the slightest unease, mighty king! I will devour Rama and his ragtag Vanaras myself.' Having worked themselves into a frenzy, the Rakshasas drew their weapons and brandished them menacingly in rage, ready to set out right away.

Vibhishana was the only voice of reason amidst the sycophants who sought favour through flattery. He differed strongly from the others in his opinion and begged them to put down their weapons and take their seats. Believing that it was neither justifiable nor meritorious to abduct another man's wife, he said respectfully, 'My dear brother, keep in mind that the shastras advise resorting to deadly force only after exhausting all nonviolent options.[15] In securing our safety, we have not yet considered the possibility of a peaceful resolution, and we are already talking about jumping to the final recourse of deadly conflict. Also, I feel we are grossly underestimating the enemy in our complacency. It is never advisable to strike a foe of greater might. You saw the power of Hanuman, and he was just the messenger! Rama has a reputation for being extremely valorous, and it is unwise to dismiss him as a puny mortal arbitrarily.'

'Moreover, he was not the initial aggressor, and we must admit that our actions precipitated his retaliation. Rama killed Khara and Dushana in self-defence and sent Hanuman here only because you aggrieved him by stealing his wife. Please take my advice; it is not prudent to make an adversary of such a formidable person. I speak out of love for you, with nothing but your welfare at heart, so I earnestly request you to give my words serious consideration. Do not succumb to self-destructive anger at what Hanuman did, but rather heed it as a warning to abandon unrighteousness in favour

---

[15] This is the concept of Ahimsa. It differs from pacifism as it accepts the necessity of violence against evil if all else fails.

of dharma. Sita's presence in Lanka poses a threat to us all. I feel you should return her to Rama, who is her lawfully wedded husband, as this is the only way to save us all from doom.'

Vibhishana's counsel was not to Ravana's liking, and finding his minions' advice more pleasing to his ego than the wise words of his righteous brother, he abruptly dismissed the assembly. Although he had elicited his ministers' guidance, all Ravana was really seeking was an endorsement of his own plans.

Many are against injustice but do nothing if it does not touch them personally. Yet, some fight injustice even at the risk of personal harm. Vibhishana fell in the latter category. The immorality of Sita's abduction weighed heavily on his mind, and he spent a sleepless night tossing and turning, troubled by the possible repercussions of Ravana's terrible wrongdoing. Early the following day, Vibhishana decided to visit Ravana privately in the hope of encouraging him to see reason. Praying for better luck in his efforts than he had at the assembly, he entered the palace, passing Brahmins chanting Vedic hymns while pouring offerings into the fire. When he approached his brother, he duly paid him his respects before taking a seat as indicated.

Attempting to get Ravana into a compliant mood, Vibhishana began with praise. 'You are immensely powerful and a scorcher of foes, but I fear Sita spells Lanka's doom. Ever since you brought her here, evil omens have been observed. Look at the holy fire; it is shrouded in smoke and does not burn brightly as it should. Reptiles have invaded our kitchens and sacrificial altars, and ants swarm over the sacred oblations. Cows are withholding their milk, and the other domestic animals, horses, elephants, camels and donkeys, show signs of restlessness. Large flocks of crows have taken to the tops of buildings, cawing loudly, and vultures are sighted circling ominously above. I hear the inauspicious call of hyenas and wolves at our city gates and am concerned that these signs warn of impending misfortune. Everyone in Lanka believes that you should not have abducted Sita, but nobody dares to speak the truth for fear of falling out of favour with you. I hope you will not be annoyed at my earnest advice, which I feel I must impart to you for your welfare. I beg you to reconsider your decision and send Sita back to Rama. I have no vested interest in giving you this counsel, so please understand my motives in coming to you.'

Ravana listened to Vibhishana silently but was bent on keeping Sita. He found the unsolicited advice unpalatable and snapped irritably, 'Rama will never get Sita back! You have no reason to fear any calamity. How can Rama win against me when the Devas, who are more powerful than him, have failed? Quite honestly, I feel that your worries are blown out of proportion, and any apprehension on your part is totally unwarranted.' Saying this, Ravana scornfully dismissed Vibhishana with the wave of his hand.

If Vibhishana hoped to discourage his brother from the perilous path he was treading, unfortunately, his words had the opposite effect[16]. On being presented with the truth, Ravana's mind became even more fixated on Sita, and later that morning, he called a special assembly of his ministers to discuss how he could secure her for himself. He arrived at the meeting hall amidst jubilant cheers, in a splendid chariot with female attendants fanning him adoringly, holding a spotless white umbrella over his head. Soon, all of the kingdom's dignitaries filed into the room, including Ravana's brothers Vibhishana and Kumbhakarna, bowing low before taking their seats according to protocol. Kumbhakarna's presence at the assembly was a rare occurrence. He was a mighty giant who had always been by Ravana's side till he found himself in a strange predicament. Due to a curse by Brahma,[17] he now slept for six months, waking up only for one day to eat before going back to sleep again for the next six months. On this day, he happened to be awake.

Ravana sat on his golden throne under his royal canopy with his brow anxiously furrowed. There was a hushed silence in the hall as everyone respectfully waited for him to speak. His first order of business was to instruct Prahasta to secure Lanka's periphery. He asked for messengers to be sent forthwith to mobilize the army by going to each house and calling every soldier back to active duty. All four military divisions were stationed at the boundary for maximum protection, outside and along the inner perimeter of the city walls. Then, addressing the assembly, Ravana said: 'We have been through a lot together over the years, both in good times and bad, and your counsel has always ensured Lanka's success. As my closest confidants, you already know our current predicament, as I have discussed it with you at length. Kumbhakarna, who is here today, is the only one who has not been briefed, since he was asleep.'

Turning to him, Ravana continued, 'I abducted Rama's wife Sita from Janasthana to teach him a lesson but have fallen madly in love with her. I have, in truth, become a slave to Janaka's exquisite daughter. From her beautiful

---

[16] This is a well-known psychological tendency; where contradictory facts only serve to strengthen a person's stance, blocking out anything that differs from entrenched opinion.

[17] The circumstances that led to this curse are described in the Epilogue.

face to her dainty feet, no one in the three worlds comes close to Sita, but despite wooing her ardently, she refuses to come to my bed. When I first brought her here, Sita stubbornly clung to the hope that her husband would rescue her and requested that I give her one year, a wish which I generously granted.[18] However, I am getting increasingly restless and am tired of waiting as she obstinately rejects my advances. While I am driven mad with passion, Sita remains devoted to Rama and will not have anything to do with me. Now, because of an impudent Vanara, Rama knows she is here, and I am certain he plans to recover her. Please assist me in deciding on an appropriate course of action whereby I can get rid of Rama and Lakshmana so that I can keep Sita for myself.'

Hearing his brother's lovesick plea, Kumbhakarna flew into a rage and admonished him with harsh words: 'Why are you seeking advice now? The time for deliberation was before you committed such an impulsive and unworthy act. Actions carried out in haste without the benefit of good counsel are inevitably a cause for repentance later. You have blundered terribly by going against dharma and are lucky that Rama has not killed you already.' Then, abruptly softening his tone, Kumbhakarna continued, 'However, since you are my brother, you are dear to me despite your folly, and I will always stand by you, even though I know you are in the wrong. I solemnly affirm that, if needed, I will drink their blood before the two brothers can draw a single arrow. Now free yourself from all worries; relax and enjoy yourself! Drink the finest wine and live without fear, knowing that you can count on me to kill Rama if that is what is required for you to be happy.'

One of Ravana's generals, Mahaparshwa, quickly seized the opportunity to ingratiate himself. He said obsequiously, 'You are all-powerful, and no one can prevent you from getting what you want, so what is stopping you from enjoying Sita by force? After accomplishing the arduous task of stealing a honeycomb from a dangerous forest, should you not enjoy the honey? Go ahead and fulfil your desire, knowing your loyal followers will take care of the fallout. In any case, I do not put much faith in the strategies of sama, dana or bheda, and prefer the option of danda to settle a problem.'

Ravana was pleased to hear Mahaparshwa's flattering words, but with a wistful look, revealed why he had not touched Sita without her consent so far. 'There is a very good reason why I have not forced myself on Janaki

---

[18] Ravana misrepresents the facts to Kumbhakarna, saying that Sita asked for a year. On the contrary she had said she would never agree to submit to him.

despite my intense desire for her. Some years ago, I was infatuated by a beautiful Apsara, and I ravished her against her will. To redress her grievance at my actions, Brahma pronounced a dire punishment that my head would split into a hundred pieces if I ever laid hands on another woman without her permission. Therefore, I need Sita to come to me willingly. Rama must be killed so that she stops waiting for him. I won this city from Kubera, and I vanquished Indra, so there is no reason why I cannot defeat someone insignificant like Rama. Once he is removed, I am sure it will be easy to bring Sita around.' Hearing Ravana, all assembled nodded in agreement and cheered loudly, except for one person.

Vibhishana listened to the discussion with much discomfort, growing increasingly perturbed with every word exchanged. Finally, he could not hold himself back any longer and said, 'Whoever gave you the ill advice of stealing another man's wife did not have your interest at heart. Sita is, in effect, like a five-headed serpent around your neck, leaving you vulnerable to being struck at any moment. Return her quickly before the mighty Vanaras destroy Lanka and Rama's arrows exterminate us all. I am afraid I must disagree with what has been proposed by the members of this council. Prahasta underestimates our opponent's strength, and Kumbhakarna indulges in boastful talk, not realizing that he is incapable of withstanding Rama's powerful arrows.'

Prahasta quickly interjected in defence of his stance, 'We have no fear of the Devas, so why should we be afraid of Rama, a mere human being?'

Vibhishana replied admonishingly, 'You brag about our strength without appreciating that none of our mighty warriors can match Rama; not even Ravana himself! Rama is a person who abides by dharma and is more powerful than the Devas, so you have good reason to fear him. It is as difficult to win against Rama as it is for an unrighteous person to enter heaven. Besides, all of you who have benefitted from Ravana's generosity should guide him to take the righteous path rather than fuel the violent and tempestuous side of his nature. Our king is mercurial; he takes decisions in haste without due consideration, and your ill advice only enables his weakness instead of protecting him from it. Friends who cannot be trusted to give sound counsel are worse than enemies. A true minister speaks judiciously in the ruler's interest without merely mouthing what he wants to hear. I beseech you, O king, for the good of Lanka, return Sita!'

Indrajit laughed out aloud and said mockingly, 'Uncle, why do you utter such cowardly words? You are the only one in our family who lacks our race's mettle and shrinks in fear of two petty humans. In my opinion, they can easily be dealt with by any ordinary Rakshasa, but if required, I am confident that I can finish them off without expending any effort. Have you forgotten that I crushed Indra's pride and brought him to his knees? I even pulled out his elephant Airavata's tusks and flung him to the ground, so I find your consternation meaningless.'

Vibhishana grew angry with his boastful nephew and reproached him sharply for his conceit. 'You speak like an inexperienced boy who lacks good sense. Not only are you ignorant, but worse still, you are violent and evil-minded. Strength without virtue is brutish and leads to damnation. Instead of protecting your father, you are propelling him to his destruction. I do not think you are fit to be part of this distinguished council, whose duty is to guide the king with appropriate advice for his personal welfare and the benefit of the kingdom. At this time, the most suitable course of action would be to remedy the great wrong he committed. We should return Sita honourably and placate Rama by offering him reparations in the form of gold and precious stones.'

By this time, Ravana was fed up with Vibhishana's dissidence. As a scholar of the shastras, he knew that his brother's advice was prompted by dharma, but Vibhishana's insistence on returning Sita had become a festering sore. Also, hearing the high praise lavished on Rama did not help the situation. Bent on pursuing his irreligious desires against good judgement, Ravana lashed out viciously, castigating his brother in open court. 'You are a traitor! You pretend to care for my well-being, but your talk shows you are duplicitous, and it is obvious that you are devoted to my enemy and not to me. You live under my roof partaking of food and drink granted by my magnanimity, and yet you glorify Rama. I can only conclude that you are envious of my position and are against my interests. An outright enemy is better than one who pretends to be a friend, cunningly lying in wait for an opportunity to strike. You call yourself my well-wisher, but all the while, you act to my detriment.

'A rival who has his eye on power can never appreciate the king's greatness, even if he is an able ruler and a follower of dharma. You disingenuously talk ill of me because you have designs on the throne and are waiting to take over in anticipation of my downfall. One must fear people like you who give bad advice. I am highly regarded in all three worlds, and you are clearly jealous of my success. The love showered on an ungrateful person does not touch his heart any more than water on a lotus petal that slides off before it can collect. Friendship with you is as empty as thunder in autumn that heralds no rain, indicating one thing outwardly but pointing to something else inside. All the affection I have shown you is pointless, reminding me of an elephant that smears itself with mud after bathing in fresh water. Similarly, you enjoy my favour and then throw muck on me.

'You have absolutely no loyalty, like a bee that flits from one flower to another, seeking nectar wherever it perceives greater benefit. In my opinion, you are a terrible blot on our clan! It is said that wild elephants know that they have more to fear from the tame ones of their own kind, who disloyally work with hunters, than from weapons or snares. If you were not my brother, I can assure you that I would have ordered you to be put to death for speaking to me so insolently. You are a complete disgrace, not only to our family but to the entire Rakshasa race. Get out of my sight before you force me to do anything I regret.'

Vibhishana was deeply offended by the hurtful accusations hurled at him because he had spoken out of genuine concern for his brother and the kingdom. He felt slighted for trying to save Ravana from disaster and realized that their relationship was irretrievably broken. There could be no meeting of minds, as he stood firmly on the side of justice, and Ravana was vehemently opposed to it. Rising in the air with his mace in hand, he prepared to depart with four loyal supporters: Anala, Panasa, Pramati and Sampati.

Taking his leave, he said indignantly, 'You have chastised me severely, but being my elder brother, you are like a father, so you have that right. However, your behaviour is unrighteous, so I have no choice but to disassociate from you like one is forced to abandon a burning house. Sadly, you surround yourself with fawning toadies who validate what you want to hear, though you desperately need advisers concerned about your welfare, who are not scared of telling you what is truly for your benefit. While it is atypical in this court for someone to speak for your good at the risk of upsetting you, it is even more unusual for you to pay heed to such rare advice when given. I spoke out of an abundance of affection, but you have deliberately misunderstood my intentions. It is unfortunate that you prefer to follow the imprudent recommendations of servile creatures who hang around you in expectation of favours instead of one who tells you the uncomfortable truth. I do not wish to see you killed by Rama's arrows, but since you find no value in my efforts to save you, I am leaving you to your own devices. At this point,

I can only pray that good sense dawns on you, and that you correct yourself before it is too late. You may think you are invincible, but remember, even the mighty fall.[19] As I take my leave of you, I want you to know that I wish you and my fellow Rakshasas well.'

---

[19] Vibhishana is reminding Ravana that the body is anitya or impermanent. Only the Self/Atman within, is nitya or undying. In the Katha Upanishad 1.26, Nachiketa rejects Yama's offers of material pleasure saying: 'These pleasures last but until tomorrow and they wear out the vital powers of life. How fleeting is all life on Earth!' In the Chandogya Upanishad 6.11.3 Uddalaka says: 'Just so, dear one, when death comes and the self departs from the body, the body dies but the self dies not.'

Chapter 25

Vibhishana Seeks Asylum

Within an hour of the fracas in Ravana's court, Vibhishana and his followers were spotted hovering in the sky near Rama's camp. The five well-armed Rakshasas with shining armaments looked ominous, and Sugriva and his fellow Vanaras presumed they had come in hostility. They hurriedly plucked out giant trees and boulders and stood ready to defend themselves in response to the perceived threat. Then Vibhishana addressed them, speaking clearly and unemotionally. 'I have come from the kingdom of the evil king Ravana; I am his younger brother. Ever since he abducted Sita from Janasthana, I have tried to persuade him to return her, but he has stubbornly rejected my advice. Today he openly insulted me with false allegations, so I have left my wife and children and have come here seeking Rama's protection. Please report my arrival to him, whom I know to be the refuge of those in need, and tell him that I am waiting to see him.'

Sugriva hastened to Rama and Lakshmana with the news of Vibhishana's arrival and said breathlessly, 'An enemy has unexpectedly turned up at our doorstep, asking for asylum. Rakshasas are not trustworthy, so I fear this one is here with some nefarious purpose in mind. He may be a covert agent, and after winning our confidence, he may try to sow seeds of dissension amongst us or find an opportune moment to destroy us. As you know, Rakshasas have extraordinary abilities; they can fly, make themselves invisible or change their form at will. They do not hesitate to use their magical powers to achieve their purpose, even if it means being deceitful, especially in battle, so we must be cautious in dealing with this so-called asylum seeker. It is safe to rely on trusted friends like the various Vanaras whom I have mobilized, or even hire assistance to bolster our intrinsic strength if necessary, but we must be circumspect about someone who has come as a defector from the rival

270

camp. It is too great a risk; besides, he is the brother of our arch-enemy, and I strongly feel we should kill him and his companions to pre-empt them from doing us any harm.'

Rama replied, 'It is proper for you as a friend to offer advice in a critical situation, but I would like to take the opinion of the others as well.' Turning to the rest of the Vanaras who had assembled before him, he said, 'All of you have heard Sugriva, but I would also like to have your individual suggestions before deciding on a course of action.'

Angada said, 'I do not think we should assume Vibhishana to be untrustworthy just because he is from the enemy camp, but at the same time, there is reason to be suspicious. Let us devise a test to ascertain the truth behind his sudden arrival.'

Sarabha agreed, suggesting that they depute a spy to find out more details. Jambavan, the old bear king, also expressed doubts about the legitimacy of the asylum seeker. He said, 'Rama, you are a wise leader in seeking the views of your team, so I will tell you what I honestly feel. I must admit I am very cynical about Vibhishana and find it odd that he has deserted his own brother to find favour with his enemy. The way he has chosen to show up abruptly is also dubious, and I can't help feeling that his motives are questionable.' Mainda added, 'I agree with Jambavan, most especially since Vibhishana is the brother of our sworn enemy. We must interrogate and vet him thoroughly rather than take his story at face value.'

Hanuman alone differed from the other Vanaras in his assessment and said to Rama, 'At the outset, I would like to say that you are like Brihaspati in wisdom and know best. While I understand the concerns of my fellow Vanaras and do not intend to put down their views, I must state that there is an inherent fallacy in their arguments. It is impossible to determine Vibhishana's true intentions by questioning him because a clever person could artfully dodge being found out; and if he is sincere, he may feel insulted. Watching his actions is also not tenable. To test him, we would necessarily have to accept him into our fold and entrust him with a duty. Sending spies to conduct a background check is not viable either, because there is no time to do this with him waiting outside. My friends are bothered about the suddenness of his arrival, but I submit that when a person seeks asylum, it is by nature impromptu and rarely planned for an appropriate time. In my judgement, Vibhishana sees you as an ally. He knows you killed Vali and recognizes that Sugriva benefited by aligning himself with you, so I have a hunch that he might be seeking similar assistance to be made king. Therefore, I think it is safe to accept him without concern about his straightforwardness. I do not share my friends' distrust of Vibhishana, primarily because his demeanour and speech display sincerity.[1] It is not easy to camouflage one's true feelings without a trace of dissemblance, which makes me believe he has genuinely come here in protest of his brother's sinfulness. Although it is my considered opinion that you accept Ravana's brother as one of us, the final decision lies with you.'

Rama listened carefully to every perspective presented, and after thinking for a while, said, 'I value everyone's advice because I know your sentiments are prompted by devotion to my welfare. However, after weighing the pros and cons of the various suggestions, I have concluded that we should give Vibhishana the benefit of the doubt and take the risk of accepting him. He has sought refuge with us, and it is my policy to accept anyone who seeks my protection.'

Sugriva was perturbed to hear this and warned, 'Be careful, Rama! He has betrayed his brother, and one who is capable of turning against his own blood cannot be trusted.'

To allay Sugriva's concerns, Rama explained his rationale in detail. Replying gently, he said, 'Dear friend, all brothers are not like Bharata, who received the kingdom on a platter but turned it down because of his love for me, and all friends are not loyal like you. Animosity between close relatives and neighboring nations is only too common an occurrence.[2] We should not distrust Vibhishana based on this and reject him solely because of his discord with his family members.

'I am not of the Rakshasa clan, and I do not intend to rule Lanka, so when Ravana is killed, Vibhishana will be king anyway. If he is honest, there may be a strategic advantage to having him on our side; if he turns out to be treacherous, I can assure you I will deal with him swiftly. At this moment, I feel strongly inclined to accept him because he has sought shelter in me, and an Ikshavaku never rejects anyone seeking security. Our shastras teach us that turning away a refugee who arrives at your door is a great sin. The person who fails to offer protection to one who has sought safety with folded hands earns infamy and is despised by the world. There is a story about a dove who

---

[1] 'The internal working of the mind is perceived through aspect, motions, gait, gestures, speech, changes in the eye, and of the facial expression.' Manusmriti 8.25–26.

[2] Rama subtly references Sugriva's fallout with his brother Vali.

sacrificed himself to a hungry hunter who came to his abode, although the very same hunter had killed his mate. If a bird had such high values, surely, we should uphold the same? The advice of Rishi Kandu, the son of the sage Kanva, has merit as it is in accordance with dharma—whoever submits himself to you seeking refuge must be given protection even at your own peril. Why Vibhishana? Even if Ravana came to me asking for sanctuary, I would grant it to him.'

Sugriva was convinced by Rama's logic and went to fetch Vibhishana. When the ousted prince arrived, he fell at Rama's feet and said, 'Please accept me as I have exiled myself from Lanka. I have left my family and all that I own behind after my brother humiliated me. I have come to you with nothing except myself and my four friends.'

Rama welcomed him affectionately and immediately asked about his adversary's strengths and weaknesses.

Vibhishana gave him a comprehensive account, meticulously describing Lanka's defences and its heroic warriors' unique abilities. He said, 'You are up against a formidable enemy. My elder brother Ravana is immensely powerful, and coupled with that, has a blessing from Brahma, whereby he cannot be killed by a Deva, Gandharva, Naga, Rakshasa, bird or beast. My second brother Kumbhakarna is gargantuan, as big as a mountain. He is invincible and can handle numerous opponents simultaneously with ease. You might have heard about my nephew, Indrajit, Ravana's eldest son, who got his name by vanquishing Indra? He wears impenetrable armour and can magically make himself invisible, which gives him the advantage of fighting his opponent unseen. Prahasta, the army commander in chief, wears a badge of honour, having defeated Kubera's great general Manibhadra, and is assisted by stalwarts like Mahodara, Mahaparshwa and Akampana, each of whom has immense strength. Additionally, thousands of blood-thirsty Rakshasas who accompanied Ravana in his countless victories are ready to stake their lives for him.

'However, I humbly put myself at your disposal to help you defeat them and promise to stand firmly by you when you storm Lanka. Ravana's greatest weakness is his arrogance and consequent overconfidence. He is self-absorbed and commits sinful actions with impunity because no one has checked him thus far. Sadly, he does not realize that his evil deeds are steadily wasting away the spiritual merit he has previously earned through years of penance.'

Rama evaluated the information given by Vibhishana, carefully observing him as he spoke, and determined him to be trustworthy. Then, embracing his new ally, he replied, 'I understand that Ravana is mighty and has the staunch support of his people; nevertheless, I vow on my three brothers that I will not return to Ayodhya till I destroy him and his cohorts.' Then turning to Lakshmana, he said, 'Bring me some water from the sea, as I would like to crown Vibhishana king straightaway. Once we have conquered Lanka, he will be its new righteous ruler.'

Unknown to the party on the beach, they were being watched by a Rakshasa spy called Shardula. He hurried back to Ravana to inform him that Rama and Lakshmana, along with a vast Vanara army, were encamped on the other shore of the ocean. Expressing great concern at their presence, he urged Ravana to send someone to assess the threat they posed more closely.

Ravana was unsettled to hear the report, knowing their purpose was to recover Sita. Deciding to create a rift in the enemy camp, he called Shuka, one of his most trusted assistants, and asked him to give Sugriva a message, hoping it would persuade him to reconsider his alliance. Ravana's statement read: 'I consider you a brother. You are the son of the mighty Riksharaja, and like me, you are born of an illustrious line. There is no reason for any enmity between us, as the abduction of Rama's wife has not harmed you in any way. Return to Kishkindha and save yourself from unnecessary embroilment in this tussle. Partnering with the losing side is pointless as Lanka cannot be reached, and all attempts to cross the sea will be in vain.'

Shuka assumed the form of a bird and delivered the message verbatim while hovering in the air. Ravana had hoped to create discord[3] to weaken his opponents' hand, but to the contrary, on hearing his communication, the Vanaras were incensed. They pulled Shuka down in rage and punched him repeatedly, plucking out his feathers.

Shuka cried out in desperation for help, and hearing his appeal, Rama rushed to his aid, shouting, 'Stop! It is forbidden to kill a messenger, so desist from committing a dishonourable act.' A shaken Shuka was released and, fluttering back into the sky, asked, 'What message should I convey to Ravana?'

Sugriva replied angrily, 'Tell him that while I do not consider him either my friend or my foe, he has wronged someone dear to me. I have promised to stand by Rama with the fire as our witness; therefore, as far as I am concerned, Ravana deserves to die. Warn him that I intend to come to Lanka with my Vanara warriors and reduce it to ashes. He feels courageous, killing the old

---

[3] Ravana uses the strategy of bheda.

bird Jatayu, but he is unaware of Rama's might. Let Ravana know he is a fool if he thinks he can escape Rama's arrows. Frankly, he is a marked man no matter where he hides or whose protection he seeks.'

Angada noticed that Shuka was slyly assessing their army the whole time and concluded that he was not just a messenger but also a spy, so once again, the Vanaras pulled him down and began thrashing him. Rama heard his cries and came to his rescue yet again. He forbade Shuka's execution, so they detained him instead. The army felt it best to let him go only after reaching Lanka to prevent him from relaying sensitive information that would alert Ravana about their plans.

Chapter 26

Nala Setu—The Incredible Bridge

With Shuka safely in custody, crossing the sea took centre stage. Hanuman and Sugriva asked Vibhishana if he had any ideas on how they could get to Lanka, and he replied, 'Rama is a descendant of Sagara, and the ocean owes the Ikshavakus a great debt. Therefore, I think he should seek the grace of Varuna, the Ocean Deva, who will surely assist him.'

Rama, given his piety, liked the suggestion and spread a mat of kusha grass down on the beach to begin a three-day penance to propitiate Varuna. Facing east, he reverently prostrated himself on the seashore with his palms joined in supplication, resolving to either invoke the Ocean Deva or else dry up the sea with his powers. However, despite his sincere penance, three days passed, and Varuna chose not to appear. Rama, who was not easily angered, suddenly felt a rage welling up inside him[1] and declared angrily, 'Varuna has haughtily refused my request for an audience. Obviously, he has mistaken my humility for weakness and fails to appreciate gentleness. Since it appears he only respects brute force, I am left with no option but to take drastic steps and dry up the sea so the Vanaras can walk across its bed on foot.' His eyes reddened, and his nostrils flared as he asked Lakshmana to bring his bow, releasing several arrows that made the waves rock with turbulence. Still, the Ocean Deva did not appear, so he affixed the mighty Brahmastra to his bow.

Lakshmana was alarmed that Rama had opted for such an extreme measure, so holding his arm to restrain him, he said, 'Wait, it is not becoming of you to act recklessly in sudden passion. There must be another way of achieving our purpose without drying up the sea and causing harm to the innocent creatures that live in its depths.' In the same instance, the Ocean

---

[1] Valmiki depicts Rama as spiritually evolved but nonetheless human, with all the emotions that go with being mortal.

Deva appeared with folded hands. Apologizing for his earlier indifference, he said, 'Please understand my position; by its very nature, the sea is deep and challenging to traverse, and I cannot alter the natural laws of existence. However, I will point you to a shallow area where it is possible to construct a bridge. I suggest you put Nala, born through the celestial architect Vishwakarma's blessings, in charge of the project. Like his father, he has the necessary engineering expertise for the job.

'Furthermore, I promise to ensure that your army is not harmed by any creature that lives within my depths, and I will allow the stones you use to float on my surface.' Rama's temper cooled instantly, and he thanked Varuna for his help. However, he had already invoked the Brahmastra, and it could not be recalled, so he asked where he should redirect it. Varuna requested he dispatch it north-west, to a part of the ocean called Drumatulya, inhabited by evil seafaring thieves[2] who made their living by loot and plunder in those waters. Rama acceded to his request to get rid of the sinners, and the powerful missile landed there, rendering the place a desert.[3]

When Nala was nominated to build the bridge, he remembered his mother's benediction that she would have a son with the same abilities as his father, Vishwakarma. With this confidence, he set to work immediately on the staggering job of engineering a causeway across the sea. The Vanaras were eager to serve Rama and started gathering the building materials. To begin with, they went into the surrounding forests and brought giant trees to lay a foundation over the shallow ridge that rose from the seabed in the area indicated by Varuna. Next, they dug out huge boulders the size of elephants, transporting them to the shore using improvised mechanical devices, and put them on top of the bed of logs. Then, as a finish layer, they created a surface consisting of smaller stones that were smooth and flat. Strings on either side of the proposed bridge helped keep its boundary to ensure it was even. Everyone put in their best effort, and by the first day, a span of 14 yojanas was complete. By the second day, they had added another 20 yojanas; on the third day, working industriously, the bridge was extended by 21 yojanas; and on the fourth day, still toiling furiously, the Vanaras built another 22 yojanas. Finally, on the fifth day, they finished the last 23 yojanas right up

---

[2] Pirates.

[3] Thought to be the Thar Desert.

to Mount Suvela[4] on the opposite shore. In five days, the Vanaras, under the leadership of Nala, miraculously constructed a stupendous bridge that spanned the ocean; it was 100 yojanas long and ten yojanas wide. The feat was indeed an unprecedented civil engineering marvel that linked two land masses.[5] From above, it looked like the parting of a woman's hair; nay, it looked like the Milky Way in space.

The jubilant army marched across to Lanka amidst a tumultuous din that drowned out the sound of the sea, and as they arrived on the other side, their clamour reached the residents of the city on the hill. Vibhishana and his four friends had already gone ahead and were waiting on the shore to fend off any unexpected assault. Nature marked the arrival of the Vanaras, with omens indicating large-scale destruction and loss of life. The wind was dusty and clouds rained red blood. The behaviour of animals and birds heralded an impending calamity and a ring of fire[6] encircled the moon. The great war to follow would exemplify the unending battle between dharma and adharma pitted against each other through the ages, which would undoubtedly be fought many a time again in the future.

Rama organized the army in the Garuda formation[7] to protect against attack and then released Shuka. He flew straight to Lanka, moaning about his plight, but Ravana laughed at the sight of him and said, 'You look terrible! What on earth happened to you? Who plucked out your feathers?' Shuka related his sorry tale, complaining bitterly that the Vanaras were a violent uncultured lot. He spoke of how they had roughed him up and said the Rakshasas could never associate with such awful creatures any more than they could with the Devas. He informed Ravana that Rama had constructed a bridge across the ocean and was camped dangerously close on the seashore

---

[4] Suvela is identified with Mihintale Hill near Anuradhapura, Sri Lanka.

[5] This bridge (setu) constructed with logs and stones over a ridge, exactly as mentioned in the Ramayana, still exists today. Although it is submerged due to rising sea levels, it is clearly visible through satellite imagery, between the southern shore of India (Dhanushkodi) and Sri Lanka (Talaimannar). Since the bridge was built by Nala, Rama called it the Nala Setu. Later it was referred to as the Rama Setu, and during the British rule of India it was renamed Adam's Bridge. Although there is no clear consensus on the measurement of a yojana, the bridge (35 km long and 3.5 km wide) is in the same 10:1 ratio stated in the Ramayana.

[6] Lunar eclipse.

[7] Shaped like the mighty bird Garuda.

with a massive army. Expressing great fear at the ferocious Vanara hordes clamouring outside, he implored Ravana to make peace by returning Sita to avoid unnecessary military engagement with such a powerful force.

Ravana was incensed at Shuka for daring to suggest the return of Sita. He yelled, 'No matter what I am up against, nothing will make me part with Sita! I will fight against the Devas, Gandharvas and the whole world to keep her and cannot wait for my arrows to claim Rama, and for my army to rout his monkey troops completely. Although they have achieved the impossible by crossing the sea to threaten me, they will not leave Lanka alive. Arrows will fly from my bow as deftly as my fingers play on the strings of my veena. How did they have the audacity to come here despite being aware of my might? Surely they know that I defeated the Devas and that my arrows are like venomous snakes that destroy everything in their path!' With this, Shuka was summarily dismissed, and his namesake was summoned to go with a companion called Sarana to spy on the Vanara camp. Ravana instructed them to find out everything they could, bringing him a full report. He wanted information about the enemy numbers, the leaders, their strength and the weapons they had at their disposal.

Shuka and Sarana assumed the guise of two Vanaras, hoping to mingle unnoticed in the enemy ranks. They viewed the multitudes that had camped on the shore extending into the mountains and surrounding woodlands, but before they could even begin counting, Vibhishana spotted them. He saw through their disguise, and grabbing them by the scruff of their necks, threw them before Rama. With their palms joined, the pair stood before him, shivering and shaking, and admitted they were agents sent by Ravana to assess his strength. Being spies and not messengers, they fully expected to be put to death, so they were surprised when Rama smiled and said magnanimously, 'If you have evaluated everything here to your satisfaction, feel free to return. If not, Vibhishana will show you around further, and when you go back, tell Ravana to meet me in battle tomorrow at daybreak. He proved his cowardice by stealing my wife, so let us see if he has the courage now to face the wrath of my arrows!'

The two hurried back to their king in trepidation and declared, 'We infiltrated the enemy camp as you commanded and found their strength to be immense. It is our considered opinion that hostility is not advisable in this instance. Rama, Lakshmana, Sugriva and Vibhishana alone can achieve victory against Lanka, even without the rest of the army. No, we stand corrected; just Rama alone is enough! He is pious and charming, but do not let his placid demeanour fool you, because he is not an adversary to be taken lightly. We strongly recommend that you return Sita and call a truce.'

Ravana shouted in fury, 'Never! Sita stays with me. You are afraid because of the ill-treatment you received when the Vanaras interrogated you, and it looks like they have broken your spirit with their torture. However, I am unfazed, knowing I am invincible and beyond defeat. Now come with me to the watch post on the roof of the palace, where we have a panoramic view so that you can point out the enemy leaders to me.'

Shuka and Sarana did as ordered. Sarana spoke first, describing the Vanara stalwarts. 'Among the legions stretching as far as the eye can see, the Vanara facing Lanka, roaring loudly and surrounded by 1,00,000 warriors, is the commander-in-chief Nila, the son of Agni. The one ready for combat, flexing his muscles and lashing his tail in a fury, is Kishkindha's crown prince Angada, son of the mighty Vali. Nala, under whose guidance the bridge was built, stands yonder, itching for battle. See the brave Shweta with his silvery hue; Chanda, followed by thousands, is the white one with long golden hair. There stands Kumuda, a mighty commander from Mount Samrochana, on the banks of the river Gomti. Rambha, tawny like a lion with his long mane, is from the Vindhyas. Sarabha commands a Vanara force called the Viharas from the Salveya Mountain. The gigantic one whose roar sounds like a kettledrum is from the Pariyatra range, and his name is Panasa. Vinata is massive; he is on the shore with a large company.

'The valiant sons of Yama—Gavaya, Gaja, Gavaksha, Gandhamadana and Sushena—are looking threateningly in our direction. Hara is known for his ferocity. He has a long tail with yellow-brown and white hair. See Dhumra, the commander of the bears, the colour of black collyrium, with his contingent hailing from Mount Rikshavan. Standing beside him is his brother, the wise Jambavan, who even helped Indra in his battles and received many powerful blessings in return. The grandfather Samnandana is yet another powerful commander, whom even Indra could not defeat. Krathana comes from Mount Kailasha. He took birth to help the Devas against the Asuras. Pramathi, the mighty general from the caves of Mount Mandara, is a force to contend with, as powerful as the wind. Kesari is a general from Sumeru, where the trees are always laden with fruit and honeycombs. From the Sarvari Meru Mountain region come brown, white, coppery-faced and yellow Vanaras with pointed fangs and sharp claws, as vicious as tigers. They are the ones with upright tails and grey eyes. There stands the mighty

Shatabali, who is ever worshipful of the sun god, and is keen to use his powers to destroy Lanka.'

Then Shuka took over the commentary. He added, 'The two you see standing there who look alike are Mainda and Dwividha; none can equal them in combat as they have sipped the heavenly nectar of longevity. The other notable warriors are Sumukha, Durmukha, Vegadarshi, Jyotirmukha, Hemakunta and Durdhara. How can I not mention the towering Hanuman, the son of Vayu with whom you are already acquainted? He set our city alight, and the fire is still not fully extinguished. The tall dark-complexioned man with lotus eyes standing beside him, who has mastery of every weapon, is Rama. The devoted Lakshmana is the fair one to his right, with a broad chest and curly locks. He is a replica of Rama, an immensely skilled warrior, and would not hesitate to give up his life for his brother. Vibhishana, whom you threw out, stands to his left and has joined them, as you can see, with the four other Rakshasas who defected with him. Rama has already anointed him the future monarch of Lanka. The king of the Vanaras, Sugriva, who stands in the centre, is the mighty Vali's identical brother and shares his prowess. There are millions of formidable Vanaras ready to lay down their lives and fight to the bitter end to destroy you. Defeating them will be no small feat, so it is best to make peace and avoid war.'

The sight of the forbidding Vanara force and the betrayal he felt at seeing his brother Vibhishana aligned with them, filled Ravana with vengeance. His unfortunate underlings bore the brunt of his irascible temper as he bellowed furiously, 'It is not appropriate for you to praise my enemies when you work for me and live off my munificence. I ought to put you fools to death, but I am showing leniency by sparing you in recognition of your past service. Get out of my sight because it is clear you do not know how to conduct yourselves before your king, and as far as I am concerned, you are not just stupid but also totally incompetent.' After Shuka and Sarana slunk out in shame, Ravana summoned another group of spies under Shardula, and asked them to bring back intelligence on Rama's next move.

They, too, disguised themselves as Vanaras and entered the camp. Once again, Vibhishana apprehended them, and as before, Rama let them go out of compassion. A bedraggled Shardula ran to Ravana and said, 'O King, the army is camped all around Mount Suvela, but we were unable to find out much. They have posted fierce guards on all sides, and we barely entered before Vibhishana and his four Rakshasa friends discovered us. The Vanaras thrashed us soundly, and we were spared only because of Rama's generosity. He is very powerful and, having filled up the sea with rocks, now stands at our door in preparation for battle with his mighty bow and formidable army arranged in the Garuda formation. I think it is preferable to return Sita to avoid conflict with Rama.'

Ravana was adamant not to return Sita under any circumstances and asked about each enemy warrior again. Shardula dutifully described the valour of the most notable amongst them, just as Shuka and Sarana had done. The reaffirmation of their strength troubled Ravana, and he decided to call his ministers for advice.

Chapter 27

War Is Imminent

With Vibhishana's departure, there was no one to give Ravana sincere guidance; and with Rama at his doorstep, he decided to hurry Sita into acceptance. If they were married, it would be too late for Rama to rescue her. Believing his attempts so far at playing fair had failed, Ravana decided it was time to resort to trickery to win Sita over. He summoned a Rakshasa called Vidyutjiva, skilled in the art of magic, and ordered him to use his powers to simulate Rama's bow and severed head. Vidyutjiva accordingly conjured up a replica dripping with blood that bore a startling likeness to Rama and was rewarded handsomely for his efforts. Ravana then went to see Sita, hoping to deceive her into accepting him. She was sitting with her head bent low, when he strode up to her and announced with great aplomb, 'You have spurned my advances thus far only because you were waiting for your husband to rescue you, but now you can give up your false hopes because he has been killed and will not be coming here. My army stealthily attacked the enemy camp while they slept, and my commander Prahasta cut off Rama's head with his sword. Sugriva, Hanuman, Jambavan, Angada, Mainda, Dwividha, Panasa, Kumuda and many other powerful Vanaras were also killed, and Lakshmana, along with the other survivors, was forced to flee. As the stragglers escaped, some were crushed by my elephants, some were struck down as they ran, while others jumped into the sea, drowning themselves. Now that your husband is no more, marry me and become my chief queen.' Ravana had the artificial head placed in front of Sita and scornfully threw the fake bow on the ground to authenticate his words.

The imitation head was so realistic that it deceived Sita. She carefully examined the eyes, nose, ears and hair, and let out a heart-rending scream. 'O Kaikeyi, are you satisfied now that Rama is dead? He did you no harm, yet you sent him here to meet his end. Kaushalya has lost her noble son in an attempt to rescue me. Alas! I am the cause of his demise.' In her anguish, she fell to the ground in a faint. When she recovered, she stroked the decapitated head lovingly and mourned, 'O Rama, I do not know how this misfortune could have transpired because the astrologers predicted you would have a long life, and being a virtuous woman, I thought I would never face the sorrow of widowhood. How could a dauntless warrior like you have been killed so easily? My beloved husband, when you took my hand in marriage, we vowed eternal togetherness. Now that you have left me, I have no wish to live and must join you. Three of us left Ayodhya, but sadly only one will return. I must surely have committed a great sin in my previous life to be going through the excruciating pain of losing you.' Looking beseechingly at Ravana, she implored, 'You threatened to put me to death, so I beg you to do it right away so that I am united with my husband.'

At that moment, an attendant arrived with an urgent message from Prahasta, forcing Ravana to leave abruptly. Strangely, the head and bow instantly vanished with him.

A kindly attendant called Sarama felt sorry for Sita in her misery. As soon as Ravana departed, she picked her up from the ground and said kindly, 'Dry your tears, dear lady; I can assure you that your husband has not been killed. Ravana used sorcery to play a cruel trick on you because, as you know, it is impossible to kill Rama in his sleep. The truth is that Ravana is terrified, because he did not expect Rama to cross the sea. The huge Vanara army camped outside the city walls has him so worried that he is huddled with his ministers to find a way to handle the threat. Hark the beating of war drums and the flourish of trumpets mobilizing the Rakshasa army! As we speak, elephants and horses are being readied for battle. If Rama were no more, what would be the need for this? Ravana tried to bluff you with an elaborate charade because he realizes the risk of losing you. Your days in captivity are coming to an end, and soon you will be reunited with your husband. He will loosen the braid you have worn in austerity all these months, and you will rest your head on his shoulder once more. If you wish, I can go secretly to Rama and deliver a message to him from you.'

Sarama's words were therapeutic, and they soothed Sita like the dry earth soaking up the first rain. She heaved a sigh of relief that Rama was still alive, but rather than send a message to him, she felt it was preferable for Sarama to determine what plans Ravana was hatching. Accordingly, Sarama snooped around the palace; reporting back on the conversations she had eavesdropped on, she said, 'Sita, Ravana's counsellors and even his mother Kaikasi are advising him to return you to your husband, but he is adamant and will not be swayed. He is determined to keep you as long as he has breath in his body, like a miser who holds on to his treasure.'

Back in the palace, Ravana's maternal grand-uncle Malyavan stood on his terrace, gazing at the multitudes of Vanaras outside the city gates. As he listened to the deafening clamour of their war cries, he felt a deep sense of foreboding and decided to make a final effort to get his stubborn nephew to see reason. Broaching the subject gingerly, he said, 'A prudent king enjoys a long and prosperous reign. It is not always apt to embark on aggression when faced with an enemy.[8] If you are less powerful or, for that matter, equally matched, it is often pragmatic to make peace. You are under attack only because you abducted Sita, so I advise you to return her honourably and call a truce. Remember, the person with dharma on his side always wins in the end.[9] In this instance, you are the one who stands to lose by embracing unrighteousness, whereas Rama is walking the noble path to victory. Unfortunately, you do not see it because you are absorbed in yourself[10] and do not realize the great injustice you are doing to others in the process. Over the years, the countless persons you have harmed have cursed you with doom, including many rishis vested with enormous spiritual power. Remember, grandsire Brahma's boon does not safeguard you from human beings or Vanaras. Recently I have been tormented by frightening dreams auguring Lanka's destruction and have witnessed many inauspicious portents that make me concerned for the future of our race. Rama is not an ordinary person, because only someone exceptional could have built a bridge across

---

[8] 'For when two parties engage in violence, experience teaches victory and defeat are uncertain; therefore, one should avoid confrontation.' Manusmriti 7:199

[9] 'Satyameva Jayate' in the Mundaka Upanishad 3.1.6 'Truth alone triumphs, not untruth.' This was adopted as India's motto. In the other great Indian epic, the Mahabharata, the same conviction is repeated as: 'Yatho Dharmastatho Jayah'—Where there is dharma, there is victory.

[10] Over-attachment to the body as a result of ego and self-absorption is deluding, as it causes a person to seek joy in transient pleasures, at the expense of spiritual progress. 'Ignorant of their ignorance, yet wise in their own esteem, those deluded men, proud of their vain learning, go round and round like the blind led by the blind. Far beyond their eyes hypnotized by the world of sense, opens the way to immortality.'—Katha Upanishad 2.5

the ocean. He is so powerful that it almost seems he is Vishnu in a human form![11] Take my advice, son, and make peace.'

Ravana looked away in defiance; completely disregarding Malyavan's words, he refused to see that the old man had spoken for his good. The well-meaning advice irked Ravana; rolling his eyes, he retorted in annoyance, 'I have no value for such useless counsel. I find your words of praise for my enemy toxic, and it makes me wonder whose side you are on. You insult me by decrying my strength. How can you say Rama is more powerful than I am? He was thrown out of his kingdom by his father and has no support except from a bunch of lowly forest-dwellers. They are sure to be wiped out in no time. I have made up my mind; I may break, but I will not bend! Having secured a woman as beautiful as Lakshmi for myself, why would I give her up for fear of a vagrant? Rama may have managed to throw a bridge over the sea by some fluke and come here, but I can assure you he will not return alive.'

Malyavan left in disgust, realizing nothing would convince someone so intransigent; meanwhile, Ravana summoned Prahasta to arrange for the security of the city's gates. Virupaksha would command the central post, Prahasta would guard the eastern entrance, and Mahaparshwa, along with Mahodara, would defend the southern gate. Indrajit would be stationed at the western entry, and Ravana decided to proceed to the most vital northern portal himself with Shuka and Sarana.

Meanwhile, Vibhishana and his four followers took the form of birds to scope out the military arrangements underway in Lanka. Returning with valuable intelligence, they briefed Rama on the enormous firepower that his army faced. All the gateways were heavily fortified with troops, and Ravana himself was at the northern entrance with 10,000 elephants, 20,000 horses and hordes of ferocious soldiers. Since Vibhishana had recently come from Ravana's court where sycophancy ruled, he felt uncomfortable describing the opponent's strength and apologetically added, 'I hope you do not get upset when I speak of the enemy's power? It is not my intention to sing their praises but only to prepare you and incite your fury against them.' However, unlike Ravana, Rama welcomed the information and used it to deliberate on the deployment of his own army, carefully planning their strategic placement in laying siege to the city. Sugriva, Jambavan and Vibhishana would handle the central command so that they could be called upon as needed. He ordered

---

[11] Malyavan is speaking from experience. His encounter with Vishnu is narrated in the Epilogue.

Nila to take a large force and tackle Prahasta at the eastern gate. Likewise, Angada would proceed to the southern gate, taking on Mahaparshwa and Mahodara. Finally, Rama put Hanuman in charge of the western gate where Indrajit was stationed. He himself decided to go with Lakshmana to meet Ravana at the principal entrance in the north.

With this plan of action in place, Rama and the Vanaras climbed to the top of Mount Suvela to survey Lanka. There they waited out the beautiful full moon night,[12] and finally, at daybreak, beheld the shining city ten yojanas wide and twenty yojanas long atop the Trikuta Mountain. Rama's heart ached as he thought of his beloved Sita imprisoned behind the tall walls. She was almost within reach and yet so far! As the team scanned the heavy fortifications, they saw Ravana seated grandiosely above the northern gate. A regal umbrella was held over his head, while servants stood on either side, fanning him reverently. He presented a picture of majesty, adorned in heavy ornaments and dressed in fine clothing embroidered with gold thread. His broad battle-scarred chest was smeared with sandalwood paste. Sitting haughtily atop the rampart, the villainous king looked as imposing as a dark rain cloud.

Ravana's pompous demeanour filled Sugriva with sudden rage. Like an arrow shot from a bow, he leaped onto the rampart and pounced on him, tearing off his crown and throwing him to the ground. Ravana was caught off guard and exclaimed furiously, 'You are called Sugriva, the one with the beautiful neck, but once I am done with you, you will be remembered as Hinagriva, the one who lost his neck!' He picked Sugriva up and flung him down with great force, but unaffected by the impact, Sugriva bounced right back up like a ball as the two began to wrestle. Equally matched in strength, they fought with the ferocity of a lion and tiger, dripping with perspiration as they pressed against each other. As the encounter continued, they threw mighty punches, moving around in circles, crouching like cats and jumping on each other, zigzagging and ducking artfully to dodge blows. They scratched and clawed till sweat mingled with blood ran down their bodies. The fight was utterly deadlocked for a long time, with no one emerging victorious. Then, realizing that he could not win a fair battle against his opponent's raw strength, Ravana decided to invoke his dark powers.

Sugriva perceived his move and leaped back to his camp in a trice, feeling invigorated at having given Ravana a sound thrashing. The Vanaras were

---

[12] Based on astronomy the date was 12 October 5076 BCE. See Bala, Saroj, *Ramayan Retold with Scientific Evidences* (Prabhat Prakashan, 2019).

elated at his achievement, but Rama was not pleased. Embracing Sugriva, he scolded, 'It was not wise for you to have acted so impulsively without conferring with me. You are a king, and you have a duty to your people. It was not prudent to put yourself in the frontline as you just did. A leader is not expendable, so exposing yourself to the danger of being killed was a very ill-advised move. Had Ravana got the better of you, I could not have borne the sorrow of your death, but luckily your reckless escapade ended well, and you have returned unharmed.' Sugriva replied sheepishly, 'I realize I acted in haste, but I was overcome by rage to see the man who carried away your wife and caused you so much grief sitting smugly with a smirk on his face.' Hearing Sugriva, the Vanaras felt a surge of pride at his bravery and cheered loudly.

It was time for the war to begin, so the army descended from the mountain and poised itself for the offensive. However, before initiating an attack, Rama wanted to give peace one last chance, as dharma demanded that every effort be made to avert unnecessary bloodshed.[13] He chose Angada to deliver his ultimatum for Ravana to return Sita or else prepare for death in battle. Instructing him accordingly, Rama said, "Go forth to Lanka as my emissary and tell Ravana that Brahma's boon has made him far too brazen. His arrogance has made him a nuisance to the inhabitants of all three worlds, and unless he changes his ways, the time for retribution has arrived. Ask him to return Sita, whom he stole deceitfully, or meet me in combat. Like Yama, I stand ready to administer justice for all those who have suffered at his hands. If Ravana does not surrender, tell him to take a last look at his beautiful kingdom, for I will surely kill him in battle and place Vibhishana on his throne."

Angada went boldly to Ravana's court and introduced himself as the late Vanara king Vali's son. He dutifully delivered Rama's message, but as might have been anticipated, the attempt to avert a bloody conflict failed. Ravana, sitting imperiously in his court with his ministers, was enraged at Rama's precondition to avoiding a war. He ordered his men to seize the insolent messenger and put him to death, but fortunately, Angada managed to brush them off. He then leaped to the top of the palace, shattering its dome before returning to Rama.

---

13 Manusmriti chapter 7.198–200 advises conciliation first before embarking on bloodshed. This is also the principle of Ahimsa—to use the least violent option available.

Chapter 28

War Begins

With no hope left to prevent bloodshed, war became inevitable. Rama and his army were forced to lay siege to Lanka. Ravana deployed double the troops to defend the gates, and the opposing sides fought furiously, reminiscent of the battles of yore between the Devas and the Asuras. The Vanaras surrounded the city; they threw logs and boulders into the moat and scaled the ramparts, raising battle cries of 'Jai Sri Rama!'[1] Following their battle plan, they stormed the gates, and before long, Virabahu, Subahu, Nala and Panasa took command of them. The mighty Shatabali besieged the southern entrance, and Tara's father Sushena fought the Rakshasas at the western portal. At the northern gate, Lakshmana, Rama and Sugriva fought along with Gavaksha and his gigantic, black-faced, long-tailed Golangula troops. Mighty warriors duelled with each other as the hostilities raged in full fury and the clamour of war drums, horns and conches filled the air.

In the melee, Angada wounded Indrajit, knocking him down from his chariot, forcing him to make a speedy retreat and disappear from the battlefield. Sampati was victorious against Prajangha. Gaja took on Tapana, and Nila dealt a blow to Nikumba with his own chariot wheel. Sugriva struck down Praghasa with a tree, and Lakshmana incapacitated Virupaksha with a single arrow. Nala gouged out the eyes of Pratapana. Rama beheaded Agniketu, Durdharsa, Mithraghna and Yajnakopa. Mainda brought down Vajramusti with his fist, and Dwividha finished off Asaniprabha with a giant sala tree. Sushena toppled Vidyunmali off his chariot and crushed his head with a rock. As evening approached, Rama wounded six more powerful Rakshasas—Yajnashatru, Mahaparshwa, Mahodara, Vajradamshtra, Shuka

---

[1] Victory to Rama! Rama was an embodiment of dharma so it implies victory to dharma.

289

and Sarana—with his flaming arrows, but they managed to slip away from the battlefield, escaping with their lives.

Blood flowed copiously in the gruesome engagement, and though bodies piled up on both sides, the Vanaras initially had the upper hand. They assailed the Rakshasas with trees and boulders, using their sharp teeth and razor-like claws to counter a variety of lethal weapons effectively. Then, fortunes suddenly shifted towards the end of the day when the Rakshasas became invigorated with the approaching dusk. Indrajit, who had retreated earlier, resumed fighting, ignobly choosing to remain unseen.[2] Using the unfair advantage of invisibility, he viciously rained arrows on the Vanaras, decimating hundreds of them. Then he employed his mystical powers to direct a missile of poisonous serpent arrows called the Nagapasha at Rama and Lakshmana. Since they could not see their assailant, the valiant brothers were unprepared for his assault and swooned, immobilized by the deadly weapon. With not an inch of space between the arrows that covered their bodies, they lay helpless, embedded with circular-headed Naracas, half-sized Ardhanaracas, teeth-like Vatsadantas, Simhadamstras and razor-headed Ksuras. The Vanara heroes became distraught at the unexpected turn of events and tried desperately to locate Indrajit, but he stayed safely hidden from view. Then they heard his booming voice sneering that even Indra did not have the power to see him. He gloated, revelling in the victory of bringing down the two scions of Raghu, thereby avenging his uncles, Khara and Dushana. Finally, aiming a parting shot of arrows at Hanuman and Angada, he triumphantly left the battlefield to convey the good news of his success to his father.

The morale of the Vanaras sank to a low ebb, and Sugriva wept bitterly, thinking his friends had perished. However, Vibhishana was more discerning and saw that they were just unconscious. Consoling Sugriva, he said, 'Your despair is unnecessary; Rama and Lakshmana are still alive and can be resuscitated. Ups and downs are inevitable in a battle, and you should not get disheartened just because the enemy has had a brief winning streak. A leader sets an example to others; giving in to despondency is bound to affect the confidence of the rank and file negatively. Now pull yourself together while I rally the troops.' Vibhishana reassured the Vanaras that their side had only

---

[2] Fighting unseen was against the rules of battle. 'When a kingdom goes to war, it should not strike with concealed weapons, nor use poisons, nor any that cause conflagrations.' Manusmriti 7:90

experienced a minor setback that would be reversed soon, and asked them to guard Rama and Lakshmana till the princes recovered consciousness.

Meanwhile, in Lanka, Indrajit proudly announced to his father that his confidence in him was not misplaced; he had won the war on the first day by eliminating Rama and Lakshmana. Ravana jumped up from his seat in excitement and hugged his favourite son close, kissing his forehead tenderly. He thanked Indrajit profusely for his achievement and ordered the city to be festively decorated with flags and garlands to proclaim his success. Ravana then excitedly sent for Trijata and asked her to take Sita over the battlefield in the Pushpaka Vimana to see Rama's dead body for herself. He surmised that once she lost hope of reuniting with her husband, Sita would voluntarily come to him.

Sita looked down woefully from the air and could not contain her grief at the sight of Rama and Lakshmana lying supine on the battlefield. They seemed as lifeless as corpses; their bodies stuck with as many arrows as quills on a porcupine. She cried out in pain at the thought of Kaushalya, who was counting the days for her precious son to return, and bemoaned that the fortunetellers were terribly mistaken in predicting that Rama would live a long life and perform many yagnas as a king. Sita was mad with grief and lamented that all the prophecies that she would bear sons and not be widowed were now belied. The two motionless bodies filled her with horror, and she was perplexed at how such an unfortunate situation could possibly have arisen when both princes possessed the knowledge of every astra. It seemed unbelievable to her that they had crossed the mighty ocean only to perish in a tiny puddle, as small as the imprint of a cow's hoof.

Trijata, on the other hand, had her doubts about the situation. She comforted Sita, saying that it did not appear to her that Rama and Lakshmana were dead. If this were the case, the Vanara soldiers would have scattered, but instead, the army was vigilantly standing guard. The princes were undoubtedly still alive, as it would be pointless to protect lifeless bodies. To reassure Sita, she said, 'O Maithili, your good nature and flawless character have endeared you to me. I would never say anything to deceive you, so trust me when I tell you that I am certain Rama and Lakshmana are not dead. The Pushpaka is a divine vehicle and would not have brought you here as a widow to witness such a tragedy. Also, note the faces of your husband and his brother are still shining with the glow of life, devoid of pallor. Do you see that the Vanaras are not mourning? If a leader dies, the army displays a lack of purpose and disperses from the scene. Here, to the contrary, the soldiers are guarding

Rama and Lakshmana carefully, alert even to the slightest movement of a blade of grass.' Trijata's logic made sense to Sita, and in relief, she folded her hands and said gratefully, 'May your words be true, Trijata!'

Rama slowly regained consciousness, but he was still affected by the poison of the Nagapasha and unable to move. His first thoughts were for Lakshmana, lying comatose on the ground. Seeing him in a cold, senseless condition, Rama cried out in pain, 'My life has no purpose without Lakshmana! Even though Sita is unrivalled in her dedication as a wife, there could possibly be another woman who is as virtuous as her somewhere in the three worlds, but I can say with complete certainty that no other brother exists anywhere who displays the peerless devotion of Lakshmana. What face will I show Mother Sumitra, who sent her valiant son to assist me in my exile? Lakshmana was my closest confidant and the wisest counsellor anyone could hope to have. He stood by me through all my trials and tribulations, sharing my sorrow and providing emotional support in my weakest moments. I have sinned in allowing him to succumb to death while serving me. I can only redeem myself by following him to the land of Yama. Alas, I spoke too soon in promising Vibhishana the throne of Lanka! Sugriva, I regret that thousands of Vanaras have sacrificed themselves on my account. Ravana is sure to finish off the rest of you, so I suggest you disband the army and go back home with those who remain alive.'

Meanwhile, Vibhishana, who had returned, also became despondent and said tearfully, 'I feel crushed to see two mighty warriors reduced to a helpless condition by my nephew's unethical tactics. It appears Ravana has won! I had hoped to rule Lanka, but a far cry from that, now it seems we are all as good as dead.' Hearing this, Sugriva turned to his father-in-law Sushena and said, 'Return to Kishkindha with Rama, Lakshmana and the Vanaras. I will stay here and complete the unfinished business of rescuing Sita and placing Vibhishana on the throne.' But, Sushena, a skilled physician, did not feel all was lost as yet. He advised Sugriva not to despair prematurely as there was still a possibility of reviving Lakshmana. He reminded him of how Brihaspati, the guru of the Devas, had used two herbs—Sanjeevakarani and Vishalyakarani—to resuscitate fallen warriors and insisted they should not give up before exhausting every possible option.

As he spoke, the night sky lit up, and Vishnu's charioteer Garuda, the splendid king of the birds, appeared. A tremendous gust of wind heralded his arrival, and the ocean became turbulent with the flapping of his enormous wings. The trees shook, and the snakes on the island slithered away in alarm, desperately seeking shelter. Garuda saw Rama and Lakshmana poisoned by the venom of snakes and decided to come to their aid. As he touched their bodies, they became whole again, and the lethal toxin that coursed through their veins was dispelled. Freed from their shackles, the two princes arose with their strength redoubled. Expressing his deepest gratitude to the mighty eagle, Rama said appreciatively, 'Thanks to your grace, we are saved, but who are you, divine being who shines with such splendour? My heart warms to behold you as if I am seeing my father.'

The eagle replied, 'My name is Garuda. Consider me a friend; I rushed here as soon as I heard of your situation. The virulence of the Nagapasha is deadly, and only I can negate its effects. You are magnanimous even to your enemies, but I would like to warn you that Rakshasas do not share your straightforward nature. Beware of them in battle! Unlike you, they have no compunctions about stooping to underhanded means to win. At the same time, take courage in knowing that ultimately you will be victorious against Ravana and all the Rakshasas; no man will be left in Lanka; only women and children will remain.' Garuda then circled Rama and flew up into the sky. Turning to bless him before disappearing, he said, in a strangely cryptic way, that Rama would understand their special relationship[3] in time.

By now it was dawn, and there was great merriment in the camp over Rama and Lakshmana's recovery. The Vanaras screeched loudly, jumping around, thumping their tails in joy, and beating tom-toms in delight. Ravana heard the raucous celebration and wondered about the exuberance since Rama and Lakshmana had been reported dead, and their followers were expected to be mourning. He grew worried that something had gone awry and sent his spies to find out more. They returned to say that the brothers who had been presumed dead had not only miraculously survived but looked rejuvenated, displaying renewed vigour like war elephants who had shaken off their chains. The colour drained from Ravana's face as he asked himself how anyone could have survived the unfailing Nagapasha. Though dejected at his short-lived victory, he was sure he could fix the problem and summoned Dhumraksha, 'The Smoky-Eyed One', to deal with the enemy and bring them to their knees.

Dhumraksha sallied forth through the western gate amidst great fanfare. He led a large brigade of warriors armed to the hilt with maces, swords, spears, cudgels, battle axes, lances, slingshots and nooses. They were well

[3] Garuda being Vishnu's vehicle had a special relationship with his avatar.

protected by armour and supported by countless elephants and chariots, but fortune did not appear to favour them. Ill omens foretold their doom. A vulture alighted on Dhumraksha's chariot, a headless torso landed before him, red rain showered down, and they were shrouded momentarily in darkness. Hanuman and his troops stationed in the west were waiting eagerly for combat, and a terrible battle ensued. The dreadful cacophony of twanging bows, crushed chariots, trumpeting elephants, neighing horses and the plaintive moaning of the injured rent the air. Many Vanaras perished, struck by arrows, their limbs torn apart by sharp weapons; yet they fought on tirelessly, using their physical strength to inflict heavy casualties on the Rakshasa army. They smashed the enemy's chariots and smote down their elephants, attacking with giant tree trunks and boulders, ripping their bodies apart.[4] Dhumraksha came to his people's rescue, showering the Vanaras with arrows. Hundreds lay dead in his wake. Hanuman was enraged to see his side taking a beating and rushed to stop the carnage. He seized a large rock and flung it at Dhumraksha's chariot, shattering it to pieces. Then he wiped out large numbers of Rakshasas wielding a massive tree that he used to bash their heads to a pulp. Meanwhile, Dhumraksha, who had dodged the boulder that destroyed his chariot, jumped to the ground and struck Hanuman's head with his mace. However, the blow was no deterrent and served only to enrage Hanuman further. He picked up another giant boulder, and hurling it with great force, crushed Dhumraksha, killing him instantly. Seeing their commander fall, the Rakshasas retreated in fear behind the city walls.

Ravana was exasperated to hear that Dhumraksha had been killed. Sighing heavily, he called upon another fierce Rakshasa called Vajradamshtra, named after his powerful canines and ordered him to deal with the Vanara threat. Vajradamshtra set out through the southern gate, where Angada was posted, and like Dhumraksha, took a large battalion of fierce fighters, well-armed with deadly weapons. Once more, there were unfavourable indications as meteors fell from the sky and jackals howled. Yet again, a raging battle ensued in which countless warriors on both sides lost their lives, and mangled corpses littered the battlefield. Finally, Vajradamshtra faced Angada in a contest that resembled an encounter between a lion and an elephant. Vajradamshtra shot several arrows, and Angada retaliated with fury. Although injured all over and bathed in blood, Angada fought relentlessly. He hurled a tree at

---

[4] While the Rakshasas had sophisticated weapons, the Vanaras relied only on their sharp nails, teeth and sheer strength.

Vajradamshtra, who managed to shatter it to pieces. Then Angada broke off a colossal crag and threw it at Vajradamshtra's chariot, flattening the vehicle. Seizing another boulder, he struck Vajradamshtra's head, causing his opponent to vomit blood and lose consciousness. When he recovered, Vajradamshtra rushed at Angada and hit him on the chest with his mace. As the two wrestled, they looked as frightening as Mars and Mercury colliding. They kicked and kneed each other, inflicting heavy blows with their fists, delivering mighty chops with the sides of their palms. After fighting for a long time, when they were both exhausted and covered in blood, Angada seized an opportunity; grabbing a sword, he lopped off his opponent's head in one stroke. While the Vanaras exulted in their victory, the Rakshasas fled the battlefield in dismay to report their commander's death to Ravana.

Vajradamshtra's death had Ravana confounded, and he was frustrated that two of his most powerful commanders had been worsted by mere monkey men. So, this time, he called on Akampana—'The Unshakeable'—in whom he had the utmost confidence. Akampana mounted a huge chariot decked with gold and jewels. He shone like the sun, and his voice boomed like thunder. He set out confident of victory, but suddenly his left eye twitched, and the day that had been fine so far became cloudy and windy, auguring misfortune.

Nevertheless, he led his forces with great ferocity and massacred many brave Vanaras. Stiff resistance was put up by Kumuda, Nala, Mainda and Dwividha as they butchered the Rakshasas in large numbers. Seeing his kith and kin falling, Akampana charged to their defence, driving his chariot amidst the Vanara ranks, ceaselessly raining arrows on them. Hanuman came to the rescue, but a hail of arrows assailed him, and he looked like a hill covered in ashoka trees aflame with blood-red flowers. Nevertheless, he advanced undaunted towards Akampana, brandishing a large aswakarna tree that he had uprooted, clearing elephants and chariots in his path as he made his way. When Hanuman had Akampana in his reach, he delivered a mighty blow to the general's head. As the Rakshasa fell to the ground, his terrified troops ran back to Lanka in a panic to deliver the news of their defeat.

Ravana could not believe that the enemy had taken out Akampana, but he was confident they would not prevail against his powerful commander-in-chief, Prahasta. Placing enormous faith in Prahasta's military expertise, Ravana said, 'The city stands beleaguered by the enemy. I believe that it can only be saved by the likes of you, Kumbhakarna, Indrajit, Nikumbha or myself. I am certain that in the face of your assault, the untrained and fickle-minded Vanaras will flee in terror, and weakened without their support, Rama and Lakshmana will be forced to accept defeat. Please suggest whatever strategy is needed to win, even if you think it is unpalatable to me.' Prahasta replied, 'In the past, views were expressed in the council suggesting that Sita be returned to avoid bloodshed, but that did not happen, and war is upon us. Now it is too late to turn back, so the only course of action left is to forge ahead. You have bestowed numerous honours on me during my many years of service, rewarding me handsomely with untold riches. I want you to know that you have my undying loyalty. I am prepared to give my life for you if necessary.' Bowing reverently, he took his leave of Ravana, with his mind intent on success.

Prahasta performed a fire ritual invoking Agni and sought the blessings of the Brahmins before setting out through the eastern gate. He departed with much pageantry to the roll of kettledrums and the blast of conches, declaring with great certitude, 'The vultures will be pleased with my efforts today, for I intend to provide them with a feast of Vanara bodies!' Four trusted aides—Narantaka, Kumbhahanu, Mahanada and Samunata—accompanied him, and he looked like Yama amidst his massive battle array. Seeing him, Rama smiled and asked who had come this time. Vibhishana explained that Prahasta was Ravana's right-hand man, his powerful commander-in-chief, well versed in military tactics. He had brought one-third of Lanka's army, so the assault that followed was brutal. Blood flowed on the battlefield like a river carrying broken weapons, entrails and body parts. It was a gruesome engagement, and though there were incalculable losses on both sides, Prahasta and his four trusted soldiers exacted a heavier toll on the Vanara forces. The casualties lay scattered like fallen leaves, pierced by arrows, halved by swords or beheaded by discuses.

Then fortuitously, the tide turned. Dwividha got the opportunity to strike down Narantaka. Durmukha took on Samunata and killed him. Jambavan smashed Mahanada's chest with a boulder, while Tara vanquished Kumbhahanu. Their deaths infuriated Prahasta, and he began to devastate the Vanaras. Seeing his brave soldiers in the mire, disembowelled and lying hacked to pieces, Nila jumped into the fray. He rushed belligerently towards Prahasta and was instantly met by a volley of arrows that struck him all over. Mindless of his injuries, he advanced heroically, smashing Prahasta's grand chariot and bow. The two fought frantically like bull elephants in rut, and finally, after a hard-fought clash, Nila emerged victorious, bashing in Prahasta's head. Bleeding profusely, the mighty Prahasta lay lifeless amongst the corpses on the battlefield, and the Rakshasa army retreated in terror, dispirited at the loss of their leader.

Ravana found the death of Prahasta, the highest-ranking general in his army, extremely disconcerting. He was rattled at the defeat of his valorous commander-in-chief, and crushed at losing a loyal friend. Realizing it had to take a mighty enemy to kill Prahasta, who had easily vanquished Indra's forces, it dawned on him that he had grossly underestimated the Vanaras' strength. Ravana decided that the time had come for him to enter the war and teach his antagonists a lesson. He appeared on the battlefield in a splendid chariot drawn by the finest steeds, blazing like fire in his resolve to annihilate Rama and every Vanara in his army. Mighty Rakshasa warriors accompanied him, and he was given a grand send-off to the flourish of drums and cheers of victory that sent shivers down the spines of the Vanaras. Vibhishana pointed out Ravana and the generals he had carefully stationed to protect the city gates—Indrajit, Atikaya, Mahodara, Trishira, Pishacha and Kumbha. In their majestic chariots decorated with flags bearing their emblems, they looked intimidating, presenting a grim picture. Each was valorous, well versed in the art of warfare and ready to die for their king.

Seeing Ravana up close for the first time, Rama was impressed by the splendorous image he presented. He had a mighty presence like the Lord of Death himself, but rather than being intimidated, Rama was eager to engage him in battle. He was pleased that Ravana had finally appeared on the scene and was keen to punish him for Sita's abduction. Ravana wasted no time beginning his attack, falling on the Vanara army like a whale leaping into the ocean, raining lethal arrows as he cut through them. Sugriva challenged him by tearing off a mountain peak and hurling it, but he was no match for the mighty Rakshasa, who dexterously repelled it and hit him back with a fiery shaft resembling Indra's thunderbolt. As the Vanara king fell groaning to the ground, the Rakshasa army cheered excitedly. Vanara titans Gavaksha, Gavaya, Sushena, Rishabha, Jyotirmukha and Nala rushed forward in defence, but their blows were in vain as Ravana sent them all reeling to the ground.

The Vanaras ran to Rama seeking protection, but as he seized his bow, Lakshmana joined his palms and said, 'You need not go; I am enough to deal with the situation. Please allow me to destroy this sinner who is the very personification of evil. I am convinced that I can subdue him and eliminate the terror he spreads.'

Rama agreed to the request, cautioning Lakshmana to be very careful, and he valiantly went forth. In the meantime, Hanuman jumped in front of Ravana to stop the slaughter of his fellow Vanaras. He threatened, 'Your boon protects you from almost all creatures, but Vanaras are not included. You have lived long; now prepare to die at my hands!' Ravana scoffed at the challenge and shouted back nonchalantly, 'Feel free to use all your power against me in your attempt to attain fame. However, know that you will not succeed, so prepare to perish!'

Hanuman did not appreciate Ravana's arrogance and taunted him with the reminder that he had killed his son Akshakumara, who had displayed similar bluster. This boast provoked Ravana to land a punch on his chest, and the impact sent Hanuman staggering. Steadying himself, he struck back, and Ravana shook like a mountain in an earthquake. On recovering, he exclaimed, 'Well played, monkey; that was a good shot,' and Hanuman replied, 'Unfortunately, it was not good enough to kill you. Try hitting me again so I can deliver you to death's door this time.' Ravana clenched his right fist and pounded Hanuman on the chest again with great force, sending him reeling to the ground. Having incapacitated Hanuman, he set his sights on Nila. As they battled, Hanuman revived himself; he was ready to resume fighting but thought it improper to interfere in a duel between two warriors. Unable to subdue Ravana with his assault of boulders and trees that was quickly countered, Nila reduced himself in size and jumped onto his chariot, hoping to attack the Rakshasa king at close quarters. He leaped atop Ravana's flagpole, jumped upon his bow, and even onto the great crown on his head, till finally, Ravana used the Agniastra to repel him. It knocked Nila out, but luckily, spared him from incineration since he was the son of the Fire Deva and enjoyed his protection.

Galvanized by his defeat of so many valorous Vanaras, Ravana rushed to take on Lakshmana, who tried to challenge him. He roared, 'Though you have not made a wise decision in appearing before me, I am glad to have you in my sights at last. Today, you will get a taste of my prowess.' Lakshmana replied sarcastically, 'True warriors don't brag! I am familiar with your great valour, which you displayed when you abducted Sita! Your destruction of the Vanaras in this battle ends here.' In the fight that followed, the two warriors exchanged arrow for arrow and seemed equally matched for a while.

Ravana dispatched seven arrows, which Lakshmana thwarted. Enraged at being stymied, he attacked again, and this time hit Lakshmana on the forehead, causing him to stumble to the ground. However, he struggled to his feet, and using his powerful Ksura, Ardhachandra, Karni and axe-headed Bhalla arrows, destroyed Ravana's bow, injuring him severely. Though badly wounded and without his bow, Ravana was undeterred. He picked up his unfailing Brahma spear and hurled it at Lakshmana, striking him on his chest. Brahma's weapon was too powerful for Lakshmana to withstand, and he lost consciousness. Overjoyed at his success, Ravana jumped off his chariot to carry Lakshmana away as a prize. However, no matter how much he tried, he could not lift him off the ground. Hanuman saw Lakshmana fall and rushed at Ravana, hammering him with his fists. The blows were so violent that Ravana dropped to his knees, and blood oozed from his mouth and ears as he swooned. Then Hanuman lifted Lakshmana, who miraculously felt light as a feather,[5] and as he did so, the divine weapon automatically returned to its master.

Meanwhile, Ravana had regained consciousness and was ready on his chariot to fight again. Rama advanced boldly towards him but did not have a chariot. Hanuman offered himself as a vehicle so that Rama could be on par with his opponent. Climbing on to Hanuman's shoulders, Rama challenged Ravana with the thunderous twang of his bowstring, proclaiming sternly, 'By striking down Lakshmana with your spear, you have invited death today. You will not find refuge from my wrath anywhere in the three worlds and are doomed to meet the same fate as your kinsmen in Janasthana.' Ravana released his arrows on Hanuman, and enraged at seeing his loyal soldier hurt, Rama fired back with a thunderbolt, knocking Ravana down and destroying his chariot. Next, seizing a crescent-shaped arrow, Rama tore off Ravana's magnificent diadem, and it fell next to him, humbled in the dirt. Then speaking magnanimously to the defeated king, who resembled a defanged serpent writhing on the ground, Rama said, 'Although I intended to kill you today in retribution for all the evil you have done, my principles do not permit me to execute someone injured and defenceless without a weapon. There is no valour in killing a helpless person. You fought hard and displayed inordinate skill on the battlefield, so go home and rest. Come back tomorrow once you have recouped your strength so I can defeat you in fair combat.' Exhausted and embarrassed, the mighty Rakshasa king, who had overcome the Devas dragged himself back to Lanka minus the royal trappings of his grand chariot, able charioteer, swift steeds and sans his dazzling crown.

---

[5] The spear was a divine weapon, so though it did its job in hitting the target, it recognized Lakshmana's piety and weighed his body down so Ravana could not lift him.

Chapter 29

Kumbhakarna

Ravana had been brought to his knees and, in a fate worse than death, pardoned by his adversary. The blow to his pride was bitter, and the humiliation stung him even more than his physical wounds. Crestfallen at being vanquished, he recalled the furious onslaught of Rama's arrows and felt unnerved for the first time in his life. Ravana remembered that he had been given immunity from death at the hands of every creature, except for human beings, and today it was troubling that he had been bested by one. His mind dwelled on the damnation heaped on him by those he had wronged over the years. The Ikshavaku king Anaranya had declared that a man born in his house would exterminate him and his line. The pious anchoress Vedavati, whom he tried to violate, had cursed him while immolating herself, prophesizing that she would be reborn to cause his death. He wondered if Sita could have returned as her? Shiva's consort Parvati had foretold that Ravana's end would be because of a woman, and Nandi[1] had warned him that Vanaras would bring about his downfall. Ravana had outraged the modesty of so many women, and when he molested the Apsaras, Rambha and Punjikasthala, they had tearfully cried that a woman would be his undoing.[2] Recalling the countless people who wished him ill, Ravana's head began to spin. It made him feel faint-hearted, and he decided it would be best for him to avoid facing Rama the following day. Instead, it would be far more expedient to send someone impossible to defeat, and the person he had in mind was Kumbhakarna.

Rousing Kumbhakarna would be no easy task, as he was in deep slumber after his recent day awake nine days ago, when he had attended

---

[1] Shiva's faithful attendant whom Ravana had insulted.

[2] Ravana's long history of abuse is told in the Epilogue.

the council. His home was a vast subterranean cavern, eight yojanas on each side, where he lay outstretched on a massive bed, snoring loudly with his mouth open. His body was covered in bristles, and his breath smelled putrid, with remnants of blood and fat from his last meal decaying in his unrinsed mouth. His head was adorned with a crown and his arms were decorated with massive gold armlets. He exhaled with the force of a powerful cyclone, and it was hard to stand in his presence without being blown away. Ravana's ministers ordered attendants to bring in piping hot food to tempt Kumbhakarna's olfactory senses. They fetched his favourite fare—meat, blood and wine—laying out a carnivorous feast of deer, buffalo and wild boar, along with heaps of rice and all kinds of delectable dishes that smelled inviting. When that did not awaken him, they burnt incense, rubbed him with sandal paste and dabbed perfume under his nose, but he continued to snore loudly. Wringing their hands, they shouted, blowing conches and banging on kettledrums as loud as they could, forcing everyone in Lanka to cover their ears, but Kumbhakarna's sleep was unbroken. Then the aides began striking him with mallets and prodding him with spears. They even had horses, camels, donkeys and elephants tread on him, yet he did not stir. Finally, in desperation, they climbed on his body, pulled his hair and bit his ears, pouring buckets of cold water over him, and then, at last, Kumbhakarna opened his eyes, inhaling the scent of the banquet laid out for him. He stretched, yawning repeatedly, his eyes still bleary with sleep, and began to devour the food hungrily.

When every platter was empty, he thundered, 'Why have I been woken up prematurely? There must be a very pressing reason for this intrusion; I hope my brother the king is well and not in any danger? Have the Devas attacked again?'

The minister Yupaksha replied, 'The threat is not from the Devas. The city is sinking under siege from Rama and his army of monkey men. We have never been defeated in the past but face a serious emergency now. Many of our valiant military commanders have been killed, morale is at a low, and even Ravana himself escaped with his life only because of Rama's magnanimity. So, as a last resort, he asked us to wake you up to assist him in dealing with the enemy.'

Kumbhakarna bathed, dressed, feasted again, quaffing pitchers of wine, and declared he would head to the battlefield right away. However, the ministers advised that it would be better to go to Ravana's palace to receive his orders, so he made his way there.

Kumbhakarna touched his brother's feet, and Ravana, in turn, clasped him warmly to his bosom. Relieved to see him, Ravana said, 'Since you have been asleep, you are unaware of a significant development that has taken place since we met at the council. Rama and his Vanara army unexpectedly made it across the sea and launched an attack on us. We have battled them for the last few days but have suffered heavy losses; our exchequer is depleted, and our soldiers are demoralized. I had no option but to wake you because you are the only one who can save Lanka. I have never begged anyone for anything before, but I know you love me, so I implore you for your help in this dire situation.'

Kumbhakarna was angry that Ravana had allowed hostilities to escalate to the point of war and berated him for the missteps that had put the kingdom in such a precarious position. 'This danger was anticipated,' he said vexedly. 'I told you before and I reiterate that you committed a dastardly act by stealing another man's wife. Now, inevitably, you are reaping the consequences of your sinful behaviour! A king should always exercise self-control, carefully weighing the outcome of his actions before plunging headlong into an undertaking that puts his people at risk. Anything done rashly without due deliberation necessarily ends in disaster, like a yagna conducted by an impious person. According to the rules of statecraft, a king achieves victory only if he marries the 'three with the five'. First, he must choose when it is appropriate to wage war; second, he must have a good assessment of his position; and third, he must be aware of the enemy's strength. Once these are determined, he should deliberate with experts and develop a comprehensive strategy with winning tactics, mobilizing the necessary resources for his success. By proceeding methodically like this, taking the right opportunity to strike, and at the same time keeping his defence secured, he obtains the desired result.

'Unfortunately, your obsession with Sita has caused you to focus solely on sensual pleasures to the exclusion of good sense. Our shastras instruct us that while it is natural to have material desires and pursue wealth, all actions must always be conducted within the framework of dharma. If your pursuit of kama or artha conflicts with dharma, you know it must be abandoned. Several members of your inner circle offered you impolitic advice, leading you down the wrong path, but you should have known better and excluded them from your discussions. Unfortunately, you did not heed the warning of our younger brother Vibhishana and instead favoured the unwholesome counsel of flatterers. I have to say you have brought this unnecessary misfortune on yourself, and your obduracy has landed Lanka in a terrible mess.'

Ravana frowned and replied peevishly, 'Why are you preaching to me in this pedantic manner when I am facing my biggest crisis? You keep harping on the past, but what has already happened cannot be changed at this point. There is no benefit derived from moralizing about what I should have or could have done. Besides, I woke you up to help me defeat the enemy, not to hear you opine on my behaviour. If you have any brotherly affection for me, use your strength to defeat my enemies and correct the course I have embarked on. I am in a tough position and am counting on you; after all, a true benefactor is one who helps in times of need.'

Kumbhakarna was moved by Ravana's woeful appeal and quickly soothed his irritation, assuring him of his complete loyalty. He knew his brother was at fault; nonetheless, he went against his better judgement and agreed to assist him. Offering his unconditional support, Kumbhakarna said indulgently, 'It is my fraternal fondness that makes me put aside my principles to assist you, despite knowing that you are on the wrong side of dharma. I care for you deeply and promise to protect you from harm as long as I live. See what happens today! Be assured that I will vanquish Rama and Lakshmana to fulfil your desire for Sita. Hanuman will pay dearly for having set Lanka on fire; I will eat him first and then devour every monkey in the Vanara army. So do not feel stressed; forget your troubles and relax; go enjoy some good wine and the company of your consorts. Take it from me that the battle is as good as won.' Then with strange prescience, he added, 'I will go alone, and Rama will reach you only after he manages to kill me.'

Hoping to ingratiate himself with Ravana in light of Kumbhakarna's criticism, a relative called Mahodara said, 'Kumbhakarna, you are wrong in saying that the king did not follow dharma out of ignorance. A person as eminently learned as Ravana is fully aware of right and wrong, but at the same time, he is not foolishly idealistic. You are but a lad and do not see that dharma does not guarantee any benefit in one's lifetime. So long as we achieve happiness in this world, what does righteousness matter? I suggest we employ trickery to bring Sita around. If we make her believe that Rama is dead by proclaiming victory and distributing gifts, she will feel vulnerable and have no alternative but to submit to our king. Women are fickle and fall prey to temptation easily when they feel insecure. Avoid going to battle; there is no need to expend the energy of our army and risk losing lives.'

Kumbhakarna felt annoyed and ridiculed Mahodara's proposition as outrageous. Reprimanding him sternly, he replied, 'It is people like you who have put us in this unfortunate position with misguided advice. You led the king away from dharma, and now I have to fix the damage you have done by going to the battlefield.' Likewise, Ravana chastised Mahodara for speaking like a coward afraid to fight; then, bolstered by a new lease of life derived from Kumbhakarna's support, he praised his brother profusely. Ravana was sure Kumbhakarna would bring him Rama's head, making all past losses seem like trifles, and sent him out with complete confidence, anticipating nothing but success.

Kumbhakarna was so colossal that the earth shook with every step he took. The Vanaras caught a glimpse of him towering above the city walls even before he entered the battlefield and trembled in fear. Terrified at the sight of this mountain-like creature, who could very well serve as a flag post for the whole world, they ran to Rama in dread. No one had ever seen anyone like him before, and Rama turned to Vibhishana for elucidation.

Vibhishana confirmed that the gargantuan Rakshasa was his elder brother, Kumbhakarna, blessed with enormous strength from birth. His gigantic size made him invincible against anyone he encountered, and had earned him many victories against the Devas, Yakshas, Nagas, Gandharvas, Kinnaras and other Rakshasa chieftains. He spoke of Kumbhakarna's voracious appetite; the giant devoured hundreds of animals in one sitting. To stop him from divesting the Earth of all living creatures, Indra attacked Kumbhakarna with his thunderbolt, but that did not affect him. Unfazed by the powerful weapon, he ripped off a tusk from Indra's elephant Airavata, striking him in the chest with it. In trepidation, Indra sought the help of Brahma. Seeing the damage Kumbhakarna's insatiable appetite was doing to the Earth, Brahma made use of a suitable opportunity, casting a spell on him to sleep forever. Ravana was aghast at the terrible pronouncement, and begged their grandfather to show mercy, pleading that the punishment was too severe. Brahma reconsidered and amended the penalty so that Kumbhakarna would sleep for six months, wake up for a day to eat, and slumber again for another six months. Vibhishana added that Kumbhakarna's untimely awakening indicated that Ravana was desperate, but it did not diminish the threat before them.

By this time, the Vanaras were petrified and needed rallying, so Vibhishana advised that the troops be informed that the giant was not a living being but a mechanical device. He felt they would be less frightened if they saw him as some kind of contraption, so Rama instructed Nila to gather the army and organize them in battle formation.

Meanwhile, back in Lanka, Kumbhakarna grabbed his spear and announced to Ravana, 'I will go alone. I don't need anyone else because I am perfectly capable of dealing with the Vanaras myself.' However, Ravana insisted that an army accompany him, warning that the Vanaras had shown themselves to be spunky and defeating them single-handed could be tricky. He personally dressed Kumbhakarna in fine ornaments and protective armour that made him look as unassailable as Narayana himself when he set out. Taking leave of his elder brother, Kumbhakarna circled him reverently and stepped over the city walls with his colossal legs, uttering a deafening war cry that sent chills down the spines of the Vanaras. Although beset by inauspicious omens like his left arm and eye throbbing and a meteor crashing to obliterate the sun's brilliance, Kumbhakarna was like death itself on the battlefield. A hundred bow-lengths in girth and 600 in height, he plowed through the enemy formation brandishing a club and trampling vast numbers of hapless Vanaras under his humungous feet. The sight of the behemoth rumbling towards them, setting the earth aquiver with his strides, was terrifying. As he laid waste to everyone in his path, the Vanaras ran helter-skelter in fear.

Young Angada displayed exemplary leadership in rounding up the fleeing troops, mustering their courage with stirring rhetoric. He enjoined the panicking Vanaras to show bravery, shouting, 'How can you turn your backs and escape like cowards when you come from such illustrious families! Only lily-livered creatures exhibit such spinelessness. Do not let this artificial ogre frighten you into becoming weaklings so you earn the scorn of your wives. What happened to your boastful talk about vanquishing the enemy? Remember, if we succeed, we will achieve glory in this world, and if we are martyred on the battlefield, we will attain heaven. Join me in contending with this impediment in our path to victory; together, I know we can finish him off.' At last, Angada managed to pull the army together with a fighting spirit to win or lay down their lives in the attempt. His rousing words restored their pluck, and the errant soldiers reassembled to meet the enormous challenge that loomed ahead.

The Vanaras struck Kumbhakarna with large trees and hurled colossal boulders at him, but he hardly felt their blows. When Dwividha flung a massive rock, he effortlessly averted it, and it smashed the chariots and elephants behind him instead. Kumbhakarna continued to cause havoc, crushing and even eating the Vanaras whole, when Hanuman flew up, striking him with a powerful blow. Kumbhakarna was stunned for a fraction of a moment and then threw a spear at Hanuman's chest, causing him excruciating pain that made him cry out in agony before blacking out. Five stalwarts of the Vanara army—Rishabha, Sarabha, Nila, Gavaksha and Gandhamadana—tried their best to impede Kumbhakarna's advance, but they were all rendered senseless. Thousands of courageous Vanaras jumped on him, biting and clawing viciously, and though they covered every inch of his body like trees on a mountain, he shook them off with ease and continued his rampage of terror, drenching the earth in blood. Angada bravely tried to tackle him, but fell unconscious when he was hit by Kumbhakarna's fist.

Sugriva could not stomach his people falling like flies and flung a boulder at Kumbhakarna's chest, but all efforts to repulse him were in vain. The boulder shattered on contact, and roaring angrily, Kumbhakarna countered the attack by hurling a gigantic spear. Luckily, Hanuman had recovered by this time, and bounding towards the weapon, caught it midflight and broke it in half on his thigh. Inflamed at being thwarted, Kumbhakarna ripped off a piece of a mountain and struck Sugriva with it, making him lose consciousness. The Rakshasas rejoiced at the sight of the fallen Vanara king, and Kumbhakarna scooped up his hostage and carried him off the battlefield in the crook of his arm. Hanuman considered expanding himself to extricate Sugriva from Kumbhakarna's clutches, but decided against it since he was confident of Sugriva's ability to free himself. Furthermore, he felt it would be better for the army's morale if their king found a way out of his captivity without any extraneous intervention.

Kumbhakarna strode triumphantly into Lanka with the enemy king's limp body tucked under his arm like a rag doll. As he walked down the main street, he was greeted with great honour. The people applauded his victory, sprinkling him with scented water and showering him with puffed rice confetti. As the refreshing droplets fell on Sugriva's face, he slowly regained consciousness. Then, feeling outraged at being taken prisoner so unceremoniously, he deftly freed himself, clawing his captor with his sharp nails and biting off his earlobes and nose. Kumbhakarna plucked Sugriva off and dashed him to the ground in rage, but he bounced back up unhurt and made off to his camp before he could be caught again.

However, the joy of Sugriva's escape was short-lived. Deprived of his nose and ears and piqued by his hostage's flight, Kumbhakarna re-entered the battlefield with the ferocity of a tornado. Heads burst open, limbs were torn off and bodies crushed in the terrible carnage he inflicted with his massive club. Overpowered and unable to put up a defence, the helpless Vanaras once again ran pell-mell in horror. Kumbhakarna was so unstoppable that even when Lakshmana jumped into the fray, completely covering him with his deadly arrows, Kumbhakarna was unaffected and said disdainfully, 'You have shown great valour in facing me, and I am impressed by your courage, but I consider it a waste of time contending with the likes of you. You are too measly an opponent; besides, it is your brother Rama I seek to conquer, not you. Once I have killed him, everyone else is as good as dead.' Whereupon Lakshmana pointed to Rama and said, 'You have indeed been invincible so far, but we are eager to see how you fare against Rama, the mighty son of Dasharatha whose valour is unmatched in all three worlds.'

As Kumbhakarna rushed madly towards Rama, he was met with arrows empowered by Rudra that dug into his chest, forcing him to drop his mace. Blood poured from his body, and, infuriated at being stymied, he used his hands and fists to vent his anger on the Vanaras. Kumbhakarna seized a mountain peak and hurled it at Rama, but he split it into tiny pieces with seven arrows that flew swiftly from his celebrated bow. Several Vanaras jumped on the giant to weaken him, but he dusted them off disdainfully. Then, licking his lips that were wet with blood, Kumbhakarna advanced towards Rama, his eyes red with rage, shouting, 'Don't equate me with the ordinary Rakshasas you have encountered before. No one has defeated me in the past, and no one will do so in the future. I stand here assailed by your entire army, deprived of my nose and ears, but I feel no pain. Today you will witness my fury for yourself before I send you to the land of Yama!'

Kumbhakarna's bluster prompted Rama to release his plumed arrows as powerful as thunderbolts. They were like the one he used to pierce the seven sala trees to prove himself to Sugriva and then to kill Vali, but they did nothing to Kumbhakarna, who continued to press forward unconcerned. He seemed utterly unmindful of the assault, like the earth when it is lashed by torrential rain. At this point, Rama realized Kumbhakarna could not be killed with arrows, and more powerful weapons would be needed to end the destruction he was causing. So, he summoned the missile presided over by Vayu, which sailed through the air and severed Kumbhakarna's right arm. Nonplussed at losing his limb, Kumbhakarna uprooted a palmyra tree with his left arm and rushed forward. Rama responded promptly by invoking the missile of Indra. It cut off Kumbhakarna's left arm, which flew past, still holding onto the tree, crushing many unfortunate warriors beneath it as it landed. Though he had lost both arms, Kumbhakarna continued to charge ahead in a mad frenzy, so using two crescent-shaped arrows, Rama cut off his legs. Then he sealed Kumbhakarna's mouth with his golden plumed shafts and invoked the Aindrastra to finish him off. The dazzling missile blazed forth at tremendous speed, illuminating the ten directions with its brilliance as it swiftly tore off the Rakshasa's enormous head. The force of the impact carried it past the city walls where it fell, demolishing portions of the defences and levelling many tall buildings. The headless torso landed in the sea, crushing giant sea creatures before sinking to the depths.

The death of Kumbhakarna was celebrated with great jubilation in the Vanara camp, while in Lanka, the mood was dismally sombre. Ravana, overcome with grief, fainted when he heard that the unthinkable had happened and his indomitable brother was no more. On recovering, he wailed in bereavement, 'How could you have been defeated, my heroic brother whom even lightning could not touch? Now, unfortunately, you have gone without removing the thorn that pricks my heart! Without you by my side, I am certain to perish as Vibhishana warned. Alas! Ill fortune has descended upon me ever since I expelled him. I am so full of misery that strangely, even Sita means nothing to me at this moment. If Rama cannot be killed, I should end my life and join you, my dear brother.'

No one had witnessed Ravana in such a depressed state ever before, so his faithful sons Trishira, Atikaya, Devantaka and Narantaka did their best to encourage his fighting spirit again. Trishira said, 'Although it is hard to accept that our invincible uncle has left us, you should not lose hope and succumb to grief. Father, let me remind you that you are a peerless warrior who conquered all three worlds, so do not give in to sorrow like a common man. We still have a lot of firepower at our disposal, and there is no reason to despair that all is lost. You possess many powerful weapons, including the infallible Shakti spear from Brahma, and besides, you have valorous sons like us who will fight for you to the bitter end. Together we will surely defeat the enemy and restore your dignity.'

Trishira's words cheered Ravana; suffused with renewed optimism, he glowed with pride and blessed his valiant sons with success in their endeavour. Intent on victory, they left with their uncles Mahaparshwa and Mahodara, who accompanied them for support.

Chapter 30

The Fall of Indrajit

The two armies met in a deadly conflict yet again, the Vanaras armed with trees and boulders and the Rakshasas equipped with powerful weapons. Before long, the battlefield was littered with corpses, making it challenging to tread anywhere without stepping on a body or into the large pools that had formed as the warriors bled. Lance in hand, Narantaka raged through the Vanara forces on horseback with the ferocity of the wind, leaving hundreds dead in his wake. As they scattered in terror, Sugriva directed Angada to tackle Narantaka. Angada approached the heavily armed Rakshasa with nothing but his claws and teeth and boldly challenged him. 'Fight with someone who is your equal! Hurl your spear at me instead of taking delight in killing those who are weaker than you.' Narantaka glowered and bit his lip in rage as his mighty weapon flew from his hands, breaking on his opponent's chest. Unfazed, Angada struck down Narantaka's horse, forcing him to the ground. Within moments the two were locked in hand-to-hand combat, pummelling each other violently. Narantaka landed a blow on Angada's skull, throwing him off balance, but he was no match for the Vanara's physical strength. In return, Angada pounded him with such ferocity that his fists sank deep into Narantaka's chest, splitting it wide open.

Devantaka was horrified to see his brother fall and raced towards him. Angada hurled a tree to prevent him from advancing, but Trishira intervened, riding on his chariot, cutting the tree to pieces. He joined his brother in the attack, along with his uncle Mahodara, seated on a massive elephant. Nila and Hanuman noticed Angada was outnumbered by three Rakshasa warriors and came to his aid. In no time, Hanuman smashed Devantaka's head to pulp. When Trishira assailed him with arrows in retaliation, Hanuman flung a boulder at him. Trishira broke it into pieces, and though Hanuman

309

continued his attack, tossing giant trees to subdue him, he once again destroyed them. Finally, Hanuman sprang upon Trishira's horse in a fury and brought it down like a lion would an antelope. Trishira was infuriated at the setback and hurled a spear at Hanuman's chest, wounding him severely. Aggravated by the injury, Hanuman punched him in the abdomen with all his might. Then, snatching Trishira's sword, the mighty Vanara swiftly beheaded him with a single deadly stroke.

Meanwhile, Nila killed Mahodara, crushing him and his elephant with a large boulder. Mahaparshwa duelled with Rishabha and struck him with his mace in a separate encounter, causing him to bleed heavily. Rishabha's lips quivered in resentment as he fought back, forcefully grabbing the offending weapon and sending Mahaparshwa reeling to the ground. Then suddenly, Mahaparshwa leaped to his feet and returned the blow. Rishabha momentarily lost his footing, tottering back, but in seconds he jumped forward, smashing Mahaparshwa with his own mace so hard that his teeth fell out of his head, and he was no more.

Now Atikaya[1] was the only one left standing. As his name suggested, he was huge and resembled his uncle Kumbhakarna. The Vanaras trembled at the sight of him, deathly afraid that another enormous ogre had appeared to torment them. Vibhishana explained to Rama that Atikaya was also an accomplished warrior apart from his gigantic size. He had a massive bow bent in three places and was equal to his father Ravana in strength. Vibhishana added that his nephew was decent and dutiful, always respectful to his elders, well-versed in the Vedas and the art of statecraft. Atikaya's extensive knowledge of many astras and his training to fight using various means—riding an elephant, a horse or even on foot—made him a formidable opponent. This valiant son of Ravana, from his junior queen Dhanyamalini, was protected by divine armour that made him invincible. Vibhishana advised that although Atikaya was an upright person, making it a pity to kill him, quick action was needed to meet the threat he posed before it was too late, and he did irretrievable damage to the Vanara army.

Seeing his troops floundering and his brothers and uncles slaughtered, Atikaya began to lay waste to the Vanaras. But they were not his real target; he considered it beneath his dignity to waste his energy on ordinary foot soldiers and tore through their ranks on his chariot trying to reach Rama. Lakshmana stopped him along the way, standing stubbornly in his path with

---

[1] Ati means great, and kaya means body. Hence Atikaya means one with a large body.

his bow drawn. But belittling him, Atikaya said mockingly, 'I do not want to waste my time with someone who is not my equal. Compared to me, you are just an inexperienced boy, so don't be foolhardy; put down your bow and save yourself from an untimely death.'

Lakshmana flushed at the insult and replied indignantly, 'Bragging without proving yourself does not make you a hero. Do not crow about your prowess till you face my arrows. In your arrogance, you underestimate me, not knowing that I will be the one to claim your life on this battlefield.'

As the battle raged on, the two warriors fought furiously, exchanging deadly arrows as each countered the other's attack. At one point, Lakshmana struck Atikaya on the forehead, causing him to shake violently. When he recovered, Atikaya said graciously, 'I must admit that was a praiseworthy shot.' The fighting continued, and the battle remained deadlocked, graduating from arrows to astras. Despite his valiant attempts, Lakshmana was frustrated that he could not make a chink in Atikaya's armour. Finally, the impasse ended when Vayu whispered a secret to Lakshmana, telling him that Atikaya's impenetrable armour was a gift from Brahma, so he could only be killed by the weapon that Brahma presided over. At once, Lakshmana invoked the fiery Brahmastra, which Atikaya found impossible to resist; it deftly severed his head, which rolled abruptly to the ground with its crown.

The loss of his four brave sons that day threw Ravana into the depths of despair. He mourned their passing and could not understand how two ordinary mortals and a bunch of forest-dwellers could have destroyed so many of his powerful Rakshasas. Ravana sighed heavily, flummoxed that every champion warrior he sent out had been killed, and wondered how Rama and Lakshmana had survived Indrajit's inexorable Nagapasha. He could not fathom what uncanny power had so inexplicably saved them from the jaws of death and worried that he had no one left on his side to send out. It appeared his strategy would need to shift from attack to defence, so Ravana immediately ordered increased vigilance of the city gates and reinforced security at the Ashoka Garden.

Indrajit approached Ravana as he sat brooding and weeping for his departed sons. He hero-worshiped his father and could not bear to see his grief-stricken state, so speaking comfortingly, he said, 'Father, all is not lost! You still have me; I will reverse all our setbacks and ensure that you achieve victory. To this day, I have never let you down on any task you have assigned me, so please have confidence in my abilities. I vow to restore the pride of Lanka by tearing Rama and Lakshmana to shreds.'

Encouraged by Indrajit's brave words, Ravana felt re-energized, and his heart overflowed with love for his valiant son. Blessing him with success, he said, 'I pray for your victory, my heroic child. You are my pride and joy, my equal in every way, and I know no one can defeat you.'

Before setting out, as was his custom, Indrajit conducted an occult fire ritual summoning demonic forces to bless him with success. Clad in red, he tore off the head of a black ram, pouring its blood into the flames with a long iron ladle, charging his weapons and imbuing himself with dark magical powers. Then, with a massive force of Rakshasas following him, he went forth in his magnificent chariot, which moved as fast as the wind. It was fully equipped with many powerful weapons, and riding out of Lanka to the blaring of conches and the thunderous beat of kettledrums, Indrajit looked daunting. When he reached the battlefield, he adopted his favourite tactic of disappearing behind the clouds, and from there, he let loose a salvo of arrows on the Vanara army powered by the Brahmastra. Particularly seeking out the leaders, Indrajit pierced Gandhamadana with eighteen arrows, struck Nala with nine, Mainda with eight, Gaja with five and Jambavan with ten. Even the dauntless Nila, Sugriva, Rishabha, Dwividha and Angada were brought down. His formidable shafts struck terror as they fell unceasingly everywhere, as inescapable as incessant drops of water beating down from a dark rain cloud. The assault was more than the Vanara army could withstand, and unable to see their foe, they were reduced to sitting targets, unable to return fire. It was a horrific massacre, and soon the air was filled with the screams of dying Vanaras, pierced and lacerated, helpless in their inability to retaliate. After disabling every enemy leader and completely decimating the army, Indrajit turned his attention to Rama and Lakshmana, covering them with arrows. Grievously injured, they too dropped down unconscious on the battlefield.

The day ended in catastrophe for the Vanaras; they were completely wiped out in a bloodbath, and the only ones left standing were Vibhishana and Hanuman.[2] In the darkness, the two scoured the battlefield for survivors with flaming torches in hand and came upon Jambavan. Vibhishana knelt beside him to check for a pulse and asked, 'Noble sir, are you still alive?' The aged bear king was barely clinging to life, and replied weakly, 'I seem to have lost my sight, but I recognize your voice to be that of Vibhishana. Pray tell me if Hanuman lives.'

---

[2] The Epilogue explains their immunity to the Brahmastra.

Vibhishana was surprised that he asked only about Hanuman, and inquired curiously, 'Yes, he is safe, but why do you enquire only after him and not about Rama and Lakshmana or any of the others?'

Jambavan promptly replied, 'Valiant Rakshasa, if Hanuman lives, there is hope; if not, we are all as good as dead even if we are breathing.' As Hanuman clasped his feet, the bear king felt a new lease of life enter his battered body. Putting his arm on Hanuman's shoulder, he said, 'You are the only one who can save us now! Cross the sea urgently and go to the Himalaya Mountains. Between the lofty peaks of Mount Rishabha and Mount Kailasha is a shining hill covered with medicinal herbs. Four plants there glow like lamps, which you must bring here as fast as possible to revive our fallen warriors. The first is the Mritasanjivani, which restores the dead. Another called the Vishalyakarani heals wounds after a weapon is extracted and the third one, Suvarnakarani, mends skin, reinvigorating the body. The fourth herb, the Sandhani, can rejoin severed limbs and fractured bones. Come back post-haste, as we have limited time in which they can be effective.'

Hanuman sprang into the air from the peak of Mount Trikuta towards the Himalayas, flying with the speed of his father Vayu to procure the medications. Covering an enormous distance, he passed over the sea and then rivers, hills and dales, cities and forests, finally alighting at his destination. The mountain[3] was full of medicinal herbs, just as Jambavan had described, and many of them glowed in the dark, but they closed and hid in fear, threatened by an intruder. Time was short, and not wanting to make a mistake by bringing the wrong plants, Hanuman tore off the peak and leaped with it into the air back to Lanka.[4] The Vanara army inhaled the extraordinary herbs, and magically, before daybreak, everyone recovered.

The powerful medicinal potions rejuvenated the Vanara army; invigorated by the magical herbs and raring to seek retribution for Indrajit's unfairness, they decided to torch Lanka. Surrounding the walls, they set fire to the gates and the tall buildings. Before long, a raging inferno rapidly consumed the

---

[3] Dunagiri Mountain in Uttarakhand. Interestingly, the villagers of Dunagiri have still not forgiven Hanuman! They do not worship him because he defaced their mountain by plucking off a part of it.

[4] Ritigala in Sri Lanka correspondingly has Himalayan herbs that are different from the local vegetation. Local people use them for their medicinal properties to cure skin diseases and to heal wounds. See Bala, Saroj, *Ramayan Retold with Scientific Evidences* (Prabhat Prakashan, 2019).

armoury and much of the city's great riches. The insatiable flames burnt stocks of weapons, piles of sandalwood, silks, woollens, gold and jewels, reddening the sky and reflecting a crimson hue on the sea. Ravana was in utter disbelief, astounded that his enemies had returned from the dead. At the end of his tether, he sent Kumbhakarna's sons Kumbha and Nikumbha, along with Yupaksha, Sonitaksha, Prajangha and Kampana, out to battle. Although they fought hard, the Vanara army, energized with magical herbs, soon overpowered them.

Angada hurled a boulder at Kampana, killing him. When Sonitaksha came forward, he snatched his sword and sliced his shoulder, temporarily incapacitating him. Yupaksha accosted Angada in his chariot with Prajangha and Sonitaksha, who had recovered and closed in with his mace. Seeing Angada assailed unfairly by three warriors, Mainda and Dwividha deftly positioned themselves on either side to protect him. In the bitter fight that ensued, Angada knocked off Prajangha's head with his fist. Mainda crushed Yupaksha to death, and Dwividha clawed Sonitaksha's face and dashed him to the ground. When Kumbha, the mighty son of Kumbhakarna, saw them fall, he pitched into the fight, shooting Dwividha with an arrow, so he dropped to the ground with his legs outstretched. Mainda came to his brother's rescue with a boulder but was also vanquished. Kumbha even subdued Angada, who was pelting him with rocks and trees. Seeing Angada in trouble, Sugriva jumped into the fray, but Kumbha's energy was flagging by this time. Not wanting to battle unfairly, Sugriva advised him to rest and engage with him once he recovered. When he returned to fight, they wrestled for a long time, and finally, Sugriva struck Kumbha on his chest, killing him. Seeing his elder brother perish, Nikumbha rushed angrily at Sugriva with his spiked club, but Hanuman intercepted him and took the blow on his chest. The weapon broke on impact, and the two fought with their fists. Ultimately, Hanuman pounced on Nikumbha, and taking hold of his neck, twisted his head and tore it off his body.

Ravana erupted like a volcano, outraged at yet another defeat, and sent Makaraksha, the son of Khara, to avenge the death of his cousins. Makaraksha considered himself as powerful as his departed father and felt honoured to have the opportunity to prove himself. His ire was directed principally at Rama. Simmering with pent-up anger at the death of his father in Janasthana and intent on seeking revenge, Makaraksha scowled at Rama and declared furiously, 'I am burning with so much rage that your end is nigh. Unfortunately, I was not present at Janasthana to help my father, but

I have wanted to put an end to you ever since the day you slew him. Luckily, you are before me now, and by sending you to the abode of Yama, my long-cherished desire will finally be fulfilled.'

Rama laughed at his outburst and said calmly, 'No one wins on the battlefield merely with boastful rhetoric. I am ready for your challenge. You just admitted that I defeated your father and 14,000 Rakshasas, so it is not wise to be overconfident about your victory.' In the duel that followed, deadly arrows were exchanged; both warriors were wounded, and considerable blood was shed, but in the end, Rama released the Agniastra, and Makaraksha was no more.

By this time, Lanka had lost almost all its brave sons, so, gnashing his teeth, Ravana had no choice but to send Indrajit out again. He entered the battlefield for the third time with the command to kill Rama and Lakshmana using any means, fair or foul. Indrajit felt invigorated by performing a ritual that suffused him with magic powers from sacrificing a goat to the Rakshasas' venerated deity. Then, he used his usual ploy of fighting under the cloak of invisibility, silently raining arrows while remaining hidden. Vowing to rid the Earth of Vanaras and take out the two who made a pretence of being hermits, Indrajit sprayed Rama and Lakshmana with arrows till their bloodied bodies resembled two kimsuka trees aflame with bright red blossoms. Although the brothers tried their best to fire in the general direction of the onslaught, they were powerless against their invisible enemy. Frustrated by their impotence, Lakshmana asked if he could release the Brahmastra against all the Rakshasas, as it would latch onto its target even if it could not be seen. However, Rama was not amenable to this suggestion, and said firmly, 'Resorting to large-scale genocide would be unconscionable. Exterminating an entire race, including those not engaged in battle, in retribution against one individual is not judicious.' He stressed the immorality of attacking in certain situations, saying it was particularly unethical to strike someone who had not caused harm. Also egregious was aggression towards a person hiding in fear, one who had surrendered, had his back turned while fleeing or was drunk and not in his senses.[5] Instead, he proposed a surgical strike by using a weapon that would target Indrajit alone.

Indrajit anticipated Rama's move and withdrew to Lanka to devise a new strategy. Employing sorcery, he conjured up an illusion of Sita to inflict extreme mental anguish on Rama, hoping to deal a devastating blow to him.

---

[5] Manusmriti chapter 7.91–93 covers these points, documenting battle etiquette.

The charade required him to be visible, so he did not risk appearing before Rama at the northern portal. Instead, he approached Hanuman through the western gate, knowing that he would inform Rama. The image of Sita was so realistic in appearance with her long braid and emaciated face that Hanuman immediately rushed to her aid. As he came near, Indrajit caught her hair, and drawing his sword, began striking at the apparition while she cried out, 'O Rama, O Rama.' Tears rolled down Hanuman's cheeks as he shouted in disgust, 'How can you treat a woman in this barbaric manner? Despite being the descendant of a Brahmin, you are an evil and uncultured creature, and your behaviour is completely contrary to that of an arya. What harm has Maithili done that you inflict such pain on her? You will undoubtedly rot in hell with others like you who commit atrocities against women.'

Indrajit sniggered, 'You are right in stating that it is ignoble to kill a woman, but all is fair in war if it inflicts pain on the enemy. Rama came here for Sita, and if she is no more, he will perish, finding his efforts to be in vain. Then I will kill all of you, including my traitorous uncle Vibhishana.' Saying this, he sliced the image diagonally from shoulder to hip, and blood gushed out of the stricken body. Having fooled the Vanaras successfully, Indrajit roared in victory and left the battlefield for the temple of Nikumbhila to perform a special ritual that would make him invincible.[6]

A very shaken Hanuman ran dripping with perspiration to Rama to narrate the shocking event he had just witnessed. When he delivered the news that the one they were fighting to save had been killed, Rama fainted in distress. Lakshmana sprinkled water to revive him, and cradling his head, wailed in despair, 'My sinless brother, despite your unfailing adherence to dharma at every instance, you face one calamity after another. It seems fortune does not smile on the virtuous and instead favours those who wield power, despite their wickedness. If we infer that unrighteousness does not win, Ravana should have perished long ago, but he continues to prosper. Dharma appears to be the recourse of the weak and timid. So far, we have relied solely on moral means to achieve our goal, but now I think the time has come to fight fire with fire. In this world, it seems might alone triumphs, so we must use all methods available to us to destroy Indrajit, Ravana and their Rakshasa followers.'

In the meantime, Vibhishana rushed to the scene, interjecting breathlessly, 'I am certain that the killing of Sita that Hanuman witnessed was just an

---

[6] Indrajit's ritual is explained in the Epilogue.

illusion. Indrajit used his mystic powers to delude you, no doubt to break your spirit. Ravana would never allow anyone to harm Sita, because he is still hoping to make her his wife. Indrajit is his father's lackey and would never do anything against his wishes, so I assure you she is safe. While his trick has succeeded in distracting you, he is in all probability performing a powerful sacrifice to Nikumbhila. He does this to guarantee his success and must be prevented from completing the ritual; otherwise, you will never be able to destroy him. Lakshmana, do not waste another moment in pointless grief over a false charade and come with me quickly so that you can stop Indrajit's dangerous sacrifice.'

Rama was still in a daze believing he had lost Sita forever. He asked Vibhishana to repeat what he said, and as he did so, Vibhishana insisted that they had very little time to avert a catastrophe. Lakshmana took his elder brother's blessings, circled him clockwise and departed with Vibhishana and the Vanara army. When they reached the temple of the Rakshasa deity Nikumbhila, they saw the ritual in progress. Indrajit was seated invisibly in front of the flame, shielded by scores of Rakshasa warriors. Acting on Vibhishana's advice, the Vanaras attacked the guards, so Indrajit would be forced to defend them, and in doing so, would have to reveal himself, abandoning the ritual midway. Hanuman was smarting at being deceived, and vented his rage on the Rakshasas, slaughtering them indiscriminately. Just as Vibhishana envisaged, Indrajit had no option but to leave the ritual incomplete to protect his soldiers. As he advanced towards Hanuman, Lakshmana twanged his bow to challenge him, and devoid of his cloak of invisibility, Indrajit was on equal footing for the first time.

Much to his chagrin, he saw Vibhishana and lambasted him with harsh words, 'Shame on you, Uncle! You are a traitor! As my father's brother, you ought to think of me as your own son, yet you have betrayed me to my enemy. You have no loyalty to your blood, serving those who seek to harm us instead. Your treachery towards your kin is contemptible, and in bringing Lakshmana here, you have failed in your duty to your family and deserve nothing but disdain.'

Glaring angrily, Vibhishana retorted, 'You lack etiquette and have a habit of speaking insolently to your elders! It is well known that I have always followed the path of righteousness despite being born a Rakshasa. Although I am your father's brother, and the same blood runs in my veins, I cannot support his evil actions. All his life, he has committed one injustice after another, stealing property that he has no right over, and abducting women for his pleasure, including the wives of others. Evil, like a burning house, must be abandoned! Unfortunately, my attempts to make Ravana correct his ways were futile. I love my family, but I cannot stand by them if they go against dharma because one who turns a blind eye to injustice is as guilty as those committing it. Now that you are in Lakshmana's field of vision, you will not survive.'

Scowling, Indrajit quickly jumped onto his chariot, drawn by spirited black steeds impatiently pawing the ground; addressing Lakshmana, he jeered, 'Today, you will breathe your last! You seem to have forgotten that I rendered you senseless twice before, but today the job will be completed when I kill you. After that, jackals and vultures will feast on your body, and your brother will have nothing but your head.' Lakshmana did not have a chariot, so he sat on Hanuman's shoulders. Then, looking like the rising sun above a hillock, he shouted back, 'I look forward to seeing how you fare when you face your opponent squarely instead of unscrupulously hiding from sight. I do not want to waste my breath on you, so go ahead and show me your prowess.'

A pitched battle between Lakshmana and Indrajit followed. In the tempestuous conflict, each mighty warrior pierced and lacerated the other. The two armies even stopped fighting to watch the combat in awe. Every move Indrajit made, Lakshmana countered, and vice versa, continuing in this manner for a long time, neither one tiring nor retreating. The spent arrows piled up around them like blades of kusha grass, yet the contest had no end in sight. Then Lakshmana got the upper hand when he managed to strike Indrajit's horses, severing his charioteer's head with a thunderbolt called Bhalla. Indrajit had never experienced such a setback; he dismounted and went to Lanka, returning in minutes with a new chariot to resume the battle.

The engagement took on even more frightening proportions as they exchanged deadly missiles. Lakshmana deployed the Varunastra, and Indrajit deflected it with the Rudrastra. Indrajit attacked him with the Agniastra, but Lakshmana used the Suryastra to divert it. Then, Indrajit seized a formidable missile of the demons that could destroy almost any weapon, but Lakshmana called upon the Maheshwarastra, which it could not withstand. This back-and-forth went on interminably, both combatants like two mighty bull elephants perfectly matched in strength, till Lakshmana fitted his bow with the missile presided over by Indra. Then, invoking its powers with an appeal to dharma, he said, 'If Rama, the son of Dasharatha, is virtuous and deserving of victory, let this weapon put an end to this ruthless son of Ravana.' He drew the bowstring to his ear and released the deadly arrow with great force. Charged with the power of dharma, the missile found its mark. The battle was over! Indrajit lay decapitated, and his head, with its iron helmet and gold earrings, rolled unceremoniously to the ground.[7]

Lakshmana was exhausted after continuously battling for three days; his body was punctured with deep gashes, bleeding profusely. Though severely injured, he hobbled to Rama, leaning on Vibhishana, excited to convey the good news. The Vanara army was in high spirits, relieved that the threat of Indrajit was gone forever. Indra and the Devas felt similar jubilation as they celebrated in their celestial abode. Rama lovingly embraced his brother. Kissing his forehead, he lavished so much praise on him, commending his victory over Indrajit, that Lakshmana felt abashed.

By now, Lakshmana was gasping and haemorrhaging dangerously, so Sushena quickly took charge and tended to his wounds, administering an elixir of Vishalyakarani nasally. Meanwhile, Rama prepared himself for Ravana's appearance on the battlefield. Now that the Rakshasa king had lost all his foremost warriors, he would have no choice but to show himself.

---

[7] Indrajit was killed on 23 November 5076 BCE according to the sky view. See Bala, Saroj, *Ramayan Retold with Scientific Evidences* (Prabhat Prakashan, 2019).

Chapter 31

The World Is Rid of Ravana

When Ravana heard that Vibhishana had assisted Lakshmana in killing Indrajit, the shock was too much for him, and he collapsed. He lay unconscious for a long time, and when he came to his senses, he was horrified at the news. Indrajit's death completely broke him, and he could not digest what he heard. Sobbing loudly, he groaned, 'I always disregarded Yama, but today I am forced to acknowledge him. My invincible child, my precious son, and heir, you defeated Indra, and even death feared you. How could Lakshmana have killed you when you swore to extract the thorn of the enemy from my side? While the Devas and rishis are celebrating, I am devastated and choked with emotion at losing you. I know you have reached the highest plane of heaven, but that is no consolation for an anguished father like me. You have abandoned your consorts, your mother Mandodari and me, making life meaningless for us. It was your duty as my eldest son to perform my funeral, but instead, in a cruel twist of fate, I will be conducting yours.'

Then suddenly, his unbearable pain transformed into a violent rage. Everyone around Ravana trembled to see the fire in his eyes as he glared and gnashed his teeth ferociously. Frothing at the mouth, he thundered, 'I performed rigorous penance for years to please Brahma and was not only granted protection from all beings but was given impenetrable armour and a mighty bow. Bring them to me so I can destroy those two wretched brothers.' Then, twisted by his anguish, he suddenly changed his mind and announced, 'Indrajit slaughtered a likeness of Sita to hurt Rama. I will kill the real Sita right now and make his hoax a reality, so Rama experiences the inexorable pain I am feeling.' Saying this, he stormed out towards the Ashoka Garden, sword in hand, with Mandodari and minsters following at his heels.

When Ravana approached, Sita shrank in fear at the baleful look in his bloodshot eyes, betraying his infernal intention. She knew he was blinded by rage at his son's death and was sure she had only moments to live. Thoughts of Rama flooded her mind, and for an instant, she wondered if she had made a mistake by insisting that her husband rescue her instead of escaping from Lanka with Hanuman. However, it was not her time to die! A wise minister called Suparshwa bravely interceded and was able to restrain Ravana. He pleaded, 'You are the son of a Brahmin,[1] the brother of Kubera and a Vedic scholar in your own right, who has practised austerities for years. How can you throw away all the piety you have earned by committing the heinous act of killing a helpless woman? It is far more appropriate to vent your anger on Rama. If you kill him in battle, you will achieve fame and simultaneously fulfil your desire to have Sita. Thirteen days of the war are over, go out tomorrow and defeat your enemies gloriously in battle.'

Mercifully, Suparshwa's words had the effect intended. Dissuaded from acting impulsively, Ravana returned to his palace.

However, Ravana did not wait till the next day to avenge his son. Instead, he went straight to his Assembly Hall and summoned the remaining leaders of his army, imploring them with folded hands to go to the battlefield right away. He said, 'March on the enemy with whatever is left of our army and focus solely on Rama. Take every elephant, horse, chariot and foot soldier and surround him. Attack him together and assail him with arrows just as the monsoon showers torrential rain. If you fail to kill him, I will make sure I do so myself tomorrow when he is weakened.'

Once again, the Rakshasas and the Vanaras were embroiled in a raging battle. Blood flowed like a river as the Vanaras tore off heads and slashed their enemy with their sharp teeth and claws. The Rakshasas returned their assault with maces, darts, swords and axes, slicing the Vanaras to pieces until Rama took up the challenge, completely routing them. In under two hours, he destroyed the entire Rakshasa army using the Gandharvastra,[2] which threw them into confusion, causing their minds to play tricks on them. A barrage of arrows flew from Rama's bow so swiftly that they were a blur,

---

[1] Ravana was the son of a Brahmin, but not one himself because he took up the profession of a Kshatriya. In Vedic times, varna was not by birth.

[2] The weapon of Chitrasena, the chief of the Gandharvas. It had a hallucinogenic effect, creating the illusion that the wielder of the weapon was everywhere.

and the Rakshasas could only surmise how fast his fingers were moving by the thousands of soldiers being felled. They were as unaware of Rama's presence as one is of the real self, deluded by the physical body.[3]

The few that survived ran back to Lanka carrying the tale of the trouncing they had received, borne out by the battlefield littered with the corpses of dead Rakshasas and carcasses of horses and elephants. Plaintive wails rent the air as Lanka mourned its dead. Rakshasa women screamed in anguish, cursing the hideous Surpanakha for bringing about the destruction of their men by setting her lustful eyes on Rama. They sorrowed that Ravana had erred dreadfully by abducting Sita, and condemned him for rejecting Vibhishana's wise advice to return her. As they grieved the loss of their husbands and sons, they cried inconsolably that there was no hope for the Rakshasa race anymore. Ravana sighed in irritation, his resentment aggravated by the hysterical lamentations that emanated from every house in the city. He felt outraged at the loss of faith in him that his people expressed, and their doleful cries drove him insane with anger. Finally, smouldering with rage at his failure, he decided to confront Rama himself to avenge the deaths of all the Rakshasas who had lost their lives.[4]

The sovereign of Lanka donned his armour and left in a ferocious mood through the northern gate with his last three generals—Mahodara, Mahaparshwa[5] and Virupaksha—marshalling the few forces and weapons that remained. His magnificent chariot was made of gold, studded with jewels and equipped with every conceivable weapon. The earth shook as it rolled menacingly onto the battlefield, its arrival announced by the deafening sound of blaring conches and booming kettledrums. At that moment, an eclipse obscured the sun, birds screeched and jackals howled. Clouds rained blood and the horses inopportunely stumbled. Ravana's left eye twitched, and

---

[3] The idea that the body deludes one from knowing one's true Self within is central to Vedic philosophy.
'Hidden in the heart of every creature exists the Self, subtler than the subtlest, greater than the greatest. They go beyond all sorrow who extinguish their self-will and behold the glory of the Self . . . ' Katha Upanishad 2.20

[4] Ravana enters the battlefield on the no moon day 24 November 5076 BCE. See Bala, Saroj, *Ramayan Retold with Scientific Evidences* (Prabhat Prakashan, 2019).

[5] Though they share the same names as Ravana's cousins, Mahodara and Mahaparshwa, who were killed earlier, these are generals.

he shivered at the doom these inauspicious signs foretold; then, disregarding the warning, he went madly forth to his death.

Along with his generals, Ravana unleashed his pent-up fury on the Vanaras. Heads were lopped off, hearts pierced, skulls smashed and many were blinded or had their limbs sliced from their bodies. The brute force of the Vanaras was no match for the sophisticated weapons wielded by the Rakshasas, and they perished in large numbers. Sugriva saw his followers being savagely slaughtered and leaped into the fray armed with a tree. The Vanara commanders joined him, carrying giant boulders, which they showered like hailstones to beat back the enemy. As the Rakshasas fell under the onslaught, Virupaksha came to their rescue with his bow, riding on a gigantic elephant. His arrows pierced Sugriva, wounding him severely, but the brave Vanara continued fighting, oblivious of his injuries. He struck Virupaksha's elephant with great force, causing it to fall back and sink to the ground. Forced to leap off the injured animal, Virupaksha advanced towards Sugriva, drawing his sword. Sugriva hurled a rock at him, but he nimbly jumped aside, inflicting a wound that made the Vanara king black out for a few minutes. As Sugriva sprang to his feet, they continued to fight, grappling with each other in physical combat. Ultimately, Sugriva landed a mighty blow on Virupaksha's temple with the force of a thunderbolt, which caused blood to pour out from the nine apertures[6] in his body.

As the battle raged on, numbers dwindled on both sides as fast as water evaporates in the baking heat of a hot summer day. Rallying Mahodara, Ravana hollered, 'Now my hopes rest on you for victory. Exterminate my enemy in recompense for all that I have done for you.' Mahodara dutifully began his assault, charging out on his chariot towards the Vanaras, cutting them to pieces. Sugriva threw a boulder at him, but he managed to shatter it, injuring Sugriva with his arrows. Then by chance, Sugriva spotted an iron bludgeon lying on the ground and struck down Mahodara's horses, forcing him to fight on foot. They battled intensely, one with a mace and the other with a bludgeon, till both weapons collided and broke. The battle continued with fists, until the two combatants were utterly exhausted. Finally, Mahodara picked up a sword and shield that lay abandoned, and Sugriva did likewise. As they parried, jumping from right to left and left to right, Sugriva was

---

[6] In the shastras, the body is compared to a city with nine gates because it has nine openings—two eyes, two nostrils, two ears, one mouth, one genital opening and one anal orifice

eventually able to cut off his opponent's head, and seeing it roll off with its earrings and helmet; the Vanaras exulted in delight.

Mahaparshwa's eyes turned crimson with rage to see his kinsman decapitated. He attacked the Vanara army like a tornado, hacking off their heads and limbs just as the wind detaches fruit from a tree in a gale. Angada rushed to protect them, flinging an iron cudgel at Mahaparshwa that stunned him, and he fell to the ground in a daze along with his charioteer. Jambavan smashed his chariot and horses with a boulder, so he had no option but to fight without them when he recovered. Enraged, Mahaparshwa assailed Jambavan and Angada repeatedly with his arrows. Angada hurled a club at him, knocking off his helmet and breaking his bow. Incensed at the attack, Mahaparshwa threw an axe at Angada, but he managed to sidestep it so that it just missed his shoulder. He then rushed at Mahaparshwa and punched him with his fist, tearing his chest open. Cries of victory arose from the Vanara army as they cheered in celebration.

Ravana had lost his last three generals and could not stand the thought of his impending defeat. So, his rantings took on a poetic expression as he doubled down on his inimical intent, vowing he would fell Rama, the tree, to get Sita, the fruit.

He advanced ferociously in search of him, eliminating the Vanaras in his path with a missile presided over by Rahu.[7] When Lakshmana tried to block his way, Ravana promptly bypassed him in his single-minded quest to hunt down Rama. Then, there was Rama himself, standing resolutely in his path with his giant bow. Ravana immediately released a salvo of flaming arrows, but Rama countered them with his crescent-shaped Bhallas. They battled fiercely, evoking terror in the hearts of the onlookers. Both warriors were experts, moving deftly as they circled each other on the battlefield. There were so many arrows flying back and forth with such incredible velocity that the sky looked as it does during the monsoon, overcast with flashes of lightning.

The conflict was cataclysmic, like the one in the past between Indra and Vritrasura.[8] Ravana's arrows nicked Rama's forehead, but the adrenaline in

---

[7] Rahu is associated with deception and the dark side. It is a shadow planet marking the point where the moon cuts the path of the sun every month, the north lunar node. Though not a physical entity, it is considered a planet in Vedic astrology because of its influence on human life.

[8] Vritrasura was a powerful Asura whose sole purpose was to kill Indra. He had a boon whereby he could not be killed by any weapon, wet or dry, made of wood or metal. Indra

his veins prevented him from feeling his injuries. Then, reciting a sacred mantra, he directed Rudra's fearsome missile at Ravana. It fell on him with great force, but Ravana was protected from its effects by his impenetrable armour. Enraged at the assault, he retaliated with missiles powered by demonic forces; they were like the claws of lions and tigers, the beaks of vultures and falcons, the fangs of wolves and hyenas, and wide-mouthed hissing serpents. However, Rama fended them off with the Agniastra, incinerating them before they could cause him injury.

Infuriated that his weapon was foiled, Ravana summoned the Asura Maya's missile. It flew from his bow with the force of a gale carrying maces, clubs, pikes, mallets and thunderbolts. Rama did not flinch; in turn, he deployed the missile of the Gandharvas, completely obliterating the threat. Then, with his eyes flashing, Ravana used the Suryastra, which was like a large discus imbued with the power of the sun. The sky lit up as it sailed through the air, but drawing from his extensive arsenal, Rama was once again able to nullify it. Frustrated, Ravana pierced Rama with ten sharp arrows, and in return, was bombarded by numerous shafts.

Meanwhile, Lakshmana was concerned about Rama fighting on foot and shot seven arrows that tore Ravana's standard and beheaded his charioteer. Then, seizing five more, he split Ravana's bow while Vibhishana smote down his horses with his mace. Ravana, seething with anger, leaped down from his chariot and flung a flaming javelin at his brother. Lakshmana staved it off with his arrows, splitting it into three pieces that fell like meteors from the sky.

Hurling the mighty Shakti javelin fashioned by Brahma, Ravana yelled, 'You will pay for saving Vibhishana's life with your own. This unfailing dart cannot be resisted and will pierce your heart today.' The weapon sailed through the air striking Lakshmana in the chest. Swooning from the impact, he fell to the ground, grievously wounded and covered in blood. When no one could extract the spear impaled in his body, Rama pulled it out, and entrusting him to Sugriva and Hanuman; he said, 'Take care of Lakshmana while I deal with this sinful Rakshasa. Only one of us will survive today; the world will either see the end of him or me.' Incensed by what Ravana had done to Lakshmana, Rama attacked him vehemently with a continuous spate of deadly arrows that he could not repel, and fearing for his life, Ravana took to his heels, escaping from the battlefield like a cloud dispelled by a gale.

---

used the Vajra made of bones from the great sage Dadhichi, in a harrowing battle where he finally killed Vritrasura.

Lakshmana lay in the dust soaked in blood, dangerously close to death, and Rama could not bear the thought of losing him. Dropping his bow, he exclaimed in anguish, 'I shudder to see my beloved brother, who is my very heartbeat, in this precarious state. No brother in the world is as loyal as Lakshmana, and he is dearer to me than my own life. Lakshmana has always stood faithfully by my side, offering me solace in my darkest times, and without him, life is hollow. I feel overcome by guilt because he followed me to the forest, and I led him to death. How will I face the reprimand of our mothers if I go back to Ayodhya without him? I do not have the will to continue fighting, as, without Lakshmana, victory would be meaningless. If he goes to the land of Yama, I will have to join him.'

Sushena came forward and said comfortingly, 'Grief is clouding your mind and weakening you. Although Lakshmana's condition is grave, he is not dead. His heart still beats, his face has not lost its colour and his body is not cold.' He then said to Hanuman, 'Go again quickly to the medicinal mountain which you put back and bring me the herbs Jambavan previously asked for that grow on its southern peak.'

Hanuman set out immediately, and as before, did not want to make a mistake by bringing the wrong herbs, so he picked up a chunk of the mountain and brought it to Lanka. Sushena expertly administered the medication to Lakshmana through his nostrils, and soon, his wounds healed as though they had never existed. Rama was relieved to see his beloved brother saved from the jaws of death, and embracing him, said fondly, 'If you had died, nothing would have mattered to me anymore, not even victory.'

Lakshmana, the keeper of Rama's conscience, chided, 'It is not befitting of you to speak in this manner like a weak person. You vowed to kill Ravana and rescue Sita, and you have never gone back on your word. Nothing would make me happier than to see him die at your hands today, so gird your loins and destroy him before the day is out.'

Ravana returned to the battlefield in a shiny new chariot, even more magnificent than the earlier one. The Devas were dismayed looking down at the unfair contest. Ravana towered menacingly over Rama, who stood barefoot on the ground with nothing but his bow. Indra summoned his trusted charioteer Matali, and quickly sent him to Rama with his personal chariot to put the two warriors on an equal footing. Matali appeared on the battlefield with his hands folded, and said to Rama, 'Indra has sent me here with his chariot to help you achieve victory. I have also brought his mighty bow, several powerful arrows, an invincible javelin and a gleaming coat of armour. Allow me to be of service to you as your charioteer, so you can rid the three worlds of Ravana's tyranny.' Rama was grateful for the assistance and walked around the chariot clockwise, ascending it to begin one of the mightiest conflicts that ever took place.

Time seemed to stand still as deadly missiles were exchanged. Ravana released the Gandharva missile and several others, which Rama met effortlessly. Ravana then let loose his venomous serpent arrows that sped through the air with flaming coils. Seeing them headed directly towards him, Rama called upon the Garuda missile that turned into hundreds of golden eagles devouring the serpents and rendering them ineffective. Goaded by his failure, Ravana targeted Rama with a volley of arrows, injuring Matali and tearing Indra's standard. When Rama returned fire, Ravana picked up his formidable spear that rivalled the thunderbolt in its fury, shouting menacingly, 'This infallible weapon is sure to strike you down today, taking your life like that of your younger brother.' It flamed through the air in a halo of lightning, emitting a thunderous sound, consuming the arrows that Rama sent to curtail it. Then Rama seized the javelin sent by Indra. It lit up the sky like a meteor and split Ravana's weapon asunder. Before he could respond, Rama pierced Ravana's chest and struck him all over his body, shouting, 'You have flouted all norms of decency with your unethical conduct, so now prepare to reap the fruit of your deplorable deeds. You call yourself a hero, but you lost any claim to that honour when you sneakily carried my wife away like a thief behind my back. Your behaviour is shameful! It is unbefitting of an arya to deceive a helpless woman, forcibly laying hands on her. If you had genuine courage, you would have faced me at Dandaka, but I suppose you feared meeting the same fate as your cousin Khara. Nevertheless, you stand before me now, and by the end of the day, vultures will feed on your entrails.'

Wounded and bleeding, Ravana slipped off his seat and collapsed in exhaustion. His charioteer, alarmed and concerned for his safety, quickly whisked him away from the battlefield. When Ravana came to his senses, he clenched his jaws and lashed out, bellowing furiously, 'Who gave you the authority to remove me from the battle? You seem to be acting on behalf of my enemy, to make me look gutless and cowardly. Sadly, you have not conducted yourself as an arya and have shown yourself to be completely untrustworthy by embarrassing me in this dreadful manner. If you want to redeem yourself in my eyes, take me back to the battlefield at once.'

The hapless charioteer was surprised at Ravana's outburst. In trepidation, he hastened to justify his decision, saying, 'I did not act out of disloyalty or a lack of confidence in your abilities. I sped you away only because I was concerned for your safety. I did not for a moment think your adversary was stronger than you, but when I saw your exhaustion and the fatigue of the thirsty horses, I felt it my responsibility as your charioteer to help you to regain your strength. I was only performing my duty to the best of my ability. As you know, a charioteer exercises his discretion in deciding when to advance, when to retreat and when to hold firmly in position. In my defence, all I can say is that I acted out of the deepest affection and regard for you.' Ravana was placated by the charioteer's explanation, and commending his loyalty, asked to be taken back to the battlefield.

In the meanwhile, Rama was waiting anxiously to resume the battle. He was immersed in thought, wrestling with the dilemma of how to inflict a death blow on Ravana—for every time he thought Yama had claimed him, he would miraculously revive again. While Rama was preparing for Ravana's return, Sage Agastya manifested himself before him through his spiritual powers. In the role of a guru, he said, 'You are engaged in an arduous battle, so I came here to offer my support. I will teach you a special mantra, a divine formula for success, to empower you and ensure your victory. The Aditya Hridayam[9] is intended to invoke the power of the cosmic intelligence symbolized by the sun,[10] the source of light and the giver of life. Chanting this mantra with concentration will bless you with the good fortune to succeed against your enemy.'

Agastya vanished as quickly as he had appeared, and facing the sun, Rama chanted the hymn with solemn reverence.

Brimming with exuberance, Ravana re-entered the battlefield with renewed vigour. Bent on proving his valour, he came careening towards Rama at great speed. Seeing his rapid advance, Rama said to Matali, 'You do not need any special instruction; as Indra's charioteer, you are highly accomplished, so I will leave the job of driving the chariot in your expert hands while I concentrate entirely on the enemy who is rushing here with such impetuosity.' Matali accordingly drove the chariot swiftly forward,

---

[9] Aditya is another name for the sun and Hridayam is heart. The hymn venerates the sun as a glorious manifestation of the cosmic consciousness called God.

[10] The same cosmic consciousness that powers the sun is present in all beings. 'The Self in man and in the Sun are one. Those who understand this see through the world and go beyond the various sheaths of being, to realize the unity of life.' Taittiriya Upanishad 2.8.1

raising great clouds of swirling dust. Ravana began shooting arrows, and Rama answered them with Indra's bow. As the two fought, everyone else on the battlefield stopped fighting and stood gaping at the mighty contest. Even the Devas watched with bated breath. Just as there is no simile for the vastness of the sea or sky, the intensity of this battle had no comparison to anything that had taken place before.

Ill omens followed Ravana's chariot, and Lanka in the background looked enshrouded in darkness. Thus far, the battle had raged on almost without a break for seven days and seven nights, with the two mighty warriors pitted against each other, demonstrating their expertise in warfare. Rama was intent on killing Ravana, while he, in turn, was unwavering in his determination to fight to the bitter end regardless of the consequences. Ravana fixed an arrow to his bow and aimed it at Rama's standard, but Matali expertly manoeuvred the chariot, so it pierced the earth instead. Rama retaliated, targeting Ravana's banner, tearing it down. This move injured Ravana's pride, and he let loose a hail of arrows that pierced Rama's horses, but the valiant steeds neither flinched nor faltered. Infuriated by their composure, Ravana used his magical powers to rain clubs, discuses, mallets, pikes and axes. However, Rama remained unruffled and easily thwarted the attack, releasing hundreds of arrows in rapid succession. Ravana then fired a fresh volley of shafts, and Rama struck back with equal fury. The sky was entirely covered by the hail of arrows colliding with one another in a furious trade of blow for blow. The standoff between the contenders continued interminably as their charioteers exhibited exceptional battle skills, moving in circles, darting forward and suddenly retreating.

Then, at last, the endless duel that had gone on for so long reached its climax as the eyes of the arch-rivals met. For an instant, they were face to face, and their horses stood muzzle to muzzle, an image encapsulating the eternal tussle between dharma and adharma. Rama released four sharp arrows that forced Ravana's horses back. Infuriated, Ravana retaliated, wounding Rama, but he did not shrink. Ravana was irritated at not debilitating Rama and attacked Matali, but he too remained unshaken. The assault on his charioteer incensed Rama, and he responded aggressively, bombarding Ravana's chariot with thousands of arrows. Ravana returned fire with a shower of maces and mallets, and the tumultuous struggle that followed was witnessed breathlessly by all. The bystanders shuddered at the spectacle as the contest continued, and the contenders remained frustratingly deadlocked. Rama wondered why the weapons he had used so successfully in the past were ineffective against

Ravana. Every time he struck Ravana's head, the Rakshasa king would magically revive as if a new one had grown in its place!

Then Matali advised, 'Gallant prince, I notice you are fighting defensively. The time has come for you to go on the offensive and finish off Ravana decisively. I suggest you use the Brahmastra as a last resort.'

Rama drew the unfailing arrow Rishi Agastya had gifted him in Dandaka and summoned the mighty Brahmastra, which never missed its mark. It was the creation of Brahma for Indra, with the power of the wind in its wings and the might of the sun in its fiery head. While its shaft was like ether, its weight could be likened to Mount Mandara and Meru combined.[11] Rama stretched his bow, charging the arrow with the incantation of a sacred mantra, and it flew swiftly, hurtling through the air with tremendous force, lighting up the sky in all directions. In moments it split open Ravana's chest, going through his body and sticking into the ground, before returning meekly to Rama's quiver, drenched in blood. There was a roar of exultation as Ravana's bow slipped from his hands, and he fell to the ground like the Asura Vritra at the hands of Indra. The Devas showered flowers from above and cheers of 'Well done! Bravo!' echoed loudly as the world rejoiced. Peace seemed to descend on the Earth; the breeze was gentle, and even the sun's rays turned mellow in acknowledgment of the righteous victory.

[11] The Brahmastra was a weapon of mass destruction. J. Robert Oppenheimer who developed the atomic bomb seems to have had this opinion based on his interest in Sanskrit literature. When asked at a lecture at Rochester University if the bomb exploded during the Trinity test of the Manhattan Project was the first one to be detonated, he replied 'Well, yes; in modern times of course.'

Chapter 32

The Aftermath

Vibhishana could not help feeling sorrowful at the sight of Ravana lying lifeless on the battlefield. He had always disapproved of his brother's ways, and his head told him that Ravana had met a fitting end; nonetheless, Ravana was of his blood, and Vibhishana's heart ached that he could not prevent him from destroying himself. Crying out in pain, he exclaimed, 'O my brother, you were erudite, a valiant warrior, a skilled statesman, and at one time, even the embodiment of dharma; yet you threw it all away for nothing. Now, as I had feared, you lie on the ground, bereft of your royal status, all because you refused to see reason though I begged you so earnestly. Instead of heeding my words, you were perversely driven by an immoral mania for a married woman, relying on the false counsel of Prahasta, Indrajit, Kumbhakarna, Atikaya and Narantaka; and with them, you have come to a tragic end. While you lie here outstretched and motionless in the dust, Lanka has lost all its glory. The great kingdom you built is in ashes. How I wish you had realized in time that you could not have defeated Rama and averted this needless calamity.'

Rama, who loved his own brothers dearly, empathized with Vibhishana's pain and tried to console him. He said, 'While your grief is understandable, Ravana's death was necessary for the good of the world. Though he was my adversary, he was a skilled warrior who was hard to defeat. Ravana died on the battlefield after putting up stiff resistance, and our shastras tell us that a Kshatriya who dies in battle achieves a place in heaven.[1] Now that he is no

---

[1] Heaven and hell in Vedic philosophy are temporary states of existence between births, experienced in proportion to the good or evil done during one's lifetime. Death on the battlefield would allow a Kshatriya to experience time in heaven. Also, heaven is not the ultimate goal as reaching it doesn't prevent rebirth. True liberation is Moksha.

more, remember all his strengths, for he had many, and put the evil he did behind you.'

Vibhishana replied, 'My brother was very accomplished. He was a scholar who had mastered the Vedas and dutifully practised religious austerities. He was also very generous, always rewarding those who served him handsomely and donating liberally to the Brahmins. I want to give him a grand state funeral with full adherence to all the sacred rites.'

Rama smiled at Vibhishana and said kindly, 'Let it be so! I feel no hatred towards Ravana because all enmity ends with death once the body is no more.[2] The funeral must be conducted with due honour to help his spirit on its onward journey.'

Ravana's many wives rushed onto the battlefield, their eyes wet with tears and their hair dishevelled. They felt unprotected like uprooted creepers as they fell on his body, cradling his head and embracing him tenderly. Sobbing bitterly, they cried, 'O noble arya, your death has made us widows. You were a brave warrior who defeated the Devas and Gandharvas; how could you have been killed by a mere mortal who came here on foot? If only you had heeded Vibhishana's advice, you would not be lying here today. When you brought Sita to Lanka, we all feared she would be the cause of your undoing, but you refused to see it.'

Mandodari, Ravana's beautiful first wife, the mother of his favourite son Indrajit, was inconsolable. Grief-stricken, she lamented in pain, 'O King, why do you lie motionless on the cold earth, unresponsive to me, your faithful companion? You were the mightiest being in the three worlds,

---

[2] In Vedic belief, the indwelling spirit (Atman) is no different from the divine consciousness and therefore untarnished and immortal. It is only the body that is flawed and perishable.

'The all-knowing Self was never born, nor will it die. Beyond cause and effect, this Self is eternal and immutable. When the body dies, the Self does not die.' Katha Upanishad 2.18

'The Self is everywhere. Bright is the Self, indivisible, untouched by sin, wise immanent and transcendent.' Isha Upanishad.8

In the Mandukya Upanishad, the body is associated with three states: waking, dreaming and deep sleep. Beyond these lies the real Self or Turiya, the superconscious state not dependent on the body. This fourth state is eternal whereas the other three are temporary. When the body is no more, only the fourth state remains. This is what Rama is referring to when he says all enmity must end with the death of the body, as only Brahman remains.

and everyone from the Devas in Swarga[3] to the rishis in the forest shook
before you, yet you lie here dead at the hands of a mortal, wandering in
the woods. Many years of penance earned you great discipline over your
senses, and the resulting merit took you to the highest pinnacle of success,
but unfortunately, your obsession with Sita made you lose your self-control,
and now you have become a victim of the ill-fated destiny you created. No
ordinary human being could have defeated you, so I must believe someone
mighty like Vishnu assumed the form of Rama to carry out this deed. The
signs of Rama's divinity were evident when he killed your cousin Khara and
his entire army single-handedly and when his messenger Hanuman burnt
down our city. I begged you repeatedly not to further hostilities with him,
pleading with you to return Sita, but tragically, you ignored me. Your
depraved infatuation with another man's wife has brought about your doom
and the downfall of Lanka. It was not right to steal Sita from her husband as
you did. She is as devoted to Rama as Arundhati is to Vasishta and Rohini to
Chandra, so you have been dealt due retribution for your sinful actions. In
the end, the doer of dharma achieves happiness while the one who perpetrates
adharma necessarily suffers. While you are cold and lifeless, Vibhishana has
attained prosperity, for, in dharma alone, there is victory.[4]

'You had numerous consorts, many far more fetching than Sita, but your
craze for her so blinded you that you did not notice them. I do not think
I am in any way less comely than the princess of Mithila, less accomplished
or of lower birth, but you pushed me aside to pursue her. Alas! You invited
your end and my misfortune by bringing her here. Your handsome face with
its sharp nose and striking features that once vied with the sun in brilliance is
now pallid, and your fiery eyes do not sparkle anymore. No one will see your
charming smile or hear your witty banter again. I, the daughter of Mayasura,
was proud to be your wife and the mother of our valiant son Indrajit, fully
secure that I had a protector who could not be vanquished. Yet now you lie
pierced with so many arrows that it is hard even to embrace you. How could
death come to one who had defeated Yama? It is painful to see you in the
dust when you have always lain on silken couches.

'The death of my beloved son Indrajit at the hands of Lakshmana was
unbearable for me, but today I feel completely undone by widowhood. I see
nothing but bleakness ahead; your partner Mandodari is in great anguish and

---

[3] Abode of the Devas.

[4] The ultimate victory of dharma is the message of the Ramayana and all the shastras.

has no wish to go on without you. In this nadir of grief, I cannot help but feel that you have been brought down by the curses heaped on you by the countless women you abused. The saying that a pious woman's tears do not fall on the earth in vain has proved true. How could one so valorous commit the cowardly act of stealing the wife of another behind his back? Vibhishana's warning to you has unfolded in the tragic denouement of the battle today. You disregarded him and paid no heed to Maricha, Kumbhakarna, Malyavan and my father Mayasura, who tried to counsel you. Lanka has perished; its wealth is no more; its menfolk are dead, and the women have no one to support them. The empty shell of your body is all that remains while your spirit has gone onward, embedded with the impressions of the good and bad deeds you committed in your life.[5] I know your death was the inevitable result of your unworthy behaviour, yet my love for you as your devoted wife fills me with great unhappiness, and my heart is in pieces.'

Her emotions spent after this long eulogy, Mandodari fell in a swoon. As her co-wives lifted her, one of them remarked stoically, 'Compose yourself! The fortune of kings is never steady, so we must accept our destiny.'

Rama felt sorry to see Mandodari's grief, and asked Vibhishana to begin preparations for the funeral so that Ravana's wives could have closure. However, Vibhishana began to have second thoughts, feeling it would be hypocritical for him to officiate at Ravana's death ceremonies. He had lost respect for the brother who had abandoned righteousness and now worried if it was appropriate for him to conduct such a person's final rites. To clear Vibhishana's confusion about his duty, Rama counselled him, saying, 'I understand your anger at Ravana's evil ways, but with his death, he has paid for his sins. Despite all his transgressions, he also had many good qualities, and in recognition of those, he deserves a proper funeral. Also, remember that your help secured my victory, so you need to perform Ravana's last rites to win the people's acceptance. All acrimony must end when the body ceases to exist, so my advice to you is to forgive his sins and feel the same brotherhood for him as before. Do your duty as Ravana's only surviving male relative and perform his funeral without delay in accordance with the shastras for the peace of his soul.'

---

[5] 'For when we die neither father, nor mother, nor spouse, nor children, nor relations continue with us as companions; spiritual merit alone remains.' Manusmriti 4.239

Vibhishana took Rama's wise advice, and a grand funeral was held, consigning the once-glorious King of Lanka to the blazing flames of a sandalwood pyre.

Oddly, after the cremation was over, Rama did not rush to Sita as might have been expected. Instead, he bade farewell to Matali, releasing the divine chariot lent by Indra. Then he embraced Sugriva, expressing his most profound gratitude, and asked Lakshmana to organize Vibhishana's coronation. The Vanaras fetched pots of seawater, and in a ceremony conducted by Lakshmana following the prescribed ordinances, Vibhishana was officially crowned King of Lanka. Rama did not participate in the celebration because he was still in exile. Since he was not permitted to enter a city, he asked Hanuman to give a message to Sita, saying, 'Take Vibhishana's permission and go to Lanka. Please convey my gratitude to Sita for her devotion and find out how she is doing. I would like you to assure her that Lakshmana and I are well. Inform her that she is free and need not fear Ravana any longer, and let me know what she says.'

Hanuman accordingly went to the Ashoka Garden. Sita was sitting unbathed and forlorn under a tree, looking as miserable as the first time he saw her. Approaching her with folded hands, Hanuman said, 'Rama sends you his greetings and wants to assure you that all is fine with Lakshmana and him. He is concerned about your well-being and is grateful for your steadfast devotion and faith in him, which helped his victory over Ravana. Rama wants you to know that he spent sleepless nights in his endeavour to regain you, even building a bridge to cross the ocean. Now his mission stands fulfilled. Vibhishana is the new lord of Lanka, so you are as safe here as if you were in your own home.'

Overjoyed and choking with emotion, Sita was unable to speak. Finding her voice, at last, she said, 'My joy is so great to hear of my husband's victory that I was tongue-tied for a moment! Unfortunately, I can give you nothing that can be deemed adequate recompense for bringing me such wonderful news. I am so grateful that even the entire store of gold, silver and precious stones in the three worlds would be insufficient to express my gratitude.'

Hanuman thanked her for her generous praise and said humbly, 'Your recognition and Rama's victory mean more to me than any amount of wealth.'

Sita admired his humility and remarked in appreciation, 'You are indeed a worthy son of your father, Vayu. Not only are you strong and brave, but you are also refined, calm and humble, and your knowledge of the shastras makes you conduct yourself with utmost grace.'

Then, Hanuman spotted Sita's guards hovering in the vicinity and grew angry. He said, 'Please give me your permission to punish these wretches who have caused you so much grief with a sound thrashing.'

Sita replied at once, 'There is no point being angry with those who were merely carrying out their master's orders. They did not act of their own volition, and I feel no hatred towards them. Everything that has happened to me is because of my own actions, for karma does not let any misdeed go unpunished.[6] Therefore, one must always be virtuous regardless of the behaviour of others, as a good character is one's best ornament. Remember the story of the man, the bear and the tiger? While walking through a forest, a man once climbed a tree to escape a tiger, only to find a bear seated there. The tiger asked the bear to act as a forest brother and push the man down, but the bear refused, saying that his dharma prevented him from betraying someone who had arrived at his abode seeking refuge.'

'Time passed, and the bear nodded off to sleep. The cunning tiger then tried to make a deal with the man to shove the bear down. He said that his hunger would be satisfied by eating the bear instead, so he would spare the man. The ungrateful man selfishly did the tiger's bidding, but the bear saved himself by hanging onto a lower branch. The tiger then asked the bear to give up the man who had proved to be so treacherous. The magnanimous bear refused, and when the tiger asked why he continued to protect the man who was unworthy of his kindness, the bear replied that a noble soul never commits an evil act in return for one committed against him. It is a virtue to show compassion to those who have wronged us, so please forgive the guards.'

As Hanuman was leaving, Sita told him to tell Rama that she longed to see him, and Hanuman faithfully conveyed her message. Hearing Sita's words, Rama became pensive with a faraway look on his face. Tears welled up in his eyes, and he sighed heavily as he wrestled with a difficult dilemma. Then, with his eyes downcast, drawing a deep breath, he said to Vibhishana, who was standing by him, 'Please could you bring Sita here? I would like her to bathe, dress, ornament herself and come here without delay.'

When Vibhishana told Sita that Rama wanted to see her, she wanted to leave immediately and was surprised that he had asked her to adorn herself. Nevertheless, she did as he requested; she bathed, groomed her hair and

---

6 Karma involves accountability, not just random fate.

dressed in fine clothes and jewellery before ascending the grand palanquin Vibhishana had arranged for her.

At last, the moment Sita had waited for all these months arrived, as she approached her beloved Rama's presence. When Vibhishana informed Rama that Sita had come, he said, 'Let her get down from the palanquin and walk here.' Strangely his face did not show the happiness that everyone expected. The truth was that his mind was racked by conflicting emotions, feeling joy, misery and anger simultaneously. The sight of his precious wife after their long separation filled his heart with supreme gladness, but at the same time, his elation at seeing her was marred by the misery that he would not be able to accept her back unconditionally as he would have liked. Rama's exile was almost over, and he would return to Ayodhya to rule in a matter of days. He was concerned that the people would malign Sita's character and feared they would not welcome back a queen who had scandalously spent so many months in the home of another man, even if it were not of her choosing. Coupled with helplessness, he also felt a tinge of anger at the unfair allegations Sita had levelled against Lakshmana when she accused him of looking at her with unclean eyes. Her offensive words had not only caused a pure and innocent soul more pain than could be imagined, but had been the impetus for her tragedy.

As the palanquin was set down, the Vanaras rushed forward, straining their necks to catch a glimpse of the woman for whom so many had given their lives, while Vibhishana tried to disperse them, instructing his guards to drive them back with sticks. Rama was annoyed to see this and interceded, saying testily, 'These are my people, so why are you chasing them away? A woman does not need to be protected from the world by walls or veils. Her character alone is her shield.' Sita climbed down from the palanquin with her heart overflowing with love and walked coyly towards Rama as the onlookers watched eagerly, anticipating a happy reunion. However, Rama behaved totally out of character! Instead of rejoicing at seeing Sita, his countenance was unnaturally grave.

Adopting a formal attitude, he said coldly, 'Noble lady, after expending significant effort, I finally killed your abductor and delivered you from his clutches. The insult that destiny dealt you is now righted, and the vow I made to free you stands fulfilled today. My mission was fruitful thanks to Hanuman, who crossed the ocean, Sugriva and his Vanaras, who fought for you, and Vibhishana, who abandoned his sinful brother to help me. I rescued you out of my Kshatriya duty and for the reputation of my noble house, not out of love for you. Your character stands in doubt, besmirched in the eyes of the world, and your purity is like a bright lamp before a blind man.[7] O daughter of Janaka, now that you are liberated from imprisonment, you are free to go anywhere you like because our relationship can be no more. You have been with another man for months; he squeezed you in his arms and held you on his lap when he bore you away, looking at you every day with lustful eyes, so how can I take you back? I have thought about this at length, and since we cannot go back to the way we were, I can only suggest that you go someplace of your choosing in the four corners of this world or live under the brotherly protection of Lakshmana, Bharata, Shatrughana, Sugriva or Vibhishana. You have such divine beauty; do you think it is believable that Ravana did not touch you?'

Sita had never heard Rama utter an unkind word to her before, let alone so publicly, and could not believe what she was hearing. The unfairness of his words was hurtful, cutting like sharp arrows piercing her ears, just as her mean allegations had felt to Lakshmana that fateful day in the forest. She broke down and wept bitterly for a long time, unable to respond; but Sita, an assertive woman, refused to let the aspersions cast on her character go undefended. Determined to vindicate herself, she wiped her tears and said in a faltering voice, 'Your words are unfair and unbefitting of an arya; they are, in fact, totally unbecoming of a refined person like you. You speak to me callously like an uncultured man addressing a common woman. From your insinuations, it appears you doubt me based on the bad conduct of a few indecent women in society, but you cannot attribute the vulgarity of some to the whole gender. If I was touched while being abducted, it was against my will, resulting from helplessness brought on by destiny. As a prisoner, my body was not in my sway, but my mind was totally in my control, and I can say with utmost surety that it never wavered for a moment. It causes me untold misery that you doubt me, despite knowing me so well for all these years.'

---

[7] By using the analogy of a bright lamp before a blind man, Rama indicates that though Sita is pure, her purity will not be seen by the world. He makes it clear that Sita is faultless, and the problem lies with the onlookers.
'As the sun, who is the eye of the world, cannot be tainted by the defects in our eyes, or by the objects it looks on, so the one Self, dwelling in all, cannot be tainted by the evils of the world.' Katha Upanishad 2.2.11

'Why did you give me false hope by sending Hanuman with the message that you would rescue me? If I had known your true feelings about me at that time, I would have given up my life then. All the trouble you took to come here, making the arduous journey across the sea and endangering yourself by waging a war that took the lives of so many, was entirely unnecessary. It appears you are consumed by petty anger, attributing the frailties of womankind to me, but I am not an ordinary woman; I was born from the earth and have never deviated from immaculate conduct. I am disheartened to see that you have forgotten the promise of "panigrahanam" taken at our marriage, when my father put my hand in yours. We vowed everlasting togetherness, and I am not sure why you are displaying such small-mindedness in brushing aside my devotion with a cruel repudiation of my chastity!'

Then, looking at Lakshmana, Sita implored, 'Do me the favour of preparing a pyre, for I see no other remedy for this calamitous situation that has befallen me. I wish to prove my character and absolve myself of the false allegations levelled at me. Unfortunately, I have been denounced publicly by my husband, who doubts me, and there is no option but to let Agni arbitrate on my purity.' Lakshmana was bewildered by the bizarre situation that was unfolding. He looked desperately to Rama for direction, but Rama stood stony-faced, looking like Yama at the dissolution of the universe. Then recognizing the acquiescence indicated in Rama's facial expression, Lakshmana reluctantly prepared the pyre.

Sita walked clockwise around Rama with her head bent low as she approached the blaze. With folded hands, she prayed, 'I was cruelly separated from my husband and forced to live in the house of another man, but my loyalty did not waver. If my mind never deviated from Rama, shield me from harm. If I am chaste despite my husband's misgivings, save me. Protect me if I have never strayed in speech, thought or action. May the deities that preside over the sun, moon, wind, Earth and all the Devas who are witnesses to my purity, safeguard me.' Then circling the fire, she boldly entered it, offering herself as an oblation of ghee poured into a sacrificial flame. While the crowd gasped in shock, Rama was in an unenviable position of impotence. Although he knew the fire would not touch Sita because of her incomparable purity, he was distressed at the pain she naturally felt hearing him reject her. Yet, at the same time, he knew it was the only way Sita could rid herself of social stigma and had no alternative but to allow her to go through the ordeal of proving herself to appease the world.

As Rama stood looking on with tears in his eyes, the Devas descended in
their aerial chariots. The king of the Yakshas, Kubera, arrived, as did Yama,
Indra, Varuna, Shiva and Brahma. They joined their palms in salutation,
and honouring Rama as the foremost amongst them, questioned why he had
turned his back on Sita. Rama, who regarded himself as an ordinary human
being, the son of Dasharatha, was surprised to be called a Deva. When he
asked who he really was, Brahma said, 'The truth is that you are Narayana
himself, the one who wields the Sudarshan, who carries the bow Saranga
and the sword Nandaka. You are the imperishable spirit who is infinite and
beyond time. You are the conqueror of enemies, whom the rishis call their
refuge; the one who incarnated as the single-tusked boar and the divine dwarf
Vamana; the supreme one who takes birth over and over to vanquish evil.
Your teachings are the Vedas; you are the intelligence behind the mind and
the consciousness that animates all beings. You are the preserver, the four-
armed Hari, the mystic sound "Om", and the reason the Universe exists. Sita
is your divine consort Lakshmi, and you are eternal, truth, consciousness,
bliss. You pervade the universe, and your power permeates everything,
including the sky, the mountains and rivers.[8] You are the entire cosmos; the
Earth symbolizes your strength, fire your wrath and the moon your calmness.
You took a human form to destroy Ravana and have achieved the purpose for
which you were born.'

Hearing Brahma's words, Agni, the Deva of fire, emerged from the pyre
with Sita, like a father carrying his daughter to safety in his arms. Miraculously
she was untouched by the burning flames. Her lovely face framed by wavy
locks had an ethereal glow, and she looked as beautiful as when she had
stepped in. Then Agni, the universal witness, spoke to Rama and said, 'Here
is your Sita, the princess of Videha! She is a blessed woman of irreproachable
conduct who has never been unfaithful in word, thought, or deed or guilty
of even an inappropriate glance. Although detained for months, she kept

---

[8] The Vedic concept of God is the supreme consciousness that dwells in all creation
(discussed in detail in the Appendices). All beings are divine, however, the nature and
purpose of an avatar is different from ordinary people. As an avatar, Rama was not
born due to the bondage of karma, but in freedom for the purpose of re-establishing
righteousness on Earth.
'Just as a spider spins its web, and draws it again, as plants sprout from the earth, as hair
grows from the body, the whole creation springs from Brahman and unto it returns.'
Mundaka Upanishad 1.1.7

her mind focused on you through every mental torture she suffered, and every temptation offered. She is beyond seduction, completely spotless in character and you must accept her back because she does not deserve any unkind treatment.'

Rama replied tenderly, 'I never doubted Sita even for a moment and implicitly believe her to be a woman of exemplary character. I love her dearly and know she is completely devoted to me, just as I am to her. Painful as it has been for both of us, this trial was, unfortunately, necessary to redeem Sita of any taint in the eyes of others since she lived in Ravana's house for almost a year. I was helpless in stopping her from proving her purity, for I knew that tongues would wag with unpleasant gossip unless Sita publicly demonstrated her virtue. In my opinion, she possesses such exalted spiritual merit that she is as pure as fire herself, and Ravana could not have violated her even if he wanted. I can never divorce my heart from Sita; she is as inextricable from me as sunlight is from the sun or as a good man is inseparable from his honest reputation.' Thus, the long nightmare was finally over for Rama and Sita, and though never parted in spirit, they were reunited once again in person.

Hearing Rama's tribute of undying love, Shiva said, 'O broad-chested, lotus-eyed one with mighty arms, you have achieved the purpose of your birth by dispelling the darkness Ravana had cast over the entire universe. However, you still have unfinished work on earth and can ascend to heaven only after completing it. Comfort Bharata and your mothers by returning to rule Ayodhya and bring glory to the Ikshavaku dynasty. Your father is here from Swarga, the realm of Indra, and would like to speak with you.'

Dasharatha descended in a fine chariot. Putting his arm around Rama, he said, 'I am proud of your success in vanquishing your enemies and in honourably completing the fourteen years of exile you unhesitatingly accepted to go through on my account. Though Kaikeyi's words are still imprinted on my heart, seeing you and Lakshmana today, I am completely rid of the sorrow I suffered in my corporeal form. My worthy son, I now know the true purpose for which you were born and the destiny you came with to destroy Ravana. Kaushalya and the people of Ayodhya will finally have the good fortune of seeing you consecrated as king. May you have a long and prosperous rule and henceforth live happily with your brothers."

Rama joined his hands and requested his father, 'Please be gracious to my mother Kaikeyi and to Bharata, whom you disowned in a temper. Reconsider your feelings and accept them back, so that they are not adversely affected by your anger.'

Dasharatha said, 'So be it,' and then addressed Lakshmana. 'You have earned great spiritual merit by your devoted service to Rama and Sita. I am very proud of you and know you will reap the appropriate reward for your good deeds.' Finally, before departing, Dasharatha fondly gave Sita his parting advice. 'Dear daughter, forgive Rama for pretending to disavow you, and do not bear a grudge towards him for it. He only did it for your welfare, to ensure that your purity, which he was sure about, would be demonstrated to the rest of the world. Choosing to undergo a difficult test by fire is a testament to your character and places you on a pedestal as an ideal for all women. You require no instruction on doing what is right; nevertheless, indulge me when I ask you to continue your steadfast devotion to your husband.'

The Devas were pleased with Rama for delivering them from Ravana, and Indra asked if there was a favour he could grant in return. Rama said earnestly, 'Many brave Vanaras and bears gave up their lives for me. If you wish to bestow something on me, please bring them back to life so they can return to their loved ones. Also, in eternal gratitude to them, may the land where they live always be plentiful with flowers, fruit and roots in every season, and may the rivers that flow near them continually provide them with fresh water.' The mighty Indra replied, 'Although what you ask for is difficult to grant, we cannot refuse you, and you will have your wish.' So, the dead Vanaras and bears were restored to life as if they had woken up from a deep slumber, and blessing Rama, Sita and Lakshmana, the Devas returned to their abode.

Chapter 33

The Return to Ayodhya

The Vanaras celebrated heartily that night, while Rama and Lakshmana indulgently observed their merriment. The following day Vibhishana came to Rama with a kind offer and said, 'I have brought a few talented female attendants with me, who are skilled in aromatherapy and the administration of various kinds of luxurious baths. They can help you wash and dress in fresh garments, so I hope you will take the opportunity to relax and unwind after all the hardship you have endured.'

Rama was touched by Vibhishana's thoughtfulness but politely declined. He said, 'Unfortunately, I cannot afford to spare any time for self-indulgence as my mind is far too restless to think of respite at this moment. The task of returning to Ayodhya at the earliest must take priority, knowing that my brother Bharata is anxiously waiting for me. Let Sugriva and the Vanaras avail of the relaxation you have so kindly offered, and instead, tell me how I can get back home quickly. The journey by foot is long and tedious and would take many days.'

Vibhishana was eager to help, and said generously, 'You will be able to reach Ayodhya in a day if you take the Pushpaka Vimana that Ravana stole from our brother Kubera. It is ready and waiting at your service, but do me the honour of being my guest in Lanka for a few days before leaving.' Rama felt warmed by his hospitality and thanked Vibhishana for his friendship; but apologized again for turning down his invitation, insisting that he was determined to return to Ayodhya immediately, having made Bharata a commitment to be back precisely after fourteen years, not a day later.

Vibhishana summoned the massive Pushpaka Vimana. It was as huge as a hill, and Rama looked at it in awe; it was made of gold with seats of cat's-eye jewels and could travel anywhere at will. When Vibhishana asked if there was anything else he could do for him, Rama said, 'Reward the Vanaras with gold and precious stones, since their efforts helped you attain the throne of Lanka, and it is proper for you to show them your gratitude. It is the mark of a good leader to make those who serve him feel appreciated, and this generosity on your part will go a long way in earning their respect.'

Then, carrying Sita in his arms, Rama climbed the long staircase into the aerial chariot with Lakshmana. At the top of the stairs, he turned and fondly bid farewell to everyone, thanking Vibhishana for his friendship and expressing his deepest gratitude to Sugriva and the Vanaras for all they had done for him. Suddenly, Vibhishana, overcome by the pangs of separation, exclaimed emotionally, 'Take us with you to Ayodhya. We would love to see your beautiful city with its charming gardens and witness the grandeur of your coronation.' Sugriva seconded him with the backing of the Vanaras, who said they would return home after the celebration. Rama was thrilled with the suggestion, declaring that nothing would give him greater joy, so everyone excitedly boarded the vimana as it headed for Ayodhya.

The Pushpaka Vimana resembled a beautiful swan. As it rose majestically into the sky like a giant bird, soaring noisily through the air, Rama pointed out all the landmarks of his journey to Sita. Behind them stood Mount Trikuta, on which the beautiful city of Lanka, built by Vishwakarma, was perched, and below them, the muddy battlefield, which had witnessed so much carnage, and where Ravana had ultimately met his end. They flew past the spectacular bridge, the incredible Nala Setu, which the mighty son of Vishwakarma had thrown over the roaring sea, and the golden peak of Mount Mainaka, which rose from the ocean to offer Hanuman a place to rest. Rama showed Sita the shore where the Vanara army had camped and where he had invoked Varuna. This place was where the Sethubandha had been indicated to him, the spot where the bridge construction began. Rama added that the beach was also where he had first met Vibhishana after Ravana expelled him.

As they neared Kishkindha, the abode of the Vanaras amid lush forests, Sita said magnanimously, 'I would love to take Tara, Ruma and all the Vanara wives with us to Ayodhya.' And so, the vimana descended, and the women excitedly climbed in joining their husbands. As the happy group continued, they passed Rishyamukha, where Rama first became acquainted with Sugriva, and the beautiful lake Pampa, where Shabri had welcomed him to Matanga's hermitage. Rama recalled how sorrowful he had been at the time, pointing out to Sita the spot where he had killed Kabandha and, further ahead, where

Jatayu had lain dying trying to save her. They flew over Panchavati, where Khara had been defeated. Then, passing the ashrams of the sages—Agastya, Suteekshna, Sarabhanga and Atri—they crossed Chitrakoota, where Bharata had come to meet them. Soon they neared the confluence of the Ganga and Yamuna, where they had stopped for a night fourteen years ago at the ashram of Rishi Bharadwaja. In the distance was Ayodhya with its tall buildings, shining as spectacularly as Amravati, and Rama exclaimed happily, 'There is no greater joy than returning home to one's motherland!' The sight of Ayodhya filled the Vanaras with curiosity, and they rushed to the windows craning their necks to look outside.

Rama wanted to pay his respects to the esteemed Rishi Bharadwaja, so the vimana alighted. He had begun his exile with the blessings of the venerated sage and wished to end it the same way. It was the lunar month of Chaitra on the fifth day of the waxing moon, and their fourteen years were complete. Rama asked the rishi if he knew whether Ayodhya continued to prosper, if his mothers were well, and if Bharata was ruling righteously. Bharadwaja expressed great joy that Rama had completed his exile successfully and assured him that all was good in Ayodhya, adding that Bharata was eagerly waiting for his return. Remembering his sadness at the commencement of Rama's exile, Bharadwaja felt elated to see him safely back after overcoming all obstacles in completing his duty. He invited Rama to rest the night at his hermitage before proceeding to Ayodhya, and not wishing to refuse the holy sage, Rama accepted his hospitality.

Bharadwaja then offered to grant Rama a wish, so he asked the great rishi to use his yogic powers to fill the trees with fruit for the Vanaras to enjoy, and instantly the forest for three yojanas became bountiful, abundant with fruit and honeycombs. As the Vanaras feasted, Rama asked Hanuman to go on a special mission. He said, 'I would like you to go to Ayodhya via Shringaverapura. First, convey the news of my return to my dear friend Guha and then proceed to Ayodhya. I would like you to inform Bharata that I have completed my exile and am on my way back with my new friends. Update him on all that has happened over the last fourteen years, including Sita's abduction and rescue. While you narrate these incidents, carefully observe his facial expressions and tone of voice. If you notice the slightest trace of displeasure in him, from having grown attached to power ruling for many years, I will not stand in his way by taking back the kingdom. In case you detect anything adverse in his feelings, however small, quickly bring back this intelligence to me so that I can decide my next step.'

Hanuman assumed a human form and set out at once. After stopping at Shringaverapura and delivering the tidings of Rama's safe return to Guha, he went on to Ayodhya, where he found Bharata in his hut at Nandigrama on the outskirts of the city. Hanuman was shocked to see the awful state he had reduced himself to, pining for his brother. Bharata was emaciated from fasting; his hair was matted, and he was dressed as a hermit with a black deerskin around his waist. His body was ravaged by his abstemious existence, eating meagrely and practising austerities for fourteen years. Hanuman's first impression of Bharata was that he looked saintly, like the embodiment of dharma with the spiritual effulgence of a Brahmarishi.

Hanuman joined his hands and said, 'The brother whom you sorrow for so much is at Rishi Bharadwaja's ashram. I am Hanuman, his servant, and have been sent ahead with a message from him. Abandon your misery; Rama is well, and after completing his exile successfully, is returning to Ayodhya tomorrow, along with Sita and Lakshmana in the auspicious hour of Pushya.'

This news was the first Bharata had heard about Rama in a long while, and he was so overjoyed that he fainted. When he recovered, Hanuman told him about all the events that had taken place since his meeting with Rama at Chitrakoota, carefully observing Bharata's face to pick up any hint of disgruntlement. However, it was evident that he felt nothing but happiness hearing that Rama was returning home. Hugging Hanuman, Bharata said with tears streaming down his face, 'I don't know if you are human or a Deva, but your arrival is a mission of mercy to me. You have given me the best information I could ever hope to receive, and I want to reward you with a hundred thousand cows, 100 villages and sixteen beautiful brides.'[1]

Bharata ordered the people of Ayodhya to organize a grand reception for Rama. The entire city was illuminated with rows of oil lamps. Every street, crossroad and building shone brightly. Brahmins recited the Vedas, and music filled the air. There were festoons of flower garlands hung throughout, and the citizens gathered eagerly to welcome their prince back. Shatrughana assembled thousands of workers to level the ground from Nandigrama to Ayodhya. Every house's threshold was decorated with designs drawn with coloured rice powder, and the streets were strewn with flower petals and sprinkled with water, so that they would not be dusty. Flags were hoisted, and the army with its elephants, horses and chariots came out in grand pageantry to salute Rama. Vaishyas carried garlands, and the entire

---

[1] This comment indicates that Hanuman was human, not a monkey.

population of the city was breathless with excitement. Kaushalya, Sumitra, Kaikeyi and all Dasharatha's consorts went to Nandigrama. Bharata placed Rama's wooden sandals on his head and carried the royal white umbrella as he waited impatiently to receive him. When there was no sign of Rama for a while, Bharata began to get restless and asked Hanuman if he had made a mistake in his communication. Hanuman smiled, saying there was no cause for concern, and assured him that Rama was undoubtedly on his way. Then, at last, they sighted the vimana, and as it descended, the exuberant crowd burst into cheers.

Bharata rushed ahead and touched his forehead to Rama's feet as soon as he alighted, and there was a loving reunion as the four brothers embraced one another. Rama touched the feet of his mothers and paid his respects to Guru Vasishta. Bharata hugged Sugriva, declaring him their fifth brother for all he had done. He embraced Vibhishana and thanked him profusely, for without his allegiance, Rama would not have achieved victory. The people looked on agog with their hands folded above their heads, looking like a vast lotus field. Not wanting to keep the Pushpaka Vimana longer than necessary, Rama commanded it to fly back to Kubera, its rightful owner.

Then Bharata took the sandals that had sat on the throne for fourteen years and placed them at Rama's feet. He said reverently, 'I am now returning your kingdom to you. You gave it to me to honour my mother's wishes, and I have held it in trust on your behalf all this time. As you instructed, I have cared for the people and grown the treasury, the army and granaries tenfold, but I can no longer bear the burden of the crown. Now that you are home, I feel my purpose is accomplished, so I am handing the reins back to you. This vast kingdom, whose authority extends far and wide all over the earth, is rightfully yours, and at long last, it is time for you to enjoy the fruit of the grand tree planted for you by our ancestors. Let us not waste a moment; I request you to dress in finery so that you can be crowned immediately.'

In preparation for his accession to the throne, Rama bathed and adorned himself in regal raiment, exchanging his hermit's garb for royal robes and glittering ornaments. Barbers took charge of his matted locks, expertly untangling and trimming them, and he was adorned with garlands and smeared with sandalwood paste. Meanwhile, the future empress Sita was dressed by Rama's mothers. Kaushalya also personally attended to the wives of the Vanaras, applying makeup and clothing them in finery. Bharata, Lakshmana, Shatrughana, Vibhishana and Sugriva also bathed and got ready for the big event, donning fancy attire. The minister Sumantra brought a splendid chariot to take Rama to the city. Bharata took the horses' reins himself, while Shatrughana held the white umbrella over Rama's head, and Lakshmana and Vibhishana fanned him. Sugriva rode alongside on the grand Shatrunjaya, followed by the rest of the Vanaras in a convoy of elephants. As the procession passed through the city to blaring conches and the roll of drums, the people shouted felicitations, showering turmeric-stained rice confetti and flower petals on them. When Rama reached his father's palace, the grand abode of his predecessors, the queen mothers were waiting for him. Greeting them, he turned to Bharata and said, 'Please ensure that all our guests are comfortable and well looked after. I want Sugriva housed in my personal residence, lavishly studded with pearls and cat's-eye, with a beautiful garden attached.'

Bharata arranged for the hospitality of the Vanaras and then said to Sugriva, 'Please may I request you to ask your Vanaras to bring holy waters from all the seas for the coronation?' At his instruction, the Vanaras immediately set out with gold vessels. Jambavan brought water from the eastern sea, Gavaya from the western region, Rishabha from the Southern Ocean and Hanuman from the Arctic in the north. The other Vanaras went in all directions collecting water from 500 rivers. The pots were placed before Vasishta, who would conduct the ceremony. As Rama ascended the throne in full regalia with Sita by his side, all the Devas and the rishis assembled to watch. The holy waters were sprinkled, and the coronation mantras were recited from the Vedas. Vasishta took the ancestral crown fashioned for the seventh Manu,[2] Vaivaswata, the son of Surya, that had rested on the head of every king of the Solar dynasty, and placed it on Rama.

On behalf of the Devas, Indra gave Rama a pearl necklace of immense beauty and asked Vayu to present him with a garland of 100 gold lotuses. The Gandharvas sang, and the Apsaras danced in honour of the occasion. Rama distributed 1,00,000 horses and cows and 100 bulls in charity to the Brahmins. He further donated 300 million gold coins and precious jewels to the people. Then he bestowed on Sugriva an exquisite garland of gold with sparkling gems. Angada was given a pair of armlets made of cat's-eye and encrusted with diamonds and other precious stones. Rama put the pearl

---

[2] After every dissolution, civilization restarts with a Manu or progenitor. The Earth is in the seventh cycle of regeneration; the last dissolution being the flood. The seventh Manu was Vaivaswata, to whom Rama traced his ancestry. He was also the author of the Manusmriti or the Code of Manu.

necklace gifted by Indra around Sita's neck, but she unclasped it and said she wished to give it to one of the Vanaras instead. Rama was pleased with her suggestion and said, 'Bestow it on him whose good qualities please you the most.' Without hesitation, Sita gifted it to Hanuman in fitting recognition of his courage, loyalty, modesty, humility, wisdom, learning, judgement, competence and unparalleled resolve. All the Vanaras and Vibhishana were rewarded handsomely for their service, and when they returned to their homes, they felt materially and spiritually enriched by their association with Rama.

After the guests left, Rama asked Lakshmana to rule by his side as prince regent, as he had initially offered when Dasharatha proclaimed him heir apparent, but Lakshmana did not accept. He felt it was only fair for Bharata to hold this position, so the latter was declared Rama's successor instead.

Rama ruled for many years, and the glory of his sovereignty was unsurpassed by any other king. He performed numerous sacrifices promoting his illustrious house's fame, including the Paundarika, the Ashwamedha and the Vajapeya.[3] Rama's focus was always on his people's welfare, and he donated incalculable amounts of wealth to charity during his reign. There was peace during Rama's rule, and it is said no widows lamented the untimely death of their husbands. There was no threat from wild animals, snakes or disease. It was an era of ideal governance that resulted in prosperity and plenty. People lived as they did in the golden age of Kritayuga[4] when dharma, represented by the bull, stood on all four legs. Crime and mendacity were unknown and no one suffered any harm. Everyone was devoted to righteousness, following the shining example set by their cherished king, and people lived long, happy lives. Even nature acknowledged the piety of Rama's rule; trees fruited bounteously, the rains fell appropriately in season and the winds were always gentle. Brahmins, Kshatriyas, Vaishyas and Shudras—the followers of the four professions—lived together in social harmony, free from avarice or strife, each performing their duties with utmost sincerity. Thus, it is believed Rama ruled for 11,000 years.[5]

---

[3] The highest form of Soma sacrifice performed by kings for prosperity. It also incorporated many kinds of sports, including chariot racing.

[4] Also known as Satyayuga, the golden epoch in which people displayed the highest virtue. The best of the four yugas.

[5] This is obviously an exaggeration! We have to consider the duration of Rama's reign based on the concept of divine time, where one divine day is equal to one human year. To

Valmiki encourages people to listen to the story of the Ramayana and imbibe the lessons it portrays. He advocates that its philosophy of life is eternally valid because it flows from the universal truths of the Vedas, purifying the mind. Valmiki's great poetic masterpiece advises the path of 'Sanatana Dharma' in Rama's footsteps, always upholding righteousness. A place in heaven is assured to those who scrupulously adhere to ethical action, choosing truth and goodness over selfish motives, as noble conduct negates past evil deeds. The admirable story of Rama's journey through life brings wisdom and maturity even to a cursory reader, who does not delve deeply into its Vedic tenets. As the great sage concludes, if a Brahmin emulates Rama, he naturally betters his scholarship, a Kshatriya becomes a more able protector, a Vaishya a more successful businessman, and a Shudra attains higher satisfaction from his service;[6] for in dharma, there is always victory.

arrive at the correct duration of Rama's rule, we need to divide 11,000 by 360 lunar years which is 30.5 years. Since Rama was considered divine, his 30.5 years were like 11,000 human years in achievement for an ordinary person.

[6] Discrimination was unknown in Vedic society, and contrary to the common notion today, the Varna system was not hierarchical. Service should not be confused with servitude. Shudras were the bulk of society and included all those who provided their skills to society in return for a fee or wage, including servants, engineers, doctors, artisans, etc.

BOOK 7
Epilogue

Chapter 34

The Ancestry of the Rakshasas

After Rama's coronation, all the great sages of the land arrived in Ayodhya to offer felicitations. Kaushika, Yavakrita, Gargya, Galava and Kanva came from the east. Swastyatreya, Namuchi, Pramuchi, Sumukha and Vimukha, led by Agastya, came from the south. Narsangu, Kavasa, Dhaumya, Kauseya and their disciples came from the west. Kashyapa, Atri, Vishwamitra, Gautama, Jamadagni and Bharadwaja joined Vasishta to represent the seven seers of the north. When the doorkeeper announced them, Rama was delighted to be blessed by their high-minded company and welcomed them with great reverence. Once seated, the rishis expressed their deepest gratitude to him for getting rid of Ravana and his vicious cohorts Prahasta, Vikata, Virupaksha, Mahodara, Akampana and Kumbhakarna. However, strangely, they remarked that the greatest service rendered to the world was the slaying of the conjurer Indrajit, who was far more dangerous than his father. Rama was surprised that the rishis considered Indrajit the most malevolent of the Rakshasas and asked why his death was so essential.

Agastya explained, smiling, 'Indrajit was dangerous because he was undefeatable in battle, but to understand our comment fully, you must know the story of his ancestry and the boon bestowed on his father.' He then proceeded to speak of Ravana's birth and the history of the Rakshasas.

Long ago, there lived an eminent Brahmin called Pulastya, the mind-born son of the creator Brahma. He was full of piety and performed austerities in the ashram of Trinabindu on the slopes of Mount Meru. Unfortunately, he found it impossible to focus effectively on his penance because a group of young maidens had made a habit of singing and dancing noisily in the vicinity of the ashram, disturbing his concentration. To be rid of them, Pulastya announced that anyone who came within his sight would instantly become pregnant and hearing this, the damsels fled in fear. However, Trinabindu's daughter missed hearing Pulastya's pronouncement and inadvertently appeared before him, searching for her friends. Since she disturbed him while he was chanting the Vedas, she became pregnant. Frightened at the changes in her body indicating that she was with child, the girl confided in her father. Aided by his yogic vision, Trinabindu realized what had happened. To set things right, he took her to Pulastya and asked him to marry her, saying she was a virtuous girl who would assist him in his rituals. Pulastya agreed to his request, and they were married.

A son was born to them in time and was named Vishrava, since he was conceived when his mother heard the Vedas recited. The boy was devoted to righteousness and equalled his father in all good qualities. Vishrava was firm in his adherence to truth, strictly observing good conduct and self-discipline. At the same time, he was sincere in his scholarship and saintly in his detachment from sensual pleasures. Rishi Bharadwaja heard about Vishrava's piety and gave his beautiful daughter Devavarnini in marriage to him. In due course, they had a boy whom they called Vaishravana, meaning the son of Vishrava. He grew up to be as virtuous as his father and later became famous as Kubera. Vaishravana performed strict penance for years, living on water and air alone. His austerity pleased Brahma, who offered him a boon. Vaishravana asked to be one of the protectors of the world's four quarters and the custodian of wealth. Brahma already had three overseers—Yama for the south, Indra for the east and Varuna for the west—so he added Vaishravana as the guardian of the north. In recognition of his effort, he also presented him with a flying chariot called the Pushpaka Vimana that enabled him to travel anywhere he wished, like the Devas.

Vaishravana returned to his father and told him about the honour he had received and asked to be directed to a place where he could reside peacefully without interfering with anyone or being disturbed himself. Pulastya advised him to go to Lanka in the south, a beautiful city on the Trikuta Mountain built by the celestial architect Vishwakarma for the Rakshasas. He said it was as lovely as Amravati, surrounded by golden ramparts, studded with gems, and protected by advanced mechanical weapons. Since it was currently unoccupied, abandoned by the Rakshasas who had fled to the netherworld in fear of Vishnu, Vaishravana would be able to live there in peace and comfort.

Vaishravana, better known as Kubera, established himself in Lanka and made it a prosperous kingdom. He lived there happily for many years and would take his vimana to visit his parents now and again. Rama was surprised that the Rakshasas lived in Lanka before Kubera. He said, 'I am intrigued by the story so far! Who were the Rakshasas, and why did Vishnu force them to abandon Lanka?

Agastya continued with his narrative. Brahma created many sons to look after the waters of the world. One group agreed to protect the waters, and the other said they would treat the waters as sacred. The protectors became known as Rakshasas, and the worshippers were called Yakshas. Among the Rakshasas, two mighty brothers, Heti and Praheti, were leaders. Praheti decided to renounce the world, retiring to a life of penance. Heti, on the other hand, wanted to have offspring and pursue material prosperity, so he married the sister of Yama, a woman called Bhaya. They had a son called Vidyutkesha. When he was of marriageable age, his father wedded him to the daughter of Sandhya, whose name was Salakantakata. In due course, she conceived a child, and when the time came for the delivery, she went to the Mandara Mountain to give birth. A boy was born to her, but she was not a woman with maternal feelings, and considering the child a burden to her enjoyment, she abandoned him there. Shiva and Parvati happened to be flying overhead on their bull Nandi and stopped when they heard the pitiful wailing of the newborn. Parvati felt compassion for the helpless infant, so to save him, Shiva immediately turned him into an adult and gave him a city in the sky to establish himself. The sudden emancipation caused the boy, Sukesha, to become arrogant, and soon he vied with Indra for power and prestige.

Meanwhile, a Gandharva called Gramani was impressed with Sukesha's power and gave his daughter Devavati to him in marriage. They had a loving relationship, and Devavati revelled in her husband's prosperity and affection for her, just as a pauper receiving great wealth. Soon they were blessed with three sons: Malyavan, Sumali and Mali. They grew up powerful, but unfortunately, were not pure-minded, and their behaviour deteriorated day-by-day like a neglected disease. Finally, realizing that the path to ultimate supremacy could only be achieved through penance, the three went to Mount Meru and embarked on severe austerities. Many years passed, and eventually, Brahma appeared before them and granted them three wishes; they requested: invincibility, longevity and a deep fraternal bond. Now pleased with their new powers, the brothers were keen to establish themselves and approached the celestial architect Vishwakarma to build them a city. He directed them to occupy a Lanka as their capital. It was a splendid place which he had built at the command of Indra, 100 yojanas long and 30 yojanas wide, high on the Trikuta Mountain. It was so beautiful that it competed with Indra's Amravati in magnificence.

At that time, there lived a Gandharva woman called Narmada who had three lovely daughters personifying modesty, prosperity and fame. She was looking for husbands for them and decided it would be advantageous to give her girls in marriage to the three Rakshasa brothers. Malyavan married Sundari and begat sons Vajramushti, Virupaksha, Durmukha, Suptaghna, Yajnakopa, Matta and Unmatta, all devilish in nature. They also had a daughter named Anala. Sumali's wife Ketumati, whose face was as lovely as the moon, gave birth to the famous warriors Prahasta, Akampana, Vikata, Kalikamukha, Dhumraksha, Danda, Suparshwa, Samrahdi, Praghasa and Bhasakarna; she also had four pretty girls—Raka, Pushpotkata, Kaikesi and Kumbhinasi. The third brother, Mali, was married to Vasudha, who was particularly good-looking and had beautiful eyes like lotus petals. Her sons Pramati, Anala, Panasa and Sampati would later become ministers to Vibhishana.

Over time the brothers became increasingly power-hungry, filled with arrogance by Brahma's boons. They began a reign of terror with their followers, attacking other kingdoms and creating mayhem wherever they went. The Devas could not vanquish them and went to Lord Shiva to ask for his assistance. He acknowledged they had a reason to be aggrieved but declined to help because of the association with Sukesha, his foster child. Instead, he suggested that they seek refuge in Vishnu. Accordingly, the Devas approached the great Narayana with folded hands and complained that the brothers terrorized the world from their base in Lanka. They were greatly relieved to secure Vishnu's intervention when he agreed that the Rakshasas had become an incorrigible menace and promised his protection.

When news of Vishnu's proposed involvement in bringing peace to the world came to be known, Malyavan warned his brothers to stand down rather than incur the wrath of Narayana. However, Mali and Sumali opposed him, arguing that their penance afforded them invincibility, so there was no reason to be afraid of taking on anyone, even if it happened to be Vishnu himself. Therefore, gathering their forces, they arrogantly set out to wage war on the Devas and consequently were met by Vishnu mounted on Garuda, armed with his discus, sword and bow. The Rakshasas surrounded him like dark rain clouds lashing down all sides of a hill with torrential rain, but they were like moths to a flame.

Vishnu blew his famous conch, the Panchajanya, and hundreds of arrows flew from his bow Saranga, decimating large numbers of the enemy and causing many to flee in terror. Sumali rode forward on his chariot to block Vishnu with a shower of arrows, but his charioteer's head was severed, forcing the horses to run amuck in confusion. Mali came to his brother's rescue and struck Garuda on the forehead with his mace, causing him to turn around in apparent retreat. The Rakshasas took this as acceptance of defeat and roared in glee. However, their celebration was premature; to protect his loyal charioteer, Vishnu released his discus. It illuminated the skies, swiftly severing Mali's head, which rolled unceremoniously to the ground. Malyavan then hurled the Shakti spear that struck Vishnu in the chest. Pulling it out, he flung it back, and Malyavan swooned. He attacked Vishnu with a spiked club on recovering, but Garuda repulsed him, flapping his wings with fury, creating a storm. Blown away by the force of the gale, Malyavan and Sumali fled with their remaining soldiers to a region of the netherworld called Rasatala, where they remained in hiding for many years.

After a long time of living in exile, one day, Sumali reappeared from the netherworld with his daughter Kaikesi. He was in search of a suitable husband for her to father powerful children to redeem the Rakshasas. By chance, he happened to see Kubera in all his splendour, visiting his father in his Pushpaka Vimana, and immediately set his sights on Vishrava as the one for his daughter. Sumali hoped that equally accomplished children begotten through him would save their race, so at her father's direction, Kaikesi appeared before Vishrava that evening as he was performing a yagna, pouring oblations into the holy fire. Then, with her eyes cast down at her feet, she started to scratch the earth with the tip of her big toe to draw his attention. The sage stopped his ritual, and noticing a girl as lovely as the moon standing before him, inquired who she was and what she wanted. She folded her hands respectfully and replied, 'Your spiritual powers should indicate to you why I have come, but even so, let me tell you my name is Kaikesi, and I am here at my father's command.'

Vishrava meditated for a moment and instantly knew that she was there to marry him in the hope of producing powerful offspring. He agreed to Kaikesi's wishes but warned that in her eagerness to have progeny by him, she had approached him at an inauspicious hour, so the children born of their union would, unfortunately, be ruthless and demonic in nature. This pronouncement frightened Kaikesi, and she asked if Vishrava could use his powers to ameliorate the outcome somehow. Vishrava consoled her with the assurance that her youngest son would be different from his siblings and a follower of dharma, so they were married. In due course, Kaikesi gave birth to a fearsome-looking boy called Dashagriva[1] on a day beset with ill omens and the eerie howling of jackals. Later he would be known by the name Ravana, the one who makes the world cry! Next came the enormous Kumbhakarna who would roam the earth, divesting it of life to satisfy his rapacious appetite. He was followed by a hideous daughter called Surpanakha, and finally, the couple was blessed with the even-minded Vibhishana.

One day, Kubera came to visit his father in his Pushpaka Vimana. His glory dazzled Kaikesi, and seeing his eminence, she taunted Dashagriva, saying he paled in comparison to his half-brother. His mother's words filled Dashagriva with envy, and he swore to her that he would make her proud of him by outshining Kubera in acclaim. So, he took his two younger brothers to the mountains, and the three embarked on severe austerities. Kumbhakarna meditated under the burning summer sun, subjecting himself to scorching heat surrounded by fire; in the monsoon, he knelt on one knee drenched in the rain, and in winter, he stood neck-deep in icy water. Vibhishana endured years of standing on one leg continuously with an intense focus on the cosmic consciousness, and Dashagriva put his body through extreme hardship without food, offering nine of his heads one by one to the sacred fire. Just as he was about to sacrifice the tenth head, Brahma appeared and asked him to choose a boon so his penance would not be in vain.[2] In response, Dashagriva asked for immortality, death being the ultimate enemy of all creatures.

However, Brahma could not grant this wish, which went against the natural laws of existence. When asked to modify his demand, Dashagriva folded his hands and said, 'Grant me immunity from death at the hands of any bird or beast; and from Nagas, Yakshas, Daityas, Danavas, Rakshasas, Gandharvas and Devas. I have no reason to be concerned about a threat from

---

[1] Literally Dashagriva is one with ten necks, but metaphorically it refers to one who has the knowledge of ten heads.

[2] The ten are not literal heads, but represent the ten fields of knowledge he had mastered: the four Vedas and the six Vedangas.

other inconsequential creatures like humans as they are as puny as straw.' Brahma granted him his boon[3] and restored the nine sacrificed heads.[4] He then turned to Vibhishana and asked what he wanted. Vibhishana requested that he always remain virtuous and rooted in dharma while being immune to harm from the Brahmastra.[5] Brahma granted his desire, and in recognition of his piety, also gave him an additional boon of longevity. Then, as Brahma was about to ask Kumbhakarna his wish, the Devas said that it would be dangerous to grant him anything that made him more powerful because he was already denuding the world of life with his voracious appetite. They sent the goddess Saraswati to manipulate his tongue, so he asked for the boon of endless sleep, and Brahma said, 'So be it!'

When Sumali heard about Dashagriva's achievement of invincibility, he decided it was time to emerge from the netherworld for good. He arrived on earth with his clan, including Maricha, Prahasta, Virupaksha and Mahodara. Joyfully embracing his grandson, he expressed gratitude to him for ridding the Rakshasas of their fear of Vishnu and urged him to reclaim Lanka from his half-brother, becoming its ruler. Dashagriva hesitated since Kubera was, after all, his elder brother, but Prahasta argued that Dashagriva should not allow his brotherly feelings to interfere with recovering the pride of the Rakshasas. Arguing forcefully for the Rakshasa cause, he said, 'Rivalry between relatives is not unusual, as we very well know from the sons of Diti and Aditi. Although both were wives of Kashyapa, there is no love lost between their sons, the Devas and the Daityas. It is the way of the world to seek power regardless of sentiment, so do not let familial feelings impede you from achieving your objectives. It is paramount that the Rakshasas regain superiority once more, so you must put aside any considerations that frustrate this goal.'

It did not take much to convince Dashagriva; propelled by his newly acquired invulnerability and innate avarice for power, he readily agreed to the plan. Using the diplomatic protocol of sama, he sent Prahasta to Lanka with a courteous message, requesting Kubera to vacate it, stating its original

---

[3] Brahma granting a boon is symbolic of getting the result of the effort put in to achieve a goal.

[4] Figurative of nine branches of knowledge.

[5] This boon protected Vibhishana from the Brahmastra released by Indrajit when it devastated the entire Vanara army.

owners, the Rakshasas, wanted it back. Kubera was not adversarial by nature, so he did not resist. His only entreaty was a request to discuss the matter with his father. When Kubera asked Vishrava for advice regarding his eviction, he acknowledged that Dashagriva had acted unfairly, but told Kubera to avoid conflict since his brother had a vicious streak. Instead, Vishrava suggested setting up a new kingdom by the Mandakini near Mount Kailasha in the Himalayas. In deference to his father's advice, Kubera nobly gave up Lanka without contest and left for the north, where he established the glorious city of Alaka.

Chapter 35

The Power of Ravana and Meghnad

After ousting Kubera, Ravana occupied Lanka and was consecrated as its ruler Lankesh, the king of the Rakshasas. Once this was done, he arranged his sister Surpanakha's marriage with Vidyutjiva, the son of the Danava chief Kalaka. On his return home, while passing through a forest, Ravana came across Mayasura, one of the sons of Diti, and his attractive daughter Mandodari. Struck by the young woman's beauty, Dashagriva asked who they were and what they were doing wandering in the woods. Narrating his story, Mayasura said he was married to a beautiful Apsara called Hema, and they lived together happily for many years in a magical golden cave of diamonds and lapis lazuli that he created for her using his magical powers.[1] Sadly, fourteen years ago, she returned home to the court of Indra, leaving behind two sons, Mayavi and Dhundhubi, and a beautiful daughter Mandodari, who accompanied him. Mayasura had brought up the girl without his wife and was now looking for a suitable husband for her. Then he asked who Ravana was, and he replied proudly, 'I am the son of Vishrava, the grandson of Pulastya and great-grandson of Brahma.' Hearing his illustrious ancestry, Mayasura decided he had finally found a fitting groom for his daughter, so Mandodari and Dashagriva were married on the spot with a fire he kindled as witness. Mayasura presented his new son-in-law with the mighty Shakti javelin he had acquired through gruelling penance to Brahma, which incidentally was the one that very nearly killed Lakshmana. After securing a wife for himself, the Rakshasa king arranged his brothers' marriages. He got Kumbhakarna married to Vajrajwala, the granddaughter

---

[1] This is the same cave the southern Vanara search team stumbled upon.

of the Asura king Bali, and Vibhishana to Sarama, the virtuous daughter of
the Gandharva king Sailusha.

In due course, Mandodari gave birth to a son whom they named Meghnad
because his lusty cry at birth sounded like the rumbling of thunder. Meghnad
was brought up with much love and affection and later became famously
known as Indrajit. Meanwhile, Kumbhakarna, who had been ordained to
endless slumber, requested a suitable abode where he could rest undisturbed,
so Dashagriva had a cozy subterranean cave built for him where he would be
comfortable in all seasons. While Kumbhakarna slept, his brother engaged in
military conquests to prove his might. Ravana laid waste to the lands of the
Devas, Nagas and Gandharvas and mercilessly tormented the rishis. He even
devastated the celestial Nandana Grove.

Soon the news of Dashagriva's nefarious exploits reached Kubera. Being
the elder, he felt it was his duty to correct his younger brother. Kubera sent
a messenger to Lanka to remind Dashagriva about his noble lineage and
asked him to cease his offensive behaviour that was tarnishing their family
name. Giving his own example, Kubera also communicated how even a
minor transgression could sometimes entail severe punishment. Kubera once
made the mistake of staring enviously at Parvati, which burnt his left eye;
in atonement, he undertook severe austerities, finally winning Lord Shiva's
protection. He hoped his words would encourage his brother to give up
villainy, but sadly his communication did not have the desired effect. Instead
of taking Kubera's counsel in the caring spirit with which it had been given,
Dashagriva felt insulted. His eyes turned red with anger, and he threatened
the hapless messenger with dire consequences, thundering furiously, 'Neither
you nor that brother of mine deserves to live. He does not have my welfare
at heart, and I do not care to hear him preaching about right and wrong. He
flaunts his friendship with Shankara[2] to taunt me, but he will regret it. I vow
to conquer the three worlds and send the guardians of the four quarters to
their death.' Saying this, he slew Kubera's envoy on the spot and asked the
Rakshasas to feast on his flesh. Then, intent on teaching his brother a lesson,
he set out for Kubera's abode in the Himalayas with six valiant commanders,
Mahodara, Prahasta, Maricha, Shuka, Sarana and Dhumraksha. When they
attacked Kubera's kingdom, his general Manibhadra and his people, the
Yakshas, put up a valiant defence, but they were completely routed.

---

[2] Another name for Shiva, like Maheshwara, Rudra and Mahadeva.

Although Dashagriva was severely wounded, he was saved from succumbing to his injuries by his boon of invincibility and went in search of Kubera. Once again, Kubera tried to reason with him. He talked about the bad karma earned by evil actions, reminding Dashagriva that one reaps what one sows, but was compelled to use force when his efforts failed. He deployed the Agniastra and the Varunastra on Dashagriva, but he was unharmed by them, protected by his boon. In turn, Dashagriva seized a giant club and stuck Kubera on the head, rendering him senseless. After vanquishing his brother, he usurped his golden aerial chariot, the Pushpaka Vimana, which could be commanded by the mind, and flew back to Lanka.

On the way, when the vimana passed a thicket of reeds in the vicinity of Mount Kailash where Lord Shiva's son Kartikeya was born, it suddenly came to a standstill. As Dashagriva was wondering why it had stopped, Shiva's faithful attendant Nandi appeared and commanded sternly, 'Turn back; no one is allowed in these hallowed precincts as it is the home of Lord Shankara.'[3]

Hearing this, Dashagriva shook with rage and asked insolently, 'Who is Shankara to stop me?' Then he laughed, jeering at Nandi's appearance, which he likened to a Vanara. Nandi felt offended and cursed him, saying, 'Since you mock me as a Vanara, let me tell you that those who look like me will be the cause of your destruction. Vanaras will humble your pride one day; I could kill you now, but it is far better that your misdeeds catch up with you to teach you a lesson.' Dashagriva stepped out of his vimana and replied arrogantly, 'I will pull up this mountain, which is blocking me. Shiva does not know my powers or who he is dealing with.' Saying this, he put his hands under the mountain and began to lift it. The movement caused it to shake violently, and Parvati lost her footing and slipped, clutching Maheshwara for support. Outraged by his insolence, Mahadeva pressed the hill down with his big toe and its weight crushed Dashagriva's arms. He howled so loudly that all three worlds wept, deafened by his cries and his frightened ministers advised, 'Propitiate Shiva and seek his forgiveness, as none other than he can help you out of this situation.'

Dashagriva began singing hymns of glory to the Lord of Kailasha,[4] hoping to extricate himself from the mess. After many years, Mahadeva finally

---

[3] To this day no one sets foot on Mount Kailasha, and strangely all attempts to climb the mountain have been unsuccessful.

[4] Shiva is the lord of Kailasha.

appeared in answer to his prayers and said, 'I am pleased with your devotion and your penitence. Since you caused the inhabitants of the three worlds to cry in pain with your ear-piercing screams, henceforth, you will be known as Ravana, the one who roars.' Shiva asked him to leave in peace, releasing his arms and restoring them to their original form. Before departing, Ravana requested Shiva to grant him a weapon if he was pleased with his devotion and was handed a gleaming sword called Chandrahasa. Shiva said, 'Take this sword but remember, it will automatically return to me if you misuse it.'[5] Ravana went back to Lanka chastened but not cured of his arrogance. He immediately re-engaged in his evil reign of terror, killing indiscriminately, and mad with power, he began appropriating women for his pleasure.

Once, while roaming the earth in his Pushpaka Vimana, Ravana noticed a beautiful maiden with matted locks deep in meditation. She was seated in the lotus position, dressed in the skin of a blackbuck. Seeing her loveliness, Ravana, an inveterate womanizer, was overcome with lust and approached her with corrupt intentions. He asked curiously, 'What is someone as comely as a goddess doing here wasting her youth in needless austerities? Whose daughter are you, and to whom are you married?' The woman replied, 'My name is Vedavati, and I am the daughter of a Brahmarishi called Kusadhwaja, the son of Brihaspati. Many admirers sought my hand in marriage, but my father did not accept any of them as he wanted me to focus on Narayana. My heart is set on Vishnu, and I am engaged in meditation to attain his grace. An angry suitor, a Daitya called Shambhu, killed my father; overcome by grief, my mother joined him on his funeral pyre, so I was left alone. Through my spiritual powers, I know who you are and would like to ask you to leave, O son of Vishrava, for I do not want to have anything to do with you.'

Ravana was not deterred by Vedavati's rejection and pressed her further, saying, 'Beautiful lady, penance is only for old women, not for someone young and lovely like you. Youth is a brief interlude in life; it can easily fade away without enjoyment. Therefore, I suggest you give up this pointless meditation and come with me to Lanka and be my wife. Vishnu cannot equal me in valour, power or in any other way.'

Vedavati was outraged and spurned his proposition, but Ravana could not accept being refused, so he grabbed her by her hair to take her by force.

---

[5] Although Valmiki does not mention it, it is believed that Ravana used the Chandrahasa on Jatayu while committing the immoral act of abducting Sita, so it returned to Shiva. He does not use it in the war, perhaps because he no longer owned it.

However, he had not contended with Vedavati's yogic powers, which she used to transform her hand into a sword, cutting herself loose. Then defiled by Ravana's unclean touch, she burst into flames. However, before giving up her body, she issued a warning. 'I will not curse you as it will take away from the precious spiritual merit I have worked so hard to earn, but I will surely take birth again as a woman who will be the cause of your downfall.' Agastya said to Rama, 'Vedavati returned as the daughter of Janaka found in a furrow, your wife in this life, who precipitated Ravana's death.'

After Vedavati immolated herself, Ravana ascended his vimana to roam the world again. Seeking new confrontations to establish his dominance, he came across the powerful king Maruta and decided to challenge him to prove his authority. It so happened that Maruta was performing a yagna with the Devas. When they saw the Pushpaka approaching, the Devas fled the scene, disguising themselves as animals, knowing they were powerless against Ravana. Indra took the form of a peacock, Yama turned himself into a crow, Varuna became a swan, and Kubera transformed into a chameleon.

Ravana barged in on the yagna and challenged Maruta to fight with him or accept his authority. Maruta was surprised at the intrusion and asked, 'Who are you?' Ravana replied arrogantly, 'How do you not know me? Who can be ignorant of my strength? I am the powerful Rakshasa Ravana who defeated my brother Kubera and seized the Pushpaka Vimana.' Maruta said scornfully, 'Having performed such a wicked deed, it is shocking that you dare to boast about it.' He grabbed his sword to teach Ravana a lesson, but his priest Samvarta, the brother of Brihaspati, barred his way. Blocking Maruta, he said, 'Do not engage in violence during a yagna as it is inauspicious. Moreover, the ritual cannot be left incomplete, or it will spell the destruction of your dynasty. In any case, victory in battle is always uncertain, so avoid inviting unnecessary bloodshed.'

Maruta threw down his weapons in obedience and peacefully continued his yagna. Since he did not resist, Ravana claimed victory over him. He did not harm Maruta but picked up a few sages and drank their blood to show his might. When he left, the Devas shed their disguises. In gratitude, Indra blessed peacocks to have no fear of snakes and to dance every time he showered rain. Yama gave crows the benediction of being protected from disease. Varuna affectionately said swans would be charming, always pure white and enjoy the water he presided over. Kubera expressed his thankfulness to the chameleon, giving him a golden hue.

In his unbridled quest for power, Ravana continued his blood-thirsty conquests, challenging Kshatriya kings all over the earth to fight or surrender. One of the kings he threatened was Anaranya of Ayodhya. They fought bitterly, and though Ravana was struck with 800 arrows, he did not perish. In turn, he dealt a death blow to Anaranya with his open palm, but before he collapsed, the dying king said prophetically, 'I do not consider myself defeated by you because I have succumbed to the vagaries of fate, of which you were merely an instrument. If I have led a virtuous life, there will be one born in my great house who will kill you and avenge the Ikshavakus.'

Ravana was relentless in terrorizing mortals on earth, so one day Narada appeared before him. When Ravana asked why he had come, Narada said, 'You are enormously powerful and have achieved dominion over the earth, but you are wasting your time on humans, who are frail creatures. There is no glory in killing those who are weak and subject to old age and death anyway. In the end, they all go to Yama, so if you want to prove your valour, try your luck at conquering him instead.'

Ravana laughed and said, 'I have already established my supremacy over the earth and was on the way to Rasatala[6] to secure my rulership of the three worlds.' Narada dissuaded him, saying, 'Why do you concern yourself with minor victories? Instead of going to Rasatala, defeat Yama and claim the ultimate achievement.'

Ravana's ego was stirred, and he said haughtily, 'Your advice is timely! Consider Yama's defeat as good as accomplished; I will turn southwards and tackle the mighty son of Surya; in any case, I had vowed to defeat the four guardians of the world.'[7] Narada was sure Ravana would not be able to vanquish Yama, who struck terror in all three worlds. After all, he was the Lord of Death, who wielded the rod of chastisement, the ultimate dispenser of judgement. Yama was time itself, and with what instrument other than time could time be conquered?

After their talk, Narada transported himself to Yama's abode to inform him that Ravana was on his way and waited to observe what happened. Then suddenly, the sky lit up as the Pushpaka Vimana arrived. When Ravana entered Yamaloka, he saw the aftermath of earthly existence before his eyes.

---

[6] One of the realms of the underworld inhabited by the Daityas, the sons of Diti and Rishi Kashyapa.

[7] Yama is the guardian of the south, Indra of the east, Kubera of the north, and Varuna of the west.

Woebegone creatures were experiencing the hellish consequences of their misdeeds, wailing and begging for mercy. Juxtaposed with this horror, good souls enjoyed a peaceful existence amidst music in large mansions, reaping the fruit of their meritorious actions.[8] Ravana started to free all those being punished for their evil actions, incurring the wrath of the servants of Yama. They arrived in hordes and attacked the vimana, but it magically repaired itself as soon as any part of it got broken due to its divine origin. Ravana retaliated, invoking the Pashupatastra[9] of Shiva, roaring in victory as he reduced Yama's army to ashes. When Yama realized his forces had been defeated, he was enraged. He called for his chariot and appeared before Ravana with Kaladanda, the personification of his unfailing rod of chastisement by his side. Though the Rakshasa ministers were fearful and fled at the sight of the lord of death, Ravana was undaunted, and a bitter battle ensued for seven days and nights. When Ravana struck Yama with thousands of arrows, Kaladanda begged, 'Let me loose, and he will cease to exist. When the end of the time comes, I destroy everything, so this Rakshasa is no contest for me. Leave him to me, Dharmaraja;[10] as you know, no one can stand the glare of my eye.'

Yama picked up the Kaladanda and was about to strike Ravana when Brahma manifested himself before him and cried, 'Stop! I have given Ravana a boon; you will falsify my word by killing him, as you are a Deva. Also, your Kaladanda will cause the world's dissolution before it is time, destroying everyone, so it is inappropriate to use it now. Therefore, you must recall your rod of punishment immediately to keep the sanctity of my boon.' Yama was forced to accede to the grandsire's wishes; vanishing from the battlefield in frustration, he said, 'If Ravana can't be slain, there is no point in my remaining here.' Ravana, however, was overjoyed, thinking Yama had retreated in fear and instantly proclaimed himself the victor.

His apparent success in conquering Yama, the most feared of the Devas, made Ravana feel upbeat, and burgeoning with pride, he mounted his flying chariot and proceeded to Rasatala. To reach it, he had to go below the ocean, past Bhogvati, the land of the serpent men, the Nagas. There he subdued their king Vasuki and went on to the city of Manimayi, the abode of giants called

---

[8] Heaven and hell are temporary states in Vedic philosophy, endured between births in proportion to earthly deeds.

[9] One of the most powerful weapons that was impossible to resist.

[10] Another name for Yama meaning lord of righteousness/justice.

Nivatakavacas. More than a year elapsed as they battled, and the two sides were dreadfully deadlocked. Once again, Brahma appeared and reminded the Nivatakavacas that his boon protected Ravana, so they made a peace treaty with their adversary before a sacred fire as witness. Ravana stayed as an honoured guest with them for a whole year and mastered various magic arts. After a pleasurable sojourn, he went on to Rasatala and reached a city called Ashmanagra, the home of Surpanakha's husband, inhabited by Daityas[11] called the Kalakeyas. Ravana attacked and defeated them, even cutting his own brother-in-law Vidyutjiva to pieces when he stood up to him to protect his people along with 400 Daityas.

After these victories, Ravana arrived at the beautiful abode of Varuna, the Deva of water. Recognizing the divine cow Surabhi, he circled clockwise around her to pay his respects before battling Varuna's army. Announcing himself boldly, Ravana said, 'Tell your master that I seek to challenge him, so he should either come out and fight or stand down in defeat with folded hands.' In response, the sons of Varuna came forward on their father's behalf with two generals, Gau and Puskara. In the fierce encounter that followed, Varuna's army was defeated. His sons retreated, but when they saw Ravana getting back on his vimana, they returned on equal footing in aerial chariots. In a fierce attack, they inflicted substantial damage on the Rakshasas till Mahodara came to the rescue and took down the horses yoked to their chariot with his mace. The fighting continued, but without their chariot, Varuna's sons were easily defeated by Ravana and had to be removed from the battlefield incapacitated. When Ravana once again challenged[12] Varuna to come out and battle with him, one of his ministers, Prabhasa, replied, 'Varuna is not here. He is visiting Brahmaloka at present. You have vanquished his sons, so there is nothing further to gain by tarrying here any longer.' Hearing this, Ravana declared victory over Varuna and joyfully returned to Lanka.

On his way back, invigorated by his numerous triumphs, Ravana roamed the earth, kidnapping the daughters and wives of kings, rishis, Devas, Nagas, Gandharvas, Yakshas and Danavas. He picked up any woman who appealed to him and added her to his collection of belles. The women shivered in fear as Ravana slaughtered their families and bundled them into the Pushpaka.

[11] Offspring of Diti.

[12] "Desire is never extinguished by the enjoyment of what is desired; it just grows stronger, like a fire that flares up fed by clarified butter." Manusmriti 2.94

In the torment of captivity, helpless and terrified, they bathed the vimana in tears, heaping curses on Ravana that a woman would bring about his death.

As soon as Ravana returned to Lanka, Surpanakha threw herself at his feet and tearily questioned why he had ruined her life by making her a widow. Feeling guilt-ridden, he consoled his wailing sister with loving words of appeasement and said, 'Please don't feel insecure about your future. I will make up for your loss by ensuring that you are always well cared for and protected. In the heat of battle, I killed your husband by mistake, thinking him to be a foe. I have an outpost in the Dandaka Forest called Janasthana, where you can reside comfortably from now on under the protection of our cousin Khara. He is the son of our mother's dear sister and is exceptionally powerful, so I know you will be safe with him.' Thus, Ravana installed Surpanakha under Khara's guardianship with a battalion of 14,000 Rakshasas, and that was how she came to live in Janasthana.

After rehabilitating his sister, Ravana headed to the Nikumbhila Grove, where he saw his favourite son Meghnad performing a sacrifice. He was dressed in black deerskin with a staff in one hand and a water pot in the other, looking fearsome. When Ravana asked what he was doing, Meghnad did not respond, as he was engrossed in the ritual, so his guru Shukracharya replied instead. 'Your Highness, please allow me to explain. Your son has performed seven demanding sacrifices perfectly and has gained immense power as a result. He successfully conducted the Agnistoma, Ashwamedha, Bahusuvarnaka, Rajsuya, Gomedha and Vishnava and has just finished the one to invoke Maheshwara. The last yagna was particularly difficult to perform, and due to his stupendous effort, he received special benedictions, including a divine aerial chariot that can go anywhere at its master's will, a cloaking trick called Tamasi Maya by which he can make himself invisible to anyone, including the Devas, and an invincible bow with a quiver of inexhaustible arrows. He is finishing up the final rituals so he can be of service to you.' Ravana felt Meghnad could have gained the same favours by propitiating Brahma and was displeased that he had invoked some of their adversaries. However, he rationalized that it was a means to an end, and what was done already could not be undone, so he waited, and they went back to the palace together.

The countless women Ravana had abducted were huddled together in fright, terror-stricken at being viciously plucked away from their families. When Vibhishana saw their wretched condition, he spoke out strongly on their behalf to Ravana. 'It was not right to take these women by force. Your roving eye has not only served to bring disrepute to our clan, but your sins have ironically rebounded on our own family. While you were busy abducting these unfortunate women, an Asura called Madhu similarly kidnapped our cousin Kumbhinasi from our inner quarters. Since she is the granddaughter of Malyavan, she is a sister to us through our aunt Anala. When Kumbhinasi was snatched, I was engrossed in rigorous penance; Indrajit was engaged in performing yagnas, and Kumbhakarna was asleep, so we could not protect her.' Ravana was outraged at Madhu's temerity and set out to avenge the insult to his family immediately. He woke up Kumbhakarna, and along with Meghnad and a large army, set out to confront the offending Asura. Thirsting for battle to establish his superiority over the three worlds, he was thereafter determined to challenge Indra, his arch-enemy, the king of the Devas.

Ravana could not find Madhu anywhere upon entering his city, but Kumbhinasi saw her brother and rushed forward, falling at his feet. He raised her gently and said, 'Have no fear, dear sister. I am here to rescue you.' Kumbhinasi cried, 'You said I should have no fear, so I beg you spare my husband because there is no greater sorrow for a woman than widowhood.' Although taken against her will, she was married now and viewed losing her husband as an even bigger misfortune than being abducted. Ravana felt compassion for her, perhaps because he had just dealt with a wailing Surpanakha, so he pardoned Madhu and asked for his help in his upcoming war against the Devas. Kumbhinasi persuaded her husband to assist her brother, and Ravana availed of their hospitality for the night before setting out with Madhu the next day to defeat Indra.

On their way to Devaloka, Ravana set up camp with his army in the vicinity of Mount Kailasha on the slopes of the Himalayas near Kubera's abode. As everyone settled down for the night, Ravana stayed awake, enjoying the pristine beauty of his surroundings in the silvery moonlight. The trees were resplendent with blossoms, and an uncontrollable passion stirred within him as he observed the Kinnara lovers and heard the sweet music of the Apsaras. It was a balmy evening, and intoxicated with desire gazing at the full moon, Ravana sighed, overpowered by concupiscence. Just then, a beautiful Apsara called Rambha, with the glow of a goddess, happened to pass by. She presented a pretty picture dressed in delicate garments, lavishly ornamented and adorned with flowers. As soon as Ravana saw her, he sprang to his feet, filled with lust. Leering at Rambha, he grabbed her hand and asked, 'Where are you going at this late hour, lovely lady? Whose presence are you planning to grace with your beauty? There is none more powerful than I, so stay here,

O lady of shapely hips and full breasts like gold pitchers. Forget your plans and come engage in the sport of love with me!'

Rambha replied in a timid voice, quaking in fear to hear his words, 'You should not speak to me in this lewd manner. I am like a daughter-in-law to you, and I look upon you as a respected family elder.' Ravana was surprised and retorted that she could not be his daughter-in-law because she was not married to his son. Rambha clarified that she was the beloved of his nephew, Nalakubera, the son of his brother Kubera. She added that she was on her way to meet him and admonished Ravana for looking at her lustfully. Ravana scoffed at her argument, sneering that Apsaras were like harlots, never espoused to one person, and therefore, she was in no way a daughter-in-law to him. Saying this, he pinned her down on a rock and ravaged her against her will. Outraged by the harrowing experience, Rambha ran to Nalakubera, dishevelled and ashamed. Weeping bitterly, she told him about the horrible ordeal she had experienced and her helplessness in resisting the attack, being a woman with less physical strength than a man. Nalakubera was enraged to hear what Ravana had done, and using his yogic powers, picked up some water in his left hand and pronounced a curse ordaining Ravana's head to split into pieces if he ever violated a woman without her consent again. Brahma endorsed the pronouncement, and from that day, Ravana was careful never to force himself on any woman.

After the incident with Rambha, Ravana went on to Indra's realm. He believed he had had achieved victory over Kubera, Yama and Varuna, so the guardian of the east was the only one left to conquer. Hearing the loud clamour of the Rakshasa army approaching, Indra put on his armour and readied his forces for battle. He was not afraid of confronting Ravana, but the Devas were powerless against his boon of invincibility, so Indra asked Vishnu for assistance. However, Vishnu was also helpless because Brahma's word had to be respected. Moreover, he explained that he could never retreat without destroying the enemy and since that option was not available to him, he suggested that the Devas deal with the Rakshasas themselves.

Vishnu urged them to face Ravana bravely but promised to cause his death at the appropriate time. Accordingly, the Devas, including the twelve Adityas, the eight Vasus, the eleven Rudras, and the forty-nine Maruts, went forth to meet the Rakshasas led by their intrepid commanders Maricha, Prahasta, Mahaparshwa, Mahodara, Akampana, Nikumbha, Shuka, Sarana, Samhrada, Dhumaketu, Mahadamstra, Ghatodara, Jambumali, Maharada, Virupaksha, Suptaghna, Yajnakopa, Durmukha, Dushana, Khara, Trishira,

Karaviraksa, Suryasatru, Mahakaya, Atikaya, Devantaka and Narantaka. They even had the support of the powerful Sumali, Ravana's grandfather, who lost no time venting his fury on his old enemies. He forced the Devas to scatter in all directions, and witnessing the terrible destruction he was wreaking, the eighth Vasu named Savitra entered the fray. A hair-raising conflict took place, in which ultimately Savitra was victorious. He overthrew Sumali's chariot and smashed his head with a mace so hard that he was reduced to dust.

Meghnad was infuriated by his great grandfather's death and provoked by the sight of the fleeing Rakshasas, he quickly drove his chariot towards the enemy ranks to seek revenge. The Devas trembled as he advanced menacingly in their direction, but Indra's son Jayanta bravely stepped forward to meet the challenge. A mighty conflict ensued between the son of the Rakshasa and the son of the Deva, who appeared equally matched as they hurled potent weapons, each managing to injure the other's charioteer. However, Meghnad invoked his boon of invisibility, creating mayhem amongst the Devas. He shot arrows from an unseen vantage point and caused his opponents to fall or scatter in fear. Jayanta's maternal grandfather Puloma feared for his grandson's life, so he appeared on the battlefield and expeditiously spirited him away to his abode in the depths of the sea.

Meanwhile, Kumbhakarna unleashed havoc on the rest of the army, mercilessly using his teeth, hands, feet and any weapon he could lay his hands on. When Jayanta disappeared, the Devas began to retreat, so to rally them, Indra asked his charioteer Matali to lead him into the battle. At this point, Ravana asked Meghnad to stand down and decided to meet Indra in a duel. Indra knew he could not kill Ravana, as Brahma's boon protected him, so he headed to another part of the battlefield to avoid confronting him. Ravana followed in hot pursuit but was surrounded by the army of the Devas and found himself in a precarious situation. Witnessing this, Meghnad rushed to his father's aid, using his illusory powers to cloak himself. He plunged the battlefield into darkness and penetrated deep into the ranks of the Devas. Only three persons could see anything: Ravana, Meghnad and Indra. Meghnad injured Matali, then showering Indra with arrows, bound and captured him. Having taken the king of the Devas captive, he declared triumphantly to Ravana, 'The Devas are crushed, so let us return! We have won by taking their King prisoner, so there is no need to exert ourselves any further.' Ravana was full of admiration for his son and lavished him with abundant praise. Glowing with pride, he said, 'You are the glory of our race, blessed with unequalled might, and in today's victory against the Devas, you have surpassed yourself in my eyes. Take Indra with you in your chariot to Lanka while I follow with my ministers.' Thus, the Rakshasas returned to Lanka victorious.

Meanwhile, Brahma was highly perturbed by Indra's capture and appeared before Ravana with an entreaty to release him, saying, 'Your son showed great valour on the battlefield. His skills are even greater than yours, and having beaten Indra, he will be known as Indrajit from now onwards. With your victory over the Devas, you have succeeded in your goal of establishing your supremacy over the three worlds, so now I suggest you release your prisoner. I will give Meghnad a boon in consideration of my request.' Indrajit requested immortality, but as in the case of his father, Brahma asked him to modify his demand, as no living being could be granted immunity from death. Indrajit then said, 'In that case, give me a conditional benediction of immortality. Grant me invincibility if I successfully complete a special fire sacrifice before setting out for battle. Through your blessings, let a divine chariot appear from the fire and lead me to a certain victory, giving me complete protection from death at the hands of my enemies. May I only be killed if I fail to finish the ritual.' Brahma bestowed this benediction, and in exchange, Indra returned to Devaloka, but his release came at a high price, as Indrajit became undefeatable. Absolute power has a tremendously corrupting influence, so Indrajit's death at the hands of Lakshmana was an outstanding achievement, crucial for world peace. Indra had his freedom, but he was very dejected at his defeat, so Brahma reminded him that he had brought the punishment on himself due to his transgression with Ahalya. Brahma had created a blemishless woman he gave in marriage to Gautama; in violating her, Indra had set a precedence for a crime never committed before. His ignoble actions invited the repercussion of him falling into the clutches of his enemy, as every deed has an inescapable consequence.

Concluding the story of Indra's defeat, Agastya said, 'Such was the extraordinary power of Indrajit, who vanquished the mighty king of the Devas!' Rama was amazed to hear of Ravana's victories and asked curiously, 'Was there no one to stop this marauding Rakshasa, or was everyone forced to submit to him?' Agastya nodded and told him about Ravana's encounter with Kartaviryaarjuna, the mighty king of the Haihayas. One day Ravana arrived at the city of Mahishmati, and in his customary bluster, sought to challenge its ruler Kartaviryaarjuna. He was told that the king was not present in the town at that time, so he left, stopping at the river Narmada that flowed nearby. Ravana bathed in its limpid waters and prepared to worship the golden Shivalinga he always carried with him, placing it on an altar of sand on the riverbank. Suddenly, the river's course was diverted from west to east, flooding his altar. Bewildered by the strange occurrence, he sent Shuka and Sarana to find the cause. They walked towards the west for about half a yojana when they came upon a humungous man with flowing hair sporting in the river with several beautiful women. He resembled a sala tree and seemed inebriated from the redness in his eyes. His 1,000 massive arms were outstretched, forming a dam that blocked the river's flow, causing it to flood its banks.

Shuka and Sarana rushed back to inform Ravana, and when they narrated what they had witnessed, he said, 'This must be Kartaviryaarjuna.' He was eager to take him on and hastened to confront him. Reaching the spot, Ravana issued a challenge to the ministers standing guard and said, 'Let the king of the Haihayas know that I, Ravana, am here to battle with him.'

The ministers replied, 'This is not an appropriate time for you to seek a trial of strength as our king is intoxicated; moreover, he is relaxing in the company of his consorts. Wait till tomorrow if you want the opportunity of a duel, as we cannot allow you to get past us for an encounter today.'

Their stance angered Ravana, and he immediately attacked the ministers. Kartaviryaarjuna stepped out of the water outraged, like a giant bull elephant ready to embark on a rampage. Prahasta tried to intercept him but was struck down. Seeing him fall unconscious, Maricha, Shuka, Sarana, Mahodara and Dhumraksha fled from the scene. Ravana then tackled Kartaviryaarjuna himself, and the two warriors fought like Bali and Indra of yore. In the combat, Kartaviryaarjuna hit Ravana on the chest with a mace. Ordinarily, the blow would be enough to kill anyone, but protected by his boon, Ravana merely sank to the ground. Then, like a tiger leaps on a deer, Kartaviryaarjuna pounced on him, and seizing him like Garuda scooping up a snake, took him prisoner. When Pulastya heard that his grandson had been captured, he appeared in Mahishmati out of an abundance of paternal affection to secure his release. Kartaviryaarjuna recognized the revered sage and received him with due honour, asking how he could be of service to him. Pulastya begged for Ravana's freedom, so in deference to his wishes, Kartaviryaarjuna released him unconditionally, and the two made a pact of friendship before the fire.

Chapter 36

The Story of Hanuman

Despite being chastened by Kartaviryaarjuna, Ravana's hunger for power was unabated, and he continued ranging over the planet seeking confrontation to establish his pre-eminence. One day he arrived at Kishkindha looking for Vali. The Vanaras told him to wait for a while as Vali had just left for the Southern Ocean to offer his customary Sandhya Vandana. He was expected to return only after paying due obeisance at all four seas, in the north, west, east and south, as was his daily practice. Pointing to a pile of bones, the Vanaras indicated that this was what remained of the foolish ones who crossed Vali, but Ravana was so impatient to prove them wrong that he got into his Pushpaka and set out to find his potential opponent. Alighting at the Southern Ocean, he saw Vali immersed in worship and furtively approached from behind. Vali noticed him from the corner of his eye but continued with his rituals, unfazed like a lion when a rabbit enters its presence.

As Ravana crept up from behind, Vali seized him, nonchalantly tucking him under his arm while he finished his prayers. Then with a struggling Ravana in tow, he sprang into the air with extraordinary speed and headed towards the Western Ocean to perform his worship there. He did the same at the other two seas, repeating his mantras at the Northern and Eastern Oceans. When Vali finally returned home, he dumped Ravana on the outskirts of Kishkindha and demanded to know why he had come. Ravana, shaken by the experience and recognizing Vali as the mightier of them, addressed him respectfully, saying, 'I sought to challenge you and establish my superiority in the fight, but I am left gaping in awe at your enormous strength. Only three beings could have jumped to the four oceans at the speed you travelled: the mind, the wind and Garuda. Now that I have seen your power, I want us to be allies. You will be a brother to me and enjoy half of all that I own, and we will never harm each other henceforth.' Vali agreed, so they lit a fire and walked around it, cementing their association.

Agastya explained that this was how the great Ravana, who vanquished the Devas, was overpowered by the Vanara Vali and pledged undying friendship to him. While acknowledging Vali's strength, Rama replied that, in his opinion, Hanuman was even more powerful and wondered why he had not intervened when Vali ill-treated Sugriva. Surprised by this aberration in his behaviour, Rama said, 'Hanuman has many admirable qualities. Heroism, capability, courage, intelligence, sagacity, diplomacy, alacrity and prowess are intrinsic to his nature. He crossed the ocean to Lanka after successfully overcoming all obstacles in his path. He found Sita and destroyed a fourth of Ravana's army, reducing Lanka to ashes. I have not heard of anyone else with such amazing exploits to his credit. If I have achieved victory today, it is largely due to Hanuman. Without his efforts, I would not have been reunited with Janaki, so I am perplexed that he did not intercede in the same way to help Sugriva when Vali falsely exiled him? Please enlighten me, revered sage, on the reason for this.'

Continuing his narrative, Agastya said, 'All that you have stated about Hanuman is indeed accurate. Though blessed with unparalleled strength, speed and intelligence, he was cursed to forget his powers.' Agastya went on to tell Hanuman's story: A Vanara called Kesari from the mountain of Sumeru married a beautiful woman named Anjana. She was artificially impregnated by Vayu and gave birth to an adorable but mischievous child called Sundara. Once when he was hungry, he mistook the sun for a mango and soared up into the sky to get it. As he ascended, it began to get hotter and hotter, but his father, Vayu, protected him, shielding him from the sun's rays. It also happened to be the time of an eclipse, and Rahu was proceeding towards the sun to obscure it. When Rahu saw Sundara, he was intimidated to have a competitor, so he reported the matter to Indra. Indra immediately mounted his elephant Airavata and went with Rahu to check out the contender. Bolstered by Indra's support, Rahu headed towards the sun once more, but Hanuman started to chase him in his inquisitiveness. Rahu was terrified and shouted to Indra for help, so he came forward on Airavata. Now, out of impishness, Hanuman started towards Indra, ignoring Surya and Rahu. Indra felt provoked by his advance and released his vajra. It struck Sundara, sending him hurtling down, and he lay motionless on a mountain with a broken jaw. Due to this deformity, he got the name Hanuman.

Seeing his son on the verge of death, Vayu was enraged and withdrew to a cave with him. The Devas were faced with a catastrophe, as all earthly beings began to perish, deprived of vital breath. To remedy the situation, Brahma appeared at the spot where Vayu had taken Hanuman. He lovingly stroked the boy, resuscitating him like a withered plant rejuvenated by water. Brahma prophesied that the child would perform great deeds in the future, and to pacify Vayu so he would begin circulating again, he asked all the Devas to bestow Hanuman with special benedictions. Indra gave him a garland of lotuses, saying that he would be called Hanuman henceforth, and since his vajra had broken Hanuman's jaw, he would never be harmed by it henceforth. Surya gave him one-hundredth of his brilliance and promised to be his guru. He also agreed to instil in Hanuman such supreme knowledge of the shastras that his intelligence and command of the Sanskrit language would be unmatched. As a result, he became a 'navavyakarna' pundit, a master of nine works of grammar. No one could equal Hanuman in his grasp of the Vedas and Vedangas, and he could be compared only to Brihaspati in the depth of his learning. Varuna guaranteed that death would not come to him from water, and Yama blessed him with long life, free from disease. Kubera proclaimed that his mace would not harm Hanuman, and he would never tire in battle. Shiva granted immunity from his weapons, and Vishwakarma affirmed that none of his creations would ever destroy the son of Vayu. Brahma, too, blessed Hanuman with the boon of longevity, and said no weapon he presided over would hurt the son of the Wind Deva.[1] He added that Hanuman would be invincible in battle, have the ability to change his form at will and fly at great speed anywhere he wanted.

Vayu was satisfied with the reparations, and taking Hanuman back to his mother, told her about the powers he had been given.

However, Hanuman became a prankster with his new-found abilities and continually troubled the sages with his mischief. Despite being repeatedly disciplined by his parents, he would interrupt yagnas and other rituals, break the sages' ladles, and scatter their offerings. Finally, at their wit's end, unable to tolerate the unruly child's nuisance any longer, the rishis cursed him to forget his powers for a very long time. However, they promised that the memory of his capabilities would return when he was reminded about them at a critical juncture, necessary to achieve an important purpose. At that

---

[1] Hanuman was immune to the Brahmastra, so he was unaffected when Indrajit used it on the Vanara army.

point, Kishkindha was ruled by a valiant Vanara called Riksharaja, who had two sons, Vali and Sugriva. When the king passed away, Vali succeeded him, and Sugriva became the crown prince. There was a close bond between Sugriva and Hanuman from boyhood, as exists between the wind and fire. When hostilities arose between the brothers, Hanuman stood by his friend through his troubles, unaware of his own powers, only recalling them only when Jambavan reminded him.

Then, concluding his story, Agastya said it was time for him and the other sages to leave. Rama bid them farewell and said that he hoped they would do him the honour of returning soon, as he planned on conducting many yagnas for his people's welfare.

A month had passed since Rama was coronated, and the great rishis took their leave. The other guests, too, returned to their kingdoms laden with generous gifts of gold and jewels. Janaka went back to Mithila, respectfully escorted by Bharata. While departing, he praised Rama's adeptness as a ruler but refused the presents he offered, saying he would prefer to leave them for his daughter instead. Rama bid Yudhajit farewell, thanking him for his support, and sent him safely back to Kekaya with Lakshmana. Yudhajit, too, did not accept any benefaction, saying, 'Let your treasury be enhanced!' Rama then embraced the King of Kashi, Pratardana, a strong ally, and said goodbye to him, along with the 300 other rulers who had assembled to honour him. When the kings returned to their kingdoms, they sent many precious gifts to Ayodhya to show their appreciation, including horses, elephants, vehicles, gold, jewels and livestock. However, Rama did not keep anything for himself, distributing all he received amongst Vibhishana, Sugriva and the Vanaras in appreciation of their service.

Rama especially honoured the valiant Angada and the glorious Hanuman, for whom he had a special affection. He adorned them with the best of ornaments he was wearing in gratitude. Then praising the other Vanaras, Rama said they were as dear to him as his own brothers and rewarded them handsomely for their support. Finally, after two months had passed, Rama hugged Sugriva and told him to return to his duties in Kishkindha. Recalling his promise to Vali, Rama reminded Sugriva to treat Angada kindly and urged him to appropriately honour and please all the loyal Vanaras who had been willing to lay down their lives for him. Before leaving, Hanuman prostrated himself before Rama and said, 'May my name always be associated with yours as your ardent devotee. I pray your story spreads far and wide throughout the world and hope that I hear it being retold for as long as I live, as listening to it will satisfy my longing to see you.'

Rama gave Hanuman a heartfelt hug, thanking him profusely, and said, 'It will be as you say, O greatest of Vanaras. I am deeply indebted to you for all you have done for me. Your name will stay alive for as long as my story abides in the world as one who rendered me invaluable service. Even if I give up my life for one of the favours you have done for me, I will still not be able to repay you fully as countless others would be left unrequited!' In special recognition, Rama took off a string of pearls he was wearing with a cat's-eye pendant in the centre and fastened it on Hanuman's neck. With that, the Vanaras left for Kishkindha in a tearful parting. Then, turning to Vibhishana, Rama hailed him as a knower of dharma and sent him back to Lanka. He bade him to rule the Rakshasas as a just king, always inclined to righteousness.

Chapter 37

The Sorrow of Separation

After the prolonged celebrations ended and the guests were gone, life returned to normal in Ayodhya. The kingdom continued to prosper, and all was well for a long while. Then, Rama was surprised one day when the Pushpaka Vimana that he had handed back to Kubera appeared at his service, with the message that Kubera wished him to keep it as his personal vehicle. The kind gesture touched Rama, but true to his nature of never taking undue advantage, he sent it back, saying that he would request its use if he ever needed it.

As the vimana departed, Bharata praised the kingdom's happy state under his brother's able rule. People led long, fruitful lives without illness, and women gave birth without labour pains. The rains were timely, the winds were mild, and overall contentment marked life in the towns and the countryside. Rama was pleased that his people were satisfied and carefree, as this was the goal towards which he continually strived. Finally, life was felicitous for him in every way. He had successfully completed his strenuous days of exile, and having got rid of Ravana, was now happily reunited with his beloved wife. The terrible war with the Rakshasas was over, and righteous rule was now established in Lanka under Vibhishana. Rama felt enriched by the true friendship he had made with the Vanaras, and after fourteen long years, he was together at last with his three brothers, whom he loved so much. His days were spent entirely in discharging his royal administrative duties, and in the evenings, he would enjoy his leisure time with Sita, relaxing in their beautiful garden adorned with majestic ashoka trees.

It was a private retreat with lush foliage. Numerous trees of all varieties, both ornamental and fruit-bearing, were painstakingly tended by expert gardeners. There were serene ponds with fragrant lotuses, and comfortable benches and bowers, cathartic at the end of a long day. Rama re-energized himself in Sita's company amidst these peaceful surroundings. They enjoyed music recitals and dance performances together, and in this idyllic manner, two years passed in what seemed like a twinkling.

Then, to add to the happiness of his picture-perfect life, Sita told Rama she was with child. As a doting husband, he was overjoyed and asked her if she had any desire he could fulfill. Smilingly contentedly, Sita said, 'All my wishes are satisfied in our relationship, but I do miss the quietude of the tranquil hermitages we lived in during our exile. Since you ask, I would like to spend some time at the ashrams on the banks of the Ganga, or at least stay for a night to offer my obeisance and get blessings for our child.' Promising to arrange for her visit the next day, Rama left for his official chamber to listen to the daily reports of public opinion, gathered by his secret agents, Vijaya, Madhumatta, Kashyapa, Mangala, Kula, Suraji, Kaliya, Bhadra, Dantavaktra and Sumagadha. But little did he know, a terrible storm was brewing that would overturn his happiness forever!

Rama always kept abreast of his citizens' views by appointing spies to mingle in the marketplace. He valued their feedback and would meet with them every day without fail to find out the true feelings that prevailed in the kingdom. On that particular day, it so happened that when Rama asked about the general sentiment in Ayodhya, one of his secret agents, a washerman called Bhadra, reported with folded hands, 'Everyone is happy; the people adore you, especially praising your victory over evil in killing Ravana.' However, Rama was very perceptive; sensing that Bhadra was holding something back, he pressed him to speak freely. He insisted on knowing if the people felt even the slightest negativity about him or anyone in his family—be it Bharata, Lakshmana, Shatrughana or anyone else close to him.

Along with his people's positive comments, Rama felt it was also essential to hear their criticism, so he could proactively correct anything that might be amiss. Put on the spot, Bhadra said reluctantly, 'If you insist, I will tell you both the good and the bad that is being discussed. As the people gather at the crossroads and marketplaces, they applaud you for building a bridge across the sea and saving the world from Ravana's atrocities, but they gossip that you went against custom, bringing your wife back though she lived in the home of another man for almost a year. They censure you for this act as it goes against accepted morality. Since the king sets the standard for appropriate social conduct, the people feel your behaviour creates a dangerous precedent in dealing with similar situations.'

Rama was crushed to hear that his people were disgruntled with him. He asked the others present if the discontentment was widespread or just a stray comment made in passing, and they all sadly confirmed that it was indeed what the people felt at large. The peace that had prevailed for the last two blissful years was shattered in an instant, and Rama's mind churned with emotion yet again in his life, wrestling with opposing dharmas that pulled him asunder. On the one hand was his duty as a husband, and on the other, his duty as a king. He did not doubt Sita himself for a moment, and when he brought her back, he had hoped fervently that her ordeal by fire would pre-empt this very situation from arising. But, unfortunately, his attempt at shielding Sita from suspicion in the minds of others had failed. The people felt he was setting a bad example by tacitly indicating the acceptability of taking back an adulterous wife. Rama knew a true leader had to be selfless, thinking primarily of those who looked up to him above his own happiness or that of his family. He was painfully aware of the great responsibility of holding a position of power, and his mind was filled with unbearable anguish. In this instance, his personal welfare and that of his precious Sita were at odds with his subjects' interests, and it was an awful dilemma where whatever action he chose would result in terrible consequences.

Rama's choices in tackling this dreadful predicament were challenging, as no recourse assured an optimal outcome for everyone. Agonizing over the possible alternatives, he ruled out ignoring his people's concerns because, as the highest administrator in the land, he was accountable to them. An option was to abandon Ayodhya. If he gave up the kingdom and returned to the forest with Sita, he would be upholding his responsibility as a husband, but it would be a dereliction of duty as a leader, an action that ensured only his personal happiness and not that of his subjects. Then there was the possibility of removing Sita from her position as his queen. He could send her back to Mithila and remarry to please his subjects, but his deep love and commitment to her made this choice impossible. There seemed to be only one remedy left, and though it was thoroughly repugnant to him, it was the least egregious.[2] After much internal deliberation, Rama decided to speak with his brothers and asked his doorman to call the three princes.

---

[2] Rama's decision to separate from Sita continues to be the subject of much discussion with arguments for and against the choice he made. However, it is important to see the situation in the light of rajdharma that required a king to rule by example. A righteous king was not supposed to live by different moral standards than the common man just

They arrived immediately with their palms joined humbly in respect, concerned at the unexpected summons. Seeing Rama's grim face, they instantly sensed something was amiss. He looked pallid and had a disconcerted countenance devoid of lustre, comparable to an eclipsed moon, a withered lotus or the dimness of the setting sun. Rama embraced his brothers with tears rolling down his cheeks and asked them to take their seats. Then composing himself, he said in a tortured voice, 'My dearest brothers, you are everything to me; I consider you my very life. All three of you are intelligent and learned in the teachings of the shastras, so I do not have to explain the intricacies of dharma to you. However, a certain devastating situation has arisen that I would like to inform you about and tell you how I have decided to address it. Despite my confidence in Sita's purity and unwavering conviction about her fidelity, my initial fear that the people might doubt her has regrettably materialized. Although Agni declared Sita's character spotless, and though she is entirely faultless beyond any doubt, unfortunately, she is being looked upon as scandalous and unfit to be queen. The citizens blame me for setting a bad example as a leader in accepting her back and have been discussing the pernicious influence of my behaviour on society. Never have I experienced such terrible misfortune that has cut me to my very core. I have struggled with this dreadful conundrum, and in the end, despite knowing that nothing can ever tarnish Sita in my eyes, I am forced to separate from her. I do this with a heavy heart to satisfy my people, who feel I have wronged them as their king by keeping my wife in her royal position just because I have the final say in the matter. I am torn to pieces, as you know what Sita means to me. Yet, the censure of my citizens cannot be disregarded.'

'Lakshmana, tomorrow morning, please take Sita in a chariot driven by Sumantra to the hermitages along the Ganga, as she has expressed a desire to visit them; but do not bring her back. Leave her in the care of Valmiki in his retreat on the banks of the Tamasa.[3] This instruction is not a request but an order, so please do not argue with me. I have arrived at this decision with great difficulty, and I do not want to waver in my resolve. Sita has mentioned

---

because his position afforded him the power of being above social norms or the law of the land. In this case, Rama was torn between two dharmas, his rajdharma—kingly duty and his patidharma—duty as a husband. He could not perform both, and sacrificed his marriage and personal happiness for the good of the kingdom. The complexity of dharma is discussed in more detail in the Appendices.

[3] A tributary of the Ganga.

that she wants to spend some time at the ashrams, as she has always loved the serenity and wholesome existence there, so in a way, you will be fulfilling her wishes.'

Lakshmana was thunderstruck at what he was hearing, but despite his misgivings, he had no choice but to do as commanded. For Rama, voluntarily giving up his precious wife was the most difficult choice he had to make in life. In contending with conflicting dharmas as a husband and a king, ultimately, he chose to uphold his royal duty, putting his people above himself. He was so sure that this was a sacrifice Sita and he had to make for the greater good of the kingdom that uncharacteristically, he did not discuss the matter with her, his brothers or counsellors, lest his willpower to follow through with what he considered his dharma weakened.

After a restless night with his heart racing and his brain in a fog, the following day, Lakshmana asked Sumantra to ready a chariot drawn by the best horses and fitted with comfortable seats. When he told Sita that Rama had asked him to take her to the ashrams of the rishis as she had desired, she was delighted to be going and dressed excitedly, taking along expensive ornaments to gift to the wives of the sages. As they were on their way, Sita's right eye twitched, and a shiver ran down her spine, making her exclaim anxiously, 'O Lakshmana, I suddenly feel unsettled by ill omens and am overwhelmed with a strange feeling of foreboding. I hope nothing happens to harm your brother. I pray my mothers-in-law remain in good health and all goes well for the people.' Saying this, she folded her hands and prayed. Lakshmana could not look her in the eye, and with his head down, fighting back his tears, he muttered in a muted voice, 'May everything indeed be well.'

That night they rested at an ashram by the banks of the Gomti, setting out again the following day at dawn. By afternoon they reached the Ganga, which was in full spate, and there Lakshmana began crying bitterly, giving vent to his pent-up feelings. Sita was surprised at the unexpected outburst of emotion and asked what had happened to cause him so much grief for no apparent reason. Presuming Lakshmana was saddened at his separation from Rama, she chided him gently, 'I know you find it hard to be parted from your brother, but we are only staying away for two nights. As you know, I also love Rama immensely; he is dearer to me than my own life, but I am not unduly distressed at being away for such a short time. Now stop this childishness and take me across the Ganga quickly to meet the sages so I can complete the task of gifting the ornaments I brought for their wives. After spending the night, we will return to Ayodhya, as I too look forward to being with my charming lotus-eyed husband again.'

Lakshmana wiped his tears and hailed a boatman to ferry them across. Leaving Sumantra behind with the chariot, he helped Sita into the boat and did his best to remain composed during the ride. When they disembarked on the other side of the river, it was time for him to disclose the reason behind his strangely melancholic mood that day. Trembling nervously, Lakshmana covered his face with his hands and dolefully told Sita the truth about the unpalatable task entrusted to him.

It was perhaps the worst moment of Lakshmana's life. He fell at Sita's feet, and at first, all he could do was ask for forgiveness. 'Please pardon me for doing what I have been ordered to do. I honestly feel death would have been preferable to the burden of this distasteful duty.' Sita was bewildered by his odd behaviour and asked in concern, 'What is the matter? You have been very out of sorts since we left. Is all well with the king? I do not understand what is causing you so much anxiety and insist that you tell me the truth.' Fumbling for words, Lakshmana somehow found the strength to say, 'O daughter of Janaka, with a heavy heart, I must convey to you that the king heard a malicious report that the people were slandering you for living in Lanka with Ravana for so many months. I cannot bring myself to mention what their scurrilous words impugned specifically, but suffice to say that they blamed Rama for setting the wrong example in taking you back after your abduction. The king could not ignore their condemnation, and though he was totally broken, especially knowing that you are faultless, he asked me to leave you in the ashram of Brahmarishi Valmiki. I believe you desired to spend time with the sages, so though it is natural to feel aggrieved at this calamitous turn of events, take comfort in prayer and the tranquillity of your holy surroundings. Valmiki was a friend of our father, and I have no doubt he will ensure that you are well cared for.'

Lakshmana's words pierced Sita's heart, and she slumped to the ground, remaining unconscious for a while. When she recovered, she said in a woebegone voice, 'O Lakshmana, I think the creator fashioned me solely to experience one sorrow after another, as I am the very embodiment of suffering! I do not know what sins I have committed in my past life, but I must have done something terrible for which my husband has discarded me, despite my impeccable conduct and steadfast adherence to dharma. I happily lived in the ashrams when we were in exile because I was with

Rama, but I am not sure I can live without him in the shame of being cast out of my home. What will I tell the sage when he asks me why I was abandoned? I would have jumped into the Ganga right now, but I am carrying a child, so that option is closed to me in my present condition.' Then, gathering herself with her characteristic resilience, Sita said, 'Lakshmana, I bear you no ill will, so do not feel guilty for doing what the king has ordered. Do as Rama has instructed and leave me here to endure the grief that appears to be my lot to undergo in this lifetime.

'However, before you depart, I would like you to listen to my words and convey a message from me on your return. Bow to my mothers-in-law on my behalf and give them and the king my greetings. Apprise the king who values dharma so much that I am chaste and will always be devoted to him. Tell him that I know he believes in me and that I recognize he has abandoned me prompted by the people's accusations, fearing the infamy of ignoring his rajdharma. Make sure Rama understands that I do not mind any hardship that has to be borne by the body and that I support him if personal sacrifice is necessary to earn back the trust of the people.' Sita understood the responsibility of her role as a queen, and that leadership involved sacrifice; still, as a wife, she was deeply hurt and made that clear while saying farewell to Lakshmana. She said tearfully, 'Before you go, take a good look at my pregnant belly and note the condition in which I have been forsaken.'

Lakshmana hung his head in shame, and taking leave of Sita, circled her, saying, 'O auspicious one, I cannot do what you ask. I have never looked beyond your feet, so how can I raise my eyes to look at you now?' He left with these words, crossing the river to the other side, where Sumantra was waiting. Lakshmana ascended the chariot but could not depart; he kept turning back to look across the river gazing at the poignant picture of Sita alone and helpless.

Sita sobbed uncontrollably as she sat forlornly on the banks of the river, unclear about her future. Disciples from Valmiki's ashram heard her, and seeing her pitiful condition, ran to their master. They blurted out anxiously, 'A regal-looking lady whom we have not seen before is sitting alone crying by the river. She is as beautiful as Devi Lakshmi and seems to be of royal birth, but she is in great sorrow for some reason and needs help. Please, master, go to her aid!'

Valmiki, who had the gift of divine vision, already knew through his yogic powers what had transpired and quickly went to Sita. His students followed him with offerings traditionally bestowed on an honoured guest.

When Valmiki reached her presence, he spoke kindly in a gentle voice. 'Welcome, chaste lady! Through the strength of my austerities, I know you are the daughter-in-law of Dasharatha, the beloved wife of Rama and the virtuous daughter of Janaka. The reason you are here is also known to me. Blessed one, I am aware of the whole truth about you, so there is no need for you to explain anything to me. You have done no wrong, so take courage in this difficult situation. My ashram is nearby. Several pious women practise their penance next door and will look after you and treat you as their daughter, so be comforted that you have a new home.'

Hearing the sage's kind words, Sita felt immense gratitude and fell at his feet. Valmiki led her to the lady anchorites, who bowed and asked what they could do for him. Entrusting Sita to their care, he said, 'This lady is Rama's wife, Sita, who has been abandoned for no fault of hers. It is my duty to protect her, so I would like you to look after her for me. Make sure you shower her with affection and treat her with great honour as she is worthy in every way of the highest respect.' Having thus arranged for Sita to be comfortable, Valmiki returned to his hermitage.

Lakshmana watched till Sita left with Valmiki, and he could see her no more. Then on the way back, overcome by incredible sadness, he vented his feelings to Sumantra. 'What greater grief could Rama face than being forced to abandon his virtuous wife who is so dear to him? I can only put this unmitigated disaster down to the vagaries of destiny. I know that Rama will suffer far more now than from the misfortune of his exile or even the terrible trauma he went through when Janaki was abducted. There appears to be no merit in this cruelty, even if it was done to satisfy the aspersions cast on Sita by the people.'

Sumantra, who had been one of Dasharatha's closest confidants, counselled Lakshmana in his despondency. Explaining the inevitability of the events that had taken place, he said, 'Don't be aggrieved at what has happened to Maithili, as it could not have been averted. All this was foretold long ago. The great sage Durvasa predicted to your father in my presence that while bringing joy to others, Rama would himself experience little happiness in life. He forewarned that Rama would face separation from all those he loved the most at some point, not just Sita but also Bharata, Shatrughana, and even you. I was sworn to silence on this matter, so I have never spoken of it, but seeing your distraught state of mind, I feel compelled to disclose what I heard. Please keep my words to yourself and do not mention them to anyone else, not even to your brothers.'

Lakshmana promised to keep his confidence, and intrigued by the prophecy, urged Sumantra to tell him more. Sumantra continued, 'Many years ago, the glorious son of Atri, the sage Durvasa spent the rainy season visiting Vasishta. It so happened that your father went to see his guru at that time and naturally met with Durvasa. They chatted about various matters, and knowing Durvasa's divine powers to see the future, Dasharatha enquired, "Pray tell me, great master, how long will my lineage continue? Will Rama and my other sons be blessed with long lives? What insight can you give me on Rama's progeny? I am keen to know the future of my family." Durvasa replied, "To answer your questions, I must give you the background to what I have to say. In ancient times, a band of Daityas sought shelter in Rishi Bhrigu's ashram, and his wife Khyati[4] took them under her protection. Vishnu asked her to give them up as they were dangerous antisocial elements, but she refused. To get past her and teach the Daityas a lesson, Vishnu was forced to sever Khyati's head, although she was a woman. When Bhrigu saw his wife lying dead, he was grief-stricken and cursed Vishnu in a fit of anger to take birth as a human and experience the pain of separation from his wife. As soon as he uttered the terrible pronouncement, he instantly felt remorseful and begged forgiveness. However, Vishnu welcomed the curse saying it would ultimately be for the good of the world. Rama is Vishnu in human form, and though he will rule for many years, the curse is destined to take effect in his life. He will perform numerous sacrifices and have two sons by Sita, but according to the prophecy, they will not be born in Ayodhya or crowned his successors there."'

Then Sumantra said, 'Having recounted this, Durvasa spoke no more. I remember these prophecies very clearly, and I know events will not go otherwise, so do not bemoan what is unalterable, Lakshmana. Try to cultivate fortitude to deal courageously with the things we cannot change in life.'

As they camped on the banks of the Gomti again that night, Lakshmana felt some relief hearing the respected elder's wise advice.

By noon the next day, they arrived in Ayodhya, and Lakshmana met Rama with the events of the last few days weighing heavily on him. Rama was sitting dolefully on his throne, driven to distraction by helplessness, a picture of ineffable sadness, his mind clearly far away from his official duties. Tears welled up in his eyes as Lakshmana clasped his feet and said with folded hands, 'In accordance with the order given to me by thy noble self, I left the

---

[4] The mother of Shukracharya, the guru of the Asuras.

pure-minded Janaki at the ashram of Valmiki on the banks of the Tamasa. Now I am back to serve at your feet and await your next command.'

Rama was broken-hearted and dazed, so as he had done on so many previous occasions, Lakshmana tried to cheer him up. He said, 'Don't grieve, brother! Destiny plays out its hand in inexplicable ways at times. An intelligent person like you knows this, so do not give way to sorrow. Everything in this mortal life perishes and comes to an end at some point, so we must practise detachment from the effects of suffering to weather the adversities that come upon us. Ultimately every meeting ends in parting as our time on earth is transient like a bubble. You have great self-discipline, so I know you have the fortitude to control your grief. The scandal that made you give up Maithili may not be over, and as a man of prominence, you could face gossip again on another front. Therefore, having taken the hard step of abandoning Sita, summon your courage and gather your strength in dealing with this crisis.'

Chapter 38

Tales about Dharma

Lakshmana's words calmed Rama's troubled mind, and he said, 'It's hard to find a well-wisher as caring as you. Nothing can take away my pain, but I feel stronger in dealing with it now. I have been remiss in attending to my royal duties for four days, so please tell my ministers that I am more in control of myself and ready to hold court again. As the past teaches us, a ruler who neglects attending to his kingdom's administration incurs terrible sin, even if he is otherwise virtuous. Long ago, there lived a king called Nriga, who was truthful and pure. Once, at a yagna, he donated millions of cows with their calves in charity. It so happened that a cow belonging to a poor Brahmin strayed into a herd marked for donation, and the king mistakenly gave it away. The Brahmin was distraught, as his family was afflicted by hunger without the cow. He searched everywhere and finally found her in another Brahmin's cowshed in a place called Kanakala.[1] Recognizing his cow, he called her by her name, and she came trotting to him with her calf. However, as he led the cow away, the Brahmin who had received her as a gift rushed after him angrily. They argued over ownership of the cow, and when they could not arrive at a suitable resolution, they decided to take their grievance to the king. As it happened, Nriga was busy with other matters and neglected his royal duty to dispense justice in the dispute. The two Brahmins waited patiently for days, yet he did not see them. Angered that the king had disregarded his responsibility by ignoring them, they cursed him to turn into a lizard and live alone in a cave till Narayana delivered him in one of his avatars on earth. Nriga's punishment is a lesson that a king must always

---

[1] Near Haridwar in Uttarakhand.

ensure he holds court, promptly addressing every single complaint brought before him.'

Lakshmana was surprised that such a harsh penalty was meted out to a good king like Nriga for a relatively minor infraction, and asked about his reaction towards the Brahmins. Rama said the king handled his sentence pragmatically, graciously accepting his fault. He gave the kingdom to his son Vasu and asked for three caves to be built with smooth floors, where he would live in the atonement of his transgression until he was freed from the curse. One shelter was to protect him from the rain, a second to keep him warm in winter and a third to escape the heat of summer. He also ordered a pleasant garden with perennially flowering plants to be created a yojana-and-a-half around the caves. He told Vasu to be firm in dharma and learn from his example, where an earth-shattering curse had been inflicted for a seemingly trivial violation. He said, 'Do not grieve for me, as destiny is the outcome of what we create for ourselves in this life or another and cannot be altered. We each get to experience exactly what is due to us whether it is good or bad.' Then he left and resided in the cave in his new form.

Rama continued, 'Now you have heard the story of Nriga, but if you are interested, I will tell you another one that illustrates a similar morality.' Lakshmana was eager to hear more and said he could never tire of listening to such astonishing anecdotes, so Rama obliged him by narrating the tale of the great King Nimi to whom King Janaka traced his ancestry. 'There was a brave and pious king called Nimi, the twelfth son of Ikshavaku. He established a glorious city called Vaijayanta near the ashram of Rishi Gautama and ruled as a just and able monarch. One day, he decided to conduct a lengthy sacrifice and requested Vasishta to be the chief priest, supported by Arti, Angira and Bhrigu. Vasishta was already committed to performing a yagna for Indra, and asked Nimi to wait for its conclusion before he officiated at another. However, Nimi was impatient, and when Vasishta left for Indra's abode, the king asked Gautama to perform the ritual instead. When Indra's yagna finished, Vasishta came to Vaijayanta to take up Nimi's yagna, but found it was already in progress. He felt slighted and tried to get an audience with Nimi to express his displeasure. However, Nimi was not available, and though Vasishta waited a long time, the king did not appear. Angered at being disregarded, he cursed Nimi for ignoring him and pronounced that his spirit would depart from his body, rendering him lifeless.'

'It happened that the king was asleep, and when he woke up and heard what had happened, he was angry at the unfair curse as he did not know his guru was waiting. In turn, he impulsively cursed Vasishta back. Nimi said, "Since you cursed me unjustly when I was not aware of your presence, your body, too, will become devoid of your spirit." As a result, they both lost their lives.'

Lakshmana asked incredulously, 'How did these two great people regain their lives again?' Rama went on to say, 'Vasishta approached Brahma and recounted how he had been deprived of his body and was now a spirit. He could not complete his karma in a disembodied form, so he pleaded with the grandsire to bestow him with another body to finish the earthly work left to accomplish.' Brahma said that Vasishta would not be born of a woman; instead, he would create an adult body for him from the combined seed of Varuna and Mitra. The ethereal Vasishta immediately went to seek Varuna. At that time, Mitra shared Varuna's position as King of the Sea of Milk, and was present there. The celestial Apsara Urvashi happened to be sporting in the seawater with her companions, and when Varuna saw her, he was smitten with desire. He asked her to engage in union with him, but she declined, claiming to be committed to Mitra already. Varuna then asked to satisfy his desire vicariously by dropping his semen into a golden pot she was carrying, if not through physical union. Urvashi was pleased with this plan, saying her relationship with Mitra hindered her from acting on her attraction to Varuna. The pot already had Mitra's semen in it, so when Urvashi went to him, he was outraged at her dalliance with Varuna and punished her to take a mortal birth. In her human form, she became the wife of Pururava, the king of Kashi. Urvashi lived on Earth till she completed the term of her punishment. She gave birth to Ayu, who in turn fathered Nahusha, who ruled Devaloka for a while when Indra was removed from his post.'

Lakshmana still did not know how Vasishta and Nimi were re-embodied and asked what had happened to them. Rama said, 'Brahma created two brilliant Brahmins out of the semen in the pot. The first one was the esteemed Agastya, and the second was Vasishta, the family priest of the Ikshavaku dynasty. This is the story of how Vasishta was reborn in a new body, but let me continue from where I left off, on Nimi. His death was a blow to his kingdom as he did not have a male heir. In desperation, his ministers embalmed his body while deciding what to do. Finally, they asked Bhrigu to perform a yagna to restore Nimi's life. As the sacrifice was nearing completion, the Devas asked Nimi's spirit to return to his physical body. However, he no longer felt any attachment to his former human self and requested instead to live as air in the eyelids of all creatures. This is the reason why the time taken for the blink of an eye is called a 'nimisha'. When Nimi could not be resuscitated, Bhrigu performed another yagna, churning the dead body to produce an heir artificially. The child born as a result was called Mithi or one born of churning. He was the first Janaka; his capital city Mithila was named after him. Mithi's kingdom came to be known as Videha, or land of the king born of the disembodied one.'

Hearing these incredible stories, Lakshmana remarked that a noble person like Nimi should not have lost control of himself and cursed his guru. Rama nodded and said, 'Forgiveness is undoubtedly an essential quality for a person in a position of authority. Of all the vices, anger is perhaps the most difficult to conquer, as you will see from the story of Nahusha's son, Yayati. Yayati had two wives: Sharmishta, the granddaughter of Diti, a princess of the Daitya race, whom he loved dearly, and Devayani, the daughter of Bhrigu's son Shukracharya, whom he did not care for as much. Sharmishta's son was called Puru, and Devayani's was called Yadu, but Yayati favoured Puru just as he did his mother. Yadu was upset with Devayani when he grew into a youth for tolerating the neglect meted out by Yayati, especially since she was born of the noble Bhargava lineage. He suggested that they throw themselves in the fire and get out of the way, so the king could be happy with his favourite wife and son, whom he cherished so much. He ranted that he was ready to give up his life rather than live without his father's love, even if his mother wanted to continue putting up with discrimination.

'Devayani was so overcome by sorrow to hear his words that she thought of her father in desperation. Shukracharya, a powerful rishi, heard her call of distress through his yogic powers and manifested himself before her. Seeing his beloved daughter in misery, he inquired solicitously about her problem. Devayani replied that she was unhappy because she and her son were neglected and despised by her husband. Not wishing to live anymore, she expressed a desire to end her life by consuming poison, drowning in water or entering a blazing fire, adding woefully, "If a tree is not looked after and dies, all the creatures that live on it also necessarily die."

'Shukracharya was enraged at Devayani's plight and pronounced a curse on Yayati. "Son of Nahusha, you have insulted me by neglecting my daughter, and for your irresponsibility towards her, you will lose your vigour and libido, turning old and decrepit instantly."

'Yayati was horrified at losing his youthfulness. He felt it was too early to be robbed of sensual pleasures and appealed to Yadu to accept his old age in exchange for his youth. Yadu scoffed at his request and refused outright. He reminded his father that he had caused him nothing but grief, so he should ask his favourite son instead. When Yayati approached Puru, he readily agreed, and Yayati enjoyed the joys of youth for many more years. Finally, when he was satiated with life and ready for Vanaprastha, he restored Puru's youthfulness once again and took back the curse of old age from him. He was so pleased with Puru's sacrifice that he honoured him by anointing him as his successor. As for Yadu, he banished him and cast a curse on him that he would produce evil offspring who would disregard him as he had done his father. Thus, Puru ruled Kashi righteously while Yadu's progeny inhabited the Krauncha Forest as lawless beings.' As Rama concluded his narration, the sun began to set, and the sky was enveloped in an orange glow. Before retiring for the night, he stressed to Lakshmana how important it was for a king to grant an audience to whoever came to see him seeking relief, never keeping anyone waiting.

The following day after completing his morning worship and rituals in the forenoon, Rama appeared in court before the whole assembly, including his ministers, counsellors, various chiefs and statesmen who conducted the day-to-day affairs. He asked Lakshmana to check if any petitioners were waiting to see him. Lakshmana went to the gate and returned to say no one was there. He attributed the lack of complaints to Rama's steady hand. Everything was so orderly in the kingdom that hardly any grievances required redressal. While Rama was pleased to hear this, he asked Lakshmana to check again to make sure. Accordingly, Lakshmana went out once more, and this time he saw an injured dog. The dog was whining as if in need of help, so Lakshmana asked him to explain his problem. The dog miraculously replied in a human tongue and said he wished to speak directly to Rama about his troubles, as he looked upon him as the refuge for all beings. When Lakshmana asked the dog to accompany him to see Rama, he refused, saying that his species was generally not allowed in hallowed places like temples, the assembly of kings or yagna grounds, and he did not want to enter the palace without specific permission. Lakshmana hurried inside to convey this to Rama, who said without hesitation, 'Bring the dog here without delay because he obviously has a pressing matter that he wants me to resolve.'

When the dog came before him, Rama noticed a deep laceration on his head and asked him to state what he could do for him without fear. The dog replied respectfully, 'The king is responsible for the protection of dharma by ensuring it is steadfastly adhered to in his kingdom. In his role as the dispenser of justice, he safeguards righteousness since a kingdom without dharma is doomed. We each reap the consequences of our actions, and the result of our conduct is the only thing we take with us when we die. O King, you are the very embodiment of dharma, so I hope you will not be angry with me at what I have to say.' Rama assured the dog that he could speak frankly without any worry, so the animal continued with his story. 'I have come to you because a king needs to be aware of what is happening in his kingdom so that he can adjudicate impartially. A Brahmin called Sarvarthasiddha, who was begging for alms, struck me severely with his staff though I did not offend him in any way.'

Hearing this, Rama immediately asked his guards to summon the Brahmin. When he arrived, Rama asked why he had shown needless violence towards the dog, who had not caused him any harm. Rama said, counselling the Brahmin, 'Anger is the deadliest of all enemies.[2] It obliterates all the good deeds that one may have done in the past. A wise man, therefore, learns to abandon anger. When our senses are out of control, they are like unruly horses yoked to a chariot, running amok. They need to be reined in with an expert charioteer's skill, so that one never inflicts pain on anyone. It is important always to practise good thoughts, good words and good deeds, because the sharpest of swords, the most venomous of snakes and even the bitterest enemy who harbours undying hatred towards you cannot do as much damage to you as your own lack of self-control. Now tell me why you hit this poor dog.'

The Brahmin honestly confessed that he struck the dog in anger. He said, 'I was out begging for food, but the hour for charity was over, so I was left hungry. The dog was obstructing my path, and when I asked him to move, he looked at me with an impertinent expression. I was famished at the time and in an irritable mood, so I admit I lost control and struck him with my stick, venting my anger on him. I realize that I committed an offence against an innocent creature, and I am ready for any punishment you deem appropriate. I want to atone for my wrongdoing to save myself from hell.'[3]

Rama turned to his ministers and advisers and said, 'You have heard the details of the case. According to dharma, a king must impose a penalty

---

[2] 'At all stages of life, in the beginning, the middle and the end, keep away from the evils of violent anger.' Sama Veda 307

[3] In Vedic belief, hell/naraka is a state of suffering experienced by the subtle body after death for earthly transgressions. Like heaven/swarga, it is a temporary interlude before rebirth. There is no concept of eternal damnation in Vedanta.

for a crime committed,[4] so what do you suggest?' After discussing the matter, the advisers stated that the shastras protected Brahmins from capital punishment[5] but did not prevent them from being censured in other ways, with the ultimate judgement about the nature of the sentence resting with the king. Hearing this opinion, the dog interceded and said, 'You asked what you could do for me; therefore, it is my plea that you punish this Brahmin by making him the head priest of the Kalanjara order.' Rama agreed to this puzzling request, and the Brahmin was sent off in style on an elephant to take on his new position as head priest. After he departed, the bemused ministers exclaimed in astonishment that the Brahmin had been rewarded with a promotion in status rather than reprimanded for his misdeed. Rama replied that he was sure the dog had an excellent reason for his unusual demand and asked him to explain his perplexing request.

The dog said, 'In my previous birth, I was the head priest of that order. I was a good leader, and my conduct was exemplary. I shared all the donations I received equally with my fellow sages. I was honest and kind to everyone, especially my subordinates, yet I was reborn as a dog for some small misdemeanour I may have committed. What do you think would be the fate of someone predisposed to cruelty if he is placed in the same position? Though it may not appear like it, the Brahmin has been condemned, not exonerated, by being exalted to a high position. Since there is great accountability that goes with power, henceforth, he cannot afford to falter in his behaviour as he did with me.' Then, satisfied with the judgement, the dog asked for permission to go his way, departing with the message that leadership demands responsibility, as a leader's job essentially comprises service to others. Also, being in a position of authority involves sacrifice, and sacrifice often entails suffering. Having completed his experience on Earth in the form of a dog,[6] this great soul went to Kashi and gave up his body by fasting to death.

---

[4] 'The king should impose a fine in direct proportion to the amount of pain caused when someone strikes a person or animal causing injury.' Manusmriti 8.286

[5] In recognition of a Brahmin's learning, he was exempt from the death penalty, but he could be punished in other ways. Manusmriti 8.380 advocates banishment as an alternative punishment. Exile was considered as bad as a death sentence in those times.

[6] This episode illustrates the Vedic concept of unity in all creation. The supreme spirit manifests in different forms, but the consciousness within each remains the same, whether the form is a Brahmin or a dog. Every aspect of God's creation is divine.

Chapter 39

Shatrughana and Lavana

Rama and Lakshmana always enjoyed each other's company, and one pleasant spring evening, as was their usual practice, they sat conversing on various matters before retiring for the night. The following day, when Rama was holding court, he was told that 100 hermits who lived on the banks of the Yamuna, led by the Bhargava Chavana, were waiting at the gate to see him. Rama asked for them to be ushered in, and they entered with offerings of fruit and pots of sacred water. After receiving them with due honour and offering them seats, Rama said, 'I am at your service. What can I do for you?'

Grateful that he was so forthcoming, the sages said they had come to him for protection. Requesting Rama's assistance, they pleaded, 'A Daitya called Lavana, the son of Madhu through Ravana's cousin sister Kumbhinasi, is harassing us. Madhu had practised severe austerities dedicated to Lord Shiva and was granted a powerful weapon fashioned from his trident. Imbued with the might of the great Mahadeva, it could reduce anyone or anything to ashes in an instant. Madhu requested that the weapon remain in his family forever, passing from one generation to the next. Shiva could not grant his wish, as the trident had to be earned by merit. However, as a compromise, he said that the weapon would be available to Madhu's successor, and as long as anyone held it in his hand, he would be immune from death. Lavana inherited the kingdom after Madhu and the divine trident, but unfortunately, he has a vicious disposition and uses it to torment the innocent. Now, Lavana has set his sights on us and attacks us mercilessly. We have come here hoping you can free us of his cruelty, like you rid the world of his uncle, Ravana.'

Rama agreed to assist them and said with folded hands, 'Tell me everything about Lavana. I would like to know where he lives and the

smallest details of his habits and conduct.' The holy men replied that Lavana
was bloodthirsty and avaricious. He killed animals indiscriminately to satisfy
his appetite but particularly enjoyed dining on the flesh of sages. They
described him as evil incarnate, and stated that he lived in Madhuvana by
the Yamuna. After giving the rishis his solemn assurance that Lavana would
be eliminated, Rama discussed the matter with his brothers to decide who
would do the job. Bharata immediately volunteered, but Shatrughana offered
to go instead. He was concerned that Bharata had already undergone much
hardship, living abstemiously as a renunciate and managing the kingdom in
Rama's absence. Rama accepted Shatrughana's proposal and announced his
intention to consecrate him as King of Madhuvana, to take over the domain
after removing Lavana. This was necessary to establish orderly rule there, as
it was considered an injustice to depose a king and leave his subjects without
protection.

Hearing Rama's command, Shatrughana regretted having spoken. He
felt uncomfortable about accepting a position of kingship as the youngest
of them and voiced his concern that it did not feel right to supersede his
elder brothers. Addressing Rama, Shatrughana said, 'I was presumptuous,
stepping in to undertake what Bharata had already agreed to do, so please
forgive me for the audacity of my offer. However, you are my senior,[1] and
the shastras place me under obligation to follow your orders, so I must do as
you ask.' Despite Shatrughana's reservations, there was no jealousy amongst
the brothers, so they put his protests aside, and he was crowned king of
Madhuvana amidst much pomp and splendour.

After the ceremony, Rama carefully briefed Shatrughana on his assignment
and gave him a celestial arrow that never missed its mark. It was the very one
that Vishnu had used to destroy Madhu and Kaitabha in his epic battle with
them.[2] Rama reminded Shatrughana of Lavana's formidable trident charged
with the power of Shiva, which made him invincible. Apparently, Lavana
carried the unfailing weapon all the time and was rarely seen without it. Since
he could only be killed when he did not have it in his possession, Rama advised
Shatrughana to wait by the gate when Lavana was out hunting with only
ordinary weapons, intercepting him before he entered the city. He ordered,
'Take 4000 horses, 2000 chariots, and 100 elephants. Carry a million gold

---

[1] 'The eldest brother should support his younger brothers as a father, and in duty they
should also behave like sons to the eldest brother.' Manusmriti 9.108

[2] The story of Madhu and Kaitabha is told in the Bhagavatha Purana.

coins and enough wealth, so the army is well-fed and looked after. They must be kept in high spirits, so remember to address them frequently to boost their morale. Also, take a few traders from the city with goods for sale so that you do not fall short of revenue. However, when you fight Lavana, make sure to go alone, not to invite suspicion, as he cannot be killed if he is prepared. Cross the Ganga with your army before the monsoons start to make it easier to get to the other side. When the summer is over, and the rains are about to begin, it would be the right time to mount your offensive.'

Shatrughana sent his army ahead, instructing them where to camp to avoid causing inconvenience to the local people in the area. Shortly after giving these orders, he set out himself, reverently circling his brothers, the three mothers and Guru Vasishta. Since the army had already departed, he travelled alone. In two nights, Shatrughana reached the vicinity of the Ganga, where he halted at the ashram of Valmiki and requested shelter for the night before continuing his journey towards the west.

The sage welcomed him and said warmly, 'My ashram is always open to the clan of Raghu.[3] I consider it an honour to have the privilege of extending my hospitality to you.' After dinner, Shatrughana noticed a magnificent sacrificial altar nearby and asked how it came to be built, so Valmiki narrated the story of an Ikshavaku called Virasaha, the son of Sudasa. Since he was the son of Sudasa, he was also called Saudasa. The young prince enjoyed hunting even as a boy. One day, he saw two Rakshasas in the forest, who had taken on the form of tigers, unfairly killing deer in large numbers to satisfy their voracious appetites. Angered by the injustice of the slaughter, Saudasa struck down one of the Rakshasas with his arrow. Then his anger abated, and he spared his companion. However, the surviving Rakshasa became wrathful and said, 'Since you have killed my friend who did you no wrong, I vow to take vengeance for his death.'

Years went by, and Saudasa became king, assuming the title Mitrasaha. He was an able ruler and once performed an Ashwamedha yagna here in this very spot under the auspices of Vasishta. It lasted many years, and he built this grand altar for the purpose.

At the end of the sacrifice, the vengeful Rakshasa came to Saudasa in the guise of Vasishta. He told him that he had almost completed the yagna, and as a special request, he wished to be fed meat in the traditional feast that was to follow. The Rakshasa knew Saudasa would find his demand strange,

---

[3] Shatrughana's great grandfather.

so he asked him not to question his motives. The king was bewildered by the unusual instruction, but he dutifully obeyed and asked his head cook to prepare the flesh. Then the Rakshasa cunningly disguised himself as the cook and presented an expertly crafted meat dish, except he used human flesh. As was the custom marking the successful completion of a sacrifice, the king and his wife Madayanti personally served Vasishta, but he detected that human flesh was being put on his plate and, infuriated, cursed the king in anger. "Since you have thought it fit to offer me this sacrilegious meat, may it be the food on which you live from now on.'

Oblivious of the Rakshasa's deception, the king was under the impression that he had merely followed his guru's command, so naturally, he was outraged. He scooped up some water in his hand and was about to pronounce a counter-curse when his wife held him back. Begging him to show restraint, she said, 'A guru must always be regarded with veneration, and though he cursed you, you should not do the same.'[4] Her timely intervention prevented the king from acting rashly, and he poured the vitriol-suffused water on his feet, which became discoloured like stone. In repentance, Saudasa threw himself before Vasishta and recounted why he had offered him the meat. When they realized that the Rakshasa had tricked them, Vasishta said regretfully, 'I uttered the words in a temper, but I am unable to retract them. However, I will amend my curse to last only twelve years; moreover, you will not remember your hardship to be disgusted by it.' After hearing this unfortunate tale, Shatrughana said goodnight and retired to a special guest hut prepared for him.

That very night, Sita gave birth to twin boys. At midnight, Valmiki received intimation of the delivery with a request to bestow his blessings on the newborns to protect them from malevolent influences. The sage immediately went to see the beautiful babies, who shone with brilliance like their father. Then, picking up a fistful of darbha grass, he chanted mantras for their protection. The tips of the grass were called kusha, and the stalks, lava. Valmiki handed the consecrated grass that he had infused with protective powers to an old ascetic woman and told her to brush the first-born child with the tips, naming him Kusha. Similarly, he asked her to use the stalks on the younger child, giving him the name Lava. He declared that they would

---

[4] 'The guru, the father, the mother and an elder brother must never be treated with disrespect, especially by a learned person, though one be grievously offended by them.' Manusmriti 2:225.

attain fame bearing those names, and the woman duly did as directed. After that, the anchoresses began singing the glory of Rama and the Ikshavaku clan, and hearing them, Shatrughana woke up and went hurriedly to the hut. He was delighted to see the boys and congratulated Sita, saying, 'God be thanked for the two lovely boys you have brought into the world!'

The following day Shatrughana rose early, departing after his morning worship. Seven nights later, he arrived on the banks of the Yamuna at the ashram of the sages who had sought Rama's help. While there, he asked for more information on the enemy, including any special knowledge about the fearsome trident. The Sage Chavana said, 'Many stories are associated with the deadly weapon, but one is significant because it involved an Ikshavaku.' Elaborating, he said, 'Ayodhya was once ruled by a king called Mandatta, a mighty warrior. After bringing the whole world under his control, Mandatta proceeded to establish his authority over Devaloka. When he arrived there, Indra cleverly asked why he wanted to bring Devaloka under his sway when a part of the earth ruled by Lavana, the son of Madhu, was still unconquered. Mandatta returned to earth and sent a messenger to Lavana, declaring that he wished to challenge him, but in response, Lavana devoured the emissary even before he had finished speaking. When the envoy did not return, the king went himself, launching a fierce attack. But Lavana merely hurled his trident at Mandatta and instantly incinerated him, along with his entire army. The strength of the trident is immeasurable; however, I have no doubt you will kill Lavana tomorrow if you tackle him when he is out hunting without his infallible weapon.'

Lavana was in the habit of going out early every morning in search of food to satisfy his rapacious appetite. Remembering Rama's advice, Shatrughana waited for him with his bow near the city's eastern gate. Lavana returned around midday with a large heap of animal carcasses, and on seeing Shatrughana, sneered, 'Many buffoons like you have sought to confront me and failed. Even so, the food I gathered today is insufficient to meet my needs, so it is fortuitous that you have presented yourself to me.' Shatrughana was incensed by the insult and roared, 'I am the son of Dasharatha, Rama's younger brother and the destroyer of all foes. I, Shatrughana, will not let you live.' Lavana laughed mockingly and said, 'I hold your lineage in utter contempt! You are puny men as weak as straw, but if you want to die by foolishly challenging me, so be it. Let me get my weapon.' However, Shatrughana barred his path and said, 'Now that I am here, you cannot leave like a coward without duelling with me. Only a simpleton allows his enemy to walk away, so take a good look at the world around you as it will be your last.' Lavana gnashed his teeth in anger. He began uprooting trees and hurling them with great force, but Shatrughana cut them to pieces with his arrows. Then, Lavana managed to strike Shatrughana on his head, and he fell unconscious. Presuming him to be dead, Lavana started gathering up the animals he had killed. Meanwhile, Shatrughana recovered, letting loose the arrow imbued with the power of Vishnu that Rama had given him. In an instant, it tore open Lavana's chest, boring deep into the earth before it returned to its quiver. The Devas, the rishis and the whole world rejoiced as the dreadful agent of darkness was eliminated; as for the trident, having fulfilled the terms of its duty, it flew back to Shiva.

The slaying of Lavana pleased the Devas, and led by Indra, they offered Shatrughana a boon of his choice. Remembering Rama's orders for him to settle the kingdom, he said, 'My wish is for this capital of Madhu, called Madhura,[5] to become a thriving city.' The Devas granted him his wish, and the half-moon-shaped city by the banks of the Yamuna flourished under Shatrughana's able leadership. In twelve years, he accomplished a lot. People of all four varnas lived peacefully. The harvests were plentiful. Traders did brisk business, and the treasury was overflowing. The city boasted many large mansions and beautiful gardens; Lavana's grand white palace was further embellished to become even more magnificent. Then, having fulfilled his assignment successfully, Shatrughana felt it was time for him to return to Ayodhya. He proceeded with a small retinue of 100 chariots, halting at Valmiki's ashram on the way back. He and his men were received warmly, and as before, after their meal, they chatted late into the evening with the sage, who told them many fascinating stories. Valmiki was full of praise that Lavana's tyranny was finally over. Kissing Shatrughana's forehead in a fatherly gesture, he said, 'The death of Ravana rid the world of great torment, no doubt, but it took strenuous effort, whereas you performed the almost impossible task of killing Lavana with ease. What you have achieved is truly creditable; I witnessed how you did it as I was with Indra at the time, watching from above. I am so proud of your stupendous achievement!'

After an enjoyable evening of good company when everyone had retired to their huts, they were surprised to hear mellifluous tunes filling the ashram. Angelic voices sang Rama's story to the accompaniment of string and percussion instruments, precisely as the events of his life had taken

---

[5] The city of Mathura today.

place. The poetry was in beautifully composed Sanskrit verse, perfectly rendered to melody. The astonished army was entranced; thinking they were dreaming, the soldiers asked Shatrughana to find out more about it from the sage. However, he put it down to an unusual occurrence, the likes of which happened in holy places. Nevertheless, the song of Rama's deeds had a profound impact on him, and Shatrughana spent a restless night yearning to see his brother again. He rose early, and after bidding farewell to Valmiki, left for Ayodhya.

When he arrived, Rama was in his assembly, surrounded by his courtiers. Shatrughana entered, bowing low, and said with folded hands, 'I have completed the task you gave me. Lavana is no more, and the city is settled anew, but I am not happy there. Bereft of your company for twelve years, I have missed you terribly. I do not wish to stay away from you any longer. Therefore, have mercy on me and allow me to return permanently to Ayodhya.'

Rama embraced his younger brother lovingly and said, 'Kshatriyas do not have the luxury of giving in to sentimentality like this, as our duty often obligates us to live away from home for long periods. You are the ruler of Madhura now, and a king's primary responsibility is to serve his people. While you must go back to your kingdom and uphold your dharma, you are, of course, always welcome to visit me from time to time. You are very dear to me, and I would not say I like being parted from you either, but it is not right for a king to abandon his duties. So, stay a week with me and then return to Madhura with the forces that you brought with you.'

Although Shatrughana was unhappy at leaving, he understood that dharma had to take precedence over all else, and dutifully returned to Madhura after seven days had elapsed.

Chapter 40

Rama Visits Agastya

Much time went by after Shatrughana's visit, and life continued uneventfully as Rama ruled Ayodhya with the assistance of Bharata and Lakshmana. One day, an elderly Brahmin turned up unexpectedly at the palace gates, carrying the body of his deceased child in his arms. Since premature death was unknown in the kingdom, he cried that some evil deed must have resulted in this unnatural occurrence. The Brahmin ranted that anomalies like this only happened when the king was negligent of his duties, and threatened that he and his wife would give up their lives on Rama's doorstep unless the situation was remedied. Rama was disturbed by the complaint and summoned his advisers Vasishta and Vamadeva, including other sagacious counsellors Markandeya, Maudgalya, Kashyapa, Katyayana, Jabali, Gautama and Narada, and asked them for their advice in resolving the matter.

Narada said, 'In Kritayuga,[1] dharma stood on all four legs as Brahmins performed penance for unselfish purposes that benefited society at large. Now, in Tretayuga, immorality has crept into society, so dharma has lost one leg. Kshatriyas also perform penance, not always with a pure intention,[2] as in Kritayuga. In Dwapara to come, dharma will lose one more leg, and in Kaliyuga, it will totter unsteadily on one limb as all varnas practise austerities

---

[1] Krita means accomplished, so Kritayuga was the age of spiritual accomplishment. In Vedic philosophy, time is viewed as cyclical. There are four yugas (depending on the level of dharma practised), that keep repeating endlessly. In Kritayuga, dharma represented by the bull stands on all four legs, so it is an age of righteousness. In Tretayuga, one leg is lost, so there is some deterioration in dharma. In Dwaparayuga, dharma balances on two legs, while in Kaliyuga, it barely stands on one leg, so unrighteousness prevails.

[2] As in the case of Ravana's penance, 'rajasa tapas', which was for his own aggrandizement.

solely for self-aggrandizement rather than for an altruistic goal. There is a man currently performing penance for an impure purpose in your kingdom, and his sinful intentions are reflected in unnatural happenings like the untimely death of the young boy. The king shares one-sixth of the merit accrued from his people's piety, so he must ensure that no one in his kingdom engages in austerities with an impious intention. I suggest that you find the person who is pursuing an immoral goal and punish him, so that the child comes back to life.'

Hearing Narada's advice, Rama asked Lakshmana to console the Brahmin and have the child's body preserved in a vat of oil, so that it did not decompose. Then, he summoned the Pushpaka Vimana and left with his sword and bow in search of the culprit. Rama flew west over dense, verdant forests, carefully scanning the terrain. However, he did not see anything untoward in that direction. Next, he went northwards to the snow-capped Himalayas and then eastwards, but did not notice anything unusual there either. Finally, going southwards, by a lake on the northern slope of the Saivala Mountain, he sighted an ascetic hanging upside down, smeared with blood and engaged in severe penance. Rama landed the vimana near him and asked who he was, and more importantly, the purpose for which he was subjecting himself to such rigorous penance. The ascetic replied, 'I am a Shudra[3] called Shambuka. The truth is that I wish to go to heaven with my body intact, and I am performing this penance to become powerful enough to conquer the kingdom of the Devas and establish myself as its ruler.' When Rama heard Shambuka's nefarious purpose, which contravened the world's natural order resulting in imbalance, he unsheathed his sword and severed his head.[4] The Devas showered him with flowers, and when Indra offered

---

[3] The story of Shambuka is considered by many scholars to be an interpolation as it is contradictory to Rama's usual behaviour of engaging in discussion first to avoid bloodshed. Also, there is criticism levelled by those who see the Shambuka incident as a 'caste-based' killing, arguing he was killed because he was a Shudra. However, this is a misinterpretation, since Shambuka is killed for performing 'tamasic tapas', austerities for an evil purpose, rather than for being a Shudra. A correct interpretation of the incident must be taken in context, considering the spirit of the text. Misreading Rama's intentions and weaponizing the deed to drive an agenda is harmful. There are numerous cases of Shudras engaging in 'sattvic tapas' or righteous penance, as in the case of the boy Dasharatha killed, Rishi Matanga and even Valmiki himself.

[4] Disruption of 'Rtha'—natural laws in the order of the universe, creating disorder—'nirrti', was immoral. The Rig Veda says: 'Rtam satyam dharmam'—Cosmic laws are

him a boon for saving them, Rama said, 'If you are pleased with my service, then may the child of the Brahmin come back to life.' That very moment, the boy was resuscitated and was reunited with his joyful parents. Indra then said to Rama, 'May auspiciousness always be with you. We are on our way to visit the saintly Rishi Agastya, who has just finished an arduous twelve-year penance in water. We would like you to join us in congratulating him on his achievement.'

Rama followed them in his vimana to the ashram of the great sage born from a pot, and after the Devas left, prostrated himself before him. Happy to see Rama, Agastya said, 'I have the greatest respect for you on account of all your virtuous qualities. Do spend one night at my ashram as my honoured guest and return home at dawn tomorrow.' Handing Rama a dazzling ornament fashioned by Vishwakarma, he said affectionately, 'This beautiful jewel was gifted to me, but since it is considered meritorious to give away a treasured possession, I would like you to have it. Please accept it from me as I think there is none more worthy than you to be adorned by it.'

Hesitating to take the gracious present, Rama said, 'Respected master, it would not be appropriate for me to accept your generosity. Kshatriyas are the ones meant to give charity, and it is frowned upon for them to take things from others, most especially from Brahmins.'

Agastya understood Rama's concern and explained why he wanted him to accept the gift. He said, 'At the beginning of Kritayuga, there were no kings. When Indra was installed in Devaloka, human beings felt they, too, needed a ruler to protect them, so they requested Brahma to establish a monarch on earth. Brahma asked the guardians of the four quarters to donate a part of their powers, and thus Kshupa was created. As such, a king commands by the power of Indra that is vested in him. He nourishes by the kindness of Varuna. He is charitable by the munificence of Kubera and dispenses judgement by the authority of Yama. Therefore, O King, know that you are invested with the guardians' authority and should not refuse this gift from me. It will help me rather than benefit you, as it is for my deliverance that I am bestowing it on you.'

---

eternal truths and following them is dharma. Rtha was believed to create peace, stability and harmony. According to the Atharva Veda 14.1.1, 'The ever-true principles of cosmic order alone sustain the balance of Mother Earth.' Shambuka's penance was selfish and aimed at disrupting the natural cosmic flow. It was detrimental to intrinsic world order as he would have created disharmony by doing something unnatural against the laws of existence.

Accepting the ornament, Rama asked Agastya how it came into his possession, so he told him the story. 'The jewel came to me in a miraculous way. Long ago, there was a large swath of uninhabited forest devoid of animals and birds. However, it was a peaceful place abundant with fruits and flowers, so I decided to practise austerities there. Amidst it, I came across a beautiful lake covered in lotuses, and unlike the rest of the desolate forest, many flocks of birds frequented this spot. The water was clear and refreshing to drink because the lake was free of moss and weeds. Nearby was a charming hermitage, but strangely, it was deserted. I spent the night there and went to the lake early in the morning to perform my worship. To my surprise, I saw the fresh, undecayed corpse of a magnificent man floating in the water. As I sat on the shore in bewilderment at this mysterious place, a celestial vimana landed. It was yoked with swans and spectacular in appearance. A divine being was seated on a throne inside, waited upon by bejewelled attendants. Some were singing and some played instruments like the mridangam, veena and panava. Apsaras were dancing and fanning the man who shone with an ethereal glow. He rose from his seat, descended from his craft and headed purposefully towards the corpse. Then to my horror, he started gorging hungrily on it. After consuming the cadaver, he sipped water, bathed in the lake and returned to his aircraft.

'The disgusting sight I had just witnessed so revolted me that I could not contain my curiosity and asked him who he was. He looked like a Deva, but what he had just done was totally abhorrent. The man replied that he was bound by the inescapable consequences of his past life that forced him to endure this misery despite having attained an otherwise blissful state. He explained that in days gone by, a king called Sudeva ruled Vidarbha.[5] He had two sons, one from each of his two wives. In his mortal body, this otherworldly being had been the elder son Shweta, and was crowned king after his father. He ruled righteously for many years following dharma, and when he retired, he came to this spot to practise austerities. After many years of penance, Shweta shed his body and attained Brahmaloka. However, despite reaching this high realm of heaven, where there was supposed to be infinite bliss, he still experienced intense hunger and thirst.[6] When he asked Brahma what he

---

[5] The region is now the current state of Maharashtra.

[6] Vedic philosophy speaks of fourteen levels of consciousness experienced: seven heavenly realms of increasing bliss, and seven hellish realms of increasing torment. These are not physical locations, but 'lokas' or states of existence.

could do to satisfy his craving, the grandsire replied that he would have to eat his own flesh. Shocked at hearing this, Shweta inquired what he had done to be subjected to such an awful punishment despite achieving a place in the highest heaven through his good deeds.

'Brahma replied that though Shweta had indeed performed extraordinary penance in his corporeal form, he had only nourished himself. He was so focused on his own salvation that he did not give anything in charity. Since he did not accrue any merit from satisfying others, he could not reap complete contentment in his afterlife. As a result of his earthly negligence, Shweta was bound by the urge to return to his corpse, continually consuming it, and though he had eaten it for years, his hunger never diminished. He was told that he would have the opportunity to be relieved from his plight when I came to the forest, so begging me to save him from his misery, he handed me this magical ornament in charity, saying it could fulfil any desire. I received the gift to free him, and as soon as I took it in my hands, the corpse in the lake vanished, and the effulgent being felt peace at last.'

Rama was amazed to hear this mysterious story, but wondered why the lush forest Shweta chose for retirement was devoid of birds and beasts. Agastya replied, 'In Kritayuga, Manu was the ruler of the Earth, and his first-born son was called Ikshavaku. Before Manu gave up his body through samadhi,[7] he placed Ikshavaku on the throne and said he would be the founder of all the royal dynasties on earth. He instructed his son to govern by the rule of law and be careful never to inflict an unnecessary sentence on anyone just because he was vested with enormous power. Manu emphasized that it was a king's duty to administer justice, as punishment rightly meted out in accordance with the law assured the king a place in heaven. Ikshavaku, your noble ancestor, had many sons. They were all high-minded except the youngest, who was crooked by nature. His father called this rotten son Danda, meaning punishment, and to get him out of the way, he sent him to rule the forest land between the Vindhya and Saivala Mountains. There he founded a city called Madhumanta, and invited Shukracharya to be his chief priest.

'Danda ruled for many years, and one day in spring, in the beautiful month of Chaitra, he happened to see an enchanting maiden in the woods near Shukracharya's ashram. As soon as his eyes fell on her, he felt overpowered by uncontrollable lust and asked, "What is your name, beautiful one? Whose

---

[7] State of spiritual union with the supreme consciousness.

daughter are you? I ask because I find myself hopelessly infatuated by you."
The girl replied, "My name is Araja, and I am the daughter of Shukracharya.
I live with my father in his ashram, here in the forest. Do not lay your hands
on me by force, as I am an unmarried maiden. Furthermore, my father is
your guru, and if he is angered, he will cause you infinite suffering. Since
you desire me, ask my father for my hand in an honourable way, and I am
sure he will give me to you in marriage." Danda was burning with passion,
and matrimony was not on his mind. He clasped his hands above his head
and said, "Bestow yourself on me without any delay. I am not afraid of the
consequences, not even of death." Saying this, he satisfied his carnality by
violating the girl, and left for his palace.

'When Shukracharya returned to his ashram and found Araja weeping
in humiliation, he was infuriated. He told his disciples to leave the forest
immediately and pronounced a curse that his anger would burn the
intemperate Danda and his entire kingdom to a cinder in seven days for
this heinous deed. He added that Indra would pour ash on the forest for
100 yojanas, destroying all forms of life. Then, telling Araja to remain in the
ashram, practising austerities, he protected the area around the lake from his
curse so that she would be safe, ensuring that the animals and birds there
would also survive unaffected. Thus, while Danda's kingdom was destroyed,
the ashram remained as holy as it had always been, and the region surrounding
it became known as Dandakaranya.[8] In time, life returned to the forest, and
rishis began to do their penance again in Janasthana.'

Agastya concluded his anecdote by saying, 'I have answered all your
questions, and now it's time for our Sandhya worship.' Rama went to the
lake with him. After spending the night, as Rama took leave of the sage the
following day, he said, 'I feel fortunate to partake of your hospitality and am
much enlightened by you. I look forward to visiting again to purify myself
in your noble company.' Blessing him, Agastya replied, 'You are very modest
because it is you who confers sanctity on all creatures by your presence.
You are the salvation of all mortals, and even if someone interacts with you
briefly, they are cleansed and become fit to enter heaven. So go in peace and
rule with dharma.'

Blessed by the sage, Rama prostrated himself before him and left in the
Pushpaka Vimana, arriving in Ayodhya by midday.

---

[8] Dandakaranya means forest of the punished.

Chapter 41

Lava and Kusha

Upon returning to Ayodhya, Rama immediately sent the vimana back to Kubera and told his doorman to inform Bharata and Lakshmana that he wished to see them. When they arrived, he updated them on all that had happened and said he was thinking of performing the Rajasuya[1] yagna to reinforce dharma in all lands. Inviting their opinion on this, Rama reminded them that Mitra, the slayer of foes, attained a place with Varuna by performing the Rajasuya. Soma similarly achieved renown in all three worlds by conducting it. Hearing this, Bharata folded his hands and said, 'O saintly one, you are rooted in dharma, which brings everlasting fame. All the other kings on earth look to you for protection and regard you as their father. Since you are the refuge for all creatures, it is my humble submission that you refrain from this endeavour that could cause unnecessary resentment.[2] The world is already under your command, and the Rajasuya will only provoke needless animosity.'

Rama was grateful for his advice and said, 'I am happy to receive such sensible guidance. You have expressed great maturity in your sentiments, and I see the pointlessness of going ahead with the Rajasuya. One must never do anything that causes unnecessary pain to anyone. It is important to accept wise counsel even if it comes from someone younger in age, so I will follow your advice.'

Lakshmana remained silent while Bharata spoke, but after his elder brother had finished, he asked Rama to consider the Ashwamedha sacrifice

---

[1] The Rajasuya Yagna was an elaborate fire ritual performed by the most powerful kings to establish their kingdom's dominion.

[2] The Rajasuya involved collecting significant tribute from other rulers.

instead, as it washed away all sins.[3] He elaborated on its great merits and how Indra had offered an Ashwamedha in repentance for slaying Vritra when he had committed the sin of killing a Brahmin. Rama smiled at Lakshmana's suggestion and said, 'What you say about the value of performing the Ashwamedha is true. I know of another story that corroborates what you have said. In times of yore, a great king called Ila ruled the prosperous kingdom of Bahalika. He had brought most of the world under his dominion and was a benevolent and able administrator. One day in the month of Chaitra, he went out hunting with his attendants. He killed many animals, but despite the large-scale slaughter of numerous creatures, he was not satisfied, and driven by greed, proceeded deeper into the forest, searching for more prey.'

'He accidentally stumbled into an area where Shiva and Parvati were relaxing, enjoying the beautiful season. It so happened that Shiva decided to take on the form of a female companion to sport in the waterfalls with Parvati. Simultaneously, every male in the vicinity transformed to the female gender, including King Ila and the men in his hunting party. After a while, Shiva changed back to his original form, but the other altered males did not regain their masculinity. Mortified at his metamorphosis into a woman, Ila threw himself at Shiva's feet and begged for help.'

'Since Ila's transformation was retribution for his greed, Shiva offered him any wish of his choosing, except the return of his manhood. But the king did not want anything else, so he begged Parvati to show compassion. Parvati replied that she and Shiva were like two halves of a whole, so she could only give him half of his request. Ila then asked if he could be male and female in alternate months. Parvati granted him this boon, and to ease his distress, further added that he would not remember being a man when he was in his female body, and vice versa.'

Bharata and Lakshmana were amazed at the story and wanted to know how Ila had managed to live with this strange affliction. Rama replied, 'Ila had become a breathtakingly beautiful woman with no memory of her life as a man. She was wandering in the forest with her companions when they came upon a lovely lake, and in it stood Budha, the son of Soma, practising penance. He looked so handsome that the arrows of Kamadeva struck Ila. She descended into the water, frolicking in it to attract Budha's attention. When Budha opened his eyes, he saw a woman of incredible beauty before him and instantly wanted to make her his wife. He got out of the lake and

---

[3] Lakshmana perhaps had the sin of abandoning Sita on his mind.

asked the other women to tell him more about her, and if she was married. They replied that she was not wedded yet and roamed around the forest with them like a free spirit, but their response did not satisfy Budha's curiosity. He still had unanswered questions, so he invoked his yogic powers, and his divine insight revealed precisely who Ila was and how he had acquired a woman's body. Budha wanted to be alone with Ila, so he asked her companions to depart and inhabit the mountain slopes as Kimpurushas.[4]

'When they had left, Budha introduced himself to Ila as the son of Soma, and asked her to accept him as her partner. Since Ila was also smitten by him, she acquiesced sweetly, saying she was unattached and happy to oblige. Thereafter, they spent the days happily absorbed in each other's company, but when a month passed, Ila woke up in bed as a male. Since he had no memory of his female form, Ila was bewildered about how he had got there. Seeing Budha performing his penance in the lake, Ila approached him, remembering coming to this spot with his retinue and wondering what had happened to them. Budha replied that Ila's followers had perhaps perished, but he had survived, sheltering in the hermitage, and had been asleep this whole time. Budha added that Ila could continue to live with him if he wished. Surprisingly, Ila had no desire to return to his earlier life; however, he said he needed to go back to anoint his son Sashabindu as the new king. Budha suggested that he dwell in the forest for a year, after which he would contrive something for his good. Ila agreed, alternating between being male and female every month. When he was male, the two would engage in lengthy philosophical discussions, and when he turned female, they would be lost to the world in physical pleasures.'

'Nine months later, Ila gave birth to a son called Pururava,[5] who looked exactly like his father, Budha. After a year, Budha remembered his promise to Ila and summoned various rishis, including Samvarta, Chavana, Aristanemi, Pramodana, Modakara and Durvasa. When they arrived, he told them what had happened and asked them what could be done to help Ila regain his manhood permanently. Ila's father also came with Pulastya, Kratu, Vasatkara and Omkara. As they discussed various options, he suggested that the situation be resolved through worshipping Shiva, since the problem

---

[4] A tribe whose members had lion heads and human bodies. Kimpurusha means: "Is it human?"

[5] Founder of the Lunar/Chandravanshi dynasty. His descendant Bharata was a mighty emperor and India is named Bharat after him.

had arisen by annoying him. It was agreed that there was no better way to propitiate Shiva than the Ashwamedha. Accordingly, they performed the grand ritual, and Shiva was pleased. When he offered a boon in appreciation, the sages asked that Ila's manhood be restored permanently. On returning home, Ila gave Bahalika to Sashabindu and established a new kingdom called Pratishtana. When he passed away, his son Pururava, born through Budha, became his successor. Just as Indra had redeemed himself of sin through the great Ashwamedha, Ila regained his manhood because of its purifying powers.'

Once Rama decided to perform the sacrifice, it took enormous preparation to get under way. The Ashwamedha was a laborious yagna that took a whole year and was hugely expensive. Rama asked Lakshmana to invite Vasishta, Vamadeva, Kashyapa, Jabali and the Brahmins who were experts in conducting the yagna, to select a horse with all the appropriate qualities considered auspicious and set it loose. He then asked him to invite Sugriva and the Vanaras, Vibhishana, the Rakshasa courtiers from Lanka, kings from all over the land, rishis engaged in penance and learned Brahmins. The preparations included arranging dancers, singers and actors to provide entertainment for the guests, and constructing a grand pavilion on the holy banks of the Gomti in the Naimisha Forest area. Through the Vedic rites of this great sacrifice, Rama wished to establish peace and goodwill in the land. They needed 1,00,000 bullocks to carry unbroken rice and 10,000 to transport sesame, beans, grains, pulses, ghee, salt, black gram, sandalwood logs and other requirements. Bharata was sent in advance, carrying gold and silver, and merchants were asked to establish themselves there to supply goods. Artisans of all trades were hired to build a temporary settlement, and cooks were engaged to cater the best of food to the attendees. All arrangements were to be of the highest standard with no expense spared. Rama also ordered a golden statue of Sita to take her place as no yagna could be conducted in the absence of a wife, and he had refused to take another one.

The grand sacrifice lasted a year and the enthusiasm did not let up for a moment the entire time. Large mounds of gold, silver and precious ornaments were distributed, and no one could recall any yagna previously performed in history as lavish as this one. The stallion guarded by Lakshmana roamed freely and returned after a year unobstructed, and the ceremonies drew to a close. Valmiki and his disciples were attendees at this grand affair. They had set up a few huts near the sacrificial area, and various kings present at the event would drop by to pay their respects to the sage. Amongst his students were Sita's sons, two young boys, gifted with mellifluous voices, whom he had taught the story of Rama's life. Now that the sacrifice was nearing completion, Valmiki asked them to recite the epic ballad publicly to the crowds on the main roads and thoroughfares. He told them to sing near the residential quarters of rishis and Brahmins, and especially in the presence of Vasishta, Vamadeva, Kashyapa and Jabali, who were conducting the sacrifice. They were also instructed to recite in the neighbourhood of the visiting dignitaries and by Rama's palace gates.

Valmiki gave his students baskets of delicious fruit to sustain themselves so they would not be fatigued, and their voices would not falter. He enjoined them to oblige if the king asked them to perform for him, reminding them to observe all the rules of music they had learned. They were to sing twenty cantos at a time in their melodious voices, adhering to the section divisions. Valmiki warned the boys not to display any greed or desire for wealth, as sages who lived on fruits and roots had no use for money. He advised that if Rama asked who they were, they should tell him they were Valmiki's disciples. Then giving them a veena and his blessings, he directed them to sing the Ramayana joyfully from their hearts, beginning with the opening verse, never forgetting to show their utmost respect to the king who was a father to all. After delivering this brief, Valmiki became silent and the twins went to bed excitedly, looking forward to their first public performance the next day.

The sons of Maithili rose early; they bathed and performed their morning worship and went into the streets singing the story of Rama as their guru had instructed. Their minds were fixed firmly on their task, and their golden voices accompanied by the dulcet notes of the veena were enchanting to all. They were as handsome as their father, and the people could not help noticing the striking resemblance. Having learned the 24,000 verses by heart, the boys sang with confidence precisely as taught, impressing everyone they encountered with their extraordinary talent. When they sang for a large group of sages who had vowed silence, even they could not help exclaiming, 'Excellent, most excellent,' on hearing the sweet sound of the first poetry ever composed.

The delighted sages gifted the young singers with whatever little they could in appreciation of their exceptional talent. Some presented them with water pots, while others offered bark garments, deerskin, sacred thread, strings of prayer beads, girdles made of grass and vessels to keep holy ingredients. One sage even gave them a special axe to chop wood. If they had nothing to offer, they blessed the youths with long lives, for no one had ever heard anything so marvellous before. As Valmiki had rightly envisaged, when news of the boys reached the court, Rama requested them to sing before him at his assembly. He invited the presence of great sages, kings, scholars, grammarians, astronomers, learned Brahmins well versed in Vedic rituals, music experts, and even those who knew the Samudrika Shastra and could read bodily signs. Linguists proficient in different languages, masters of logic, artists, dancers and musicians, those knowledgeable in politics and policy, and pundits of Vedanta[6] also attended.

The boys sang before the distinguished audience, mesmerizing them with their marvellous rendition of Rama's life story. Wonderstruck, they whispered to each other that the boys looked just like Rama, aside from their matted hair and hermit's clothes. Once the singers had recited twenty cantos, they paused, and Rama asked Bharata to reward them with 18,000 gold coins and anything else they wished. Everyone was astonished when they refused, politely saying that they were hermits, who lived in the forest and had no use for silver and gold. Rama then asked, 'Who are you remarkable young men and who is your guru? How long is the whole story?' The boys replied, 'We are disciples of the venerable Sage Valmiki. O King, this story of your life consists of 24,000 verses. It contains 100 legends and is told in 500 cantos, divided into six books and an epilogue. We will gladly sing it to you in its entirety over the next few days if you wish.'

Rama and his court listened spellbound to the epic story of his life sung by the boys over the days that followed, and his heart melted when he realized that they were his sons. Twelve years had passed since he had abandoned Sita, and her absence still tortured him as much as it did on the sad day he had sent her away. Nevertheless, Rama had remained steadfast in his devotion, never looking at another woman despite their long separation. He now conjectured that if Sita swore to her purity before the assembly, the citizens might be ready to accept her back as their queen, so he sent a message to Valmiki:

Many years have elapsed since Sita left Ayodhya. If she is willing, I would like her to clear her name by taking an oath proclaiming her innocence of the charges levelled at her, so she is freed from taint. With time, I feel the people have mellowed, and I am sure that if Maithili swears to her purity before the assembly, convincing them of her virtue, they will be ready to accept her as their queen once again.

---

[6] The philosophy of the Vedas, the essence of Vedic teachings.

When the envoy conveyed Rama's message to Valmiki, he replied, 'Inform the king it will happen as he desires. Sita will come to the assembly tomorrow.'

Rama was overjoyed and eagerly awaited Sita's return, feeling confident that the people would be satisfied with her assertion of purity.

The next day all the eminent sages assembled: Vasishta, Vamadeva, Jabali, Kashyapa, Vishwamitra, Dirghata, Durvasa, Pulastya, Shakti, Bhargava, Vamana, Markandeya, Maudgalya, Garga, Chavana, Shatananda, Bharadwaja, Narada, Parvata and Gautama. Representatives of the four varnas—Kshatriyas, Shudras, Vaishyas and learned Brahmins—took their seats. The atmosphere was solemn and the air was thick with tension as everyone sat silently in anticipation of Sita's declaration of chastity. All eyes turned to Valmiki as he entered the hall with Sita following behind, her teary face downcast and her hands folded respectfully.

The audience burst into spontaneous applause, and then there was a hushed silence as the great sage spoke. Addressing Rama, he said, 'O son of Dasharatha, let me present before this assembly the virtuous Sita, who has never wavered in her adherence to dharma. You abandoned her near my hermitage twelve years ago, prompted by the censure of wagging tongues. She is prepared to swear to her innocence of the unfair aspersions sullying her good name, so please permit her to speak. Her twin boys are yours, and I affirm this as the tenth son of Pracheta, who never utters an untruth.

'As you know, I have practised austerities for many years, and I am willing to stake the merits of all my penance if Maithili is at fault in any way. I gave her shelter in my ashram, knowing her innocence through the divine vision bestowed on me by my spiritual powers. She is pure, both in body and mind. Therefore, I am confident of stating unequivocally before everyone that Sita is sinless in her conduct and completely devoted to you.'

Overwhelmed with emotion at seeing his beautiful wife after so many years, Rama folded his hands and said, 'O holy master, I know Sita is indeed as pure as you say. If any lingering reservations still prevail in anyone's mind, your words should be sufficient to dispel them. I never lost faith in Sita and was distraught that the people decried me for bringing her back, so I beg you not to add the crime of distrust to my sin of sending her away. Despite Sita's trial by fire before the Devas, which proved her purity beyond doubt, I was unable to ignore public opinion when my people felt I had wronged them. I considered it my foremost duty as a king to be answerable for my actions to the citizens of Ayodhya, so I was forced to abandon my wife even though she was blameless. For this transgression, I beg forgiveness, fully aware that her children Kusha and Lava are my sons. However, before we are reunited again, I would be grateful if Sita reasserts her chastity for the benefit of everyone here. The assembly waited eagerly in anticipation of Sita's affirmation, and the Devas looked down on the scene from above.'

At that moment, a gentle breeze bearing a divine fragrance wafted through the room. Sita glanced briefly at the crowd assembled. She was dressed like an ascetic in simple ochre clothing and spoke with her hands folded and eyes cast down. 'If it is true that I have never envisioned anyone other than Rama as my husband, let Mother Earth Madhavi give me refuge. May she accept me if I have been devoted in thought, word and deed to my husband. If I speak the truth that I have been completely faithful to Rama, I ask Mother Earth to take me within her.'[7] Suddenly, the earth split open, and a celestial throne borne by divine serpents emerged. On it was seated Mother Earth, and in the blink of an eye, she gathered Sita in her arms, and placing her by her side, she descended into her depths as the Devas showered flowers. The assembly was left gaping in amazement, stunned by the unexpected turn of events. Stupefied at what they had just witnessed, not a single person moved nor did anyone speak a word. The crowd remained frozen for a long while as they stared at Rama in shock, waiting for his reaction.

Heartbroken, Rama leaned on a wooden staff for support, his body weak with emotion. The joy of reuniting with Sita was cruelly snatched from him, and shedding tears of sorrow laced with anger, he finally spoke with his head bent down. 'A misfortune of great magnitude, beyond what I have ever experienced, has occurred. It was unbearable for me to see Sita vanish forever before my very eyes. I rescued her from Lanka, so I will surely recover her from the depths of the Earth. O Goddess of the Earth, hand me back my Sita. I consider you my mother-in-law because you gave Sita to King Janaka, so I earnestly request you return her to me. If you cannot do this, open up again and take me to the otherworld, so we can be together. I am maddened by grief, so if you do not oblige, I will have no choice but to use force.'

---

[7] Sita chose to be swallowed up by the earth as an ultimate sacrifice. It is important to understand that she did not spurn Rama, acting out of hurt pride or a sense of injured ego. Sita knew the fickleness of mob mentality only too well, and she did not want Rama to face a moral dilemma yet again if the people accepted her temporarily and changed their minds later.

Following Rama's tirade, Brahma's voice resounded through the hall: 'O Raghava, great descendant of Raghu, shed your grief and stop ranting and raving in anger. Remember your true primordial self and the agreement you made with the Devas to assist them by taking birth in a human form. Control your mind, knowing that you are the incarnation of Vishnu. The sinless Sita has gone back to her heavenly realm and will be reunited with you there once again. Let your sons Kusha and Lava sing the final book concluding the epic poem you have been listening to these last few days. It is the first poem ever composed,[8] and you are the protagonist of whose joys and sorrows it sings. It is the truth exemplifying the Veda,[9] and through it, the world will forever remember you and your admirable life. Compose yourself now as you listen to the rest of your story that has not yet taken place. However, be careful to ensure that only you hear this part, which foretells your future.' In response, Rama dismissed the assembly, and taking his sons, walked away with them to the leafy hut he was staying in for the yagna.

The following day, he asked them to sing the remainder of the story without hesitation about its content. They sang from the point where Sita returned briefly before entering the bowels of the earth and how Rama, filled with emptiness, would have no peace of mind. All the guests soon returned to their homes, and Rama continued to rule with Sita enshrined in his heart. He never remarried, and though he lived many years performing innumerable yagnas, he conducted them with Sita's statue by his side. Rama's rule was known as 'Ramrajya', where the kingdom prospered, reaching great heights. The rains were timely, and the people were happy. There was contentment all around, and natural calamities and illness were unknown. After some years, having reached a ripe old age, Kaushalya passed away peacefully, surrounded by her loved ones. Then not long after her demise, Sumitra and Kaikeyi, having spent prayerful lives, followed. Rama honoured their memory by donating a large amount of wealth in their names and performed special yagnas for their peace.

---

[8] The Ramayana is referred to as 'adi kavya' or first poem.

[9] The Ramayana illustrates the deep philosophy of the Vedas, making it accessible to the common man.

Chapter 42

The End of Rama's Reign

One day, Bharata's maternal uncle Yudhajit, now the King of Kekaya, sent his guru Garga to Ayodhya laden with gifts, including 10,000 horses, blankets, fine clothing, precious gems and ornaments, to deliver a message. Rama heard about the arrival of the respected son of Angiras and went out to formally welcome him as he neared the city. After inquiring about the king's welfare, Rama received his communication. The rishi said, 'Your uncle Yudhajit has sent you a message for the aggrandizement of your kingdom. There is a beautiful region on the banks of the river Sindhu, currently inhabited by three million Gandharvas, who are the descendants of Sailusha. He would like you to help him defeat them and establish two cities in that region, to benefit your illustrious house.' Rama understood that Yudhajit wanted Bharata's line to continue as rulers, since Ayodhya did not pass on to them as it should have per Dasharatha's promise to Ashwapati.

He asked Bharata to lead his sons, Taksha and Pushkala, in battle and conquer the region as advised by their uncle. Rama ordered him to establish two cities for his sons and only return after installing them as rulers, and properly settling them. Then, he consecrated the princes as kings in advance and sent them off with an army accompanied by their father and Garga. Yudhajit joined them with his troops, and a fierce battle took place. After many days of fighting, Bharata invoked the missile of Yama called Samvarta, and claimed victory over the territory. Two cities were founded, Takshasila[1] for Taksha east of Sindhu, and Pushkalavata for Pushkala[2] to the west of the great river. In five years, they developed into well-established kingdoms,

---

[1] Taxila in Pakistan.

[2] Peshawar in Pakistan.

teeming with commerce and prosperity. The cities had delightful gardens, busy marketplaces and opulent multi-storeyed mansions reminiscent of Ayodhya. Once this was done, having completed his assignment, Bharata returned. Then, Rama turned to Lakshmana and said his two sons, Angada and Chandraketu, should have their own kingdoms, too. Therefore, he asked Lakshmana to conduct a survey and locate a suitable area they could annex without causing any offence, so that the princes could be consecrated as kings. Bharata advised that there was such a place, the region of Karupata,[3] which could easily be secured for Angada and Chandraketu. Lakshmana set out with the princes and established Angadiya and Chandrakanta, returning to Ayodhya after one year.

The years rolled by: Rama, Bharata and Lakshmana ruled Ayodhya with dharma as their guide, while Shatrughana ruled righteously in Madhura. Then, one day after many years had elapsed, Kala, or time personified, came to Rama's palace in the guise of a hermit. When Lakshmana inquired who the visitor was and what he could do for him, he said, 'Please announce my arrival to Rama. I am here on important business as the emissary of a powerful sage to discuss a private matter with him.'

Lakshmana dutifully informed Rama and escorted the hermit to his presence on his instruction. Rama received the unexpected guest with honour, offering him a golden seat, and inquired about his message. The hermit replied, 'I cannot talk openly as my communication is confidential. We must conduct our discussion behind closed doors, so a third person does not hear our exchange. If anyone disturbs us, gleaning even the slightest knowledge of our conversation, you must order him to be put to death. I will speak if you agree to these terms.' Rama accepted, and to ensure they would not be interrupted, told Lakshmana to send away the doorman and stand guard himself.

Once they were alone, Rama asked the visitor to speak as he was eager to hear what he had to say. The hermit said, 'O King of the world, I am Kala, time, your son in your cosmic form, and am here on behalf of the grandsire Brahma. I am the destroyer of all things, and Brahma has sent me to remind you of the reason you took birth as the son of Dasharatha. Your human avatar was to protect the world by ridding it of Ravana, thereby re-establishing righteousness. You chose a duration of 11,000 years to achieve your purpose, and I am here to inform you that the period is now completed.

---

[3] In eastern India—the area now comprising of Bihar, Odisha and West Bengal.

If you wish to continue living on Earth, of course, it is your prerogative, but the time you allotted yourself is over, and the Devas are eagerly awaiting your return.'

Rama laughed and said, 'I am delighted that you have come, and I am pleased with the message you have brought. I was born in human form for the benefit of the world, and since my goal has been achieved, I am ready to go back.[4] In fact, you have come just as I was contemplating this very matter myself, so I am happy to do as the grandsire says.'

Just then, the famous sage Durvasa arrived and demanded to see Rama urgently. Knowing Rama could not be disturbed, Lakshmana fell at his feet and said, 'Holy master, I can fulfil whatever you need. Rama is in a private meeting, so it might be some time before he is free to see you.' Durvasa, known for his temper, was enraged at being asked to wait. In a heated tone of voice, he thundered, 'Son of Sumitra, inform Rama this very instant that I am here. If you delay one minute longer, I shall curse Ayodhya, Rama and all your progeny.'

Lakshmana knew the consequences of interrupting Rama's meeting with the mysterious hermit, but felt it better for him to perish rather than all Ayodhya. Opening the door tentatively, he said, 'Rishi Atri's son, the esteemed Durvasa, is here and insists on an audience with you immediately.' Rama hurriedly sent Kala away and came out to meet Durvasa. When he asked what he could do for him, Durvasa said, 'I have just completed 1000 years of penance, and I am here so you can help me break my fast with your hands.'

After being served as requested, Durvasa left satisfied; but Rama paled, overcome by grief, remembering his promise to Kala, as Lakshmana was his heartbeat outside his body. As he deliberated miserably on what to do, Lakshmana said, 'Do not grieve for me, brother of mighty arms, because this parting is preordained. I insist you kill me without a qualm, as those who do not keep their word incur terrible sin. If you care for me and wish to show me grace, do your duty and follow through with your commitment.'

---

[4] In Vedic philosophy, everyone is born for a particular purpose. Though not applicable in the case of a divine avatar who has no karmic bondage, for ordinary people, this is based on 'prarabhdha karma' chosen to be experienced in their current lifetime. Once karma is exhausted, the spirit automatically casts off the body. More on this in the Appendices.

Rama was distraught and sought the counsel of his guru Vasishta to resolve this terrible dilemma. Vasishta advised calmly, 'I have known this for a long time because your separation from Lakshmana was prophesied. By abandoning him, you will fulfil your promise to Kala, but on the other hand, if you break your word, dharma will perish, and irreparable harm will be done to society. Therefore, in my opinion, it would be best if you gave up Lakshmana for the sake of the world.'

Hearing his advice, Rama turned to Lakshmana and declared before the assembly, 'Son of Sumitra, I must renounce you to preserve dharma, so from this moment, I dismiss you from my presence forever. Banishment is as severe a sentence as death for those of honour, so I will not be going back on my word.'

Lakshmana left without hesitation. He did not turn back or even go home to bid farewell to his family; instead, he proceeded in great haste to the Sarayu. Bathing to cleanse himself, he sat down in meditation on the riverbank. Then, established in yoga, he entered a state of samadhi, suspending his breath to cast off his body willingly. The Devas showered Lakshmana with flowers for his exemplary adherence to dharma, and his spirit entered heaven, restored to its state as one-fourth of the energy of Vishnu.

Lakshmana's death left Rama feeling empty. He announced to his assembly that he wanted to coronate Bharata and depart from the world. Hearing him, all those present prostrated before him, while Bharata fell unconscious, unable to take the shock. When he recovered, he said, 'I do not want the kingdom, as I have no use for it without you. Divide it between Kusha and Lava, consecrating them rulers of north and south Kosala. Also, send messengers to Shatrughana to tell him about your decision.' Vasishta then said, 'Your subjects are at your feet; as a king, you answer to them and must do as they wish.'

When Rama asked the people to speak, they said they would like to accompany him wherever he went, whether to the forest, the mountains, the river or the ocean. Rama agreed and anointed his sons, each as rulers of the northern and southern regions of the kingdom. He divided his wealth between them and, kissing them on the forehead, sent them off to establish themselves. Kusha's beautiful city at the foot of the Vindhyas was called Kushavati,[5] and Lava's capital became famous as Lava Sravasti.[6] Messengers

---

5 Kushinagar near Gorakhpur, Uttar Pradesh.

6 Lahore in Pakistan.

went to Shatrughana to inform him of all that had transpired. They rode
without halting and reached Madhura in three days. When Shatrughana
heard what had happened, he split his kingdom between his two sons,
Subahu and Shatrughati, and after crowning them rulers of Madhura and
Vidisha, respectively, departed in a single chariot for Ayodhya. He bowed
before Rama and said, 'I have given my kingdom to my sons and am now
here to join you unfettered by responsibility. This time you must not refuse
because I hate to disobey your orders.' Rama smiled indulgently and said, 'As
you wish.'

Meanwhile, Sugriva heard the news and, crowning Angada king of
Kishkindha, arrived with some of the Vanaras. Similarly, hearing about
the development, Vibhishana also reached Ayodhya. They, too, insisted on
joining him. Rama agreed to Sugriva accompanying him, but told Vibhishana
that he could not give up his body for as long as he had subjects to care for
in Lanka. Instead, Rama requested him to take the Ikshavaku family deity
Jagannath with him, so it could continue to be venerated. Having dissuaded
Vibhishana from accompanying him, he turned to Hanuman and said,
'Do not break your vow of listening to my story wherever it is sung,' and
Hanuman worshipfully replied that he would stay alive for as long as Rama's
story abided. Rama told Jambavan, Mainda and Dwividha to live till the
advent of Kaliyuga, and to the rest, he said, 'You may come with me if you
like.' Bidding his five dear friends farewell, Rama set out on his final journey
the following morning.

Dressed in fine silk, Rama proceeded to the Sarayu. Vasishta performed
the rituals for his departure from the world, and the chief priest took the fire
from the Agnihotra,[7] along with the umbrella from the Vajapeya sacrifice.
Rama walked in silence, holding a fistful of kusha grass in his hand. All
at once, Lakshmi appeared to his right, Mother Earth to his left, and in
front walked the goddess of all enterprise. Every weapon Rama had possessed
took a human form and accompanied him. The four Vedas followed as four
Brahmins, joined by Gayatri, Omkara and Vasatkara, and the doors of heaven
were flung wide open. Bharata, Shatrughana, Sugriva and all the people of
Ayodhya were part of the procession. After walking a yojana-and-a-half, they
arrived at the river. As Rama entered its swirling waters, the sky brightened,
and Brahma welcomed him back, surrounded by the Devas, whose vimanas
lit up the sky. A fragrant breeze blew, and flowers showered down as Rama

---

[7] Daily fire lit in Vedic households.

gave up his body in the river, taking his original form as Vishnu. Then he
requested Brahma to allot a deserving place in heaven to all who accompanied
him. Sugriva became one with Surya, and all the other Devas who took birth
as Vanaras to help in the battle against adharma merged with their celestial
forms. Everyone who entered the Sarayu with Rama went on to everlasting
bliss.[8] Ayodhya was abandoned and lay desolate, only reinhabited many
years later.

The story of Rama's life has a purifying effect on those who hear it. By
emulating his steadfast adherence to dharma, all sins are dispelled. One who
recites the Ramayana is worthy of receiving cloth, cows and gold. Hearing
even one canto of the Ramayana with reverence is like performing 1000
Ashwamedha sacrifices and 10,000 Vajapeyas. He who heeds the lessons of
the Ramayana gains the same benefit as going on pilgrimage to holy places
like Prayag, rivers like the Ganga, forests like Naimisha and hallowed grounds
like Kurukshetra. The Ramayana shows the path to 'dharma, artha, kama,
moksha',[9] and its study ensures a place with Vishnu as it is an unsurpassed
illustration of the Gayatri.[10]

Thus ends the Ramayana of Valmiki.[11]

---

[8] They achieved Moksha, so they were liberated from the cycle of birth and death.

[9] The four goals of human life—Purushartha, discussed in the Appendices.

[10] The unity of the indwelling spirit in all creatures as the same universal consciousness,
called God, is the message of the Gayatri.

[11] Many scholars question the authenticity of the Epilogue (Uttarakanda), insisting
that Valmiki's work ends with Rama's coronation. There is compelling evidence for this
opinion, based on the abrupt change in style and tone in Book 7. The Epilogue is more
in line with fantastical Puranic stories, than with Valmiki's factual narrative. Also, the
chapter on Rama's coronation ends with an invocation to listen to the Ramayana, citing
the benefits derived from hearing about Rama's exemplary life. This seems to suggest that
the subsequent verses were appended to the main story at a later time for a moralistic
purpose.

namaste

The divine light in me honours the divine light in you

ekam sat vipra bahuda vadanti

Truth is one though the wise call it by many names

Rig Veda

Appendices

The Historicity of Rama—
Man or Myth?

Although many today dismiss Rama's existence as entirely mythical, his historicity was never in question till about 200 years ago. Valmiki's Ramayana has always been referred to as 'itihas', which means—it so happened. Rama was eulogized through the ages as the great king of Ayodhya, whose reign was marked by peace and prosperity. His rule is immortalized as the golden age of 'Ramrajya'. This long-cherished belief was challenged in the 1800s with the advent of colonialism, when Western Indologists removed Rama from the annals of history, relegating him to mythology. In 1818, J.S. Mill wrote *The History of British India*, asserting that the Ramayana was pure fantasy and all Vedic texts mere flights of imagination. Then, in 1835, Thomas Babington Macaulay introduced the Indian Education Act, which replaced Sanskrit with English, dismantling and then replacing the traditional education system with one entirely European in thought. The new act was a turning point in public opinion as it rewrote the history of India from a colonial point of view, condensing the nation's historical timeline and discarding much of its antiquity.

Macaulay famously said, 'We must at present do our best to form a class who may be interpreters between us and the millions whom we govern; a class of persons, Indian in blood and colour, but English in taste, in opinions, in morals, and in intellect.' He believed in the pre-eminence of the English language, as we see from his statement on Indian education. 'I have no knowledge of either Sanscrit or Arabic. But I have done what I could to form a correct estimate of their value. I have read translations of the most celebrated Arabic and Sanscrit works. I have conversed, both here and at home, with men distinguished by their proficiency in the Eastern tongues. I am quite ready to take the oriental learning at the valuation of the orientalists themselves. I have never found one among them who could deny that a single shelf of a good European library was worth the whole native literature of India and Arabia. The intrinsic superiority of the Western literature is indeed fully admitted by those members of the committee who support the oriental plan of education.'

Macaulay further remarked on Vedic spiritual heritage: 'Our English schools are flourishing wonderfully. The effect of this education on the Hindus is prodigious . . . It is my belief that if our plans of education are followed up, there will not be a single idolator among the respectable classes in Bengal thirty years hence.'

Over the years, educated Indians gradually became distanced from Sanskrit and could only access their ancient texts in English. Since Western scholars did the translations, they interpreted Sanskrit works through a colonial lens due to either malice or ignorance, and what resulted was often far removed from the actual meaning.

Regarding Sanskrit literature's historical and scientific value, Macaulay scoffed: 'The question now before us is simply whether, when it is in our power to teach this language (English), we shall teach languages in which, by universal confession, there are no books on any subject which deserve to be compared to our own, whether, when we can teach European science, we shall teach systems which, by universal confession, wherever they differ from those of Europe differ for the worse, and whether, when we can patronize sound philosophy and true history, we shall countenance, at the public expense, medical doctrines which would disgrace an English farrier, astronomy which would move laughter in girls at an English boarding school, history abounding with kings thirty feet high and reigns 30,000 years long, and geography made of seas of treacle and seas of butter.'[1] Decades of indoctrination resulted in the intellectual colonization of educated Indians, who developed a distorted idea of the timeline and content of their heritage. Rama was one of the casualties of this Westernization of thought, and was soon revered purely as a Hindu deity, not as a ruler who once existed. Although his return home after killing Ravana is still celebrated exuberantly every year in India, Rama's existence has sadly been consigned to the fantasy world of imagination.

However, despite the prevailing scepticism today, there is significant evidence to demonstrate that Rama was a historical figure and that the basic events of his life occurred. Valmiki draws attention to the epic's veracity in the opening verses of the Ramayana itself, where he begins by revealing that

---

1 Thomas Babington Macaulay, 'Macaulay's Minute on Education', 2 February 1835.

it is a contemporaneous account. He states his purpose, which is to compose a biography singing the praise of an exceptionally righteous man based on reality, not fiction. The Ramayana begins with a question: Valmiki asks his guru, Narada, if an exceptionally righteous person exists in their time; someone who upholds dharma at every instance. Narada's answer is Rama.

Detractors allude to the work's fantastical elements, overlooking that the Ramayana was composed in epic style. Although there is a natural hyperbole associated with the genre and some interwoven storytelling, these aspects of the composition should not be used to quibble about the essential historicity of events described. Rama, for instance, was supposed to have ruled for 11,000 years, which is poetic licence to mean a long time! The ancient rishis did not author fiction for public entertainment. Instead, they used actual historical events to illustrate dharma, by narrating stories that depicted righteous action. Some parables in the Ramayana may not have historicity, like the story of Rama and the dog and the killing of Shambuka, which appear to have been added primarily to explain the subtlety of dharma. But, despite the apparent exaggeration and the interpolations that have crept into the text over time, there is strong proof that the major incidents described took place.

Due to advancements in science, many aspects of Valmiki's work are verifiable today and have been corroborated as factual. Interestingly, the Ramayana offers more proof for Rama having lived than is available for many in history, unquestioningly accepted as historical figures. Yet, the doubt cast committing the Ramayana to mythology is so firmly entrenched now, that it has become an orthodoxy hard to overturn even with strong substantiation of the story's authenticity.

Here are some pertinent facts to consider:

* Until quite recently, the Ramayana was never treated as a fairy tale but as the biography of a man whose exemplary life was told as an inspiring story to demonstrate the philosophy of the Vedas.[2] It was considered an authentic account composed by someone who had witnessed Rama's life first-hand. Valmiki even offered shelter to Sita and raised her children

[2] 'dharmārtha-kāma-mokṣāṇām, upadeśa-samanvitam pūrva-vṛtta-kathā-yuktam itihāsaṃ pracakṣate.'—Historical events told as a story to illustrate to society the right pursuit of the goals of life: dharma, artha, kama, moksha.

in his hermitage. Therefore, in the event of a contradiction between Valmiki's Ramayana and other narratives of Rama's life, Valmiki's version is accepted as accurate. Over the centuries, many retellings of the Ramayana were written in local languages as embellished versions of the original story. Many of these works are devotional expressions, not historical accounts, like Valmiki's composition. Nevertheless, the basic narrative remains the same in all these renditions, the most famous being Goswami Tulsidas's Ramcharitmanas. We cannot ignore the literary evidence of Rama's existence any more than similar textual proof for Alexander and other European figures.

- It is remarkable that every site associated with Rama is geographically correct, exactly where it is today, and many have the same name, including Ayodhya on the southern banks of the Sarayu, where Valmiki described it situated. Ayodhya means unconquerable, and though it is now an ordinary city, its name continues, memorializing its past Ikshavaku glory. To this day, all the places Rama visited retain the memory of his stay, evidenced by temples and local folklore honouring him. Panchavati, for example, is modern-day Nashik. 'Nasika' means nose, indicating this is where Lakshmana cut off Surpanakha's ears and nose. Kishkindha is Hampi, and during the British rule, it was chronicled that certain forest tribes in the area called themselves Vanaras and had a monkey as a symbol on their flag.[3] Many areas in Sri Lanka are associated with the Ramayana, including Sigiriya, Nuwara Eliya, Ella and Bandarawala.

- The most significant archaeological evidence of Rama's historicity is the Rama Setu, built by Nala, now called Adam's Bridge, which connects India with Sri Lanka precisely in the location mentioned in the Ramayana. Dr Badrinarayanan, former director of the Geological Survey of India, conducted extensive research at the site from 2004 to 2005 and found the bridge a manufactured structure. His study concluded that the boulders were not marine in origin but brought from elsewhere and placed over a naturally existing sandy ridge. Further, the bridge was dated back to 7000 years ago, corresponding with the era of Rama, and was deemed too symmetrical to be natural. The Ramayana says the construction was done by placing boulders on a shoal, which is exactly the case. Interestingly, the bridge is 35 km long and 3.5 km wide, in the same 10:1 ratio mentioned by Valmiki—100

---

[3] This is mentioned in the book *Historical Rama* by D.K. Hari and Hema Hari.

yojanas long and 10 yojanas wide. Ocean levels 7000 years ago were lower than today, indicating that the bridge was above water, though now it lies shallowly submerged. Dr Rajiv Nigam, of the National Institute of Oceanography, Goa, in his paper, 'Sea Level Fluctuations During the Last 15,000 Years and their Impact on Human Settlement', points out that 7000 years ago, sea levels were three meters lower than today, the exact depth at which the bridge currently lies.[4]

- Valmiki describes real places, and the fauna and flora associated with each region from Ayodhya to Sri Lanka perfectly match the native landscape. The Ramayana elaborately details every location, devoting passage after passage to extol each area's natural beauty. The narrative mentions specific plant and animal names, and it is hard to accept that the author could have been so accurate about far-off places based solely on imagination. Sugriva's detailed description of world geography when he dispatches the Vanaras to the four quarters of the earth is intriguing. He even seems to mention the Paracas Candelabra in South America and its exact purpose, though its origin is shrouded in mystery today. Also, noteworthy is Sugriva's remark about only being able to sight Agastya (Canopus) from south of the Vindhyas, because we know it was not yet visible from northern India 7000 years ago due to a phenomenon called the precession of the equinoxes.

- The mighty rivers of India—the Sutlej (Shutudri), Beas (Vipasha), Ganga, Yamuna, Mandakini, Narmada, Godavari and so on—are placed where they are today, including the Saraswati, which dried up by 1900 BCE due to tectonic activity and failing monsoons, indicating that Rama lived when it was still perennial and flowing from the Himalayas to the Arabian Sea. Bharata crossed the Saraswati and other rivers in their exact order when he journeyed home from Kekaya in the north-west to Ayodhya in the east. Valmiki tells us all human enterprise came to a standstill during the rainy season, accurately describing the heavy precipitation in the fifth millennium BCE, before the monsoon began weakening approximately 2000 years later.

- The Vedic rishis were skilled astronomers, and Valmiki date-stamps at least ten significant events in Rama's life, starting with his birth, giving a detailed description of the precise planetary positions at the time.

---

[4] Saroj Bala has done extensive research on the historical proof of Rama in her book, *Rama Retold with Scientific Evidences*.

When fed into planetarium software (Planetarium Gold or Stellarium), this sky information reveals the specific date when such a formation occurred. Based on this, Rama was born on 10 January 5114 BCE.[5] Other references to astral events can be similarly dated, for example, the solar eclipse described during Rama's war with Khara. The chronology of events dated by the Planetarium Gold software follows Valmiki's exact timeline without any deviation.

Calendar date based on Planetarium software (BCE)	Valmiki Ramayana event consistent with the timeline in the story
10 January 5114	Rama was born in Chaitra
11 January 5114	Bharata was born
4 January 5089	Coronation eve when Rama was twenty-five
7 October 5077	War with Khara when a solar eclipse was viewed at Panchavati/Nashik
3 April 5076	Vali is killed
12 September 5076	Hanuman visits Lanka
14 September 5076	Hanuman returns after burning Lanka
20 September 5076	Vanara army sets forth for Lanka. Lakshmana describes the sky formation
12 October 5076	Vanara army reaches Lanka
4 December 5076	Ravana is killed
2 January 5075	Rama's return to Ayodhya after fourteen years at age thirty-nine

• The genealogy of the Solar dynasty, the Suryavanshis, is well documented and clearly traced, beginning with the first king Ikshavaku, till Rama, and for generations after him. In addition, there are cross-references to

---

[5] Many scholars have agreed on the 5114 BCE date, including Pushkar Bhatnagar, Saroj Bala, D.K. Hari and Hema Hari, and Jayasree Saranathan.

many of the kings in other Vedic texts. For instance, Rama's descendant, Brihadbala, fought in the Mahabharata on the side of the Kauravas in 3139 BCE. While sceptics argue that Valmiki concocted a fictitious family tree, it is far-fetched to believe this is possible. The specific achievements of many kings in the line are cited in multiple accounts, in the proper sequence of their existence, showing consistency across different works.

- It is relevant to note that Al Biruni, who came to India in 1030 with Mahmud Ghazni as a chronicler, documented in his travelogue 'Kitab ul Hind' that Rama, the son of Dasharatha, built the bridge across the ocean from the southern tip of the Indian continent to Lanka.[6] This statement shows that Rama was considered historical.

- The Mughal king Humayun's wife, Hamida Banu, was fascinated by the Ramayana and commissioned a pictorial edition. Her son, Akbar, had it translated into Persian, and minted commemorative coins believing Rama to have been a great monarch who ruled the land, obviously not just a Hindu deity who was a figment of the imagination.[7]

- There is a cultural continuity of Indian customs from Rama's time to the modern-day, including birth, death, marriage and other ceremonies. The citizens of Ayodhya welcomed Rama home with pomp and splendour, and remarkably Deepavali, the festival of lights commemorating his victorious return, is still celebrated every year on the day it occurred, just as the citizens of Ayodhya did millennia ago.

- Versions of Rama's story exist in many countries besides India, including Myanmar, Indonesia, Cambodia, Vietnam, Laos, Philippines, Nepal, Sri Lanka, Thailand, Malaysia, Japan, Mongolia and China. It is unlikely that these reproductions of the Ramayana would have sprung up in admiration of an imaginary figure, and far more credible that the life of a real person inspired them. Notably, Thailand's royal family traces its lineage to Rama, and all the kings still carry his name. In Korea, the royal matrilineal line is believed to go back to Rama's descendant: a princess called Suriratna from Ayodhya.

- In the Indus/Saraswati River basin area, ruins show planned cities like Ayodhya described in the Ramayana: archaeology has unearthed multi-storeyed houses with courtyards constructed neatly in rows, wells, fire altars, granaries, water storage and towns with a brick-lined underground

---

[6] Hari, D.K., and Hari Hema D.K., *Historical Rama*, 2nd edition (Sri Sri Publications Trust, 2011).

[7] Ibid.

drainage system. Birhana, in the Fatehabad district of Haryana, excavated between 2003 and 2006, is the oldest site, dating back as far as 7570 BCE.

Based on data from literary, archaeological and geographical sources, including cultural corroboration, it is evident that the Ramayana is not a myth but the true story of a great man and ancient ancestor of humanity.

Memorable Lines from
the Valmiki Ramayana

'*Those who know dharma say truth is the highest dharma.*'—Book 2, Ayodhyakanda. Ironically, this is said by Kaikeyi to Dasharatha, when trying to persuade him to keep his promise and exile Rama.

'*Happiness is not always secured.*'—Book 2, Ayodhyakanda. Rama says this to Kaikeyi, on seeing his father in a state of dejection when summoned by him on the coronation day.

'*Once Rama gives his word, it is final, and he does not equivocate.*'—Book 2, Ayodhyakanda. Rama to Kaikeyi, promising to keep his father's word.

'*One who has taken the wrong path should be disciplined, even if he is a guru, parent or elder in age or learning.*'—Book 2, Ayodhyakanda. Lakshmana says this to Rama, encouraging him to resist their father's unfair promise to Kaikeyi.

'*Destiny is hard to overcome.*'—Book 2, Ayodhyakanda. Rama to Lakshmana, who rages about the unfairness of Rama's exile.

'*Only the timid and weak leave things to destiny, the valiant who have a strong mind never seek shelter in fate.*'—Book 2, Ayodhyakanda. Lakshmana's response to Rama, when Rama says some events in life occur due to what is preordained, so Kaikeyi and their father should not be blamed.

'*He who, having parted with an excellent elephant, seeks to retain the tether is indeed a fool.*'—Book 2, Ayodhyakanda. Rama says this when Dasharatha wants to send him to the forest equipped with all comforts.

'*A veena is of no use without its strings, and a chariot is useless without wheels. Similarly, a wife who is bereft of her husband cannot be happy even if she has a hundred sons.*'—Book 2, Ayodhyakanda. Sita to Kaushalya, asserting fidelity to her marriage vows and devotion to Rama despite his changed circumstances.

'Grief destroys one's courage, it effaces learning, it eradicates one's everything. There is no enemy greater than grief!'—Book 2, Ayodhyakanda. Kaushalya says this, apologizing to Dasharatha for speaking harshly to him while sorrowing about Rama's exile.

'No life is expunged before the appointed hour.'—Book 2, Ayodhyakanda. Kaushalya says this in grief, wishing for death when Rama leaves and regretting that it does not come before its time.

'There is no deity more powerful than time.'—Book 2, Ayodhyakanda. Bharata to Guha and others, when he sees the humble grass bed where Rama slept at Shringaverapura.

'O blessed lady; a doer surely reaps the fruit of his deeds based on the nature of good or evil he has perpetrated.'—Book 2, Ayodhyakanda. Dasharatha says this to Kaushalya, while narrating his secret about having killed a hermit boy in his youth by mistake.

'The night that has passed does not return.'— Book 2, Ayodhyakanda. Rama to Bharata, trying to convince him that he cannot return to Ayodhya till he finishes his exile, persuading his brother to accept the situation.

'Only a person's conduct and character proclaim whether he is well-born or otherwise, whether he is truly honest or just pretends that he is unblemished.'—Book 2, Ayodhyakanda. Rama chastising Jabali for suggesting that he disregard his father's promise because Dasharatha is no more.

'People are as repelled by a liar as they are by a serpent.'—Book 2, Ayodhyakanda. Rama to Jabali, on the importance of being ethical.

'It is difficult for children to repay the debt owed to their mother and father for the enormous effort put into raising them.'—Book 2, Ayodhyakanda. Rama to Vasishta, stressing the need to uphold his father's pledge in response to his plea to return to Ayodhya.

'Splendour would sooner depart from the moon, nay the Himalaya Mountain would sooner shed its snow, and the ocean would sooner transgress its limits than I shall violate my father's pledge.'—Book 2, Ayodhyakanda. Rama to Bharata, when insisting on keeping his word though Bharata begs him to take back the throne.

'Prosperity flows from dharma; dharma is the source of happiness, and by following dharma, one gets everything. Dharma is the essence of this world.'—Book 3, Aranyakanda. Sita to Rama, advising him against unnecessary violence when he agreed to help the rishis by exterminating the Rakshasas.

'He who oppresses other created beings, who is hard-hearted and perpetrates sinful deeds cannot survive even if he is the ruler of the three worlds . . . The perpetrator of a sinful deed inevitably reaps its terrible consequence when the time comes just as a tree bears fruit in the appropriate season.'—Book 3, Aranyakanda. Rama, issuing a warning to Khara, who had spent his life torturing innocent sages, that his actions were about to catch up with him.

'There is no greater sin than coveting another man's wife.'—Book 3, Aranyakanda. Marichi to Ravana, when he tries to dissuade the latter from his plan of abducting Sita.

'It is easy to find those who speak agreeable words to your liking, but it is rare to find one who speaks for your good even though it may be unpalatable.'—Maricha to Ravana, pleading with him to heed sensible advice.

'One should only lift what one can carry. One should only eat what one can digest. Similarly, why perform an act that earns neither merit nor glory, and only costs you dearly?'—Book 3, Aranyakanda. Jatayu to Ravana, when he tries to reason with the Rakshasa king to return Sita.

'One who is bent on courting death does not take kindly to the wise advice of well-wishers.'—Book 3, Aranyakanda. Sita to Ravana, telling him to return her to Rama to avoid provoking reprisal in the form of his death.

'Suffering is natural with regard to human beings.'—Book 3, Aranyakanda. Lakshmana to Rama, telling him that everyone is afflicted by sorrow at some time or the other in life, so suffering must be borne with fortitude.

'There is no greater strength than enthusiasm. There is nothing unattainable by those who are determined, no matter how difficult.'—Book 4, Kishkindhakanda. Lakshmana to Rama, who is despondent about losing Sita.

'Whether it be in times of happiness or sorrow, a friend is one who provides support.'—Book 4, Kishkindhakanda. Sugriva to Rama, assuring Rama of his friendship when he hears the story of Sita's abduction.

'The vilest among men is he who, having pledged his word to return a favour to someone who has helped him in the past, disappoints him by forgetting his

promise.'—Book 4, Kishkindhakanda. Rama to Lakshmana, when he sends him to remind Sugriva to follow through on his promise to help find Sita.

'There is no atonement for one who is ungrateful!'—Book 4, Kishkindhakanda. Lakshmana to Sugriva, admonishing him for not keeping his promise.

'To err is human; there is none who has not erred at some point.'—Book 4, Kishkindhakanda. Sugriva to Lakshmana, apologizing for his delay in starting the search for Sita.

'Having an untiring zeal, skill to perform the job and an unflagging spirit in the face of difficulty is the path to success.'—Book 4, Kishkindhakanda. Angada to his team members, who were losing heart in their mission.

'One should not allow one's mind to be overcome by melancholy. Despondency is very destructive and kills a man like an angry serpent kills a child.'—Book 4, Kishkindhakanda. Angada to the Vanaras, when they are faced with the vast ocean that appears impossible to cross.

'Compassion is the highest virtue.'—Book 5, Sundarakanda. Sita says this to Hanuman, when she asks him to tell Rama not to delay in rescuing her.

'One who is angry loses the power to discriminate between right and wrong both in speech and action. There is no crime an enraged person is incapable of committing or abuse that he is incapable of uttering.'—Book 5, Sundarakanda. Hanuman to himself, when he muses on his rashness in burning Lanka without securing Sita's safety.

'Like a flowing river, what has gone will never come back.'—Book 5, Sundarakanda. Ravana to Sita, when persuading her to submit to him.

'Wise men say victory is achieved through good counsel.'—Book 6, Yudhakanda. Ravana to his ministers, when he asks for their advice following Hanuman's destruction of Lanka.

'Even when veiled, one's innermost thoughts reflect on one's face, and they are hard to conceal no matter how hard one tries.'—Book 6, Yudhakanda. Hanuman to Rama, when Hanuman argues in favour of accepting Vibhishana.

'Those who are truly valiant do not roar in vain, like thundering clouds bereft of rain.'—Book 6, Yudhakanda. Kumbhakarna to Ravana as he sets out to face Rama.

'One should never underestimate the power of the enemy.'—Book 6, Yudhakanda. Vibhishana to Ravana, when the Rakshasa ministers boast about Ravana's superiority over Rama.

'The tears of virtuous women do not fall on the ground in vain.'—Book 6, Yudhakanda. Mandodari, when she laments Ravana's misdoings while weeping over his body.

'The wise should never undertake any action that causes harm to the world.'—Book 7, Uttarakanda. Rama to Bharata, when he takes his advice and decides not to perform the Rajasuya sacrifice.

The Sixteen Attributes of Rama
Mentioned by Valmiki

1- **Gunavan**: Principled/virtuous.

2- **Viryavan**: Valorous.

3- **Dharmajnya**: An upholder of dharma.

4- **Kritajanya**: Grateful.

5- **Satyavakya**: Truthful.

6- **Dhridavrata**: Resolute/determined.

7- **Charitrena Cha Yukta**: One of stellar character.

8- **Sarva Bhuteshu Hita**: One who thinks about the whole world's welfare.

9- **Vidhvan**: Learned and scholarly.

10- **Samartha**: Capable/adept.

11- **Eka Priyadarshana**: Singularly good-looking.

12- **Atmavan**: One who has self-control and is hence courageous.

13- **Jita Krodha**: One who is not prone to anger or has control over anger.

14- **Dyutiman**: One who radiates brilliance.

15- **Anasuyaka**: Never jealous or fault-finding.

16- **Bibhyatideva**: Feared even by the Devas when provoked in war. Someone not to be taken lightly.

The Vedic Concept of God

The popular notion that the Vedic people were polytheists who worshipped many gods cannot be further from the truth. Such a simplistic impression comes from ignorance of Vedic philosophy, which sees God as one universally present supreme reality that expresses itself in a plurality of forms. 'Ekam Sat Vipra Bahuda Vadanti: God is one, whom the wise call by many names.' (Rig Veda 1.164.46)

The most lucid explanation of the Vedic concept of God, referred to as Brahman (though the name is unimportant), is found in the Taittiriya Upanishad. In verse 2.1, the Upanishad says: Brahman, is 'Satyam—reality, Gyanam—knowledge, Anantam—infinity.' The Veda further asserts that the one who realizes this achieves everything because, 'The knower of Brahman achieves the highest.'

So, who or what is Brahman?

Brahman is pure consciousness. The word Brahman means that which expands limitlessly, so it is a name attributed to infinite consciousness. Brahman is not an entity; it does not have a gender, nor is it constrained to a specific abode, yet we constantly feel its presence. Brahman is existence, the ultimate reality of the universe. Since this power is not an object, it is not visible, but we perceive it by its expression, continually experiencing it as awareness.

How then can we describe this elusive infinite existence? Brahman is identified by three qualities—'Satyam, Gyanam and Anantam'—and each of these enigmatic words is loaded with meaning.

Satyam means reality or truth. The Upanishads say that Brahman (God) is the singular truth behind the Universe. All creation exists within this reality (Sat) as an expression of Brahman. Just as individual waves have a tentative form but are inseparable and undifferentiated from the ocean, so too, every creature emanates from Brahman and exists only because

445

of Brahman. Simply put, the glory of the supreme reality is seen in all beings and every splendorous manifestation of nature. The beauty of the sunset, bubbling brooks, verdant forests and the marvel that transforms a caterpillar into a butterfly or a tiny seed into a giant tree are nothing but expressions of Brahman. Everything we see around us (including ourselves) borrows existence from Brahman/pure consciousness. A wave cannot exist without the ocean; similarly, nothing in the world is independent of Brahman, and all life is but an appearance of Brahman. Differences are superficial as divinity lies in all matter equally despite its multiple manifestations. Vedanta uses the analogy of gold and ornaments to illustrate that creation is inseparable from the creator. Brahman is like gold, which is the basis of any piece of jewellery made of it, whether a bangle, necklace or ring. Although each object has a specific design and purpose, the underlying substance, gold, is the same in its various forms. All are created from gold; when melted, they dissolve back into gold.

Similarly, Brahman is the ultimate reality, and all matter is but an image, just like the ornaments or a reflection in a mirror that have no separate existence. Like gold ornaments, we see the one consciousness expressed in numerous names and forms, all derived from the same essence. Despite the apparent diversity of matter around us due to the manifesting power of Brahman called Maya, a oneness of spirit or unity of existence binds all creation. As the Chandogya Upanishad 3.14.1 says, 'This Universe comes forth from Brahman, exists in Brahman, and will return to Brahman. Verily all is Brahman.'

Anantam means limitless or endless. Brahman is infinite, therefore not restricted by space, time or form. Brahman is omnipresent and does not occupy a particular location or area, which means God is everywhere. Brahman is eternal, not constrained by time, and ever-present without beginning or end. Since Brahman is not confined to a specific form or shape that differentiates one material thing from another, God pervades the world without object limitation. Therefore, since there is nothing apart from Brahman, all creation is one with Brahman. The first line of the Isha Upanishad puts this beautifully: 'Ishavasiyam Idam Sarvam'. Consciousness pervades the entire universe. It is the imperishable force within all humans, animals, plants, the power behind the sun, the moon and all aspects of nature. If creation is like a string of pearls, the thread is Brahman.

The non-duality between Brahman and creation is expressed in four Mahavakyas or great aphorisms in the Upanishads:

1. **Prajnanam Brahman:** Consciousness is Brahman. Rig Veda, Aitareya Upanishad 3.3

2. **Tat Tvam Asi:** You are that (Brahman). Sama Veda, Chandogya Upanishad 6.8.7
3. **Ayam Atma Brahman:** The Self is Brahman. Atharva Veda, Mandukya Upanishad 1.2
4. **Aham Brahmasmi:** I am Brahman. Yajur Veda, Brihadaranyaka Upanishad 1.4.10

Drawing from the conclusion that no part of creation is independent of Brahman, the Vedas say the imperishable inner Self, the sense of existence within, called the Atman, is no different from pure consciousness or God. Therefore, the body is merely a reflection of consciousness and not the actual reality. It is simply an instrument of consciousness, a tool that provides the means to experience life. We tend to identify ourselves entirely with our physical form because we are unaware of the Atman, but we actually have a cosmic identity beyond the mind or body that is unborn, unchanging and undying. Though the Atman/Consciousness/God cannot be seen, it reveals itself as the light illuminating every experience, even the most mundane. In Vedic philosophy, enlightenment is defined as shedding attachment to the individual body-mind complex and identifying with the sentience within. Therefore, a spiritually evolved person sees divinity as the expression of consciousness, identical for every creature, whether it be a gnat or a human being. The namaste greeting symbolizes this view, saying, 'The divinity in me bows to the divinity in you.' Since all creation is essentially believed to be a manifestation of the One, unity of existence and universal harmony is the key message of the Vedas.

Gyanam means knowledge, the third attribute of Brahman, cosmic intelligence. All knowledge is based on consciousness, the unseen source of all perception, as there can be no experience without it. Therefore, consciousness powers our understanding and is the root of wisdom. Vedanta refers to it as the knower through which the world is known. Just as we know we have eyesight because we can see, the proof of inner consciousness is awareness. The Vedas maintain that realizing the true non-dual Self by negating individual ego, seeing oneself in every being and every being as oneself is attaining Brahman. This awareness of the deepest inner self as divine is the highest wisdom, as through it, worldliness is shed, and the ultimate bliss of becoming one with the Universe is achieved. Vedic Philosophy believes that actual knowledge is never gleaned through blind faith, so the path to God-realization (Brahmagyana) is through 'sravanam, mananam, nidhidhyasan': listening, analysing logically and finally experiencing for oneself.

'The knower of that Supreme Brahman verily becomes Brahman.'
Mundaka Upanishad 3.2.9

'Brahman is not grasped by the eye, nor by speech, not by other senses,
nor by penance or good works. The mind becomes pure through the clarity
of knowledge; thereupon in meditation, one beholds that (Brahman) that is
indivisible.' Mundaka Upanishad 3.1.8

'Like the butter hidden in milk, pure consciousness resides in every
being; that ought to be constantly churned out with the churning rod of the
mind.' Amritabindu Upanishad

The Devas should not be confused with God, nor are they gods or demi-
gods as often mistakenly described. They are beings of light, elemental powers
symbolizing the numerous aspects of the supreme consciousness. Brahman
can be invoked in any of these manifestations as each is an expression of the
same, all-pervading Paramatma/God. He who discards his limited identity
and understands that every facet of creation represents the whole, seeing
divinity in all creatures, is a pandit.

Brahma, Vishnu and Mahesh/Shiva are symbolic representations of the
cosmic functions of creation, sustenance and dissolution. Brahma is pictured
as the creator whose feminine counterpart, Saraswati, symbolizes knowledge/
learning. Preservation is visualized in the form of Vishnu alongside Lakshmi,
symbolic of prosperity. Shiva represents dissolution, and his consort Parvati
(Prakriti/Maya), stands for the manifesting power of consciousness, but all
are the same Brahman, none intended to be viewed separately.

Similarly, other Devas, too, represent various aspects of Brahman.

Brihaspati	Scholarship
Indra	Rain
Varuna and Mitra	Water
Yama	Death
Agni	Fire
Vayu	Air
Surya	Sun
Kubera	Wealth
Vishwakarma	Building and engineering
Ashwini twins	Medicine

In Vedic philosophy, Brahman is one, and everything is Brahman, so the formless supreme consciousness can be worshipped in any image favoured by a devotee. Since it is difficult for most to focus on the concept of unmanifested infinity not perceived by the senses, a deity serves as an icon of worship, an object to anchor the mind and assist concentration on something difficult to grasp without a tangible aid. Colonizers who subjugated India over the ages demonized idol worship because they considered equating a stone with God abhorrent. However, their disgust resulted from a gross misunderstanding of the truth, as the very basis of Vedic belief is that the reality called God cannot be objectified. It rises above petty differences to state that we do not have a limited identity; each of us is an aspect of the cosmos. The idol functions only as a symbol of divinity, just as a flag today is symbolic of the country it represents. When we salute the flag, we honour the nationhood it denotes, not the cloth.

Summary of the Vedic concept of God:

- Belief in one all-encompassing infinite divinity, or universal consciousness/God, from which all creation emanates regardless of race, religion or even species. Just as we cannot attribute the terms 'yours' or 'mine' to the sun, which shines on everyone alike, there can be no concept of 'your God' or 'my God' based on different religions. In the words of the Maha Upanishad, 'Vasudaiva Kutumbakam': The world is one family. The Vedas advocate that all beings are united in the brotherhood of oneness, so a realized person sees Brahman everywhere and in everything. 'Ekam Evadvitiyam Brahman': Brahman is one without a second (Infinity is only one). Chandogya Upanishad 6.2.2.

- Vedic philosophy is inherently secular; going a step further, it is not just tolerant but inclusive of different forms of worship as equally relevant. There are no 'others' or heretic non-believers. On the contrary, diversity is embraced because of the fundamental belief that infinite consciousness manifests in various shapes, each one worthy. For this reason, the word secular was not initially included in the Indian Constitution. It was deemed unnecessary in a Hindu-majority country where the religion itself is intrinsically secular, and the plurality of worship is respected.

- God is not constrained by the dictates of a particular religion. In the Vedic viewpoint, all sincere prayers fall at the feet of the same supreme consciousness, no matter the form in which that power is envisaged.

This recognition of one reality with countless manifestations, each pointing to the self-same Almighty, obviates the need for conversion. Just as all rivers ultimately flow into the ocean, so too do all virtuous paths lead to the same truth. Therefore, based on the conviction that all righteous ways lead to the same place, the concept of religious imperialism is absent. Thus, the names and forms in which we envisage God become irrelevant, as finally, they refer to one consciousness that does not change depending on the lens through which it is viewed.

- Rituals performed venerating a deity may appear irreligious to an uninformed onlooker, but these are never meant to be directed at the physical object itself, but the supreme consciousness it represents. Deities are a way of worshipping the unmanifest through the manifest. The great rishis may have been able to meditate on an infinite formless reality, but it is not easy for an ordinary person to contemplate what the senses cannot readily perceive.

- Faith in God is not demanded because God is realized through introspection and personal spiritual discovery, not through religious dogma, unquestioning belief or fear of hell. Philosophical inquiry is encouraged in Vedanta. Most of the Upanishads are in the form of a dialogue with a student asking questions. Scepticism is considered an essential stage in spiritual growth, never frowned upon because doubt is necessary for the evolution from ignorance to enlightenment. In Vedic philosophy, God is not a jealous entity that demands blind faith or fanatical following, but a sublime power to be experienced through realization.

- Therefore, the Vedic guru only illuminates the path to God realization and never forces his student to accept his teachings without individual conviction, as genuine knowledge comes from self-discovery, not imposed ideas. The Vedas do not prescribe a mandated path to liberation, as every individual is a spiritual seeker on a personal quest. In the words of the Atharva Veda, 'Do not be led by others, awaken your own mind, amass your own experience, and decide for yourself your own path.'

What Is Dharma?

Dharma comes from the root 'dhri', which carries the sense of upholding. So, it means that by which society is sustained, preventing it from disintegrating. Dharma is not a religion. The Vedic people did not follow religion as we understand it today; instead, they had a philosophy of noble living called Sanatana Dharma that guided their actions. While the English word for Sanatana is 'everlasting', there is no good translation for Dharma, though it is loosely considered righteousness.

Sanatana Dharma has no beginning defined by a founder as it essentially espouses timelessly held values. These principles of harmonious living are universally accepted ethics by all people regardless of race or religion, so strictly, Sanatana Dharma cannot be defined as a religious faith. It is not an exclusive club of followers, as its central precept is the concept of unity enshrined in the Vedas. This idea of oneness comes from the belief that there is one supreme reality, Brahman, and every animate and inanimate object is an expression of that truth. Since all creation is viewed as part of the same infinite, formless, nameless, indefinable consciousness, all aspects of the Universe are seen as inextricably bound together in a web of interdependence.

Following the path of dharma involves a holistic attitude, casting aside selfishness and conducting all actions for the universal good, rather than only for one's egotistical satisfaction. The Ramayana is a beautiful treatise on Sanatana Dharma and explores its intricacies throughout the narrative. For instance, the repeated references to environmental protection stress the importance of coexistence and respecting the laws of nature for overall peace and harmony. Thus, the destruction of forests or pollution of the Earth is against dharma, as such selfish actions disturb nature's balance, resulting in climate change and dangerous consequences, like storms or droughts.

Sanatana Dharma is eternally relevant, because it is not restricted to social norms that inevitably vary through the ages, but deals with enduring principles as valid today as they were yesterday. There are no commandments associated with its practice, only broad ethical standards advocating empathy and selflessness in the quest for universal well-being.

The Manusmriti, an ancient guide to social conduct, mentions ten guidelines for dharmic action. These are:

1	**Dhriti**	Inner strength, patience or fortitude in handling life's challenges
2	**Kshama**	Forgiveness of wrongs done to one
3	**Damah**	Self-disciple and not falling prey to uncontrolled desires
4	**Asteya**	Honesty. Not taking anything that does not belong to you
5	**Shaucha**	Cleanliness. Purity of mind and body
6	**Indriya Nigraha**	Control of the senses rather than being ruled by them
7	**Dhi**	Discriminative reasoning power. The ability to be judicious
8	**Vidya**	Spiritual knowledge
9	**Satyam**	Truthfulness
10	**Akrodha**	Control of anger

Actions performed keeping these principles in mind tend to be meritorious. However, they are only recommendations because life can be complex, often presenting conflicting dharmas. Sanatana Dharma emphasizes conscience over religious mandates. For instance, although telling the truth is considered righteous, there may be occasions when lying is dharma. To give an example from recent history, in Nazi Germany, if a Christian were hiding Jews and the Gestapo came knocking at the door, telling a lie to save innocent lives would be dharma, and paradoxically, telling the truth, in this case, would be adharma. Therefore, the right thing to do is based on the situation, not prescribed rules. In the Ramayana, we see many ethical dilemmas, occasions where conflicting dharmas are depicted, notably in the slaying of Tataka, the killing of Vali, the abandonment of Sita and the Shambuka episode.

A Summary of Sanatana Dharma:

1. Sanatana Dharma is not a religion but a spiritual philosophy that arises from the Vedas, advocating timeless values based on the unity of all creation.

2. It has no founder, rigid laws, or particular form of God that must be followed to remain a member.

3. There is no formal initiation process for non-believers to be converted to Sanatana Dharma or excommunication because it encompasses all humanity regardless of individual belief. In this aspect, while being the oldest in the world, Vedic philosophy is the most forward-thinking, including everyone under its umbrella, irrespective of personal faith. Furthermore, followers are seekers on a spiritual journey; they are not believers in diktats laid down as sacrosanct by any organization, so there is no concept of proselytizing or conversion by coercion or allurement.

4. Dharma has an expansive meaning because dharmic action is highly nuanced. It varies based on context and is not easily definable.

5. Practising Sanatana Dharma in every action makes a person gradually evolve to a higher level of consciousness. It is believed that virtuous living through purity of behaviour frees one from an unhealthy attachment to the body. Such a person is a 'jivanmukta', one who identifies with the indwelling Atman and is, therefore, always at peace, liberated from suffering during life. Eventually, this leads to moksha, freedom from the endless cycle of rebirth.

6. Sanatana Dharma involves individual self-realization through contemplation and introspection. It does not demand unquestioning faith, as true spirituality comes from acquiring knowledge, not following a rigid belief system. Therefore, heresy, apostasy and blasphemy are alien to its practice.

7. Contrary to popular opinion, Sanatana Dharma is not polytheistic in outlook, as it believes that one consciousness/God envelopes the universe. The One, infinite, all-knowing God—true existence, all-pervading consciousness and the source of eternal bliss (Sat Chit Ananda)— appears in countless forms. The peace invocation of the Isha Upanishad expresses this sentiment beautifully: 'Om poornam adah poornam idam,

poornaat poornam udachyate, poornasya poornam aadaay, poornam evaa vashishyate.' Consciousness (God) is infinite, and all creation is infinite (flowing from consciousness/God) because taking a part of infinity does not diminish infinity.

8. The essential message of Santana Dharma is peaceful coexistence and harmonious living with all manifestations of Brahman/consciousness, including plants, animals and Mother Earth. Therefore, a person who practises Sanatana Dharma has no contempt for anyone else based on the form in which they see God, and hence has no motive to hate others.

The Doctrine of Karma and Rebirth

The word 'karma' tends to evoke the idea of punishment. Although retribution may be an aspect of karma, the term does not mean punishment, as popularly believed. Karma comes from the root 'kri', which means to act or do, and translates as acts or deeds. In the Vedic view, every action (karma) has a corresponding repercussion (karma), whether good or bad. Therefore, karma is both the cause and the consequence of exercising our free will. The results of conscious decisions made in the past shape our destiny perforce. This doctrine of natural justice and accountability is a hallmark of all Indic religions—Hinduism, Buddhism, Jainism and Sikhism. Karma is the inevitable outcome of a self-created fate, so it places a sense of responsibility on the doer, differentiating it from fatalism. According to dharma, virtuous actions lead to pleasant experiences, and wicked actions conducted out of adharma result in future unhappiness.

Karma, both good and bad, is associated only with human beings because it results from the individual determination that drives decisions and deeds. Animals do not accrue karma because they act purely on instinct and lack the discernment to exercise choices in their behaviour. For instance, a tiger cannot choose to adopt ahimsa and become a vegetarian as a human being can. Since individual actions generate karma, we decide our destiny ourselves; it is not randomly foisted on us by some higher power. Specific positive and negative experiences are inevitable in life as our own earlier actions have predetermined them. However, the destiny we face is not associated with powerlessness, as we have autonomy in dealing with current events to shape future karma. Self-created destiny and free will intertwine in a lifetime, but ultimately, we are responsible for our fortune, with only ourselves to hold accountable. The Vedas leave no doubt about this.

'The Atman (the true self) is immortal. Every mortal body is enlivened by the Atman in accordance with its previous actions (karma).' Rig Veda 1.164.30

'The immortal Atman is ceaselessly associated with the mortal body in every birth and rebirth that results from our own actions. We, humans, have comprehended the one (physical body) but have not understood the other (the Atman free from the body).' Rig Veda 1.164.38

'Man eats what he cooks. That is, he reaps what he sows.' Atharva Veda 12.3.48

There are four aspects to karma:

1. Sanchita karma is the entire store of karma from all past lives. Quite literally, our accumulated baggage!
2. Prarabhda karma refers to the specific experiences chosen to be experienced and expiated in the current lifetime. It is the purpose for which birth in the present body occurred.
3. Kriyaman karma consists of the new karma created in the ongoing life while dealing with the prarabhda karma accompanying birth.
4. Agami karma is the karma accrued in the current birth that adds to accumulated sanchit karma to be experienced in the future.

In Vedic philosophy, heaven and hell are transitory; they are temporary realms of existence between births, experienced in proportion to the dharma or adharma accumulated during a lifetime. Therefore, the rishis taught that the spirit's ultimate quest is not heaven but moksha. It is to exist permanently in a disembodied divine state liberated from the endless cycle of birth and death, only achieved when all karma is shed. Till then, there is no escape from the bondage of rebirth. The Vedic goal is to expiate past karma without creating new karma. However, spirituality and worldly life are not mutually exclusive, so becoming an ascetic or retiring from society is unnecessary to avoid generating binding karma. Cultivating a saintly attitude while continuing one's routine work is possible. In fact, the Vedas teach that abandoning one's duty creates a karmic debt.

The path to liberation is available to everyone by adopting an attitude of Karmayoga in performing daily duties. Karmayoga is not merely following rituals and religious obligations like going to a temple or saying prayers dutifully. It is non-egotistical, unselfish behaviour born from the belief that Brahman pervades the universe.[1] 'The wise man beholds all beings in the

---

[1] 'The wise innocent man, engrossed in selfless service to mankind, is ever dear to God. He attains oneness with God.' Rig Veda 6.2.2

self and the self in all beings; for that reason, he does not hate anyone (Isha Upanishad 6). If this concept of universal oneness influences every action, it is impossible to commit adharma and create bad karma. In upholding dharma at every instance, Rama is a shining example of a Karmayogi, renouncing the desire for personal gain and always putting the collective good ahead of himself. In his selfless service and personal sacrifice, he lived spiritually amidst the busyness of life. 'Those who give charity and look after the welfare of others are ever happy.' Sama Veda 285.

The Purpose of Human Existence—Purushartha

Purushartha is an essential concept in Sanatana Dharma. It refers to the four goals of human existence expounded in the Vedas:

1	**Dharma**	Righteous conduct that brings about peace and harmony
2	**Artha**	Material prosperity and economic security
3	**Kama**	Fulfilment of desires, including sensual enjoyment
4	**Moksha**	Liberation from karma and therefore from rebirth

In the Vedic view, the ultimate aim of human life is to achieve moksha, liberation from rebirth. The endless cycle of birth and death is bondage, marked by suffering, and freedom from that cycle is the attainment of eternal bliss. Rebirth occurs in one physical body after another as part of spiritual evolution, to learn lessons acquired only through experiences in an embodied form.

However, the Vedas recognize that economic goals and material pleasures are natural endeavours that drive human existence. Therefore, they do not propound renouncing the world but rather living a balanced life, as prosperity and fulfilment of desires are essential for a robust society. Instead of embarking on formal asceticism, doing one's duty while mentally giving up selfish desires is considered the path to spiritual growth. Thus, Vedic philosophy sees no sin in aspiring for wealth (artha) and pleasure (kama) for a limited period, during the stage of Grihastha, if such pursuit is in sync with dharma. However, when kama or artha are selfishly chased solely for personal benefit, the balance of existence is disrupted, resulting in destruction. For instance, if a few trees are cut down to build a settlement and new saplings are planted in their place, it is an example of pursuing artha with dharma.

But, on the other hand, if the earth is denuded of forests on a large scale without restitution, the greed of such selfish action creates binding karma.

Righteous action while remembering oneself as a manifestation of pure consciousness—Aham Brahmasmi—leads to harmonious living, as upholding dharma while pursuing artha and kama paves the way to achieving moksha. Conversely, striving for artha and kama without dharma chains us in karmic shackles. Vedic philosophy emphasizes that economic prosperity and sensual desires must always be reined in by the tenets of dharma to ensure the purity of action, spiritual growth and ultimate liberation. Ravana demonstrates this lesson as an example of someone who pursued desire without dharma and therefore perished.

Yoga

Yoga means 'union'. The word is derived from 'yuj' which means to join or unite, and therefore, refers to connecting with the cosmic consciousness, merging the finite with the infinite to experience ultimate bliss. The ancient sage Patanjali compiled the essence of yoga derived from Vedic philosophy in his famous Yoga Sutras. These pithy threads of knowledge comprise 195 aphorisms that illuminate the path to attaining a higher state of consciousness. Patanjali describes eight steps to achieving divine connection, becoming one with the ultimate reality and freeing oneself from human limitations. During the yogic state of samadhi, the living being attains Kaivalya—aloneness, total detachment from the material world, merging with the cosmic intelligence to experience divine ecstasy, the achievement of heaven on earth. The body is disconnected from the external world; instead, there is full inner awareness. 'The pure soul, cleansed through the control of breath and meditation, soon attains salvation and becomes one with God through yogic samadhi.' Atharva Veda 6.51.1

Unfortunately, yoga is mainly associated with physical fitness today, though it is far more than an exercise regimen. Yoga is a process of spiritual wellness that unites the human being with the cosmic reality. It is both the means of achieving this union and the state of meditation in which it is experienced. Patanjali's sutras help to rid over-identification and attachment with the body-mind complex, the cause of suffering, by attaining a state of higher consciousness.

The eight steps to achieving Yogic Samadhi are:

1. **Yama**: Restraints—Five disciplines in behaviour

1	**Ahimsa**	Choosing the path of least violence
2	**Satya**	Truthfulness
3	**Asteya**	Honesty. Not taking anything that does not belong to you
4	**Brahmacharya**	Continence or control over sexual impulses
5	**Aparigraha**	Not hoarding out of greed

2. **Niyama**: Five personal observances

1	**Shaucha**	Cleanliness. Purity of mind and body
2	**Santosha**	Contentment
3	**Tapas**	Discipline. Austerity
4	**Svadhyaya**	Introspection
5	**Ishwara Pranidhana**	Contemplation on the higher power of universal consciousness

3. **Asana**: Mastering physical postures to control the body as a prerequisite to stilling the mind.
4. **Pranayam**: Practising breath control, essential for calming the mind and effective concentration.
5. **Pratyahara**: Sense withdrawal; achieving command over the five sense organs by drawing attention inward.
6. **Dharana**: Focused concentration. Maintaining a continuous stream of thought by fixing the mind on an object, often a preferred deity, but it could be anything else. A mantra is usually chanted to assist mental attention.
7. **Dhyana**: Complete absorption in meditation. This intense single-pointed focus is only possible when the mind is ready and cleansed of impurity through stages one to six.
8. **Samadhi**: Enlightenment attained through a transcendental state where the oneness of being and integration with all creation is experienced. Samadhi is disconnecting from time, matter and space to connect fully

with the supreme consciousness. It is divine ecstasy where the individual ego is wholly effaced, resulting in union with God. In the words of the Chandogya Upanishad, 'There is no joy in the finite; there is joy only in the infinite.'

Patanjali describes the state of yoga as 'Chitta Vrithi Nirodha', where all the kleshas/impediments to spirituality are removed. The mind is decluttered of vrittis—impressions (formed over lifetimes) that impede divine spiritual union.

The five kleshas are as follows:

1	**Avidya**	Delusion. Ignorance of the oneness of creation
2	**Asmita**	Egoism, or notion of self that arises from over-identification with the individual body-mind complex
3	**Raga**	Intense attachments
4	**Dwesha**	Intense aversions
5	**Abhinivesha**	Obstinacy in not seeing the truth of the inner Self as eternal, which results in clinging to life and a fear of death

In yoga, detachment from the physical flesh-and-bone body, becoming established in the indwelling Spirit is a blessed state. Attainment of this level of higher consciousness causes altered brain functioning, as we see in the rishis, who achieved miraculous powers through samadhi. However, it must be clarified that their supernatural abilities were not the purpose of attaining samadhi but a natural outcome of connecting with the ultimate reality.

Who Were the Vedic People?

Voltaire said, 'I am convinced everything has come down to us from the banks of the Ganges—astronomy, astrology, metempsychosis, etc . . . It is very important to note that some 2500 years ago, Pythagoras went from Samos to the Ganges to learn geometry . . . But he would certainly not have undertaken such a strange journey had the reputation of the Brahmins' science not been long established in Europe.'[1] He was not alone in this view; like him, the world had accepted India as the centre of knowledge and the source of wisdom for centuries. But then, suddenly, the identity of the Vedic people came into question in the nineteenth century when colonialists noticed that Greek and Latin shared a commonality with Sanskrit. Moreover, they discovered Sanskrit was of greater antiquity and the root of many European languages.

The prevailing milieu of imperialism automatically led to the assumption that this rich mother language must have had a Western origin, and like English, was imported into India at some point in time. As a result, it was speculated that Sanskrit, Greek and Latin were sister languages that developed from a common 'Proto Indo-European' origin. This hypothetical source language was assumed to have been spoken by a people in a homeland around the Russian Steppes before they split up, with some going west to Europe and others south-east towards Persia and India. The thesis asserted race based on language, an impossible deduction on linguistics alone without supporting evidence from other fields of study. Given the paucity of any factual corroboration, the theory's genesis appeared to stem from racial arrogance that prevented colonizers from accepting that a highly refined language such as Sanskrit could have originated in the East, from where its influence spread elsewhere.

---

[1] Voltaire, 'Lettres sur l'origine des sciences et sur celle des peuples de l'Asie' (Letter of 15 December 1775).

Nevertheless, Sanskrit and the Vedic culture's Western origin gained widespread acceptance. Soon, it was universally acknowledged without question and even internalized by Indians since the ruling power controlled the narrative. Today, new analytic tools have spurred a raging debate on the subject, but despite the preponderance of evidence to prove otherwise, the core of this outdated belief is still broadly accepted. One school maintains that the Vedic people were foreigners who replaced India's culture, while the other insists that they were indigenous to the Indian civilization.

The notion of the Western origin of Sanskrit emerged when a British administrator named William Jones travelled to Calcutta in 1780. Since he was a judge, he began to study the language to understand native Hindu law. Jones was a linguist and an accomplished scholar in Greek and Latin. When he delved into Sanskrit, he was surprised by the excellence of its grammar and remarked, 'The Sanscrit language, whatever be its antiquity, is of a wonderful structure; more perfect than the Greek, more copious than the Latin, and more exquisitely refined than either, yet bearing to both of them a stronger affinity, both in the roots of verbs and the forms of grammar, than could possibly have been produced by accident; so strong indeed, that no philologer could examine them all three, without believing them to have sprung from some common source, which, perhaps, no longer exists; there is a similar reason, though not quite so forcible, for supposing that both the Gothic and the Celtic, though blended with a very different idiom, had the same origin with the Sanscrit; and the old Persian might be added to the same family.' The description of the Sanskrit language as 'exquisitely refined' was spot on. Sanskrit, or more correctly Samskritam (a combination of samyak—well/proper and kritam—done), means refined language. This realization marked the beginning of Western interest in Sanskrit and correspondingly, in the origin of the Vedic people.

In 1847, the British East India Company hired a philologist, Max Mueller, to translate the Vedas specifically to make the Hindu intelligentsia dismiss them as barbaric, backward and fanciful. The hope was that the changed attitude of a few influential groups would soon spread throughout Indian society, liberating it from its perceived paganism. Mueller was not a missionary but seemed to have a religious zeal. We realize this intent in his letters. He wrote to his wife: ' . . . I feel convinced, though I shall not live to see it, that this edition of mine and the translation of the Veda will hereafter tell to a great extent on the fate of India, and on the growth of millions of souls in that country. It is the root of their religion, and to show them what that root is, I feel sure, the only way of uprooting all that has sprung from it during the last 3,000 years.' (Oxford, 9 December 1867)

Along the same lines, Mueller wrote to the theologian Chevalier Bunsen, 'India is much riper for Christianity than Rome or Greece were at the time of St Paul. The rotten tree has for some time had artificial supports . . . For the good of this struggle, I should like to lay down my life, or at least to lend my hand to bring about this struggle . . . I do not at all like to go to India as a missionary; that makes one dependent on the parsons . . . I should like to live for ten years quite quietly and learn the language, try to make friends, and see whether I was fit to take part in a work, by means of which the old mischief of Indian priestcraft could be overthrown and the way opened for the entrance of simple Christian teaching . . . ' (25 August 1856)

The disdain for Vedic philosophy with which Mueller embarked on his translation of the Vedas is apparent.

'The ancient religion of India is doomed, and if Christianity does not step in, whose fault will it be?' (Written to the Secretary of State for India, the Duke of Argyll, 16 December 1868)

'The worship of Shiva or Vishnu and the other popular deities, is of the same, nay, in many cases of a more degraded and savage character than the worship, of Jupiter, Apollo and Minerva; it belongs to a stratum of thought which is long buried beneath our feet, it may live on like the lion and the tiger but the mere air of free thought and civilized life will extinguish it.' (Westminster Lectures on Missions, December 1873)

Excerpts from Mueller's letters express his opinion that the culture of the Aryans brought by earlier European conquest sorely needed replacement. In a communication to the Duke of Argyll, he wrote, 'India has been conquered once, but India must be conquered again, and that second conquest should be a conquest by education. Much has been done for education of late, but if the funds were tripled and quadrupled, that would hardly be enough . . . A new national literature may spring up, impregnated with Western ideas, yet retaining its native spirit and character . . . A new national literature will bring with it a new national life, and new moral vigour. As to religion, that will take care of itself. The missionaries have done far more than they themselves seem to be aware of.'

With this mindset, Mueller propounded the famous Aryan Invasion Theory (AIT) in the mid-nineteenth century, based on two main factors: racial eminence and comparative linguistics. Alleging the Vedic people's European origin, he claimed that a band of tall, fair-skinned nomadic pastoralists from the Russian Steppes, called the Aryans, crossed the Himalayas on horse-driven chariots in 1500 BCE. Being a superior race, they subjugated the unsophisticated dark-skinned aboriginals, whom they pushed south of the Vindhyas to become the Dravidians. The colonizing Aryan invaders then settled in the north and civilized the land, completely eradicating the local culture. They imposed Sanskrit and the Vedic lifestyle on the natives and were responsible for all ancient Sanskrit literature. According to Mueller, the conquering Aryan race began composing the Vedas soon after their arrival, starting with the Rig Veda, which he dated at 1200 BCE. They also formed the Vedic caste system, declaring themselves the upper-caste Brahmins and the natives the lower-caste Shudras. This hypothesis implied that Brahmins and Shudras were of different racial ancestry, and since genetic study was unknown at the time, the supposition was accepted as fact.

Then, in the 1920s, Mohenjo-Daro and Harappa, dating back to 3000 BCE, were excavated. Although the discovery of these highly advanced urban civilizations demonstrated that the indigenous people were far from unsophisticated aboriginals as previously believed, surprisingly, it did little to cast doubt on the Aryan Invasion Theory. Instead, the narrative was neatly amended to fit the new information suggesting that the Indus Valley inhabitants, although evolved, were the peaceful dark-skinned pre-Vedic natives. They fled south when the Aryans, who had a technological edge in the form of horse-driven chariots unknown to the locals, attacked and defeated them. As a result, the prevailing culture was entirely replaced by an imported Vedic one indicating the invaders' superiority.

The concept of Aryan supremacy fuelled white nationalism in Europe. Hitler notably adopted the false narrative of a master race, along with a distortion of the word Arya and the holiest of Vedic symbols, the Swastika. Finally, in the latter part of the twentieth century, when archaeological evidence proved conclusively that no invasion had occurred, the theory was modified to a peaceful migration and then further amended to a 'trickling in'. Despite the many iterations of how the Vedic culture came to India, whether by violent invasion, peaceful migration or people trickling in, the core assertion has remained that in 1500 BCE, foreigners replaced the pre-Vedic local culture and language of North India with their own. The claim that the Vedic culture was imported rather than indigenous is still touted, though it is refuted by literature, archaeology and science.

Motivating Factors for the AIT at Inception:

1. Hubris: The thought that the language of a subjugated people was the source of most European languages, including English, was abhorrent to imperialists.

2.	In his 1650 work, 'The Annals of the Old Testament', Archbishop James Ussher propounded that the first day of creation was 23 October 4004 BCE. Most Christian scholars firmly held this belief during the colonization of India, and the Vedic civilization did not fit into this. According to the Biblical timeline, a highly evolved people could not have lived thousands of years before the Earth was supposed to have come into existence. Furthermore, the ecclesiastic chronology insisted that God destroyed the whole world by a flood around 2348 BCE, so the Vedic civilization posed a considerable problem. To tie in with Biblical events, Mueller fixed the anomaly by ascribing 1500 BCE for the Aryan invasion when Sanskrit and the Vedic culture ostensibly came to India.

The Aryan Invasion Theory was politically convenient. It served to divide and rule, effectively controlling the natives by justifying British colonization with an ancient precedent. The concept of invading Aryans was fed to the Indian population through the Westernization of education, beginning with Thomas Babington Macaulay's Indian Education Act of 1835. While the theory had apparent advantages for the ruling power, many Indians also embraced it, as it put them on the same racial footing as their rulers. The idea that foreigners displaced native Indians had far-reaching effects. It effectively divided the nation, with north and south Indians believing they were racially, linguistically and culturally distinct from each other. The ancient varna system's meritocracy was also replaced with birth-based caste and Brahmin eminence based on their perceived superior Caucasian ancestry.

There are four central tenets of the Aryan Invasion/Migration Theory. These are:

1.	The Aryans were a race whose original homeland was the Russian Steppes, or thereabouts, deduced from the concentration of Indo-European languages and its central location that facilitated spread in all directions.
2.	The invaders/migrants were males who arrived on horse-drawn chariots hitherto unknown to the locals.
3.	The invaders/migrants brought Sanskrit and the Vedic culture to north-west India, as the similarity between Indo-European languages points to a common origin.
4.	The invading/immigrant race displaced the natives from North India and pushed them south of the Vindhyas.

In light of all the multidisciplinary evidence that has recently emerged, is it plausible that Sanskrit works like the Ramayana resulted from an imported culture? How does the proof for the Aryan Invasion/Migration Theory stack up under scrutiny?

Literary Evidence

There is no reference in the entire gamut of Vedic literature to support invaders or migrants supplanting the local culture. In fact, the word 'arya' in Sanskrit refers to a noble-minded, culturally refined person, not to ethnicity, so anyone could be called an arya depending on their conduct. For instance, in the Ramayana, Tara lamenting Vali's death, refers to him as an aryaputra, son of an arya, though he is a Vanara. Western Indologists picked out the word from the Rig Veda and falsely ascribed it to denote a superior white race. Similarly, Dasyu does not have a racial connotation either. The term simply alluded to the enemy, considered ignoble. In the famous battle of the ten kings described in Book 7 of the Rig Veda, the Puru-Bharata clan are the aryas or noble people, and their enemy clansmen, like the Anu and the Druhyu, are called dasyus/dasas. Puranic literature tells us that the five main tribes (Anu, Druhyu, Puru, Yadu and Turvashu) were related, with a common ancestry going back to a king named Yayati, so they were not racially different from one another.

If the native Harappans were the dasyus forced south of the Vindhyas, it is surprising that Tamil Sangam literature does not demonstrate any resentment regarding their supposed displacement nor record the slightest hint of hostility towards the people of the north. The greatest Tamil kings, the Cholas, trace their ancestry to the Solar dynasty's King Shibi from the north.[2] Agastya, considered the father of the Tamil language, was a northerner greatly revered in the south. There is absolutely no evidence of a north–south divide in Vedic times; on the contrary, the entire land from the Himalayas to the southern sea is united in a common civilizational heritage. We see this oneness clearly depicted in the Ramayana.

While Vedic literature does not speak of a distant motherland or share any memory of rivers or mountains outside India and Afghanistan, it depicts a deep connection with the Sapta Sindhu (seven rivers) and profound veneration for the geography of the area. The Nadistuti Sukta in the Rig

---

[2] Shibi ruled in the Swat region.

Veda, Book 10.75 defines the Vedic homeland by referencing the rivers to include the land stretching from the Ganga in the east to the Indus in the west. The Veda also points explicitly to an east-west migration of culture,[3] not west to the east, as would be expected if it had been composed of migrants entering from the north-west. The earliest part of the Rig Veda, Book 6, mentions only the Ganga, Yamuna and Saraswati, marking the Rig Vedic homeland's western boundary. The next composition, Book 3, describes Sudasa, the Bharata king, performing the Ashwamedha in the Saraswati area. Subsequently, in Book 7, we have the historical war of the ten kings, where Sudasa (moving westwards) fights on the banks of the Parushuni/Ravi against enemy clans from the vicinity of the Asikni/Chenab.[4]

Based on this textual evidence, the old Rig Vedic heartland from where the culture spread to other areas can firmly be placed in the Saraswati–Yamuna–Ganga area. In the later books, as Shrikant Talageri notes, we see a westward expansion of the civilization by the gradual introduction of rivers in Pakistan and Afghanistan. Rivers beyond the Indus first appear in the newer Book 4, when Sudasa's descendants fight the battle of Varsagira on the Sarayu/Harioiu (not the one in Ayodhya), which is a tributary of the Indus. Notably, the reference to Sapta Sindhu only occurs much later in Book 8 and not before. In his research, Talageri also points to the same progression from east to west when analysing the mention of places, lakes and animals native to each area. The Vedas depict a settled culture of agriculturalists who cherished and eulogized their ancestral land, not newly entering nomadic invaders or migrants. In fact, evidence of agriculture and the domestication of animals dates to the eighth millennium BCE in the Gangetic plains,[5] Indus–Saraswati basin and the Mehrgarh sites.

Although there is absolutely no mention of an influx of people from outside India in any Vedic text, many references do point to outward migration. For example, when the Puru-Bharatas established dominance in the Rig Vedic battle of the ten kings, some of the defeated tribes migrated westwards towards Persia and territories beyond. Western Indologists wrongly portrayed this war between related clans inhabiting north India to depict the struggle between invading aryans and native dasyus because of an incorrect

---

[3] Shrikant G. Talageri, *The Rigveda and the Avesta: The Final Evidence* (Aditya Prakashan, 2008).

[4] Rig Veda Books 6, 3 and 7 are the oldest, followed by Books 4 and 2. Books 5, 1, 8, 9 and 10 are classified as newer books.

[5] Shitala Prasad Singh, 'Early Centres of Origin of Agriculture in the Middle Ganga Plain', *American International Journal of Research in Humanities, Arts and Social Science* (2014).

understanding of the two terms to indicate race rather than qualities. When the Bharata king Sudas defeated the ten kings on the banks of the Ravi, the enemy 'dasyus', the Druhyu and Anu, fled. The Anu moved westwards into Persia and the Druhyus north to modern-day Afghanistan and Central Asia.

Another migration recorded in Puranic literature is when the Druhyu king Angara was driven out of Punjab into Afghanistan by Mandhatta of the Ikshavaku dynasty. Subsequently, Angara's successor Gandhara named the new kingdom after himself. The Puranas state that the sons of the later Druhyu king Pracetas migrated out farther to Central Asia, regions that came to be known as Uttara Kuru and Uttara Madra, where they founded various prosperous kingdoms. After that, mention of the Druhyus fades, as they ceased to be part of the Vedic homeland. However, the land was well known; Sugriva refers to Uttara Kuru in the Ramayana when he tells the Vanaras not to go past it as the region beyond was unexplored. Another intriguing piece of information is that the Celtic Druids are believed to have been the priestly Druhyu.

A later Vedic text, the Baudhayana Srautasutra 18.44, mentions the migration of the Pururava[6] and Urvashi's sons. It says Ayu goes eastwards, and his people are the Kuru-Panchalas and Kashi-Videhas, while Amavasu migrates westward to Gandhara,[7] Parsu[8] and Aratta.[9] The Bogazkoy tablets of Turkey, traced to the fourteenth century BCE, refer to Vedic deities like Indra, Mitra and Varuna, showing that the culture had spread there. The Rig Veda 3.53.5 speaks of travelling to other lands for trade. 'O thou, powerful one like Indra! There are riches in your as well as in other lands. By travelling on nimble steeds, seek out those destinations that are treasure troves of fortune.'

The Vedas were composed gradually over many centuries, as is evident from the changes in vocabulary and grammar from the earliest part of the Rig Veda to later texts. The archaic Vedic Sanskrit is thousands of years earlier than 1200 BCE. Max Mueller picked the 1200 BCE date because he claimed the Aryans arrived in 1500 BCE, and the Rig Veda was presumed to be a pre-Iron Age text, which could not have been composed later. However, the

---

[6] Chandravanshi Dynasty, the offspring of Budha and Ila.

[7] Afghanistan.

[8] Persia.

[9] Armenia–Azerbaijan area.

period between 1500 and 1200 BCE is insufficient to explain the vast gulf in language across the books. A pertinent reference from the Ramayana shows it was composed before the Atharva Veda was separated out as the fourth Veda. When Rama meets Hanuman, he praises him as a master of all three Vedas—Rig, Yajur and Sama—but does not include the Atharva Veda. If Rama is dated to the fifth millennium BCE, then the three Vedas existed long before then.

Geological Evidence

The Archaeological Society of India has identified more than 2000 Harappan sites in the Punjab, Haryana, Uttar Pradesh, Rajasthan and Gujarat areas, mainly concentrated along the dry Saraswati paleochannel, now called the Ghaggar. The Saraswati is given enormous importance in the Rig Veda and is referenced seventy-two times. It is glorified as 'Ambitame, Naditame and Devitame' (Rig Veda 2.41.16), the best mother, the best river and the best goddess. The Rig Veda 7.95.2 hails the Saraswati as the 'Mother of Floods' flowing from the Himalayas to the western (Arabian) sea.

'The river Saraswati has shattered the mountain peaks with her fast and powerful waves, just as easily as one uproots lotus stems; let us invoke her who strikes what is far and near, with holy hymns and prayers.' (Rig Veda 6.61.2)

Rig Veda 7.36.6 describes her forceful flow. 'Coming together, glorious, loudly roaring—Saraswati, Mother of Floods, the seventh—with copious milk with fair streams, strongly flowing, full swelling with the volume of their water.'

For years, sceptics dismissed the Saraswati as a mythical river, but the American Landsat discovery of its dry paleochannel and subsequent geological studies have conclusively proved its existence in the precise location described in Vedic literature. Excavations show that the Saraswati supported numerous Harappan-type settlements along its banks for thousands of years till it lost its water supply. Tectonic activity around 3500 BCE deprived the river of its source, and subsequently, it also lost its tributaries, the Sutlej and the Yamuna. The once-mighty river was reduced to a monsoonal stream that completely dried up by 1900 BCE due to climate change, and the people naturally migrated away. The Vedas mirror the loss; while the Rig Veda describes the Saraswati as a forceful river, the Atharva Veda deifies her as a goddess because the river was only a memory by then. The supposed Aryans could not have settled in north India in 1500 BCE and composed the Rig

Veda in 1200 BCE praising the Saraswati that was virtually non-existent by
that time. When a river dries up, outward migration is more logical than an
inward one. Descriptions of the Saraswati's powerful flow in the Rig Veda
indicate its composition when the river was in its prime thousands of years
before 1200 BCE. Research shows this date was not later than 5000 BCE at a
minimum and likely around 8000 BCE or even a few millennia earlier, closer
to the early Holocene.

Genetic Evidence

The invasion/migration theory assumed different racial ancestries for north
and south Indians based on skin colour and facial features, but recent genetic
studies have shown no significant contribution from Central Asia to the
Indian gene pool in the last 10,000–15,000 years[10] To quote from a paper
by some of the foremost population geneticists, 'Results show that Indian
tribal and caste populations derive largely from the same genetic heritage of
the Pleistocene southern and western Asians and have received limited gene
flow from external regions since the Holocene.'[11] Others like Oppenheimer,
Sahoo and Danino also confirm the lack of evidence for European genetic
influence in their research.

Moreover, there is no significant genetic difference between north Indians
and south Indians, Brahmins and Shudras, to indicate a racial distinction.[12]
Therefore, colour difference generalizations must be ascribed to geographical
location and other factors, not genetics. It is utterly implausible that a
handful of people migrating in small numbers could have totally supplanted

---

[10] Sengupta, S., et al. (2006). 'Polarity and Temporality of High-Resolution
Y-Chromosome Distributions in India Identify Both Indigenous and Exogenous
Expansions and Reveal Minor Genetic Influence of Central Asian Pastoralists', *American
Journal of Human Genetics*.

[11] Kivisild, T., Rootsi, S., Metspalu, M., Mastana, S., Kaldma, K., Parik, J., Metspalu,
E., Adojaan, M., Tolk, H., Stepanov, V., Gölge, M., Usanga, E., Papiha, S., Cinnioğlu,
C., King, R., Cavalli-Sforza, L., Underhill, P., & Villems, R. (2003). 'The Genetic
Heritage of the Earliest Settlers Persists Both in Indian Tribal and Caste Populations'. \
American Journal of Human Genetics 72(2), pp. 313–32.

[12] Sharma, S., Rai, E., Sharma, P. et al. (2009) 'The Indian Origin of Paternal Haplogroup
R1a1* Substantiates the Autochthonous Origin of Brahmins and the Caste System,' *J
Hum Genet* 54, pp. 47–55.

a thriving civilization, teeming with people, and that too without leaving any archaeological trace of their origin.[13]

The discovery of the prevalence of the R1a1 paternal Y-haplotype from Eurasia to India created excitement amongst advocates of the migration theory, who believed that the Aryan gene had been found. However, concentration does not necessarily confirm either origin or spread. While the R1a1 is present in Central Asians and north Indians, it is also seen in south Indians and found in remarkably high concentration in tribes like the Sahariyas of Central India and the Chenchus of Andhra.[14] A 2015 genome-wide study indicates that the R1 is an ancient haplotype, bifurcating into R1a and R1b about 25,000 years ago. Regarding the Z93 paternal genetic imprint, the study says, 'Datations show that the Z93 Pakistani-Indian group is the most ancient (about 15,5 K years); in Europe, the Eastern populations are the most ancient (about 12,5 K years) and the Northern ones the most recent (about 6,9 K years)'.[15] Conspicuously, it is mostly missing from western Europe, where one branch from the common homeland supposedly migrated. India's genetic diversity is second only to Africa, and Indian genes are amongst the most ancient, so it is likely that the R1a1 originated in India and travelled west. Populations have migrated in and out of India over millennia, and genetic transfer is natural, but there is no evidence of any large-scale resettlement resulting in total cultural transformation. It is vital to view genetic data in conjunction with other studies and not in isolation, as genes are not markers for language or heritage. Archaeology and textual evidence show a continuity of local culture that was not uprooted and replaced.

Archaeological Evidence

Archaeology indicates that the Harappans were the Vedic people, seen in the unbroken continuity of tradition. Relics dating back thousands of years before 1500 BCE, found in Harappan settlements along the Indus

---

[13] Premendra Priyadarshi points out that the migrating population would have had to be four times the native one to overwhelm it genetically.

[14] Sharma, S., Rai, E., Sharma, P. et al. (2009) 'The Indian Origin of Paternal Haplogroup R1a1* Substantiates the Autochthonous Origin of Brahmins and the Caste System,' *J Hum Genet* 54, pp. 47–55.

[15] Lucotte, Gerard. *The Major Y-Chromosome Haplotype XI - Haplogroup R1a in Eurasia*, Hereditary Genetics, Walsh Medical Media

and Saraswati, show the Vedic nature of these civilizations. Excavations in Mohenjo-Daro and Harappa and more recently along the erstwhile Saraswati in Rakhigarhi,[16] Birhana,[17] Banawali,[18] Lothal,[19] Dholavira[20] and Kalibangan[21] have unearthed figures in yoga postures, figurines of women with vermilion in the parting of their hair, the Swastika symbol of well-being, the holy asvatta tree, the Om symbol, Vedic fire altars, representations of the Namaste greeting, the Shivalinga and Pashupatinath. According to B.B. Lal, former director general of the Archaeological Survey of India, the Harappans and the Vedic people were the same. Interestingly, the description of Ayodhya in the Ramayana, which is considered a Vedic text, closely matches the well-planned Harappan ruins with water reservoirs, well laid out roads, underground drainage, multi-storeyed buildings with staircases, courtyards, granaries and wells. Also, Vedic altars were constructed of brick, and the Harappans were expert brickmakers. While discussing Harappan cities, it is noteworthy that there are no such settlements in the south where the displaced people allegedly moved, replacing what they lost.

Proponents of Aryan migration argue that the colonizers brought the horse and chariot to India in 1500 BCE, as they came from a 'horse culture'. This conclusion was based on references to horses in the Rig Veda and the absence of horses depicted on Harappan seals. However, the reasoning is not sound because the Harappan seals show bulls but not cows, and it is absurd to assume they did not have cows. The hypothesis is further proved incorrect by the excavations in Sinauli, Uttar Pradesh, east of the Rig Vedic area, conducted in 2018, where chariots dating back to 2100 BCE were found. Also, skeletal horse remains were discovered in 1974 at Surkotada by A.K. Sharma of the Archaeological Survey of India. These were carbon-dated to 2000 BCE and verified by the world-renowned zoologist Sandor Bokonyi, an authority on horse bones. He confirmed that they belonged to a domesticated horse, based on the effect of the bit on the teeth:

---

[16] Rakhigarhi 6500 BCE. The largest Harappan site excavated. It shows remarkable continuity of building style and pottery.

[17] Birhana 7570 BCE, the oldest excavated Harappan site.

[18] Banawali 2500 BCE. Typical well-planned fortified Harappan township.

[19] Lothal 2400 BCE. Harappan port city that facilitated trade.

[20] Dholavira 3000 BCE. Famous for its ingenious water management system.

[21] Kalibangan 2700 BCE. Shows ploughed agricultural fields dated to 2800 BCE.

'The occurrence of true horse (*Equus caballus L.*) was evidenced by the enamel pattern of the upper and lower cheek and teeth and by the size and form of the incisors and phalanges (toe bones).' Since then, horse bones and teeth have been found in several Harappan sites. Finally, there is no evidence of increased horse/chariot remains pertaining to the period after 1500 BCE to show that they were brought in after that date.

Supporters of Aryan migration use the references to horses and chariots in the Rig Veda to suggest that it was composed after the arrival of the Aryans in 1500 BCE. However, it is evident that the native population was familiar with the horse and chariot long before that date. The Bhimbetka cave paintings depicting horses go back 10,000 years. Excavations of so-called pre-Vedic settlements, like Kalibangan, Banawali and Rakhigarhi, unearthed models of terracotta chariots with painted spoked wheels, indicating the people of the time were familiar with such objects. Based on geological evidence of the Saraswati River, the Rig Veda was in existence well before 5000 BCE, showing that the horse and chariot could not have been later imports. In the 1940s, the British archaeologist Mortimer Wheeler bolstered Max Mueller's invasion theory, proposing the destruction of the native Indus civilizations by invaders with horse/chariot technology when he found some thirty skeletons with injuries in Mohenjo-Daro. Since Indra was called Purandara in the Rig Veda, wrongly translated as the destroyer of forts, Wheeler concluded that the allusion was to the massacre of the Harappans. 'Pura' actually means settlement or habitation, and 'Dara', stream, so Purandara was the destroyer of towns by floods.[22] Irrespective of all this, Wheeler's assumption proved false when George Dales ascertained in 1964 that the bones lay buried in different layers and could not be attributed to a single event.

The Harappans were expert mariners, who traded with distant places, exporting various goods, including cotton fabric, jewellery, beads, gems, ivory and copper. This fact is proven by Harappan seals found as far as Mesopotamia and Sumeria. They would undoubtedly have been familiar with horses in the area, so the notion that these people were blindsided by

---

[22] Indra is the rain deity, bringing heavy rainfall that caused rivers to flood their banks, destroying nearby settlements. Indra is also known as Purandara or 'destroyer of villages.' Priyadarshi, Premendra. *In Quest of the Dates of the Vedas: Comprehensive Study of the Vedic and the Indo-European Flora, Fauna and Climate in Light of the Information Emerging from the Disciplines of Archaeology, Archaeo-Botany, Geology, Genetics and Linguistics for the Last 10,000 Years.*

horses defies logic. It is unclear what the Harappans imported because only a few cylindrical Mesopotamian seals have been found in their settlements. Perhaps they brought in consumables like wine, but it could well have been horses.[23] There is a corroborating reference in the Ramayana that Ayodhya got horses from Central Asia and bred them locally. Many marine references in the Vedas stand in sharp contradiction to the landlocked Steppe people who were not seafarers and relate more to the Harappans. Trading seals of the Indus-Saraswati valley in Mesopotamia and Central Asia prove this connection, and one can logically assume merchants also carried the Vedic culture with them.

According to the Aryan Migration Theory, the Russian Steppe people separated into three branches after a sojourn in Central Asia. One went to Mesopotamia, which explained the Mittani rulers who had Vedic names; another went to Persia and produced the Avesta; the third came to India and composed the Vedas. By this supposition, as Talageri points out, the Sumerian Mittani inscriptions should share similarities with the earlier books of the Rig Veda, which were composed closer to the time the three branches were together. Instead, they share commonality with the later books, indicating that the culture spread from India (not from the Russian Steppe) to Mesopotamia. Also, the Mittani kings' names are a chronological marker for when such names were prevalent and are found only in the new books of the Rig Veda, and their art has the peacock motif, which is distinctly Indian.

The new field of astroarchaeology provides dates from Sanskrit literature that specify sky formations for significant events, and based on this, Rama's birth occurred in 5114 BCE. The Ramayana describes the Saraswati as one of the mighty rivers that Bharata had to cross on his return from Kekaya, showing that it was still in full flow at the time. The descriptions of the Saraswati can be used to trace historical events. Based on the Saraswati evidence and the fact that Rama refers only to the Rig, Sama and Yajur Vedas, we can conclude that the three were composed much earlier than the Ramayana and could not have been the work of invaders starting 1200 BCE. Interestingly, in the Mahabharata, ascribed to the third millennium BCE, the Saraswati River is described as drying up and disappearing in certain areas long before 1500 BCE, the supposed date of the Aryan arrival.

---

23 Sanyal, Sanjeev, *Land of the Seven Rivers: A Brief History of India's Geography* (Penguin Random House India, 2013).

Cultural Continuity

While the linguistic Aryan invasion/migration theory insists that an overhaul of indigenous culture occurred in 1500 BCE, archaeology traces an unbroken Vedic cultural continuity from Harappan times to the current day. As the famous archeologist, John Marshall wrote in his introduction to *Mohenjo-Daro and The Indus Civilization*: 'Taken as a whole, their (Harappan) religion is so characteristically Indian as hardly to be distinguishable from still living Hinduism or at least that aspect of it which is bound up with animism and the cults of Siva and Mother Goddess—still two most popular worships.'

Some of the continuing traditions:

1. Hindu women still wear the tilak or bindi and vermilion in the parting of their hair.
2. Bangles worn right to the upper arm, as depicted in the Harappan dancing girl, are still fashionable amongst villagers in Rajasthan and Gujarat.
3. Items of jewellery like the decorative waist chain, or cummerbund, were worn till recently, and anklets are still in vogue.
4. The Swastika symbol of well-being continues to be a holy sign for Hindus.
5. Figurines depicting the Namaste greeting, symbolizing the Vedic belief of the God within, show that the Harappans had the same greeting as today.
6. There have been figurines found in yoga positions.
7. Fire altars abound in excavated Harappan settlements, although pujas have replaced yagnas in modern times.
8. Traditional bullock carts and boats have the same design as in Harappan times.
9. Terracotta toys like those in villages today have been found in the Indus-Saraswati sites.
10. The Shivalinga continues to be worshipped.
11. There is continuity in food habits too. Pots from the Saraswati sites contained turmeric which is still used today. Even tandoors have been found.
12. All rivers and mountains in India have Vedic names without exception. No pre-Vedic name remains, which means that the foreign Aryans wiped out all traces of the prior civilization as if they had never

existed. This is not typical in situations of population replacement, as demonstrated in the recent example of the United States, where many places and rivers are still called by native American names.

Conclusion

In his later years, Max Mueller changed his mind on Vedic antiquity, finally admitting that his dates were purely speculative. 'It is quite clear that we cannot fix a terminum a quo, whether the Vedic hymns were composed 1000 or 2000 or 3000 years, BCE no power on earth will ever determine.'[24] For the Aryan Invasion/Migration Theory to stand, the Rig Veda composed in 1200 BCE must hold, but all evidence proves otherwise, taking it back to at least 8000 BCE or even earlier.

Sadly, Mueller's arbitrary date is still widely accepted, as the myth he propounded has become conventional wisdom. The indoctrination was so pernicious that even today, after seventy-five years of independence from Britain's imperial rule, educated Indians still cling to the false narrative they were taught and sadly continue to instruct children in the same flawed theory in schools. While the linguistic connection between Sanskrit and most European languages has universal consensus, the unidentified Proto-Indo European language remains pure speculation, so one must conclude that the mother language was Sanskrit or its archaic form developed in India.

Eurocentric colonialists had a vested interest in propounding that Sanskrit was borrowed from the West as it was not advantageous for the natives they ruled to be of a highly evolved culture. However, though they are long gone, political interests and academic bias continue to mire the debate. There is overwhelming multidisciplinary evidence supporting the birth of Sanskrit, and the Vedic civilization, in the Sapta Sindhu basin, the Rig Vedic homeland, with no convincing proof that the native culture was displaced. Interestingly, the location of Harappan settlements excavated coincides precisely with the territory described in the Rig Veda and has similar characteristics. Nevertheless, the vast majority still adhere to the fallacy peddled in the nineteenth century, showing how hard it is to dispel entrenched ideas.

---

[24] Mueller, Max, *Collected Works*, Vol II, p. 91.

Shastras—Shruti and Smriti

Shastras are literally 'instruments of knowledge'. Traditional Vedic education covered eighteen vidhyas or fields of study.

- The Four Vedas
- The Six Vedangas
- The Four Upavedas
- The Four Upangas

The Vedas are sacred texts called 'Shruti', or divinely heard wisdom unchanging with time. Veda is derived from the root 'vid', meaning to know, so the Vedas are books of knowledge, not a code of religious laws.

'Knowledge of eternal truth (Brahman) leads to eternal peace and bliss.' (Yajur Veda 40.14)

'The divine wisdom of the Vedas leads to material and spiritual advancement.' (Sama Veda 98)

There are four Vedas composed in Sanskrit suktas or hymns, meticulously passed down through the ages from teacher to student through memorization and oral recitation. Amazingly, not one syllable has been altered over the centuries, and they are chanted today precisely as they were thousands of years ago. There is no specific author of the Vedas, nor is there a date of origin attributed to them. These ancient texts are called 'anadi', without beginning, and 'apurushaya', not authored by man, because they were divine revelations to sages in a higher state of consciousness over many centuries. The Vedas are abstruse, philosophically dense texts that are difficult to comprehend without a deep understanding of Vedic spirituality and a thorough knowledge of the Vedangas, Upavedas and Upangas. Learning Sanskrit alone is insufficient to interpret the Vedas correctly; therefore, English translations by modern Indologists often tend to be inaccurate and misleading.

The Four Vedas are:

1. **The Rig Veda** is the first Veda and the oldest literature in existence. 'Rik' means to praise, and it contains hymns of adoration to Vedic deities like Agni, Indra and Soma, manifestations of the supreme consciousness. It also includes the Gayatri Mantra, the holiest of hymns. The ten books of the Rig Veda are not arranged chronologically. Books 6, 3 and 7 are the earliest. Books 2 and 4 come next, and the rest (Books 5, 1, 8, 9 and 10) are later compositions.

2. **The Yajur Veda** is the Veda of worship. 'Yajur' derives from 'yajus', meaning worship or sacrifice. It describes the rituals for yagnas and serves as a guidebook for priests. The text contains two streams of thought, the Krishna Yajur Veda and the Shukla Yajur Veda.

3. **The Sama Veda**, the shortest of the Vedas, is meant to be sung. It is the Veda of melodies and chants. Sama comes from 'saman', which means song, and is considered the Veda of devotion. Sama Veda is the source of Indian classical music.

4. **The Atharva Veda** is the newest. Atharva is derived from 'atharvan', priest of fire, so the Atharva Veda is the knowledge of fire rituals for everyday life. It also contains teachings on medicine as well as statecraft.

Each Veda has four parts:

1. **The Samhitas:** Collections of mantras, foundation hymns of praise and rituals.

2. **The Brahmanas:** Liturgical explanation of the Samhitas. They are a guide to practices/ yagnas.

3. **The Aranyakas:** Explanation of the philosophy behind Vedic rituals and sacrifices. 'Aranyaka' means from the forest, as these were contemplations on the Brahmanas conducted in the woods.

4. **The Upanishads:** 'Upanishad' means 'approach to dispel darkness'. The student sat by his guru, seeking enlightenment through knowledge. The Upanishadic quest is to understand the truth, removing the veil of ignorance that obscures the innermost Self. The guru's role was to illumine and provide guidance, as it was believed that true wisdom was acquired through individual experience, not

by following a belief system. There are 108 Upanishads spread over the four Vedas, but ten are held most significant as the great sage Adi Shankaracharya wrote commentaries on them. The Upanishads are the essence of Vedic spiritual philosophy; therefore, they are also called Vedanta. They explore the nature of reality, the inner self and its relationship with Brahman, the universal consciousness.

The Vedangas are the supplementary branches of study without which it is impossible to understand the true meaning of the Vedas. The following are the six Vedangas:

1. **Shiksha:** Phonetics/pronunciation
2. **Chandas:** Prosody/poetic meter
3. **Vyakarana:** Grammar
4. **Nirukta:** Etymology
5. **Kalpa:** Instructions for rituals
6. **Jyotisha:** Astronomy, including astrology

The four Upavedas are disciplines of applied knowledge. Though these texts do not deal directly with philosophy, they arise from the tenets of the Vedas. These are:

1. **Ayurveda:** The science of health and well-being based on the Atharva Veda.
2. **Dhanurveda:** The science of warfare based on the Rig Veda. This field of study is mentioned in Vedic texts but is mostly lost today. Rama was a master of Dhanurveda.
3. **Gandharvaveda:** The study of music and dance based on the Sama Veda.
4. **Arthashastra:** A treatise on economics and wealth management based on the Yajur Veda.

Just as the six Vedangas help decipher the Vedas, the four Upangas serve to understand the Vedangas. These are:

1. **Nyaya:** Logic.
2. **Mimamsa:** This means the desire to know. It explores the philosophy of rituals.

3. **Puranas:** Deal with the creation of the universe, the cycle of time, human history and the genealogy of notable kings. The stories are meant to illustrate Vedic philosophy and combine history with mythology.

4. **Dharma Shastras:** Also called Smritis. They are texts that codify social conduct inspired by the philosophy of the Vedas. Unlike the Vedas, considered eternal and unchanging, the smritis were written for a specific time and place. Like a constitution, they require a periodical amendment to suit changed circumstances in society and are not meant to be followed blindly by future generations. The Indian Constitution is only seventy-odd years old but has already been amended 106 times, showing that codes change even in a short period. There are many smritis, but the oldest and most comprehensive is the Manusmriti. Unfortunately, the Manusmriti is much maligned today due to incorrect translations into English that do not capture its true intent. Also, changed social norms over thousands of years have made parts of it obsolete. Additionally, various interpolations have crept into the text over the centuries, detracting from the original. However, despite this, many aspects of the Manusmriti continue to be relevant.

The Vedic Varna System

When discussing Vedic society and especially Hinduism today, the first thing that comes to mind is caste, but surprising as it may seem, the Vedic people did not have a caste system! In fact, no Vedic text mentions the practice in its current birth-based form. The word 'caste' was wrongly ascribed to the Vedic 'varna system', due to a misunderstanding of its purpose and meaning by European colonialists. 'Varna' comes from the Sanskrit root 'var', which means to cover, group, colour, classify, describe or choose. Unlike caste, assigned by birth, varna was based on profession and used to identify people according to their function in the community. It was related to a person's innate aptitude to perform a particular job rather than parentage.

On the other hand, 'caste', derived from Portuguese 'casta', indicates breeding rather than vocation and is quite different from varna. Also, the varna system was not stratified like hierarchical caste, which related to family identity and lineage. Varnas were simply occupational classifications to sustain an orderly and prosperous society where each person performed his duty according to his 'svadharma', or responsibility, depending on his specific role in the community. On the other hand, European society was rigidly class and lineage-oriented, and perhaps they interpreted the varna system in the same light as a caste-based system.

In Vedic times, a hierarchy where one varna was superior to another was entirely absent. A person's occupation or varna was not determined by birth but by intrinsic qualities and innate talent. As the Yajur Veda says in 16.15, 'All men are equal in brotherhood. There is no one small and no one big.' The story of Satyakama Jabala in Chapter 4 of the Chandogya Upanishad clearly illustrates this. Satyakama was the son of a single mother called Jabala, a servant woman. He was keen to learn from a guru and asked his mother about his father to introduce himself properly. His mother replied that she was uncertain about his paternity, so she advised him to take her name and call himself Satyakama Jabala. The boy approached a guru called Haridrumata Gautama and requested to be accepted as his student. When the guru asked him about his antecedents, Satyakama replied that he could not say because he did not know his father and went by Satyakama Jabala. The guru was impressed by the boy's honesty and immediately accepted him as his disciple. He asserted that Satyakama displayed truthfulness and was, therefore, a true Brahmin by nature. Satyakama Jabala later became a celebrated sage, though he was born to a Shudra woman out of wedlock.

These are the natural attributes conducive to the choice of Varna:

- **Brahmins:** Ahimsa, forgiveness, self-control, purity, austerity, tolerance, honesty, knowledge, contemplation.
- **Kshatriyas:** Strength, splendour, heroism, confidence, determination, courage, generosity, resourcefulness, leadership.
- **Vaishyas:** A propensity for trade and commerce, talent for making money flow through society by generating wealth, harnessing natural resources, farming, herding and so on.
- **Shudras:** General workers who had an aptitude for providing a service to benefit society based on their skills. This varna included artisans, architects, engineers, charioteers, barbers, blacksmiths, carpenters, cart makers, fishermen, potters, household servants and so on, all valuable members of Vedic society. The Taittiriya Samhita of the Krishna Yajur Veda pays homage to Shudras. 'We salute the carpenters and the cart makers. We salute the potters and the blacksmiths. We salute the bird hunters and the fishermen. We salute the arrow makers and the bow makers.' The Shukla Yajur Veda 18.48 has the prayer: 'O Lord fill the Brahmins with light, Kshatriyas with light, Vaishyas with light and Shudras with light. May we have love towards all.' The thirteenth chapter of the Shatapatha Brahmana reveres the work of Shudras, comparing their hard work to the penance of rishis. 'Shudras are like ascetics. Their hard work increases the wealth and tapas of society.' The following verse from the Atharva Veda 19.62.1 indicates that all varnas were equally respected: 'May all noble people admire me. May kings and Kshatriyas admire me. May the Shudras and Vaishyas admire me. May all look at me with admiration.'

In Vedic society, varna was chosen based on an individual's propensity to perform a particular function. Therefore, the son of a Brahmin did not automatically become a Brahmin. He had to earn the qualification, much like the son of a professor cannot call himself one today unless he achieves the title through his own effort. Moreover, a Brahmin was not just an educated person but also one who lived an austere life of piety associated with the occupation and a role model of morality. He was poor in material wealth and rich in knowledge. While it was usual and customary for professions to pass down from father to son, varna was not determined by birth alone; this practice sprung up more recently. The following verse from the Rig Veda 3.8.4 on the sacred thread ceremony or initiation into learning (dvija or twice-born) notably does not mention varna because anyone could gain knowledge and become a dvija. 'This youth, suitably dressed, graceful, brilliant as the rising sun, has a promising future, reborn through education as a scholar. O sages, who have noble thoughts and are seekers of divinity, help him rise to great heights.'

There are numerous examples of people adopting a different varna than their parents. In the Ramayana, the boy Dasharatha accidentally killed says he was not of Brahmin parentage but was performing the Sandhya Vandana and studying the Vedas, perhaps becoming a Brahmin as a result. Ravana was born to a Brahmin father but became a Kshatriya. Vishwamitra was a Kshatriya, who became a great rishi through austerities. Similarly, the sage Matanga was born of a Shudra father yet became a revered sage. Shabri was of humble birth but was respected as a knower of Brahman, having attained Brahmagyana. Even Valmiki, who composed the Ramayana, was not always a respected rishi, but previously a hunter who had turned to robbery.

The Gotra System further debunks the narrative of varna assigned by birth. Gotra means cow-shed and refers to a clan under a common umbrella that traces its paternal Y chromosome lineage to the same ancestor. The descendants of seven great sages—Gautama, Bharadwaja, Vishwamitra, Jamadagni, Kashyapa, Atri and Vasishta—form the gotras. Over time, many sub-gotras sprang up from the original seven, as we see today. Individuals who share a gotra are considered related, so endogamous marriage within a gotra is frowned upon. Since everyone has a gotra, different varnas, in effect, belong to the same extended family.

The varna system is first mentioned in the Purusha Suktam, Rig Veda 10.90. Purusha, in Vedic philosophy, refers to the universal consciousness that pervades the entire universe; unfortunately, the word was mistranslated as an entity. Therefore, when the Veda says Brahmins emanated from the mouth, Kshatriyas from the arms, Vaishyas from the thighs and Shudras from the feet, the varnas were wrongly interpreted hierarchically, indicating that the Brahmins were at the top and Shudras at the bottom. The actual meaning is that all four varnas originate from the same infinite universal consciousness, and while they display specific qualities conducive to their function, they are all equally important, just as all parts of the body are crucial in their respective roles. The feet are no less important than the mouth, and the thighs are not inferior to the arms. No varna was considered lowly, impure or untouchable. Such discrimination was impossible in a culture that believed in the oneness of all creation. Purusha, or consciousness being infinite, has no higher or lower aspect. Shudras were compared to feet because they supported the rest of society with their service, just as the feet bear the body. The very earth the Vedic people revered was also born of the cosmic being's feet, according to the same Purusha Suktam. In the Ramayana, Sumantra was a Shudra because he was a charioteer by profession, but he was Dasharatha's closest adviser and most trusted minister.

Manusmriti 8.335–338 on punishment places the highest penalty on Brahmins, as the learned should know better.

'No father, teacher, friend, mother, wife, brother, son, nor personal priest should go unpunished by the king if they do not keep within their duty.' (8.335)

'Where another common man would be fined one karshapana, the king shall be fined 1000; that is the established rule.' (8.336)

'For theft, the punishment of a Shudra should be eight times (the value of the stolen object), that of a Vaishya sixteen-fold and that of a Kshatriya thirty-two.' (8.337)

'But of a Brahmin, it is sixty-four, or a full hundred or even twice sixty-four times, for he knows about virtues and vices.' (8.338)

The four varnas are inherent to any society and exist in modern times, too. Educators, scientists and other such learned people are comparable to Brahmins, though Brahmins were held to a much higher standard of behaviour in Vedic times. Those in the government, police and military responsible for protecting the populace are Kshatriyas. People engaged in business and commerce are Vaishyas and the rest, who provide general services, are Shudras. A society tends to hold in high status those who possess what it values the most. In our modern world, that place is given to people with wealth and power, Vaishyas and Kshatriyas. However, unlike today, in Vedic times, knowledge was revered, so Brahmins were considered paramount in Vedic society. They were esteemed scholars who lived pious, unselfish lives for society's benefit, and their sacrifice was deeply respected. Brahmins enjoyed a special status on account of their wisdom and purity of mind. It was considered a great sin to kill a Brahmin because they lived frugally on charity, devoted to learning, contemplation and others' welfare, not because of their birth.

Unfortunately, the previously fluid varna system degenerated into a rigid birth-based caste system over the last few hundred years. The main impetus for this was colonization, where varna was used to divide and rule by enacting laws based on a person's so-called caste. For instance, The Land Alienation Act of 1900, and the Punjab Preemption Act of 1913, stated which castes could own land. Some castes were criminalized, living on the fringes of society, while others were given preferential treatment in terms of jobs. The current version of varna associated with caste by birth began in the middle of the nineteenth century with the British census that divided Hindu society into castes by family. By the 1901 census of India, Herbert Hope Risley, a British administrator, institutionalized caste by dividing the Hindu population into four castes by confusing varnas with jatis. Whereas varna is associated with choice, jati means 'thus born'. There were hundreds of jatis or birth-based endogamous tribes and communities, similar to guilds, with nothing to do with varna. By force-fitting all the jatis into the four varnas, the varna system also became hereditary.[1] This new classification further distorted the varna system, which was already losing its original fluidity; it ceased to be egalitarian, becoming an inflexible, oppressive caste-based practice that morphed into one of the greatest evils ever to exist. Also, previously unheard of, a fifth caste called untouchables sprang up, downtrodden and treated with contempt as low class and unclean. The Vedas do not sanction untouchability as discrimination of any kind is censured. In Vedic times impurity was based solely on a fall from dharma, not varna.

The following selection of lines reflects the equality of all human beings:

'Never insult those who are in any way physically disabled, nor those devoid of knowledge, nor the aged, nor those who have no beauty or wealth, nor those who are of low social standing.' (Manusmriti 4:141)

'He who recognizes the Atman in all created beings becomes equal-minded towards all and reaches the highest state, Brahman.' (Manusmriti 12.125)

---

[1] Sharma, Pt Satish K., *Caste, Conversion, A Colonial Conspiracy: What Every Hindu & Christian Needs to Know about Caste* (Notion Press, October 2021).

'The face of truth is covered by the glittering cover of gold. The Purusha—the ultimate source of conscious life that shines in the sun is here in me. I am that Om, the Supreme Reality.' (Yajur Veda 40.17)

'Likewise, may I speak these beneficent words to all people assembled here; to the Brahmin and the Kshatriya, to the Shudra and the Vaishya, to kin and aliens alike.' (Yajur Veda 26.2)

'No mortal is higher or lower, nor is anybody of middle status. All are nobly born and possess outstanding characteristics, progressing through their effort by utilizing the natural resources from Mother Earth for the welfare of all.' (Rig Veda 5.59.6)

'May all members of society have a common objective. May their hearts beat as one, and their minds think as one, so that with their combined energies and diverse skills, they may accomplish the common good.' (Rig Veda 10.191.4)

'Not one of you is small, not one a feeble child. All of you are truly great.' (Rig Veda 8.30.1)

'One who looks upon all living beings as part of the Universal Consciousness, seeing one spirit in all creation, is never deluded.' (Yajur Veda 40.6)

The Atharva Veda sums it up best: 'All are equal in birth and death. Differences arise only during the interval. The emperor and the beggar are both born naked; they sleep equally silently; they bow out without leaving their new address. Then how can their reality be different? There can be no doubt on this score. All are basically the same.'

The Four Stages of Vedic Life—
Ashramas

Vedic life was divided into four stages called ashramas to aid in leading a spiritual existence. These were Brahmacharya, Grihastha, Vanaprastha and Sanyasa.

1. **Brahmacharya**, or student life, was the first stage associated with a single-minded focus on acquiring knowledge. It covered formal education from ages five to twenty-five and comprised strict discipline under a guru. Vedic scholarship was not designed merely to impart skills like today but to build moral fibre that would result in a spiritual approach to life. It was a God-conscious education that taught the oneness of creation and universal brotherhood. Students observed celibacy and lived in the gurukul, the home of their spiritual master, serving him regardless of their social status. This service taught respect and humility. They learned the Shastras, both Shruti[1] and Smriti,[2] science, philosophy, logic, ethics, archery and practical everyday chores. The strength of character was developed through control over the senses and mind. A guru never charged a fee; as a Brahmin he lived on charity, and his duty was to serve society with his knowledge. Education was free, and students paid what they could in the form of 'dakshina'.[3]

2. **Grihastha** was the second phase, associated with family life. It began with marriage after Brahmacharya and continued for the next quarter

---

[1] Shruti refers to the Vedas—divine revelations heard by rishis in deep meditation.

[2] Smritis are the texts on codes of conduct like the Manusmriti. These are most relevant to society at the time they are written and need to be amended over time to suit the norms of the age, much like the Constitution of a country.

[3] Offering or gift.

till age fifty. In Vedic society, a husband and wife saw themselves as spiritual partners and best friends. A wife was considered the other half of her husband, 'ardhangini',[4] so there was no concept of women being inferior. Grihastha involved maintaining a household, earning a living and raising children. It was a limited period that allowed for the pursuit of artha and kama within the boundaries of dharma. Selfishness was to be avoided with five daily duties—the study of the Vedas, service to elders and remembrance of ancestors, feeding animals, offering hospitality to unexpected guests and respecting the environment, symbolized by the Devas. This stage was allotted to earning an income that facilitated charity to the Brahmins and support to the other ashramas. Grihasta was also the only stage when varna was relevant.

3. **Vanaprastha** was the third quarter of life between ages fifty and seventy-five. It was the retirement stage, marked by a withdrawal from worldly life after handing over duties and obligations to the next generation. Renouncing artha and kama was considered necessary in the human spiritual journey to avoid excessive attachment to materialism. This stage was associated with social service, when spiritual practice replaced professional goals and sensual pleasures. The aim was to detach oneself from the burden of daily affairs and engage in contemplation. Thus, Vanaprastha was a preparation for the final stage of life.

4. **Sanyasa** covered the last quarter of life between ages seventy-five and hundred. It involved total renunciation, living a solitary existence and giving up all relationships for the reclusive life of an ascetic. At this stage, the sole concern was concentrating on the attainment of moksha. It was a period of meditation and purification of existence through austerity. The mind did not dwell on indulgences or sense gratification; sanyasa was a complete detachment from worldliness in preparation for departure from the earth.

---

[4] From ardha meaning half and anga meaning body.

Vedic Food Habits

In Vedic life, food, like all forms of matter, was classified into three categories based on 'gunas', or fundamental qualities affecting the body and mind. Ayurveda considers diet as one of the most vital sources of well-being.

Food was classified by its nature as follows:

1. **Sattva:** These foods are of the highest quality as they are healthful, full of goodness and do not excite the senses. Sattva foods are fresh and obtained without injury to animals: whole grains, fruit, vegetables, lentils, milk and milk products. A sattvic diet is humane; it makes a person pure-minded because it is compassionate and does not generate excessive emotion. Brahmins generally consumed a sattvic diet as they understood the oneness of creation.

2. **Rajas:** Foods in this category incite passion. They are spicy, rich, stimulating and cause hyperactivity of the mind and body. Rajas foods are hard to digest, so it was advised to consume them in moderation. They include certain meats, fish, chicken, eggs and vegetables cooked to indulge the senses, including onion and garlic. Eating a predominantly Rajas diet aggravates tendencies of aggression and domination. Therefore, it was associated with Kshatriyas.

3. **Tamas:** These foods are associated with ignorance, decay and disease. They are toxic and cause dullness and lethargy. Thus, these foods were recommended to be avoided to live a healthy life. Impure meat, alcohol and stale food are examples of tamas.

Like all aspects of Vedic life, food habits were influenced by the spiritual message of oneness and harmony. For this reason, vegetarianism was encouraged, as Ahimsa, the principle of doing the least harm, freed a person of karmic debt. However, meat consumption was not prohibited, as Vedic philosophy advocates freedom of choice and attaining wisdom through self-realization, not rigidly following prescriptive commandments. Here are some verses on the subject:

'One can never obtain meat without causing injury to living beings . . . one should, therefore, abstain from meat. Reflecting on how meat is obtained and on how embodied creatures are tied up and killed, one should avoid eating any kind of meat . . . (Manusmriti 5.48–49)

'There is no sin in eating meat or drinking wine or in sexual union as this is how living beings engage in life, but disengagement yields great fruit.' (Manusmriti 5.56)

'By not harming any living being, one becomes eligible for immortality.' (Manusmriti 6.60)

'Those who see all beings as pervaded by one consciousness, experience oneness with them.' (Yajur Veda 40.7)

'O teeth! You eat rice, you eat barley, you eat gram and you eat sesame. These cereals are specifically meant for you. Do not kill those who are capable of being fathers and mothers.' (Atharva Veda 6.140.2)

'Having no ill-feeling for any living being, in all manners possible and for all times is called ahimsa, and it should be the desired goal of all seekers.' (Patanjali Yoga Sutras, 2.30)

In Vedic texts, references to rice, wheat and barley suggest that cereals formed an essential part of the diet. Vedic people also ate curd, ghee and other dairy products, lentils, fruit, vegetables and meat. Although not mandatory, Brahmins generally adopted a sattvic diet to support tranquillity of mind and abstain from causing injury. This practice continues till today. Turmeric was an essential spice mentioned in Vedic literature, and excavated cooking pots from Saraswati sites show its use. Vedic shastras stress moderation, so animal flesh was eaten in small quantities as a side dish and was not the centre of the plate even if consumed.

Some mistranslations of Vedic texts advocate the prevalence of beef-eating in Vedic times, but this is false. Sanskrit words have multiple meanings depending on grammar and the context of use. A cursory knowledge of the language is dangerous and can completely change the meaning in translation. There is enormous reverence for cows throughout Vedic literature and an emphatic injunction against killing them. They are identified with Aditi and are a symbol of motherhood.

'A guru, a teacher, a father, a mother, a Brahmin, a cow and a yogi should never be killed.' (Manusmriti 4.162)

'I speak to those of knowledge: do not harm the innocent cow, for in so doing, you are harming the earth and Mother Nature.' (Rig Veda 8.101.15)

Vedic literature shows that the cow has a special status, and it was considered sinful to cause it harm. While the Vedic people cherished and valued the cow, it is a misconception to believe they worshipped it. The cow was revered for many reasons, but not because it was equated with God. Cattle were a source of livelihood and the wealth of society. Milk provided nourishment, so the cow was likened to a mother. Clarified butter or ghee was used as a cooking medium and an offering in yagnas. Cow dung provided fuel, manure and plaster for huts. Bulls ploughed fields and were vital in agriculture. Bullock carts were also a means of transport. It is thankless to kill an animal that gives so much and repay its kindness with death. Ingratitude was one of the greatest sins in Vedic times. Rama mentions this when Sugriva forgets his promise to help find Sita.

The Vedic people owed so much gratitude to the animal that the Vedas refer to it as 'aghanya', an innocent creature that should never be killed under any circumstances.

'The aghanya cows and bulls bring you prosperity.' (Yajur Veda 12.73)

'Those who feed on human flesh, horses and those who destroy milk-giving aghanya cows deserve punishment.' (Rig Veda 10.87.16)

Every household had cows, and they were treated like family in the same way we treat our pet dogs today. The thought of eating a cow was as horrific to Vedic people as eating dogs in modern times.

The entire Hymn 28 in Book 6 of the Rig Veda is dedicated to the sanctity of the cow.

The hymn asks everyone to ensure that cows are happy and healthy, blessing those who care for cows. Cows are revered for giving sustenance and bringing prosperity, so the Veda directs people never to kill them. If cows are healthy and happy, men and women also keep fit and prosperous.

Yagnas—Vedic Fire Sacrifices

Yagna is derived from 'yaj', which means worship or honour. At a ritualistic level, a yagna involved a sacrificial fire (Agni) into which offerings were made while chanting mantras. Agni was believed to carry the prayers to higher powers like Indra and Varuna, thereby bringing prosperity. The ceremonial practice of a yagna was meant to enact the profound philosophy of the Vedas to bring about transformation and renewal.

'Agni, may we be able to perform all types of auspicious and benedictory yagnas freely and without impediment, so that the deities who protect us may readily and generously help us grow.' (Rig Veda 1.89.1)

Ritualistic yagnas form part of the Karma Kanda of the Vedas, the liturgy section, as opposed to the Gyana Kanda, which deals with philosophy, where the mind is symbolically the altar. We see this in the Chandogya Upanishad, which equates a personal attitude of sacrifice with an abstract yagna, a higher form of worship.

'Now what people call yagna is really Brahmacharya (the disciplined life of a student of sacred knowledge), for only by personal sacrifice does one obtain the Self.' (Chandogya Upanishad 8.5.1)

The Svetasvatara Upanishad Verse 1.5.14 speaks of yagna as the inner cleansing of oneself:

'By making one's own body as the lower friction sticks, the syllable Om as the upper friction sticks, then practising the friction of meditation, one may realize God who is hidden within, as it were.'

In the ceremonial yagna of the Karma Kanda, a fire was lit in an altar of specific dimensions called a yagna vedi and offerings like ghee, milk, grains and soma were made. The ritualistic enactment of the spiritual philosophy of the Vedas served to remove negativity through purification and a prayer for prosperity:

'May my paddy and rice, my barley, my beans and my sesame, and my sesame, my mung beans, and my legumins, my millet, my wild grains and my wheat, my lentils and all other grains grow and be plentiful by sacrifice (yagna).' (Shukla Yajur Veda 18.12)

Yagnas are not conducted anymore, but the Vedic wedding ceremony is one that continues to be performed today.

The word sacrifice for yagna can be misleading because it conjures up the image of killing. Causing harm to any creature contradicts the fundamental teaching of Vedic philosophy. Although some passages can be misconstrued to suggest this, it is hard to believe that the Vedas encourage animal sacrifice. Perhaps the practice resulted from an erroneous interpretation; the philosophy behind the ritual got lost along the way, and its original intention as a 'mock enactment'[1] began to be followed in a literal sense. Shankaracharya, credited with the revival of Vedic philosophy, strongly condemned blind adherence to rituals as he walked the length and breadth of India, asserting that all forms of life are divine. The Vedas are cryptic and difficult to decipher because the same word has multiple interpretations and cannot be taken literally. Many analogies have a symbolic connotation alluding to a subtler meaning that may appear paradoxical on a cursory reading. For example, the Gomedha does not advocate killing a cow, the Purushamedha is not a human sacrifice and the Pitramedha was not the ritualistic killing of the father, though they can translate as such word for word.

The fire in a yagna stands for purity, and it is our base animalistic instincts, like greed, pride, anger etc. that are sacrificed. The animal is symbolic. At the end of the Ashwamedha, it became a practice to kill the horse because it represented royal sway, pride and the unruly senses, but the Vedas do not necessarily suggest a literal killing. For example, note the following line from the Yajur Veda:

'Imam ma himsirekashafam pashum kanikradam vaajinam vaajineshu.' (Yajur Veda 13.48)

The translation is: 'Do not slaughter this one-hoofed animal that neighs and is fastest of the fast.'

Consider the following verse from the Shatapatha Brahmana:

Raashtram vaa ashwamedha
Annam hi gau
Agnirvaa ashwah
Aajyam medhah

—Shatapatha 13.1.6.3

---

[1] Kak, Subhash, *The Asvamedha: The Rite and Its Logic*, first edition (New Delhi: Motilal Banarsidass, 2002).

Here 'ashwa' symbolizes the power of the kingdom, and the word 'medha' indicates its intellect or mental strength, not slaughter. It also stands for consolidation of the empire.

Therefore, the Ashwamedha Yagna was meant to be a symbolic ritual dedicated to the kingdom's glory, well-being and prosperity. By figuratively killing the horse that stood for royal power, any false pride resulting from subduing a vast number of kingdoms was destroyed.

Women in Vedic Society

Although Vedic society was patriarchal, women enjoyed great respect, and several references in Vedic texts indicate that they held a high status. 'Fathers, husbands, brothers, and brothers-in-law who wish for great good fortune should revere and adorn their women.' (Manusmriti 3.55)

Violence towards women was looked upon with abhorrence. A girl child was never considered a burden, and many verses in the Vedas praise daughters. For example, Rig Veda 10.159.3 describes a daughter as refulgent, and 8.31.8 says it is a blessing to have both sons and daughters.

Men were expected to treat all women courteously. 'Addressing a woman who is another man's wife and not related by birth, one should say lady or good woman or sister.' (Manusmriti 2.129). Manusmriti, in 2.138, speaks about being gracious and giving women the right of way on the street. God, the ultimate power, was perceived as a union of male and female energy, and the feminine aspect of the divine was considered as worthy of reverence as the male form.

The powers of the Vedic Trinity—Brahma, Vishnu and Shiva—are incomplete without their female counterparts, Saraswati, Lakshmi and Parvati. In marriage, a bride was considered a treasure to be cherished. 'Where the wife is radiant and happy, the whole house is heaven-like, but if she is unhappy, all will appear like hell.' (Manusmriti 3.62)

A husband and wife were viewed as two halves of a whole; neither one was superior or inferior. The word for wife, 'ardhangini', expresses this equality. Atharva Veda 14.2.71 says, 'O wife, if I am the male aspect (Purusha), you are the female aspect (Prakriti) of the same. If I am Samaveda (song), you are Rigveda (verse).' The Vedic people acknowledged the inherent physical differences in men and women, so while celebrating the oneness of spirit, they valued each gender's unique attributes, never forgetting that both emanate from the same cosmic consciousness.

Women were not forced into marriage and always had the final say, even if the alliance was arranged. 'But it would be better for a daughter, even though she has reached puberty, to stay in the house until she dies than for him (the father) to give her to a man with no good qualities,' (Manusmriti 9.89)

Marriages by choice were commonplace in the ancient customs of Swayamvara[1] and Gandharvavivah.[2] In the family, a woman was the mistress of the household and was referred to as 'samraghi' or empress of her domain.

Further, it was believed that a society could only prosper if the women were treated with respect. 'Yatra nari astu pujyante, ramante tatra devataa.' The deities delight in places where women are revered (Manusmriti 3.56). The mistreatment of women was considered a great sin. This belief is repeated throughout the Ramayana.

After marriage, women retained their parental identity, evident in the various names of Sita: Janaki, Maithili and Vaidehi. Men were often known by their mothers. Lakshmana, for instance, is also called Soumitra, son of Sumitra, and Hanuman is referred to as Anjaneya, son of Anjana. A wife was not expected to obey her husband blindly but to act as a friend and guide in life, a moral compass. We see Sita fulfilling this duty when she is concerned about Rama's promise to exterminate the Rakshasas from Dandakaranya. A wife's role was so crucial that a yagna required her presence and could not be fruitful without her. Rig Veda 10.85.46 speaks about women taking a leading role in society, and Atharva Veda 2.36.3 says, 'May this bride become the queen of the house of her husband and enlighten all.'

Education was as open to girls as it was to boys, though they were homeschooled and did not live away in a gurukul.

'The youthful girl who graduates from Brahmacharya obtains a suitable husband.' (Atharva Veda 11.5.18)

'Parents should gift their daughters' intellectuality and the power of knowledge when she leaves for her husband's home. They should give her a dowry of knowledge.' (Atharva Veda 14.1.6)

The Vedas describe many women as Brahmavadinis;[3] those who attained the highest level of philosophical knowledge. Rig Veda 10.191 speaks of the right of every human being to study the Vedas, and many female

---

[1] Ceremony where several eligible suitors were invited, and the bride garlanded the man of her choice.

[2] Marriage where two individuals fall in love and marry.

[3] One who speaks about Brahman, an expounder of the Veda.

seers contributed to Vedic hymns. Ghosha, Godha, Maitreyi, Anasuya, Lopamudra and Gargi were some of the acclaimed women scholars of the past. Kshatriya women even learned martial arts, as we see in the case of Kaikeyi in the Ramayana. Kaushalya is described as 'mantravid' or learned in mantras. Vedavati, who Ravana tried to have his way with, was a female ascetic who meditated in solitude just as a male rishi would. In the Brihadaranyaka Upanishad, sage Yagnavalkya had two wives, and while Katyayani preferred household duties, the other wife, Maitreyi, was of superior intelligence and chose to pursue higher learning. Gargi was a famous philosopher in the court of Janaka who debated on an equal footing with her male counterparts, and the Yoga Yagnavalkya is a dialogue between her and the famous sage. The Yajur Veda 20.84 appreciates women as educators: 'May the scholarly woman (represented by Saraswati) purify our lives with her knowledge, noble actions, and guidance.'

In their domestic role of giving birth and raising offspring, women were honoured as custodians of morality and valued for their contribution to the continuity of humankind. 'Women give birth to the next generation. They enlighten the home. They bring fortune and bliss. Hence women are synonymous with prosperity.' (Manusmriti 9.26)

The Vedas place the mother on a pedestal and demand that she be given the highest respect. 'The teacher (acharya) is ten times more venerable than an instructor (upadhyaya), the father a hundred times more than the teacher, but the mother a thousand times more than the father.' (Manusmriti 2:145)

Kaushalya refers to this when she asks Rama not to leave for the forest and accept her command over keeping his father's promise.

'The mother is great! I pray for her happiness.' (Rig Veda 1.159.2)

'Matrdevo bhava': Respect your mother as a Deva. (Taittiriya Upanishad 1.11.2)

Society placed the responsibility for a woman's welfare on the men in the family, so she was never neglected. 'A father who does not marry his daughter to a deserving groom deserves condemnation. A husband who does not fulfil the just demands of his wife deserves condemnation. A son who does not take care of his widowed mother deserves condemnation.' (Manusmriti 9.4)

Women were never cloistered behind walls or hidden by veils. This practice was unknown in Vedic times and came about much later. Women had the right to their own wealth and property, as Lakshmana points out in the case of Kaushalya, who was financially independent.

A woman's right to property is protected in the following lines:

'A daughter is equivalent to a son. In her presence, how can anyone snatch away her right over the property?' (Manusmriti 9.130)

'If a person has no wife or kin, his wealth should be distributed equally among his brothers and sisters. If the elder brother refuses to give the other brothers and sisters their due share, he is punishable by law.' (Manusmriti 9. 212-213)

'A daughter alone has the right over the personal property of her mother.' (Manusmriti 9.131)

Women participated in society as independent individuals, not appendages, and had the right to remarry in certain circumstances, including ill-treatment and abandonment, if the husband was convicted of a crime or passed away. When Rama is exiled, Vasishta suggests Sita should rule in his place, holding the highest position in the land, pointing to the power women shared and their equality in society. Yajur Veda 10.26 speaks of a queen's active role in governance. Women spoke their minds freely, and their power is evident in the interaction between Kaikeyi and Dasharatha when she insists on having her way. Sita was no milquetoast and is depicted by Valmiki as a strong woman with a mind of her own. She decides to go with Rama despite his reluctance, and when she is rejected after being rescued, she stands her ground.

While Vedic women had great freedom and men were taught to treat them with respect, this changed after the first millennium CE with the arrival of Mahmud Ghazni and the subsequent Arab, Turk and Mughal subjugation of India. The old ways changed forever. Over 40,000 temples were destroyed,[4] and great universities like Nalanda, Sharada Peeth, Vikramshila and countless others were burnt to the ground. Nalanda is said to have housed so many manuscripts that it smouldered for three months. The invaders came to loot the wealth of India, but their religious zeal sought to wipe out Vedic culture, viewing idolaters as sinners. In perhaps the worst massacre ever, spanning several centuries, it is estimated from the perpetrators' chronicles that as many as eighty million men were slaughtered, and their womenfolk carried off and sold in the markets of Central Asia.[5] Disrespecting the women of a defeated

---

[4] Goel, Sita Ram, *Hindu Temples – What Happened to Them*, 2 volumes (Voice of India, 1990).

[5] Lal, K.S., *Growth of Muslim Population in Medieval India (A.D. 1000-1800)* (New Delhi: Research Publications in Social Sciences, 1973); *Kitab-I-Yamini*, translated by Rev. James Reynolds from the Persian version of the contemporary Arabic chronicle of Al Utbi (London: W.H. Allen and Co., 1848).

enemy kingdom was alien to Vedic philosophy and never encountered before. To protect themselves from a fate worse than death, Rajput wives famously immolated themselves en masse, performing jauhar to preserve their chastity. Buried in the annals of history lie boastful records of ethnic cleansing, like Timur Lang's slaughter of a hundred thousand Hindus in a single day.

Unfortunately, women lost the liberties that they had once enjoyed. Gradually equality was replaced with various repressive cultural practices far removed from the original Vedic philosophy. The purdah system began, which kept women veiled and hidden from sight. Society began to view them as a liability, and ills like prepubescent[6] child marriage, female infanticide, forced sati and ill-treatment of widows crept in, destroying the egalitarian society of the past.

---

[6] A girl child began to be viewed as such a great liability that she was married off as quickly as possible. If she was prepubescent, she remained with her parents till she reached puberty.

Respect for Guests, Elders
and Brahmins

Aside from affording women high standing in society, the Vedic civilization particularly honoured unexpected guests who turned up, elders and the learned.

The Taittiriya Upanishad 1.11.2 instructs people to 'see the divine in your mother, father, teacher, and a random visitor'. The word for an uninvited guest is 'atithi', which means one who arrives without notice or an unexpected visitor. It was considered uncouth to turn away anyone who arrived at the door without offering food and water. Sita follows this tradition of hospitality when Ravana comes to her hut in the guise of a wandering sage. Vedic custom advocated feeding a stranger who arrived out of the blue even if it meant staying hungry oneself. The Atharva Veda says, 'For the success and fulfilment of a yagna, partake of the food after the guests have eaten. This is the right way.'

Utmost respect was shown to parents as givers of life. 'He whose mother and father are not properly served and honoured, meets with worries and woes; while he whose mother and father are held in high esteem, achieves bliss and wins admiration among his friends and virtuous people.' (Rig Veda 4.6.7)

Rama alludes to the debt children owe their parents when he refuses to return to Ayodhya despite Vasishta's request. There are many verses in the Vedas about respecting parents, especially celebrating mothers. Along with parents, all seniors in age were venerated. Atharva Veda 3.30.5 instructs, 'Be respectful to elders,' and Manusmriti 2.137 says, 'A very old Shudra deserves more respect than anyone else regardless of their wealth, lineage, age, actions, or knowledge.' Manusmriti 2.121 emphasizes that 'one who habitually salutes and treats the elderly well thrives in four ways: long life, knowledge, fame, and strength'.

Vedic Brahmins lived abstemiously, never dealing with money, and were deeply venerated for their scholarship and exemplary conduct. They lived meagrely on charity, single-mindedly focused on knowledge and service to society. Therefore, killing such a self-sacrificing person was considered a heinous crime that resulted in a terrible loss to the community. A Brahmin was a guru and commanded enormous respect in his role of imparting wisdom. 'Guru' comes from 'gu', darkness and 'ru', remover, so he was revered for showing the light. The following mantra expresses the importance given to a guru:

'Gurur Brahma, Gurur Vishnuh, Gurur Devo Maheshwarah; Guruh Sakshat Parabrahma, Tasmai Shri Gurave Namah.'

'The Guru is Brahma; the Guru is Vishnu; the Guru is Shiva. Indeed, the Guru is the Supreme Absolute. To that Guru, I offer my reverent salutations.'

A guru was not just a teacher but also a knower of Brahman, a true Brahmin, a pure-minded sacrificing individual, who had achieved self-realization and liberation from materialism. The Ramayana depicts the importance of the guru throughout. Manusmriti 2.148 states that a guru is responsible for a person's true birth, as knowledge is immortal, living on when the body is no more.

The Vedic Concept of Time

Today, the world believes in the Western concept of time, seeing it as linear, but this is not how time was always viewed. The Vedic people saw time entirely differently, as cyclical, repeating endlessly in four epochs called yugas. Ancient Indian astronomers studiously observed stellar movements and had advanced knowledge of the heavens. The rishis were not flat-earthers; they knew the earth was round. Thousands of years ago, they spoke about the earth's rotation, that it travelled around the sun, that the moon orbited around our globe, and that the Solar System revolved around the centre of the Milky Way. The Sanskrit word for our planet is 'jagat', which indicates that it is in motion. They even knew about the precession of the equinoxes and theorized that the sun orbited around a dual star, a concept that modern astronomers are now exploring.

The rishis inferred that the motion of astral bodies influenced human consciousness and derived the idea of dharma yugas based on the effect of the Solar System's revolution around the sun's binary star and orbit around the centre of the galaxy. They determined that the sun took 24,000 years to complete one cycle. This period also approximates the time taken for the Earth's axis to make a complete circle tracing through the constellations of the Zodiac in the precession of the equinoxes. The Vedic rishis hypothesized that the sun revolved around the galactic centre, called Vishnu nabhi,[1] the seat of Brahma, associated with creative power. While orbiting elliptically around its star, the sun takes 12,000 years to move away from Vishnu nabhi and another 12,000 to trace its path back. The sages concluded that human virtue, intellect, knowledge, lifespan and physical stature expanded or reduced based on this trajectory. Therefore, four waxing yugas comprising

---

[1] Vishnu's navel.

12,000 years trace an ascent to a higher level of consciousness, and similarly, four waning yugas mark a decline to a lower level of consciousness.[2]

The four yugas are:

1. **Kritayuga or Satya yuga (4800 years):** The Golden Age of perfection marked by truth, righteousness, wisdom and love, where dharma, represented by a bull, stands on all four legs: Tapas—austerity, Saucha—cleanliness, Satyam—truth and Daya—compassion. This epoch is when the Solar System is closest to Vishnu nabhi, making it an age of peace when dharma is at 100 per cent; all people have purity of mind and are in touch with their inner selves.

2. **Tretayuga (3600 years):** The Silver Age when morality declines by a quarter and dharma loses one leg. Rama lived during this yuga. It is the age of thought when people use mental powers to perform amazing feats.

3. **Dwaparayuga (2400 years):** The Bronze Age, when human spirituality reduces by half, and dharma is left with only two legs. While virtue diminishes to a large degree, with selfishness on the rise, it is also the age of energy and innovation. The other great Indian epic, the Mahabharata, takes place in this yuga when Vishnu incarnates as Krishna.

4. **Kaliyuga (1200 years):** The Iron Age of darkness, when negative forces overshadow goodness and dharma limps on one leg. This low point in human virtue occurs when the Solar System is furthest from Vishnu nabhi, resulting in the age of materialism.

The other way of looking at time is at a cosmic level as Divya Yugas or divine epochs. One day of divine time is considered one human year, so a cycle of four yugas, is 12,000 years x 360 = 43,20,000 years. This figure is remarkably close to the scientific estimate of the earth being approximately 4.54 billion years old. Seen as Divya Yugas, Kritayuga/Satyayuga lasts 17,28,000 years, Treta 12,96,000 years, Dvapara 8,64,000 years and Kaliyuga 4,32,000 years.

A 1000 four-yuga cycles make a Kalpa, one day of Brahma, at the end of which the world is destroyed and recreated, continuing the yuga cycle.

'The Hindu religion is the only one of the world's great faiths dedicated to the idea that the cosmos itself undergoes an immense, indeed an infinite,

---

[2] The Holy Science – Sri Yukteswar, 1894.

number of deaths and rebirths. It is the only religion in which the time scales correspond to those of modern scientific cosmology. Its cycles run from our ordinary day and night to a day and night of Brahma, 8.64 billion years long. Longer than the age of the Earth or the sun and about half the time since the Big Bang.'[3]

---

[3] Carl Sagan, *Cosmos* (Random House, 1980).

YUGA CHART

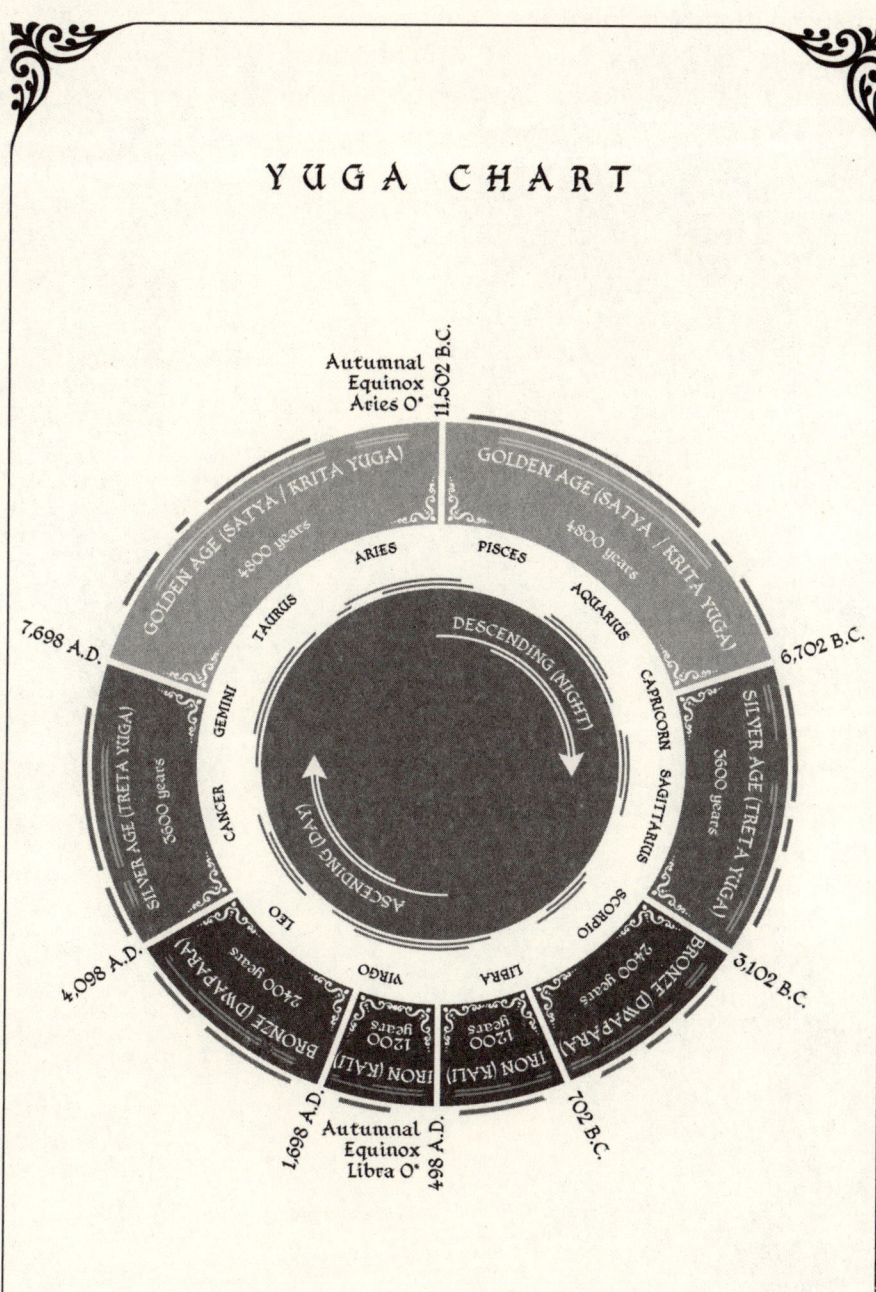

The Story of Valmiki

Valmiki's story is found in the Skanda Purana. It tells us that the great sage who composed the Ramayana was not always a revered ascetic. His real name was Ratnakara, and he was given the name Valmiki, 'the one who emerged from an anthill', only later in life when he attained enlightenment. Valmiki's life story is intriguing. Although born to Rishi Prachetasa, he was lost in the forest in early childhood and adopted by a hunter. His foster parents brought him up with affection and initiated him into their vocation. When he came of age, he married a woman from the same community and fathered many children. Although Ratnakara was a skilled hunter, he found it difficult to feed his family and took to robbery to supplement his income.

Ratnakara was greatly feared, as he would mercilessly attack and kill unsuspecting travellers to steal their possessions. One day, the esteemed sage Narada passed through the jungle, and Ratnakara waylaid him. This encounter was a life-changing event for Ratnakara. Narada had nothing valuable on his person to hand over and asked the young man why he was engaged in a life of crime instead of earning an honest living. When Ratnakara said he was doing it for his family because he had many mouths to feed, Narada asked if his loved ones would share the bad karma he was accumulating with his evil deeds. When Ratnakara said he was sure they would, Narada suggested he check with them to confirm his understanding. Tying the sage to a tree, Ratnakara went to find out, but to his dismay, his family said he was doing his duty in providing for them, so they did not feel responsible for his actions. This rejection changed Ratnakara forever; he hurried back to Narada and fell at his feet, begging him for a way to atone for all the crimes he had committed in his ignorance. Narada became his guru and instructed him to meditate single-mindedly on the divine consciousness, chanting the Lord's name to expiate his sins. Ratnakara remained absorbed in concentration for so many years that an anthill formed around him.

Finally, Narada appeared before Ratnakara again, and clearing the anthill, proclaimed him Valmiki. Brahmagyana[1] had wholly transformed the cruel bandit, and he lived a life of penance from then on. Valmiki set up his ashram on the banks of the Tamasa and gave refuge to Sita when she was abandoned. During this time, he composed the Ramayana and taught it to Rama's sons, Lava and Kusha.

---

[1] Knowledge of Brahman.

Rama's Ancestry

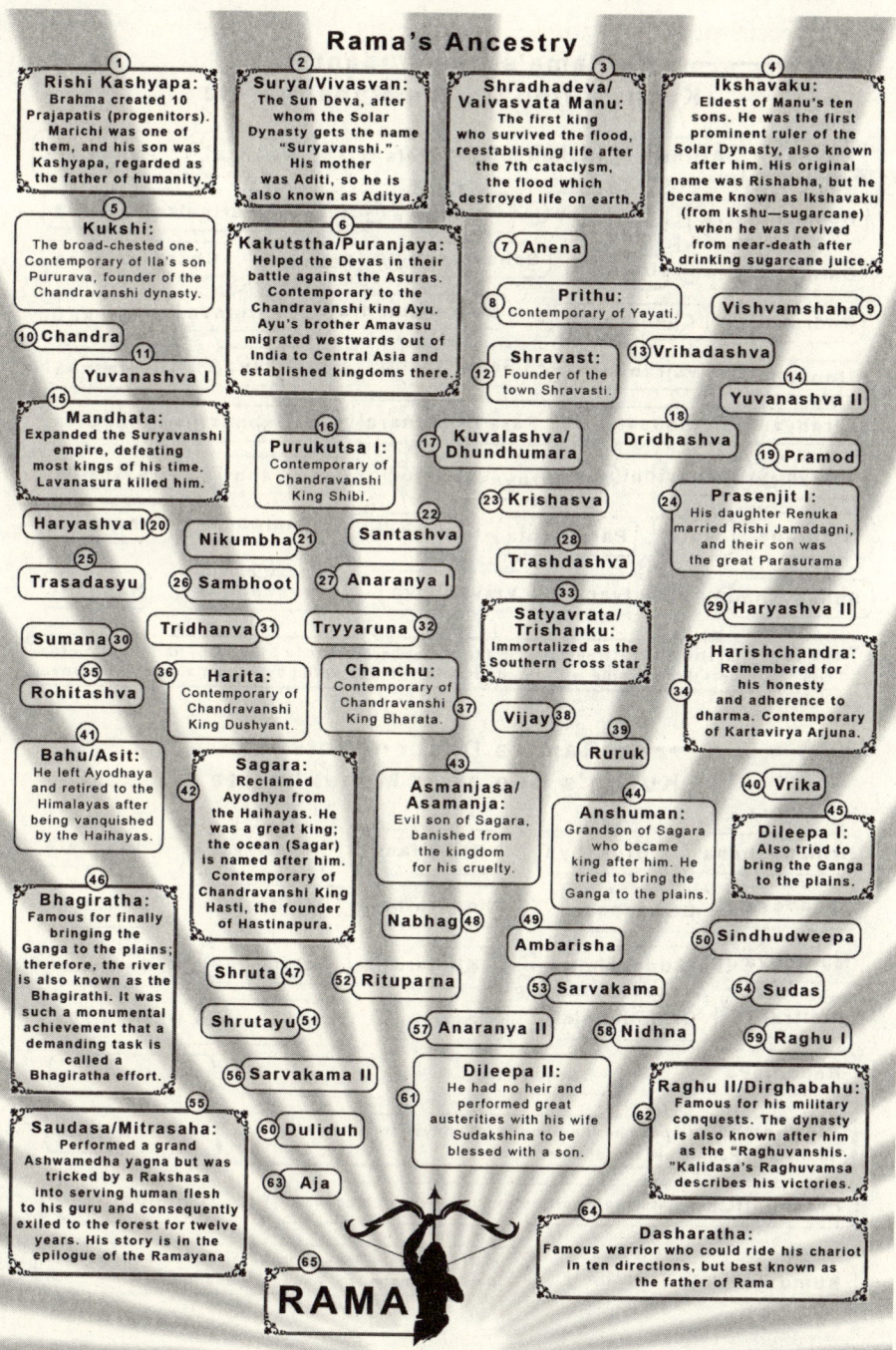

1. **Rishi Kashyapa:** Brahma created 10 Prajapatis (progenitors). Marichi was one of them, and his son was Kashyapa, regarded as the father of humanity.

2. **Surya/Vivasvan:** The Sun Deva, after whom the Solar Dynasty gets the name "Suryavanshi." His mother was Aditi, so he is also known as Aditya.

3. **Shradhadeva/Vaivasvata Manu:** The first king who survived the flood, reestablishing life after the 7th cataclysm, the flood which destroyed life on earth.

4. **Ikshavaku:** Eldest of Manu's ten sons. He was the first prominent ruler of the Solar Dynasty, also known after him. His original name was Rishabha, but he became known as Ikshavaku (from ikshu—sugarcane) when he was revived from near-death after drinking sugarcane juice.

5. **Kukshi:** The broad-chested one. Contemporary of Ila's son Pururava, founder of the Chandravanshi dynasty.

6. **Kakutstha/Puranjaya:** Helped the Devas in their battle against the Asuras. Contemporary to the Chandravanshi king Ayu. Ayu's brother Amavasu migrated westwards out of India to Central Asia and established kingdoms there.

7. Anena

8. **Prithu:** Contemporary of Yayati.

9. Vishvamshaha

10. Chandra

11. Yuvanashva I

12. **Shravast:** Founder of the town Shravasti.

13. Vrihadashva

14. Yuvanashva II

15. **Mandhata:** Expanded the Suryavanshi empire, defeating most kings of his time. Lavanasura killed him.

16. **Purukutsa I:** Contemporary of Chandravanshi King Shibi.

17. Kuvalashva/Dhundhumara

18. Dridhashva

19. Pramod

20. Haryashva I

21. Nikumbha

22. Santashva

23. Krishasva

24. **Prasenjit I:** His daughter Renuka married Rishi Jamadagni, and their son was the great Parasurama

25. Trasadasyu

26. Sambhoot

27. Anaranya I

28. Trashdashva

29. Haryashva II

30. Sumana

31. Tridhanva

32. Tryyaruna

33. **Satyavrata/Trishanku:** Immortalized as the Southern Cross star

34. **Harishchandra:** Remembered for his honesty and adherence to dharma. Contemporary of Kartavirya Arjuna.

35. Rohitashva

36. **Harita:** Contemporary of Chandravanshi King Dushyant.

37. **Chanchu:** Contemporary of Chandravanshi King Bharata.

38. Vijay

39. Ruruk

40. Vrika

41. **Bahu/Asit:** He left Ayodhaya and retired to the Himalayas after being vanquished by the Haihayas.

42. **Sagara:** Reclaimed Ayodhya from the Haihayas. He was a great king; the ocean (Sagar) is named after him. Contemporary of Chandravanshi King Hasti, the founder of Hastinapura.

43. **Asmanjasa/Asamanja:** Evil son of Sagara, banished from the kingdom for his cruelty.

44. **Anshuman:** Grandson of Sagara who became king after him. He tried to bring the Ganga to the plains.

45. **Dileepa I:** Also tried to bring the Ganga to the plains.

46. **Bhagiratha:** Famous for finally bringing the Ganga to the plains; therefore, the river is also known as the Bhagirathi. It was such a monumental achievement that a demanding task is called a Bhagiratha effort.

47. Shruta

48. Nabhag

49. Ambarisha

50. Sindhudweepa

51. Shrutayu

52. Rituparna

53. Sarvakama

54. Sudas

55. **Saudasa/Mitrasaha:** Performed a grand Ashwamedha yagna but was tricked by a Rakshasa into serving human flesh to his guru and consequently exiled to the forest for twelve years. His story is in the epilogue of the Ramayana

56. Sarvakama II

57. Anaranya II

58. Nidhna

59. Raghu I

60. Duliduh

61. **Dileepa II:** He had no heir and performed great austerities with his wife Sudakshina to be blessed with a son.

62. **Raghu II/Dirghabahu:** Famous for his military conquests. The dynasty is also known after him as the "Raghuvanshis." Kalidasa's Raghuvamsa describes his victories.

63. Aja

64. **Dasharatha:** Famous warrior who could ride his chariot in ten directions, but best known as the father of Rama

65. RAMA

Rama's Descendants
Kusha's line till the Mahabharata

Kusha (1) — Atithi (2) — Nishadha (3) — Nala II (4) — Nabhas (5) — Pundarika (6)

Ksemadhanva (7) — Devanika (8) — Ahinagu (9) — Ruru (10) — Paripatra (11) — Sala (12)

Dala (13) — Bala (14) — Uktha (15) — Sahasrasva (16) — Para II (17) — Chandravaloka (18)

Rudraksh (19) — Chandragiri (20) — Bhanuchandra (21) — Srutayu (22) — Uluka (23)

Unnabha (24) — Vajranabha (25) — Sankhana (26) — Vyusitasva (27) — Visvasaha (28)

Hiranyanabha Kausalya (29) — Para III (Atnara) (30) — Brahmistha (31) — Putra (32)

Pusya (33) — Arthasidhi (34) — Dhruvasandhi (35) — Sudarsana (36) — Agnivatna (37)

Sighraga (38) — Maru (39) — Parsusruta (40) — Susandhi (41) — Amarsana (42) — Mahasvana (43)

Sahasvana (44) — Visrutvana (45) — Visvabhava (46) — Visvasahava (47) — Nagnajit (48)

Taksaka (49) — **Brihadbala** (50): Ironically, in the Mahabharata war in 3139 BCE, he fought on the unrighteous side with the Kauravas and was killed by Arjuna's son, Abhimanyu.

Rama's Descendants
Kusha's line after Mahabharata

Brihadkshana (1) — Urukshya (2) — Brihadasva (3) — Prativyoma (4) — Divakara (5)

Sahadeva (6) — Brihadasva (7) — Bhanuratha (8) — Pratitashva (9) — Supratika (10)

Marudeva (11) — Sunakshatra (12) — Kinnara (13) — Antariksha (14) — Suvarna (15)

Amitrajit (16) — Brihadbhaja (17) — Dharmin (18) — Kritanjaya or Dhananjaya (19)

Rananjaya (20) — Sanjaya (21) — Sakya (22) — Suddhodana (23)

Siddhartha (24): He became the Buddha and never ruled the kingdom, so his son Rahula became the next king. — **Rahula** (25)

Prasenajit (26): His sister was married to Bimbisara of Magadha. — Kahudraka (27)

Kumdaka (28) — Suratha (29) — **Sumitra** (30): The last known king in the Ikshavaku Dynasty, ousted by Mahapadmananda.

The Message of the Ramayana

The Ramayana teaches the secular message of universal harmony achieved through a spiritual approach to life. These are some of the main lessons it instils:

1. **Integrity:** Cultivate righteousness based on the qualities Rama displayed. Do what is right even if it is inconvenient.
2. **Fortitude:** Recognize that life has ups and downs, bearing misfortunes with courage and forbearance.
3. **Recognize Good Advice:** Corrupt counsel or company can have terrible consequences. This is evidenced by the evil influence of Manthara on Kaikeyi and the wrong guidance of Surpanakha and Ravana's ministers. The Ramayana highlights the value of good advice and the importance of recognizing it. Vali suffered because he ignored Tara, whereas Rama benefited from Lakshmana's advice not to succumb to anger or despondency.
4. **Inner Strength:** True character manifests itself in times of adversity. Rama was reduced to a pauper, moments from inheriting one of the greatest kingdoms on earth. Yet he gave up everything without complaint to honour his father's promise.
5. **Selflessness:** Detachment from material pleasures, 'aparigraha', is the path to peace and happiness. Bharata was handed the kingdom but refused to accept it because his principles were stronger than his desire for material gain.
6. **Equality:** View everyone equally. Rama had the quality of 'sousheelyam', and never differentiated between people based on their social status. Despite his royal birth, Guha, a tribal, and Hanuman, a forest dweller, were his dearest friends.

7. **Ahimsa:** Live by ahimsa and do the least harm possible. Only exercise the option of violence after exhausting all attempts at non-violence. Rama tried to achieve a peaceful resolution with Ravana until the end and resorted to war only when left with no alternative. However, it is essential to note that ahimsa differs from pacifism. Violence is deemed just when there is no other choice, as it restores dharma in a moral battle or dharmayudha.

8. **Personal Responsibility:** We hold our destiny firmly in our hands based on the choices we make. Karma is the law of causality, and consequences naturally follow our actions, depending on whether we do good or evil. As Mandodari rightly said in her eulogy, Ravana perished because of his own sinful actions.

9. **Keep Good Company:** There is excellent value in good associations. Rama gained wisdom from the erudite company of the rishis, and his friendship with Vibhishana and the Vanaras was mutually beneficial.

10. **Avoid Egotism:** Wealth and power can have a corrupting influence if we are not careful. Sugriva almost fell into the trap but luckily heeded the good advice he was given. Ravana, on the other hand, was destroyed by his egotism.

11. **Dharma Is Contextual:** Dharma is complex, and righteous action depends on the situation. For example, Rama killed Vali when he was fighting someone else, which is typically considered unrighteous, but in the circumstances, it was the only possible action to restore dharma because Vali was sinful and could not be killed in direct combat. Sometimes, depending on the context, one dharma must be sacrificed to uphold another for the greater good. When Rama abandoned Sita, he placed his duty as a king above that as a husband.

12. **Focus on the Imperishable:** When we die, we carry only dharma and the effect of our deeds (karma) with us. All material objects are left behind, yet we foolishly attach more importance to temporary things that are irrelevant in the long run.

13. **Leadership Matters:** Virtuous leaders are crucial in building dharmic civilizations, like Rama's Ayodhya and Vibhishana's Lanka.

14. **Win the Inner Battle:** Our greatest enemies lie within us. These are kama—selfish desires, krodha—anger, moha—attachment, lobha—greed, madha—pride and matsarya—envy. Life is a constant battle against these dark forces. The conflict between Rama and Ravana,

dharma and adharma, can be viewed metaphorically in this light, as we each have aspects of Rama and Ravana within.

15. **The World Is a Family:** The Ramayana teaches unity. Many creatures share the same planet, so we must learn to respect all life forms, never taking more from the earth than we put back. The theme of environmental conservation runs strongly throughout the Ramayana. Additionally, while uniting the people from the Himalayas to the Indian Ocean in civilizational nationhood, the epic also includes the whole world with its message of coexistence. 'Live in complete harmony with nature. Experience the grace of God in the splendour of the universe. Be blessed by God's reassuring love. The sweet dawn will sweeten your soul, the dazzling midday sun will set your heart aflutter, and the serene music of your soul will guide you towards peace and prosperity. And when the day's task is over, you will sleep in the lap of Mother Nature. All the deities will be favourable to you.' Yajur Veda 34.37

16. **Truth Prevails:** Truth and dharma eventually triumph, even if adharma appears to win temporarily. In the words of the Mundaka Upanishad, 'Satyameva Jayate': Truth is always victorious.

RAMA'S JOURNEY

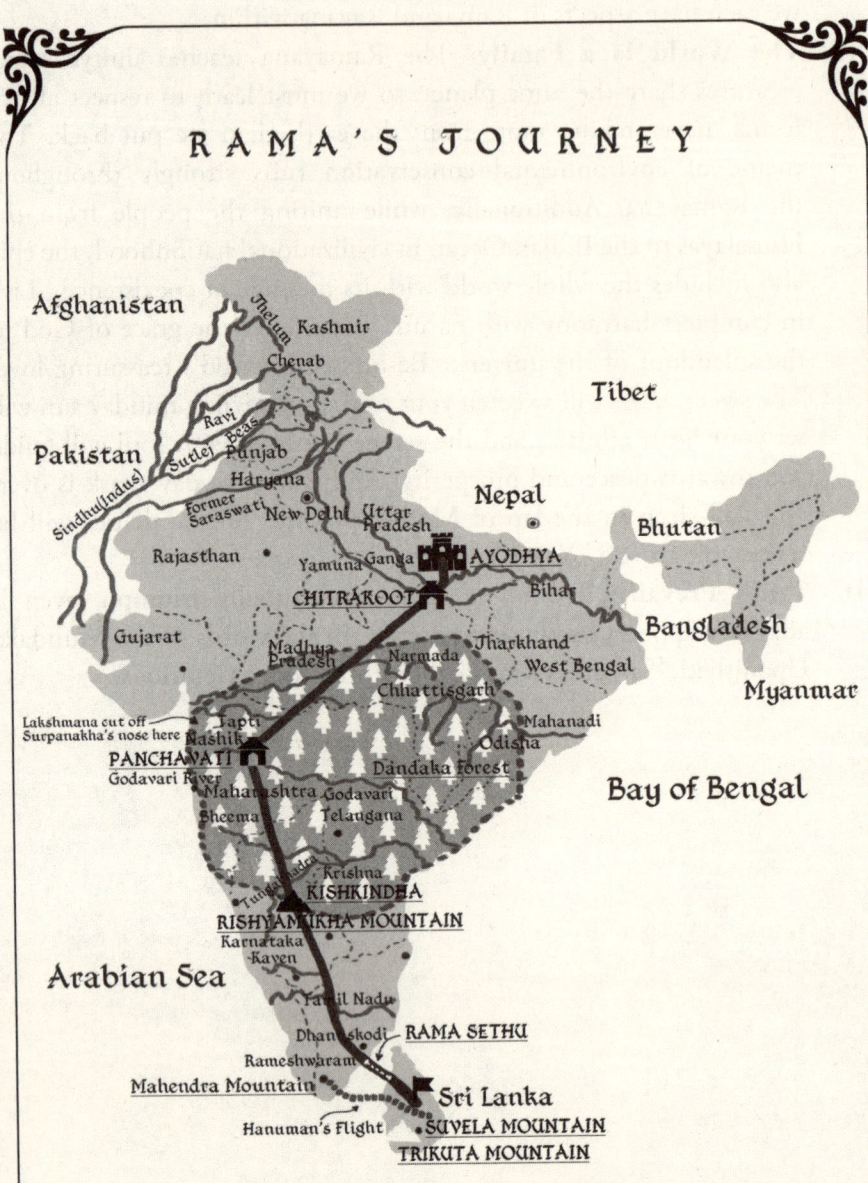

Afghanistan

Kashmir

Jhelum

Chenab

Tibet

Pakistan

Ravi

Beas

Sutlej

Punjab

Sindhu/Indus

Haryana

former Saraswati

New Delhi

Uttar Pradesh

Nepal

Bhutan

Rajasthan

Yamuna Ganga

AYODHYA

CHITRAKOOT

Bihar

Bangladesh

Gujarat

Madhya Pradesh

Narmada

Jharkhand

West Bengal

Myanmar

Chhattisgarh

Mahanadi

Lakshmana cut off Surpanakha's nose here

Tapti

Nashik

PANCHAVATI

Godavari River

Dandaka Forest

Odisha

Maharashtra

Godavari

Bheema

Telangana

Bay of Bengal

Tungabhadra

Krishna

KISHKINDHA

RISHYAMUKHA MOUNTAIN

Karnataka

Kaveri

Arabian Sea

Tamil Nadu

Dhanushkodi

RAMA SETHU

Rameshwaram

Mahendra Mountain

Hanuman's Flight

Sri Lanka

SUVELA MOUNTAIN

TRIKUTA MOUNTAIN

INDIAN OCEAN

Bibliography

Acharya, Pt Sri Rama Ramanuja. *The Laws of Manu for the 21ˢᵗ Century: Compiled and Edited by Pt Sri Rama Ramanuja Acharya*. Srimatham. http://www.srimatham.com/uploads/5/5/4/9/5549439/manu_for_modern_times.pdf

Bala, Saroj. *Ramayan Retold with Scientific Evidences*. Prabhat Prakashan, 2019.

Buhler, George. *The Laws of Manu*. Pinnacle Press, 2017.

Chavda, A.L. *The Aryan Invasion Myth: How 21st Century Science Debunks 19th Century Indology*. Self-Published, Chavda, A.L., 2017.

Danino, Michel. *Genetics and the Aryan Debate*, Bulletin of the Indian Archaeological Society, Archaeology Online. https://www.archaeologyonline.net/artifacts/genetics-aryan-debate

Danino, Michel. *The Lost River: On the Trail of the Sarasvati*. Penguin Random House India, 2010.

Debroy, Bibek, trans. *The Valmiki Ramayana* (Vols. 1–3). Penguin Random House India, 2017.

Doniger, Wendy. *The Laws of Manu*. Penguin Random House India, 2000.

Doniger, Wendy. *The Rig Veda*. Penguin Books India, 1994.

Dutt, M. N., trans. *Manusmriti*. Chowkhamba Vidyabhawan, 2020.

Gambhirananda, Swami. *Eight Upanishads*. 2ⁿᵈ edition. Vedanta Press and Bookshop, 1957.

Giri, Sri Yukteswar. *The Holy Science*. First published, 1894.

Hari, D.K., and Hari Hema D.K. *Historical Rama*. 2ⁿᵈ edition. Sri Sri Publications Trust, 2011.

Hari, D.K., and Hari Hema D.K. *Ramayana in Lanka*. 1ˢᵗ edition. Sri Sri Publications Trust, 2010.

Ishwaran, Eknath. *The Upanishads*. 2ⁿᵈ edition. Nilgiri Press, 2007.

Kak, Subhash. *The Asvamedha: The Rite and Its Logic*. Motilal Banarsidass Publishers, 2004.

Kishore, Dr B.R. *Atharvaveda*. Diamond Pocket Books (P) Ltd., 1998.

Kishore, Dr B.R. *Samveda*. Diamond Pocket Books (P) Ltd., 1998

Kishore, Dr B.R. *Yajurveda*. Diamond Pocket Books (P) Ltd., 1998.

Kivisild, T., et al. 'The Genetic Heritage of the Earliest Settlers Persists Both in Indian Tribal and Caste Populations', *American Journal of Human Genetics*, American Society of Human Genetics, https://www.ncbi.nlm. nih.gov/pmc/articles/PMC379225/

Knapp, Stephen. *Proof of Vedic Culture's Global Existence*. BookSurge Publishing, 2009.

Lal, B.B. *Rama: His Historicity, Mandir and Setu, Evidence of Literature, Archaeology and Other Sciences*. Hardback edition. Aryan Books International, 2019.

Lal, B.B. *The Rigvedic People: 'Invaders'?/'Immigrants'? or Indigenous? Evidence of Archaeology and Literature*. Aryan Books International, 2015.

Lucotte, Gerard. *The Major Y-Chromosome Haplotype XI - Haplogroup R1a in Eurasia*, Hereditary Genetics, Walsh Medical Media, https:// www.walshmedicalmedia.com/open-access/the-major-ychromosome-haplotype-xi--haplogroup-r1a-in-eurasia-2161-1041-1000150.pdf

Malhotra, Rajiv, and Babaji, Satyanarayana Dasa. *Sanskrit Non-Translatables: The Importance of Sanskritizing English*. Amaryllis, 2020.

Mueller F. Max, and Mueller, Georgina Adelaide. *The Life and Letters of the Right Honourable Friedrich Max Mueller*, Internet Archive, 6 February 2008. https://archive.org/details/lifelettersofrig01mluoft/mode/2up

Nikhilananda, Swami. *The Upanishads—A New Translation (Vols. 1–4)*. 7th edition. Self-Published, Ramakrishna–Vivekananda Centre, NY, 2016.

Oak, Nilesh Nilkanth. *The Historic Rama*. Self-Published, CreateSpace Independent Publishing Platform, 2014.

Oppenheimer, Stephen. *Out of Africa's Eden: The Peopling of the World*, Academia.edu, https://www.academia.edu/13015970/Out_of_Africas_Eden_The_peopling_of_the_world

Ostler, Nicholas. *Empires of the Word: A Language History of the World*. Harper Perennial, 2006.

Pande, Vikrant, and Kulkarni, Neelesh. *In the Footsteps of Rama: Travels with the Ramayana*. Harper Collins Publishers, 2021.

Priyadarshi, Premendra. *In Quest of the Dates of the Vedas: Comprehensive Study of the Vedic and the Indo-European Flora, Fauna and Climate in Light of the Information Emerging from the Disciplines of Archaeology, Archaeo-Botany, Geology, Genetics and Linguistics for the Last 10,000 Years*. Partridge India, 2014.

Radhakrishnan, S. *The Principal Upanishads*. 31st impression. Harper Collins, 2019.

Ram, Dr Tulsi, trans. *The Four Vedas (Vols. 1–8)*. 2013 edition, Arsh Sahitya Prachar Trust, 2013.

Sahoo S., Singh A., Himabindu G., Banerjee J., Sitalaximi T., Gaikwad S., Trivedi R., Endicott P., Kivisild T., Metspalu M., Villems R., Kashyap V. K. *A Prehistory of Indian Y Chromosomes: Evaluating Demic Diffusion Scenarios*, National Library of Medicine, https://www.ncbi.nlm.nih.gov/pmc/articles/PMC1347984/

Sanyal, Sanjeev. *Land of the Seven Rivers: A Brief History of India's Geography*. Penguin Random House India, 2013.

Sengupta, S., et al. 'Polarity and Temporality of High-Resolution Y-Chromosome Distributions in India Identify Both Indigenous and Exogenous Expansions and Reveal Minor Genetic Influence of Central Asian Pastoralists', *American Journal of Human Genetics*, (2006) American Society of Human Genetics, https://www.cell.com/ajhg/fulltext/S0002-9297(07)62353-2

Sharma, Pt Satish K. *Caste, Conversion, A Colonial Conspiracy: What every Hindu & Christian needs to know about Caste*. Notion Press, 2020.

Sharma, S., Rai, E., Sharma, P. et al. 'The Indian Origin of Paternal Haplogroup R1a1* Substantiates the Autochthonous Origin of Brahmins and the Caste System,' *J Hum Genet* 54 (2009): 47–55, https://www.nature.com/.

Shastry, Shiv. *Aryan Invasion Myth or Fact?: Uncovering the Evidence*. Self-Published, Shastry, Shiv. 2021.

Singh, Dr Shitala Prasad. 'Early Centres of Origin of Agriculture in the Middle Ganga Plain', *American International Journal of Research in Humanities, Arts and Social Sciences*, International Association of Scientific Innovation and Research (IASIR), http://iasir.net/AIJRHASSpapers/AIJRHASS14-432.pdf

Srimad Valmiki—Ramayana: With Sanskrit Text and English translation (Vols. 1 & 2). Geeta Press Gorakhpur, January 2020.

Srimad Valmiki Ramayana, Valmiki Ramayana, http://www.valmikiramayan.net/

Talageri, Shrikant G. *The Rigveda and The Avesta: The Final Evidence*. 3rd reprint. Aditya Prakashan, 2008.

Vidyalankar, Pandit Satyakam. *The Holy Vedas: A Golden Treasury*. Hind Pocket Books (A Penguin Random House Company), 2019.